Strategic Management Process

Business Ethics, Social Responsibility, and Environmental Sustainability

SIMPLE AND STRAIGHTFORWARD APPROACH TO STRATEGIC PLANNING

Implement Strategies— Management Issues Chapter 7

Implement Strategies— Marketing, Finance, Accounting, R&D, and MIS Issues Chapter 8

Measure and Evaluate Performance Chapter 9

Global/International Issues

Strategy Implementation

Strategy Evaluation

USED TO INTEGRATE AND ORGANIZE ALL CHAPTERS IN THIS TEXT

MyManagementLab®

MyManagementLab is an online assessment and preparation solution for courses in Principles of Management, Human Resources, Strategy, and Organizational Behavior that helps you actively study and prepare material for class. Chapter-by-chapter activities, including study plans, focus on what you need to learn and to review in order to succeed.

Visit **www.pearsonglobaleditions.com/mymanagementlab** to learn more.

Strategic Management Concepts
A Competitive Advantage Approach

Fourteenth Edition

Global Edition

Fred R. David

Francis Marion University

Florence, South Carolina

PEARSON

Boston   Columbus   Indianapolis   New York   San Francisco   Upper Saddle River
Amsterdam   Cape Town   Dubai   London   Madrid   Milan   Munich Paris   Montréal   Toronto
Delhi   Mexico City   São Paulo   Sydney   Hong Kong   Seoul   Singapore   Taipei   Tokyo

Editorial Director: Sally Yagan
Senior Acquisitions Editor: Kim Norbuta
Senior Acquisitions Editor, Global Edition: Steven Jackson
Editor, Global Edition: Leandra Paoli
Director of Editorial Services: Ashley Santora
Editorial Project Manager: Claudia Fernandes
Director of Marketing: Maggie Moylan
Senior Marketing Manager: Nikki Ayana Jones
Marketing Manager, International: Dean Erasmus
Marketing Assistant: Ian Gold
Senior Managing Editor: Judy Leale
Production Project Manager: Ilene Kahn

Senior Operations Supervisor: Arnold Vila
Operations Specialist: Cathleen Petersen
Creative Director: Blair Brown
Design Supervisor: Janet Slowik
Senior Art Director: Kenny Beck
Cover Designer: Jodi Notowitz
Interior Designer: Dina Curro
Cover Illustration: © James Thew-Fotolia.com
Senior Media Project Manager, Editorial: Denise Vaughn
MyLab Product Manager: Joan Waxman
Media Project Manager, Production: Lisa Rinaldi
Full-Service Project Management: Integra

Pearson Education Limited
Edinburgh Gate
Harlow
Essex CM20 2JE
England

and Associated Companies throughout the world

Visit us on the World Wide Web at:
www.pearson.com/uk

© Pearson Education Limited 2013

ISBN 13: 978-0-273-76760-2
ISBN 10: 0-273-76760-7

British Library Cataloguing-in-Publication Data
A catalogue record for this book is available from the British Library

10 9 8 7 6 5 4 3 2 1
16 15 14 13 12

Typeset in 10/12 Times by Integra
Printed and bound by Courier Kendallville in The United States of America

The publisher's policy is to use paper manufactured from sustainable forests.

To Spikes and Aubie David—
for fifteen years of love.

Brief Contents

Contents

Chapter 4 The Internal Assessment 122

Chapter 5 Strategies in Action 160

Manufacturing Firms

FOOD PROCESSING
1. Kraft Foods Inc. — 2009, Kristopher J. Blanchard
2. Hershey Company — 2009, Anne Walsh and Ellen Mansfield

PERSONAL CARE
3. Procter & Gamble Company — 2011, Alen Badal
4. Estée Lauder Companies, Inc.— 2011, Sharynn M. Tomlin

HEALTH CARE
5. Bristol-Meyers Squibb — 2011, Gail J. Robin
6. Pfizer, Inc. — 2009, Vijaya Narapareddy

BEVERAGES
7. Dr Pepper Snapple Group, Inc. — 2011, Joseph S. Harrison
8. PepsiCo — 2009, John and Sherry Ross

COMPUTERS
9. Dell, Inc. — 2011, Matthew Baker and Anne M. Walsh
10. Apple, Inc. — 2011, Mernoush Banton

AUTOMOTIVE
11. Harley-Davidson, Inc. — 2009, Carol Pope and Joanne Mack
12. Ford Motor Company — 2009, Alen Badal

Service Firms

AIRLINES
13. United Continental Holdings, Inc. — 2011, Charles M. Byles
14. Ryanair Holdings, plc — 2011, Charles M. Byles

COMMERCIAL BANKS
15. Wells Fargo Corporation — 2009, Donald L. Crooks, Robert S. Goodman, and John Burbridge
16. E*TRADE Financial Corporation — 2011, Amit J. Shah and Michael L. Monahan

FOOD DELIVERY
17. Krispy Kreme Doughnuts (KKD) — 2009, John Burbridge and Coleman Rich
18. Starbucks Corporation — 2011, Marlene M. Reed and Rochelle R. Brunson

HOSPITALITY AND ENTERTAINMENT
19. Walt Disney Company — 2009, Mernoush Banton
20. Merryland Amusement Park — 2009, Gregory Stone

INTERNET BASED
21. Yahoo! Inc. — 2009, Hamid Kazeroony
22. eBay Inc. — 2009, Lori Radulovich

RETAIL STORES
23. Gap, Inc. — 2011, Sharynn M. Tomlin
24. Wal-Mart Stores, Inc. — 2009, Amit J. Shah and Michael L. Monahanat

OFFICE SUPPLY STORES
25. Staples, Inc. — 2011, William J. Donoher
26. Office Depot, Inc. — 2011, Wayne E. Smith

Preface

Why the Need for This New Edition?

The world is dramatically different than it was two years ago. The global economic recovery has created a business environment that is quite different and more complex than it was when the previous edition of this text was published. Thousands of businesses are now flourishing and consumers are again buying discretionary products. Tight credit markets remain, as do high unemployment and high food prices, but millions of new entrepreneurs have entered the business world globally. Democracy is taking hold in the Middle East, and China has replaced Japan as the world's second largest in gross domestic product. Business firms today are leaner and meaner than ever, so gaining and sustaining competitive advantage is harder than ever. Intense price competition, rapid technological change, and social networking have altered marketing to its core. Opportunities and threats abound today all over the world, including Africa. This new edition reveals how to conduct effective strategic planning in this new world order.

Since the prior edition, thousands of liquidations, bankruptcies, divestitures, mergers, alliances, and partnerships captured the news. Private equity firms returned to the spotlight by taking hundreds of firms public and acquiring hundreds more. Corporate scandals highlighted the need for improved business ethics and corporate disclosure of financial transactions. Downsizing, rightsizing, and reengineering contributed to a permanently altered corporate landscape. Thousands of firms began doing business globally, and thousands more closed their global operations. Thousands prospered, and yet thousands failed in the last two years as more industries commoditized, making strategic management an even more important factor in being successful. Long-held competitive advantages, such as print media, news, and entertainment, eroded in recent years, and new avenues for competitive advantage formed. This new edition captures the complexity of this new business environment.

There is less room for error today in the formulation and implementation of a strategic plan. This new edition provides an effective approach for developing a clear strategic plan. Changes made in this edition are aimed squarely at illustrating the effect of new business concepts and techniques on strategic-management theory and practice. Due to the magnitude of recent changes affecting companies, cultures, and countries, every page of this edition has been updated. This textbook is one of the most widely read strategic-management books in the world, perhaps the most widely read. This text is now published in 10 languages.

What Is New in This Edition?

This 14th edition is positioned to be the leader and best choice globally for teaching strategic management. Here is a summary of what is new in this edition:

- Chapter 11, "Global/International Issues," is expanded 70 percent. There is extensive new coverage of cultural and conceptual strategic-management differences across countries. Doing business globally has become a necessity in most industries because nearly all strategic decisions today are affected by global issues and concerns. Every case company in this edition does business globally, providing students ample opportunity to evaluate and consider international aspects of doing business.
- An updated Cohesion Case on Adidas (2011)—this is one of the most successful, well-known, and best managed global companies in the world—students apply strategy concepts to Adidas at the end of each chapter through new Assurance of Learning Exercises.
- New or improved Assurance of Learning Exercises appear at the end of all chapters to apply chapter concepts; the exercises prepare students for strategic-management case analysis.
- A new "Special Note to Students" paragraph is provided at the end of every chapter to guide students in developing and presenting a case analysis that reveals recommendations for how a firm can best gain and sustain competitive advantage. The whole notion of how to gain and sustain competitive advantage is strengthened throughout this edition. Note the brand new subtitle heading for this book: "A Competitive Advantage Approach."
- A brand-new boxed insert at the beginning of each chapter showcases a company doing strategic management exceptionally well.
- Nearly all brand-new examples throughout the chapters.
- Extensive new narrative on strategic management theory and concepts in every chapter to illustrate the new business world order.
- New review questions at the end of each chapter.
- Brand-new color photographs bring this new edition to life and illustrate companies and concepts.
- All new current readings at the end of each chapter; new research and theories of seminal thinkers in strategy development, such as Ansoff, Chandler, Porter, Hamel, Prahalad, Mintzberg, and Barney, are provided in the chapters; practical aspects of strategic management, however, are still center stage and the trademark of this text.
- Chapter 10, "Business Ethics/Social Responsibility/Environmental Sustainability," is expanded 40 percent, providing extensive new coverage of ethics and sustainability because this text emphasizes that "good ethics is good business." Unique to strategic-management texts, the sustainability discussion is strengthened to promote and encourage firms to conduct operations in an environmentally sound manner. Respect for the natural environment has become an important concern for consumers, companies, society, and AACSB-International.

Chapters: Time-Tested Features

This edition continues to offer many special time-tested features and content that have made this text so successful for over 20 years. Historical trademarks of this text that are strengthened in this edition are described below.

- This text meets AACSB-International guidelines that support a practitioner orientation rather than a theory/research approach. It offers a skills-oriented approach to developing a vision and mission statement; performing an external audit; conducting an internal assessment; and formulating, implementing, and evaluating strategies.
- The author's writing style is concise, conversational, interesting, logical, lively, and supported by numerous current examples throughout.
- A simple, integrative strategic-management model appears in all chapters and on the inside front cover of the text. This model is widely used for strategic planning among consultants and companies worldwide. At the start of each chapter, the section of the comprehensive strategy model covered in that chapter is highlighted and enlarged so students can see the focus of each chapter in the basic unifying comprehensive model. One reviewer said, "One thing I have admired about David's text is that he follows the fundamental sequence of strategy formulation, implementation, and evaluation. There is a basic flow from vision/mission to internal/external environmental scanning to strategy development, selection, implementation, and evaluation. This has been, and continues to be, a hallmark of the David text. Many other strategy texts are more disjointed in their presentation, and thus confusing to the student, especially at the undergraduate level."
- A Cohesion Case follows Chapter 1 and is revisited at the end of each chapter. This Cohesion Case allows students to apply strategic-management concepts and techniques to a real organization as chapter material is covered, which readies students for case analysis in the course.
- End-of-chapter Assurance of Learning Exercises effectively apply concepts and techniques in a challenging, meaningful, and enjoyable manner. Several exercises apply text material to the Cohesion Case, textual material to a college or university, and send students into the business world to explore important strategy topics. The exercises are relevant, interesting, and contemporary.
- There is excellent pedagogy in this text, including notable quotes and objectives to open each chapter, and key terms, current readings, discussion questions, and experiential exercises to close each chapter.
- There is excellent coverage of strategy formulation issues, such as business ethics, global versus domestic operations, vision/mission, matrix analysis, partnering, joint venturing, competitive analysis, governance, and guidelines for conducting an internal/external strategy assessment.
- There is excellent coverage of strategy implementation issues such as corporate culture, organizational structure, outsourcing, marketing concepts, financial analysis, and business ethics.
- A systematic, analytical approach is presented in Chapter 6, including matrices such as the SWOT, BCG, IE, GRAND, SPACE, and QSPM.
- The chapter material is again published in a four-color format.

Instructor's Resource Center

At www.pearsonglobaleditions.com/david, instructors can access a variety of print, digital, and presentation resources available with this text in downloadable format. Registration is simple and gives you immediate access to new titles and new editions. As a registered faculty member, you can download resource files and receive immediate access and instructions for installing course management content on your campus server.

If you ever need assistance, our dedicated technical support team is ready to help with the media supplements that accompany this text. Visit http://247.pearsoned.com/ for answers to frequently asked questions and toll-free user support phone numbers.

The following supplements are available for download to adopting instructors:

- Instructor's Manual
- Case Instructor's Manual
- Test Bank
- TestGen® Computerized Test Bank
- PowerPoints

Videos on DVD

Exciting and high-quality video clips help deliver engaging topics to the classroom to help students better understand the concepts explained in the textbook. Please contact your local representative to receive a copy of the DVD.

Author Website

The Strategic Management Club Online at www.strategyclub.com contains templates and links to help students save time in performing analyses and make presentations look professional.

Special Note to Professors

Thank you for considering this text. This new edition provides exceptionally up-to-date coverage of strategic-management concepts, theory, research, and techniques. Every sentence and paragraph has been scrutinized, modified, clarified, deleted, streamlined, updated, and/or improved to enhance the content and caliber of presentation. The basic structure of this edition stays with 11 chapters, but there are many new examples, concepts, readings, exercises, and review questions in every chapter—and an updated Cohesion Case on Adidas. The improvements in readability and coverage are dramatic. Every chapter features strategic-management concepts and practices presented in a clear, focused, and relevant manner with hundreds of new examples integrated throughout.

The skills-oriented, practitioner perspective that historically has been the foundation of this text is enhanced and strengthened in this edition. New and expanded coverage of strategic-management theories and research in the text reflect companies' new perspective on doing business. To survive and prosper in this global economic recovery, organizations must build and sustain competitive advantage. This text is now trusted around the world to provide future and present managers the latest skills and concepts needed to effectively formulate and efficiently implement a strategic plan—a game plan, if you will—that can lead to sustainable competitive advantage for any type of business.

The reviewers and I believe you will find this edition to be the best strategic-management textbook available for communicating both the excitement and value of strategic management. Concise and exceptionally well organized, this text is now published in English, Chinese, Spanish, Thai, German, Japanese, Farsi, Indonesian, Indian, and Arabic. A version in Russian is being negotiated. On five continents, this text is widely used in colleges and universities at both the graduate and undergraduate levels. In addition, thousands of companies, organizations, and governmental bodies use this text as a management guide, making it perhaps the most widely used strategic planning book in the world.

This textbook meets all AACSB-International guidelines for the strategic-management course at both the graduate and undergraduate levels, and previous editions have been used at more than 500 colleges and universities.

A Sample of Universities Presently Using This Textbook

You can trust this textbook to meet all your needs. Although very widely used around the world, a sample of colleges and universities using the prior (13th) edition of this text in English in the United States is given here:

Albany State University	Eastern Oregon University
Alcorn State University	Eastern Washington University
Alvernia University	East Stroudsburg University
Ambassador College	Elmhurst College
American International College	Faulkner University
Anderson University	Florida Institute of Technology
Angelo State University	Fort Valley State College
Aquinas College	Francis Marion University
Bellevue University	Fresno Pacific University
Belmont Abbey College	Frostburg State University
Benedictine University	George Fox University
Briar Cliff University	Georgetown College
Brooklyn College	George Washington University
California State University–Long Beach	Georgia Southwestern State University
California Lutheran University	Hampton University
Carnegie Mellon University	Harding University
Catawba College	Hofstra University
Central Connecticut State University	Indiana University–Kokomo
Central Washington University	Indiana Wesleyan University
Chatam University	Iona College
Chicago State University	Jackson Community College
Claflin University	Jamestown College
Clarion University of Pennsylvania	John Brown University
Clarkson College	Johnson & Wales University–Charlotte
Cleveland State University	Johnson & Wales University–Denver
Columbia College	Johnson & Wales University–Providence
Concordia University	Kansas State University
Delaware State University	Keene State College
Depaul University–Loop Campus	Kellogg Community College
Dominican University	La Salle University
Eastern Michigan University	Limestone College

Loyola College, Bush Center

Loyola University, Maryland

Madonna University

Marshall University

Mercer University

Mesa State College

Miami-Dade College

Middle Georgia College

Millersville University

Millsaps College

Morgan State University

Morrison College of Reno

Mount Hood Community College

Murray State University

New England College

New Mexico State University

New York University

North Carolina Wesleyan College

Norfolk State University

North Central College

Northwest Arkansas Community College

Oakland University

Ohio Dominican University

Ohio State University–Main Campus

Oklahoma State University

Oral Roberts University

Pace University–Pleasantville

Palm Beach State College

Park University

Penn State University–Abington

Penn State University–University Park

Philadelphia University

Point Park University

Queens College of CUNY

Quinnipiac University

Rider University

Robert Morris College

Roger Williams University

Saint Cloud State University

Saint Leo University

Saint Mary's College

Saint Xavier University

Sam Houston State University

San Antonia College

Savannah State University

Seton Hall University

Siena Heights University

South Carolina State University

Southern New Hampshire University

Southern University–Baton Rouge

Southern Utah University

Southern Wesleyan University

Southwest Baptist University

St. Bonaventure University

St. Joseph College

St. Louis University

St. Thomas University

Texarkana College

Texas A&M University–Commerce

Texas A&M University–Texarkana

Texas Tech University

Three Rivers Community College

Troy University–Dothan

Troy University–Main Campus

Troy University–Montgomery

University of Alabama–Birmingham

University of Arkansas–Fayetteville

University of Colorado–Boulder

University of Hawaii–Manoa

University of Louisiana–Monroe

University of Maine–Augusta

University of Maine–Fort Kent

University of Maryland–College Park

University of Miami

University of Michigan–Flint

University of Minnesota–Crookston

University of Mobile

University of Nevada–Las Vegas

University of New Orleans

University of North Texas–Dallas

University of Pennsylvania

University of San Francisco

University of Texas–El Paso

University of Texas–Pan American

University of Texas–San Antonio

University of The Incarnate Word

University of Toledo

University of Nevada–Reno

University of New Orleans

University of North Texas

University of Toledo

Valley City State University

VCCS

Virginia State University

Virginia Tech–Blacksburg

Wagner College

Washington University

Webster University

Western Connecticut State University

Western Kentucky University

Western Michigan University

Widener University

William Jewell College

Williams Baptist College

Winona State University

Winston-Salem State University

Acknowledgments

Many persons have contributed time, energy, ideas, and suggestions for improving this text over 14 editions. The strength of this text is largely attributed to the collective wisdom, work, and experiences of strategic-management professors, researchers, students, and practitioners. Names of particular individuals whose published research is referenced in this edition of this text are listed alphabetically in the Name Index. To all individuals involved in making this text so popular and successful, I am indebted and thankful.

Many special persons and reviewers contributed valuable material and suggestions for this edition. I would like to thank my colleagues and friends at Auburn University, Mississippi State University, East Carolina University, and Francis Marion University. I have served on the management faculty at all these universities. Scores of students and professors at these schools helped shape the development of this text. Many thanks go to the following 23 reviewers whose comments shaped this 14th edition:

Moses Acquaah, The University of North Carolina at Greensboro

Charles M. Byles, Virginia Commonwealth University

Charles J. Capps III, Sam Houston State University

Neil Dworkin, Western Connecticut State University

Jacalyn M. Florn, University of Toledo

John Frankenstein, Brooklyn College/City University of New York

Bill W. Godair, Landmark College, Community College of Vermont

Carol Jacobson, Purdue University

Susan M. Jensen, University of Nebraska at Kearney

Dmitry Khanin, California State University at Fullerton

Thomas E. Kulik, Washington University at St. Louis

Jerrold K. Leong, Oklahoma State University

Trina Lynch-Jackson, Indiana University

Elouise Mintz, Saint Louis University

Raza Mir, William Paterson University

Gerry N. Muuka, Murray State University

Lori Radulovich, Baldwin-Wallace College

Thomas W. Sharkey, University of Toledo

Frederick J. Slack, Indiana University of Pennsylvania

Daniel Slater, Union University

Jill Lynn Vihtelic, Saint Mary's College

Michael W. Wakefield, Colorado State University–Pueblo

Don Wicker, Brazosport College

Individuals who develop cases for the North American Case Research Association Meeting, the Midwest Society for Case Research Meeting, the Eastern Case Writers Association Meeting, the European Case Research Association Meeting, and Harvard Case Services are vitally important for continued progress in the field of strategic-management. From a research perspective, writing strategic-management cases represents a valuable scholarly activity among faculty. Extensive research is required to structure strategic-management cases in a way that exposes strategic issues, decisions, and behavior. Pedagogically, strategic-management cases are essential for students in learning how to apply concepts, evaluate situations, formulate a "game plan," and resolve implementation problems. Without a continuous stream of updated cases, the strategic-management course and discipline would lose much of its energy and excitement.

Professors who teach this course supplement lecture with simulations, guest speakers, experiential exercises, class projects, and/or outside readings. Case analysis, however, is typically the backbone of the learning process in most strategic-management courses across the country. Case analysis is almost always an integral part of this course.

Analyzing strategic-management cases gives students the opportunity to work in teams to evaluate the internal operations and external issues facing various organizations and to craft strategies that can lead these firms to success. Working in teams gives students practical experience solving problems as part of a group. In the business world, important decisions are generally made within groups; strategic-management students learn to deal with overly aggressive group members and also timid, noncontributing group members. This experience is valuable as strategic-management students near graduation and enter the working world full time.

Students can improve their oral and written communication skills as well as their analytical and interpersonal skills by proposing and defending particular courses of action for the case companies. Analyzing cases allows students to view a company, its competitors, and its industry concurrently, thus simulating the complex business world. Through case analysis, students learn how to apply concepts, evaluate situations, formulate strategies, and resolve implementation problems. Instructors typically ask students to prepare a three-year strategic plan for the firm. Analyzing a strategic-management case entails students applying concepts learned across their entire business curriculum. Students gain experience dealing with a wide range of organizational problems that impact all the business functions.

The following people wrote cases that were selected for inclusion in this 14th edition. These persons helped develop the most current compilation of cases ever assembled in a strategic-management text:

Dr. M. Jill Austin, Middle Tennessee State University

Dr. Alen Badal, The Union Institute

Matthew Baker, La Salle University

Dr. Mernoush Banton, Florida International University

Dr. Rochelle R. Brunson, Baylor University

Laura Buckner, Middle Tennessee State University

Dr. John J. Burbridge, Elon University

Dr. Charles M. Byles, Virginia Commonwealth University

Mary R. Dittman, Francis Marion University

Dr. William (Bill) J. Donoher, Missouri State University

Joseph S. Harrison, University of Richmond

Dr. Michael L. Monahan, Frostburg State University

Dr. Vijaya Narapareddy, University of Denver

Dr. Lori Radulovich, Baldwin-Wallace College

Dr. Deana M. Raffo, Middle Tennessee State University

Dr. Marlene Reed, Baylor University

Dr. Coleman R. Rich, Elon University

Dr. Gail J. Robin, Baker College

Dr. Amit J. Shah, Frostburg State University

Dr. Wayne E. Smith, Argosy University

Dr. Sharynn M. Tomlin, Angelo State University

Dr. Anne M. Walsh, La Salle University

Ralph I. Williams Jr., Middle Tennessee State University

I especially appreciate the wonderful work completed by the 14th edition ancillary authors as follows:

Case Instructor's Manual—Forest R. David

Instructor's Manual—Amit J. Shah

Test Bank—Maureen Steddin

PowerPoints—Brad Cox

Scores of Pearson employees and salespersons have worked diligently behind the scenes to make this text a leader in strategic management. I appreciate the continued hard work of all those professionals, such as Sally Yagan, Kim Norbuta, Claudia Fernandes, and Ilene Kahn.

I also want to thank you, the reader, for investing the time and effort to read and study this text. It will help you formulate, implement, and evaluate strategies for any organization with which you become associated. I hope you come to share my enthusiasm for the rich subject area of strategic management and for the systematic learning approach taken in this text.

Finally, I want to welcome and invite your suggestions, ideas, thoughts, comments, and questions regarding any part of this text or the ancillary materials. Please call me at 910-612-5343, e-mail me at freddavid9@gmail.com, or write me at the School of Business, Francis Marion University, Florence, SC 29501. I sincerely appreciate and need your input to continually improve this text in future editions. Your willingness to draw my attention to specific errors or deficiencies in coverage or exposition will especially be appreciated.

Thank you for using this text.

Fred R. David

Pearson wish to acknowledge and thank the following people for their involvement in the Global Edition:

Dr. Yoosuf A. Cader, Zayed University, United Arab Emirates
Dr. Olivier Furrer, Radboud University Nijmegen, The Netherlands
Dr. Victor Goh Yuan Sheng, Singapore Management University, Singapore
Dr. David Li, The Hong Kong Polytechnic University, Hong Kong
Dr. Patrick L. McClelland, American University of Sharjah, United Arab Emirates
Prof. Hester Nienaber, UNISA, South Africa
Dr. James Small, The University of Tilburg, The Netherlands
Dr. Sreenivasan Jayashree, Multimedia University, Malaysia

About the Author

Dr. Fred R. David's February 2011 *Business Horizons* article titled "What Are Business Schools Doing for Business Today?" is changing the way many business schools view their curricula. Dr. David is the sole author of two mainstream strategic-management textbooks: (1) *Strategic Management: Concepts and Cases* and (2) *Strategic-Management Concepts*. These texts have been on a two-year revision cycle since 1986, when the first edition was published. These texts are among the best if not the best-selling strategic-management textbooks in the world and have been used at more than 500 colleges and universities, including Harvard University, Duke University, Carnegie-Mellon University, Johns Hopkins University, the University of Maryland, University of North Carolina, University of Georgia, San Francisco State University, University of South Carolina, and Wake Forest University.

This textbook has been translated and published in Chinese, Japanese, Farsi, Spanish, Indonesian, Indian, Thai, German, and Arabic and is widely used across Asia and South America. It is the best-selling strategic-management textbook in Mexico, China, Peru, Chile, and Japan, and is number two in the United States. Approximately 90,000 students read Dr. David's textbook annually as well as thousands of businesspersons. The book has led the field of strategic management for more than a decade in providing an applications/practitioner approach to the discipline.

A native of Whiteville, North Carolina, Fred David received a BS degree in mathematics and an MBA from Wake Forest University before being employed as a bank manager with United Carolina Bank. He received a PhD in Business Administration from the University of South Carolina, where he majored in General Management with an emphasis in Strategic Management. Currently the TranSouth Professor of Strategic Management at Francis Marion University (FMU) in Florence, South Carolina, Dr. David has also taught at Auburn University, Mississippi State University, East Carolina University, the University of South Carolina, and the University of North Carolina at Pembroke. He is the author of 153 referred publications, including 41 journal articles and 56 proceedings publications. David has articles published in such journals as *Academy of Management Review*, *Academy of Management Executive*, *Journal of Applied Psychology*, *Long Range Planning*, and *Advanced Management Journal*.

Dr. David received a Lifetime Honorary Professorship Award from the Universidad Ricardo Palma in Lima, Peru. He delivered the keynote speech at the 21st Annual Latin American Congress on Strategy hosted by the Centrum School of Business in Peru. He has provided an eight-hour Strategic Planning Workshop to the faculty at Pontificia Universidad Catolica Del in Lima, Peru, and an eight-hour Case Writing/Analyzing Workshop to the faculty at Utah Valley State College in Orem, Utah. He has received numerous awards, including FMU's Board of Trustees Research Scholar Award, the university's Award for Excellence in Research given annually to the best faculty researcher on campus, and the Phil Carroll Advancement of Management Award, given annually by the Society for the Advancement of Management (SAM) to a management scholar for outstanding contributions in management research. Dr. David serves on the Board of Directors of SAM. He has given collegiate graduation commencement addresses several times at Troy University.

List of cases available in the Concepts and Cases version of *Strategic Management: A Competitive Advantage Approach* (ISBN: 978-0-273-76748-0).

Case Information Matrix

Case Company	Stock Symbol	Headquarters City, State	Web Site URL Address	#Employees	Profits/ Revenues/% (2010) (in millions)
Cohesion Case: Adidas Group	ADS (Frankfurt Stock Exchange)	Herzogenaurach, Germany	www.adidas.com	42,541	567/11,990/4.7*
MANUFACTURING FIRMS					
Food Processing					
1. Kraft Foods, Inc.	KFT	Norfield, IL	www.kraft.com	127,000	4,114/49,207/8.4
2. Hershey Co.	HSY	Hershey, PA	www.hersheys.com	11,300	509/5,671/8.9
Personal Care					
3. Procter & Gamble Co.	PG	Cincinnati, OH	http://www.pg.com	127,000	12,736/78,938/16.1
4. Estée Lauder Companies	EL	New York, NY	http://www.elcompanies.com	31,200	478/7,795/6.1
Health Care					
5. Bristol-Meyers Squibb	BMY	New York, NY	http://www.bms.com	28,000	3,102/19,484/15.9
6. Pfizer, Inc.	PFE	New York, NY	www.pfizer.com	106,500	8,257/67,809/12.1
Beverages					
7. Dr Pepper Snapple Group, Inc.	DPS	Plano, TX	http://www.drpeppersnapple.com	19,000	528/5,636/9.4
8. PepsiCo, Inc.	PEP	Purchase, NY	www.pepsico.com	294,000	6,320/57,838/10.9
Computers					
9. Dell, Inc.	DELL	Round Rock, TX	http://www.dell.com	94,300	2,635/61,494/4.3
10. Apple, Inc.	AAPL	Cupertino, CA	http://www.apple.com	46,600	14,013/65,225/21.5
Automotive					
11. Harley-Davidson, Inc.	HOG	Milwaukee, WI	www.harlety-davidson.com	6,900	146/4,859/3.0
12. Ford Motor Co.	F	Dearborn, MI	www.ford.com	164,000	6,561/128,954/5.1
SERVICE FIRMS					
Airlines					
13. United Continental Holdings, Inc.	UAL	Chicago, IL	www.unitedcontinentalholdings.com	86,000	253/23,229/.01
14. Ryanair Holdings, plc	RYAAY	Dublin, Ireland	http://www.ryanair.ie	7,168	413/4,043/10.2
Commercial Banks					
15. Wells Fargo Corp.	WFC	San Francisco, CA	www.wellsfargo.com	263,800	12,362/93,249/13.3
16. E*TRADE Financial Corp.	ETFC	New York, NY	http://www.etrade.com	2,962	−28/2,077/−.01

Case Company	Stock Symbol	Headquarters City, State	Web Site URL Address	#Employees	Profits/ Revenues/% (2010) (in millions)
Food Delivery					
17. Krispy Kreme Doughnuts	KKD	Winston-Salem, NC	www.krispykreme.com	2,640	7.6/361/2.1
18. Starbucks Corp.	SBUX	Seattle, WA	http://www.starbucks.com	137,000	945/10,707/8.8
Hospitality and Entertainment					
19. Walt Disney Co.	DIS	Burbank, CA	www.disney.com	150,000	3,963/38,063/10.4
20. Merryland Amusement Park	N/A	Kansas City, MO	N/A	N/A	N/A
Internet Based					
21. Yahoo!, Inc.	YHOO	Sunnyvale, CA	www.yahoo.com	13,600	1,231/6,324/19.5
22. eBay, Inc.	EBAY	San Jose, CA	www.ebay.com	17,700	1,800/9,156/19.7
Retail Stores					
23. Gap, Inc.	GPS	San Francisco, CA	http://www.gapinc.com	135,000	1,102/14,197/7.7
24. Wal-Mart Stores, Inc.	WMT	Bentonville, AR	www.walmartstores.com	2.0m	16,389/421,849/3.9
Office Supply Stores					
25. Staples, Inc.	SPLS	Farmingham, MA	http://www.staples.com	54,149	881/25,545/3.4
26. Office Depot, Inc.	ODP	Boca Raton, FL	http://www.officedepot.com	41,000	34/11,633/0.3

*Conversation Rate 1.40 USD = 1 Euro

List of cases available in the Concepts and Cases version of *Strategic Management: A Competitive Advantage Approach* (ISBN: 978-0-273-76748-0).

Case Description Matrix

Topical Content Areas (Y = Yes and N = No) Case Company	1 2 3 4 5 6 7 8 9 10 11 12 13 14
Cohesion Case: Adidas Group	Y Y Y Y Y Y Y Y Y Y Y Y N Y Y

MANUFACTURING FIRMS

Food Processing

1. Kraft Foods, Inc.	Y Y N Y Y Y Y Y Y Y N N N
2. Hershey Co.	Y Y Y Y Y Y Y Y Y Y Y N N N

Personal Care

3. Procter & Gamble Co.	Y Y Y Y Y N Y Y Y N Y N N N
4. Estée Lauder Companies	Y Y Y Y N N Y Y Y N N N N N

Health Care

5. Bristol-Meyers Squibb	Y Y Y Y Y N Y Y Y N N N N N
6. Pfizer, Inc.	Y Y Y Y Y Y Y Y Y N N N Y N

Beverages

7. Dr Pepper Snapple Group, Inc.	Y Y Y N Y Y Y Y Y N Y Y N N
8. PepsiCo, Inc.	Y N Y N Y Y Y Y Y N N Y Y N

Computers

9. Dell, Inc.	Y Y Y Y Y N Y Y Y N N N N N
10. Apple, Inc.	Y Y Y Y Y N N Y Y N N N N N

Automotive

11. Harley-Davidson, Inc.	Y Y Y Y Y Y Y Y Y Y N N N Y N
12. Ford Motor Co.	Y Y Y Y Y Y Y Y Y N Y N Y N

Topical Content Areas (Y = Yes and N = No)
Case Company

1 2 3 4 5 6 7 8 9 10 11 12 13 14

SERVICE FIRMS

Airlines

Company	1	2	3	4	5	6	7	8	9	10	11	12	13	14
13. United Continental Holdings, Inc.	Y	Y	Y	Y	Y	Y	Y	Y	Y	N	N	Y	N	N
14. Ryanair Holdings, plc	Y	Y	Y	Y	Y	Y	Y	Y	N	N	N	Y	N	Y

Commercial Banks

Company	1	2	3	4	5	6	7	8	9	10	11	12	13	14
15. Wells Fargo Corp.	Y	Y	Y	Y	Y	Y	Y	Y	N	N	Y	N	Y	N
16. E*TRADE Financial Corp.	Y	Y	Y	Y	Y	N	Y	Y	Y	Y	Y	N	N	N

Food Delivery

Company	1	2	3	4	5	6	7	8	9	10	11	12	13	14
17. Krispy Kreme Doughnuts	Y	N	Y	Y	Y	Y	Y	Y	Y	N	N	N	Y	N
18. Starbucks Corp.	Y	Y	Y	Y	Y	Y	Y	Y	Y	Y	N	N	N	N

Hospitality and Entertainment

Company	1	2	3	4	5	6	7	8	9	10	11	12	13	14
19. Walt Disney Co.	Y	Y	Y	Y	Y	N	Y	Y	Y	N	Y	N	N	Y
20. Merryland Amusement Park	Y	Y	Y	Y	Y	Y	Y	Y	Y	Y	Y	Y	N	Y

Internet Based

Company	1	2	3	4	5	6	7	8	9	10	11	12	13	14
21. Yahoo!, Inc.	Y	Y	Y	N	Y	Y	Y	Y	Y	Y	Y	N	Y	N
22. eBay, Inc.	Y	Y	Y	Y	Y	Y	Y	Y	Y	Y	N	Y	N	Y

Retail Stores

Company	1	2	3	4	5	6	7	8	9	10	11	12	13	14
23. Gap, Inc.	Y	Y	Y	N	Y	Y	Y	Y	Y	N	N	N	N	N
24. Wal-Mart Stores, Inc.	Y	Y	Y	N	Y	Y	Y	Y	Y	N	N	N	Y	N

Office Supply Stores

Company	1	2	3	4	5	6	7	8	9	10	11	12	13	14
25. Staples, Inc.	Y	Y	Y	Y	Y	Y	Y	Y	Y	N	N	Y	N	N
26. Office Depot, Inc.	Y	Y	Y	Y	Y	Y	Y	Y	Y	Y	Y	Y	N	N

1. Year-end 2008 or 2010 Financial Statements Provided?
2. Organizational Chart Provided?
3. Does Company Do Business Outside the United States?
4. Is a Vision or Mission Statement Provided?
5. Business Ethics Issues Included?
6. Sustainability Issues Included?
7. Strategy Formulation Emphasis?
8. Strategy Implementation Emphasis?
9. By-Segment Financial Data Included?
10. Firm Has Declining Revenues?
11. Firm Has Declining Net Income?
12. Case Company Appears in Text for First Time Ever?
13. Case Company Appeared in Prior Edition and Updated Now?
14. Firm Headquartered Outside the United States?

"NOTABLE QUOTES"

"If we know where we are and something about how we got there, we might see where we are trending—and if the outcomes which lie naturally in our course are unacceptable, to make timely change."
—*Abraham Lincoln*

"Without a strategy, an organization is like a ship without a rudder, going around in circles. It's like a tramp; it has no place to go."
—*Joel Ross and Michael Kami*

"Plans are less important than planning."
—*Dale McConkey*

"The formulation of strategy can develop competitive advantage only to the extent that the process can give meaning to workers in the trenches."   —*David Hurst*

"Most of us fear change. Even when our minds say change is normal, our stomachs quiver at the prospect. But for strategists and managers today, there is no choice but to change."
—*Robert Waterman Jr.*

"If a man takes no thought about what is distant, he will find sorrow near at hand. He who will not worry about what is far off will soon find something worse than worry."
—*Confucius*

"Integrity = Longevity"
—*Michael Johnson, CEO of Herbalife*

The Nature of Strategic Management

1

CHAPTER OBJECTIVES

After studying this chapter, you should be able to do the following:

1. Describe the strategic-management process.

2. Explain the need for integrating analysis and intuition in strategic management.

3. Define and give examples of key terms in strategic management.

4. Discuss the nature of strategy formulation, implementation, and evaluation activities.

5. Describe the benefits of good strategic management.

6. Discuss the relevance of Sun Tzu's *The Art of War* to strategic management.

7. Discuss how a firm may achieve sustained competitive advantage.

ASSURANCE OF LEARNING EXERCISES

Assurance of Learning Exercise 1A
Examine Recent and Future
Acquisitions for Nokia

Assurance of Learning Exercise 1B
Gathering Strategy Information
on Adidas AG

Assurance of Learning Exercise 1C
Getting Familiar with SMCO

Assurance of Learning Exercise 1D
Becoming a Certified
Strategic Planner

Assurance of Learning Exercise 1E
Strategic Planning at
Nestlé

Assurance of Learning Exercise 1F
Interviewing Local Strategists

When CEOs from the big three American automakers, Ford, General Motors (GM), and Chrysler, showed up without a clear strategic plan to ask congressional leaders for bailout monies, they were sent home with instructions to develop a clear strategic plan for the future. Austan Goolsbee, one of President Obama's top economic advisers, said, "Asking for a bailout without a convincing business plan was crazy." Goolsbee also said, "If the three auto CEOs need a bridge, it's got to be a bridge to somewhere, not a bridge to nowhere."[1] This textbook gives the instructions on how to develop a clear strategic plan—a bridge to somewhere rather than nowhere.

This chapter provides an overview of strategic management. It introduces a practical, integrative model of the strategic-management process; it defines basic activities and terms in strategic management.

This chapter also introduces the notion of boxed inserts. A boxed insert at the beginning of each chapter reveals how some firms are doing really well competing in a weak global economy. The firms showcased are prospering as their rivals weaken. Each boxed insert examines the strategies of firms doing great amid high unemployment, rising interest rates, unavailability of credit, rising consumer demand, and intense price competition.

The boxed insert beginning each chapter showcases excellent strategic management. The first company featured for excellent performance is Nokia.

Excellent Strategic Management Showcased

NOKIA CORPORATION

Headquartered in Helsinki, Finland, Nokia is the world's leading supplier of mobile phones, fixed telecom networks, and related customer services. About 1.4 billion people globally connect to one another with a Nokia voice-optimized mobile phone or an Internet-connected smartphone. Nokia customers also have access to maps and navigation, a growing catalog of digital music, and an online Apps store. In fact, Nokia's NAVTEQ is a leader in comprehensive digital mapping and navigation services, and Nokia Siemens Networks is one of the leading providers of telecommunications infrastructure hardware, software and professional services globally.

Given that Nokia is continuously developing its digital mapping services, it is no surprise that they are a founding member of the Car Connectivity Consortium. Established in March 2011, Nokia joined eleven other companies to develop global standards and solutions for smartphone and in-vehicle connectivity. The 'Terminal Mode' standard allows high-performing mobile devices to connect to vehicle-based systems such as digital displays, steering wheel buttons, and car audios systems. Founding members include vehicle manufacturers Daimler, General Motors, Honda, Hyundai Motor Company, Toyota, and Volkswagen; system suppliers Alpine and Panasonic; and consumer electronics makers LG Electronics, Nokia and Samsung.

With increasing competition from the likes of Apple and Blackberry, Nokia has been making important strategic decisions. Its joint venture with Siemens, Nokia Siemens Networks, paid $975 million in

cash for the acquisition of the wireless network infrastructure assets of Motorola Solutions in April, 2011. The acquisition strengthened the company's position in North America and Japan, adding approximately 6,900 employees across 52 countries. The acquisition covers a number of research and development facilities, including sites in the United States, China, Russia, India, and the UK.

Source: Based on information at www.nokia.com.

Adidas is featured as the new Cohesion Case because it is a well-known global firm undergoing strategic change and is very well managed. By working through Adidas related Assurance of Learning Exercises at the end of each chapter, you will be well prepared to develop an effective strategic plan for any company assigned to you this semester. The end-of-chapter exercises apply chapter tools and concepts.

What Is Strategic Management?

Once there were two company presidents who competed in the same industry. These two presidents decided to go on a camping trip to discuss a possible merger. They hiked deep into the woods. Suddenly, they came upon a grizzly bear that rose up on its hind legs and snarled. Instantly, the first president took off his knapsack and got out a pair of jogging shoes. The second president said, "Hey, you can't outrun that bear." The first president responded, "Maybe I can't outrun that bear, but I surely can outrun you!" This story captures the notion of strategic management, which is to achieve and maintain competitive advantage.

Defining Strategic Management

Strategic management can be defined as the art and science of formulating, implementing, and evaluating cross-functional decisions that enable an organization to achieve its objectives. As this definition implies, strategic management focuses on integrating management, marketing, finance/accounting, production/operations, research and development, and information systems to achieve organizational success. The term *strategic management* in this text is used synonymously with the term *strategic planning*. The latter term is more often used in the business world, whereas the former is often used in academia. Sometimes the term *strategic management* is used to refer to strategy formulation, implementation, and evaluation, with *strategic planning* referring only to strategy formulation. The purpose of strategic management is to exploit and create new and different opportunities for tomorrow; *long-range planning*, in contrast, tries to optimize for tomorrow the trends of today.

The term *strategic planning* originated in the 1950s and was very popular between the mid-1960s and the mid-1970s. During these years, strategic planning was widely believed to be the answer for all problems. At the time, much of corporate America was "obsessed" with strategic planning. Following that "boom," however, strategic planning was cast aside during the 1980s as various planning models did not yield higher returns. The 1990s, however, brought the revival of strategic planning, and the process is widely practiced today in the business world.

A strategic plan is, in essence, a company's game plan. Just as a football team needs a good game plan to have a chance for success, a company must have a good strategic plan to compete successfully. Profit margins among firms in most industries are so slim that there is little room for error in the overall strategic plan. A strategic plan results from tough managerial choices among numerous good alternatives, and it signals commitment to specific markets, policies, procedures, and operations in lieu of other, "less desirable" courses of action.

The term *strategic management* is used at many colleges and universities as the title for the capstone course in business administration. This course integrates material from all business courses. The Strategic Management Club Online at www.strategyclub.com offers many benefits for strategic management students.

Stages of Strategic Management

The *strategic-management process* consists of three stages: strategy formulation, strategy implementation, and strategy evaluation. *Strategy formulation* includes developing a vision and mission, identifying an organization's external opportunities and threats, determining internal strengths and weaknesses, establishing long-term objectives, generating alternative strategies, and choosing particular strategies to pursue. Strategy-formulation issues include deciding what new businesses to enter, what businesses to abandon, how to allocate resources, whether to expand operations or diversify, whether to enter international markets, whether to merge or form a joint venture, and how to avoid a hostile takeover.

Because no organization has unlimited resources, strategists must decide which alternative strategies will benefit the firm most. Strategy-formulation decisions commit an organization to specific products, markets, resources, and technologies over an extended period of time. Strategies determine long-term competitive advantages. For better or worse, strategic decisions have major multifunctional consequences and enduring effects on an organization. Top managers have the best perspective to understand fully the ramifications of strategy-formulation decisions; they have the authority to commit the resources necessary for implementation.

Strategy implementation requires a firm to establish annual objectives, devise policies, motivate employees, and allocate resources so that formulated strategies can be executed. Strategy implementation includes developing a strategy-supportive culture, creating an effective organizational structure, redirecting marketing efforts, preparing budgets, developing and utilizing information systems, and linking employee compensation to organizational performance.

Strategy implementation often is called the "action stage" of strategic management. Implementing strategy means mobilizing employees and managers to put formulated strategies into action. Often considered to be the most difficult stage in strategic management, strategy implementation requires personal discipline, commitment, and sacrifice. Successful strategy implementation hinges upon managers' ability to motivate employees, which is more an art than a science. Strategies formulated but not implemented serve no useful purpose.

Interpersonal skills are especially critical for successful strategy implementation. Strategy-implementation activities affect all employees and managers in an organization. Every division and department must decide on answers to questions such as "What must we do to implement our part of the organization's strategy?" and "How best can we get the job done?" The challenge of implementation is to stimulate managers and employees throughout an organization to work with pride and enthusiasm toward achieving stated objectives.

Strategy evaluation is the final stage in strategic management. Managers desperately need to know when particular strategies are not working well; strategy evaluation is the primary means for obtaining this information. All strategies are subject to future modification because external and internal factors are constantly changing. Three fundamental strategy-evaluation activities are (1) reviewing external and internal factors that are the bases for current strategies, (2) measuring performance, and (3) taking corrective actions. Strategy evaluation is needed because success today is no guarantee of success tomorrow! Success always creates new and different problems; complacent organizations experience demise.

Strategy formulation, implementation, and evaluation activities occur at three hierarchical levels in a large organization: corporate, divisional or strategic business unit, and functional. By fostering communication and interaction among managers and employees across hierarchical levels, strategic management helps a firm function as a competitive team. Most small businesses and some large businesses do not have divisions or strategic business units; they have only the corporate and functional levels. Nevertheless, managers and employees at these two levels should be actively involved in strategic-management activities.

Peter Drucker says the prime task of strategic management is thinking through the overall mission of a business:

...that is, of asking the question, "What is our business?" This leads to the setting of objectives, the development of strategies, and the making of today's decisions for tomorrow's results. This clearly must be done by a part of the organization that can see the entire business; that can balance objectives and the needs of today against the needs of tomorrow; and that can allocate resources of men and money to key results.[2]

Integrating Intuition and Analysis

Edward Deming once said, *"In God we trust. All others bring data."* The strategic-management process can be described as an objective, logical, systematic approach for making major decisions in an organization. It attempts to organize qualitative and quantitative information in a way that allows effective decisions to be made under conditions of uncertainty. Yet strategic management is not a pure science that lends itself to a nice, neat, one-two-three approach.

Based on past experiences, judgment, and feelings, most people recognize that *intuition* is essential to making good strategic decisions. Intuition is particularly useful for making decisions in situations of great uncertainty or little precedent. It is also helpful when highly interrelated variables exist or when it is necessary to choose from several plausible alternatives. Some managers and owners of businesses profess to have extraordinary abilities for using intuition alone in devising brilliant strategies. For example, Will Durant, who organized GM, was described by Alfred Sloan as "a man who would proceed on a course of action guided solely, as far as I could tell, by some intuitive flash of brilliance. He never felt obliged to make an engineering hunt for the facts. Yet at times, he was astoundingly correct in his judgment."[3] Albert Einstein acknowledged the importance of intuition when he said, "I believe in intuition and inspiration. At times I feel certain that I am right while not knowing the reason. Imagination is more important than knowledge, because knowledge is limited, whereas imagination embraces the entire world."[4]

Although some organizations today may survive and prosper because they have intuitive geniuses managing them, most are not so fortunate. Most organizations can benefit from strategic management, which is based upon integrating intuition and analysis in decision making. Choosing an intuitive or analytic approach to decision making is not an either–or proposition. Managers at all levels in an organization inject their intuition and judgment into strategic-management analyses. Analytical thinking and intuitive thinking complement each other.

Operating from the I've-already-made-up-my-mind-don't-bother-me-with-the-facts mode is not management by intuition; it is management by ignorance.[5] Drucker says, "I believe in intuition only if you discipline it. 'Hunch' artists, who make a diagnosis but don't check it out with the facts, are the ones in medicine who kill people, and in management kill businesses."[6] As Henderson notes:

> The accelerating rate of change today is producing a business world in which customary managerial habits in organizations are increasingly inadequate. Experience alone was an adequate guide when changes could be made in small increments. But intuitive and experience-based management philosophies are grossly inadequate when decisions are strategic and have major, irreversible consequences.[7]

In a sense, the strategic-management process is an attempt both to duplicate what goes on in the mind of a brilliant, intuitive person who knows the business and to couple it with analysis.

Adapting to Change

The strategic-management process is based on the belief that organizations should continually monitor internal and external events and trends so that timely changes can be made as needed. The rate and magnitude of changes that affect organizations are increasing dramatically, as evidenced by how the global economic recession has caught so many firms by surprise. Firms, like organisms, must be "adept at adapting" or they will not survive.

For 30 years, Lowe's Company and Home Depot Inc. have been and remain fierce competitors trying to adapt better than the other to changing consumer needs. Home Depot is the larger firm and is reporting faster growing revenues and profits, but Lowe's CEO Robert Niblock says his company is moving quickly to showcase tools and appliances on the Internet as expertly as in stores. Lowe's revenues are about $49 billion annually compared to Home Depot's $68 billion. Home Depot's CEO Frank Blake has recently added 19 centralized distribution centers so store workers can spend more time waiting on shoppers. Both firms are hiring thousands of part-time workers, transitioning away from full-time employees, to keep labor costs down and create a price competitive advantage.

The second-largest bookstore chain in the United States, Borders Group, declared bankruptcy in 2011 as the firm had not adapted well to changes in book retailing from traditional bookstore shopping to customers buying online, preferring digital books to hard copies, and even renting rather than buying books. Borders is second in number of stores behind Barnes & Noble, which also is struggling to survive in an industry rapidly going digital and moving away from brick-and-mortar stores. Based in Ann Arbor, Michigan, Borders Group operates 676 stores nationwide, but was on the brink of financial collapse before being acquired in July 2011 by Direct Brands, a division of Phoenix, Arizona–based Najafi Companies.

To survive, all organizations must astutely identify and adapt to change. The strategic-management process is aimed at allowing organizations to adapt effectively to change over the long run. As Waterman has noted:

> In today's business environment, more than in any preceding era, the only constant is change. Successful organizations effectively manage change, continuously adapting their bureaucracies, strategies, systems, products, and cultures to survive the shocks and prosper from the forces that decimate the competition.[8]

Online social networking, rising food prices, and high energy prices are external changes that are transforming business and society today. On a political map, the boundaries between countries may be clear, but on a competitive map showing the real flow of financial and industrial activity, the boundaries have largely disappeared. The speedy flow of information has eaten away at national boundaries so that people worldwide readily see for themselves how other people live and work. We have become a borderless world with global citizens, global competitors, global customers, global suppliers, and global distributors! U.S. firms are challenged by large rival companies in many industries. To say U.S. firms are being challenged in the automobile industry is an understatement. But this situation is true in many industries.

The need to adapt to change leads organizations to key strategic-management questions, such as "What kind of business should we become?" "Are we in the right field(s)?" "Should we reshape our business?" "What new competitors are entering our industry?" "What strategies should we pursue?" "How are our customers changing?" "Are new technologies being developed that could put us out of business?"

The Internet has changed the way we organize our lives; inhabit our homes; and relate to and interact with family, friends, neighbors, and even ourselves. The Internet promotes endless comparison shopping, which thus enables consumers worldwide to band together to demand discounts. The Internet has transferred power from businesses to individuals. Buyers used to face big obstacles when attempting to get the best price and service, such as limited time and data to compare, but now consumers can quickly scan hundreds of vendor offerings. Both the number of people shopping online and the average amount they spend is increasing dramatically. Digital communication has become the name of the game in marketing. Consumers today are flocking to blogs, short-post forums such as Twitter, video sites such as YouTube, and social networking sites such as Facebook, Myspace, and LinkedIn instead of television, radio, newspapers, and magazines. Facebook and Myspace recently unveiled features that further marry these social sites to the wider Internet. Users on these social sites now can log on to many business shopping sites with their IDs from their social site so their friends can see what items they have purchased on various shopping sites. Both of these social sites want their members to use their IDs to manage all their online identities. Most traditional retailers have learned that their online sales can boost in-store sales as they utilize their websites to promote in-store promotions.

Key Terms in Strategic Management

Before we further discuss strategic management, we should define nine key terms: competitive advantage, strategists, vision and mission statements, external opportunities and threats, internal strengths and weaknesses, long-term objectives, strategies, annual objectives, and policies.

Competitive Advantage

Strategic management is all about gaining and maintaining *competitive advantage.* This term can be defined as "anything that a firm does especially well compared to rival firms." When a firm can do something that rival firms cannot do, or owns something that rival firms desire, that can represent a competitive advantage. For example, having ample cash on the firm's balance sheet can provide a major competitive advantage. Some cash-rich firms are buying distressed rivals. For example, Dish Network Corp. in mid-2011 acquired (for $1 billion) the satellite company DBSD North America based in Reston, Virginia, which was operating under bankruptcy protection. The acquisition gave Dish Network access to varied broadband spectrums. Dish Network is also trying to acquire bankrupt satellite operator Terrestar Networks, which would allow Dish Network to launch mobile video or satellite Internet services.

Having less fixed assets than rival firms also can provide major competitive advantages in a global recession. For example, Apple has no manufacturing facilities of its own, and rival Sony has 57 electronics factories. Apple relies exclusively on contract manufacturers for production of all of its products, whereas Sony owns its own plants. Less fixed assets has enabled Apple to remain financially lean with virtually no long-term debt. Sony, in contrast, has built up massive debt on its balance sheet.

CEO Paco Underhill of Envirosell says, "Where it used to be a polite war, it's now a 21st-century bar fight, where everybody is competing with everyone else for the customers' money." Shoppers are "trading down," so Nordstrom is taking customers from Neiman Marcus and Saks Fifth Avenue, T.J. Maxx and Marshalls are taking customers from most other stores in the mall, and Family Dollar is taking revenues from Wal-Mart.[9] Getting and keeping competitive advantage is essential for long-term success in an organization. In mass retailing, big-box companies such as Wal-Mart, Best Buy, and Sears are losing competitive advantage to smaller stores, so there is a dramatic shift in mass retailing to becoming smaller. For example, Best Buy opened 150 of its small-format Best Buy Mobile stores in 2011. Home Depot is selling off portions of its parking lots to fast-food chains and auto repair shops. Sears in Greensboro, North Carolina, just leased 34,000 square feet of its space to Whole Foods Market, which is set to open in 2012. As customers shift more to online purchases, less brick and mortar is definitely better for sustaining competitive advantage in retailing. Even Wal-Mart began in mid-2011 to open Wal-Mart Express stores of less than 40,000 square feet each, rather than 185,000-square-foot Supercenters. Office Depot's new 5,000-square-foot stores are dramatically smaller than their traditional stores.

Normally, a firm can sustain a competitive advantage for only a certain period due to rival firms imitating and undermining that advantage. Thus it is not adequate to simply obtain competitive advantage. A firm must strive to achieve *sustained competitive advantage* by (1) continually adapting to changes in external trends and events and internal capabilities, competencies, and resources; and by (2) effectively formulating, implementing, and evaluating strategies that capitalize upon those factors.

An increasing number of companies are gaining a competitive advantage by using the Internet for direct selling and for communication with suppliers, customers, creditors, partners, shareholders, clients, and competitors who may be dispersed globally. E-commerce allows firms to sell products, advertise, purchase supplies, bypass intermediaries, track inventory, eliminate paperwork, and share information. In total, e-commerce is minimizing the expense and cumbersomeness of time, distance, and space in doing business, thus yielding better customer service, greater efficiency, improved products, and higher profitability.

The social network company Myspace was acquired in June 2011 by Specific Media based in Irvine, California. Previously owned by Beverly Hills-based News Corp., Myspace is being battered by the rapid rise of rival Facebook. Myspace's customer base dropped to 80 million at the start of 2011 from well over 100 million a year earlier, while Facebook customers at the same time numbered 500 million, up from about 350 million. Analyst Jeremiah Owyang at market research firm Altimeter Group said: "The end was in sight for Myspace before former CEO Chris DeWolfe left. The company did not innovate for years, while Facebook did. It comes down to culture and leadership. Myspace did not evolve its business model. It stuck with its young demographic, and made minimal changes until it was too late."[10]

Strategists

Strategists are the individuals who are most responsible for the success or failure of an organization. Strategists have various job titles, such as chief executive officer, president, owner, chair of the board, executive director, chancellor, dean, or entrepreneur. Jay Conger, professor of organizational behavior at the London Business School and author of *Building Leaders,* says, "All strategists have to be chief learning officers. We are in an extended period of change. If our leaders aren't highly adaptive and great models during this period, then our companies won't adapt either, because ultimately leadership is about being a role model."

Strategists help an organization gather, analyze, and organize information. They track industry and competitive trends, develop forecasting models and scenario analyses, evaluate corporate and divisional performance, spot emerging market opportunities, identify business threats, and develop creative action plans. Strategic planners usually serve in a support or staff role. Usually found in higher levels of management, they typically have considerable authority for decision making in the firm. The CEO is the most visible and critical strategic manager. Any manager who has responsibility for a unit or division, responsibility for profit and loss outcomes, or direct authority over a major piece of the business is a strategic manager (strategist). In the last five years, the position of chief strategy officer (CSO) has emerged as a new addition to the top management ranks of many organizations, including Sun Microsystems, Network Associates, Clarus, Lante, Marimba, Sapient, Commerce One, BBDO, Cadbury Schweppes, General Motors, Ellie Mae, Cendant, Charles Schwab, Tyco, Campbell Soup, Morgan Stanley, and Reed-Elsevier. This corporate officer title represents recognition of the growing importance of strategic planning in business. Franz Koch, the CSO of German sportswear company Puma AG, was promoted to CEO of Puma in mid-2011. When asked about his plans for the company, Mr. Koch said on a conference call "I plan to just focus on the long-term strategic plan."

Strategists differ as much as organizations themselves, and these differences must be considered in the formulation, implementation, and evaluation of strategies. Some strategists will not consider some types of strategies because of their personal philosophies. Strategists differ in their attitudes, values, ethics, willingness to take risks, concern for social responsibility, concern for profitability, concern for short-run versus long-run aims, and management style. The founder of Hershey Foods, Milton Hershey, built the company to manage an orphanage. From corporate profits, Hershey Foods today cares for over a thousand boys and girls in its School for Orphans.

Vision and Mission Statements

Many organizations today develop a *vision statement* that answers the question "What do we want to become?" Developing a vision statement is often considered the first step in strategic planning, preceding even development of a mission statement. Many vision statements are a single sentence. For example, the vision statement of Stokes Eye Clinic in Florence, South Carolina, is "Our vision is to take care of your vision."

Mission statements are "enduring statements of purpose that distinguish one business from other similar firms. A mission statement identifies the scope of a firm's operations in product and market terms."[11] It addresses the basic question that faces all strategists: "What is our business?" A clear mission statement describes the values and priorities of an organization. Developing a mission statement compels strategists to think about the nature and scope of present operations and to assess the potential attractiveness of future markets and activities. A mission statement broadly charts the future direction of an organization. A mission statement is a constant reminder to its employees of why the organization exists and what the founders envisioned when they put their fame and fortune at risk to breathe life into their dreams.

External Opportunities and Threats

External opportunities and *external threats* refer to economic, social, cultural, demographic, environmental, political, legal, governmental, technological, and competitive trends and events that could significantly benefit or harm an organization in the future. Opportunities and threats are largely beyond the control of a single organization—thus the word *external*. A few opportunities and threats that face many firms are listed here:

- Availability of capital can no longer be taken for granted.
- Consumers expect green operations and products.
- Marketing moving rapidly to the Internet.
- Commodity food prices are increasing.
- Political unrest in the Middle East is raising oil prices.
- Computer hacker problems are increasing.
- Intense price competition is plaguing most firms.
- Unemployment and underemployment rates remain high.
- Interest rates are rising.
- Product life cycles are becoming shorter.
- State and local governments are financially weak.
- Turmoil and violence in Mexico is increasing.
- Winters are colder and summers hotter than usual.
- Home prices remain exceptionally low.
- Global markets offer the highest growth in revenues.

The types of changes mentioned above are creating a different type of consumer and consequently a need for different types of products, services, and strategies. Many companies in many industries face the severe external threat of online sales capturing increasing market share in their industry.

Other opportunities and threats may include the passage of a law, the introduction of a new product by a competitor, a national catastrophe, or the declining value of the dollar. A competitor's strength could be a threat. Unrest in the Middle East, rising energy costs, or social media networking could represent an opportunity or a threat.

A basic tenet of strategic management is that firms need to formulate strategies to take advantage of external opportunities and to avoid or reduce the impact of external threats. For this reason, identifying, monitoring, and evaluating external opportunities and threats are essential for success. This process of conducting research and gathering and assimilating external information is sometimes called *environmental scanning* or industry analysis. Lobbying is one activity that some organizations utilize to influence external opportunities and threats.

Internal Strengths and Weaknesses

Internal strengths and *internal weaknesses* are an organization's controllable activities that are performed especially well or poorly. They arise in the management, marketing, finance/accounting, production/operations, research and development, and management information systems activities of a business. Identifying and evaluating organizational strengths and weaknesses in the functional areas of a business is an essential strategic-management activity. Organizations strive to pursue strategies that capitalize on internal strengths and eliminate internal weaknesses.

Strengths and weaknesses are determined relative to competitors. *Relative deficiency or superiority is important information.* Also, strengths and weaknesses can be determined by elements of being rather than performance. For example, a strength may involve ownership of natural resources or a historic reputation for quality. Strengths and weaknesses may be determined relative to a firm's own objectives. For example, high levels of inventory turnover may not be a strength to a firm that seeks never to stock-out.

Internal factors can be determined in a number of ways, including computing ratios, measuring performance, and comparing to past periods and industry averages. Various types of surveys also can be developed and administered to examine internal factors such as employee morale, production efficiency, advertising effectiveness, and customer loyalty.

Long-Term Objectives

Objectives can be defined as specific results that an organization seeks to achieve in pursuing its basic mission. *Long-term* means more than one year. Objectives are essential for organizational success because they state direction; aid in evaluation; create synergy; reveal priorities; focus coordination; and provide a basis for effective planning, organizing, motivating, and controlling activities. Objectives should be challenging, measurable, consistent, reasonable, and clear. In a multidimensional firm, objectives should be established for the overall company and for each division.

Strategies

Strategies are the means by which long-term objectives will be achieved. Business strategies may include geographic expansion, diversification, acquisition, product development, market penetration, retrenchment, divestiture, liquidation, and joint ventures. Strategies currently being pursued by some companies are described in Table 1-1.

Strategies are potential actions that require top management decisions and large amounts of the firm's resources. In addition, strategies affect an organization's long-term prosperity, typically for at least five years, and thus are future-oriented. Strategies have multifunctional or multidivisional consequences and require consideration of both the external and internal factors facing the firm.

Annual Objectives

Annual objectives are short-term milestones that organizations must achieve to reach long-term objectives. Like long-term objectives, annual objectives should be measurable, quantitative, challenging, realistic, consistent, and prioritized. They should be established at the corporate, divisional, and functional levels in a large organization. Annual objectives should be stated in terms of management, marketing, finance/accounting, production/operations, research and

TABLE 1-1 **Sample Strategies in Action in 2011**

Skype

Headquartered in Luxembourg and acquired by Microsoft Corporation in 2011, Skype offers software applications that enable users to make voice calls over the Internet as well as video conferencing, instant messaging, and file transfer. Wildly popular among people who regularly make international calls, Skype audio conferences support up to 25 people at a time, including the host. Skype 3.0, recently released for Apple's iOS platform, offers video chat for the iPhone, iPad, and iPod Touch devices. Skype recently acquired Qik, a mobile video streaming and storage company, and partnered with Sony and Panasonic to create Skype-ready Blu-ray players. Skype now accounts for more than 25 percent of all international calls, up from 13 percent in 2009. The mobile-based video call market is expected to exceed $1 billion by 2015.

Sbarro Inc.

The fast-food Italian eatery located in many mall food courts around the world is struggling to survive and swamped in debt. Based in Melville, New York, Sbarro is closing weak stores among its 1,000 total in 40 countries, including Qatar, Egypt, and New Zealand. Sbarro has hired bankruptcy and restructuring lawyers to help the firm survive as many consumers have switched, for various reasons, to other mall fast food choices, such as Chick-fil-A. Sbarro needs a clear strategic plan to survive.

Target Corp.

The Minneapolis-based mass retailer expanded into Canada for the first time in 2012, converting about 150 of its acquired Zellers stores into Target stores. With 1,752 stores in the United States, Target is a latecomer to Canada; Wal-Mart and Sears have been in Canada for years. Most of Target's new Canadian stores will be in highly urban areas such as Vancouver, Montreal, Ottawa, Edmonton, and Calgary. Reportedly about 70 percent of Canadians are already familiar with the Target brand.

Caesars Entertainment

Formerly named Harrah's Entertainment, this gaming company for the first time ever is establishing noncasino hotels in Asia, following in the footsteps of its major competitor MGM Resorts International. Both firms are shut out from gaining gambling licenses to operate in Macau and Singapore. Since the U.S. gaming market remains sluggish, Caesars is anxious to take advantage of high growth in China, India, and Vietnam. Caesars plans initially to "manage rather than own" the hotels that soon will use its brand name across Asia.

development, and management information systems (MIS) accomplishments. A set of annual objectives is needed for each long-term objective. Annual objectives are especially important in strategy implementation, whereas long-term objectives are particularly important in strategy formulation. Annual objectives represent the basis for allocating resources.

Policies

Policies are the means by which annual objectives will be achieved. Policies include guidelines, rules, and procedures established to support efforts to achieve stated objectives. Policies are guides to decision making and address repetitive or recurring situations.

Policies are most often stated in terms of management, marketing, finance/accounting, production/operations, research and development, and MIS activities. Policies can be established at the corporate level and apply to an entire organization at the divisional level and apply to a single division, or they can be established at the functional level and apply to particular operational activities or departments. Policies, like annual objectives, are especially important in strategy implementation because they outline an organization's expectations of its employees and managers. Policies allow consistency and coordination within and between organizational departments.

Substantial research suggests that a healthier workforce can more effectively and efficiently implement strategies. Smoking has become a heavy burden for Europe's state-run social welfare systems, with smoking-related diseases costing well over $100 billion a year. Smoking also is a huge burden on companies worldwide, so firms are continually implementing policies to curtail smoking. Table 1-2 gives a ranking of some countries by percentage of people who smoke.

Hotel/motels in the United States are rapidly going "smoke-free throughout" with more than 13,000 now having this policy. The American Hotel and Lodging Association says there are 50,800

TABLE 1-2   Percentage of People Who Smoke in Selected Countries

Country	Percentage
Greece	50
Russia	High
Austria	
Spain	
U.K.	
France	
Germany	
Italy	
Belgium	
Switzerland	Low
USA	19

Source: Based on Christina Passariello, "Smoking Culture Persists in Europe, Despite Bans," *Wall Street Journal*, January 2, 2009, A5.

hotel/motels in the United States with 15 or more rooms. All Marriotts are now nonsmoking. Almost all car rental companies are exclusively nonsmoking, including Avis, Dollar, Thrifty, and Budget. These four rental car companies charge a $250 cleaning fee if a customer smokes in their rental vehicle.

The Strategic-Management Model

The strategic-management process can best be studied and applied using a model. Every model represents some kind of process. The framework illustrated in Figure 1-1 is a widely accepted, comprehensive model of the strategic-management process.[12] This model does not guarantee success, but it does represent a clear and practical approach for formulating, implementing, and evaluating strategies. Relationships among major components of the strategic-management process are shown in the model, which appears in all subsequent chapters with appropriate areas shaped to show the particular focus of each chapter. These are three important questions to answer in developing a strategic plan:

Where are we now?

Where do we want to go?

How are we going to get there?

Identifying an organization's existing vision, mission, objectives, and strategies is the logical starting point for strategic management because a firm's present situation and condition may preclude certain strategies and may even dictate a particular course of action. Every organization has a vision, mission, objectives, and strategy, even if these elements are not consciously designed, written, or communicated. The answer to where an organization is going can be determined largely by where the organization has been!

The strategic-management process is dynamic and continuous. A change in any one of the major components in the model can necessitate a change in any or all of the other components. For instance, third-world countries coming online could represent a major opportunity and require a change in long-term objectives and strategies; a failure to accomplish annual objectives could require a change in policy; or a major competitor's change in strategy could require a change in the firm's mission. Therefore, strategy formulation, implementation, and evaluation activities should be performed on a continual basis, not just at the end of the year or semiannually. The strategic-management process never really ends.

Note in the *strategic-management model* that business ethics/social responsibility/ environmental sustainability issues impact all activities in the model as described in full in Chapter 10. Also, note in the model that global/international issues also impact virtually all strategic decisions today, as described in detail in Chapter 11.

FIGURE 1-1

A Comprehensive Strategic-Management Model

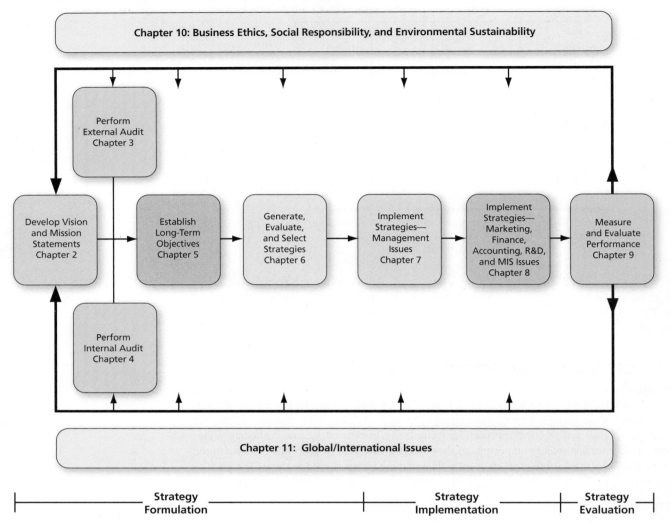

Source: Fred R. David, "How Companies Define Their Mission," *Long Range Planning* 22, no. 3 (June 1988): 40.

The strategic-management process is not as cleanly divided and neatly performed in practice as the strategic-management model suggests. Strategists do not go through the process in lockstep fashion. Generally, there is give-and-take among hierarchical levels of an organization. Many organizations semiannually conduct formal meetings to discuss and update the firm's vision/mission, opportunities/threats, strengths/weaknesses, strategies, objectives, policies, and performance. These meetings are commonly held off-premises and are called *retreats*. The rationale for periodically conducting strategic-management meetings away from the work site is to encourage more creativity and candor from participants. Good communication and feedback are needed throughout the strategic-management process.

Application of the strategic-management process is typically more formal in larger and well-established organizations. Formality refers to the extent that participants, responsibilities, authority, duties, and approach are specified. Smaller businesses tend to be less formal. Firms that compete in complex, rapidly changing environments, such as technology companies, tend to be more formal in strategic planning. Firms that have many divisions, products, markets, and technologies also tend to be more formal in applying strategic-management concepts. Greater formality in applying the strategic-management process is usually positively associated with the cost, comprehensiveness, accuracy, and success of planning across all types and sizes of organizations.[13]

Benefits of Strategic Management

Strategic management allows an organization to be more proactive than reactive in shaping its own future; it allows an organization to initiate and influence (rather than just respond to) activities—and thus to exert control over its own destiny. Small business owners, chief executive officers, presidents, and managers of many for-profit and nonprofit organizations have recognized and realized the benefits of strategic management.

Historically, the principal benefit of strategic management has been to help organizations formulate better strategies through the use of a more systematic, logical, and rational approach to strategic choice. This certainly continues to be a major benefit of strategic management, but research studies now indicate that the process, rather than the decision or document, is the more important contribution of strategic management.[14] *Communication is a key to successful strategic management.* Through involvement in the process, in other words, through dialogue and participation, managers and employees become committed to supporting the organization. Figure 1-2 illustrates this intrinsic benefit of a firm engaging in strategic planning. Note that all firms need all employees on a mission to help the firm succeed.

The manner in which strategic management is carried out is thus exceptionally important. A major aim of the process is to achieve the understanding of and commitment from all managers and employees. Understanding may be the most important benefit of strategic management, followed by commitment. When managers and employees understand what the organization is doing and why, they often feel they are a part of the firm and become committed to assisting it. This is especially true when employees also understand linkages between their own compensation and organizational performance. Managers and employees become surprisingly creative and innovative when they understand and support the firm's mission, objectives, and strategies. A great benefit of strategic management, then, is the opportunity that the process provides to empower individuals. *Empowerment* is the act of strengthening employees' sense of effectiveness by encouraging them to participate in decision making and to exercise initiative and imagination, and rewarding them for doing so.

Strategic planning is a learning, helping, educating, and supporting process, not merely a paper-shuffling activity among top executives. Strategic-management dialogue is more important than a nicely bound strategic-management document.[15] The worst thing strategists can do is develop strategic plans themselves and then present them to operating managers to execute. Through involvement in the process, line managers become "owners" of the strategy. Ownership of strategies by the people who have to execute them is a key to success!

Although making good strategic decisions is the major responsibility of an organization's owner or chief executive officer, both managers and employees must also be involved in strategy formulation, implementation, and evaluation activities. Participation is a key to gaining commitment for needed changes.

An increasing number of corporations and institutions are using strategic management to make effective decisions. But strategic management is not a guarantee for success; it can be dysfunctional if conducted haphazardly.

Financial Benefits

Research indicates that organizations that use strategic-management concepts are more profitable and successful than those that do not.[16] Businesses using strategic-management concepts show significant improvement in sales, profitability, and productivity compared to firms without systematic

FIGURE 1-2

Benefits to a Firm That Does Strategic Planning

planning activities. High-performing firms tend to do systematic planning to prepare for future fluctuations in their external and internal environments. Firms with planning systems more closely resembling strategic-management theory generally exhibit superior long-term financial performance relative to their industry.

High-performing firms seem to make more informed decisions with good anticipation of both short- and long-term consequences. In contrast, firms that perform poorly often engage in activities that are shortsighted and do not reflect good forecasting of future conditions. Strategists of low-performing organizations are often preoccupied with solving internal problems and meeting paperwork deadlines. They typically underestimate their competitors' strengths and overestimate their own firm's strengths. They often attribute weak performance to uncontrollable factors such as a poor economy, technological change, or foreign competition.

More than 100,000 businesses in the United States fail annually. Business failures include bankruptcies, foreclosures, liquidations, and court-mandated receiverships. Although many factors besides a lack of effective strategic management can lead to business failure, the planning concepts and tools described in this text can yield substantial financial benefits for any organization.

Nonfinancial Benefits

Besides helping firms avoid financial demise, strategic management offers other tangible benefits, such as an enhanced awareness of external threats, an improved understanding of competitors' strategies, increased employee productivity, reduced resistance to change, and a clearer understanding of performance–reward relationships. Strategic management enhances the problem-prevention capabilities of organizations because it promotes interaction among managers at all divisional and functional levels. Firms that have nurtured their managers and employees, shared organizational objectives with them, empowered them to help improve the product or service, and recognized their contributions can turn to them for help in a pinch because of this interaction.

In addition to empowering managers and employees, strategic management often brings order and discipline to an otherwise floundering firm. It can be the beginning of an efficient and effective managerial system. Strategic management may renew confidence in the current business strategy or point to the need for corrective actions. The strategic-management process provides a basis for identifying and rationalizing the need for change to all managers and employees of a firm; it helps them view change as an opportunity rather than as a threat.

Greenley stated that strategic management offers the following benefits:

1. It allows for identification, prioritization, and exploitation of opportunities.
2. It provides an objective view of management problems.
3. It represents a framework for improved coordination and control of activities.
4. It minimizes the effects of adverse conditions and changes.
5. It allows major decisions to better support established objectives.
6. It allows more effective allocation of time and resources to identified opportunities.
7. It allows fewer resources and less time to be devoted to correcting erroneous or ad hoc decisions.
8. It creates a framework for internal communication among personnel.
9. It helps integrate the behavior of individuals into a total effort.
10. It provides a basis for clarifying individual responsibilities.
11. It encourages forward thinking.
12. It provides a cooperative, integrated, and enthusiastic approach to tackling problems and opportunities.
13. It encourages a favorable attitude toward change.
14. It gives a degree of discipline and formality to the management of a business.[17]

Why Some Firms Do No Strategic Planning

Some firms do not engage in strategic planning, and some firms do strategic planning but receive no support from managers and employees. Some reasons for poor or no strategic planning are as follows:

- *Lack of knowledge or experience in strategic planning*—No training in strategic planning.
- *Poor reward structures*—When an organization assumes success, it often fails to reward success. When failure occurs, then the firm may punish.

- *Firefighting*—An organization can be so deeply embroiled in resolving crises and fire-fighting that it reserves no time for planning.
- *Waste of time*—Some firms see planning as a waste of time because no marketable product is produced. Time spent on planning is an investment.
- *Too expensive*—Some organizations see planning as too expensive in time and money.
- *Laziness*—People may not want to put forth the effort needed to formulate a plan.
- *Content with success*—Particularly if a firm is successful, individuals may feel there is no need to plan because things are fine as they stand. But success today does not guarantee success tomorrow.
- *Fear of failure*—By not taking action, there is little risk of failure unless a problem is urgent and pressing. Whenever something worthwhile is attempted, there is some risk of failure.
- *Overconfidence*—As managers amass experience, they may rely less on formalized planning. Rarely, however, is this appropriate. Being overconfident or overestimating experience can bring demise. Forethought is rarely wasted and is often the mark of professionalism.
- *Prior bad experience*—People may have had a previous bad experience with planning, that is, cases in which plans have been long, cumbersome, impractical, or inflexible. Planning, like anything else, can be done badly.
- *Self-interest*—When someone has achieved status, privilege, or self-esteem through effectively using an old system, he or she often sees a new plan as a threat.
- *Fear of the unknown*—People may be uncertain of their abilities to learn new skills, of their aptitude with new systems, or of their ability to take on new roles.
- *Honest difference of opinion*—People may sincerely believe the plan is wrong. They may view the situation from a different viewpoint, or they may have aspirations for themselves or the organization that are different from the plan. Different people in different jobs have different perceptions of a situation.
- *Suspicion*—Employees may not trust management.[18]

Pitfalls in Strategic Planning

Strategic planning is an involved, intricate, and complex process that takes an organization into uncharted territory. It does not provide a ready-to-use prescription for success; instead, it takes the organization through a journey and offers a framework for addressing questions and solving problems. Being aware of potential pitfalls and being prepared to address them is essential to success.

Some pitfalls to watch for and avoid in strategic planning are these:

- Using strategic planning to gain control over decisions and resources
- Doing strategic planning only to satisfy accreditation or regulatory requirements
- Too hastily moving from mission development to strategy formulation
- Failing to communicate the plan to employees, who continue working in the dark
- Top managers making many intuitive decisions that conflict with the formal plan
- Top managers not actively supporting the strategic-planning process
- Failing to use plans as a standard for measuring performance
- Delegating planning to a "planner" rather than involving all managers
- Failing to involve key employees in all phases of planning
- Failing to create a collaborative climate supportive of change
- Viewing planning as unnecessary or unimportant
- Becoming so engrossed in current problems that insufficient or no planning is done
- Being so formal in planning that flexibility and creativity are stifled[19]

Guidelines for Effective Strategic Management

Failing to follow certain guidelines in conducting strategic management can foster criticisms of the process and create problems for the organization. Issues such as "Is strategic management in our firm a people process or a paper process?" should be addressed.

Even the most technically perfect strategic plan will serve little purpose if it is not implemented. Many organizations tend to spend an inordinate amount of time, money, and effort on developing the strategic plan, treating the means and circumstances under which it will be implemented as afterthoughts! Change comes through implementation and evaluation, not through the plan. A technically imperfect plan that is implemented well will achieve more than the perfect plan that never gets off the paper on which it is typed.[20]

Strategic management must not become a self-perpetuating bureaucratic mechanism. Rather, it must be a self-reflective learning process that familiarizes managers and employees in the organization with key strategic issues and feasible alternatives for resolving those issues. Strategic management must not become ritualistic, stilted, orchestrated, or too formal, predictable, and rigid. Words supported by numbers, rather than numbers supported by words, should represent the medium for explaining strategic issues and organizational responses. A key role of strategists is to facilitate continuous organizational learning and change.

R. T. Lenz offered some important guidelines for effective strategic management:

Keep the strategic-management process as simple and nonroutine as possible. Eliminate jargon and arcane planning language. Remember, strategic management is a process for fostering learning and action, not merely a formal system for control. To avoid routinized behavior, vary assignments, team membership, meeting formats, and the planning calendar. The process should not be totally predictable, and settings must be changed to stimulate creativity. Emphasize word-oriented plans with numbers as back-up material. If managers cannot express their strategy in a paragraph or so, they either do not have one or do not understand it. Stimulate thinking and action that challenge the assumptions underlying current corporate strategy. Welcome bad news. If strategy is not working, managers desperately need to know it. Further, no pertinent information should be classified as inadmissible merely because it cannot be quantified. Build a corporate culture in which the role of strategic management and its essential purposes are understood. Do not permit "technicians" to co-opt the process. It is ultimately a process for learning and action. Speak of it in these terms. Attend to psychological, social, and political dimensions, as well as the information infrastructure and administrative procedures supporting it.[21]

An important guideline for effective strategic management is open-mindedness. A willingness and eagerness to consider new information, new viewpoints, new ideas, and new possibilities is essential; all organizational members must share a spirit of inquiry and learning. Strategists such as chief executive officers, presidents, owners of small businesses, and heads of government agencies must commit themselves to listen to and understand managers' positions well enough to be able to restate those positions to the managers' satisfaction. In addition, managers and employees throughout the firm should be able to describe the strategists' positions to the satisfaction of the strategists. This degree of discipline will promote understanding and learning.

No organization has unlimited resources. No firm can take on an unlimited amount of debt or issue an unlimited amount of stock to raise capital. Therefore, no organization can pursue all the strategies that potentially could benefit the firm. Strategic decisions thus always have to be made to eliminate some courses of action and to allocate organizational resources among others. Most organizations can afford to pursue only a few corporate-level strategies at any given time. It is a critical mistake for managers to pursue too many strategies at the same time, thereby spreading the firm's resources so thin that all strategies are jeopardized. Joseph Charyk, CEO of the Communication Satellite Corporation (Comsat), said, "We have to face the cold fact that Comsat may not be able to do all it wants. We must make hard choices on which ventures to keep and which to fold."

Strategic decisions require trade-offs such as long-range versus short-range considerations or maximizing profits versus increasing shareholders' wealth. There are ethics issues too. Strategy trade-offs require subjective judgments and preferences. In many cases, a lack of objectivity in formulating strategy results in a loss of competitive posture and profitability. Most organizations today recognize that strategic-management concepts and techniques can enhance the effectiveness of decisions. Subjective factors such as attitudes toward risk, concern for social responsibility, and organizational culture will always affect strategy-formulation decisions, but organizations need to be as objective as possible in considering qualitative factors. Table 1-3 summarizes important guidelines for the strategic-planning process to be effective.

TABLE 1-3   Seventeen Guidelines for the Strategic-Planning Process to Be Effective

1. It should be a people process more than a paper process.
2. It should be a learning process for all managers and employees.
3. It should be words supported by numbers rather than numbers supported by words.
4. It should be simple and nonroutine.
5. It should vary assignments, team memberships, meeting formats, and even the planning calendar.
6. It should challenge the assumptions underlying the current corporate strategy.
7. It should welcome bad news.
8. It should welcome open-mindness and a spirit of inquiry and learning.
9. It should not be a bureaucratic mechanism.
10. It should not become ritualistic, stilted, or orchestrated.
11. It should not be too formal, predictable, or rigid.
12. It should not contain jargon or arcane planning language.
13. It should not be a formal system for control.
14. It should not disregard qualitative information.
15. It should not be controlled by "technicians."
16. Do not pursue too many strategies at once.
17. Continually strengthen the "good ethics is good business" policy.

Comparing Business and Military Strategy

A strong military heritage underlies the study of strategic management. Terms such as *objectives, mission, strengths*, and *weaknesses* first were formulated to address problems on the battlefield. According to *Webster's New World Dictionary,* strategy is "the science of planning and directing large-scale military operations, of maneuvering forces into the most advantageous position prior to actual engagement with the enemy." The word *strategy* comes from the Greek *strategos,* which refers to a military general and combines *stratos* (the army) and *ago* (to lead). The history of strategic planning began in the military. A key aim of both business and military strategy is "to gain competitive advantage." In many respects, business strategy is like military strategy, and military strategists have learned much over the centuries that can benefit business strategists today. Both business and military organizations try to use their own strengths to exploit competitors' weaknesses. If an organization's overall strategy is wrong (ineffective), then all the efficiency in the world may not be enough to allow success. Business or military success is generally not the happy result of accidental strategies. Rather, success is the product of both continuous attention to changing external and internal conditions and the formulation and implementation of insightful adaptations to those conditions. The element of surprise provides great competitive advantages in both military and business strategy; information systems that provide data on opponents' or competitors' strategies and resources are also vitally important.

Of course, a fundamental difference between military and business strategy is that business strategy is formulated, implemented, and evaluated with an assumption of *competition,* whereas military strategy is based on an assumption of *conflict.* Nonetheless, military conflict and business competition are so similar that many strategic-management techniques apply equally to both. Business strategists have access to valuable insights that military thinkers have refined over time. Superior strategy formulation and implementation can overcome an opponent's superiority in numbers and resources.

Both business and military organizations must adapt to change and constantly improve to be successful. Too often, firms do not change their strategies when their environment and competitive conditions dictate the need to change. Gluck offered a classic military example of this:

When Napoleon won, it was because his opponents were committed to the strategy, tactics, and organization of earlier wars. When he lost—against Wellington, the Russians, and the Spaniards—it was because he, in turn, used tried-and-true strategies against enemies who thought afresh, who were developing the strategies not of the last war but of the next.[22]

Similarities can be construed from Sun Tzu's writings to the practice of formulating and implementing strategies among businesses today. Table 1-4 provides narrative excerpts from *The Art of War*. As you read through the table, consider which of the principles of war apply to business strategy as companies today compete aggressively to survive and grow.

Special Note to Students

In performing strategic management case analysis, emphasize throughout your project, beginning with the first page or slide, where your firm has competitive advantages and disadvantages. More importantly, emphasize throughout how you recommend the firm sustain and grow its competitive advantages and how you recommend the firm overcome its competitive disadvantages. Begin paving the way very early for what you ultimately recommend your firm should do over the next three

TABLE 1-4 Excerpts from Sun Tzu's *The Art of War* Writings

- War is a matter of vital importance to the state: a matter of life or death, the road either to survival or ruin. Hence, it is imperative that it be studied thoroughly.
- Warfare is based on deception. When near the enemy, make it seem that you are far away; when far away, make it seem that you are near. Hold out baits to lure the enemy. Strike the enemy when he is in disorder. Avoid the enemy when he is stronger. If your opponent is of choleric temper, try to irritate him. If he is arrogant, try to encourage his egotism. If enemy troops are well prepared after reorganization, try to wear them down. If they are united, try to sow dissension among them. Attack the enemy where he is unprepared, and appear where you are not expected. These are the keys to victory for a strategist. It is not possible to formulate them in detail beforehand.
- A speedy victory is the main object in war. If this is long in coming, weapons are blunted and morale depressed. When the army engages in protracted campaigns, the resources of the state will fall short. Thus, while we have heard of stupid haste in war, we have not yet seen a clever operation that was prolonged.
- Generally, in war the best policy is to take a state intact; to ruin it is inferior to this. To capture the enemy's entire army is better than to destroy it; to take intact a regiment, a company, or a squad is better than to destroy it. For to win one hundred victories in one hundred battles is not the epitome of skill. To subdue the enemy without fighting is the supreme excellence. Those skilled in war subdue the enemy's army without battle.
- The art of using troops is this: When ten to the enemy's one, surround him. When five times his strength, attack him. If double his strength, divide him. If equally matched, you may engage him with some good plan. If weaker, be capable of withdrawing. And if in all respects unequal, be capable of eluding him.
- Know your enemy and know yourself, and in a hundred battles you will never be defeated. When you are ignorant of the enemy but know yourself, your chances of winning or losing are equal. If ignorant both of your enemy and of yourself, you are sure to be defeated in every battle.
- He who occupies the field of battle first and awaits his enemy is at ease, and he who comes later to the scene and rushes into the fight is weary. And therefore, those skilled in war bring the enemy to the field of battle and are not brought there by him. Thus, when the enemy is at ease, be able to tire him; when well fed, be able to starve him; when at rest, be able to make him move.
- Analyze the enemy's plans so that you will know his shortcomings as well as his strong points. Agitate him to ascertain the pattern of his movement. Lure him out to reveal his dispositions and to ascertain his position. Launch a probing attack to learn where his strength is abundant and where deficient. It is according to the situation that plans are laid for victory, but the multitude does not comprehend this.
- An army may be likened to water, for just as flowing water avoids the heights and hastens to the lowlands, so an army should avoid strength and strike weakness. And as water shapes its flow in accordance with the ground, so an army manages its victory in accordance with the situation of the enemy. And as water has no constant form, there are in warfare no constant conditions. Thus, one able to win the victory by modifying his tactics in accordance with the enemy situation may be said to be divine.
- If you decide to go into battle, do not anounce your intentions or plans. Project "business as usual."
- Unskilled leaders work out their conflicts in courtrooms and battlefields. Brilliant strategists rarely go to battle or to court; they generally achieve their objectives through tactical positioning well in advance of any confrontation.
- When you do decide to challenge another company (or army), much calculating, estimating, analyzing, and positioning bring triumph. Little computation brings defeat.
- Skillful leaders do not let a strategy inhibit creative counter-movement. Nor should commands from those at a distance interfere with spontaneous maneuvering in the immediate situation.
- When a decisive advantage is gained over a rival, skillful leaders do not press on. They hold their position and give their rivals the opportunity to surrender or merge. They do not allow their forces to be damaged by those who have nothing to lose.
- Brilliant strategists forge ahead with illusion, obscuring the area(s) of major confrontation, so that opponents divide their forces in an attempt to defend many areas. Create the appearance of confusion, fear, or vulnerability so the opponent is helplessly drawn toward this illusion of advantage.

(Note: Substitute the words *strategy* or *strategic planning* for *war* or *warfare*)

Source: Based on *The Art of War* and from www.ccs.neu.edu/home/thigpen/html/art_of_war.html

years. The notion of competitive advantage should be integral to the discussion of every page or PowerPoint slide. Therefore, avoid being merely *descriptive* in your written or oral analysis; rather, be *prescriptive*, insightful, and forward-looking throughout your project.

Conclusion

All firms have a strategy, even if it is informal, unstructured, and sporadic. All organizations are heading somewhere, but unfortunately some organizations do not know where they are going. The old saying "If you do not know where you are going, then any road will lead you there!" accents the need for organizations to use strategic-management concepts and techniques. The strategic-management process is becoming more widely used by small firms, large companies, nonprofit institutions, governmental organizations, and multinational conglomerates alike. The process of empowering managers and employees has almost limitless benefits.

Organizations should take a proactive rather than a reactive approach in their industry, and they should strive to influence, anticipate, and initiate rather than just respond to events. The strategic-management process embodies this approach to decision making. It represents a logical, systematic, and objective approach for determining an enterprise's future direction. The stakes are generally too high for strategists to use intuition alone in choosing among alternative courses of action. Successful strategists take the time to think about their businesses, where they are with their businesses, and what they want to be as organizations—and then they implement programs and policies to get from where they are to where they want to be in a reasonable period of time.

It is a known and accepted fact that people and organizations that plan ahead are much more likely to become what they want to become than those that do not plan at all. A good strategist plans and controls his or her plans, whereas a bad strategist never plans and then tries to control people! This textbook is devoted to providing you with the tools necessary to be a good strategist.

Key Terms and Concepts

Annual Objectives (p. 41)
Competitive Advantage (p. 38)
Empowerment (p. 45)
Environmental Scanning (p. 41)
External Opportunities (p. 40)
External Threats (p. 40)
Internal Strengths (p. 41)
Internal Weaknesses (p. 41)
Intuition (p. 37)
Long-Range Planning (p. 35)
Long-Term Objectives (p. 41)
Mission Statements (p. 40)
Policies (p. 42)

Retreats (p. 44)
Strategic Management (p. 35)
Strategic-Management Model (p. 43)
Strategic-Management Process (p. 35)
Strategic Planning (p. 35)
Strategies (p. 41)
Strategists (p. 39)
Strategy Evaluation (p. 36)
Strategy Formulation (p. 35)
Strategy Implementation (p. 36)
Sustained Competitive Advantage (p. 39)
Vision Statement (p. 40)

Issues for Review and Discussion

1. Nokia has done very well in 2010–2011. Do you think that same strategy will be as effective going forward? Why?
2. Does Nokia have its strategic plan posted on its website? Should the company? Why or why not?
3. Compare and contrast the activities involved in strategy formulation versus strategy implementation.
4. Do you think the nature of gaining and sustaining competitive advantage for companies has permanently changed given the political and economic collapse of some Middle East and European countries?
5. There is a dramatic shift in mass retailing to become smaller. Give four reasons for this phenomena. Give four corporate examples of this.
6. Avoid being merely descriptive in your written or oral case analysis; rather, be prescriptive, insightful, and

forward-looking throughout your project. Discuss the meaning of this sentence.

7. Explain what Dale McConkey means when he says "plans are less important than planning" in the opening-chapter quotes.

8. In terms of developing a strategic plan, what does Edward Deming mean when he says "In God we trust. All others bring data."

9. Strategy formulation, implementation, and evaluation activities occur at what three hierarchical levels in a large organization?

10. What was Einstein's rationale for saying "Imagination is more important than knowledge." Do you agree with Einstein? Why?

11. What does Drucker mean when he says "I believe in intuition only if you discipline it." Do you agree with Drucker? Why?

12. Strategic management is all about gaining and maintaining competitive advantage. Explain and give three examples.

13. Based on the definition of strategists in Chapter 1, identify the top five strategists that you have ever personally spoken to and interacted with.

14. For your college or university, would collapse of the euro currency be a major threat or opportunity? Why? What is the probability in your view of such a collapse?

15. Strategic management is not a panacea for success. It can be dysfunctional if conducted haphazardly. Give five examples of potential "haphazard" aspects of the planning process.

16. Explain why an important guideline for effective strategic management is open-mindedness.

17. Explain how and why firms are today using social networking sites to gain competitive advantage.

18. Compare and contrast vision versus mission statements.

19. In your opinion, identify the top 10 external factors affecting your university. Rank your top 10 with one being most important.

20. In order of importance, rank the top six benefits of a firm engaging in strategic management.

21. In order of importance, rank the top six reasons that many firms do no strategic planning.

22. In order of importance, rank the top six guidelines to follow in conducting strategic management activities.

23. Discuss how relevant you think Sun Tzu's *Art of War* writings are for firms today in developing and carrying out a strategic plan.

24. Determine the ways and means that your college or university does strategic planning and report on these efforts to your class.

25. Go to the www.strategyclub.com website and describe the strategic planning products offered.

26. Compare and contrast the extent that strategic-planning concepts are used by companies in your country versus companies in the United States?

27. Would strategy formulation or strategy implementation concepts differ more across countries? Why?

28. Compare strategic planning with long range planning.

29. What are the three activities that comprise strategy evaluation? Why is strategy evaluation important even for successful firms?

30. Explain how a firm can achieve sustained competitive advantage.

31. Identify and give an overview of three social networking sites that firms are using to gain competitive advantage.

32. List six strategists that you know personally. Rank the six in terms of how effective you believe each person is in leading the organization he/she is associated with.

33. List six characteristics of objectives and give an example of each.

34. Conduct Internet research to determine what percentage of persons in your country smoke. What is the implication of this for firms in your country?

35. List four financial and four nonfinancial benefits of a firm engaging in strategic planning.

36. Compare business strategy and military strategy.

37. Strategic planning should be more a people process than a paper process. Explain.

38. Strategic planning should not be controlled by technicians. Explain.

39. According to Sun Tzu, warfare is based on deception. Should strategic planning be based on deception? Explain.

40. Sun Tzu says "Generally, in war the best policy is to take a state intact; to ruin it is inferior to this." Explain. Is this true in corporate strategic planning? Explain.

41. What is Nokia's competitive advantage? How can this advantage be sustained?

42. Are there any compelling reasons why the external audit and internal audit should not be conducted simultaneously?

43. Which stage of strategic management do you feel is most important? Why?

44. Should strategic planning be more open or closed, (i.e hidden or transparent)? Why?

45. Discuss the extent to which strategic planning concepts would be applicable to individuals managing their own lives.

Notes

1. Kathy Kiely, "Officials Say Auto CEOs Must Be Specific on Plans," *USA Today*, November 24, 2008, 3B.

2. Peter Drucker, *Management: Tasks, Responsibilities, and Practices* (New York: Harper & Row, 1974), 611.

3. Alfred Sloan, Jr., *Adventures of the White Collar Man* (New York: Doubleday, 1941), 104.

4. Quoted in Eugene Raudsepp, "Can You Trust Your Hunches?" *Management Review* 49, no. 4 (April 1960): 7.

5. Stephen Harper, "Intuition: What Separates Executives from Managers," *Business Horizons* 31, no. 5 (September–October 1988): 16.

6. Ron Nelson, "How to Be a Manager," *Success*, July–August 1985, 69.

7. Bruce Henderson, *Henderson on Corporate Strategy* (Boston: Abt Books, 1979), 6.

8. Robert Waterman, Jr., *The Renewal Factor: How the Best Get and Keep the Competitive Edge* (New York: Bantam, 1987). See also *BusinessWeek*, September 14, 1987, 100. Also, see *Academy of Management Executive* 3, no. 2 (May 1989): 115.

9. Jayne O'Donnell, "Shoppers Flock to Discount Stores," *USA Today*, February 25, 2009, B1.

10. Marc Saltzman, "Many Layoffs at Myspace Could Be Coming Soon," *USA Today*, January 4, 2011, 2B.

11. John Pearce II and Fred David, "The Bottom Line on Corporate Mission Statements," *Academy of Management Executive* 1, no. 2 (May 1987): 109.

12. Fred R. David, "How Companies Define Their Mission," *Long Range Planning* 22, no. 1 (February 1989): 91.

13. Jack Pearce and Richard Robinson, *Strategic Management,* 7th ed. (New York: McGraw-Hill, 2000), 8.

14. Ann Langley, "The Roles of Formal Strategic Planning," *Long Range Planning* 21, no. 3 (June 1988): 40.

15. Bernard Reimann, "Getting Value from Strategic Planning," *Planning Review* 16, no. 3 (May–June 1988): 42.

16. G. L. Schwenk and K. Schrader, "Effects of Formal Strategic Planning in Financial Performance in Small Firms: A Meta-Analysis," *Entrepreneurship and Practice* 3, no. 17 (1993): 53–64. Also, C. C. Miller and L. B. Cardinal, "Strategic Planning and Firm Performance: A Synthesis of More Than Two Decades of Research," *Academy of Management Journal* 6, no. 27 (1994): 1649–1665; Michael Peel and John Bridge, "How Planning and Capital Budgeting Improve SME Performance," *Long Range Planning* 31, no. 6 (October 1998): 848–856; Julia Smith, "Strategies for Start-Ups," *Long Range Planning* 31, no. 6 (October 1998): 857–872.

17. Gordon Greenley, "Does Strategic Planning Improve Company Performance?" *Long Range Planning* 19, no. 2 (April 1986): 106.

18. Adapted from www.mindtools.com/plrreschn.html

19. Adapted from www.des.calstate.edu/limitations.html and www.entarga.com/stratplan/purposes.html

20. Dale McConkey, "Planning in a Changing Environment," *Business Horizons*, September–October 1988, 66.

21. R. T. Lenz, "Managing the Evolution of the Strategic Planning Process," *Business Horizons* 30, no. 1 (January–February 1987): 39.

22. Frederick Gluck, "Taking the Mystique out of Planning," *Across the Board*, July–August 1985, 59.

Current Readings

Bach, David, and David Bruce Allen. "What Every CEO Needs to Know About Nonmarket Strategy." *MIT Sloan Management Review* 51, no. 3 (Spring 2010): 41–44.

Bungay, Stephen. "How to Make the Most of Your Company's Strategy." *Harvard Business Review*, January–February 2011, 132–141.

Carmeli, Abraham, and Gideon D. Markman. "Capture, Governance, and Resilience: Strategy Implications from the History of Rome." *Strategic Management Journal* 32, no. 3 (March 2011): 322–341.

Chakravorti, Bhaskar. "Finding Competitive Advantage in Adversity." *Harvard Business Review*, November 2010, 102–109.

Chen, Eric L., Ritta Katila, Rory McDonald, and Kathleen M. Eisenhardt. "Life in the Fast Lane: Origins of Competitive Interaction in New vs. Established Markets." *Strategic Management Journal* 31, no. 13 (December 2010): 1527–1547.

Christensen, H. Kurt. "Defining Customer Value as the Driver of Competitive Advantage." *Strategy & Leadership* 38, no. 5 (2010): 20.

D'Aveni, Richard A., Giovanni Battista Dagnino, and Ken G. Smith. "The Age of Temporary Advantage." *Strategic Management Journal* 31, no. 13 (December 2010): 1371–1385.

Delios, Andrew. "How Can Organizations Be Competitive but Dare to Care?" *The Academy of Management Perspectives* 24, no. 3 (August 2010): 25–36.

Geroski, P. A., Jose Mata, and Pedro Portugal. "Founding Conditions and the Survival of New Firms." *Strategic Management Journal* 31, no. 5 (May 2010): 510–529.

Giesen, Edward, Eric Riddleberger, Richard Christner, and Ragna Bell. "When and How to Innovate Your Business Model." *Strategy & Leadership* 38, no. 4 (2010): 17.

Gilad, Benjamin. "War Gaming: Virtual Reality, Real Lessons." *Strategy & Leadership* 38, no. 6 (2010): 38.

Hansen, Morten T., Herminia Ibarra, and Urs Peyer. "The Best-Performing CEOs in the World." *Harvard Business Review*, January–February 2010, 104–113.

Harris, Jeanne, Elizabeth Craig, and Henry Egan. "How Successful Organizations Strategically Manage Their Analytic Talent." *Strategy & Leadership* 38, no. 3 (2010): 15.

Hitt, Michael A., Katalin Takacs Haynes, and Roy Serpa. "Strategic Leadership for the 21st Century." *Business Horizons* 53, no. 5 (September–October 2010): 437–444.

Jacobides, Michael G. "Strategy Tools for a Shifting Landscape." *Harvard Business Review*, January–February 2010, 76–85.

Marcel, Jeremy J., Pamela S. Barr, and Irene M. Duhaime. "The Influence of Executive Cognition on Competitive Dynamics." *Strategic Management Journal* 32, no. 2 (February 2011): 115–138.

Narayanan, V. K., Lee J. Zane, and Benedict Kemmerer. "The Cognitive Perspective in Strategy: An Integrative Review." *Journal of Management* 37, no. 1 (January 2011): 305–351.

Pfeffer, Jeffrey. "Building Sustainable Organizations: The Human Factor." *The Academy of Management Perspectives* 24, no. 1 (February 2010): 34–45.

Plambeck, Nilis, and Klaus Weber. "When the Glass is Half Full and Half Empty: CEO's Ambivalent Interpretations of Strategic Issues." *Strategic Management Journal* 31, no. 7 (July 2010): 689–710.

Rollinson, Randall. "Should Strategy Professionals Be Certified?" *Strategy & Leadership* 39, no. 1 (March 2011): 39–45.

Wilson, James W., and Soren Eilertsen. "How Did Strategic Planning Help During the Economic Crisis?" *Strategy & Leadership* 38, no. 2 (2010): 5.

Weiss, Jeff, Aram Donigian, and Jonathan Hughes. "Extreme Negotiations." *Harvard Business Review*, November 2010, 66–75.

Zand, Dale E. "Drucker's Strategic Thinking Process: Three Key Techniques." *Strategy & Leadership* 38, no. 3 (2010): 23.

THE COHESION CASE

Adidas Group – 2011

Forest R. David

Francis Marion University
www.adidas-group.com

The Adidas Jabulani was the official match ball for the 2010 Federation of International Football Associations (FIFA) World Cup in South Africa. The ball represented the latest in Adidas design technology, featuring only eight 3-D panels, making the ball perfectly round and more accurate than any previous ball developed. The name Jabulani was derived from the Bantu language Zulu, which is spoken by 25 percent of the South African population. Perfectly fitting the spirit of the World Cup, Jabulani literally translated means "to celebrate." Furthermore, to celebrate the diversity of South Africa, the ball contains eleven different colors representing 1) 11 starting players on each team, 2) 11 official languages of South Africa, and 3) 11 South African tribes that make up the country.

Adidas and the Union of European Football Associations (UEFA) have extended their partnership for UEFA EURO 2012 and UEFA EURO 2016. Adidas will continue to provide the balls, equipment, staff, officials, and referees for the tournaments. Adidas has a three-decade history of sponsoring some of the largest sporting events in the world, including the EURO Championships and the World Cup and hopes this new agreement will keep the Adidas name solidified as the top brand in soccer worldwide.

Headquartered in Herzogenaurach, Germany, Adidas AG is a sports apparel and footwear manufacturer and parent company of the Adidas Group, which consists of the Reebok sportswear company, the golf company TaylorMade-adidas Golf (including Ashworth), and Rockport and other brands such as the outdoor specialist Five Ten. Besides sports footwear, Adidas also produces other products such as bags, shirts, watches, eyewear, and other sports- and clothing-related goods. The company is the largest sportswear manufacturer in Europe and the second-biggest sportswear manufacturer in the world, with Nike being the biggest.

Adidas AG consists of three main brands: Adidas, Reebok, and TaylorMade. Adidas is further broken down into Sports Performance and Sports Style, while two of Reebok's largest segments are CCM Hockey and Rockport. TaylorMade-adidas Golf segment includes TaylorMade-adidas Golf and Ashworth. Adidas Group actually consists of many subsidiaries headquartered around the world, as indicated in Exhibit 1. As indicated in Exhibit 2, Adidas had 2010 revenues of 11,990, up 15 percent from 2009.

EXHIBIT 1   Subsidiaries of Adidas Group and Their Respective Headquarters Location

Adidas Group Headquarters	Germany
Adidas International Marketing	The Netherlands
Reebok Europe	The Netherlands
Adidas North America	USA
Reebok North America	USA
TaylorMade-adidas Golf	USA
Adidas Sourcing	Hong Kong
Adidas Latin America	Panamá, Republic of Panamá

EXHIBIT 2   Adidas Financial Data (in millions of Euros)

Year	2006	2007	2008	2009	2010
Sales	10,084	10,299	10,799	10,381	11,990
EBIT	1,078	1,165	1,280	780	1,159
Net income	483	551	642	245	567
Net debt	2,231	1,766	2,189	917	221

History

At the age of 20, Adolf (Adi) Dassler was driven by a single idea when he made his first shoe. His vision was to produce the most durable and safest footwear for athletes in different sports. Dassler continued this vision until his death in 1978. His first shoe in 1920 was constructed of canvas due to few materials being available in the post-war period. By the 1930s, Dassler was making 30 different styles of shoes for 11different sports and employed around 100 workers.

After World War II, Dassler found himself once again making shoes with limited materials and in 1947, with only 47 workers, he resurrected shoe manufacturing using canvas and rubber from American fuel tanks. His brother, Rudolf, founded rival company Puma, which is headquartered in Herzogenaurach, along with Adidas. Dassler made the first post-war sports shoes in 1949 and formally registered his company Adidas, which is the first three letters of his first and last names. To this day, Adidas is still referred to as the "Three Stripes Company."

Perhaps the earliest and greatest pioneer in sports marketing, Dassler courted many famous athletes to endorse his product, such as Jessie Owens, Muhammad Ali, Franz Beckenbauer, and many other famous athletes from around the world. Along with forming relationships with athletes, Adidas received one of its biggest marketing opportunities when the German football team won the 1954 World Cup wearing Adidas shoes with screw-in studs. From this event, Adidas was able to aggressively target major sporting events as a platform to introduce new products.

After the death of Dassler in 1978 and the prospering of world-class rival Nike, Adidas struggled to keep its reputation and market share during the 1980s. In 1992, Adidas started targeting younger athletes and in 1993 hired Robert Dreyfus as CEO. In 1995, Dreyfus had the Three Stripes back on the sportswear map and listed as a new IPO on the German Stock Exchange. Continuing with their momentum, Adidas acquired Salomon Group in 2001 before divesting them in 2005 but keeping the TaylorMade Brand. In January 2006, Adidas acquired Reebok International Ltd., furthering the Adidas Group as one of the top athletic footwear, apparel, and sports hardware producers in the world.

In 2008, Adidas entered the English cricket market by sponsoring English batting star Kevin Pietersen. The following year, Adidas signed the English player Ian Bell and the Indian Player Ravindra Jadeja. Adidas produces and sells cricket bats currently available in the Incurza, Pellara, and Libro lines. Adidas manufactures the uniforms worn by both the England and the Australia cricket teams.

Source: Courtesy of adidas Group

Current Events

Adidas signed a partnership with Cricket South Africa in 2011 and the uniforms worn by the South African Cricket Team during and after the 2011 Cricket World Cup. Adidas sponsors the South Korea national cricket team. In the Indian Premier League, Adidas is the official apparel sponsor for the Mumbai Indians, Delhi Daredevils, and Pune Warriors India.

Also in 2011, for the twelfth consecutive year, Adidas AG was selected to join the Dow Jones Sustainability Indexes (DJSI), the world's first global sustainability index family tracking the performance of the leading sustainability-driven companies worldwide. In the category "Clothing, Accessories & Footwear," Adidas AG was rated as industry leader in sustainability issues and corporate responsibility for the eighth time. Adidas Group currently has more than 46,000 employees worldwide.

Adidas plans to use the UEFA EURO 2012 as a platform to achieve market leadership in Poland by 2015. In the Ukraine, where Adidas is already the clear market leader, Adidas wants to further expand its leadership position. "As the Official Partner of UEFA EURO 2012, we will use the event to reach market leadership in Poland by 2015 and take over category leadership in football in 2012," said Herbert Hainer, CEO of the Adidas Group. "This is the first time a major tournament like the UEFA EURO will be hosted by Poland and the Ukraine. We are very excited about the upcoming event and plan to leverage UEFA EURO 2012 internationally to showcase our brand and our innovative and exciting products."

Adidas is poised to succeed at the upcoming London 2012 Olympic & Paralympic Games. "As the Official IAAF Athletic Sponsor and Licensee Product Supplier, we are proud to support the world's best athletes on their road to London 2012. Our mission is clear: To provide all of our athletes with the lightest products to make them faster and help them improve their performance," said Zion Armstrong, Managing Director, Adidas Group South Korea. "With the Adizero Range, we are setting new standards in lightweight footwear not only in running but also across other categories including football, American football and basketball." At the upcoming London 2012 Olympic Games, Adidas is outfitting all volunteers, technical staff, and the officials. As the Official Partner of Team GB,

Adidas provides all British athletes in all Olympic sports with performance products. Adidas will also provide fans across the UK with both Licensed as well as Event-Branded Olympic fan wear for those upcoming games.

Adidas used the 2011 IAAF World Championships in Daegu, South Korea to showcase its leadership in innovation by outfitting athletes such as Jessica Ennis, Dayron Robles, Blanka Vlasic, Christina Obergföll, and Yohan Blake with the latest Adidas footwear. A popular new Adidas product is the Adizero Feather, the lightest everyday running shoe weighing only 160g (women's size UK 5.5). This shoe helps athletes run faster and improve their performance. Adidas currently sponsors over 500 athletes and a total of 12 federations. Adidas outfitted over 7,300 volunteers at the World Championships in Daegu.

In October 2011, in Moscow, Russia, Herbert Hainer, CEO of Adidas Group, revealed his company's growth plans for Russia/CIS. Until 2015, sales are expected to increase at a double-digit average growth rate per annum, establishing Russia/CIS among the top three markets globally for Adidas Group. Adidas's sales in Russia are expected to exceed €1 billion by 2013. "I am very pleased to announce that the Adidas Group's position in Russia/CIS is going from strength to strength. Our Group is the clear market leader, with Adidas number 1 and Reebok number 2 in the market", said

Source: Courtesy of adidas Group

Herbert Hainer, CEO. Together with North America and Greater China, Russia/CIS is one of Adidas's three key attack markets as part of its strategic business plan Route 2015. As part of that plan, these three markets are expected to contribute 50 percent of the Group's sales growth. By 2015, Adidas Group wants to achieve global sales of €17 billion and a sustainable operating margin of 11 percent. In Russia/CIS, Rockport has substantial market share in the brown shoe segment. Adidas Group expects to have over 800 stores in Russia/CIS by the end of 2011. By 2015, at least 400 stores will be added across Russia, bringing the total store number to more than 1,200. In 2012, the Ukraine, which is part of Adidas Group's Russia/CIS market, will be co-hosting the UEFA EURO 2012 together with Poland. Adidas will be the Official Sponsor, Supplier and Licensee of UEFA EURO 2012, also providing the Official Match Ball for the tournament. While Adidas Group is already the clear market leader in the Ukraine and intends to further expand this position, the company plans to reach market leadership in Poland by 2015.

Mission/Vision

The strategic-management process begins with a clear vision and mission statement. The case authors could not find a vision statement for Adidas Group. However, the current mission statement of Adidas AG is provided in their Annual Report and reads as follows:

> The adidas Group strives to be the global leader in the sporting goods industry with brands built on a passion for sports and a sporting lifestyle.

> We are committed to continuously strengthening our brands and products to improve our competitive position.

> We are innovation and design leaders who seek to help athletes of all skill levels achieve peak performance with every product we bring to market.

> We are consumer focused and therefore we continuously improve the quality, look, feel and image of our products and our organisational structures to match and exceed consumer expectations and to provide them with the highest value.

> We are a global organisation that is socially and environmentally responsible, that embraces creativity and diversity and is financially rewarding for our employees and shareholders.

> We are dedicated to consistently delivering outstanding financial results.

Product Areas

Adidas keeps track of its products sold in three main product groupings: footwear, apparel, and hardware. The company sells almost as much apparel as footwear. Note in Exhibit 3 (on page 62) that Adidas's footwear sales increased 16 percent in 2010 to 5,389 million euro. Note that Adidas's apparel sales in 2010 increased 15.4 percent to 5,380 million euro. Note also that in Exhibit 3 Adidas hardware sales increased 13.5 percent in 2010 to 1,221 million euros.

Running/Football (Soccer)

Adidas currently manufactures running shoes that include the adiStar Salvation 3, the adiStar Ride 3 (the replacement for the adiStar Cushion 6), the Supernova Sequence 4 (the replacement for the Supernova Control 10), and the Supernova Glide 3, among others. Adidas performance apparel is widely used by runners. Adidas uses kangaroo leather to make their more expensive shoes.

Adidas is a major supplier of team kits for international football teams. Adidas also makes referee kits that are used in international competition and by many countries and leagues in the world. The company has been an innovator in the area of footwear for the sport. Some of the most famous football teams in the world are currently sponsored by Adidas, which is renowned for advancing the Predator boot design developed by ex-Liverpool and Australian international player Craig Johnston. This design featured a ribbed rubber structure for the upper leather of the shoe, used to accent the movement of the ball when struck; highly skilled players claimed they were able to curve the flight of the ball more easily when wearing this new contoured design. The Predator also features the Craig Johnston-invented Traxion sole.

FIFA, the world governing body of football, commissioned specially designed footballs for use in World Cup tournaments. Adidas's Jabulani ball used in the 2010 World Cup was designed and developed by Loughborough University in conjunction with Chelsea FC. The ball, however, received much criticism from players, managers, and pundits for being too hard to control. The lighter and more aerodynamic ball led to many shots and passes being over hit. The Jabulani was widely blamed for the low numbers of long-range goals or even remotely accurate attempts in the opening stage of the tournament.

Adidas provides apparel and equipment for all teams in Major League Soccer (MLS). Adidas and Major League Soccer have an 8-year sponsorship agreement that will continue to make Adidas the official athletic sponsor and licensed product supplier for the league, and to work together to expand the developmental league for MLS through 2018.

Adidas is the longstanding kit provider to the German national football team, a sponsorship that began in 1954 and is contracted to continue until at least 2018. Adidas also sponsors the Argentine, Japanese, Mexican, Scottish, Spanish and Colombian national football teams, among others.

Tennis/Golf

Adidas sponsors many professional tennis players and recently introduced a new line of tennis rackets, including the Feather which is made for the "regular player," the Response for the "club player," and the Barricade for "tournament players." Back in November 2009, then World Number 4 Andy Murray was confirmed as Adidas's highest paid star with a 5-year contract reported to be worth $24.5 million.

Adidas sells apparel, footwear, and accessories for men, women, and youth for rookie to professional golfers. Adidas's golf equipment includes footwear, shirts, shorts, pants, skirts, outerwear, base layer and eyewear.

Basketball

Adidas is the current outfitter of all 30 franchises in the National Basketball Association and sponsors numerous players. The company recently unveiled a new NBA game jersey to be worn by all NBA players in games beginning in the 2010–2011 season. However, with the first two weeks of the U.S. basketball season cancelled and more games under threat, Adidas faces losing half its licensed NBA apparel sales, some analysts estimate Games that have been dropped from the 2011–2012 season, include defending champions Dallas Mavericks at home to the Chicago Bulls.

Basketball is a lucrative business in the United States for the world's top two sporting goods makers, Nike and Adidas, and for retailers such as Finish Line and Footlocker. Canaccord analyst

Camilo Lyon estimates basketball comprises about 30 percent of Footlocker sales and 20 percent for Finish Line. Adidas stands to lose the most from the "lockout" because it has held the license to provide NBA uniforms and apparel since 2006.

Adidas makes some $100 million in sales from licensed NBA products, with basketball products as a whole, including footwear, among its top five sporting categories. Matt Powell, analyst at SportsOneSource, recently told Reuters licensed apparel sales could halve, similar to the last lockout in the 1998–1999 season, if the season were cancelled.

Rugby/Baseball

Adidas make rugby balls and other rugby gear. They are the current kit and ball supplier to the New Zealand All Blacks, Irish Munster Rugby, the Argentinean Pumas, and the South African Stormers, and Western Province rugby union teams, among others. Adidas are also the official match ball supplier to the Heineken Cup. Unhappy with the local price of the Adidas replica All Blacks jersey, New Zealand-based All Blacks fans have asked for price cuts and begun purchasing the jersey from overseas vendors after it was revealed that the local price of $NZ220 was more than twice the price offered on some websites. Adidas has responded by enforcing cross-border agreements to stop overseas retailers from selling to New Zealand residents. It has been labelled a public relations disaster by leading New Zealand PR firms and consumer advocate groups. The largest New Zealand sportswear retailer Rebel Sport has stated it is angry and is considering selling the All Blacks Jerseys to the general public below cost. Rebel Sport recently decided not to stock the Adidas Rugby Union Jumper.

Gymnastics

Adidas gymnastics wear is available worldwide through GK Elite Sportswear. Adidas SB (skateboarding) are shoes made specifically for skateboarding. Many of the shoes Adidas previously made were redesigned for skateboarding. Adidas also produces baseball equipment and sponsors numerous players of Major League Baseball and the Nippon Professional Baseball in Japan. From 1997 to 2008, Adidas sponsored the New York Yankees.

Adidas Group Divisions

The three primary brands of the Adidas Group are Adidas, Reebok, and TaylorMade, but as indicated in Exhibit 3, the company breaks down its financial information also by Rockport and Reebok CCM-Hockey. Rockport's 2010 revenues increased 8.6 percent to 240 million euros as indicated in Exhibit 3. Note that Reebok CCM-Hockey's revenues in 2010 increased 13 percent to 200 million euros.

Adidas AG

Adidas AG is committed to providing the most technologically advanced sportswear. In this line of products, Adidas competes amongst other brands directly with Under Armour. Adidas produces an assortment of products for tennis, running, basketball, football, and other sports—products for amateur athletes, professional athletes, and all fitness-minded people. The Adidas brand breaks their products down into two primary divisions: Sport Performance and Sport Style. The Sport Performance division focuses mostly on athletes in four areas: football, running, training, and basketball. Sport Style is targeted at youth and fashion-minded people, linking the sport theme to street fashion and even high-fashion products. As indicated in Exhibit 3, Adidas's 2010 revenues increased 15.9 percent to 8,714 million euros.

Reebok

With its world headquarters in Canton, Massachusetts, Reebok is an American-inspired global brand keeping its roots in women's sports and fitness but also has expanded into men's fitness, and even has exclusive contracts with the National Football League (NFL), National Hockey League (NHL), and many major college sports teams in the United States. Purchased by Adidas Group in 2006, Reebok gives on its website its vision: "fulfilling and leading through creativity." Also, Reebok states its purpose as "being committed to corporate responsibility and enabling youth around the world to fulfil their potential through producing great and innovative products and through Reebok's Human Rights Program that aids underprivileged youth around the world meet their potential and maintain an active and healthy lifestyle." Reebok offers apparel and shoes for running, basketball, football, American football, hockey, and casual wear through Rockport, treadmills, stationary bikes, elliptical machines, and much more. Two of the companies largest segments are Reebok-CCM Hockey and Rockport. As indicated in Exhibit 3, Reebok's 2010 revenues increased 19.3 percent to 1,913 million euros.

Reebok is expanding its toning shoe category, even after the U.S. consumer watchdog called into question their health benefits. Adidas last year sold around eight million pairs of the shoes, marketed under Reebok EasyTone, and CEO Hainer said the category would be expanded as it offered good margins. Reebok in September 2011 agreed to pay $25 million to settle charges that it made unsupported claims that its toning shoes help wearers get fit faster. The Federal Trade Commission criticized advertisements by Reebok that its shoes strengthened hamstrings and calves by up to 11 percent more than regular sneakers and toned the buttocks up to 28 percent more. CEO Hainer said Reebok had changed the advertising to no longer include percentages. Adidas said at the time it did not agree with the FTC allegations and only chose to settle to avoid a legal battle.

TaylorMade

Headquartered in Carlsbad, California USA, TaylorMade is the world leader in metalwood golf clubs. Some top TaylorMade products include the R7 Quad, R9 SuperTri, Burner09 TP, and the 460 TP, just to name a few. The company markets a full line of golf clubs for all applications as well as golf gloves, hats, shoes, balls, and other apparel. Under the guidance and management of Adidas AG, in 2006 TaylorMade in 2006 became only the second brand in the golf industry to have over $1 billion USD in revenue in a single year. In 2008, TaylorMade sold their Maxfli brand to Dick's Sporting Goods. Exhibit 4 provides financial information for TaylorMade. As indicated in Exhibit 3, Adidas's 2010 revenues increased 9.4 percent to 909 million euros.

Financial Information

As indicated in Exhibit 3, the Adidas Group is doing very well but this is no guarantee for success in the future. Note that the company's sales increased 15.5 percent in 2010 to 11,990 million euros. The company's net income in 2010 increased a whopping 131 percent to 567 million euros. Also note in Exhibit 3 that the Adidas Group's financial leverage ratio dropped nicely in 2010 to 4.3 percent from 24.3 percent in 2009.

EXHIBIT 3 **Adidas Group's Consolidated Income Statement (in Millions of Euro)**

	2010	2009	2008	2007	2006[1]
Income Statement Data (€ in millions)					
Net sales	11,990	10,381	10,799	10,299	10,084
Gross profit	5,730	4,712	5,256	4,882	4,495
Royalty and commission income	100	86	89	102	90
Other operating income	110	100	103	80	55
Other operating expenses	5,046	4,390	4,378	4,115	3,759
EBITDA	1,159	780	1,280	1,165	1,078
Operating profit	894	508	1,070	949	881
Financial result	(88)	(150)	(166)	(135)	(158)
Income before taxes	806	358	904	815	723
Income taxes	238	113	260	260	227
Net income attributable to non-controlling interests	(1)	0	(2)	(4)	(13)
Net income attributable to shareholders[2]	567	245	642	551	483
Income Statement Ratios					
Gross margin	47.8%	45.4%	48.7%	47.4%	44.6%
Operating margin	7.5%	4.9%	9.9%	9.2%	8.7%
Interest coverage	10.1	3.9	7.4	6.8	5.9
Effective tax rate	29.5%	31.5%	28.8%	31.8%	31.4%
Net income attributable to shareholders as percentage of net sales[2]	4.7%	2.4%	5.9%	5.4%	4.8%
Net sales by brand (€ in millions)					
Adidas	8,714	7,520	7,821	7,113	6,626
Reebok	1,913	1,603	1,717	1,831	1,979
TaylorMade—adidas Golf	909	831	812	804	856
Rockport	252	232	243	291	293
Reebok—CCM Hockey	200	177	188	210	202

EXHIBIT 3   (Continued)

Net sales by product category (€ in millions)

Footwear	5,389	4,642	4,919	4,751	4,733
Apparel	5,380	4,663	4,775	4,426	4,105
Hardware	1,221	1,076	1,105	1,121	1,246

Balance Sheet Data (€ in millions)

Total assets	10,618	8,875	9,533	8,325	8,379
Inventories	2,119	1,471	1,995	1,629	1,607
Receivables and other current assets	2,324	2,038	2,523	2,048	1,913
Working capital	1,972	1,649	1,290	1,522	1,733
Net borrowings	221	917	2,189	1,766	2,231
Shareholders' equity	4,616	3,771	3,386	3,023	2,828

Balance Sheet Ratios

Net borrowings/EBITDA	0.2	1.2	1.7	1.5	2.1
Financial leverage	4.8%	24.3%	64.6%	58.4%	78.9%
Equity ratio	43.5%	42.5%	35.5%	36.3%	33.8%
Equity-to-fixed-assets ratio	97.4%	85.9%	73.6%	72.2%	63.5%
Asset coverage I	141.5%	137.4%	127.7%	136.1%	138.7%
Asset coverage II	97.7%	102.9%	89.1%	98.0%	102.0%
Fixed asset intensity of investments	44.6%	49.5%	48.2%	50.3%	53.2%
Current asset intensity of investments	55.4%	50.5%	51.8%	49.7%	46.8%
Liquidity I	35.5%	30.0%	10.5%	14.5%	15.8%
Liquidity II	78.2%	80.4%	55.1%	70.3%	80.4%
Liquidity III	132.4%	132.2%	109.8%	132.6%	153.7%
Working capital turnover	6.1	6.3	8.4	6.8	5.8
Return on equity[2]	12.3%	6.5%	18.9%	18.2%	17.1%
Return on capital employed[2]	20.2%	11.3%	19.8%	20.2%	17.6%

Data Per Share[3]

Share price at year-end (in €)	48.89	37.77	27.14	51.26	37.73
Basic earnings[2] (in €)	2.71	1.25	3.25	2.71	2.37
Diluted earnings[2] (in €)	2.71	1.22	3.07	2.57	2.25
Price / earnings ratio at year-end	18.0	31.0	8.8	19.9	16.8
Market capitalization at year-end (€ in millions)	10,229	7,902	5,252	10,438	7,679
Operating cash flow (in €)	4.28	6.11	2.52	3.83	3.74
Dividend (in €)	0.80[4]	0.35	0.50	0.50	0.42
Dividend payout ratio (in %)	29.5	29.8	15.1	18.0	17.7
Number of shares outstanding at year-end (in thousands)	209,216	209,216	193,516	203,629	203,537

EXHIBIT 3   (Continued)

Employees

Number of employees at year-end	42,541	39,596	38,982	31,344	26,376
Personnel expenses (€ in millions)	1,521	1,352	1,283	1,186	1,087

[1] Including Reebok, Rockport and Reebok–CCM Hockey from February 1, 2006 onwards.

[2] Includes income from continuing and discontinued operations.

[3] Figures adjusted for 1:4 share split conducted on June 6, 2006.

[4] Subject to Annual General Meeting approval.

Source: adidas Group, (mission statement) used with permission. The "3-Bars" logo is a registered trade mark of the adidas Group, used with permission.

External Issues

Apparel

Numerous external issues impact the Adidas Group, including the economy in various countries, currency rates, consumer discretionary spending, unemployment rates, tax rates, restricted credit, and much more. Customer buying patterns continue to change as the global economy slowly improves. For the apparel industry in particular, customers still ponder whether "What I have in my closet is good enough or do I have to have new items?" The degree to which apparel companies can produce products that are not just exciting or new, but actual "must-haves" among potential customers may indeed be the key to future survival and growth.

According to the S&P Industry Surveys based out of the United States, most of the retail industry will continue to suffer reduced sales over the coming years, but a few segments will outperform the otherwise lackluster forecast. The categories that are expected to outperform include: sports and exercise-based apparel, consumer electronics, prepared foods, shoes and accessories, and green goods. Aside from properly positioning products in categories forecasted to improve, companies are also offering more value-priced clothing and products to entice thrifty consumers to purchase. Luxury brands are expected to remain weak through 2014 as consumers are turning away from status symbol items. Luxury brand producers must increasingly focus on how their brands are more durable, and how they indeed offer better craftsmanship and quality. Even focusing on these attributes, luxury brands will be a tough sell in the near future. A competitor of Adidas, Under Armour, manufacturers products that promise to insulate the wearer from cold while whisking away sweat, and keep athletes cool in warm climates. Running shoes are now synchronized with computers to measure performance and fitness levels. Other advances even include t-shirts and fabrics that control odor and tagless shirts.

Footwear

Lower-cost footwear in recent years has outperformed higher-end items and this trend continues. Among shoe categories in the United States, low performance and running/jogging shoes were the leaders in footwear sales, followed by basketball and cross trainer. Due to declining footwear sales in the United States, Nike has increased its penetration into Western Europe including France, Germany, and Great Britain and recently entered new Eastern European markets such as Poland and the Czech Republic. Nike generates 60 percent of its sales outside of the United States.

With a more environmentally conscious public, many companies are focusing on green initiatives as a means of attracting customers' money. Positioning products as green brands is starting to become an effective strategy. Adidas has a detailed Sustainability Report at its corporate website.

Competitors

Nike (NKE)

Founded in 1964 by Phil Knight and legendary University of Oregon track coach Bill Bowerman, the company was originally named Blue Ribbon Sports. It 1972, Knight changed the company name to Nike after the Greek winged Goddess of Victory. Nike went public in 1980. Headquartered in Beaverton, Oregon, Nike currently has operations in over 160 countries, employs over 34,000 workers, and owns over 330 retail stores in the United States and over 330 retail stores internationally.

An expert in marketing athletic products, Nike designs and develops products for many sports and athletic applications including: running, basketball, football, American football, baseball, golf, tennis, and many more. In addition to shoes, Nike produces a wide line of apparel, athletic bags, license agreements for jerseys and apparel for professional and college athletic teams, bats, baseball gloves, golf clubs, sport balls, and many other sports-related products. In addition to the Nike brand name, the company also markets products under the brand names of Converse, Chuck Taylor, All Star, Umbro, Cole Haan, Bragano, Hurley International, and Nike Golf.

For its fiscal 2012 first quarter ending August 31, 2011, Nike's diluted earnings per share and revenue represented new records as the company enjoyed strong demand for Nike brands. Nike earnings that quarter increased 15 percent to $645 million. Nike's revenues in its fiscal 2012 first quarter increased 18 percent to $6.1 billion, up 11 percent on a currency-neutral basis. The company had increased growth in every geographic area except Western Europe, which was flat due to the negative impact from changes in the timing of shipments and comparisons to last year's strong World Cup related sales. By category, revenues were up on a currency neutral basis in all key categories except football (soccer), which had a challenging year prior comparison given the World Cup last year. Revenues from Nike's other businesses increased 10 percent as growth in Converse, Cole Haan and Nike Golf offset lower revenues at Hurley and Umbro.

Nike is altering the sales mindset of athletic apparel in China. To do so, Nike is changing the ideas of fashion and helping create a culture of everyday-citizen sports that extends beyond the country's lauded Olympic teams and professional players. Nike plans to roughly double its China sales by 2015 to reach a target of $4 billion annually. To reach this goal, Nike plans to open more stores and put a renewed focus on recreational sports such as running and snowboarding.

Under Armour (UA)

Relatively new to the athletic appeal industry, Under Armour is very popular among young athletes. The company has license contracts with some major American universities as a provider of sports appeal and jerseys to their athletic teams. What started out as just a compression t-shirt company, Under Armour now develops, markets, and distributes performance apparel, footwear, and accessories for men, women, and youth primarily in the United States, Canada, and some international countries. It offers products made from moisture-wicking synthetic fabrics designed to regulate body temperature regardless of weather conditions. The company provides products in three fit types: compression (tight fitting), fitted (athletic cut), and loose (relaxed) extending across the sporting goods, outdoor, and active lifestyle markets.

Under Armour made its name by developing products made from synthetic fabrics designed to regulate body temperature and enhance performance regardless of weather conditions. Under Armour products have grown tremendously in popularity as individuals have found that the brand offers athletic apparel and accessories that can legitimately affect and improve performance. Additionally, the brand has become recognized as a higher-end brand option for both athletic and casual attire.

Under Armour's footwear offerings include football cleats, baseball, lacrosse, and softball cleats, and slides. The company also provides baseball bats, football, golf, and running gloves, as well as hats, eye wear, bags, and many more sports accessories. Under Armour prides itself on technology and being a good corporate citizen. Three of their main technology marketing tools are HeatGear®, ColdGear® and AllSeasonGear®. As a good corporate citizen, Under Armour is a sponsor of many different cancer research foundations, wildlife conservation foundations, and educational foundations throughout the United States.

Under Armour's revenue for the second quarter of 2011 was up 42 percent from last year to $291 million. The strong showing was led by Under Armour's direct-to-consumer channel, comprising 27 percent of total revenue, with sales up 81 percent from last year. Its largest segment, apparel, was also strong, up 36 percent to $209 million. Under Armour's excellent earnings has enabled it to maintain a strong financial profile, with cash and short-term investments of $120 million against just $37 million in total debt.

Callaway Golf (ELY)

Headquartered in Carlsbad, California USA and founded in 1982 by Eli Callaway, Callaway Golf sells, designs, and manufactures golf clubs and balls worldwide. The company also sells many accessories such as golf bags, gloves, shoes, and other apparel. Callaway has always had a reputation for producing top quality products and in 1990 introduced their Big Bertha Driver. Today, Callaway's most innovative breakthrough clubs are sold under the Diablo name. All Callaway products are tested and developed with the vision of Eli Calloway himself, to make golf easier for everyone. This vision includes: hitting more fairways, hitting a slice, making the ball stop on the green, or just trying to break 100.

The mission of Callaway is simply to design and manufacture top quality golf equipment. Callaway insists that if a new product is to be marketed, then the new product must offer significant advantages over previous products and not just be a marketing ploy. Despite this strict ethical stance, Callaway has produced more than 1,100 United States patents, more than any other golf manufacturer.

Callaway's sales were down 8 percent for the first half of 2011 compared to the same period in the prior year. This decrease in 2011 was primarily due to declines in sales volume across all product categories. Callaway's gross margins as a percentage of net sales were 40 percent for the six months of 2011 compared to 43 percent for the six months of 2010. Callaway's operating expenses for the first six months of 2011 were $213.5 million (38% of net sales) compared to $207.4 million (34% of sales) for the first six months of 2010.

Callaway's net income during the first six months of 2011 decreased to a net loss of $50.7 million from net income of $31.8 million during the comparable period of 2010 and the firm's earnings per share decreased to a loss of $0.87 per share for the first half of 2011 compared to earnings per share of $0.38 for the same period in 2010.

The Armani Group

The Armani Group has over 5,000 employees and 13 factories. Based in Milan, Italy, Armani designs, manufactures, distributes, and retails fashion and lifestyle products including apparel, accessories, eyewear, watches, jewelry, fragrances, and cosmetics, and home furnishings under a range of brand names: Giorgio Armani Privé, Giorgio Armani, Armani Collezioni, Emporio Armani, AJ (Armani Jeans), EA7, A/X Armani Exchange, Armani Junior, Armani Teen, Armani Baby, and Armani Casa. Armani's exclusive distribution network includes 609 freestanding shops worldwide: 85 Giorgio Armani boutiques, 183 Emporio Armani stores, 31 Armani Collezioni stores, 180 A/X Armani Exchange stores, 22 AJ/Armani Jeans stores, 12 Armani Junior stores, 10 Giorgio Armani Accessori stores, 2 Emporio Armani Accessori stores, 14 Emporio Armani Caffes, and 28 Armani Casa stores, in 46 countries. Armani and Reebok currently have a multi-year global alliance to create a special collection of sportswear. The alliance entails Armani's EA7 and Emporio labels, with their sporty and sexy lines, joining forces with Reebok's innovation and technologies.

Conclusion

Jesse Owens, Muhammad Ali, and scores of other famous athletes have broken records in their Adidas athletic shoes. Athletic shoes are still the heart of Adidas's business, but the company's famous 3-Stripes logo appears on apparel and other sport accoutrements. As the number two maker of sporting goods worldwide, behind Nike, Adidas has many contracts with famous football and basketball athletes. Adidas today has more than 1,150 retail locations and thousands of distributors.

Adidas Group needs a clear three-year strategic plan to compete effectively against Nike, Li Ning, Under Armour, Converse, Callaway Golf, and Giorgio Armani S.p.A. Some analysts believe Adidas should acquire Armani. Do you think it would be wise for Adidas AG to acquire Armani Group, one of the leading fashion and luxury goods groups in the world?

ASSURANCE OF LEARNING EXERCISES

Assurance of Learning Exercise 1A

Examine Recent and Future Acquisitions for Nokia

Purpose

Nokia is featured in the opening chapter insert as a firm that engages in excellent strategic planning. However, Nokia recently paid $975 million in cash to acquire the wireless network infrastructure assets of Motorola Solutions. The acquisition strengthened the company's position in North America and Japan, adding approximately 6,900 employees across 52 countries. The acquisition covers a number of research and development facilities, including sites in the United States, China, Russia, India, and the UK. Often when an acquisition is made, numerous layoffs and closings result as the two firms merge operations and minimize duplicated activities and functions.

This exercise gives you practice examining the impact of an acquisition to determine appropriate changes needed to reduce extraneous costs once incurred by two firms but now by only one firm. In addition, this exercise gives you practice identifying a potential acquisition candidate.

Instructions

Step 1	Go to Nokia's website.
Step 2	Review Nokia's most recent *Form 10K* or *Annual Report*.
Step 3	Examine the change in performance variables before and after the Motorola Solutions acquisition.
Step 4	What strategic changes were made after the acquisition? What additional changes in your view are still needed?
Step 5	Conduct some research to identify another similar acquisition that would enable Nokia to become a stronger competitor. Since the continent of Africa is rapidly coming online, what firm could Nokia acquire to expand into servicing that continent?

Assurance of Learning Exercise 1B

Gathering Strategy Information on Adidas AG

Purpose

The purpose of this exercise is to get you familiar with strategy terms introduced and defined in Chapter 1. Let's apply these terms to the Cohesion Case on Adidas AG.

Instructions

Step 1	Go to http://www.adidas-group.com/en/home/Welcome.aspx which is Adidas AG's website. Click on the words Investor Relations. Then click on *Annual Report*. Print the 2010, or if available the 2011, Adidas Annual Report. This document may be quite long, so you may want to copy the document electronically. The *Annual Report* contains excellent information for developing a list of internal strengths and weaknesses for Adidas.
Step 2	Go to your college library and make a copy of *Standard & Poor's* Industry Surveys for the athletic footwear and apparel industry. This document will contain excellent information for developing a list of external opportunities and threats facing Adidas.
Step 3	Go on the Internet and find and print information about Adidas's three major competitors: Nike, Puma, and Callaway Golf.

Step 4   Using the information gathered above, on a separate sheet of paper, list what you consider to be Adidas's three major strengths, three major weaknesses, three major opportunities, and three major threats. Each factor listed for this exercise must include a %, #, $, or ratio to reveal some quantified fact or trend. These factors provide the underlying basis for a strategic plan, because a firm strives to take advantage of strengths, improve weaknesses, avoid threats, and capitalize on opportunities. Estimate the #'s as needed.

Step 5   Through class discussion, compare your lists of external and internal factors to those developed by other students and add to your lists of factors. Keep this information for use in later exercises at the end of other chapters.

Step 6   Be mindful that whatever case company is assigned to you and/or your team of students this semester, you can start to update the information on your company by following the steps listed for any publicly held firm.

Assurance of Learning Exercise 1C

Getting Familiar with SMCO

Purpose
This exercise is designed to help strategy students become familiar with the Strategic Management Club Online (SMCO). The SMCO offers templates for the case analysis exercises in this course.

Instructions

Step 1   Go to the www.strategyclub.com website. Review the various sections of this site.

Step 2   Select a section of the SMCO site that you feel will be the most useful to you in this class. Write a one-page summary of that section and why you feel it will benefit you the most.

Assurance of Learning Exercise 1D

Becoming a Certified Strategic Planner

Purpose
This exercise alerts you to the opportunity to become a Certified Strategic Planner by attending a one-day workshop given by Dr. Fred David in the United States.

Instructions

Step 1   Go to www.checkmateplan.com and click on the Certified Strategic Planner hot link. Review the material provided. If you know of anyone who may be interested in becoming a Certified Strategic Planner, refer those persons to this site.

Assurance of Learning Exercise 1E

Strategic Planning at Nestlé

Purpose
The purpose of this exercise is to give you experience investigating the strategic plan of large, publicly held firms such as Nestlé SA. An important aspect of formulating a strategic plan is to assess the strategic plans of rival firms. For this exercise, you are on the top management team of M&M Mars, a large chocolate company that competes with Nestlé in the confectionery business worldwide.

Instructions

Step 1 Go to Nestlé's website and review the company's recent *Annual Report*. List as clearly as you can the five major strategies that Nestlé is pursuing worldwide.

Step 2 Go to M&M Mars's website and determine as best you can what the privately held firm is doing worldwide to compete with Nestlé.

Step 3 Write a one-page paper that summarizes your assessment of Nestlé's strategic plan as compared to M&M Mars's strategic plan. Include whether you feel being privately held, as M&M Mars is, enables a firm to conceal its strategic plan from rival firms. Do you feel it is advantageous to keep strategies secret from shareholders, employees, creditors, suppliers, and other stakeholders? What would be the advantages of being publicly held?

Assurance of Learning Exercise 1F

Interviewing Local Strategists

Purpose

This exercise is designed to give you experience learning first hand how strategists in your city/town formulate and implement strategies. This information can be used to compare and contrast concepts presented in this textbook with practices of local strategists. Recall that strategists include owners of businesses, directors of nonprofit organizations, top managers of large firms, CEOs, presidents, and many others.

Instructions

Visit five strategists in your city. Interview them, asking the following questions. Prepare answers and report back to your professor.

1. How do you decide which strategies to implement in this organization?
2. How often do you change strategies or take a fresh look at existing strategies?
3. How many persons assist you in formulating strategies?
4. Does your organization have written mission, vision, and objective statements?
5. Is the strategic planning process in your company more secret or open in regard to process and procedure? Which approach do you feel is best? Why?

Source: D. Hurst/Alamy

"NOTABLE QUOTES"

"A business is not defined by its name, statutes, or articles of incorporation. It is defined by the business mission. Only a clear definition of the mission and purpose of the organization makes possible clear and realistic business objectives."
—*Peter Drucker*

"A corporate vision can focus, direct, motivate, unify, and even excite a business into superior performance. The job of a strategist is to identify and project a clear vision."
—*John Keane*

"Where there is no vision, the people perish."
—*Proverbs 29:18*

"The last thing IBM needs right now is a vision. (July 1993) What IBM needs most right now is a vision. (March 1996)"
—*Louis V. Gerstner Jr., CEO, IBM Corporation*

"The best laid schemes of mice and men often go awry."
—*Robert Burns (paraphrased)*

"A strategist's job is to see the company not as it is … but as it can become."
—*John W. Teets, Chairman of Greyhound, Inc.*

"That business mission is so rarely given adequate thought is perhaps the most important single cause of business frustration."
—*Peter Drucker*

"The very essence of leadership is that you have to have vision. You can't blow an uncertain trumpet."
—*Theodore Hesburgh*

The Business Vision and Mission

2

CHAPTER OBJECTIVES

After studying this chapter, you should be able to do the following:

1. Describe the nature and role of vision and mission statements in strategic management.

2. Discuss why the process of developing a mission statement is as important as the resulting document.

3. Identify the components of mission statements.

4. Discuss how clear vision and mission statements can benefit other strategic-management activities.

5. Evaluate mission statements of different organizations.

6. Write good vision and mission statements.

ASSURANCE OF LEARNING EXERCISES

Assurance of Learning Exercise 2A
Examining Potential Changes Needed in a Firm's Vision/Mission

Assurance of Learning Exercise 2B
Studying an Alternative View of Mission Statement Content

Assurance of Learning Exercise 2C
Evaluating Mission Statements

Assurance of Learning Exercise 2D
Evaluating the Mission Statement of Under Armour—a Competitor of Adidas AG

Assurance of Learning Exercise 2E
Selecting the Best Vision and Mission Statements in a Given Industry

Assurance of Learning Exercise 2F
Writing an Excellent Vision and Mission Statement for Novartis AG

This chapter focuses on the concepts and tools needed to evaluate and write business vision and mission statements. A practical framework for developing mission statements is provided. Actual mission statements from large and small organizations and for-profit and nonprofit enterprises are presented and critically examined. The process of creating a vision and mission statement is discussed. The recent economic recession resulted in many firms changing direction and thereby altering their entire vision and mission. For example, Microsoft has entered the smartphone business with Nokia, and IBM is focusing more on business analytics.

The boxed insert company examined in this chapter is Microsoft Corporation, which has a clear strategic plan.

We can perhaps best understand vision and mission by focusing on a business when it is first started. In the beginning, a new business is simply a collection of ideas. Starting a new business rests on a set of beliefs that the new organization can offer some product or service to some customers, in some geographic area, using some type of technology, at a profitable price. A new business owner typically believes that the management philosophy of the new enterprise will result in a favorable public image and that this concept of the business can be communicated to, and will be adopted by, important constituencies. When the set of beliefs about a business at its inception is put into writing, the resulting document mirrors the same basic ideas that underlie

Excellent Strategic Management Showcased

MICROSOFT CORPORATION

Headquartered in Redmond, Washington, Microsoft develops, manufactures, licenses, and supports a wide range of computer and Internet products and services. Microsoft dominates the home and business computer operating system market with its Microsoft Windows and Microsoft Office products. Microsoft has diversified into the video game industry with the Xbox 360 and into the consumer electronics industry with its Zune, MSN, and Windows Phone OS. Microsoft products are very widely used globally.

For the fiscal year ended June 30, 2011, Microsoft reported record revenue of $69.94 billion, a 12 percent increase from the prior year. Operating income, net income, and diluted earnings per share for the year were $27.16 billion, $23.15 billion, and $2.69, which represented increases of 13 percent, 23 percent, and 28 percent, respectively, when compared with the prior year. In September 2011, Microsoft raised its quarterly dividend by 25 percent, their largest dividend increase since the company started paying quarterly dividends in 2004, up from $0.16 to $0.20. Microsoft currently has 90,412 employees of which 36,107 live and work outside the United States.

Nokia, the world's largest phone maker by volume, released its first Windows Phone in late 2011. Nokia is changing its entire smartphone software platform from its own Symbian software to Microsoft's Windows Phone operating system. Microsoft's partnership with Nokia is an example of the company's excellent strategic plan for the future.

In addition, Microsoft has been developing its Microsoft Dynamics CRM range which is a software program that offers financial, customer relationship, and supply chain management solutions for businesses. Microsoft Dynamics CRM 4.0 is available in eight languages, including English, Spanish, simplified Chinese and French. The product's multitenant architecture allows for smoother and quicker deployment. Increase Ltd., a hosted Microsoft Dynamics CRM solution provider based in the United Kingdom, is very pleased

with the new Microsoft product. Microsoft Dynamics CRM 4.0's expanded global capabilities include multilanguage and multi-currency features to help support the firm's global operations.

One reason that Mark Lasswell, CRM executive sponsor and president of the Civil Infrastructure Client Group at CH2M HILL, adopted CRM 4.0 was its global capabilities to support the large-scale rollout to the company's 12 business units as well as the ability to leverage existing IT infrastructure. Microsoft Dynamics CRM 4.0 is now available for on-premise and on-demand deployments in many languages including English, simplified Chinese and Spanish. Seventeen additional languages—including Arabic, Brazilian Portuguese, Hong Kong Chinese, Japanese, Norwegian and traditional Chinese and Turkish—will be released in late 2011.

Source: Based on information at www.microsoft.com.

the vision and mission statements. As a business grows, owners or managers find it necessary to revise the founding set of beliefs, but those original ideas usually are reflected in the revised statements of vision and mission.

Vision and mission statements often can be found in the front of annual reports. They often are displayed throughout a firm's premises and are distributed with company information sent to constituencies. The statements are part of numerous internal reports, such as loan requests, supplier agreements, labor relations contracts, business plans, and customer service agreements. In a recent study, researchers concluded that 90 percent of all companies have used a mission statement sometime in the previous five years.[1]

What Do We Want to Become?

It is especially important for managers and executives in any organization to agree on the basic vision that the firm strives to achieve in the long term. A *vision statement* should answer the basic question, "What do we want to become?" A clear vision provides the foundation for developing a comprehensive mission statement. Many organizations have both a vision and mission statement, but the vision statement should be established first and foremost. The vision statement should be short, preferably one sentence, and as many managers as possible should have input into developing the statement.

Several example vision statements are provided in Table 2-1.

What Is Our Business?

Current thought on mission statements is based largely on guidelines set forth in the mid-1970s by Peter Drucker, who is often called "the father of modern management" for his pioneering studies at General Motors Corporation and for his 22 books and hundreds of articles. *Harvard Business Review* has called Drucker "the preeminent management thinker of our time."

Drucker says that asking the question "What is our business?" is synonymous with asking the question "What is our mission?" An enduring statement of purpose that distinguishes one organization from other similar enterprises, the *mission statement* is a declaration of an organization's "reason for being." It answers the pivotal question "What is our business?" A clear mission statement is essential for effectively establishing objectives and formulating strategies.

Sometimes called a *creed statement,* a statement of purpose, a statement of philosophy, a statement of beliefs, a statement of business principles, or a statement "defining our business," a mission statement reveals what an organization wants to be and whom it wants to serve. All organizations

TABLE 2-1 Vision Statement Examples

Tyson Foods' vision is to be the world's first choice for protein solutions while maximizing shareholder value. (*Author comment: Good statement, unless Tyson provides nonprotein products*)

General Motors' vision is to be the world leader in transportation products and related services. (*Author comment: Good statement*)

PepsiCo's responsibility is to continually improve all aspects of the world in which we operate—environment, social, economic—creating a better tomorrow than today. (*Author comment: Statement is too vague; it should reveal beverage and food business*)

Dell's vision is to create a company culture where environmental excellence is second nature. (*Author comment: Statement is too vague; it should reveal computer business in some manner; the word* environmental *is generally used to refer to natural environment so is unclear in its use here*)

The vision of First Reliance Bank is to be recognized as the largest and most profitable bank in South Carolina. (*Author comment: This is a very small new bank headquartered in Florence, South Carolina, so this goal is not achievable in five years; the statement is too futuristic*)

Samsonite's vision is to provide innovative solutions for the traveling world. (*Author comment: Statement needs to be more specific, perhaps mention luggage; statement as is could refer to air carriers or cruise lines, which is not good*)

Royal Caribbean's vision is to empower and enable our employees to deliver the best vacation experience for our guests, thereby generating superior returns for our shareholders and enhancing the well-being of our communities. (*Author comment: Statement is good but could end after the word "guests"*)

Procter & Gamble's vision is to be, and be recognized as, the best consumer products company in the world. (*Author comment: Statement is too vague and readability is not that good*)

have a reason for being, even if strategists have not consciously transformed this reason into writing. As illustrated in Figure 2-1, carefully prepared statements of vision and mission are widely recognized by both practitioners and academicians as the first step in strategic management. Drucker has the following to say about mission statements:

> A business mission is the foundation for priorities, strategies, plans, and work assignments. It is the starting point for the design of managerial jobs and, above all, for the design of managerial structures. Nothing may seem simpler or more obvious than to know what a company's business is. A steel mill makes steel, a railroad runs trains to carry freight and passengers, an insurance company underwrites fire risks, and a bank lends money. Actually, "What is our business?" is almost always a difficult question and the right answer is usually anything but obvious. The answer to this question is the first responsibility of strategists.[2]

Some strategists spend almost every moment of every day on administrative and tactical concerns, and strategists who rush quickly to establish objectives and implement strategies often overlook the development of a vision and mission statement. This problem is widespread even among large organizations. Many corporations in America have not yet

FIGURE 2-1

A Comprehensive Strategic-Management Model

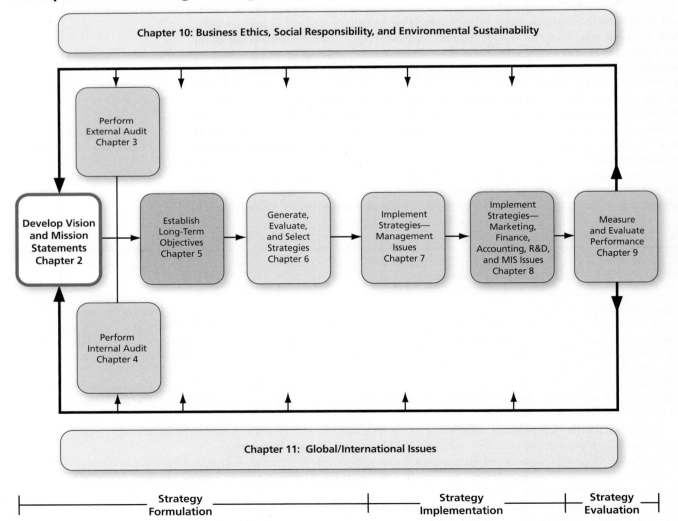

Source: Fred R. David, "How Companies Define Their Mission," *Long Range Planning* 22, no. 3 (June 1988): 40.

developed a formal vision or mission statement.[3] An increasing number of organizations are developing these statements.

Some companies develop mission statements simply because they feel it is fashionable, rather than out of any real commitment. However, as described in this chapter, firms that develop and systematically revisit their vision and mission statements, treat them as living documents, and consider them to be an integral part of the firm's culture realize great benefits. Johnson & Johnson (J&J) is an example firm. J&J managers meet regularly with employees to review, reword, and reaffirm the firm's vision and mission. The entire J&J workforce recognizes the value that top management places on this exercise, and these employees respond accordingly.

Vision versus Mission

Many organizations develop both a mission statement and a vision statement. Whereas the mission statement answers the question "What is our business?" the *vision statement* answers the question "What do we want to become?" Many organizations have both a mission and vision statement.

It can be argued that profit, not mission or vision, is the primary corporate motivator. But profit alone is not enough to motivate people.[4] Profit is perceived negatively by some employees in companies. Employees may see profit as something that they earn and management then uses and even gives away to shareholders. Although this perception is undesired and disturbing to management, it clearly indicates that both profit and vision are needed to motivate a workforce effectively.

When employees and managers together shape or fashion the vision and mission statements for a firm, the resultant documents can reflect the personal visions that managers and employees have in their hearts and minds about their own futures. Shared vision creates a commonality of interests that can lift workers out of the monotony of daily work and put them into a new world of opportunity and challenge.

The Process of Developing Vision and Mission Statements

As indicated in the strategic-management model, clear vision and mission statements are needed before alternative strategies can be formulated and implemented. As many managers as possible should be involved in the process of developing these statements because, through involvement, people become committed to an organization.

A widely used approach to developing a vision and mission statement is first to select several articles about these statements and ask all managers to read these as background information. Then ask managers themselves to prepare a vision and mission statement for the organization. A facilitator or committee of top managers should then merge these statements into a single document and distribute the draft statements to all managers. A request for modifications, additions, and deletions is needed next, along with a meeting to revise the document. To the extent that all managers have input into and support the final documents, organizations can more easily obtain managers' support for other strategy formulation, implementation, and evaluation activities. Thus, the process of developing a vision and mission statement represents a great opportunity for strategists to obtain needed support from all managers in the firm.

During the process of developing vision and mission statements, some organizations use discussion groups of managers to develop and modify existing statements. Some organizations hire an outside consultant or facilitator to manage the process and help draft the language. Sometimes an outside person with expertise in developing such statements, who has unbiased views, can manage the process more effectively than an internal group or committee of managers. Decisions on how best to communicate the vision and mission to all managers, employees, and external constituencies of an organization are needed when the documents are in final form. Some organizations even develop a videotape to explain the statements and how they were developed.

An article by Campbell and Yeung emphasizes that the process of developing a mission statement should create an "emotional bond" and "sense of mission" between the organization and its employees.[5] Commitment to a company's strategy and intellectual agreement on the strategies to be pursued do not necessarily translate into an emotional bond; hence, strategies that have been formulated may not be implemented. These researchers stress that an emotional bond comes when an individual personally identifies with the underlying values and behavior of a firm, thus turning intellectual agreement and commitment to strategy into a sense of mission. Campbell and Yeung also differentiate between the terms *vision* and *mission*, saying that vision is "a possible and desirable future state of an organization" that includes specific goals, whereas mission is more associated with behavior and the present.

Importance (Benefits) of Vision and Mission Statements

The importance (benefits) of vision and mission statements to effective strategic management is well documented in the literature, although research results are mixed. Rarick and Vitton found that firms with a formalized mission statement have twice the average return on shareholders' equity than those firms without a formalized mission statement have; Bart and Baetz found a positive relationship between mission statements and organizational performance; *BusinessWeek* reports that firms using mission statements have a 30 percent higher return on certain financial measures than those without such statements; however, some studies have found that having a mission statement does not directly contribute positively to financial performance.[6] The extent of manager and employee involvement in developing vision and mission statements can make a difference in business success. This chapter provides guidelines for developing these important documents. In actual practice, wide variations exist in the nature, composition, and use of both vision and mission statements. King and Cleland recommend that organizations carefully develop a written mission statement in order to reap the following benefits:

1. To ensure unanimity of purpose within the organization
2. To provide a basis, or standard, for allocating organizational resources
3. To establish a general tone or organizational climate
4. To serve as a focal point for individuals to identify with the organization's purpose and direction, and to deter those who cannot from participating further in the organization's activities
5. To facilitate the translation of objectives into a work structure involving the assignment of tasks to responsible elements within the organization
6. To specify organizational purposes and then to translate these purposes into objectives in such a way that cost, time, and performance parameters can be assessed and controlled.[7]

Reuben Mark, former CEO of Colgate, maintains that a clear mission increasingly must make sense internationally. Mark's thoughts on vision are as follows:

> When it comes to rallying everyone to the corporate banner, it's essential to push one vision globally rather than trying to drive home different messages in different cultures. The trick is to keep the vision simple but elevated: "We make the world's fastest computers" or "Telephone service for everyone." You're never going to get anyone to charge the machine guns only for financial objectives. It's got to be something that makes people feel better, feel a part of something.[8]

A Resolution of Divergent Views

Another benefit of developing a comprehensive mission statement is that divergent views among managers can be revealed and resolved through the process. The question "What is our business?" can create controversy. Raising the question often reveals differences among strategists in the organization. Individuals who have worked together for a long time and who think they know each other suddenly may realize that they are in fundamental disagreement. For example, in a college or university, divergent views regarding the relative importance of teaching, research, and service often are expressed during the mission statement development process. Negotiation, compromise, and eventual agreement on important issues are needed before people can focus on more specific strategy-formulation activities.

Considerable disagreement among an organization's strategists over vision and mission statements can cause trouble if not resolved. For example, unresolved disagreement over the business mission was one of the reasons for W. T. Grant's bankruptcy and eventual liquidation. As one executive reported:

> There was a lot of dissension within the company whether we should go the Kmart route or go after the Montgomery Ward and JCPenney position. Ed Staley and Lou Lustenberger (two top executives) were at loggerheads over the issue, with the upshot being we took a position between the two and that consequently stood for nothing.[9]

Too often, strategists develop vision and business mission statements only when the organization is in trouble. Of course, it is needed then. Developing and communicating a clear mission during troubled times indeed may have spectacular results and even may reverse decline. However, to wait until an organization is in trouble to develop a vision and mission statement is a gamble that characterizes irresponsible management. According to Drucker, the most important time to ask seriously, "What do we want to become?" and "What is our business?" is when a company has been successful:

> Success always obsoletes the very behavior that achieved it, always creates new realities, and always creates new and different problems. Only the fairy tale story ends, "They lived happily ever after." It is never popular to argue with success or to rock the boat. It will not be long before success will turn into failure. Sooner or later, even the most successful answer to the question "What is our business?" becomes obsolete.[10]

In multidivisional organizations, strategists should ensure that divisional units perform strategic-management tasks, including the development of a statement of vision and mission. Each division should involve its own managers and employees in developing a vision and mission statement that is consistent with and supportive of the corporate mission. Ten benefits of having a clear mission and vision are provided in Table 2-2.

An organization that fails to develop a vision statement as well as a comprehensive and inspiring mission statement loses the opportunity to present itself favorably to existing and potential *stakeholders*. All organizations need customers, employees, and managers, and most firms need creditors, suppliers, and distributors. The vision and mission statements are effective vehicles for communicating with important internal and external stakeholders. The principal benefit of these statements as tools of strategic management is derived from their specification of the ultimate aims of a firm:

> They provide managers with a unity of direction that transcends individual, parochial, and transitory needs. They promote a sense of shared expectations among all levels and generations of employees. They consolidate values over time and across individuals and interest groups. They project a sense of worth and intent that can be identified and assimilated by company outsiders. Finally, they affirm the company's commitment to responsible action, which is symbiotic with its need to preserve and protect the essential claims of insiders for sustained survival, growth, and profitability of the firm.[11]

Characteristics of a Mission Statement

A Declaration of Attitude

A mission statement is more than a statement of specific details; it is a declaration of attitude and outlook. It usually is broad in scope for at least two major reasons. First, a good mission

TABLE 2-2   Ten Benefits of Having a Clear Mission and Vision

1. Achieve clarity of purpose among all managers and employees.
2. Provide a basis for all other strategic planning activities, including internal and external assessment, establishing objectives, developing strategies, choosing among alternative strategies, devising policies, establishing organizational structure, allocating resources, and evaluating performance.
3. Provide direction.
4. Provide a focal point for all stakeholders of the firm.
5. Resolve divergent views among managers.
6. Promote a sense of shared expectations among all managers and employees.
7. Project a sense of worth and intent to all stakeholders.
8. Project an organized, motivated organization worthy of support.
9. Achieve higher organizational performance.
10. Achieve synergy among all managers and employees.

statement allows for the generation and consideration of a range of feasible alternative objectives and strategies without unduly stifling management creativity. Excess specificity would limit the potential of creative growth for the organization. However, an overly general statement that does not exclude any strategy alternatives could be dysfunctional. Apple Computer's mission statement, for example, should not open the possibility for diversification into pesticides—or Ford Motor Company's into food processing.

Second, a mission statement needs to be broad to reconcile differences effectively among, and appeal to, an organization's diverse *stakeholders,* the individuals and groups of individuals who have a special stake or claim on the company. Thus a mission statement should be *reconcilatory.* Stakeholders include employees, managers, stockholders, boards of directors, customers, suppliers, distributors, creditors, governments (local, state, federal, and foreign), unions, competitors, environmental groups, and the general public. Stakeholders affect and are affected by an organization's strategies, yet the claims and concerns of diverse constituencies vary and often conflict. For example, the general public is especially interested in social responsibility, whereas stockholders are more interested in profitability. Claims on any business literally may number in the thousands, and they often include clean air, jobs, taxes, investment opportunities, career opportunities, equal employment opportunities, employee benefits, salaries, wages, clean water, and community services. All stakeholders' claims on an organization cannot be pursued with equal emphasis. A good mission statement indicates the relative attention that an organization will devote to meeting the claims of various stakeholders.

The fine balance between specificity and generality is difficult to achieve, but it is well worth the effort. George Steiner offers the following insight on the need for a mission statement to be broad in scope:

Most business statements of mission are expressed at high levels of abstraction. Vagueness nevertheless has its virtues. Mission statements are not designed to express concrete ends, but rather to provide motivation, general direction, an image, a tone, and a philosophy to guide the enterprise. An excess of detail could prove counterproductive since concrete specification could be the base for rallying opposition. Precision might stifle creativity in the formulation of an acceptable mission or purpose. Once an aim is cast in concrete, it creates a rigidity in an organization and resists change. Vagueness leaves room for other managers to fill in the details.[12]

As indicated in Table 2-3, in addition to being broad in scope, an effective mission statement should not be too lengthy; recommended length is less than 250 words. An effective mission statement should arouse positive feelings and emotions about an organization; it should be inspiring in the sense that it motivates readers to action. A mission statement should be enduring.

All of these are desired characteristics of a statement. An effective mission statement generates the impression that a firm is successful, has direction, and is worthy of time, support, and investment—from all socioeconomic groups of people.

It reflects judgments about future growth directions and strategies that are based on forward-looking external and internal analyses. A business mission should provide useful criteria for selecting among alternative strategies. A clear mission statement provides a basis for generating and screening strategic options. The statement of mission should be dynamic in orientation, allowing judgments about the most promising growth directions and those considered less promising.

A Customer Orientation

A good mission statement describes an organization's purpose, customers, products or services, markets, philosophy, and basic technology. According to Vern McGinnis, a mission statement should (1) define what the organization is and what the organization aspires to be, (2) be limited enough to exclude some ventures and broad enough to allow for creative growth, (3) distinguish a given organization from all others, (4) serve as a framework for evaluating both current and prospective activities, and (5) be stated in terms sufficiently clear to be widely understood throughout the organization.[13]

A good mission statement reflects the anticipations of customers. Rather than developing a product and then trying to find a market, the operating philosophy of organizations should be to identify customers' needs and then provide a product or service to fulfill those needs.

Good mission statements identify the utility of a firm's products to its customers. This is why AT&T's mission statement focuses on communication rather than on telephones; it is why ExxonMobil's mission statement focuses on energy rather than on oil and gas; it is why Union Pacific's mission statement focuses on transportation rather than on railroads; it is why Universal Studios' mission statement focuses on entertainment rather than on movies. A major reason for developing a business mission statement is to attract customers who give meaning to an organization.

The following utility statements are relevant in developing a mission statement:

Do not offer me things.

Do not offer me clothes. Offer me attractive looks.

Do not offer me shoes. Offer me comfort for my feet and the pleasure of walking.

Do not offer me a house. Offer me security, comfort, and a place that is clean and happy.

Do not offer me books. Offer me hours of pleasure and the benefit of knowledge.

Do not offer me CDs. Offer me leisure and the sound of music.

Do not offer me tools. Offer me the benefits and the pleasure that come from making beautiful things.

Do not offer me furniture. Offer me comfort and the quietness of a cozy place.

Do not offer me things. Offer me ideas, emotions, ambience, feelings, and benefits.

Please, do not offer me *things*.

Mission Statement Components

Mission statements can and do vary in length, content, format, and specificity. Most practitioners and academicians of strategic management feel that an effective statement should include nine *components*. Because a mission statement is often the most visible and public part of the strategic-management process, it is important that it includes the nine characteristics as summarized in Table 2-3, as well as the following nine components:

1. *Customers*—Who are the firm's customers?
2. *Products or services*—What are the firm's major products or services?
3. *Markets*—Geographically, where does the firm compete?
4. *Technology*—Is the firm technologically current?

TABLE 2-3 Characteristics of a Mission Statement

1. Broad in scope; do not include monetary amounts, numbers, percentages, ratios, or objectives
2. Less than 250 words in length
3. Inspiring
4. Identify the utility of a firm's products
5. Reveal that the firm is socially responsible
6. Reveal that the firm is environmentally responsible
7. Include nine components customers, products or services, markets, technology, concern for survival/growth/profits, philosophy, self-concept, concern for public image, concern for employees
8. Reconciliatory
9. Enduring

5. *Concern for survival, growth, and profitability*—Is the firm committed to growth and financial soundness?
6. *Philosophy*—What are the basic beliefs, values, aspirations, and ethical priorities of the firm?
7. *Self-concept*—What is the firm's distinctive competence or major competitive advantage?
8. *Concern for public image*—Is the firm responsive to social, community, and environmental concerns?
9. *Concern for employees*—Are employees a valuable asset of the firm?[14]

Excerpts from the mission statements of different organizations are provided in Table 2-4 to exemplify the nine essential mission statement components.

Writing and Evaluating Mission Statements

Perhaps the best way to develop a skill for writing and evaluating mission statements is to study actual company missions. Therefore, the mission statements presented in Table 2-5 are evaluated based on the nine desired components. Note in Table 2-5 that numbers provided in each statement reveal what components are included in the respective documents. Among the statements in Table 2-5, note that the Dell mission statement is the best because it lacks only one component, whereas the L'Oreal statement is the worst, lacking six of the nine recommended components.

There is no one best mission statement for a particular organization, so good judgment is required in evaluating mission statements. Realize that some individuals are more demanding than others in assessing mission statements in this manner. For example, if a statement merely includes the word "customers" without specifying who the customers are, is that satisfactory? Ideally a statement would provide more than simply inclusion of a single word such as "products" or "employees" regarding a respective component. Why? Because the statement should be informative, inspiring, enduring, and serve to motivate stakeholders to action. Evaluation of a mission statement regarding inclusion of the nine components is just the beginning of the process to assess a statement's overall effectiveness.

Special Note to Students

Recall that gaining and sustaining competitive advantage is the essence of strategic management, so when presenting your vision/mission analysis for the firm, be sure to address the "self concept" or "distinctive competence" component. Compare your recommended vision/mission statement both with the firm's existing statements and with rival firms' statements in order to clearly reveal how your recommendations or strategic plan enables the firm to gain and sustain competitive advantage. Thus, your proposed mission statement should certainly include the nine components and nine characteristics, but in your vision/mission discussion, focus on competitive advantage. In other words, be prescriptive, forward-looking, and insightful—couching your vision/mission overview in terms of how you believe the firm can

TABLE 2-4 Examples of the Nine Essential Components of a Mission Statement

1. Customers

We believe our first responsibility is to the doctors, nurses, patients, mothers, and all others who use our products and services. (Johnson & Johnson)

To earn our customers' loyalty, we listen to them, anticipate their needs, and act to create value in their eyes. (Lexmark International)

2. Products or Services

AMAX's principal products are molybdenum, coal, iron ore, copper, lead, zinc, petroleum and natural gas, potash, phosphates, nickel, tungsten, silver, gold, and magnesium. (AMAX Engineering Company)

Standard Oil Company (Indiana) is in business to find and produce crude oil, natural gas, and natural gas liquids; to manufacture high-quality products useful to society from these raw materials; and to distribute and market those products and to provide dependable related services to the consuming public at reasonable prices. (Standard Oil Company)

3. Markets

We are dedicated to the total success of Corning Glass Works as a worldwide competitor. (Corning Glass Works)

Our emphasis is on North American markets, although global opportunities will be explored. (Blockway)

4. Technology

Control Data is in the business of applying micro-electronics and computer technology in two general areas: computer-related hardware; and computing-enhancing services, which include computation, information, education, and finance. (Control Data)

We will continually strive to meet the preferences of adult smokers by developing technologies that have the potential to reduce the health risks associated with smoking. (RJ Reynolds)

5. Concern for Survival, Growth, and Profitability

In this respect, the company will conduct its operations prudently and will provide the profits and growth which will assure Hoover's ultimate success. (Hoover Universal)

To serve the worldwide need for knowledge at a fair profit by adhering, evaluating, producing, and distributing valuable information in a way that benefits our customers, employees, other investors, and our society. (McGraw-Hill)

6. Philosophy

Our world-class leadership is dedicated to a management philosophy that holds people above profits. (Kellogg)

It's all part of the Mary Kay philosophy—a philosophy based on the golden rule. A spirit of sharing and caring where people give cheerfully of their time, knowledge, and experience. (Mary Kay Cosmetics)

7. Self-Concept

Crown Zellerbach is committed to leapfrogging ongoing competition within 1,000 days by unleashing the constructive and creative abilities and energies of each of its employees. (Crown Zellerbach)

8. Concern for Public Image

To share the world's obligation for the protection of the environment. (Dow Chemical)

To contribute to the economic strength of society and function as a good corporate citizen on a local, state, and national basis in all countries in which we do business. (Pfizer)

9. Concern for Employees

To recruit, develop, motivate, reward, and retain personnel of exceptional ability, character, and dedication by providing good working conditions, superior leadership, compensation on the basis of performance, an attractive benefit program, opportunity for growth, and a high degree of employment security. (The Wachovia Corporation)

To compensate its employees with remuneration and fringe benefits competitive with other employment opportunities in its geographical area and commensurate with their contributions toward efficient corporate operations. (Public Service Electric & Gas Company)

best gain and sustain competitive advantage. Do not be content with merely showing a nine-component comparison of your proposed statement with rival firms' statements, although that would be nice to include in your analysis.

Conclusion

Every organization has a unique purpose and reason for being. This uniqueness should be reflected in vision and mission statements. The nature of a business vision and mission can represent either a competitive advantage or disadvantage for the firm. An organization achieves a heightened sense of purpose when strategists, managers, and employees develop and communicate a clear business vision and mission. Drucker says that developing a clear business vision and mission is the "first responsibility of strategists."

TABLE 2-5   Example Mission Statements

Fleetwood Enterprises will lead the recreational vehicle and manufactured housing industries (2, 7) in providing quality products, with a passion for customer-driven innovation (1). We will emphasize training, embrace diversity and provide growth opportunities for our associates and our dealers (9). We will lead our industries in the application of appropriate technologies (4). We will operate at the highest levels of ethics and compliance with a focus on exemplary corporate governance (6). We will deliver value to our shareholders, positive operating results and industry-leading earnings (5). (*Author comment: Statement lacks two components: Markets and Concern for Public Image*)

We aspire to make PepsiCo the world's (3) premier consumer products company, focused on convenient foods and beverages (2). We seek to produce healthy financial rewards for investors (5) as we provide opportunities for growth and enrichment to our employees (9), our business partners and the communities (8) in which we operate. And in everything we do, we strive to act with honesty, openness, fairness and integrity (6). (*Author comment: Statement lacks three components: Customers, Technology, and Self-Concept*)

We are loyal to Royal Caribbean and Celebrity and strive for continuous improvement in everything we do. We always provide service with a friendly greeting and a smile (7). We anticipate the needs of our customers and make all efforts to exceed our customers' expectations (1). We take ownership of any problem that is brought to our attention. We engage in conduct that enhances our corporate reputation and employee morale (9). We are committed to act in the highest ethical manner and respect the rights and dignity of others (6). (*Author comment: Statement lacks five components: Products/Services, Markets, Technology, Concern for Survival/Growth/Profits, Concern for Public Image*)

Dell's mission is to be the most successful computer company (2) in the world (3) at delivering the best customer experience in markets we serve (1). In doing so, Dell will meet customer expectations of highest quality; leading technology (4); competitive pricing; individual and company accountability (6); best-in-class service and support (7); flexible customization capability (7); superior corporate citizenship (8); financial stability (5). (*Author comment: Statement lacks only one component: Concern for Employees*)

Procter & Gamble will provide branded products and services of superior quality and value (7) that improve the lives of the world's (3) consumers. As a result, consumers (1) will reward us with industry leadership in sales, profit (5), and value creation, allowing our people (9), our shareholders, and the communities (8) in which we live and work to prosper. (*Author comment: Statement lacks three components: Products/Services, Technology, and Philosophy*)

At L'Oreal, we believe that lasting business success is built upon ethical (6) standards which guide growth and on a genuine sense of responsibility to our employees (9), our consumers, our environment and to the communities in which we operate (8). (*Author comment: Statement lacks six components: Customers, Products/Services, Markets, Technology, Concern for Survival/Growth/Profits, Concern for Public Image*)

Note: The numbers in parentheses correspond to the nine components listed on page 81; author comments also refer to those components.

A good mission statement reveals an organization's customers; products or services; markets; technology; concern for survival, growth, and profitability; philosophy; self-concept; concern for public image; and concern for employees. These nine basic components serve as a practical framework for evaluating and writing mission statements. As the first step in strategic management, the vision and mission statements provide direction for all planning activities.

Well-designed vision and mission statements are essential for formulating, implementing, and evaluating strategy. Developing and communicating a clear business vision and mission are the most commonly overlooked tasks in strategic management. Without clear statements of vision and mission, a firm's short-term actions can be counterproductive to long-term interests. Vision and mission statements always should be subject to revision, but, if carefully prepared, they will require infrequent major changes. Organizations usually reexamine their vision and mission statements annually. Effective mission statements stand the test of time.

Vision and mission statements are essential tools for strategists, a fact illustrated in a short story told by Porsche's former CEO Peter Schultz:

Three people were at work on a construction site. All were doing the same job, but when each was asked what his job was, the answers varied: "Breaking rocks," the first replied; "Earning a living," responded the second; "Helping to build a cathedral," said the third. Few of us can build cathedrals. But to the extent we can see the cathedral in whatever cause we are following, the job seems more worthwhile. Good strategists and a clear mission help us find those cathedrals in what otherwise could be dismal issues and empty causes.[15]

Key Terms and Concepts

Concern for Employees (p. 82)
Concern for Public Image (p. 82)
**Concern for Survival, Growth, and
    Profitability** (p. 82)
Creed Statement (p. 75)
Customers (p. 81)
Markets (p. 81)
Mission Statement (p. 75)

Mission Statement Components (p. 81)
Philosophy (p. 82)
Products or Services (p. 81)
Reconciliatory (p. 80)
Self-Concept (p. 82)
Stakeholders (p. 80)
Technology (p. 81)
Vision Statement (p. 75)

Issues for Review and Discussion

1. Microsoft has a mission statement. Visit http://www
   .microsoft.com/about/corporatecitizenship/en-us/default
   .aspx and analyze the company's mission statement in
   light of the guidelines in Chapter 2.
2. Summarize Microsoft's successful global strategy for the
   last decade. Can that strategy be as successful in 2012 and
   2013? Explain.
3. See if you can find a vision statement for Microsoft. If
   not, write a proposed vision statement for the company.
4. Should the mission statement components vary in importance depending on type of business? If yes, how would their
   relative importance vary for Microsoft versus IKEA, a company highlighted at the beginning of Chapter 7.
5. List three things you are on a mission to accomplish in the
   next three years. How relevant is the concept of vision/
   mission to an individual in their personal and professional
   life? Explain.
6. Conduct a Google search for the key words "mission
   statement." What are the two best websites in your opinion that provides example mission statements?
7. Write a vision statement for your university. Write a vision statement for your School (or College) of Business
   within the university.
8. If you just purchased a 10-employee company, how would
   you establish a clear vision and mission?
9. Identify from the Internet six mission statement examples.
   Evaluate the six statements and bring your analysis to
   class.
10. How and why could the process of developing a vision
    and mission statement vary across countries?
11. In rank order of importance, list six benefits of having a
    clearly defined vision and mission statement.

12. Only the fairy story ends "they lived happily ever after."
    What is the relevance of this statement to the concepts
    vision and mission statement?
13. Explain the meaning and significance of the term
    "reconciliatory" in developing mission statements.
14. List the nine mission statement components. Give an ex-
    ample of each component for your college or university.
15. In order of importance, rank seven characteristics of a
    mission statement.
16. Write a vision and mission statement for a local restaurant
    in your area.
17. Write one excellent sentence for Pepsi Cola Company that
    includes four mission statement components.
18. Within a given industry, compare the mission statements
    of three companies in your country versus three compet-
    ing companies in the United States. How did they differ?
19. Does IKEA have its vision and mission statement posted
    on its website? Should the company? Why or why not?
20. How often do you think a firm's vision and mission state-
    ments should be changed? Why?
21. Explain how a mission statement can be "reconciliatory."
    Give an example.
22. Do local fast food restaurants need a mission statement
    posted in their place of business? Why or why not?
23. Find 10 mission statements on the Internet. Evaluate the
    statements in terms of six characteristics and nine
    components.
24. Referring to the end of Chapter 2, explain how a team of
    students should couch their mission statement discussion
    of slides in a presentation.
25. List the four most important characteristics of a mission
    statement for a small retail store. Explain.

Notes

1. Barbara Bartkus, Myron Glassman, and Bruce McAfee, "Mission Statements: Are They Smoke and Mirrors?" *Business Horizons*, November–December 2000, 23.
2. Peter Drucker, *Management: Tasks, Responsibilities, and Practices* (New York: Harper & Row, 1974), 61.
3. Fred David, "How Companies Define Their Mission," *Long Range Planning* 22, no. 1 (February 1989): 90–92; John Pearce II and Fred David, "Corporate Mission Statements: The Bottom Line," *Academy of Management Executive* 1, no. 2 (May 1987): 110.
4. Joseph Quigley, "Vision: How Leaders Develop It, Share It and Sustain It," *Business Horizons*, September–October 1994, 39.
5. Andrew Campbell and Sally Yeung, "Creating a Sense of Mission," *Long Range Planning* 24, no. 4 (August 1991): 17.
6. Charles Rarick and John Vitton, "Mission Statements Make Cents," *Journal of Business Strategy* 16 (1995): 11. Also, Christopher Bart and Mark Baetz, "The Relationship Between Mission Statements and Firm Performance: An Exploratory Study," *Journal of Management Studies* 35 (1998): 823; "Mission Possible," *Business Week* (August 1999): F12.
7. W. R. King and D. I. Cleland, *Strategic Planning and Policy* (New York: Van Nostrand Reinhold, 1979), 124.
8. Brian Dumaine, "What the Leaders of Tomorrow See," *Fortune,* July 3, 1989, 50.
9. Drucker, 78, 79.
10. "How W. T. Grant Lost $175 Million Last Year," *Business Week,* February 25, 1975, 75.
11. Drucker, 88.
12. John Pearce II, "The Company Mission as a Strategic Tool," *Sloan Management Review* 23, no. 3 (Spring 1982): 74.
13. George Steiner, *Strategic Planning: What Every Manager Must Know* (New York: The Free Press, 1979), 160.
14. Vern McGinnis, "The Mission Statement: A Key Step in Strategic Planning," *Business* 31, no. 6 (November–December 1981): 41.
15. Drucker, 61.
16. http://ezinearticles.com/?Elements-of-a-Mission-Statement&id=3846671
17. Robert Waterman Jr., *The Renewal Factor: How the Best Get and Keep the Competitive Edge* (New York: Bantam, 1987); *Business Week,* September 14, 1987, 120.

Current Readings

Bartkus, Barbara, Myron Glassman, and R. Bruce McAfee. "Mission Statements: Are They Smoke and Mirrors?" *Business Horizons* 43, no. 6 (November–December 2000): 23.

Church Mission Statements, http://www.missionstatements.com/church_mission_statements.html

Collins, David J., and Michael G. Rukstad. "Can You Say What Your Strategy Is?" *Harvard Business Review*, April 2008, 82.

Company Mission Statements, http://www.missionstatements.com/company_mission_statements.html

Conger, Jay A., and Douglas A. Ready. "Enabling Bold Visions." *MIT Sloan Management Review* 49, no. 2 (Winter 2008): 70.

Day, George S., and Paul Schoemaker. "Peripheral Vision: Sensing and Acting on Weak Signals." *Long Range Planning* 37, no. 2 (April 2004): 117.

Ibarra, Herminia, and Otilia Obodaru. "Women and the Vision Thing." *Harvard Business Review*, January 2009, 62–71.

Lissak, Michael, and Johan Roos. "Be Coherent, Not Visionary." *Long Range Planning* 34, no. 1 (February 2001): 53.

Newsom, Mi Kyong, David A. Collier, and Eric O. Olsen. "Using 'Biztainment' to Gain Competitive Advantage." *Business Horizons*, March–April 2009, 167–166.

Nonprofit Organization Mission Statements, http://www.missionstatements.com/nonprofit_mission_statements.html

Restaurant Mission Statements, http://www.missionstatements.com/restaurant_mission_statements.html

School Mission Statements, http://www.missionstatements.com/school_mission_statements.html

ASSURANCE OF LEARNING EXERCISES

Assurance of Learning Exercise 2A

Examining Potential Changes Needed in a Firm's Vision/Mission

Purpose

Microsoft is featured in the opening chapter insert as a firm that engages in excellent strategic planning. Microsoft has a major new product. Microsoft Dynamics CRM 4.0 is now available for on-premise and on-demand deployments in Danish, English, Finnish, Dutch, French, German, simplified Chinese and Spanish. Seventeen additional languages—Arabic, Brazilian Portuguese, Czech, Greek, Hebrew, Hong Kong Chinese, Hungarian, Italian, Japanese, Korean, Norwegian, Polish, Portuguese, Russian, Swedish, traditional Chinese, and Turkish—will be released in late 2011.

This exercise gives you practice examining the change or needed change in a company's vision and mission statements, given a change in the company's product offerings. Visit http://www.microsoft.com/about/diversity/en/us/vision.aspx, and locate Microsoft's vision and mission statements.

Instructions

Step 1   Evaluate the vision and mission statements in light of the characteristics and components in Chapter 2.

Step 2   Write improved vision and mission statements for Microsoft given:
a) shortcomings of the statements based on Chapter 2 concepts, and
b) the new Microsoft Dynamics CRM 4.0 being rolled out globally.

Assurance of Learning Exercise 2B

Studying an Alternative View of Mission Statement Content

Purpose

This exercise presents a somewhat different view of mission statements as compared to concepts presented in Chapter 2. For example, according to Bart (1997), a mission statement consists of three essential components:

1. Key market – Who is your target client/customer?
2. Contribution – What product or service do you provide to that client?
3. Distinction – What makes your product or service unique, so that the client would choose you?

For example, if you locate McDonald's mission statement on the Internet, Bart's essential components are covered in the following ways:

1. Key Market: the fast food customer world-wide
2. Contribution: tasty and reasonably-priced food prepared in a high-quality manner
3. Distinction: delivered consistently (world-wide) in a low-key décor and friendly atmosphere.

Another example, is Courtyard by Marriott, which provides travelers with economy and quality lodging. Its key components are:

1. Key Market: economy and quality minded travelers
2. Contribution: moderate priced lodging
3. Distinction: consistently perceived as clean, comfortable, well-maintained, and attractive, staffed by friendly, attentive and efficient people

Instruction

Compare and contrast the guidelines presented by Bart with the guidelines presented in Chapter 2.

Source: Based on information at 1) Christopher K. Bart. "Sex, Lies, and Mission Statements." *Business Horizons,* pp. 9–18, November–December, 1997, and 2) www.wikipedia.com.

Assurance of Learning Exercise 2C

Evaluating Mission Statements

Purpose

A business mission statement is an integral part of strategic management. It provides direction for formulating, implementing, and evaluating strategic activities. This exercise will give you practice evaluating mission statements, a skill that is a prerequisite to writing a good mission statement. The mission statement for Adidas is given below:

"The Adidas Group strives to be the global leader in the sporting goods industry with sports brands built on a passion for sports and a sporting lifestyle. We are dedicated to consistently delivering outstanding financial results. We are innovation and design leaders who seek to help athletes of all skill levels achieve peak performance with every product we bring to market.

We are consumer focused and therefore we continuously improve the quality, look, feel and image of our products and our organizational structures to match and exceed consumer expectations and to provide them with the highest value.

We are a global organization that is socially and environmentally responsible, creative and financially rewarding for our employees and shareholders.

We are committed to continuously strengthening our brands and products to improve our competitive position."

Instructions

Step 1	On a separate sheet of paper, write the nine mission statement components down the left-hand side.
Step 2	Write "yes" or "no" beside each number to indicate whether you feel the Adidas mission statement has included the respective component. For any component that you record a "no," write a good sentence to encompass that component.
Step 3	Turn your paper in to your instructor for a classwork grade.

Assurance of Learning Exercise 2D

Evaluating the Mission Statement of Under Armour—a Competitor of Adidas AG

Purpose

There is always room for improvement in regard to an existing vision and mission statement. Under Armour was founded in 1996 by former University of Maryland football player Kevin Plank. Under Armour sportswear is designed to keep athletes cool, dry and light throughout the course of a game, practice or workout. The technology behind Under Armour's diverse product assortment is complex, but the advice is simple: wear HeatGear® when it's hot, ColdGear® when it's cold, and AllSeasonGear® between the extremes (www.underarmour.com). Visit the Under Armour website and locate their mission statement.

Instructions

Step 1	On a separate sheet of paper, write the nine mission statement components down the left-hand side.
Step 2	Write "yes" or "no" beside each number to indicate whether you feel the Under Armour mission statement has included the respective component. For any component that you record a "no," write a good sentence to encompass that component.
Step 3	Turn your paper in to your instructor for a classwork grade.

Assurance of Learning Exercise 2E

Selecting the Best Vision and Mission Statements in a Given Industry

Purpose

This exercise is designed to get you familiar with existing vision and mission statements in an industry of your choosing.

Instruction

Identify 10 companies in an industry that you are interested in working in one day. Find the companies' vision and mission statements. Keep searching until you have found five vision statements and five mission statements. The statements do not have to be from the same companies. Rank your five vision statements and your five mission statements in order of attractiveness, with 1 being the best and 5 being the worst.

Assurance of Learning Exercise 2F

Writing an Excellent Vision and Mission Statement for Novartis AG

Purpose

This exercise is designed to give you practice developing from scratch or improving an existing vision and mission statement.

Instructions

Step 1   Go to the Novartis AG website and look for the company's vision statement and mission statement. Recall from Chapter 2 that companies use different names or titles for these documents.

Step 2   Prepare an improved vision and mission statement for Novartis AG whether or not you were able to find these statements on the company's website or in the firm's *Annual Report*.

"NOTABLE QUOTES"

"If you're not faster than your competitor, you're in a tenuous position, and if you're only half as fast, you're terminal."
—George Salk

"The opportunities and threats existing in any situation always exceed the resources needed to exploit the opportunities or avoid the threats. Thus, strategy is essentially a problem of allocating resources. If strategy is to be successful, it must allocate superior resources against a decisive opportunity."
—William Cohen

"Organizations pursue strategies that will disrupt the normal course of industry events and forge new industry conditions to the disadvantage of competitors."
—Ian C. Macmillan

"If everyone is thinking alike, then somebody isn't thinking."
—George Patton

"It is not the strongest of the species that survive, nor the most intelligent, but the one most responsive to change."
—Charles Darwin

"Nothing focuses the mind better than the constant sight of a competitor who wants to wipe you off the map."
—Wayne Calloway

The External Assessment

3

CHAPTER OBJECTIVES

After studying this chapter, you should be able to do the following:

1. Describe how to conduct an external strategic-management audit.

2. Discuss 10 major external forces that affect organizations: economic, social, cultural, demographic, environmental, political, governmental, legal, technological, and competitive.

3. Describe key sources of external information, including the Internet.

4. Discuss important forecasting tools used in strategic management.

5. Discuss the importance of monitoring external trends and events.

6. Explain how to develop an EFE Matrix.

7. Explain how to develop a Competitive Profile Matrix.

8. Discuss the importance of gathering competitive intelligence.

9. Describe the trend toward cooperation among competitors.

10. Discuss market commonality and resource similarity in relation to competitive analysis.

ASSURANCE OF LEARNING EXERCISES

Assurance of Learning Exercise 3A
IBM and Africa: An External Assessment

Assurance of Learning Exercise 3B
Preparing a CPM for IBM Based on Countries Rather than Companies

Assurance of Learning Exercise 3C
Develop Divisional IBM EFE Matrices

Assurance of Learning Exercise 3D
Developing an EFE Matrix for Adidas AG

Assurance of Learning Exercise 3E
The External Assessment

Assurance of Learning Exercise 3F
Developing a CPM for IBM Corporation

Assurance of Learning Exercise 3G
Developing a CPM for Adidas AG

Assurance of Learning Exercise 3H
Analyzing Your College or University's External Strategic Situation

This chapter examines the tools and concepts needed to conduct an external strategic management audit (sometimes called *environmental scanning* or *industry analysis*). An *external audit* focuses on identifying and evaluating trends and events beyond the control of a single firm, such as increased foreign competition, population shifts to the Sunbelt, an aging society, consumer fear of traveling, and stock market volatility. An external audit reveals key opportunities and threats confronting an organization so that managers can formulate strategies to take advantage of the opportunities and avoid or reduce the impact of threats. This chapter presents a practical framework for gathering, assimilating, and analyzing external information. The Industrial Organization (I/O) view of strategic management is introduced.

The Chapter 3 boxed insert company pursuing strategies based on an excellent external strategic analysis is IBM.

The Nature of an External Audit

The purpose of an *external audit* is to develop a finite list of opportunities that could benefit a firm and threats that should be avoided. As the term *finite* suggests, the external audit is not aimed at developing an exhaustive list of every possible factor that could influence the business; rather, it is aimed at identifying key variables that offer actionable responses. Firms should be

Excellent Strategic Management Showcased

IBM CORPORATION

Headquartered in Armonk, New York, IBM is a well-known multinational technology and consulting firm that manufactures and sells computer hardware and software. IBM offers infrastructure and hosting services in areas ranging from mainframe computers to nanotechnology. The company's distinctive culture and product branding has given it the nickname *Big Blue*.

In 2011, *Fortune* ranked IBM the 18th largest firm in the United States, as well as the 7th most profitable. Globally, *Forbes* ranked IBM as the 31st largest firm in the world in 2011. IBM employs more than 425,000 employees in over 200 countries, including thousands of scientists, engineers, consultants, and sales professionals.

For the second quarter of 2011, IBM's revenue increased 12 percent to $26.7 billion while its net income rose 8 percent to $3.7 billion. The company's Software revenue rose 17 percent while its Systems and Technology revenue rose 17 percent. Globally, IBM's Growth markets revenue were up 23 percent in that quarter while its business analytics revenue rose more than 20 percent in the first half of the year. The company's Smarter Planet revenue rose more than 50 percent in the first half of 2011 and its Cloud revenue on track to double in 2011.

In September 2011, IBM opened a new office branch in Luanda, Angola (Africa) as part of the company's continued geographic expansion to increase its presence in key growth markets in support of its global strategy. IBM is making huge investments in Africa and recently opened new locations in Dakar, Senegal and Dar es Salaam, Tanzania. IBM now has a direct presence in more than 20 African countries, including South Africa, Ghana, Nigeria, Kenya, Morocco, Egypt, Tunisia and Algeria. IBM already serves a number

of key clients in Central Africa, spanning sectors including telecommunications, oil and gas, finance, and government. For example in Angola, IBM is working with one of the country's major banks to help transform the institution's core banking technology infrastructure and support business growth. With a new system based on IBM Power servers and software technologies, the bank has been able to upgrade its banking services.

Also in September 2011, IBM announced the continued adoption of its smarter computing systems, software, and services across China's private and public sectors. For example, IBM is working with the China National Bureau of Statistics, Guizhou Provincial Health Department and Guizhou Mobile to help each build more advanced IT environments based on IBM's optimized system architecture, data and analytics integration, and cloud computing capabilities. Through these smarter computing initiatives, each organization will improve their operational efficiencies and end-user services.

Source: Based on information at www.ibm.com.

FIGURE 3-1

A Comprehensive Strategic-Management Model

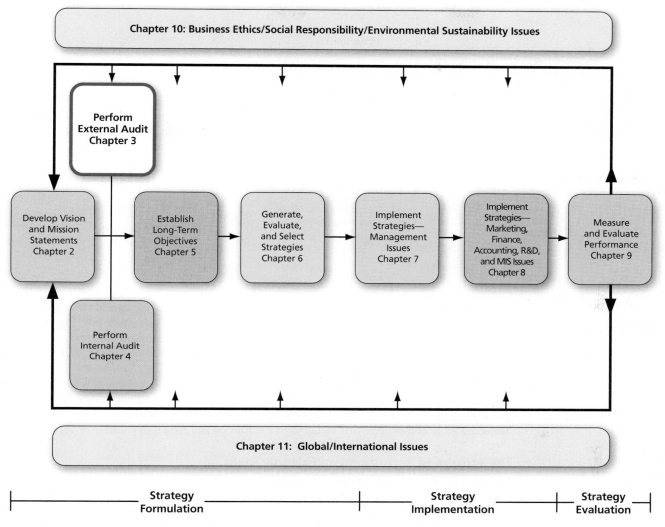

Source: Fred R. David, "How Companies Define Their Mission," *Long Range Planning* 22, no. 3 (June 1988): 40.

able to respond either offensively or defensively to the factors by formulating strategies that take advantage of external opportunities or that minimize the impact of potential threats. Figure 3-1 illustrates how the external audit fits into the strategic-management process.

Key External Forces

External forces can be divided into five broad categories: (1) economic forces; (2) social, cultural, demographic, and natural environment forces; (3) political, governmental, and legal forces; (4) technological forces; and (5) competitive forces. Relationships among these forces and an organization are depicted in Figure 3-2. External trends and events, such as rising food prices and people in African countries coming online, significantly affect products, services, markets, and organizations worldwide. The U.S. unemployment rate is about 10 percent—the most since 1945 when the country downsized from the war effort. All sectors witness high unemployment rates, except for education, health-care services, and government employment. Many Americans still resort to minimum wage jobs to make ends meet.

Changes in external forces translate into changes in consumer demand for both industrial and consumer products and services. External forces affect the types of products developed,

FIGURE 3-2

Relationships Between Key External Forces and an Organization

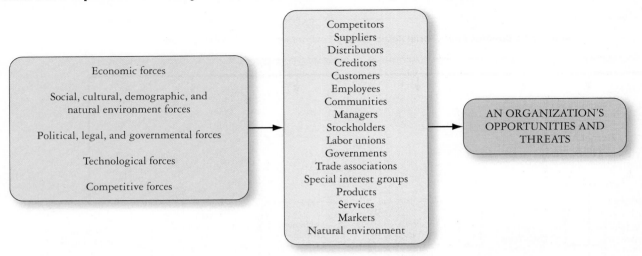

the nature of positioning and market segmentation strategies, the type of services offered, and the choice of businesses to acquire or sell. External forces directly affect both suppliers and distributors. Identifying and evaluating external opportunities and threats enables organizations to develop a clear mission, to design strategies to achieve long-term objectives, and to develop policies to achieve annual objectives.

The increasing complexity of business today is evidenced by more countries developing the capacity and will to compete aggressively in world markets. Foreign businesses and countries are willing to learn, adapt, innovate, and invent to compete successfully in the marketplace. There are more competitive new technologies in Europe and Asia today than ever before.

The Process of Performing an External Audit

The process of performing an external audit must involve as many managers and employees as possible. As emphasized in earlier chapters, involvement in the strategic-management process can lead to understanding and commitment from organizational members. Individuals appreciate having the opportunity to contribute ideas and to gain a better understanding of their firm's industry, competitors, and markets.

To perform an external audit, a company first must gather competitive intelligence and information about economic, social, cultural, demographic, environmental, political, governmental, legal, and technological trends. Individuals can be asked to monitor various sources of information, such as key magazines, trade journals, and newspapers. These persons can submit periodic scanning reports to a committee of managers charged with performing the external audit. This approach provides a continuous stream of timely strategic information and involves many individuals in the external-audit process. The Internet provides another source for gathering strategic information, as do corporate, university, and public libraries. Suppliers, distributors, salespersons, customers, and competitors represent other sources of vital information.

Once information is gathered, it should be assimilated and evaluated. A meeting or series of meetings of managers is needed to collectively identify the most important opportunities and threats facing the firm. These key external factors should be listed on flip charts or a chalkboard. A prioritized list of these factors could be obtained by requesting that all managers rank the factors identified, from 1 for the most important opportunity/threat to 20 for the least important opportunity/ threat. These key external factors can vary over time and by industry. Relationships with suppliers or distributors are often a critical success factor. Other variables commonly used include market share, breadth of competing products, world economies, foreign affiliates, proprietary and key account advantages, price competitiveness, technological advancements, population shifts, interest rates, and pollution abatement.

Freund emphasized that these key external factors should be (1) important to achieving long-term and annual objectives, (2) measurable, (3) applicable to all competing firms, and (4) hierarchical in the sense that some will pertain to the overall company and others will be more narrowly focused on functional or divisional areas.[1] A final list of the most important key external factors should be communicated and distributed widely in the organization. Both opportunities and threats can be key external factors.

The Industrial Organization (I/O) View

The *Industrial Organization (I/O)* approach to competitive advantage advocates that external (industry) factors are more important than internal factors in a firm for achieving competitive advantage. Proponents of the I/O view, such as Michael Porter, contend that organizational performance will be primarily determined by industry forces. Porter's Five-Forces Model, presented later in this chapter, is an example of the I/O perspective, which focuses on analyzing external forces and industry variables as a basis for getting and keeping competitive advantage. Competitive advantage is determined largely by competitive positioning within an industry, according to I/O advocates. Managing strategically from the I/O perspective entails firms striving to compete in attractive industries, avoiding weak or faltering industries, and gaining a full understanding of key external factor relationships within that attractive industry. I/O research provides important contributions to our understanding of how to gain competitive advantage.

I/O theorists contend that external factors and the industry in which a firm competes has a stronger influence on the firm's performance than do the internal functional issues in marketing, finance, and the like. Firm performance, they contend, is based more on industry properties such as economies of scale, barriers to market entry, product differentiation, the economy, and level of competitiveness than on internal resources, capabilities, structure, and operations. The recent global economic recession's negative impact on both strong and weak firms added credence to the notion that external forces are more important than internal.

The I/O view has enhanced our understanding of strategic management. However, it is not a question of whether external or internal factors are more important in gaining and maintaining competitive advantage. Effective integration and understanding of *both* external and internal factors is the key to securing and keeping a competitive advantage. In fact, as discussed in Chapter 6, matching key external opportunities/threats with key internal strengths/weaknesses provides the basis for successful strategy formulation.

Economic Forces

The Dow Jones Industrial Average is over 10,500, corporate profits are high, dividend increases are up sharply, and emerging markets are growing in double digits. Yet, job growth is still stymied, home prices remain low, and millions of people work for minimum wages or are either unemployed or underemployed. Strong exports of energy and grains have farm suppliers and railroads hiring, but commodity prices are up sharply, especially food, which is contributing to rising inflation fears. Many firms are switching to the extent possible to part-time rather than full-time employees to avoid having to pay health benefits. Consumer spending rebounded nicely in 2011 from 2010.

Economic factors have a direct impact on the potential attractiveness of various strategies. For example, when interest rates rise, funds needed for capital expansion become more costly or unavailable. Also, as interest rates rise, discretionary income declines, and the demand for discretionary goods falls. When stock prices increase, the desirability of equity as a source of capital for market development increases. Also, when the market rises, consumer and business wealth expands. A summary of economic variables that often represent opportunities and threats for organizations is provided in Table 3-1.

TABLE 3-1   Key Economic Variables to Be Monitored

Shift to a service economy in the United States	Import/export factors
Availability of credit	Demand shifts for different categories of goods and services
Level of disposable income	Income differences by region and consumer groups
Propensity of people to spend	Price fluctuations
Interest rates	Export of labor and capital from the United States
Inflation rates	Monetary policies
Money market rates	Fiscal policies
Federal government budget deficits	Tax rates
Gross domestic product trend	European Economic Community (EEC) policies
Consumption patterns	Organization of Petroleum Exporting Countries (OPEC) policies
Unemployment trends	
Worker productivity levels	Coalitions of Lesser Developed Countries (LDC) policies
Value of the dollar in world markets	
Stock market trends	
Foreign countries' economic conditions	

To take advantage of Canada's robust economy and eager-to-spend people, many firms are aggressively expanding operations into Canada, including TJX opening many Marshalls stores, Target opening 220 stores, Wal-Mart opening 40 supercenters, and Tanger Outlet Factory Centers opening five new stores in 2011. "Canada is one of the most economically prosperous countries in the world," said Howard Davidowitz, chairman of Davidowitz & Associates, a retail consultancy and investment-banking firm. "It has a stable currency, it did not have a banking crisis and it did not spend itself into insanity."

Trends in the dollar's value have significant and unequal effects on companies in different industries and in different locations. For example, the pharmaceutical, tourism, entertainment, motor vehicle, aerospace, and forest products industries benefit greatly when the dollar falls against the yen and euro. Agricultural and petroleum industries are hurt by the dollar's rise against the currencies of Mexico, Brazil, Venezuela, and Australia. Generally, a strong or high dollar makes U.S. goods more expensive in overseas markets. This worsens the U.S. trade deficit. When the value of the dollar falls, tourism-oriented firms benefit because Americans do not travel abroad as much when the value of the dollar is low; rather, foreigners visit and vacation more in the United States.

A low value of the dollar means lower imports and higher exports; it helps U.S. companies' competitiveness in world markets. The dollar has fallen to five-year lows against the euro and yen, which makes U.S. goods cheaper to foreign consumers and combats deflation by pushing up prices of imports. However, European firms such as Volkswagen AG, Nokia Corp., and Michelin complain that the strong euro hurts their financial performance. The low value of the dollar benefits the U.S. economy in many ways. First, it helps stave off the risks of deflation in the United States and also reduces the U.S. trade deficit. In addition, the low value of the dollar raises the foreign sales and profits of domestic firms, thanks to dollar-induced gains, and encourages foreign countries to lower interest rates and loosen fiscal policy, which stimulates worldwide economic expansion. Some sectors, such as consumer staples, energy, materials, technology, and health care, especially benefit from a low value of the dollar. Manufacturers in many domestic industries in fact benefit because of a weak dollar, which forces foreign rivals to raise prices and extinguish discounts. Domestic firms with big overseas sales, such as McDonald's, greatly benefit from a weak dollar. Table 3-2 lists some advantages and disadvantages of a weak U.S. dollar for American firms.

The improving but weak economy worldwide and depressed home prices has dramatically slowed the migration of people from country to country and from the city to the suburbs. Because people are not moving nearly as much as in years past, there is lower and lower demand for new or used houses. Thus the housing market is expected to remain sluggish well into 2012 and 2013.

TABLE 3-2   Advantages and Disadvantages of a Weak Dollar for Domestic Firms

Advantages	Disadvantages
1. Leads to more exports	1. Can lead to inflation
2. Leads to lower imports	2. Can cause rise in oil prices
3. Makes U.S. goods cheaper to foreign consumers	3. Can weaken U.S. government
4. Combats deflation by pushing up prices of imports	4. Makes it unattractive for Americans to travel globally
5. Can contribute to rise in stock prices in short run	5. Can contribute to fall in stock prices in long run
6. Encourages foreign countries to lower interest rates	
7. Raises the revenues and profits of firms that do business outside the United States	
8. Forces foreign firms to raise prices	
9. Reduces the U.S. trade deficit	
10. Encourages firms to globalize	
11. Encourages foreigners to visit the United States	

Social, Cultural, Demographic, and Natural Environment Forces

Social, cultural, demographic, and environmental changes have a major impact on virtually all products, services, markets, and customers. Small, large, for-profit, and nonprofit organizations in all industries are being staggered and challenged by the opportunities and threats arising from changes in social, cultural, demographic, and environmental variables. In every way, the United States is much different today than it was yesterday, and tomorrow promises even greater changes.

The United States is getting older and less white. The oldest members of America's 76 million baby boomers plan to retire soon, and this has lawmakers and younger taxpayers deeply concerned about who will pay their Social Security, Medicare, and Medicaid. Individuals age 65 and older in the United States as a percentage of the population will rise to 18.5 percent by 2025.

By 2075, the United States will have no racial or ethnic majority. This forecast is aggravating tensions over issues such as immigration and affirmative action. Hawaii, California, and New Mexico already have no majority race or ethnic group. For the first time ever, the number of Hispanic people surpassed the number of whites in New Mexico in the recent 2010 census data. New Mexico's population grew 13.2 percent to 2.06 million from 2000 to 2010. Also, people from the West Coast are seeking more affordable living in the Rocky Mountain states. For example, Idaho's population increased 21.1 percent from 2000 to 2010 with 1.7 million people now calling Idaho home. There is a "migration for cheaper life" across the United States.

The population of the world surpassed 7.0 billion in 2011; the United States has just over 310 million people. That leaves billions of people outside the United States who may be interested in the products and services produced through domestic firms. Remaining solely domestic is an increasingly risky strategy, especially as the world population continues to grow to an estimated 8 billion in 2028 and 9 billion in 2054.

Social, cultural, demographic, and environmental trends are shaping the way Americans live, work, produce, and consume. New trends are creating a different type of consumer and, consequently, a need for different products, different services, and different strategies. There are now more American households with people living alone or with unrelated people than there are households consisting of married couples with children. American households are making more and more purchases online.

The trend toward an older America is good news for restaurants, hotels, airlines, cruise lines, tours, resorts, theme parks, luxury products and services, recreational vehicles, home builders, furniture producers, computer manufacturers, travel services, pharmaceutical firms, automakers, and funeral homes. Older Americans are especially interested in health care, financial services, travel, crime prevention, and leisure. The world's longest-living people are the Japanese, with Japanese women living to 86.3 years and men living to 80.1 years on average. By 2050, the Census Bureau projects that the number of Americans age 100 and older will increase to over 834,000 from just under 100,000 centenarians in the United States in 2000. Americans age 65 and over will increase from 12.6 percent of the U.S. population in 2000 to 20.0 percent by the year 2050.

The aging American population affects the strategic orientation of nearly all organizations. Apartment complexes for the elderly, with one meal a day, transportation, and utilities included in the rent, have increased nationwide. Called *lifecare facilities,* these complexes now exceed 2 million. Some well-known companies building these facilities include Avon, Marriott, and Hyatt. Individuals age 65 and older in the United States comprise 13 percent of the total population; Japan's elderly population ratio is 17 percent, and Germany's is 19 percent.

Americans were on the move in a population shift to the South and Rocky Mountain states away from the Northeast and Midwest (Frostbelt), and the expensive West Coast. But the recession and housing bust nationwide has slowed migration throughout the United States. More Americans are staying in place rather than moving. New jobs are the primary reason people move across state lines, so with fewer jobs, there is less need to move. Falling home prices also have prompted people to avoid moving. The historical trend of people moving from the Northeast and Midwest to the Sunbelt and West has dramatically slowed. Hard number data related to this trend can represent key opportunities for many firms and thus can be essential for successful strategy formulation, including where to locate new plants and distribution centers and where to focus marketing efforts.

A summary of important social, cultural, demographic, and environmental variables that represent opportunities or threats for virtually all organizations is given in Table 3-3.

Political, Governmental, and Legal Forces

Federal, state, local, and foreign governments are major regulators, deregulators, subsidizers, employers, and customers of organizations. Political, governmental, and legal factors, therefore, can represent key opportunities or threats for both small and large organizations. Political unrest in the Middle East threatens to raise oil prices globally, which could cause inflation. The political overthrow of monarchies in Egypt, Tunisia, and Libya is spreading to Yemen, Jordan, Syria, and other countries as people in all nations desire liberty and freedom rather than oppression and suppression.

For industries and firms that depend heavily on government contracts or subsidies, political forecasts can be the most important part of an external audit. Changes in patent laws, antitrust legislation, tax rates, and lobbying activities can affect firms significantly. The increasing global interdependence among economies, markets, governments, and organizations makes it imperative that firms consider the possible impact of political variables on the formulation and implementation of competitive strategies.

Many countries worldwide are resorting to protectionism to safeguard their own industries. European Union (EU) nations, for example, have tightened their own trade rules and resumed subsidies for various of their own industries while barring imports from certain other countries. The EU recently restricted imports of U.S. chicken and beef. India is increasing tariffs on foreign steel. Russia perhaps has instituted the most protectionist measures by raising tariffs on most imports and subsidizing its own exports. Russia even imposed a new toll on trucks from the EU, Switzerland, and Turkmenistan. Despite these measures taken by other countries, the United States has largely refrained from "Buy American" policies and protectionist measures, although there are increased tariffs on French cheese and Italian water. Many economists say the current rash of trade constraints will make it harder for global economic growth to recover from the global recession.

TABLE 3-3   Key Social, Cultural, Demographic, and Natural Environment Variables

Childbearing rates	Attitudes toward retirement
Number of special-interest groups	Attitudes toward leisure time
Number of marriages	Attitudes toward product quality
Number of divorces	Attitudes toward customer service
Number of births	Pollution control
Number of deaths	Attitudes toward foreign peoples
Immigration and emigration rates	Energy conservation
Social Security programs	Social programs
Life expectancy rates	Number of churches
Per capita income	Number of church members
Location of retailing, manufacturing, and service businesses	Social responsibility
Attitudes toward business	Attitudes toward careers
Lifestyles	Population changes by race, age, sex, and level of affluence
Traffic congestion	Attitudes toward authority
Inner-city environments	Population changes by city, county, state, region, and country
Average disposable income	Value placed on leisure time
Trust in government	Regional changes in tastes and preferences
Attitudes toward government	Number of women and minority workers
Attitudes toward work	Number of high school and college graduates by geographic area
Buying habits	Recycling
Ethical concerns	Waste management
Attitudes toward saving	Air pollution
Sex roles	Water pollution
Attitudes toward investing	Ozone depletion
Racial equality	Endangered species
Use of birth control	
Average level of education	
Government regulation	

A political debate raging in the United States concerns sales taxes on the Internet. Wal-Mart, Target, and other large retailers are pressuring state governments to collect sales taxes from Amazon.com. Big brick-and-mortar retailers are backing a coalition called the Alliance for Main Street Fairness, which is leading political efforts to change sales-tax laws in more than a dozen states. Wal-Mart's executive Raul Vazquez says, "The rules today don't allow brick-and-mortar retailers to compete evenly with online retailers, and that needs to be addressed."

American Labor Unions

The extent that a state is unionized can be a significant political factor in strategic planning decisions as related to manufacturing plant location and other operational matters. The size of American labor unions has fallen sharply in the last decade due in large part to erosion of the U.S. manufacturing base. The single best example of this is the decline of the United Automobile Workers (UAW) as U.S. automakers and car parts suppliers went through hard times. The number of workers represented by unions in the U.S. fell from 9 percent to 6.9 percent between 2000 and 2010.

Huge declines of late in receipts of federal, state, and municipal governments has contributed to a sharp decline in the membership of public-sector unions. Organized public-sector labor issues are being debated in many state legislatures. State governments seek concessions, the

TABLE 3-4   The Most versus the Least Unionized States

	(% of Workers) Unionized	2000 to 2010 % Change in Union Membership
The Most Unionized States		
1. New York	24.2%	− 5.1%
2. Alaska	22.9%	+ 4.6%
3. Hawaii	21.8%	− 12.1%
4. Washington	19.4%	+ 6.6%
5. California	17.5%	+ 9.4%
6. New Jersey	17.1%	− 17.8%
7. Connecticut	16.7%	+ 2.5%
8. Michigan	16.5%	− 20.7%
9. Rhode Island	16.4%	− 9.9%
10. Oregon	16.2%	+ 0.6%
The Least Unionized States		
1. North Carolina	3.2%	− 11.1%
2. Georgia	4.04%	− 36.5%
3. Arkansas	4.04%	− 31.0%
4. Louisiana	4.3%	− 39.4%
5. Mississippi	4.5%	− 25.0%
6. Virginia	4.62%	− 17.9%
7. South Carolina	4.65%	+ 15.0%
8. Tennessee	4.7%	− 47.2%
9. Texas	5.4%	− 6.9%
10. Oklahoma	5.5%	− 19.1%

Source: Based on: http://247wallst.com/2011/03/10/the-states-with-the-strongest-and-weakest-unions/5/

most drastic of which may be the abolition of collective bargaining rights. Wisconsin recently passed a law eliminating most collective-bargaining rights for the state's public-employee unions. That law sets a precedent that many other states may follow to curb union rights as a way to help state budgets become solvent. Ohio is close to passing a similar bill curbing union rights for 400,000 public workers.

The Republican majority in many state legislatures and governors' offices makes the "declining public unionization" trend likely to continue. Public unions now face the kind of erosion that private unions did in the last decade. Local governments simply do not have sufficient tax receipts to support current union payrolls and benefits. Table 3-4 compares the most unionized states with the least unionized. Note that union membership overall dropped in most states from 2000 to 2010 due to private sector losses, but public sector union employees, on the other hand, have held their own.

Governments worldwide are under pressure to protect jobs at home and maintain the nation's industrial base. For example, in France, Renault SA's factory in Sandouville is one of the most unproductive auto factories in the world. However, Renault has taken $3.9 billion in low-interest loans from the French government, so the company cannot close any French factories for the duration of the loan or resort to mass layoffs in France for a year.

Local, state, and federal laws; regulatory agencies; and special-interest groups can have a major impact on the strategies of small, large, for-profit, and nonprofit organizations. Many companies have altered or abandoned strategies in the past because of political or governmental actions. In the academic world, as state budgets have dropped in recent years, so too has state support for colleges and universities. Due to the decline in monies received from the state, many institutions of higher learning are doing more fund-raising on their own—naming buildings and classrooms, for example, for donors. A summary of political, governmental, and legal variables that can represent key opportunities or threats to organizations is provided in Table 3-5.

TABLE 3-5 Some Political, Governmental, and Legal Variables

Government regulations or deregulations	Sino-American relationships
Changes in tax laws	Russian-American relationships
Special tariffs	European-American relationships
Political action committees	African-American relationships
Voter participation rates	Import–export regulations
Number, severity, and location of government protests	Government fiscal and monetary policy changes
Number of patents	Political conditions in foreign countries
Changes in patent laws	Special local, state, and federal laws
Environmental protection laws	Lobbying activities
Level of defense expenditures	Size of government budgets
Legislation on equal employment	World oil, currency, and labor markets
Level of government subsidies	Location and severity of terrorist activities
Antitrust legislation	Local, state, and national elections

Technological Forces

Papa John's International in 2012 expects to receive 50 percent of all its pizza orders through its website, up from 30 percent in 2011 and far more than the industry average of 10 percent. Technology is a key to Papa John's success as it strives to compete with Domino's Pizza and Pizza Hut. Papa John's new website is interactive, where customers can see a picture of their pizza as they decide upon toppings. Papa John's new loyalty program, called Papa Points, is promoted heavily through its new website.

Lagging behind Netflix and Redbox in technology has been disastrous for Blockbuster, which recently filed for Chapter 11 bankruptcy protection and then barely escaped liquidation before being acquired by Dish Network Corp. for $320 million. Internet streaming giant Netflix and $1 DVD movies offered by Redbox essentially forced Blockbuster to close more than 1,000 of its 3,000 stores while at the same time desperately trying to shift to digital distribution. In virtually every industry, the more technologically astute firms gain overwhelming competitive advantage over less competent rivals.

The *Internet* has changed the very nature of opportunities and threats by altering the life cycles of products, increasing the speed of distribution, creating new products and services, erasing limitations of traditional geographic markets, and changing the historical trade-off between production standardization and flexibility. The Internet is altering economies of scale, changing entry barriers, and redefining the relationship between industries and various suppliers, creditors, customers, and competitors.

Total Internet retail sales the last two months of 2010 jumped 15.4 percent compared to 2009. Purchases online of apparel at specialty stores increased 25 percent, even though people prefer to touch and try on garments.[2] Retail sales over the Internet now account for about 10 percent of all retail sales, excluding purchases of automobiles and gas.

To effectively capitalize on e-commerce, a number of organizations are establishing two new positions in their firms: *chief information officer (CIO)* and *chief technology officer (CTO)*. This trend reflects the growing importance of *information technology (IT)* in strategic management. A CIO and CTO work together to ensure that information needed to formulate, implement, and evaluate strategies is available where and when it is needed. These individuals are responsible for developing, maintaining, and updating a company's information database. The CIO is more a manager, managing the firm's relationship with stakeholders; the CTO is more a technician, focusing on technical issues such as data acquisition, data processing, decision-support systems, and software and hardware acquisition.

Technological forces represent major opportunities and threats that must be considered in formulating strategies. Technological advancements can dramatically affect organizations' products, services, markets, suppliers, distributors, competitors, customers, manufacturing processes, marketing practices, and competitive position. Technological advancements can create new markets, result in a proliferation of new and improved products, change the relative competitive cost positions in an industry, and render existing products and services obsolete. Technological changes can reduce or eliminate cost barriers between businesses, create shorter production runs, create shortages in technical skills, and result in changing values and expectations of employees, managers, and customers. Technological advancements can create new competitive advantages that are more powerful than existing advantages. No company or industry today is insulated against emerging technological developments. In high-tech industries, identification and evaluation of key technological opportunities and threats can be the most important part of the external strategic-management audit.

Organizations that traditionally have limited technology expenditures to what they can fund after meeting marketing and financial requirements urgently need a reversal in thinking. The pace of technological change is increasing and literally wiping out businesses every day. An emerging consensus holds that technology management is one of the key responsibilities of strategists. Firms should pursue strategies that take advantage of technological opportunities to achieve sustainable, competitive advantages in the marketplace.

In practice, critical decisions about technology too often are delegated to lower organizational levels or are made without an understanding of their strategic implications. Many strategists spend countless hours determining market share, positioning products in terms of features and price, forecasting sales and market size, and monitoring distributors; yet too often, technology does not receive the same respect.

Not all sectors of the economy are affected equally by technological developments. The communications, electronics, aeronautics, and pharmaceutical industries are much more volatile than the textile, forestry, and metals industries.

Competitive Forces

An important part of an external audit is identifying rival firms and determining their strengths, weaknesses, capabilities, opportunities, threats, objectives, and strategies.

For example, Tupperware Brands Corp. (TBC) produces and sells household products and beauty items. TBC competes intensely with Avon Products and Newell Rubbermaid. Tupperware parties became synonymous with American suburban life in the 1950s, when independent salespeople organized gatherings to sell their plastic containers. TBC today deploys a sales force of about 2.6 million people in about 100 countries and obtains more than 80 percent of their annual $2.3 billion revenue from outside the United States. Table 3-6 compares Tupperware with its two largest competitors. Note that TBC outperforms Avon and Rubbermaid on most criteria.

Collecting and evaluating information on competitors is essential for successful strategy formulation. Identifying major competitors is not always easy because many firms have divisions that compete in different industries. Many multidivisional firms do not provide sales and profit information on a divisional basis for competitive reasons. Also, privately-held firms do not publish any financial or marketing information. Addressing questions about competitors such as those presented in Table 3-7 is important in performing an external audit.

Competition in virtually all industries can be described as intense—and sometimes as cutthroat. For example, Walgreens and CVS pharmacies are located generally across the street from each other and battle each other every day on price and customer service. Most automobile dealerships also are located close to each other. Dollar General, based in Goodlettsville, Tennessee, and Family Dollar, based in Matthews, North Carolina, compete intensely on price to attract customers away from each other and away from Wal-Mart. Best Buy dropped prices wherever possible to finally put Circuit City totally out of business.

Seven characteristics describe the most competitive companies:

1. Market share matters; the 90th share point isn't as important as the 91st, and nothing is more dangerous than falling to 89.
2. Understand and remember precisely what business you are in.
3. Whether it's broke or not, fix it—make it better; not just products, but the whole company, if necessary.

TABLE 3-6   An Actual CPM for Tupperware

Critical Success Factors	Weight	TUPPERWARE Rating	Score	AVON Rating	Score	RUBBERMAID Rating	Score
Advertising	0.15	1	0.15	3	0.45	4	0.60
Customer Service	0.03	3	0.09	2	0.06	1	0.03
Price Competitiveness	0.05	2	0.01	3	0.15	4	0.20
Top Management Expertise	0.14	4	0.56	3	0.42	2	0.28
Product Quality	0.08	4	0.32	3	0.24	2	0.16
E-commerce	0.09	1	0.09	3	0.27	2	0.18
Financial Position	0.15	4	0.60	3	0.45	2	0.30
Customer Loyalty	0.04	4	0.16	3	0.12	1	0.04
Global Expansion	0.08	4	0.32	2	0.16	1	0.08
Sales Distribution	0.06	4	0.24	2	0.12	1	0.06
Market Share	0.08	2	0.16	4	0.32	3	0.24
Product Line Offerings	0.05	4	0.20	2	0.10	3	0.15
Total	**1.00**		**2.99**		**2.86**		**2.32**

Source: Based on information provided by Eddie Guzman and David Campbell Jr.

4. Innovate or evaporate; particularly in technology-driven businesses, nothing quite recedes like success.
5. Acquisition is essential to growth; the most successful purchases are in niches that add a technology or a related market.
6. People make a difference; tired of hearing it? Too bad.
7. There is no substitute for quality and no greater threat than failing to be cost-competitive on a global basis.[3]

TABLE 3-7   Key Questions About Competitors

1. What are the major competitors' strengths?
2. What are the major competitors' weaknesses?
3. What are the major competitors' objectives and strategies?
4. How will the major competitors most likely respond to current economic, social, cultural, demographic, environmental, political, governmental, legal, technological, and competitive trends affecting our industry?
5. How vulnerable are the major competitors to our alternative company strategies?
6. How vulnerable are our alternative strategies to successful counterattack by our major competitors?
7. How are our products or services positioned relative to major competitors?
8. To what extent are new firms entering and old firms leaving this industry?
9. What key factors have resulted in our present competitive position in this industry?
10. How have the sales and profit rankings of major competitors in the industry changed over recent years? Why have these rankings changed that way?
11. What is the nature of supplier and distributor relationships in this industry?
12. To what extent could substitute products or services be a threat to competitors in this industry?

Competitive Intelligence Programs

What is competitive intelligence? *Competitive intelligence* (*CI*), as formally defined by the Society of Competitive Intelligence Professionals (SCIP), is a systematic and ethical process for gathering and analyzing information about the competition's activities and general business trends to further a business's own goals (SCIP website).

Good competitive intelligence in business, as in the military, is one of the keys to success. The more information and knowledge a firm can obtain about its competitors, the more likely it is that it can formulate and implement effective strategies. Major competitors' weaknesses can represent external opportunities; major competitors' strengths may represent key threats.

Starwood Hotels & Resorts Worldwide recently sued Hilton Hotels Corp. for allegedly stealing more than 100,000 confidential electronic and paper documents containing "Starwood's most competitively sensitive information." The complaint alleges that two Starwood executives, Ross Klein and Amar Lalvani, resigned from Starwood to join Hilton and took this information with them. The legal complaint says, "This is the clearest imaginable case of corporate espionage, theft of trade secrets, unfair competition and computer fraud." In addition to monetary awards, Starwood is seeking to force Hilton to cancel the rollout of the Denizen hotel chain. Hilton is owned by Blackstone Group.

Hiring top executives from rival firms is also a way companies obtain competitive intelligence. Just two days after Facebook's COO, Owen Van Natta, left the company, he accepted the CEO job at Myspace, replacing then CEO and cofounder Chris DeWolfe. Van Natta had previously also been Facebook's COO, chief revenue officer, and vice president of operations. Google Inc. is losing top staff to Facebook, Twitter, and LinkedIn, which are all private companies that can lure top engineers and executives with pre-IPO stock. For example, Facebook's COO, Sheryl Sandberg, was previously Google's vice president of online sales and operations, and Facebook's VP of advertising and global operations, David Fischer, previously held that same position at Google. In 2010 alone, Facebook went from 1,000 employees to 2,000, Twitter went from 100 to 300, and LinkedIn went from 450 to 900.

Many U.S. executives grew up in times when U.S. firms dominated foreign competitors so much that gathering competitive intelligence did not seem worth the effort. Too many of these executives still cling to these attitudes—to the detriment of their organizations today. Even most MBA programs do not offer a course in competitive and business intelligence, thus reinforcing this attitude. As a consequence, three strong misperceptions about business intelligence prevail among U.S. executives today:

1. Running an intelligence program requires lots of people, computers, and other resources.
2. Collecting intelligence about competitors violates antitrust laws; business intelligence equals espionage.
3. Intelligence gathering is an unethical business practice.[4]

Any discussions with a competitor about price, market, or geography intentions could violate antitrust statutes. However, this fact must not lure a firm into underestimating the need for and benefits of systematically collecting information about competitors for strategic planning purposes. The Internet is an excellent medium for gathering competitive intelligence. Information gathering from employees, managers, suppliers, distributors, customers, creditors, and consultants also can make the difference between having superior or just average intelligence and overall competitiveness.

Firms need an effective competitive intelligence (CI) program. The three basic objectives of a CI program are (1) to provide a general understanding of an industry and its competitors, (2) to identify areas in which competitors are vulnerable and to assess the impact strategic actions would have on competitors, and (3) to identify potential moves that a competitor might make that would endanger a firm's position in the market.[5] Competitive information is equally applicable for strategy formulation, implementation, and evaluation decisions. An effective CI program allows all areas of a firm to access consistent and verifiable information in making decisions. All members of an organization—from the chief executive officer to custodians—are valuable intelligence agents and should feel themselves to be a part of the CI process. Special characteristics of a successful CI program include flexibility, usefulness, timeliness, and cross-functional cooperation.

The increasing emphasis on *competitive analysis* in the United States is evidenced by corporations putting this function on their organizational charts under job titles such as Director of Competitive Analysis, Competitive Strategy Manager, Director of Information Services, or Associate Director of Competitive Assessment. The responsibilities of a *director of competitive analysis* include planning, collecting data, analyzing data, facilitating the process of gathering and analyzing data, disseminating intelligence on a timely basis, researching special issues, and recognizing what information is important and who needs to know. Competitive intelligence is not corporate espionage because 95 percent of the information a company needs to make strategic decisions is available and accessible to the public. Sources of competitive information include trade journals, want ads, newspaper articles, and government filings, as well as customers, suppliers, distributors, competitors themselves, and the Internet.

Unethical tactics such as bribery, wiretapping, and computer hacking should never be used to obtain information. Marriott and Motorola—two U.S. companies that do a particularly good job of gathering competitive intelligence—agree that all the information you could wish for can be collected without resorting to unethical tactics.

Hilton Worldwide, Inc. is banned in 2011 and 2012 from creating a luxury "lifestyle" hotel (Denizen) under an agreement to settle a corporate-espionage lawsuit that stemmed from Hilton allegedly stealing confidential documents from rival Starwood Hotels & Resorts regarding their exclusive W Hotel. Also as part of the settlement, Hilton is paying Starwood an undisclosed amount of money.

Market Commonality and Resource Similarity

By definition, competitors are firms that offer similar products and services in the same market. Markets can be geographic or product areas or segments. For example, in the insurance industry the markets are broken down into commercial/consumer, health/life, or Europe/Asia. Researchers use the terms *market commonality* and *resource similarity* to study rivalry among competitors. *Market commonality* can be defined as the number and significance of markets that a firm competes in with rivals.[6] *Resource similarity* is the extent to which the type and amount of a firm's internal resources are comparable to a rival.[7] One way to analyze competitiveness between two or among several firms is to investigate market commonality and resource similarity issues while looking for areas of potential competitive advantage along each firm's value chain.

Competitive Analysis: Porter's Five-Forces Model

As illustrated in Figure 3-3, *Porter's Five-Forces Model* of competitive analysis is a widely used approach for developing strategies in many industries. The intensity of competition among firms varies widely across industries. Table 3-8 reveals the average gross profit margin and earnings per share for firms in different industries. Note the substantial variation among industries. For example, note that gross profit margin ranges from 59.28 percent to 24.50 percent, while EPS ranges from $2.45 to $0.18. Note that brick and mortar bookstores have the lowest EPS, which implies fierce competition in that industry. Intensity of competition is highest in lower-return industries. The collective impact of competitive forces is so brutal in some industries that the market is clearly "unattractive" from a profit-making standpoint. Rivalry among existing firms is severe, new rivals can enter the industry with relative ease, and both suppliers and customers can exercise considerable bargaining leverage. According to Porter, the nature of competitiveness in a given industry can be viewed as a composite of five forces:

1. Rivalry among competing firms
2. Potential entry of new competitors
3. Potential development of substitute products
4. Bargaining power of suppliers
5. Bargaining power of consumers

FIGURE 3-3

The Five-Forces Model of Competition

The following three steps for using Porter's Five-Forces Model can indicate whether competition in a given industry is such that the firm can make an acceptable profit:

1. Identify key aspects or elements of each competitive force that impact the firm.
2. Evaluate how strong and important each element is for the firm.
3. Decide whether the collective strength of the elements is worth the firm entering or staying in the industry.

Rivalry Among Competing Firms

Rivalry among competing firms is usually the most powerful of the five competitive forces. The strategies pursued by one firm can be successful only to the extent that they provide competitive advantage over the strategies pursued by rival firms. Changes in strategy by one firm may be met with retaliatory countermoves, such as lowering prices, enhancing quality, adding features, providing services, extending warranties, and increasing advertising.

The Internet, coupled with the common currency in Europe, enables consumers to make price comparisons easily across countries. Just for a moment, consider the implications for car dealers who used to know everything about a new car's pricing, while you, the consumer, knew very little. You could bargain, but being in the dark, you rarely could win. Now you can shop online in a few hours at every dealership within 500 miles to find the best price and terms. So you, the consumer, can win. This is true in many, if not most, business-to-consumer and business-to-business sales transactions today.

TABLE 3-8 Competitiveness Across a Few Industries (year-end 2010 data)

	Gross Profit Margin (%)	EPS ($)
Pharmaceutical	59.28	1.63
Telecommunications	57.37	0.76
Fragrances/Cosmetics	46.12	1.16
Banking	30.78	0.09
Bookstores	35.78	0.18
Food Manufacturers	30.54	0.65
Oil and Gas	32.96	1.68
Airlines	29.59	0.69
Machinery/Construction	27.53	2.45
Paper Products	24.50	1.38

Source: Based on information at www.finance.yahoo.com retrieved on May 10, 2011.

TABLE 3-9   Conditions That Cause High Rivalry Among Competing Firms

1. High number of competing firms
2. Similar size of firms competing
3. Similar capability of firms competing
4. Falling demand for the industry's products
5. Falling product/service prices in the industry
6. When consumers can switch brands easily
7. When barriers to leaving the market are high
8. When barriers to entering the market are low
9. When fixed costs are high among firms competing
10. When the product is perishable
11. When rivals have excess capacity
12. When consumer demand is falling
13. When rivals have excess inventory
14. When rivals sell similar products/services
15. When mergers are common in the industry

The intensity of rivalry among competing firms tends to increase as the number of competitors increases, as competitors become more equal in size and capability, as demand for the industry's products declines, and as price cutting becomes common. Rivalry also increases when consumers can switch brands easily; when barriers to leaving the market are high; when fixed costs are high; when the product is perishable; when consumer demand is growing slowly or declines such that rivals have excess capacity and/or inventory; when the products being sold are commodities (not easily differentiated, such as gasoline); when rival firms are diverse in strategies, origins, and culture; and when mergers and acquisitions are common in the industry. As rivalry among competing firms intensifies, industry profits decline, in some cases to the point where an industry becomes inherently unattractive. When rival firms sense weakness, typically they will intensify both marketing and production efforts to capitalize on the "opportunity." Table 3-9 summarizes conditions that cause high rivalry among competing firms.

Potential Entry of New Competitors

Whenever new firms can easily enter a particular industry, the intensity of competitiveness among firms increases. Barriers to entry, however, can include the need to gain economies of scale quickly, the need to gain technology and specialized know-how, the lack of experience, strong customer loyalty, strong brand preferences, large capital requirements, lack of adequate distribution channels, government regulatory policies, tariffs, lack of access to raw materials, possession of patents, undesirable locations, counterattack by entrenched firms, and potential saturation of the market.

Despite numerous barriers to entry, new firms sometimes enter industries with higher-quality products, lower prices, and substantial marketing resources. The strategist's job, therefore, is to identify potential new firms entering the market, to monitor the new rival firms' strategies, to counterattack as needed, and to capitalize on existing strengths and opportunities. When the threat of new firms entering the market is strong, incumbent firms generally fortify their positions and take actions to deter new entrants, such as lowering prices, extending warranties, adding features, or offering financing specials.

Potential Development of Substitute Products

In many industries, firms are in close competition with producers of substitute products in other industries. Examples are plastic container producers competing with glass, paperboard, and aluminum can producers, and acetaminophen manufacturers competing with other manufacturers of pain and headache remedies. The presence of substitute products puts a ceiling on the price that can be charged before consumers will switch to the substitute product. Price ceilings equate to profit ceilings and more intense competition among rivals. Producers of eyeglasses and contact lenses, for example, face increasing competitive pressures from laser eye surgery. Producers of sugar face similar pressures from artificial sweeteners. Newspapers and magazines face substitute-product competitive pressures from the Internet and 24-hour cable television. The magnitude of competitive pressure derived from the development of substitute products is generally evidenced by rivals' plans for expanding production capacity, as well as by their sales and profit growth numbers.

Competitive pressures arising from substitute products increase as the relative price of substitute products declines and as consumers' costs of switching decrease. The competitive strength of substitute products is best measured by the inroads into the market share those products obtain, as well as those firms' plans for increased capacity and market penetration.

For example, circulation of U.S. newspapers continues to drop drastically, with the exception of the *Wall Street Journal* and a few other bright spots. The growing popularity of free news on the web and more timely news online are two key factors negatively impacting traditional papers such as the *New York Times*, *Los Angeles Times*, and others.

Bargaining Power of Suppliers

The bargaining power of suppliers affects the intensity of competition in an industry, especially when there is a large number of suppliers, when there are only a few good substitute raw materials, or when the cost of switching raw materials is especially high. It is often in the best interest of both suppliers and producers to assist each other with reasonable prices, improved quality, development of new services, just-in-time deliveries, and reduced inventory costs, thus enhancing long-term profitability for all concerned.

Firms may pursue a backward integration strategy to gain control or ownership of suppliers. This strategy is especially effective when suppliers are unreliable, too costly, or not capable of meeting a firm's needs on a consistent basis. Firms generally can negotiate more favorable terms with suppliers when backward integration is a commonly used strategy among rival firms in an industry.

However, in many industries it is more economical to use outside suppliers of component parts than to self-manufacture the items. This is true, for example, in the outdoor power equipment industry, where producers of lawn mowers, rotary tillers, leaf blowers, and edgers such as Murray generally obtain their small engines from outside manufacturers such as Briggs & Stratton that specialize in such engines and have huge economies of scale.

In more and more industries, sellers are forging strategic partnerships with select suppliers in efforts to (1) reduce inventory and logistics costs (e.g., through just-in-time deliveries); (2) speed the availability of next-generation components; (3) enhance the quality of the parts and components being supplied and reduce defect rates; and (4) squeeze out important cost savings for both themselves and their suppliers.[8]

Bargaining Power of Consumers

When customers are concentrated or large in number or buy in volume, their bargaining power represents a major force affecting the intensity of competition in an industry. Rival firms may offer extended warranties or special services to gain customer loyalty whenever the bargaining power of consumers is substantial. Bargaining power of consumers also is higher when the products being purchased are standard or undifferentiated. When this is the case, consumers often can negotiate selling price, warranty coverage, and accessory packages to a greater extent.

The bargaining power of consumers can be the most important force affecting competitive advantage. Consumers gain increasing bargaining power under the following circumstances:

1. If they can inexpensively switch to competing brands or substitutes
2. If they are particularly important to the seller
3. If sellers are struggling in the face of falling consumer demand
4. If they are informed about sellers' products, prices, and costs
5. If they have discretion in whether and when they purchase the product[9]

Sources of External Information

A wealth of strategic information is available to organizations from both published and unpublished sources. Unpublished sources include customer surveys, market research, speeches at professional and shareholders' meetings, television programs, interviews, and conversations with stakeholders. Published sources of strategic information include periodicals, journals, reports, government documents, abstracts, books, directories, newspapers, and manuals. The Internet has made it easier for firms to gather, assimilate, and evaluate information.

There are many excellent websites for gathering strategic information, but six that the author uses routinely are listed here:

1. http://marketwatch.multexinvestor.com
2. http://moneycentral.msn.com
3. http://finance.yahoo.com
4. www.clearstation.com
5. http://us.etrade.com/e/t/invest/markets
6. www.hoovers.com
7. http://globaledge.msu.edu/industries/

An excellent source of industry information is provided by Michigan State University at http://globaledge.msu.edu/industries/ as indicated above. Industry Profiles provided at that site are an excellent source for information, news, events, and statistical data for any industry. In addition to a wealth of indices, risk assessments, and interactive trade information, a wide array of global resources are provided.

Most college libraries subscribe to Standard & Poor's (S&P's) *Industry Surveys*. These documents are exceptionally up-to-date and give valuable information about many different industries. Each report is authored by a Standard & Poor's industry research analyst and includes the following sections:

1. Current Environment
2. Industry Trends
3. How the Industry Operates
4. Key Industry Ratios and Statistics
5. How to Analyze a Company
6. Glossary of Industry Terms
7. Additional Industry Information
8. References
9. Comparative Company Financial Analysis

Forecasting Tools and Techniques

Boeing announced in early 2011 that it forecasts China to need 4,330 new commercial airplanes valued at $480 billion over the next 20 years, making China the world's second-largest airplane market after the United States. Boeing projects that China's airplane market will grow at nearly twice the rate of the rest of the industry globally. Based on these forecasts, Boeing plans to grow its 52 percent airplane market share in China by producing more single-isle jet planes.

Forecasts are educated assumptions about future trends and events. Forecasting is a complex activity because of factors such as technological innovation, cultural changes, new products, improved services, stronger competitors, shifts in government priorities, changing social values, unstable economic conditions, and unforeseen events. Managers often must rely on published forecasts to effectively identify key external opportunities and threats.

A sense of the future permeates all action and underlies every decision a person makes. People eat expecting to be satisfied and nourished in the future. People sleep assuming that in the future they will feel rested. They invest energy, money, and time because they believe their efforts will be rewarded in the future. They build highways assuming that automobiles and trucks will need them in the future. Parents educate children on the basis of forecasts that they will need certain skills, attitudes, and knowledge when they grow up. The truth is we all make implicit forecasts throughout our daily lives. The question, therefore, is not whether we should forecast but rather how we can best forecast to enable us to move beyond our ordinarily unarticulated assumptions about the future. Can we obtain information and then make educated assumptions (forecasts) to better guide our current decisions to achieve a more desirable future state of affairs? We should go into the future with our eyes and our minds open, rather than stumble into the future with our eyes closed.[10]

Sometimes organizations must develop their own projections. Most organizations forecast (project) their own revenues and profits annually. Organizations sometimes forecast market share or customer loyalty in local areas. Because forecasting is so important in strategic management and because the ability to forecast (in contrast to the ability to use a forecast) is essential, selected forecasting tools are examined further here.

Forecasting tools can be broadly categorized into two groups: quantitative techniques and qualitative techniques. Quantitative forecasts are most appropriate when historical data are available and when the relationships among key variables are expected to remain the same in the future. *Linear regression,* for example, is based on the assumption that the future will be just like the past—which, of course, it never is. As historical relationships become less stable, quantitative forecasts become less accurate.

No forecast is perfect, and some forecasts are even wildly inaccurate. This fact accents the need for strategists to devote sufficient time and effort to study the underlying bases for published forecasts and to develop internal forecasts of their own. Key external opportunities and threats can be effectively identified only through good forecasts. Accurate forecasts can provide major competitive advantages for organizations. Forecasts are vital to the strategic-management process and to the success of organizations.

Making Assumptions

Planning would be impossible without assumptions. McConkey defines assumptions as the "best present estimates of the impact of major external factors, over which the manager has little if any control, but which may exert a significant impact on performance or the ability to achieve desired results."[11] Strategists are faced with countless variables and imponderables that can be neither controlled nor predicted with 100 percent accuracy. Wild guesses should never be made in formulating strategies, but reasonable assumptions based on available information must always be made.

By identifying future occurrences that could have a major effect on the firm and by making reasonable assumptions about those factors, strategists can carry the strategic-management process forward. Assumptions are needed only for future trends and events that are most likely to have a significant effect on the company's business. Based on the best information at the time, assumptions serve as checkpoints on the validity of strategies. If future occurrences deviate significantly from assumptions, strategists know that corrective actions may be needed. Without reasonable assumptions, the strategy-formulation process could not proceed effectively. Firms that have the best information generally make the most accurate assumptions, which can lead to major competitive advantages.

Industry Analysis: The External Factor Evaluation (EFE) Matrix

An *External Factor Evaluation (EFE)* Matrix allows strategists to summarize and evaluate economic, social, cultural, demographic, environmental, political, governmental, legal, technological, and competitive information. Illustrated in Table 3-10, the EFE Matrix can be developed in five steps:

1. List key external factors as identified in the external-audit process. Include a total of 15 to 20 factors, including both opportunities and threats, that affect the firm and its industry. List the opportunities first and then the threats. Be as specific as possible, using percentages, ratios, and comparative numbers whenever possible. Recall that Edward Deming said, "In God we trust. Everyone else bring data."

2. Assign to each factor a weight that ranges from 0.0 (not important) to 1.0 (very important). The weight indicates the relative importance of that factor to being successful in

TABLE 3-10 EFE Matrix for a Local Ten-Theater Cinema Complex

Key External Factors	Weight	Rating	Weighted Score
Opportunities			
1. Rowan County is growing 8% annually in population	0.05	3	0.15
2. TDB University is expanding 6% annually	0.08	4	0.32
3. Major competitor across town recently ceased operations	0.08	3	0.24
4. Demand for going to cinema growing 10% annually	0.07	2	0.14
5. Two new neighborhoods being developed within 3 miles	0.09	1	0.09
6. Disposable income among citizens grew 5% in prior year	0.06	3	0.18
7. Unemployment rate in county declined to 3.1%	0.03	2	0.06
Threats			
8. Trend toward healthy eating eroding concession sales	0.12	4	0.48
9. Demand for online movies and DVDs growing 10% annually	0.06	2	0.12
10. Commercial property adjacent to cinemas for sale	0.06	3	0.18
11. TDB University installing an on-campus movie theater	0.04	3	0.12
12. County and city property taxes increasing 25% this year	0.08	2	0.16
13. Local religious groups object to R-rated movies being shown	0.04	3	0.12
14. Movies rented from local Blockbuster store up 12%	0.08	2	0.16
15. Movies rented last quarter from Time Warner up 15%	0.06	1	0.06
Total	**1.00**		**2.58**

the firm's industry. Opportunities often receive higher weights than threats, but threats can receive high weights if they are especially severe or threatening. Appropriate weights can be determined by comparing successful with unsuccessful competitors or by discussing the factor and reaching a group consensus. The sum of all weights assigned to the factors must equal 1.0.

3. Assign a rating between 1 and 4 to each key external factor to indicate how effectively the firm's current strategies respond to the factor, where 4 = *the response is superior*, 3 = *the response is above average*, 2 = *the response is average*, and 1 = *the response is poor*. Ratings are based on effectiveness of the firm's strategies. Ratings are thus company-based, whereas the weights in Step 2 are industry-based. It is important to note that both threats and opportunities can receive a 1, 2, 3, or 4.
4. Multiply each factor's weight by its rating to determine a weighted score.
5. Sum the weighted scores for each variable to determine the total weighted score for the organization.

Regardless of the number of key opportunities and threats included in an EFE Matrix, the highest possible total weighted score for an organization is 4.0 and the lowest possible total weighted score is 1.0. The average total weighted score is 2.5. A total weighted score of 4.0 indicates that an organization is responding in an outstanding way to existing opportunities and threats in its industry. In other words, the firm's strategies effectively take advantage of existing opportunities and minimize the potential adverse effects of external threats. A total score of 1.0 indicates that the firm's strategies are not capitalizing on opportunities or avoiding external threats.

An example of an EFE Matrix is provided in Table 3-10 for a local 10-theater cinema complex. Note that the most important factor to being successful in this business is "Trend toward healthy eating eroding concession sales" as indicated by the 0.12 weight. Also note that the local cinema is doing excellent in regard to handling two factors, "TDB University is expanding 6 percent annually" and "Trend toward healthy eating eroding concession sales." Perhaps the cinema is placing flyers on campus and also adding yogurt and healthy drinks to its concession menu. Note that you may have a 1, 2, 3, or 4 anywhere down the Rating column.

Note also that the factors are stated in quantitative terms to the extent possible, rather than being stated in vague terms. Quantify the factors as much as possible in constructing an EFE Matrix. Finally, note that the total weighted score of 2.58 is above the average (midpoint) of 2.5, so this cinema business is doing pretty well, taking advantage of the external opportunities and avoiding the threats facing the firm. There is definitely room for improvement, though, because the highest total weighted score would be 4.0. As indicated by ratings of 1, this business needs to capitalize more on the "two new neighborhoods nearby" opportunity and the "movies rented from Time Warner" threat. Note also that there are many percentage-based factors among the group. Be quantitative to the extent possible! Note also that the ratings range from 1 to 4 on both the opportunities and threats.

An External Factor Evaluation (EFE) Matrix for UPS, Inc. is provided in Table 3-11. Note that "customers outsourcing their supply chain" and "foreign currency obligations" were considered by this researcher to be the most important factors in this industry, as indicated by the 0.10 weight values. UPS does best however on opportunity #1 and #4. Overall, UPS does better internally than externally since the total score of 2.59 is a bit less than the upcoming analogous IFE Matrix in the next chapter.

TABLE 3-11 An Actual External Factor Evaluation Matrix for UPS, Inc.

Opportunities	Weight	Rating	Wt. Score
1. Europe accounts for ~50% of international revenue	0.04	4	0.16
2. Africa is becoming commercially developed	0.03	2	0.06
3. >24 alliances with Asian delivery companies	0.07	2	0.14
4. International market growing 10% faster than U.S.	0.03	4	0.12
5. Customers outsourcing up to 100% of supply chain to lower cost	0.10	3	0.30
6. Increased international usage of wireless access tracking information	0.03	2	0.06
7. Telematics technology in ~12,000 U.S. UPS vehicles	0.03	2	0.06
8. Hybrid vehicles are available to add to the growing UPS alternative fuel vehicle (AFV) fleet	0.06	3	0.18
9. Only 43.2% of employees are not affiliated with a union	0.07	2	0.14
10. Direct-to-consumer business models require delivery services to be 100% effective	0.03	2	0.06
Threats			
11. Incurred $77 million charge on foreign currency obligations	0.10	3	0.30
12. Jet and diesel fuel price variations cause fluctuations in surcharges from a 13% increase to a 21.2% decrease	0.08	3	0.24
13. Adverse currency exchange rate fluctuation (7.2% decline for the year)	0.03	2	0.06
14. FASB guidance requires re-measurement of pension and benefit plans = $44 million reduction to income	0.04	1	0.04
15. 1% change in health care cost trend rates = increase in post-retirement benefit obligation of $83 million	0.06	3	0.18
16. Joint venture partner for Dubai owns 20% put option	0.03	2	0.06
17. Undistributed earnings of non-U.S. subs ~$2.2 billion	0.05	2	0.10
18. Consumers expect "green business operations"	0.04	3	0.12
19. U.S. unemployment rates continue holding near 10%	0.03	2	0.06
20. FedEx has greater international presence (27% compared to UPS 24% of total revenues)	0.05	3	0.15
Totals	**1.00**		**2.59**

The Competitive Profile Matrix (CPM)

The *Competitive Profile Matrix (CPM)* identifies a firm's major competitors and its particular strengths and weaknesses in relation to a sample firm's strategic position. The weights and total weighted scores in both a CPM and an EFE have the same meaning. However, *critical success* factors in a CPM include both internal and external issues; therefore, the ratings refer to strengths and weaknesses, where 4 = major strength, 3 = minor strength, 2 = minor weakness, and 1 = major weakness. The critical success factors in a CPM are not grouped into opportunities and threats as they are in an EFE. In a CPM, the ratings and total weighted scores for rival firms can be compared to the sample firm. This comparative analysis provides important internal strategic information. Avoid assigning the same rating to firms included in your CPM analysis.

A sample Competitive Profile Matrix is provided in Table 3-12. In this example, the two most important factors to being successful in the industry are "advertising" and "global expansion," as indicated by weights of 0.20. If there were no weight column in this analysis, note that each factor then would be equally important. Thus, having a weight column makes for a more robust analysis, because it enables the analyst to assign higher and lower numbers to capture perceived or actual levels of importance. Note in Table 3-12 that Company 1 is strongest on "product quality," as indicated by a rating of 4, whereas Company 2 is strongest on "advertising." Overall, Company 1 is strongest, as indicated by the total weighted score of 3.15 and Company 3 is weakest.

Other than the critical success factors listed in the example CPM, factors often included in this analysis include breadth of product line, effectiveness of sales distribution, proprietary or patent advantages, location of facilities, production capacity and efficiency, experience, union relations, technological advantages, and e-commerce expertise.

A word on interpretation: Just because one firm receives a 3.20 rating and another receives a 2.80 rating in a Competitive Profile Matrix, it does not follow that the first firm is 20 percent better than the second. Numbers reveal the relative strengths of firms, but their implied precision is an illusion. Numbers are not magic. The aim is not to arrive at a single number, but rather to assimilate and evaluate information in a meaningful way that aids in decision making.

Another Competitive Profile Matrix is provided in Table 3-13. Note that Company 2 has the best product quality and management experience; Company 3 has the best market share and inventory system; and Company 1 has the best price as indicated by the ratings. Again, avoid assigning duplicate ratings on any row in a CPM.

TABLE 3-12   An Example Competitive Profile Matrix

Critical Success Factors	Weight	Company 1		Company 2		Company 3	
		Rating	Score	Rating	Score	Rating	Score
Advertising	0.20	1	0.20	4	0.80	3	0.60
Product Quality	0.10	4	0.40	3	0.30	2	0.20
Price Competitiveness	0.10	3	0.30	2	0.20	1	0.10
Management	0.10	4	0.40	3	0.20	1	0.10
Financial Position	0.15	4	0.60	2	0.30	3	0.45
Customer Loyalty	0.10	4	0.40	3	0.30	2	0.20
Global Expansion	0.20	4	0.80	1	0.20	2	0.40
Market Share	0.05	1	0.05	4	0.20	3	0.15
Total	**1.00**		**3.15**		**2.50**		**2.20**

Note: (1) The ratings values are as follows: 1 = major weakness, 2 = minor weakness, 3 = minor strength, 4 = major strength. (2) As indicated by the total weighted score of 2.50, Competitor 2 is weakest. (3) Only eight critical success factors are included for simplicity; this is too few in actuality.

TABLE 3-13 Another Example Competitive Profile Matrix

Critical Success Factors	Weight	Company 1 Rating	Company 1 Weighted Score	Company 2 Rating	Company 2 Weighted Score	Company 3 Rating	Company 3 Weighted Score
Market Share	0.15	3	0.45	2	0.30	4	0.60
Inventory System	0.08	2	0.16	1	0.08	4	0.32
Financial Position	0.10	2	0.20	3	0.30	4	0.40
Product Quality	0.08	3	0.24	4	0.32	2	.16
Consumer Loyalty	0.02	3	0.06	1	0.02	4	0.08
Sales Distribution	0.10	3	0.30	2	0.20	4	.40
Global Expansion	0.15	3	0.45	2	0.30	4	0.60
Organization Structure	0.05	3	0.15	4	0.20	2	0.10
Production Capacity	0.04	3	0.12	2	0.08	4	0.16
E-commerce	0.10	3	0.30	1	0.10	4	0.40
Customer Service	0.10	3	0.30	2	0.20	4	0.40
Price Competitive	0.02	4	0.08	1	0.02	3	0.06
Management Experience	0.01	2	0.02	4	0.04	3	.03
Total	**1.00**		**2.83**		**2.16**		**3.69**

The Competitive Profile Matrix provided in Table 3-14 was developed for UPS and compares that company to its major rival, Federal Express. Note this analysis reveals UPS to be stronger than FedEx in all areas considered except e-commerce.

Special Note To Students

In developing and presenting your external assessment for the firm, be mindful that gaining and sustaining competitive advantage is the overriding purpose of developing the opportunity/threat lists, value chain, EFEM, and CPM. During this section of your written or oral project, emphasize how and why particular factors can yield competitive advantage for the firm. In other words,

TABLE 3-14 An Actual Competitive Profile Matrix for UPS, Inc.

Critical Success Factors	Weight	UPS Rating	UPS Score	FedEx Rating	FedEx Score
Advertising	0.05	4	0.20	3	0.15
Organization Structure	0.08	2	0.16	1	0.08
Customer Service	0.10	4	0.40	3	0.30
Global Expansion	0.07	4	0.28	3	0.21
Financial Position	0.10	4	0.40	3	0.40
Employee Dedication	0.08	4	0.32	3	0.24
Management Experience	0.10	4	0.40	3	0.30
Customer Loyalty	0.10	4	0.40	3	0.30
Market Share	0.10	4	0.40	3	0.30
Product Quality	0.08	3	0.24	2	0.16
E-commerce	0.06	2	0.12	3	0.18
Price Competitiveness	0.08	4	0.32	2	0.16
Total	**1.00**		**3.64**		**2.78**

instead of robotically going through the weights and ratings (which by the way are critically important), highlight various factors in light of where you are leading the firm. Make it abundantly clear in your discussion how your firm, with your suggestions, can subdue rival firms or at least profitably compete with them. Showcase during this section of your project the key underlying reasons how and why your firm can prosper among rivals. Remember to be *prescriptive,* rather than *descriptive,* in the manner that you present your entire project. If presenting your project orally, be self confident and passionate rather than timid and uninterested. Definitely "bring the data" throughout your project because "vagueness" is the most common downfall of students in case analyses.

Conclusion

Increasing turbulence in markets and industries around the world means the external audit has become an explicit and vital part of the strategic-management process. This chapter provides a framework for collecting and evaluating economic, social, cultural, demographic, environmental, political, governmental, legal, technological, and competitive information. Firms that do not mobilize and empower their managers and employees to identify, monitor, forecast, and evaluate key external forces may fail to anticipate emerging opportunities and threats and, consequently, may pursue ineffective strategies, miss opportunities, and invite organizational demise. Firms not taking advantage of e-commerce and social media networks are technologically falling behind.

A major responsibility of strategists is to ensure development of an effective external-audit system. This includes using information technology to devise a competitive intelligence system that works. The external-audit approach described in this chapter can be used effectively by any size or type of organization. Typically, the external-audit process is more informal in small firms, but the need to understand key trends and events is no less important for these firms. The EFE Matrix and Porter's Five-Forces Model can help strategists evaluate the market and industry, but these tools must be accompanied by good intuitive judgment. Multinational firms especially need a systematic and effective external-audit system because external forces among foreign countries vary so greatly.

Key Terms and Concepts

Chief Information Officer (CIO) (p. 101)
Chief Technology Officer (CTO) (p. 101)
Competitive Analysis (p. 105)
Competitive Intelligence (CI) (p. 104)
Competitive Profile Matrix (CPM) (p. 113)
Director of Competitive Analysis (p. 105)
Environmental Scanning (p. 92)
External Audit (p. 92)
External Factor Evaluation (EFE)
    Matrix (p. 110)

External Forces (p. 93)
Industrial Organization (I/O) (p. 95)
Industry Analysis (p. 92)
Information Technology (IT) (p. 101)
Internet (p. 101)
Lifecare Facilities (p. 98)
Linear Regression (p. 110)
Market Commonality (p. 105)
Porter's Five-Forces Model (p. 105)
Resource Similarity (p. 105)

Issues for Review and Discussion

1. IBM has been very successful in the last decade? What changes in their strategies do you feel will be needed in 2012 and 2013?
2. Of the many rival firms that IBM faces, which competitor do you think IBM worries most about? Why? Prepare a CPM that includes IBM and the rival firm you identified.
3. A political debate raging in the United States concerns sales taxes on the Internet. Most states do not collect a sales tax. Brick and mortar businesses think this is unfair. How does the situation in Europe compare to the United States in terms of sales tax on items purchased online? What is the strategic implication for companies?
4. The size of American labor unions has fallen sharply in the last decade due in large part to erosion of the U.S. manufacturing base. How does the situation in Europe compare to the United States in this regard? What is the strategic implication for companies?
5. List four major reasons why some countries in Europe are struggling economically as compared to countries in Asia. What is the strategic implication for companies?
6. Does the Arab Spring that is unfolding in the Middle East represent more of an opportunity or threat to companies? Explain.
7. Identify two companies that you think would have a 1.5 total weighted score on their EFE Matrix. Why? Identify two companies that you think would have a 3.5 total weighted score on their EFE Matrix. Why?
8. Summarize what Chapter 3 says at the end regarding competitive advantage whenever someone is presenting an EFE Matrix and CPM as part of a case analysis or strategic plan.
9. List the 10 key external forces that give rise to opportunities and threats. Give a specific example of each force for your college or university.
10. Give four reasons why you agree or do not agree with I/O theorists.
11. Regarding economic variables, list in order of importance six specific factors that you feel most greatly impact your college or university.
12. Explain why U.S.-based firms such as McDonald's greatly benefit from a weak dollar.
13. Regarding social, cultural, demographic, and natural environment variables, list in order of importance six specific factors that you feel most greatly impact your college or university.
14. Regarding political, governmental, and legal variables, list in order of importance six specific factors that you feel most greatly impact your college or university.
15. Explain how wireless technology is impacting four industries.
16. Discuss the pros and cons of gathering and assimilating competitive intelligence.
17. Using Porter's Five-Forces Model, explain competitiveness for a local fast food restaurant.
18. Identify an industry in which "bargaining power of suppliers" is the most important factor among Porter's variables.
19. Develop an EFE Matrix for your college or university.
20. Distinguish between ratings and weights in an EFE Matrix.
21. List 10 external trends or facts pertaining specifically to your country that would impact companies in your city.
22. Develop a CPM for a company that you or your parents have been employed.
23. Discuss the ethics of gathering competitive intelligence.
24. Discuss the ethics of cooperating with rival firms.
25. Contact your college library. Ask if they have the S&P Industry Surveys in hardcopy in the library. If they do, print out the relevant report for a company that you are most familiar with.
26. Your boss develops an EFE Matrix that includes 54 factors. How would you suggest reducing the number of factors to 20?
27. List the 10 external areas that give rise to opportunities and threats. Give an example of each for IBM.
28. Compare the ratings in an EFE Matrix with those in a CPM in terms of meaning and definition.
29. Discuss the I/O view or approach to strategic planning.
30. List in order of importance what you are the six major advantages of a weak dollar for a U.S.-based firm.
31. List in order of importance what you feel are the six major advantages of a weak euro for a European-based firm headquartered in a country that has the euro as its currency.
32. Cooperating with competitors is becoming more common. What are the advantages and disadvantages of this for a company?
33. Regarding sources of external information, visit the www.finance.yahoo.com website and enter IBM, and click on Headlines, and identify three major new initiatives the company has undertaken.
34. Explain the difference between making assumptions and making wild guesses about future opportunities and threats facing business firms.
35. Explain how the external assessment would or should be different for non-profit organizations versus corporations.
36. Apply Porter's Five-Forces Model to IBM. What strategic implications arise in that analysis?
37. Compare and contrast competitive intelligence programs across several organizations that you are familiar.

Notes

1. York Freund, "Critical Success Factors," *Planning Review* 16, no. 4 (July–August 1988): 20.
2. Ann Zimmerman, "Gift Shoppers Flocked to the Web," *Wall Street Journal*, December 24, 2010, B1.
3. Bill Saporito, "Companies That Compete Best," *Fortune*, May 22, 1989, 36.
4. Kenneth Sawka, "Demystifying Business Intelligence," *Management Review*, October 1996, 49.
5. John Prescott and Daniel Smith, "The Largest Survey of 'Leading-Edge' Competitor Intelligence Managers," *Planning Review* 17, no. 3 (May–June 1989): 6–13.
6. M. J. Chen, "Competitor Analysis and Interfirm Rivalry: Toward a Theoretical Integration," *Academy of Management Review* 21 (1996): 106.
7. S. Jayachandran, J. Gimeno, and P. R. Varadarajan, "Theory of Multimarket Competition: A Synthesis and Implications for Marketing Strategy," *Journal of Marketing* 63, 3 (1999): 59; and M. J. Chen. "Competitor Analysis and Interfirm Rivalry: Toward a Theoretical Integration," *Academy of Management Review* 21 (1996): 107–108.
8. Arthur Thompson, Jr., A. J. Strickland III, and John Gamble, *Crafting and Executing Strategy: Text and Readings* (New York: McGraw-Hill/Irwin, 2005), 63.
9. Michael E. Porter, *Competitive Strategy: Techniques for Analyzing Industries and Competitors* (New York: Free Press, 1980), 24–27.
10. horizon.unc.edu/projects/seminars/futuresresearch/rationale.asp.
11. Dale McConkey, "Planning in a Changing Environment," *Business Horizons* 31, no. 5 (September–October 1988): 67.

Current Readings

Allio, Robert J. "In this Recession's Aftermath, CEO's Face Unique Threats and Opportunities." *Strategy & Leadership* 38, no. 4 (2010): 27.

Denning, Stephen. "Masterclass: Managing the Threats and Opportunities of the Open Corporation." *Strategy & Leadership* 38, no. 6 (2010): 16.

Holburn, Guy L. F., and Bennet A. Zeiner. "Political Capabilities, Policy Risk, and International Investment Strategy: Evidence from the Global Electric Power Generation Industry." *Strategic Management Journal* 31, no. 12 (December 2010): 1290–1315.

Ghemawat, Pankaj. "Finding Your Strategy in the New Landscape." *Harvard Business Review*, March 2010, 54–61.

Gulati, Ranjay, Nitin Nohria, and Franz Wohlgezogen. "Roaring Out of Recession." *Harvard Business Review*, March 2010, 62–69.

Haas, Martine R. "The Double-Edged Swords of Autonomy and External Knowledge: Analyzing Team Effectiveness in a Multinational Organization." *Academy of Management Journal* 53, no. 5 (October 2010): 989.

Kilduff, Gavin J., Hillary Anger Elfenbein, and Barry M. Staw. "The Psychology of Rivalry: A Relationally Dependent Analysis of Competition." *Academy of Management Journal* 53, no. 5 (October 2010): 943–969.

Lam, Shun Yin. "What Kind of Assumptions Need to be Realistic and How to Test Them: A Response to Tsang (2006)." *Strategic Management Journal* 31, no. 6 (June 2010): 679–687.

Makridakis, Spyros, Robin M. Hogarth, and Anil Gaba. "Why Forecasts Fail. What to Do Instead." *MIT Sloan Management Review* 51, no. 2 (Winter 2010): 83–95.

Ofek, Elie, and Luc Wathieu. "Are You Ignoring Trends That Could Shake Up Your Business?" *Harvard Business Review*, July–August 2010, 124–131.

Yang, Hongyan, Corey Phelps, and H. Kevin Steensma. "Learning From What Others Have Learned From You: The Effects of Knowledge Spillovers on Originating Firms." *The Academy of Management Journal* 53, no. 2 (April 2010): 371–389.

ASSURANCE OF LEARNING EXERCISES

Assurance of Learning Exercise 3A

IBM and Africa: An External Assessment

Purpose

IBM is featured in the opening chapter case as a firm that engages in excellent strategic planning. This exercise gives you practice conducting an external strategic management audit to determine if Africa is the new, best place for IBM to produce and market products and services.

In September 2011, IBM opened a new branch office in Luanda, Angola as part of the company's continued geographic expansion to increase its presence in key growth markets in support of its global strategy. IBM is making huge investments in Africa and recently opened new locations in Dakar, Senegal and Dares Salaam, Tanzania. IBM now has a direct presence in more than 20 African countries, including South Africa, Ghana, Nigeria, Kenya, Morocco, Egypt, Tunisia and Algeria. IBM already serves a number of key clients in Central Africa, spanning sectors including telecommunications, oil & gas, finance and government. For example in Angola, IBM is working with one of the country's major banks to help transform the institution's core banking technology infrastructure and support business growth. With a new system based on IBM Power servers and software technologies, the bank has been able to upgrade its banking services.

Instructions

Step 1 Research the business climate in 10 African countries mentioned prior.

Step 2 Prepare an EFE Matrix for IBM based solely on the opportunities and threats that IBM will face in doing business in the 10 African countries you chose.

Step 3 Based on your research, list the 10 African countries you selected in rank order of attractiveness for IBM to focus efforts upon. Give a one-sentence rationale for each country's ranking.

Assurance of Learning Exercise 3B

Preparing a CPM for IBM Based on Countries Rather than Companies

Purpose

Countries are similar to companies in that they compete with each other for investment dollars and economic development.

Instructions

Step 1 Revisit the research you collected and analyzed in the above exercise.

Step 2 Prepare a CPM that reveals your assessment of 6 African countries in terms of their relative strengths and weaknesses across what you deem to be the most critical success factors.

Assurance of Learning Exercise 3C

Develop Divisional IBM EFE Matrices

Purpose

IBM has four major divisions. The company faces fierce but different competitors in each segment. The external opportunities and threats that IBM face are different in each segment, so each division prepares its own list of critical external success factors. This external analysis is critically important in strategic planning because a firm needs to exploit opportunities and avoid or at least mitigate threats.

The purpose of this exercise is to develop divisional EFE Matrices that a firm could use in developing an overall corporate EFE Matrix.

Instructions

Step 1   Go to IBM's website. Review the company's most recent *Form 10K*.

Step 2   Determine and review IBM's major divisions.

Step 3   Conduct research to determine what you believe are the four major threats and the four major opportunities critical to strategic planning within IBM's business segments. Review the relevant *Standard and Poor's* Industry Survey documents for each segment.

Step 4   Develop divisional EFE Matrices for IBM. Work within a team of students if your instructor so requests but you will need an EFE Matrix for each segment.

Step 5   Prioritize the 16 threats and the 16 opportunities developed in the prior step so that corporate IBM top executives can better develop a corporate EFE Matrix.

Step 6   Let's say IBM has their operations segmented by Domestic versus Global. Based on your research, prepare an EFE Matrix for IBM's domestic operations and another EFE Matrix for IBM's Global Operations.

Assurance of Learning Exercise 3D

Developing an EFE Matrix for Adidas AG

Purpose

This exercise will provide practice developing an EFE Matrix. An EFE Matrix summarizes the results of an external audit. This is an important tool widely used by strategists.

Instructions

Step 1   Join with two other students in class and jointly prepare an EFE Matrix for Adidas AG. Refer back to the Cohesion Case and to Exercise 1B, if necessary, to identify external opportunities and threats. Use the information in the *Standard and Poor's* Industry Surveys that you copied as part of Assurance of Learning Exercise 1B. Be sure not to include strategies as opportunities, but do include as many monetary amounts, percentages, numbers, and ratios as possible.

Step 2   All three-person teams participating in this exercise should record their EFE total weighted scores on the board. Put your initials after your score to identify it as your teams.

Step 3   Compare the total weighted scores. Which team's score came closest to the instructor's answer? Discuss reasons for variation in the scores reported on the board.

Assurance of Learning Exercise 3E

The External Assessment

Purpose

This exercise will help you become familiar with important sources of external information available in your college or university library. A key part of preparing an external audit is searching the Internet and examining published sources of information for relevant economic, social, cultural, demographic, environmental, political, governmental, legal, technological, and competitive trends and events. External opportunities and threats must be identified and evaluated before strategies can be formulated effectively.

Instructions

Step 1 Select an American company or business where you recently purchased a product or previously have worked. Conduct an external audit for this company. Find opportunities and threats in recent issues of newspapers and magazines. Search for information using the Internet. Use the following websites:

http://marketwatch.multexinvestor.com
www.hoovers.com
http://moneycentral.msn.com
http://finance.yahoo.com
www.clearstation.com
https://us.etrade.com/e/t/invest/markets

Step 2 On a separate sheet of paper, list 10 opportunities and 10 threats that face this company. Be specific in stating each factor.

Step 3 Include a bibliography to reveal where you found the information.

Step 4 Write a three-page summary of your findings, and submit it to your instructor.

Assurance of Learning Exercise 3F

Developing a CPM for IBM Corporation

Purpose

Monitoring competitors' performance and strategies is a key aspect of an external audit. This exercise is designed to give you practice evaluating the competitive position of organizations in a given industry and assimilating that information in the form of a CPM.

Instructions

Step 1 Gather information about IBM Corporation. Turn back to the opening chapter boxed insert and review this information.

Step 2 On a separate sheet of paper, prepare a CPM that includes IBM and its two leading competitors.

Step 3 Turn in your CPM for a classwork grade.

Assurance of Learning Exercise 3G

Developing a CPM for Adidas AG

Purpose

Monitoring competitors' performance and strategies is a key aspect of an external audit. This exercise is designed to give you practice evaluating the competitive position of organizations in a given industry and assimilating that information in the form of a CPM.

Instructions

Step 1 Gather information from Assurance of Learning Exercise 1B. Also, turn back to the Cohesion Case and review the section on competitors.

Step 2 On a separate sheet of paper, prepare a CPM, that includes Nike, Puma, Under Armour, and Callaway Golf.

Step 3 Turn in your CPM for a classwork grade.

Assurance of Learning Exercise 3H

Analyzing Your College or University's External Strategic Situation

Purpose

This exercise is excellent for doing together as a class.

Instruction

As a class, determine your college or university's major external opportunities and threats. List 10 opportunities and 10 threats. Then, get everyone in class to rank order their factors with 1 being most important and 10 being least important. Then, gather up everyone's paper, count the numbers, and in that manner create a prioritized list of the key external opportunities and threats facing your college.

"NOTABLE QUOTES"

"Like a product or service, the planning process itself must be managed and shaped, if it is to serve executives as a vehicle for strategic decision-making."
—Robert Lenz

"The difference between now and five years ago is that information systems had limited function. You weren't betting your company on it. Now you are."
—William Gruber

"Weak leadership can wreck the soundest strategy."
—Sun Tzu

"A firm that continues to employ a previously successful strategy eventually and inevitably falls victim to a competitor."
—William Cohen

"Great spirits have always encountered violent opposition from mediocre minds."
—Albert Einstein

"The idea is to concentrate our strength against our competitor's relative weakness."
—Bruce Henderson

The Internal Assessment

CHAPTER OBJECTIVES

After studying this chapter, you should be able to do the following:

1. Describe how to perform an internal strategic-management audit.
2. Discuss the Resource-Based View (RBV) in strategic management.
3. Discuss key interrelationships among the functional areas of business.
4. Identify the basic functions or activities that make up management, marketing, finance/accounting, production/operations, research and development, and management information systems.
5. Explain how to determine and prioritize a firm's internal strengths and weaknesses.
6. Explain the importance of financial ratio analysis.
7. Discuss the nature and role of management information systems in strategic management.
8. Develop an Internal Factor Evaluation (IFE) Matrix.
9. Explain cost/benefit analysis value chain analysis, and benchmarking as strategic-management tools.

ASSURANCE OF LEARNING EXERCISES

Assurance of Learning Exercise 4A
Develop a Corporate IFE Matrix for J&J

Assurance of Learning Exercise 4B
Should J&J Deploy More Resources or Less Outside of the USA?

Assurance of Learning Exercise 4C
Apply Breakeven Analysis

Assurance of Learning Exercise 4D
Performing a Financial Ratio Analysis for Adidas AG

Assurance of Learning Exercise 4E
Constructing an IFE Matrix for Adidas AG

Assurance of Learning Exercise 4F
Analyzing Your College or University's Internal Strategic Situation

This chapter focuses on identifying and evaluating a firm's strengths and weaknesses in the functional areas of business, including management, marketing, finance/accounting, production/operations, research and development, and management information systems. Relationships among these areas of business are examined. Strategic implications of important functional area concepts are examined. The process of performing an internal audit is described. The Resource-Based View (RBV) of strategic management is introduced as is the Value Chain Analysis (VCA) concept. Johnson & Johnson (J&J) does an excellent job using its strengths to capitalize upon opportunities. Johnson & Johnson is showcased in the opening chapter boxed insert.

The Nature of an Internal Audit

All organizations have strengths and weaknesses in the functional areas of business. No enterprise is equally strong or weak in all areas. Maytag, for example, is known for excellent production and product design, whereas Procter & Gamble is known for superb marketing. Internal strengths/weaknesses, coupled with external opportunities/threats and a clear statement of mission, provide the basis for establishing objectives and strategies. Objectives and strategies are established with the intention of capitalizing upon internal strengths and overcoming weaknesses. The internal-audit part of the strategic-management process is illustrated in Figure 4-1.

Excellent Strategic Management Showcased

JOHNSON & JOHNSON (J&J)

Headquartered in New Brunswick, New Jersey, Johnson & Johnson (J&J) is a global pharmaceutical, medical devices, and consumer packaged goods manufacturer that consistently ranks at the top of Harris Interactive's National Corporate Reputation Survey. It was also recently ranked as the world's most respected company by *Barron's Magazine*.

J&J includes some 250 subsidiary companies with operations in 60 countries employing approximately 116,000 people worldwide. J&J implements a decentralized management approach as each of its operating companies functions as its own small business. Selling products in over 175 countries, J&J's brands are recognized all over the world. J&J brands include numerous household names of medications and first aid supplies such as the Band-Aid® brand line of bandages, Tylenol® medications, Johnson's baby products, Neutrogena® skin and beauty products, Clean & Clear® facial wash, and Acuvue® contact lenses.

J&J has had 27 consecutive years of adjusted earnings increases; and 49 consecutive years of dividend increases. Over the last 10 years, J&J stock generated a 4.0 percent total return for investors compared to a 1.4 percent total return for the S&P 500.

J&J had sales of $16.6 billion for the second quarter of 2011, an increase of 8.3 percent as compared to the second quarter

of 2010. Domestic sales increased only 0.1 percent, while international sales increased 15.9 percent. J&J's Worldwide Pharmaceutical sales of $6.2 billion for the second quarter represented an increase of 12.2 percent versus the prior year. Domestic sales increased 4.1 percent but international sales increased 22.6 percent. J&J's Worldwide Medical Devices and Diagnostics sales of $6.6 billion for the second quarter of 2011 represented increases of 7.2 and 13.4 percent, respectively, versus the prior year domestic and international sales.

Source: Based on information at www.jnj.com.

FIGURE 4-1

A Comprehensive Strategic-Management Model

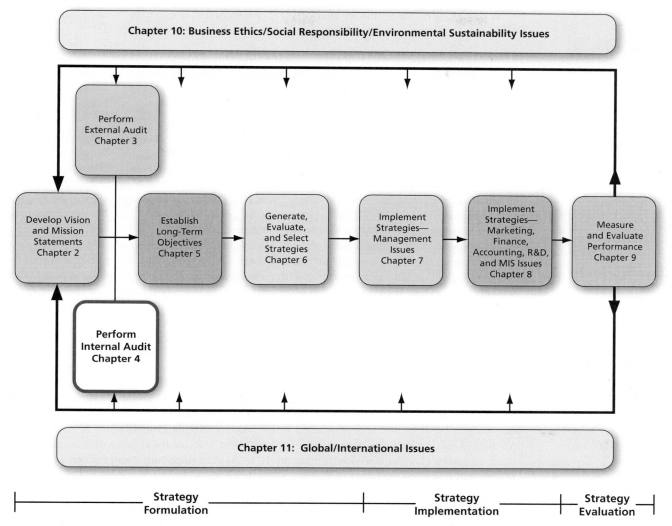

Source: Fred R. David, "How Companies Define Their Mission," *Long Range Planning* 22, no. 3 (June 1988): 40.

Key Internal Forces

It is not possible in a strategic-management text to review in depth all the material presented in courses such as marketing, finance, accounting, management, management information systems, and production/operations; there are many subareas within these functions, such as customer service, warranties, advertising, packaging, and pricing under marketing.

For different types of organizations, such as hospitals, universities, and government agencies, the functional business areas, of course, differ. In a hospital, for example, functional areas may include cardiology, hematology, nursing, maintenance, physician support, and receivables. Functional areas of a university can include athletic programs, placement services, housing, fund-raising, academic research, counseling, and intramural programs. Within large organizations, each division has certain strengths and weaknesses.

A firm's strengths that cannot be easily matched or imitated by competitors are called *distinctive competencies.* Building competitive advantages involves taking advantage of distinctive competencies. For example, the firm Research in Motion (RIM) exploits its distinctive competence in research and development by producing a wide range of innovative products. Strategies are designed in part to improve on a firm's weaknesses, turning them into strengths—and maybe even into distinctive competencies.

FIGURE 4-2

The Process of Gaining Competitive Advantage in a Firm

Weaknesses ⇒ Strengths ⇒ Distinctive Competencies ⇒ Competitive Advantage

Figure 4-2 illustrates that all firms should continually strive to improve on their weaknesses, turning them into strengths, and ultimately developing distinctive competencies that can provide the firm with competitive advantages over rival firms.

The Process of Performing an Internal Audit

The process of performing an *internal audit* closely parallels the process of performing an external audit. Representative managers and employees from throughout the firm need to be involved in determining a firm's strengths and weaknesses. The internal audit requires gathering and assimilating information about the firm's management, marketing, finance/accounting, production/operations, research and development (R&D), and management information systems operations. Key factors should be prioritized as described in Chapter 3 so that the firm's most important strengths and weaknesses can be determined collectively.

Compared to the external audit, the process of performing an internal audit provides more opportunity for participants to understand how their jobs, departments, and divisions fit into the whole organization. This is a great benefit because managers and employees perform better when they understand how their work affects other areas and activities of the firm. For example, when marketing and manufacturing managers jointly discuss issues related to internal strengths and weaknesses, they gain a better appreciation of the issues, problems, concerns, and needs of all the functional areas. In organizations that do not use strategic management, marketing, finance, and manufacturing managers often do not interact with each other in significant ways. Performing an internal audit thus is an excellent vehicle or forum for improving the process of communication in the organization. *Communication* may be the most important word in management.

Performing an internal audit requires gathering, assimilating, and evaluating information about the firm's operations. Critical success factors, consisting of both strengths and weaknesses, can be identified and prioritized in the manner discussed in Chapter 3. According to William King, a task force of managers from different units of the organization, supported by staff, should be charged with determining the 10 to 20 most important strengths and weaknesses that should influence the future of the organization. He says:

> The development of conclusions on the 10 to 20 most important organizational strengths and weaknesses can be, as any experienced manager knows, a difficult task, when it involves managers representing various organizational interests and points of view. Developing a 20-page list of strengths and weaknesses could be accomplished relatively easily, but a list of the 10 to 15 most important ones involves significant analysis and negotiation. This is true because of the judgments that are required and the impact which such a list will inevitably have as it is used in the formulation, implementation, and evaluation of strategies.[1]

Strategic management is a highly interactive process that requires effective coordination among management, marketing, finance/accounting, production/operations, R&D, and management information systems managers. Although the strategic-management process is overseen by strategists, success requires that managers and employees from all functional areas work together to provide ideas and information. Financial managers, for example, may need to restrict the number of feasible options available to operations managers, or R&D managers may develop products for which marketing managers need to set higher objectives. A key to organizational success is effective coordination and understanding among managers from all functional business areas. Through involvement in performing an internal strategic-management audit, managers from different departments and divisions of the firm come to understand the nature and effect of decisions in other functional business areas in their firm. Knowledge of these relationships is critical for effectively establishing objectives and strategies.

A failure to recognize and understand relationships among the functional areas of business can be detrimental to strategic management, and the number of those relationships that must be managed increases dramatically with a firm's size, diversity, geographic dispersion, and the number of products or services offered. Governmental and nonprofit enterprises traditionally have not placed sufficient emphasis on relationships among the business functions. Some firms place too great an emphasis on one function at the expense of others. Ansoff explained:

> During the first fifty years, successful firms focused their energies on optimizing the performance of one of the principal functions: production/operations, R&D, or marketing. Today, due to the growing complexity and dynamism of the environment, success increasingly depends on a judicious combination of several functional influences. This transition from a single function focus to a multifunction focus is essential for successful strategic management.[2]

Financial ratio analysis exemplifies the complexity of relationships among the functional areas of business. A declining return on investment or profit margin ratio could be the result of ineffective marketing, poor management policies, research and development errors, or a weak management information system. The effectiveness of strategy formulation, implementation, and evaluation activities hinges upon a clear understanding of how major business functions affect one another. For strategies to succeed, a coordinated effort among all the functional areas of business is needed. In the case of planning, George wrote:

> We may conceptually separate planning for the purpose of theoretical discussion and analysis, but in practice, neither is it a distinct entity nor is it capable of being separated. The planning function is mixed with all other business functions and, like ink once mixed with water, it cannot be set apart. It is spread throughout and is a part of the whole of managing an organization.[3]

The Resource-Based View (RBV)

Some researchers emphasize the importance of the internal audit part of the strategic-management process by comparing it to the external audit. Robert Grant concluded that the internal audit is more important, saying:

> In a world where customer preferences are volatile, the identity of customers is changing, and the technologies for serving customer requirements are continually evolving, an externally focused orientation does not provide a secure foundation for formulating long-term strategy. When the external environment is in a state of flux, the firm's own resources and capabilities may be a much more stable basis on which to define its identity. Hence, a definition of a business in terms of what it is capable of doing may offer a more durable basis for strategy.[4]

The *Resource-Based View (RBV)* approach to competitive advantage contends that internal resources are more important for a firm than external factors in achieving and sustaining competitive advantage. In contrast to the I/O theory presented in the previous chapter, proponents of the RBV view contend that organizational performance will primarily be determined by internal resources that can be grouped into three all-encompassing categories: physical resources, human resources, and organizational resources.[5] Physical resources include all plant and equipment, location, technology, raw materials, machines; human resources include all employees, training, experience, intelligence, knowledge, skills, abilities; and organizational resources include firm structure, planning processes, information systems, patents, trademarks, copyrights, databases, and so on. RBV theory asserts that resources are actually what helps a firm exploit opportunities and neutralize threats.

The basic premise of the RBV is that the mix, type, amount, and nature of a firm's internal resources should be considered first and foremost in devising strategies that can lead to sustainable competitive advantage. Managing strategically according to the RBV involves developing and exploiting a firm's unique resources and capabilities, and continually maintaining and strengthening those resources. The theory asserts that it is advantageous for a firm to pursue a strategy that is not currently being implemented by any competing firm. When other firms are unable to duplicate a particular strategy, then the focal firm has a sustainable competitive advantage, according to RBV theorists.

For a resource to be valuable, it must be either (1) rare, (2) hard to imitate, or (3) not easily substitutable. Often called *empirical indicators,* these three characteristics of resources enable a firm to implement strategies that improve its efficiency and effectiveness and lead to a sustainable competitive advantage. The more a resource(s) is rare, nonimitable, and nonsubstitutable, the stronger a firm's competitive advantage will be and the longer it will last.

Rare resources are resources that other competing firms do not possess. If many firms have the same resource, then those firms will likely implement similar strategies, thus giving no one firm a sustainable competitive advantage. This is not to say that resources that are common are not valuable; they do indeed aid the firm in its chance for economic prosperity. However, to sustain a competitive advantage, it is more advantageous if the resource(s) is also rare.

It is also important that these same resources be difficult to imitate. If firms cannot easily gain the resources, say RBV theorists, then those resources will lead to a competitive advantage more so than resources easily imitable. Even if a firm employs resources that are rare, a sustainable competitive advantage may be achieved only if other firms cannot easily obtain these resources.

The third empirical indicator that can make resources a source of competitive advantage is substitutability. Borrowing from Porter's Five-Forces Model, to the degree that there are no viable substitutes, a firm will be able to sustain its competitive advantage. However, even if a competing firm cannot perfectly imitate a firm's resource, it can still obtain a sustainable competitive advantage of its own by obtaining resource substitutes.

The RBV has continued to grow in popularity and continues to seek a better understanding of the relationship between resources and sustained competitive advantage in strategic management. However, as alluded to in Chapter 3, one cannot say with any degree of certainty that either external or internal factors will always or even consistently be more important in seeking competitive advantage. Understanding both external and internal factors, and more importantly, understanding the relationships among them, will be the key to effective strategy formulation (discussed in Chapter 6). Because both external and internal factors continually change, strategists seek to identify and take advantage of positive changes and buffer against negative changes in a continuing effort to gain and sustain a firm's competitive advantage. This is the essence and challenge of strategic management, and oftentimes survival of the firm hinges on this work.

Integrating Strategy and Culture

Relationships among a firm's functional business activities perhaps can be exemplified best by focusing on organizational culture, an internal phenomenon that permeates all departments and divisions of an organization. *Organizational culture* can be defined as "a pattern of behavior that has been developed by an organization as it learns to cope with its problem of external adaptation and internal integration, and that has worked well enough to be considered valid and to be taught to new members as the correct way to perceive, think, and feel."[6] This definition emphasizes the importance of matching external with internal factors in making strategic decisions.

Organizational culture captures the subtle, elusive, and largely unconscious forces that shape a workplace. Remarkably resistant to change, culture can represent a major strength or weakness for the firm. It can be an underlying reason for strengths or weaknesses in any of the major business functions.

Defined in Table 4-1, *cultural products* include values, beliefs, rites, rituals, ceremonies, myths, stories, legends, sagas, language, metaphors, symbols, heroes, and heroines. These products or dimensions are levers that strategists can use to influence and direct strategy formulation, implementation, and evaluation activities. An organization's culture compares to an individual's personality in the sense that no two organizations have the same culture and no two individuals have the same personality. Both culture and personality are enduring and can be warm, aggressive, friendly, open, innovative, conservative, liberal, harsh, or likable.

TABLE 4-1   Example Cultural Products Defined

Rites	Planned sets of activities that consolidate various forms of cultural expressions into one event.
Ceremonial	Several rites connected together.
Ritual	A standardized set of behaviors used to manage anxieties.
Myth	A narrative of imagined events, usually not supported by facts.
Saga	A historical narrative describing the unique accomplishments of a group and its leaders.
Legend	A handed-down narrative of some wonderful event, usually not supported by facts.
Story	A narrative usually based on true events.
Folktale	A fictional story.
Symbol	Any object, act, event, quality, or relation used to convey meaning.
Language	The manner in which members of a group communicate.
Metaphors	Shorthand of words used to capture a vision or to reinforce old or new values.
Values	Life-directing attitudes that serve as behavioral guidelines.
Belief	An understanding of a particular phenomenon.
Heroes/Heroines	Individuals greatly respected.

Source: Based on H. M. Trice and J. M. Beyer, "Studying Organizational Cultures through Rites and Ceremonials," *Academy of Management Review* 9, no. 4 (October 1984): 655.

At Google, the culture is very informal. Employees are encouraged to wander the halls on employee-sponsored scooters and brainstorm on public whiteboards provided everywhere. In contrast, the culture at Procter & Gamble (P&G) is so rigid that employees jokingly call themselves "Proctoids." Despite this difference, the two companies are swapping employees and participating in each other's staff training sessions. Why? Because P&G spends more money on advertising than any other company and Google desires more of P&G's $8.7 billion in annual advertising expenses; P&G has come to realize that the next generation of laundry-detergent, toilet-paper, and skin-cream customers now spend more time online than watching TV.

Dimensions of organizational culture permeate all the functional areas of business. It is something of an art to uncover the basic values and beliefs that are deeply buried in an organization's rich collection of stories, language, heroes, and rituals, but cultural products can represent both important strengths and weaknesses. Culture is an aspect of an organization that can no longer be taken for granted in performing an internal strategic-management audit because culture and strategy must work together.

Table 4-2 provides some example (possible) aspects of an organization's culture. Note you could ask employees/managers to rate the degree that the dimension characterizes the firm. When one firm acquires another firm, integrating the two cultures can be important. For example, in Table 4-2, one firm may score mostly 1's (low) and the other firm may score mostly 5's (high), which would present a challenging strategic problem.

The strategic-management process takes place largely within a particular organization's culture. Lorsch found that executives in successful companies are emotionally committed to the firm's culture, but he concluded that culture can inhibit strategic management in two basic ways. First, managers frequently miss the significance of changing external conditions because they are blinded by strongly held beliefs. Second, when a particular culture has been effective in the past, the natural response is to stick with it in the future, even during times of major strategic change.[7] An organization's culture must support the collective commitment of its people to a common purpose. It must foster competence and enthusiasm among managers and employees.

Organizational culture significantly affects business decisions and thus must be evaluated during an internal strategic-management audit. If strategies can capitalize on cultural strengths, such as a strong work ethic or highly ethical beliefs, then management often can swiftly and easily implement changes. However, if the firm's culture is not supportive, strategic changes may be ineffective or even counterproductive. A firm's culture can become antagonistic to new strategies, with the result being confusion and disorientation.

TABLE 4-2   Fifteen Example (Possible) Aspects of an Organization's Culture

Dimension	Low		Degree		High
1. Strong work ethic; arrive early and leave late	1	2	3	4	5
2. High ethical beliefs; clear code of business ethics followed	1	2	3	4	5
3. Formal dress; shirt and tie expected	1	2	3	4	5
4. Informal dress; many casual dress days	1	2	3	4	5
5. Socialize together outside of work	1	2	3	4	5
6. Do not question supervisor's decision	1	2	3	4	5
7. Encourage whistle-blowing	1	2	3	4	5
8. Be health conscious; have a wellness program	1	2	3	4	5
9. Allow substantial "working from home"	1	2	3	4	5
10. Encourage creativity/innovation/openmindness	1	2	3	4	5
11. Support women and minorities; no glass ceiling	1	2	3	4	5
12. Be highly socially responsible; be philanthropic	1	2	3	4	5
13. Have numerous meetings	1	2	3	4	5
14. Have a participative management style	1	2	3	4	5
15. Preserve the natural environment; have a sustainability program	1	2	3	4	5

An organization's culture should infuse individuals with enthusiasm for implementing strategies. Allarie and Firsirotu emphasized the need to understand culture:

> Culture provides an explanation for the insuperable difficulties a firm encounters when it attempts to shift its strategic direction. Not only has the "right" culture become the essence and foundation of corporate excellence, it is also claimed that success or failure of reforms hinges on management's sagacity and ability to change the firm's driving culture in time and in time with required changes in strategies.[8]

The potential value of organizational culture has not been realized fully in the study of strategic management. Ignoring the effect that culture can have on relationships among the functional areas of business can result in barriers to communication, lack of coordination, and an inability to adapt to changing conditions. Some tension between culture and a firm's strategy is inevitable, but the tension should be monitored so that it does not reach a point at which relationships are severed and the culture becomes antagonistic. The resulting disarray among members of the organization would disrupt strategy formulation, implementation, and evaluation. In contrast, a supportive organizational culture can make managing much easier.

Internal strengths and weaknesses associated with a firm's culture sometimes are overlooked because of the interfunctional nature of this phenomenon. It is important, therefore, for strategists to understand their firm as a sociocultural system. Success is often determined by linkages between a firm's culture and strategies. The challenge of strategic management today is to bring about the changes in organizational culture and individual mind-sets that are needed to support the formulation, implementation, and evaluation of strategies.

Management

The *functions of management* consist of five basic activities: planning, organizing, motivating, staffing, and controlling. An overview of these activities is provided in Table 4-3. These activities are important to assess in strategic planning because an organization should continually capitalize on its management strengths and improve on its management weak areas.

Planning

The only thing certain about the future of any organization is change, and *planning* is the essential bridge between the present and the future that increases the likelihood of achieving desired results. Planning is the process by which one determines whether to attempt a task, works out the most effective way of reaching desired objectives, and prepares to overcome unexpected

TABLE 4-3   The Basic Functions of Management

Function	Description	Stage of Strategic-Management Process When Most Important
Planning	Planning consists of all those managerial activities related to preparing for the future. Specific tasks include forecasting, establishing objectives, devising strategies, developing policies, and setting goals.	Strategy Formulation
Organizing	Organizing includes all those managerial activities that result in a structure of task and authority relationships. Specific areas include organizational design, job specialization, job descriptions, job specifications, span of control, unity of command, coordination, job design, and job analysis.	Strategy Implementation
Motivating	Motivating involves efforts directed toward shaping human behavior. Specific topics include leadership, communication, work groups, behavior modification, delegation of authority, job enrichment, job satisfaction, needs fulfillment, organizational change, employee morale, and managerial morale.	Strategy Implementation
Staffing	Staffing activities are centered on personnel or human resource management. Included are wage and salary administration, employee benefits, interviewing, hiring, firing, training, management development, employee safety, affirmative action, equal employment opportunity, union relations, career development, personnel research, discipline policies, grievance procedures, and public relations.	Strategy Implementation
Controlling	Controlling refers to all those managerial activities directed toward ensuring that actual results are consistent with planned results. Key areas of concern include quality control, financial control, sales control, inventory control, expense control, analysis of variances, rewards, and sanctions.	Strategy Evaluation

difficulties with adequate resources. Planning is the start of the process by which an individual or business may turn empty dreams into achievements. Planning enables one to avoid the trap of working extremely hard but achieving little.

Planning is an up-front investment in success. Planning helps a firm achieve maximum effect from a given effort. Planning enables a firm to take into account relevant factors and focus on the critical ones. Planning helps ensure that the firm can be prepared for all reasonable eventualities and for all changes that will be needed. Planning enables a firm to gather the resources needed and carry out tasks in the most efficient way possible. Planning enables a firm to conserve its own resources, avoid wasting ecological resources, make a fair profit, and be seen as an effective, useful firm. Planning enables a firm to identify precisely what is to be achieved and to detail precisely the who, what, when, where, why, and how needed to achieve desired objectives. Planning enables a firm to assess whether the effort, costs, and implications associated with achieving desired objectives are warranted.[9] Planning is the cornerstone of effective strategy formulation. But even though it is considered the foundation of management, it is commonly the task that managers neglect most. Planning is essential for successful strategy implementation and strategy evaluation, largely because organizing, motivating, staffing, and controlling activities depend upon good planning.

The process of planning must involve managers and employees throughout an organization. The time horizon for planning decreases from two to five years for top-level to less than six months for lower-level managers. The important point is that all managers do planning and should involve subordinates in the process to facilitate employee understanding and commitment.

Planning can have a positive impact on organizational and individual performance. Planning allows an organization to identify and take advantage of external opportunities as well as minimize the impact of external threats. Planning is more than extrapolating from the past and present into the future (long range planning). It also includes developing a mission, forecasting future events and trends, establishing objectives, and choosing strategies to pursue (strategic planning).

An organization can develop synergy through planning. *Synergy* exists when everyone pulls together as a team that knows what it wants to achieve; synergy is the 2 + 2 = 5 effect. By establishing and communicating clear objectives, employees and managers can work together toward desired results. Synergy can result in powerful competitive advantages. The strategic-management process itself is aimed at creating synergy in an organization.

Planning allows a firm to adapt to changing markets and thus to shape its own destiny. Strategic management can be viewed as a formal planning process that allows an organization to pursue proactive rather than reactive strategies. Successful organizations strive to control their own futures rather than merely react to external forces and events as they occur. Historically, organisms and organizations that have not adapted to changing conditions have become extinct. Swift adaptation is needed today more than ever because changes in markets, economies, and competitors worldwide are accelerating. Many firms did not adapt to the global recession of late and went out of business.

Organizing

The purpose of *organizing* is to achieve coordinated effort by defining task and authority relationships. Organizing means determining who does what and who reports to whom. There are countless examples in history of well-organized enterprises successfully competing against— and in some cases defeating—much stronger but less-organized firms. A well-organized firm generally has motivated managers and employees who are committed to seeing the organization succeed. Resources are allocated more effectively and used more efficiently in a well-organized firm than in a disorganized firm.

The organizing function of management can be viewed as consisting of three sequential activities: breaking down tasks into jobs (work specialization), combining jobs to form departments (departmentalization), and delegating authority. Breaking down tasks into jobs requires the development of job descriptions and job specifications. These tools clarify for both managers and employees what particular jobs entail. In *The Wealth of Nations,* published in 1776, Adam Smith cited the advantages of work specialization in the manufacture of pins:

> One man draws the wire, another straightens it, a third cuts it, a fourth points it, a fifth grinds it at the top for receiving the head. Ten men working in this manner can produce 48,000 pins in a single day, but if they had all wrought separately and independently, each might at best produce twenty pins in a day.[10]

Combining jobs to form departments results in an organizational structure, span of control, and a chain of command. Changes in strategy often require changes in structure because positions may be created, deleted, or merged. Organizational structure dictates how resources are allocated and how objectives are established in a firm. Allocating resources and establishing objectives geographically, for example, is much different from doing so by product or customer.

The most common forms of departmentalization are functional, divisional, strategic business unit, and matrix. These types of structure are discussed further in Chapter 7.

Delegating authority is an important organizing activity, as evidenced in the old saying "You can tell how good a manager is by observing how his or her department functions when he or she isn't there." Employees today are more educated and more capable of participating in organizational decision making than ever before. In most cases, they expect to be delegated authority and responsibility and to be held accountable for results. Delegation of authority is embedded in the strategic-management process.

Motivating

Motivating can be defined as the process of influencing people to accomplish specific objectives.[11] Motivation explains why some people work hard and others do not. Objectives, strategies, and policies have little chance of succeeding if employees and managers are not motivated to implement strategies once they are formulated. The motivating function of management includes at least four major components: leadership, group dynamics, communication, and organizational change.

When managers and employees of a firm strive to achieve high levels of productivity, this indicates that the firm's strategists are good leaders. Good leaders establish rapport with subordinates, empathize with their needs and concerns, set a good example, and are trustworthy and fair. Leadership includes developing a vision of the firm's future and inspiring people to work hard to achieve that vision. Kirkpatrick and Locke reported that certain traits also characterize effective leaders: knowledge of the business, cognitive ability, self-confidence, honesty, integrity, and drive.[12]

Research suggests that democratic behavior on the part of leaders results in more positive attitudes toward change and higher productivity than does autocratic behavior. Drucker said:

> Leadership is not a magnetic personality. That can just as well be demagoguery. It is not "making friends and influencing people." That is flattery. Leadership is the lifting of a person's vision to higher sights, the raising of a person's performance to a higher standard, the building of a person's personality beyond its normal limitations.[13]

Group dynamics play a major role in employee morale and satisfaction. Informal groups or coalitions form in every organization. The norms of coalitions can range from being very positive to very negative toward management. It is important, therefore, that strategists identify the composition and nature of informal groups in an organization to facilitate strategy formulation, implementation, and evaluation. Leaders of informal groups are especially important in formulating and implementing strategy changes.

Communication, perhaps the most important word in management, is a major component in motivation. An organization's system of communication determines whether strategies can be implemented successfully. Good two-way communication is vital for gaining support for departmental and divisional objectives and policies. Top-down communication can encourage bottom-up communication. The strategic-management process becomes a lot easier when subordinates are encouraged to discuss their concerns, reveal their problems, provide recommendations, and give suggestions. A primary reason for instituting strategic management is to build and support effective communication networks throughout the firm.

> The manager of tomorrow must be able to get his people to commit themselves to the business, whether they are machine operators or junior vice-presidents. The key issue will be empowerment, a term whose strength suggests the need to get beyond merely sharing a little information and a bit of decision making.[14]

Staffing

The management function of *staffing,* also called *personnel management* or *human resource management,* includes activities such as recruiting, interviewing, testing, selecting, orienting, training, developing, caring for, evaluating, rewarding, disciplining, promoting, transferring, demoting, and dismissing employees, as well as managing union relations.

Staffing activities play a major role in strategy-implementation efforts, and for this reason, human resource managers are becoming more actively involved in the strategic-management process. It is important to identify strengths and weaknesses in the staffing area.

The complexity and importance of human resource activities have increased to such a degree that all but the smallest organizations now need a full-time human resource manager. Numerous court cases that directly affect staffing activities are decided each day. Organizations and individuals can be penalized severely for not following federal, state, and local laws and guidelines related to staffing. Line managers simply cannot stay abreast of all the legal developments and requirements regarding staffing. The human resources department coordinates staffing decisions in the firm so that an organization as a whole meets legal requirements. This department also provides needed consistency in administering company rules, wages, policies, and employee benefits as well as collective bargaining with unions.

Human resource management is particularly challenging for international companies. For example, the inability of spouses and children to adapt to new surroundings can be a staffing problem in overseas transfers. The problems include premature returns, job performance slumps, resignations, discharges, low morale, marital discord, and general discontent. Firms such as Ford Motor and ExxonMobil screen and interview spouses and children before assigning persons to overseas positions. 3M Corporation introduces children to peers in the target country and offers spouses educational benefits.

Controlling

The *controlling* function of management includes all of those activities undertaken to ensure that actual operations conform to planned operations. All managers in an organization have controlling responsibilities, such as conducting performance evaluations and taking necessary action to minimize inefficiencies. The controlling function of management is particularly important for effective strategy evaluation. Controlling consists of four basic steps:

1. Establishing performance standards
2. Measuring individual and organizational performance
3. Comparing actual performance to planned performance standards
4. Taking corrective actions

Measuring individual performance is often conducted ineffectively or not at all in organizations. Some reasons for this shortcoming are that evaluations can create confrontations that most managers prefer to avoid, can take more time than most managers are willing to give, and can require skills that many managers lack. No single approach to measuring individual performance is without limitations. For this reason, an organization should examine various methods, such as the graphic rating scale, the behaviorally anchored rating scale, and the critical incident method, and then develop or select a performance-appraisal approach that best suits the firm's needs. Increasingly, firms are striving to link organizational performance with managers' and employees' pay. This topic is discussed further in Chapter 7.

Management Audit Checklist of Questions

The following checklist of questions can help determine specific strengths and weaknesses in the functional area of business. An answer of *no* to any question could indicate a potential weakness, although the strategic significance and implications of negative answers, of course, will vary by organization, industry, and severity of the weakness. Positive or yes answers to the checklist questions suggest potential areas of strength.

1. Does the firm use strategic-management concepts?
2. Are company objectives and goals measurable and well communicated?
3. Do managers at all hierarchical levels plan effectively?
4. Do managers delegate authority well?
5. Is the organization's structure appropriate?
6. Are job descriptions and job specifications clear?
7. Is employee morale high?
8. Are employee turnover and absenteeism low?
9. Are organizational reward and control mechanisms effective?

Marketing

Marketing can be described as the process of defining, anticipating, creating, and fulfilling customers' needs and wants for products and services. There are seven basic *functions of marketing:* (1) customer analysis, (2) selling products/services, (3) product and service planning, (4) pricing, (5) distribution, (6) marketing research, and (7) opportunity analysis.[15] Understanding these functions helps strategists identify and evaluate marketing strengths and weaknesses.

Customer Analysis

Customer analysis—the examination and evaluation of consumer needs, desires, and wants—involves administering customer surveys, analyzing consumer information, evaluating market positioning strategies, developing customer profiles, and determining optimal market segmentation strategies. The information generated by customer analysis can be essential in developing an effective mission statement. Customer profiles can reveal the demographic characteristics of an organization's customers. Buyers, sellers, distributors, salespeople, managers, wholesalers, retailers, suppliers, and creditors can all participate in gathering information to successfully identify customers' needs and wants. Successful organizations continually monitor present and potential customers' buying patterns.

Selling Products/Services

Successful strategy implementation generally rests upon the ability of an organization to sell some product or service. *Selling* includes many marketing activities, such as advertising, sales promotion, publicity, personal selling, sales force management, customer relations, and dealer relations. These activities are especially critical when a firm pursues a market penetration strategy. The effectiveness of various selling tools for consumer and industrial products varies. Personal selling is most important for industrial goods companies, whereas advertising is most important for consumer goods companies.

Internet advertising revenues received from firms such as Google, Amazon, Yahoo, and Facebook reached a record $12.1 billion in the first half of 2010, up more than 11 percent from the first half of the prior year, according to the Interactive Advertising Bureau. In contrast, newspaper advertising in 2010 totaled $7.3 billion, down 4.7 percent from the prior year and the lowest total since 1985.

Total advertising expenditures in the United States in 2011 is expected to be $155.2 billion, up 2.5 percent from the prior year. Global ad spending, however, is forecast to increase 4.2 percent to $470.8 billion. ZenithOptimedia expects the largest ad spending increases in the U.S. in 2011 to flow to the Internet, which is projected to increase 13 percent. One aspect of ads in a recession is that they generally take more direct aim at competitors, and this marketing practice is holding true in our bad economic times. Nick Brien at Mediabrands says, "Ads have to get combative in bad times. It's a dog fight, and it's about getting leaner and meaner." Ads are less lavish and glamorous today and are also more interactive. Table 4-4 lists specific characteristics of ads forthcoming in 2012 in response to the economic hard times many people nationwide and worldwide are facing.

Marketers spent between $2.8 and $3 million per 30-second advertising spot during the 2011 Super Bowl between the Pittsburg Steelers and Green Bay Packers. Advertising can be very expensive, and that is why marketing is a major business function to be studied carefully. Without marketing, even the best products and services have little chance of being successful.

A private company and the world's largest social network, Facebook, may epitomize where the advertising industry is going. Facebook subtly injects the advertiser's brand into the user's consciousness in order to provoke a purchase down the line by getting you to "like" the brand. Companies such as Ford, 7-Eleven, and McDonald's have recently unveiled new products on their Facebook pages. Starbucks offers coupons and free pastries to its 14 million Facebook fans. BP used its Facebook page to release statements and photos during the Gulf Oil Crisis. Anton Vincent, marketing vice president for General Mills' baking products division, says that Facebook allows a company to "leverage the loyalty" of its best customers. If you have recently gotten engaged and updated your Facebook status, you may start seeing ads from local jewelers who have used Facebook's automated ad system to target you. Facebook enables any firm today to very effectively target their exact audience with perfect advertising.[16] In performing a strategic planning analysis, in addition to comparing rival firms' websites, it is important to compare rival firms' Facebook page.

One of the last off-limit advertising outlets has historically been books, but with the proliferation of e-books, marketers are experimenting more and more with advertising to consumers as they read e-books. New ads are being targeted based on the book's content and the demographic profile of the reader. Digital e-book companies such as Wowio and Amazon are trying to

TABLE 4-4 Desirable Characteristics of Ads Today

1. Take direct aim at competitors; so leaner, meaner, and to the point.
2. Be less lavish and glamorous, requiring less production dollars to develop.
3. Be short and sweet, mostly 10- and 15-second ads rather than 30+ seconds.
4. "Make you feel good" or "put you in a good mood" because (a) ads can be more easily avoided than ever and (b) people are experiencing hard times and seek comfort.
5. Be more pervasive such as on buses, elevators, cell phones, and trucks.
6. Appear less on websites as banner ads become the new junk mail.
7. Red will overtake the color orange as the most popular ad color.
8. More than ever emphasize low price and value versus rivals.
9. More than ever emphasize how the product/service will make your life better.

Source: Based on Suzanne Vranica, "Ads to Go Leaner, Meaner in '09," *Wall Street Journal,* January 5, 2009, B8.

insert ads between chapters and along borders of digital pages. Random House says its e-books will soon include ads, but only with author approval. Global advertising expenditures are expected to grow 4.6 percent in 2011 and a bit more in 2012.

Determining organizational strengths and weaknesses in the selling function of marketing is an important part of performing an internal strategic-management audit. With regard to advertising products and services on the Internet, a new trend is to base advertising rates exclusively on sales rates. This new accountability contrasts sharply with traditional broadcast and print advertising, which bases rates on the number of persons expected to see a given advertisement. The new cost-per-sale online advertising rates are possible because any website can monitor which user clicks on which advertisement and then can record whether that consumer actually buys the product. If there are no sales, then the advertisement is free.

Product and Service Planning

Product and service planning includes activities such as test marketing; product and brand positioning; devising warranties; packaging; determining product options, features, style, and quality; deleting old products; and providing for customer service. Product and service planning is particularly important when a company is pursuing product development or diversification.

One of the most effective product and service planning techniques is *test marketing*. Test markets allow an organization to test alternative marketing plans and to forecast future sales of new products. In conducting a test market project, an organization must decide how many cities to include, which cities to include, how long to run the test, what information to collect during the test, and what action to take after the test has been completed. Test marketing is used more frequently by consumer goods companies than by industrial goods companies. Test marketing can allow an organization to avoid substantial losses by revealing weak products and ineffective marketing approaches before large-scale production begins. Starbucks is currently test marketing selling beer and wine in its stores to boost its "after 5 pm" sales.

Pricing

Five major stakeholders affect *pricing* decisions: consumers, governments, suppliers, distributors, and competitors. Sometimes an organization will pursue a forward integration strategy primarily to gain better control over prices charged to consumers. Governments can impose constraints on price fixing, price discrimination, minimum prices, unit pricing, price advertising, and price controls. For example, the Robinson-Patman Act prohibits manufacturers and wholesalers from discriminating in price among channel member purchasers (suppliers and distributors) if competition is injured.

Competing organizations must be careful not to coordinate discounts, credit terms, or condition of sale; not to discuss prices, markups, and costs at trade association meetings; and not to arrange to issue new price lists on the same date, to rotate low bids on contracts, or to uniformly restrict production to maintain high prices. Strategists should view price from both a short-run and a long-run perspective, because competitors can copy price changes with relative ease. Often a dominant firm will aggressively match all price cuts by competitors.

With regard to pricing, as the value of the dollar increases, U.S. multinational companies have a choice. They can raise prices in the local currency of a foreign country or risk losing sales and market share. Alternatively, multinational firms can keep prices steady and face reduced profit when their export revenue is reported in the United States in dollars.

Intense price competition, coupled with Internet price-comparative shopping, has reduced profit margins to bare minimum levels for most companies. For example, airline tickets, rental car prices, hotel room rates, and computer prices are lower today than they have been in many years.

PepsiCo. Inc. recently raised prices for its Tropicana juice line by up to 8 percent after the 2011 harsh winter crushed Florida's citrus crop in many places. Also due to especially cold winters hurting citrus crops, Coca-Cola Co. recently raised prices of their Minute Maid and Simply Juice brands. Fruit and vegetable prices are rising dramatically all over the world as a result not only of harsh winters, but also rising gas prices, which significantly increases the cost of transporting perishable products. The rapid rise in food commodity prices is attributed as one reason why regimes in Tunisia, Egypt, Yemen, and Libya toppled. Global populations are growing, becoming more prosperous and informed, and draining stockpiles of grain and meat.

Corn inventories are used in food, feed, and fuel, and that reserve fell to just 50 days recently, a 37-year low. Soybean stockpiles worldwide are the lowest in two decades. Consumers worldwide are seeing high food prices at supermarkets.

Distribution

Distribution includes warehousing, distribution channels, distribution coverage, retail site locations, sales territories, inventory levels and location, transportation carriers, wholesaling, and retailing. Most producers today do not sell their goods directly to consumers. Various marketing entities act as intermediaries; they bear a variety of names such as wholesalers, retailers, brokers, facilitators, agents, vendors—or simply distributors.

Distribution becomes especially important when a firm is striving to implement a market development or forward integration strategy. Some of the most complex and challenging decisions facing a firm concern product distribution. Intermediaries flourish in our economy because many producers lack the financial resources and expertise to carry out direct marketing. Manufacturers who could afford to sell directly to the public often can gain greater returns by expanding and improving their manufacturing operations.

Successful organizations identify and evaluate alternative ways to reach their ultimate market. Possible approaches vary from direct selling to using just one or many wholesalers and retailers. Strengths and weaknesses of each channel alternative should be determined according to economic, control, and adaptive criteria. Organizations should consider the costs and benefits of various wholesaling and retailing options. They must consider the need to motivate and control channel members and the need to adapt to changes in the future. Once a marketing channel is chosen, an organization usually must adhere to it for an extended period of time.

Marketing Research

Marketing research is the systematic gathering, recording, and analyzing of data about problems relating to the marketing of goods and services. Marketing research can uncover critical strengths and weaknesses, and marketing researchers employ numerous scales, instruments, procedures, concepts, and techniques to gather information. Marketing research activities support all of the major business functions of an organization. Organizations that possess excellent marketing research skills have a definite strength in pursuing generic strategies. The president of PepsiCo said,

> "Looking at the competition is the company's best form of market research. The majority of our strategic successes are ideas that we borrow from the marketplace, usually from a small regional or local competitor. In each case, we spot a promising new idea, improve on it, and then out-execute our competitor."[17]

Cost/Benefit Analysis

The seventh function of marketing is *cost/benefit analysis,* which involves assessing the costs, benefits, and risks associated with marketing decisions. Three steps are required to perform a cost/benefit analysis: (1) compute the total costs associated with a decision, (2) estimate the total benefits from the decision, and (3) compare the total costs with the total benefits. When expected benefits exceed total costs, an opportunity becomes more attractive. Sometimes the variables included in a cost/benefit analysis cannot be quantified or even measured, but usually reasonable estimates can be made to allow the analysis to be performed. One key factor to be considered is risk. Cost/benefit analysis should also be performed when a company is evaluating alternative ways to be socially responsible.

The practice of cost/benefit analysis differs among countries and industries. Some of the main differences include the types of impacts that are included as costs and benefits within appraisals, the extent to which impacts are expressed in monetary terms, and differences in the discount rate. Government agencies across the world rely on a basic set of key cost/benefit indicators, including the following:

1. NPV (net present value)
2. PVB (present value of benefits)

3. PVC (present value of costs)
4. BCR (benefit cost ratio = PVB / PVC)
5. Net benefit (= PVB − PVC)
6. NPV/k (where k is the level of funds available)[18]

Marketing Audit Checklist of Questions

The following questions about marketing must be examined in strategic planning:

1. Are markets segmented effectively?
2. Is the organization positioned well among competitors?
3. Has the firm's market share been increasing?
4. Are present channels of distribution reliable and cost effective?
5. Does the firm have an effective sales organization?
6. Does the firm conduct market research?
7. Are product quality and customer service good?
8. Are the firm's products and services priced appropriately?
9. Does the firm have an effective promotion, advertising, and publicity strategy?
10. Are marketing, planning, and budgeting effective?
11. Do the firm's marketing managers have adequate experience and training?
12. Is the firm's Internet presence excellent as compared to rivals?

Finance/Accounting

Financial condition is often considered the single best measure of a firm's competitive position and overall attractiveness to investors. Determining an organization's financial strengths and weaknesses is essential to effectively formulating strategies. A firm's liquidity, leverage, working capital, profitability, asset utilization, cash flow, and equity can eliminate some strategies as being feasible alternatives. Financial factors often alter existing strategies and change implementation plans.

Especially good websites from which to obtain financial information about firms are provided in Table 4-5.

Finance/Accounting Functions

According to James Van Horne, the *functions of finance/accounting* comprise three decisions: the investment decision, the financing decision, and the dividend decision.[19] Financial ratio analysis is the most widely used method for determining an organization's strengths and weaknesses in the investment, financing, and dividend areas. Because the functional areas of business are so closely related, financial ratios can signal strengths or weaknesses in management, marketing, production, research and development, and management information systems activities. Financial ratios are equally applicable in for-profit and nonprofit organizations. Even though nonprofit organizations obviously would not have return-on-investment or earnings-per-share ratios, they would routinely monitor many other special ratios. For example, a church would

TABLE 4-5 Excellent Websites to Obtain Information on Companies, Including Financial Ratios

1. http://marketwatch.multexinvestor.com
2. http://moneycentral.msn.com
3. http://finance.yahoo.com
4. www.clearstation.com
5. http://us.etrade.com/e/t/invest/markets
6. www.hoovers.com
7. http://globaledge.msu.edu/industries/

monitor the ratio of dollar contributions to number of members, while a zoo would monitor dollar food sales to number of visitors. A university would monitor number of students divided by number of professors. Therefore, be creative when performing ratio analysis for nonprofit organizations because they strive to be financially sound just as for-profit firms do.

The *investment decision,* also called *capital budgeting,* is the allocation and reallocation of capital and resources to projects, products, assets, and divisions of an organization. Once strategies are formulated, capital budgeting decisions are required to successfully implement strategies. The *financing decision* determines the best capital structure for the firm and includes examining various methods by which the firm can raise capital (for example, by issuing stock, increasing debt, selling assets, or using a combination of these approaches). The financing decision must consider both short-term and long-term needs for working capital. Two key financial ratios that indicate whether a firm's financing decisions have been effective are the debt-to-equity ratio and the debt-to-total-assets ratio.

Dividend decisions concern issues such as the percentage of earnings paid to stockholders, the stability of dividends paid over time, and the repurchase or issuance of stock. Dividend decisions determine the amount of funds that are retained in a firm compared to the amount paid out to stockholders. Three financial ratios that are helpful in evaluating a firm's dividend decisions are the earnings-per-share ratio, the dividends-per-share ratio, and the price-earnings ratio. The benefits of paying dividends to investors must be balanced against the benefits of internally retaining funds, and there is no set formula on how to balance this trade-off. For the reasons listed here, dividends are sometimes paid out even when funds could be better reinvested in the business or when the firm has to obtain outside sources of capital:

1. Paying cash dividends is customary. Failure to do so could be thought of as a stigma. A dividend change is considered a signal about the future.
2. Dividends represent a sales point for investment bankers. Some institutional investors can buy only dividend-paying stocks.
3. Shareholders often demand dividends, even in companies with great opportunities for reinvesting all available funds.
4. A myth exists that paying dividends will result in a higher stock price.

Most companies have ceased cutting and instead are raising their dividend payout. General Electric raised its quarterly dividend twice in 2010. Honeywell Inc. recently raised its annual dividend 10 percent to $1.33 a share while Germany's Siemens AG raised its dividend 68 percent to $3.57 a share. Siemens strives to pay out 30 to 50 percent of its net income to shareholders. S&P says there were 59 dividend increases in the fourth quarter of 2010 alone, up 25 percent from 2009. S&P expects that more than 50 percent of the S&P 500 firms will raise their dividend payout in 2011.[20]

McDonald's has raised its dividend payout for 35 years in a row, including recent years. Among all S&P 500 companies, 255 increased their dividends in 2010, up from 157 in 2009, and that trend is accelerating as firms' cash reserves grow. In addition to boosting dividend payouts, companies are also buying back their own stock more often and in larger amounts. Investors love dividends and other methods companies use to return capital to shareholders. Other companies recently raising their dividend rate are Tyco International Ltd. (to $0.25 per share per quarter from $0.21), Staples, Inc. (to $0.10 per quarter from $0.09), Prudential PLC (to 23.85 pence from 19.85), Bank of Nova Scotia (to C$0.52 from C$0.49 per share per quarter), Qualcomm Inc. (from $0.19 to $0.215 per share per quarter), and Applied Materials, Inc.(to $0.08 from $0.07 per share per quarter).

Basic Types of Financial Ratios

Financial ratios are computed from an organization's income statement and balance sheet. Computing financial ratios is like taking a picture because the results reflect a situation at just one point in time. Comparing ratios over time and to industry averages is more likely to result in meaningful statistics that can be used to identify and evaluate strengths and weaknesses. Trend analysis, illustrated in Figure 4-3, is a useful technique that incorporates both the time and industry average dimensions of financial ratios. Note that the dotted lines reveal projected ratios. Some websites, such as those provided in Table 4-5, calculate financial ratios and provide data with charts.

FIGURE 4-3

A Financial Ratio Trend Analysis

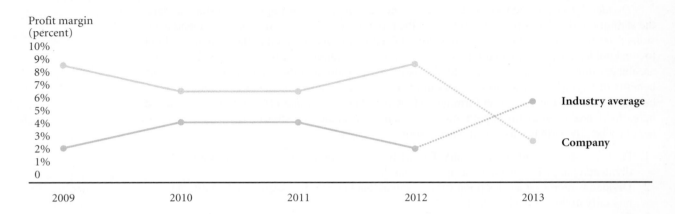

Table 4-6 provides a summary of key financial ratios showing how each ratio is calculated and what each ratio measures. However, all the ratios are not significant for all industries and companies. For example, accounts receivable turnover and average collection period are not very meaningful to a company that primarily does a cash receipts business. Key financial ratios can be classified into the following five types:

1. *Liquidity ratios* measure a firm's ability to meet maturing short-term obligations.
   Current ratio
   Quick (or acid-test) ratio

2. *Leverage ratios* measure the extent to which a firm has been financed by debt.
   Debt-to-total-assets ratio
   Debt-to-equity ratio
   Long-term debt-to-equity ratio
   Times-interest-earned (or coverage) ratio

3. *Activity ratios* measure how effectively a firm is using its resources.
   Inventory turnover
   Fixed assets turnover
   Total assets turnover
   Accounts receivable turnover
   Average collection period

4. *Profitability ratios* measure management's overall effectiveness as shown by the returns generated on sales and investment.
   Gross profit margin
   Operating profit margin
   Net profit margin
   Return on total assets (ROA)
   Return on stockholders' equity (ROE)
   Earnings per share (EPS)
   Price-earnings ratio

TABLE 4-6   A Summary of Key Financial Ratios

Ratio	How Calculated	What It Measures
Liquidity Ratios		
Current Ratio	$$\frac{\text{Current assets}}{\text{Current liabilities}}$$	The extent to which a firm can meet its short-term obligations
Quick Ratio	$$\frac{\text{Current assets minus inventory}}{\text{Current liabilities}}$$	The extent to which a firm can meet its short-term obligations without relying upon the sale of its inventories
Leverage Ratios		
Debt-to-Total-Assets Ratio	$$\frac{\text{Total debt}}{\text{Total assets}}$$	The percentage of total funds that are provided by creditors
Debt-to-Equity Ratio	$$\frac{\text{Total debt}}{\text{Total stockholders' equity}}$$	The percentage of total funds provided by creditors versus by owners
Long-Term Debt-to-Equity Ratio	$$\frac{\text{Long-term debt}}{\text{Total stockholders' equity}}$$	The balance between debt and equity in a firm's long-term capital structure
Times-Interest-Earned Ratio	$$\frac{\text{Profits before interest and taxes}}{\text{Total interest charges}}$$	The extent to which earnings can decline without the firm becoming unable to meet its annual interest costs
Activity Ratios		
Inventory Turnover	$$\frac{\text{Sales}}{\text{Inventory of finished goods}}$$	Whether a firm holds excessive stocks of inventories and whether a firm is slowly selling its inventories compared to the industry average
Fixed Assets Turnover	$$\frac{\text{Sales}}{\text{Fixed assets}}$$	Sales productivity and plant and equipment utilization
Total Assets Turnover	$$\frac{\text{Sales}}{\text{Total assets}}$$	Whether a firm is generating a sufficient volume of business for the size of its asset investment
Accounts Receivable Turnover	$$\frac{\text{Annual credit sales}}{\text{Accounts receivable}}$$	The average length of time it takes a firm to collect credit sales (in percentage terms)
Average Collection Period	$$\frac{\text{Accounts receivable}}{\text{Total credit sales/365 days}}$$	The average length of time it takes a firm to collect on credit sales (in days)
Profitability Ratios		
Gross Profit Margin	$$\frac{\text{Sales minus cost of goods sold}}{\text{Sales}}$$	The total margin available to cover operating expenses and yield a profit
Operating Profit Margin	$$\frac{\text{Earnings before interest and taxes EBIT}}{\text{Sales}}$$	Profitability without concern for taxes and interest
Net Profit Margin	$$\frac{\text{Net income}}{\text{Sales}}$$	After-tax profits per dollar of sales
Return on Total Assets (ROA)	$$\frac{\text{Net income}}{\text{Total assets}}$$	After-tax profits per dollar of assets; this ratio is also called return on investment (ROI)
Return on Stockholders' Equity (ROE)	$$\frac{\text{Net income}}{\text{Total stockholders' equity}}$$	After-tax profits per dollar of stockholders' investment in the firm
Earnings Per Share (EPS)	$$\frac{\text{Net income}}{\text{Number of shares of common stock outstanding}}$$	Earnings available to the owners of common stock
Price-Earnings Ratio	$$\frac{\text{Market price per share}}{\text{Earnings per share}}$$	Attractiveness of firm on equity markets

(continued)

TABLE 4-6   A Summary of Key Financial Ratios—continued

Ratio	How Calculated	What It Measures
Growth Ratios		
Sales	Annual percentage growth in total sales	Firm's growth rate in sales
Net Income	Annual percentage growth in profits	Firm's growth rate in profits
Earnings Per Share	Annual percentage growth in EPS	Firm's growth rate in EPS
Dividends Per Share	Annual percentage growth in dividends per share	Firm's growth rate in dividends per share

5. *Growth ratios* measure the firm's ability to maintain its economic position in the growth of the economy and industry.
Sales
Net income
Earnings per share
Dividends per share

Financial ratio analysis must go beyond the actual calculation and interpretation of ratios. The analysis should be conducted on three separate fronts:

1. ***How has each ratio changed over time?*** This information provides a means of evaluating historical trends. It is important to note whether each ratio has been historically increasing, decreasing, or nearly constant. For example, a 10 percent profit margin could be bad if the trend has been down 20 percent each of the last three years. But a 10 percent profit margin could be excellent if the trend has been up, up, up. Therefore, calculate the percentage change in each ratio from one year to the next to assess historical financial performance on that dimension. Identify and examine large percent changes in a financial ratio from one year to the next.

2. ***How does each ratio compare to industry norms?*** A firm's inventory turnover ratio may appear impressive at first glance but may pale when compared to industry standards or norms. Industries can differ dramatically on certain ratios. For example grocery companies, such as Kroger, have a high inventory turnover whereas automobile dealerships have a lower turnover. Therefore, comparison of a firm's ratios within its particular industry can be essential in determining strength/weakness.

3. ***How does each ratio compare with key competitors?*** Oftentimes competition is more intense between several competitors in a given industry or location than across all rival firms in the industry. When this is true, financial ratio analysis should include comparison to those key competitors. For example, if a firm's profitability ratio is trending up over time and compares favorably to the industry average, but it is trending down relative to its leading competitor, there may be reason for concern.

Financial ratio analysis is not without some limitations. First of all, financial ratios are based on accounting data, and firms differ in their treatment of such items as depreciation, inventory valuation, research and development expenditures, pension plan costs, mergers, and taxes. Also, seasonal factors can influence comparative ratios. Therefore, conformity to industry composite ratios does not establish with certainty that a firm is performing normally or that it is well managed. Likewise, departures from industry averages do not always indicate that a firm is doing especially well or badly. For example, a high inventory turnover ratio could indicate efficient inventory management and a strong working capital position, but it also could indicate a serious inventory shortage and a weak working capital position.

It is important to recognize that a firm's financial condition depends not only on the functions of finance, but also on many other factors that include (1) management, marketing, management production/operations, research and development, and management information systems decisions; (2) actions by competitors, suppliers, distributors, creditors, customers, and

FIGURE 4-4

A Before and After Breakeven Chart When Prices Are Lowered

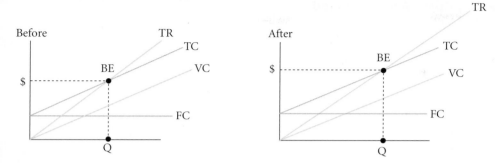

shareholders; and (3) economic, social, cultural, demographic, environmental, political, govern-mental, legal, and technological trends.

Since consumers remain price sensitive, many firms have lowered prices to compete. As a firm lowers prices, its *breakeven (BE) point* in terms of units sold increases, as illustrated in Figure 4-4. The breakeven point can be defined as the quantity of units that a firm must sell in order for its total revenues (TR) to equal its total costs (TC). Note that the before and after chart in Figure 4-4 reveals that the Total Revenue (TR) line rotates to the right with a decrease in Price, thus increasing the Quantity (Q) that must be sold just to break even. Increasing the breakeven point is thus a huge drawback of lowering prices. Of course when rivals are lowering prices, a firm may have to lower prices anyway to compete. However, the breakeven concept should be kept in mind because it is so important, especially in recession-ary times.

Notice in Figure 4-5 that increasing Fixed Costs (FC) also raises a firm's breakeven quantity. Note the before and after chart in Figure 4-5 reveals that adding fixed costs such as more stores, or more plants, or even more advertising as part of a strategic plan raises the Total Cost (TC) line, which makes the intersection of the Total Cost (TC) and Total Revenue (TR) lines at a point farther down the Quantity axis. Increasing a firm's fixed costs (FC) thus significantly raises the quantity of goods that must be sold to break even. This is not just the-ory for the sake of theory. Firms with less fixed costs, such as Apple and Amazon.com, have lower breakeven points, which give them a decided competitive advantage in harsh economic times. Figure 4-5 reveals that adding *fixed costs (FC),* such as plant, equipment, stores, ad-vertising, and land, may be detrimental whenever there is doubt that significantly more units can be sold to offset those expenditures.

Firms must be cognizant of the fact that lowering prices and adding fixed costs could be a catastrophic double whammy because the firm's breakeven quantity needed to be sold is in-creased dramatically. Figure 4-6 illustrates this double whammy. Note how far the breakeven

FIGURE 4-5

A Before and After Breakeven Chart When Fixed Costs Are Increased

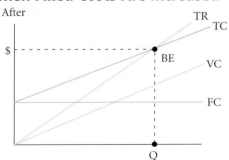

FIGURE 4-6

A Before and After Breakeven Chart When Prices Are Lowered and Fixed Costs Are Increased

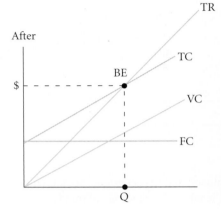

point shifts with both a price decrease and an increase in fixed costs. If a firm does not breakeven, then it will of course incur losses, and losses are not good, especially sustained losses.

Finally, note in Figure 4-4, 4-5, and 4-6 that *Variable Costs (VC)* such as labor and materials, when increased, have the effect of raising the breakeven point, too. Raising Variable Costs is reflected by the Variable Cost line shifting left or becoming steeper. When the Total Revenue (TR) line remains constant, the effect of increasing Variable Costs is to increase Total Costs, which increases the point at which Total Revenue = Total Costs (TC) = Breakeven (BE).

Suffice it to say here that various strategies can have dramatically beneficial or harmful effects on the firm's financial condition due to the concept of breakeven analysis.

There are some limitations of breakeven analysis, including the following points:

1. Breakeven analysis is only a supply side (*i.e.* costs only) analysis, as it tells you nothing about what sales are likely to be for the product at various prices.
2. It assumes that fixed costs (FC) are constant. Although this is true in the short run, an increase in the scale of production will cause fixed costs to rise.
3. It assumes average variable costs are constant per unit of output, at least in the range of likely quantities of sales.
4. It assumes that the quantity of goods produced is equal to the quantity of goods sold (i.e., there is no change in beginning or ending inventory).
5. In multi-product companies, it assumes that the relative proportions of each product sold and produced are constant (*i.e.*, the sales mix is constant).[21]

Finance/Accounting Audit Checklist

The following finance/accounting questions, like the similar questions about marketing and management earlier, should be examined:

1. Where is the firm financially strong and weak as indicated by financial ratio analyses?
2. Can the firm raise needed short-term capital?
3. Can the firm raise needed long-term capital through debt and/or equity?
4. Does the firm have sufficient working capital?
5. Are capital budgeting procedures effective?
6. Are dividend payout policies reasonable?
7. Does the firm have good relations with its investors and stockholders?
8. Are the firm's financial managers experienced and well trained?
9. Is the firm's debt situation excellent?

Production/Operations

The *production/operations function* of a business consists of all those activities that transform inputs into goods and services. Production/operations management deals with inputs, transformations, and outputs that vary across industries and markets. A manufacturing operation transforms or converts inputs such as raw materials, labor, capital, machines, and facilities into finished goods and services. As indicated in Table 4-7, Roger Schroeder suggested that production/operations management comprises five functions or decision areas: process, capacity, inventory, workforce, and quality.

Most automakers require a 30-day notice to build vehicles, but Toyota Motor fills a buyer's new car order in just five days. Honda Motor was considered the industry's fastest producer, filling orders in 15 days. Automakers have for years operated under just-in-time inventory systems, but Toyota's 360 suppliers are linked to the company via computers on a virtual assembly line. The new Toyota production system was developed in the company's Cambridge, Ontario, plant and now applies to its Solara, Camry, Corolla, and Tacoma vehicles.

Production/operations activities often represent the largest part of an organization's human and capital assets. In most industries, the major costs of producing a product or service are incurred within operations, so production/operations can have great value as a competitive weapon in a company's overall strategy. Strengths and weaknesses in the five functions of production can mean the success or failure of an enterprise.

Many production/operations managers are finding that cross-training of employees can help their firms respond faster to changing markets. Cross-training of workers can increase efficiency, quality, productivity, and job satisfaction. For example, at General Motors' Detroit gear and axle plant, costs related to product defects were reduced 400 percent in two years as a result of cross-training workers. As shown in Table 4-8, James Dilworth outlined implications of several types of strategic decisions that a company might make.

Singapore rivals Hong Kong as an attractive site for locating production facilities in Southeast Asia. Singapore is a city-state near Malaysia. An island nation of about 4 million, Singapore is changing from an economy built on trade and services to one built on information technology. A large-scale program in computer education for older (over age 26) residents is very popular. Singapore children receive outstanding computer training in schools. All government services are computerized nicely. Singapore lures multinational businesses with great tax breaks, world-class infrastructure, excellent courts that efficiently handle business disputes, exceptionally low tariffs, large land giveaways, impressive industrial parks, excellent port facilities, and a government very receptive to and cooperative with foreign businesses. Foreign firms now account for 70 percent of manufacturing output in Singapore.

In terms of ship container traffic processed annually, Singapore has the largest and busiest seaport in the world, followed by Hong Kong, Shanghai, Los Angeles, Busan (South Korea), Rotterdam, Hamburg, New York, and Tokyo. The Singapore seaport is five times the size of the New York City seaport.[22]

TABLE 4-7 The Basic Functions (Decisions) Within Production/Operations

Decision Areas	Example Decisions
1. Process	These decisions include choice of technology, facility layout, process flow analysis, facility location, line balancing, process control, and transportation analysis. Distances from raw materials to production sites to customers are a major consideration.
2. Capacity	These decisions include forecasting, facilities planning, aggregate planning, scheduling, capacity planning, and queuing analysis. Capacity utilization is a major consideration.
3. Inventory	These decisions involve managing the level of raw materials, work-in-process, and finished goods, especially considering what to order, when to order, how much to order, and materials handling.
4. Workforce	These decisions involve managing the skilled, unskilled, clerical, and managerial employees by caring for job design, work measurement, job enrichment, work standards, and motivation techniques.
5. Quality	These decisions are aimed at ensuring that high-quality goods and services are produced by caring for quality control, sampling, testing, quality assurance, and cost control.

Source: Based on R. Schroeder, *Operations Management* (New York: McGraw-Hill, 1981), 12.

TABLE 4-8   Implications of Various Strategies on Production/Operations

Various Strategies	Implications
1. Low-cost provider	Creates high barriers to entry
	Creates larger market
	Requires longer production runs and fewer product changes
2. A high-quality provider	Requires more quality-assurance efforts
	Requires more expensive equipment
	Requires highly skilled workers and higher wages
3. Provide great customer service	Requires more service people, service parts, and equipment
	Requires rapid response to customer needs or changes in customer tastes
	Requires a higher inventory investment
4. Be the first to introduce new products	Has higher research and development costs
	Has high retraining and tooling costs
5. Become highly automated	Requires high capital investment
	Reduces flexibility
	May affect labor relations
	Makes maintenance more crucial
6. Minimize layoffs	Serves the security needs of employees and may develop employee loyalty
	Helps to attract and retain highly skilled employees

Source: Based on: J. Dilworth, *Production and Operations Management: Manufacturing and Nonmanufacturing,* 2nd ed. Copyright © 1983 by Random House, Inc.

Production/Operations Audit Checklist

Questions such as the following should be examined:

1. Are supplies of raw materials, parts, and subassemblies reliable and reasonable?
2. Are facilities, equipment, machinery, and offices in good condition?
3. Are inventory-control policies and procedures effective?
4. Are quality-control policies and procedures effective?
5. Are facilities, resources, and markets strategically located?
6. Does the firm have technological competencies?

Research and Development

Apple Inc. continues to develop and sell new products such as the iPhone and iPad despite spending less on R&D over the last 10 years than rival Microsoft did even in fiscal 2010 alone.[23] Microsoft routinely spends 14 to 15 percent of its sales on R&D, or $8.7 billion in fiscal 2010, compared to Apple every year spending about 2.5 percent of its annual sales on R&D. The correlation between R&D expenditures and successful product launches is not high. Thus, firms such as Research in Motion (RIM) and Nokia are reducing their R&D expenditures, especially as a percent of sales. RIM is spending $1.35 billion in fiscal 2011 on R&D or about 6 percent of revenues, compared to Nokia spending 13.8 percent of sales in 2010.

The fifth major area of internal operations that should be examined for specific strengths and weaknesses is *research and development (R&D).* Many firms today conduct no R&D, and yet many other companies depend on successful R&D activities for survival. Firms pursuing a product development strategy especially need to have a strong R&D orientation.

Organizations invest in R&D because they believe that such an investment will lead to a superior product or service and will give them competitive advantages. Research and development expenditures are directed at developing new products before competitors do, at improving product quality, or at improving manufacturing processes to reduce costs.

Effective management of the R&D function requires a strategic and operational partnership between R&D and the other vital business functions. A spirit of partnership and mutual trust between general and R&D managers is evident in the best-managed firms today. Managers in these firms jointly explore; assess; and decide the what, when, where, why, and how much of R&D. Priorities, costs, benefits, risks, and rewards associated with R&D activities are discussed openly and shared. The overall mission of R&D thus has become broad-based, including supporting existing businesses, helping launch new businesses, developing new products, improving product quality, improving manufacturing efficiency, and deepening or broadening the company's technological capabilities.[24]

The best-managed firms today seek to organize R&D activities in a way that breaks the isolation of R&D from the rest of the company and promotes a spirit of partnership between R&D managers and other managers in the firm. R&D decisions and plans must be integrated and coordinated across departments and divisions by having the departments share experiences and information. The strategic-management process facilitates this cross-functional approach to managing the R&D function.

R&D spending at major corporations declined in 2009 for the first time in 10 years as the worldwide recession hit most firms hard. Roche Holding AG led all firms in R&D spending at $9.12 billion, followed by Microsoft at $9.01 billion and Nokia at $8.24 billion. Other large spenders were Toyota Motor at $7.82 billion and Pfizer at $7.74 billion. Interestingly absent among the top 10 R&D spenders, Apple spent about 3.1 percent of sales on R&D, roughly half the typical level for computer and electronic companies. Booz and Co. partner Barry Jaruzelski remarked that: "Apple succeeds because it has a deep understanding of consumers, is focused on its projects 'as opposed to trying to spread their bets,' and attracts superior talent."[25]

Internal and External R&D

Cost distributions among R&D activities vary by company and industry, but total R&D costs generally do not exceed manufacturing and marketing start-up costs. Four approaches to determining R&D budget allocations commonly are used: (1) financing as many project proposals as possible, (2) using a percentage-of-sales method, (3) budgeting about the same amount that competitors spend for R&D, or (4) deciding how many successful new products are needed and working backward to estimate the required R&D investment.

R&D in organizations can take two basic forms: (1) internal R&D, in which an organization operates its own R&D department, and/or (2) contract R&D, in which a firm hires independent researchers or independent agencies to develop specific products. Many companies use both approaches to develop new products. A widely used approach for obtaining outside R&D assistance is to pursue a joint venture with another firm. R&D strengths (capabilities) and weaknesses (limitations) play a major role in strategy formulation and strategy implementation.

Most firms have no choice but to continually develop new and improved products because of changing consumer needs and tastes, new technologies, shortened product life cycles, and increased domestic and foreign competition. A shortage of ideas for new products, increased global competition, increased market segmentation, strong special-interest groups, and increased government regulations are several factors making the successful development of new products more and more difficult, costly, and risky. In the pharmaceutical industry, for example, only one out of every few thousand drugs created in the laboratory ends up on pharmacists' shelves. Scarpello, Boulton, and Hofer emphasized that different strategies require different R&D capabilities:

> The focus of R&D efforts can vary greatly depending on a firm's competitive strategy. Some corporations attempt to be market leaders and innovators of new products, while others are satisfied to be market followers and developers of currently available products. The basic skills required to support these strategies will vary, depending on whether R&D becomes the driving force behind competitive strategy. In cases where new product introduction is the driving force for strategy, R&D activities must be extensive.[26]

In an effort to share huge R&D costs associated with developing hybrid and electric cars, Germany's BMW AG and France's PSA Peugeot Citroen in mid-2011 established a 50–50 joint venture to develop fuel-efficient technologies. The joint venture will develop and produce a full range of hybrid car components, such as battery packs and drivetrains, as well as software for hybrid and electric vehicles. Peugeot has a similar R&D partnership with Mitsubishi Motors

Corp., while BMW has a similar alliance with rival Daimler AG. Even fierce rivals Renault SA and Nissan Motor Co have a joint partnership to develop small electric cars—so the days of never working with rival firms is over, especially in regard to defraying heavy R&D expenditures.

Research and Development Audit

Questions such as the following should be asked in performing an R&D audit:

1. Does the firm have R&D facilities? Are they adequate?
2. If outside R&D firms are used, are they cost-effective?
3. Are the organization's R&D personnel well qualified?
4. Are R&D resources allocated effectively?
5. Are management information and computer systems adequate?
6. Is communication between R&D and other organizational units effective?
7. Are present products technologically competitive?

Management Information Systems

Nordstrom Inc. in recent years has tried to stay ahead of competitors by integrating its online and in-store inventory systems, enabling consumers to see what is available in stores near them. Nordstrom has a five-star rating system online to track what people think and say in social media forums. Nordstrom just acquired HauteLook Inc., a fast-growing, online flash sales company that offered luxury clothes at a discount.

Information ties all business functions together and provides the basis for all managerial decisions. It is the cornerstone of all organizations. Information represents a major source of competitive management advantage or disadvantage. Assessing a firm's internal strengths and weaknesses in information systems is a critical dimension of performing an internal audit.

A management information system's purpose is to improve the performance of an enterprise by improving the quality of managerial decisions. An effective information system thus collects, codes, stores, synthesizes, and presents information in such a manner that it answers important operating and strategic questions. The heart of an information system is a database containing the kinds of records and data important to managers.

A *management information system* receives raw material from both the external and internal evaluation of an organization. It gathers data about marketing, finance, production, and personnel matters internally, and social, cultural, demographic, environmental, economic, political, governmental, legal, technological, and competitive factors externally. Data are integrated in ways needed to support managerial decision making.

There is a logical flow of material in a computer information system, whereby data are input to the system and transformed into output. Outputs include computer printouts, written reports, tables, charts, graphs, checks, purchase orders, invoices, inventory records, payroll accounts, and a variety of other documents. Payoffs from alternative strategies can be calculated and estimated. *Data* become *information* only when they are evaluated, filtered, condensed, analyzed, and organized for a specific purpose, problem, individual, or time.

Even Wal-Mart recognizes the immense importance of information technology. In mid-2011 Wal-Mart acquired Kosmix, a social media technology provider that has built a platform that enables users to filter and organize content in social networks in order to connect people with information that matters to them, in realtime. Kosmix powers a site called TweetBeat, essentially a realtime social media filter for live events. Additionally, the technology is used to power RightHealth, a popular health and medical information site. Kosmix is now operating as part of a newly formed group named WalMartLabs, which is creating information technologies and businesses around social and mobile commerce to support Wal-Mart's multichannel strategy. This acquisition blurs the line between offline and online shopping.

Management Information Systems Audit

Questions such as the following should be asked when conducting this audit:

1. Do all managers in the firm use the information system to make decisions?
2. Is there a chief information officer or director of information systems position in the firm?

3. Are data in the information system updated regularly?
4. Do managers from all functional areas of the firm contribute input to the information system?
5. Are there effective passwords for entry into the firm's information system?
6. Are strategists of the firm familiar with the information systems of rival firms?
7. Is the information system user-friendly?
8. Do all users of the information system understand the competitive advantages that information can provide firms?
9. Are computer training workshops provided for users of the information system?
10. Is the firm's information system continually being improved in content and user-friendliness?

Value Chain Analysis (VCA)

According to Porter, the business of a firm can best be described as a *value chain,* in which total revenues minus total costs of all activities undertaken to develop and market a product or service yields value. All firms in a given industry have a similar value chain, which includes activities such as obtaining raw materials, designing products, building manufacturing facilities, developing cooperative agreements, and providing customer service. A firm will be profitable as long as total revenues exceed the total costs incurred in creating and delivering the product or service. Firms should strive to understand not only their own value chain operations but also their competitors', suppliers', and distributors' value chains.

Value chain analysis (VCA) refers to the process whereby a firm determines the costs associated with organizational activities from purchasing raw materials to manufacturing product(s) to marketing those products. VCA aims to identify where low-cost advantages or disadvantages exist anywhere along the value chain from raw material to customer service activities. VCA can enable a firm to better identify its own strengths and weaknesses, especially as compared to competitors' value chain analyses and their own data examined over time.

Substantial judgment may be required in performing a VCA because different items along the value chain may impact other items positively or negatively, so there exist complex interrelationships. For example, exceptional customer service may be especially expensive yet may reduce the costs of returns and increase revenues. Cost and price differences among rival firms can have their origins in activities performed by suppliers, distributors, creditors, or even shareholders. Despite the complexity of VCA, the initial step in implementing this procedure is to divide a firm's operations into specific activities or business processes. Then the analyst attempts to attach a cost to each discrete activity, and the costs could be in terms of both time and money. Finally, the analyst converts the cost data into information by looking for competitive cost strengths and weaknesses that may yield competitive advantage or disadvantage. Conducting a VCA is supportive of the RBV's examination of a firm's assets and capabilities as sources of distinctive competence.

When a major competitor or new market entrant offers products or services at very low prices, this may be because that firm has substantially lower value chain costs or perhaps the rival firm is just waging a desperate attempt to gain sales or market share. Thus value chain analysis can be critically important for a firm in monitoring whether its prices and costs are competitive. An example value chain is illustrated in Figure 4-7. There can be more than a hundred particular value-creating activities associated with the business of producing and marketing a product or service, and each one of the activities can represent a competitive advantage or disadvantage for the firm. The combined costs of all the various activities in a company's value chain define the firm's cost of doing business. Firms should determine where cost advantages and disadvantages in their value chain occur *relative to the value chain of rival firms.*

Value chains differ immensely across industries and firms. Whereas a paper products company, such as Stone Container, would include on its value chain timber farming, logging, pulp mills, and papermaking, a computer company such as Hewlett-Packard would include programming, peripherals, software, hardware, and laptops. A motel would include food, housekeeping, check-in and check-out operations, website, reservations system, and so on. However, all firms should use value chain analysis to develop and nurture a core competence and convert this

FIGURE 4-7

An Example Value Chain for a Typical Manufacturing Firm

Supplier Costs
  Raw materials
  Fuel
  Energy
  Transportation
  Truck drivers
  Truck maintenance
  Component parts
  Inspection
  Storing
  Warehouse
Production Costs
  Inventory system
  Receiving
  Plant layout
  Maintenance
  Plant location
  Computer
  R&D
  Cost accounting
Distribution Costs
  Loading
  Shipping
  Budgeting
  Personnel
  Internet
  Trucking
  Railroads
  Fuel
  Maintenance
Sales and Marketing Costs
  Salespersons
  Website
  Internet
  Publicity
  Promotion
  Advertising
  Transportation
  Food and lodging
Customer Service Costs
  Postage
  Phone
  Internet
  Warranty
Management Costs
  Human resources
  Administration
  Employee benefits
  Labor relations
  Managers
  Employees
  Finance and legal

competence into a distinctive competence. A *core competence* is a value chain activity that a firm performs especially well. When a core competence evolves into a major competitive advantage, then it is called a distinctive competence. Figure 4-8 illustrates this process.

More and more companies are using VCA to gain and sustain competitive advantage by being especially efficient and effective along various parts of the value chain. For example, Wal-Mart has built powerful value advantages by focusing on exceptionally tight inventory control, volume purchasing of products, and offering exemplary customer service. Computer companies in contrast compete aggressively along the distribution end of the value chain. Of course, price competitiveness is a key component of effectiveness among both mass retailers and computer firms.

Benchmarking

Benchmarking is an analytical tool used to determine whether a firm's value chain activities are competitive compared to rivals and thus conducive to winning in the marketplace. Benchmarking entails measuring costs of value chain activities across an industry to determine "best practices" among competing firms for the purpose of duplicating or improving upon those best practices. Benchmarking enables a firm to take action to improve its competitiveness by identifying (and improving upon) value chain activities where rival firms have comparative advantages in cost, service, reputation, or operation.

A comprehensive survey on benchmarking was recently commissioned by the Global Benchmarking Network, a network of benchmarking centers representing 22 countries. Over 450 organizations responded from over 40 countries. The results showed that:

1. Mission and Vision Statements along with Customer (Client) Surveys are the most used (77 percent of organizations) of 20 improvement tools, followed by SWOT analysis (72 percent), and Informal Benchmarking (68 percent). Performance Benchmarking was used by 49 percent and Best Practice Benchmarking by 39 percent.
2. The tools that are likely to increase in popularity the most over the next three years are Performance Benchmarking, Informal Benchmarking, SWOT, and Best Practice Benchmarking. Over 60 percent of organizations not currently using these tools indicated they are likely to use them in the next three years.[27]

The hardest part of benchmarking can be gaining access to other firms' value chain activities with associated costs. Typical sources of benchmarking information, however, include published reports, trade publications, suppliers, distributors, customers, partners, creditors, shareholders, lobbyists, and willing rival firms. Some rival firms share benchmarking data. However, the International Benchmarking Clearinghouse provides guidelines to help ensure that restraint of trade, price fixing, bid rigging, bribery, and other improper business conduct do not arise between participating firms.

Due to the popularity of benchmarking today, numerous consulting firms such as Accenture, AT Kearney, Best Practices Benchmarking & Consulting, as well as the Strategic Planning Institute's Council on Benchmarking, gather benchmarking data, conduct benchmarking studies, and distribute benchmark information without identifying the sources.

FIGURE 4-8

Transforming Value Chain Activities into Sustained Competitive Advantage

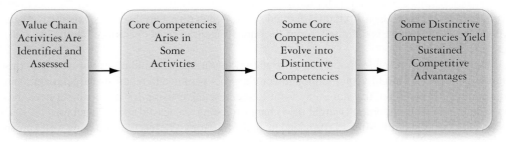

The Internal Factor Evaluation (IFE) Matrix

A summary step in conducting an internal strategic-management audit is to construct an *Internal Factor Evaluation (IFE) Matrix*. This strategy-formulation tool summarizes and evaluates the major strengths and weaknesses in the functional areas of a business, and it also provides a basis for identifying and evaluating relationships among those areas. Intuitive judgments are required in developing an IFE Matrix, so the appearance of a scientific approach should not be interpreted to mean this is an all-powerful technique. A thorough understanding of the factors included is more important than the actual numbers. Similar to the EFE Matrix and Competitive Profile Matrix described in Chapter 3, an IFE Matrix can be developed in five steps:

1. List key internal factors as identified in the internal-audit process. Use a total of from 10 to 20 internal factors, including both strengths and weaknesses. List strengths first and then weaknesses. Be as specific as possible, using percentages, ratios, and comparative numbers. Recall that Edward Deming said, "In God we trust. Everyone else bring data."
2. Assign a weight that ranges from 0.0 (not important) to 1.0 (all-important) to each factor. The weight assigned to a given factor indicates the relative importance of the factor to being successful in the firm's industry. Regardless of whether a key factor is an internal strength or weakness, factors considered to have the greatest effect on organizational performance should be assigned the highest weights. The sum of all weights must equal 1.0.
3. Assign a 1-to-4 rating to each factor to indicate whether that factor represents a major weakness (rating = 1), a minor weakness (rating = 2) a minor strength (rating = 3) or a major strength (rating = 4). Note that strengths must receive a 3 or 4 rating and weaknesses must receive a 1 or 2 rating. Ratings are thus company-based, whereas the weights in step 2 are industry-based.
4. Multiply each factor's weight by its rating to determine a weighted score for each variable.
5. Sum the weighted scores for each variable to determine the total weighted score for the organization.

Regardless of how many factors are included in an IFE Matrix, the total weighted score can range from a low of 1.0 to a high of 4.0, with the average score being 2.5. Total weighted scores well below 2.5 characterize organizations that are weak internally, whereas scores significantly above 2.5 indicate a strong internal position. Like the EFE Matrix, an IFE Matrix should include from 10 to 20 key factors. The number of factors has no effect upon the range of total weighted scores because the weights always sum to 1.0.

When a key internal factor is both a strength and a weakness, the factor should be included twice in the IFE Matrix, and a weight and rating should be assigned to each statement. For example, the Playboy logo both helps and hurts Playboy Enterprises; the logo attracts customers to *Playboy* magazine, but it keeps the Playboy cable channel out of many markets. Be as quantitative as possible when stating factors. Use monetary amounts, percentages, numbers, and ratios to the extent possible.

An example IFE Matrix is provided in Table 4-9 for a retail computer store. Note that the two most important factors to be successful in the retail computer store business are "revenues from repair/service in the store" and "location of the store." Also note that the store is doing best on "average customer purchase amount" and "in-store technical support." The store is having major problems with its carpet, bathroom, paint, and checkout procedures. Note also that the matrix contains substantial quantitative data rather than vague statements; this is excellent. Overall, this store receives a 2.5 total weighted score, which on a 1-to-4 scale is exactly average/halfway, indicating there is definitely room for improvement in store operations, strategies, policies, and procedures.

The IFE Matrix provides important information for strategy formulation. For example, this retail computer store might want to hire another checkout person and repair its carpet, paint, and bathroom problems. Also, the store may want to increase advertising for its repair/services, because that is a really important (weight 0.15) factor to being successful in this business.

Another example IFE Matrix is provided in Table 4-10 for UPS, Inc., the company well known for its brown trucks. Headquartered in Sandy Springs, Georgia, UPS delivers roughly 15 million

TABLE 4-9 A Sample Internal Factor Evaluation Matrix for a Retail Computer Store

Key Internal Factors	Weight	Rating	Weighted Score
Strengths			
1. Inventory turnover increased from 5.8 to 6.7	0.05	3	0.15
2. Average customer purchase increased from $97 to $128	0.07	4	0.28
3. Employee morale is excellent	0.10	3	0.30
4. In-store promotions resulted in 20 percent increase in sales	0.05	3	0.15
5. Newspaper advertising expenditures increased 10 percent	0.02	3	0.06
6. Revenues from repair/service segment of store up 16 percent	0.15	3	0.45
7. In-store technical support personnel have MIS college degrees	0.05	4	0.20
8. Store's debt-to-total assets ratio declined to 34 percent	0.03	3	0.09
9. Revenues per employee up 19 percent	0.02	3	0.06
Weaknesses			
1. Revenues from software segment of store down 12 percent	0.10	2	0.20
2. Location of store negatively impacted by new Highway 34	0.15	2	0.30
3. Carpet and paint in store somewhat in disrepair	0.02	1	0.02
4. Bathroom in store needs refurbishing	0.02	1	0.02
5. Revenues from businesses down 8 percent	0.04	1	0.04
6. Store has no website	0.05	2	0.10
7. Supplier on-time delivery increased to 2.4 days	0.03	1	0.03
8. Often customers have to wait to check out	0.05	1	0.05
Total	**1.00**		**2.50**

packages daily to 220 countries. Note in Table 4-10 that UPS's new Worldport expansion is considered the most important factor to success in the industry as indicated by a weight of 0.09. Also note the use of many $'s, #'s, and %'s in the factor statements. The total weighted score of 2.84 indicates that UPS is doing pretty well, but there definitely is room for improvement.

In multidivisional firms, each autonomous division or strategic business unit should construct an IFE Matrix. Divisional matrices then can be integrated to develop an overall corporate IFE Matrix.

Be as divisional as possible when developing a corporate IFE Matrix. Also, in developing an IFE Matrix, do not allow more than 30 percent of the key factors to be financial ratios, because financial ratios are generally the result of many other factors so it is difficult to know what particular strategies should be considered based on financial ratios. For example, a firm would have no insight on whether to sell in Brazil or South Africa to take advantage of a high ROI ratio.

Special Note to Students

It can be debated whether external or internal factors are more important in strategic planning, but there is no debate regarding the fact that gaining and sustaining competitive advantage is the essence or purpose of strategic planning. In the internal portion of your case analysis, emphasize how and why your internal strengths and weaknesses can be leveraged to both gain competitive advantage and overcome competitive disadvantage, in light of the direction you are taking the firm. Maintain your project's upbeat, insightful, and forward-thinking demeanor during the internal assessment, rather than being mundane, descriptive, and vague. Focus on how your firm's resources, capabilities, structure, and strategies, with your recommended improvements, can lead the firm to prosperity. Although the numbers absolutely must be there, must be accurate, and must be reasonable, do not bore a live audience or class with overreliance on numbers. Periodically throughout your presentation or written analysis, refer to your recommendations, explaining how your plan of action will improve the firm's weaknesses and capitalize on strengths in light of anticipated competitor countermoves. Keep your audience's attention, interest, and suspense, rather than "reading" to them or "defining" ratios for them.

TABLE 4-10   An Actual Internal Factor Evaluation (IFE) Matrix for UPS, Inc.

Key Internal Factors

Strengths	Weight	Rating	Wt. Score
1. Completed first phase of Worldport expansion, increasing sorting capacity 15 percent growing to 37 percent	0.09	4	0.36
2. First major airline to successfully operate a 100 percent Stage III fleet three years in advance of Federal regulations	0.07	4	0.28
3. Five out of every six UPS drivers come from part-time ranks (promotion within)	0.07	3	0.21
4. Over 4,000 UPS drivers have driven for 25 years or more without an avoidable accident	0.06	3	0.18
5. Dividends of $0.47 per share paid and increasing	0.06	4	0.24
6. Average daily volume for Next-Day Air and Deferred Products increased 2.8 percent and 4.3 percent respectively	0.06	3	0.18
7. Have yielded 1.71 percent cost and production efficiencies, improving operating margin	0.06	4	0.24
8. Owns 80 percent of joint venture headquartered in Dubai with 20 percent option to purchase	0.08	3	0.24
9. Streamlining Domestic Package segment, reducing U.S. regions from five to three and U.S. districts from 46 to 20	0.07	3	0.21
10. Purchased 130 hybrid vehicles, adding to UPS alternative fuel vehicle (AFV) fleet	0.07	4	0.28

Weakness			
11. Approximately 254,000 UPS employees are members of a union	0.03	1	0.03
12. Approximately 2,800 UPS pilots	0.03	1	0.03
13. Approximately 3,400 UPS ground mechanics	0.03	1	0.03
14. Inability to identify sufficient operating cost savings to result in at least 300 furloughs for airline pilots	0.04	1	0.04
15. Top executives diversity percentage is low (25 percent)	0.03	2	0.06
16. Over 4,000 UPS drivers have driven for more than 25 years and are now eligible for retirement	0.04	1	0.04
17. Top executives' tenure in current position five years or less	0.03	2	0.06
18. 80 percent of all UPS U.S. small package delivery services guaranteed	0.02	2	0.04
19. With ~408,000 employees, expenses relating to health and pension benefits are high	0.03	1	0.03
20. 41.7 percent of top UPS executives are cross-trained	0.03	2	0.06
TOTALS	**1.00**		**2.84**

Conclusion

Management, marketing, finance/accounting, production/operations, research and development, and management information systems represent the core operations of most businesses. A strategic-management audit of a firm's internal operations is vital to organizational health. Many companies still prefer to be judged solely on their bottom-line performance. However, an increasing number of successful organizations are using the internal audit to gain competitive advantages over rival firms.

Systematic methodologies for performing strength-weakness assessments are not well developed in the strategic-management literature, but it is clear that strategists must identify and evaluate internal strengths and weaknesses in order to effectively formulate and choose among alternative strategies. The EFE Matrix, Competitive Profile Matrix, IFE Matrix, and clear statements of vision and mission provide the basic information needed to successfully formulate competitive strategies. The process of performing an internal audit represents an opportunity for managers and employees throughout the organization to participate in determining the future of the firm. Involvement in the process can energize and mobilize managers and employees.

Key Terms and Concepts

Activity Ratios (p. 140)
Benchmarking (p. 151)
Breakeven (BE) Point (p. 143)
Capital Budgeting (p. 139)
Communication (p. 126)
Controlling (p. 133)
Core Competence (p. 151)
Cost/Benefit Analysis (p. 137)
Cultural Products (p. 128)
Customer Analysis (p. 134)
Data (p. 148)
Distinctive Competencies (p. 125)
Distribution (p. 137)
Dividend Decisions (p. 139)
Empirical Indicators (p. 128)
Financial Ratio Analysis (p. 127)
Fixed Costs (FC) (p. 143)
Financing Decision (p. 139)
Functions of Finance/Accounting (p. 138)
Functions of Management (p. 130)
Functions of Marketing (p. 134)
Growth Ratios (p. 142)
Human Resource Management (p. 133)
Information (p. 148)
Internal Audit (p. 126)

Internal Factor Evaluation (IFE) Matrix (p. 152)
Investment Decision (p. 139)
Leverage Ratios (p. 140)
Liquidity Ratios (p. 140)
Management Information System (p. 148)
Marketing Research (p. 137)
Motivating (p. 132)
Organizational Culture (p. 128)
Organizing (p. 132)
Personnel Management (p. 133)
Planning (p. 130)
Pricing (p. 136)
Product and Service Planning (p. 136)
Production/Operations Function (p. 145)
Profitability Ratios (p. 140)
Research and Development (R&D) (p. 146)
Resource-Based View (RBV) (p. 127)
Selling (p. 134)
Staffing (p. 133)
Synergy (p. 131)
Test Marketing (p. 136)
Value Chain Analysis (VCA) (p. 149)
Variable Costs (VC) (p. 144)

Issues for Review and Discussion

1. Johnson & Johnson (J&J) has been very successful in the last decade. Research J&J to see if they do strategic planning. Report back to your class on your findings.
2. Go to www.hoovers.com and enter J&J. See the list of top executives for J&J. Diagram an organizational chart for J&J.
3. Given the fifteen example (possible) aspects of an organization's culture as presented in the chapter, rate a company you are very familiar with in terms of the extent each culture item exists. Explain.
4. Rank order the seven functions of marketing in order of importance for a small hardware business.
5. Develop a quantitative problem to show that you understand cost/benefit analysis.
6. Develop a quantitative problem to show that you understand breakeven analysis.
7. For J&J, determine their most recent dividend payout amount per share. How has that amount changed over the last 12 months?
8. List some advantages and disadvantages of a company paying dividends versus reinvesting that money in the company and striving for stock price increase as the primary way to reward investors.
9. Diagram a breakeven chart for J&J. Explain how it may work for J&J.
10. J&J has historically spent more on R&D than almost any company in the world. What the major advantages and disadvantages of this strategy?

11. Perform a value chain analysis for an organization of your choice.

12. Discuss the relationship between benchmarking and value chain analysis.

13. Explain why in an IFE Matrix the ratings should be 4 or 3 for strengths and 1 or 2 for weaknesses as compared to the EFE Matrix where the ratings should be 1, 2, 3, or 4 anywhere among both the opportunities and threats.

14. Compare the financial ratio analysis for J&J at four different websites identified in the chapter. Which site do you like best? Why?

15. Conduct a Google search for value chain analysis. In a two-page report, expand on the concepts presented in the chapter.

16. What competitive advantages would Amazon have over Wal-Mart stores in doing business outside the United States?

17. How could the "process of performing an internal audit" differ across countries given varying management styles globally?

18. Why is sole reliance on financial ratios an ineffective means of deriving internal strengths and weaknesses?

19. Give an example of two resources for a fast-food chain that you believe meet the three "empirical indicators" criteria.

20. Prepare a culture assessment table as presented in the chapter for a local business that you are familiar with. In other words, rate that business on all 15 culture criteria presented. What are the implications of your ratings on the strategic planning process within that firm?

21. Why is human resource management particularly challenging for international firms?

22. List some specific characteristics of advertisements in the wake of a global economic recession.

23. How do changes in the value of the dollar affect pricing of products of global firms?

24. Historically, what has been the attitude of technology firms toward paying dividends? Give some examples.

25. Describe Singapore as a place to locate a business or begin doing business.

26. Go to the www.checkmateplan.com website and describe the strategic planning products offered.

27. Develop a value chain analysis for a large global firm and its primary rival firm.

28. Identify four major strengths and four major weaknesses of your college or university. Rank each factor in terms of importance.

29. Look up financial information about J&J. Identify three financial ratios where the firm is weak and three financial ratios the firm is strong.

30. What five cultural products do you feel are most important? Justify your selections.

31. For the company where you work or would like to work, rate the company on the 15 aspects of culture listed in the chapter.

32. Develop a breakeven chart for a company that simultaneously lays off employees and closes facilities.

33. Financial ratio analysis should be conducted on three separate fronts. What are these fronts and which is most important?

34. Explain breakeven analysis using three graphs that show changes in breakeven given: 1) a change in price, 2) a change in advertising expenditures, and 3) a change in labor costs.

35. Why is breakeven analysis such an important strategic planning concept?

36. What are the basic functions of production/operations in a large manufacturing company? Why are these factors important in an internal strategic management audit?

37. Explain benchmarking.

38. Go to the www.strategyclub.com website and review the benefits of the strategic planning software.

39. For the Adidas Cohesion Case, what do you consider to be the company's four major strengths and four major weaknesses?

40. Prepare a financial ratio analysis for Adidas. Include comparative ratios for Adidas.

41. Explain how Adidas could utilize breakeven analysis.

42. Explain how top executives of Adidas could utilize Porter's Five Forces Model to aid the firm in strategic planning.

43. Since Adidas and Puma are based in the same city, could this close proximity benefit or hinder the two firms 1) cooperating with each other on R&D, or 2) gathering and assimilating competitive intelligence on the other firm?

44. Since Adidas is so divisional, how could the company best develop a corporate IFE Matrix for various divisional IFE Matrices?

45. When is it more important to capitalize on strengths than improve on weaknesses in strategic planning?

46. Explain what 20 internal factors is a recommended number to include in an IFE Matrix, rather than 10 or 40 total.

47. Do you think the RBV view or the I/O theorists view is more important/accurate in performing a strategic analysis? What would be important implications for a business?

Notes

1. Reprinted by permission of the publisher from "Integrating Strength–Weakness Analysis into Strategic Planning," by William King, *Journal of Business Research* 2, no. 4: 481. Copyright 1983 by Elsevier Science Publishing Co., Inc.

2. Igor Ansoff, "Strategic Management of Technology" *Journal of Business Strategy* 7, no. 3 (Winter 1987): 38.

3. Claude George Jr., *The History of Management Thought*, 2nd ed. (Upper Saddle River, NJ: Prentice-Hall, 1972), 174.

4. Robert Grant, "The Resource-Based Theory of Competitive Advantage: Implications for Strategy Formulation," *California Management Review*, Spring 1991, 116.

5. J. B. Barney, "Firm Resources and Sustained Competitive Advantage," *Journal of Management* 17 (1991): 99–120; J. B. Barney, "The Resource-Based Theory of the Firm," *Organizational Science* 7 (1996): 469; J. B. Barney, "Is the

Resource-Based 'View' a Useful Perspective for Strategic Management Research? Yes." *Academy of Management Review* 26, no. 1 (2001): 41–56.

6. Edgar Schein, *Organizational Culture and Leadership* (San Francisco: Jossey-Bass, 1985), 9.

7. John Lorsch, "Managing Culture: The Invisible Barrier to Strategic Change," *California Management Review* 28, no. 2 (1986): 95–109.

8. Y. Allarie and M. Firsirotu, "How to Implement Radical Strategies in Large Organizations," *Sloan Management Review* (Spring 1985): 19.

9. www.mindtools.com/plfailpl.html

10. Adam Smith, *The Wealth of Nations* (New York: Modern Library, 1937), 3–4.

11. Richard Daft, *Management*, 3rd ed. (Orlando, FL: Dryden Press, 1993), 512.

12. Shelley Kirkpatrick and Edwin Locke, "Leadership: Do Traits Matter?" *Academy of Management Executive* 5, no. 2 (May 1991): 48.

13. Peter Drucker, *Management Tasks, Responsibilities, and Practice* (New York: Harper & Row, 1973), 463.

14. Brian Dumaine, "What the Leaders of Tomorrow See," *Fortune*, July 3, 1989, 51.

15. J. Evans and B. Bergman, *Marketing* (New York: Macmillan, 1982), 17.

16. Brad Stone, "See Your Friends," *Bloomberg Businessweek* (September 27–October 3, 2010): 65–69.

17. Quoted in Robert Waterman, Jr., "The Renewal Factor," *BusinessWeek*, September 14, 1987, 108.

18. http://en.wikipedia.org/wiki/Cost-benefit_analysis

19. J. Van Horne, *Financial Management and Policy* (Upper Saddle River, N.J.: Prentice-Hall, 1974), 10.

20. Bob Sechler and Paul Glader, "GE's Dividend Mends Further," *Wall Street Journal*, December 11–12, 2010, B4.

21. http://en.wikipedia.org/wiki/Break-even_(economics)

22. Kevin Klowden, "The Quiet Revolution in Transportation," *Wall Street Journal*, April 24, 2007, A14.

23. Martin Peers, "RIM: Less Research = More Motion," *Wall Street Journal*, March 30, 2011, C16.

24. Philip Rousebl, Kamal Saad, and Tamara Erickson, "The Evolution of Third Generation R&D," *Planning Review* 19, no. 2 (March–April 1991): 18–26.

25. James Hagerty, "R&D Spending Drops at Major Firms," *Wall Street Journal*, November 3, 2010, B4.

26. Vida Scarpello, William Boulton, and Charles Hofer, "Reintegrating R&D into Business Strategy," *Journal of Business Strategy* 6, no. 4 (Spring 1986): 50–51.

27. http://en.wikipedia.org/wiki/Benchmarking

Current Readings

Bloom, Nick, Tobias Kretschmer, and John Van Reenen. "Are Family-Friendly Workplace Practices a Valuable Firm Resource?" *Strategic Management Journal* 32, no. 4 (April 2011): 343–367.

Boyd, Brian K., Donald D. Bergh, and David J. Ketchen, Jr. "Reconsidering the Reputation-Performance Relationship: A Resource-Based View." *Journal of Management* 36, no. 3 (May 2010): 588.

Connelly, Brian L., Laszlo Tihanyi, S. Trevis Certo, and Michael A. Hitt. "Marching to the Beat of Different Drummers: The Influence of Institutional Owners on Competitive Actions." *The Academy of Management Journal* 53, no. 4 (August 2010): 723–768.

Drayton, Bill, and Valeria Budinich. "A New Alliance for Global Change." *Harvard Business Review*, September 2010, 56–65.

Hoffman, Donna L., and Marek Fodor. "Can You Measure the ROI of Your Social Media Marketing?" *MIT Sloan Management Review* 52, no. 1 (Fall 2010): 41–48.

Hopkins, Michael S. "Collaborate or Race? How to Design the Value Chain You Need." *MIT Sloan Management Review* 51, no. 2 (Winter 2010): 22–24.

Hopkins, Michael S. "The 4 Ways IT Is Revolutionizing Innovation." *MIT Sloan Management Review* 51, no. 3 (Spring 2010): 51–56.

Kraaijenbrink, Jeroen, J. C. Spender, and Aard J. Groen. "The Resource-Based View: A Review and Assessment of Its Critiques." *Journal of Management* 36, no. 1 (January 2010): 349–366.

Kunc, Martin H., and John D. W. Morecroft. "Managerial Decision Making and Firm Performance Under a Resource-Based Paradigm." *Strategic Management Journal* 31, no. 11 (November 2010): 1164–1182.

Lange, Donald, Peggy M. Lee, and Ye Dai. "Organizational Reputation: A Review." *Journal of Management* 37, no. 1 (January 2011): 153–184.

Raes, Anneloes M. L., Marielle G. Heijltjes, Ursula Glunk, and Robert A. Roe. "The Interface of the Top Management Team and Middle Managers: A Process Model." *The Academy of Management Review* 36, no. 1 (January 2011): 102–126.

Sirmon, David G., Michael A. Hitt, Jean-Luc Arregle, and Joanna Tochman Campbell. "The Dynamic Interplay of Capability Strengths and Weaknesses: Investigating the Bases of Temporary Competitive Advantage." *Strategic Management Journal* 31, no. 13 (December 2010): 1386–1409.

Vermeulen, Freek, Phanish Puranam, and Ranjay Gulati. "Change for Change's Sake." *Harvard Business Review* (June 2010): 70–78.

Zhu, Yunxia, and Jianmin Feng. "Does the Relationship Between Job Satisfaction and Job Performance Depend on Culture?" *The Academy of Management Perspectives* 24, no. 1 (February 2010): 86–88.

ASSURANCE OF LEARNING EXERCISES

Assurance of Learning Exercise 4A

Develop a Corporate IFE Matrix for J&J

Purpose

Johnson & Johnson is featured in the opening chapter case as a firm that engages in excellent strategic planning. Note that J&J has three major business segments. Each of these divisions of J&J would prepare their own IFE Matrices, which would be assimilated to develop an overall corporate IFE Matrix.

This exercise gives you practice developing divisional IFE Matrices and assimilating those into an overall corporate IFE Matrix.

Instructions

Step 1	Review J&J's most recent *Form 10K* in regards to the company's three business segments.
Step 2	Review the latest S&P *Industry Survey* for companies that produce and market personal care products.
Step 3	Develop three divisional IFE Matrices for J&J's business segments.
Step 4	Assimilate your divisional IFE Matrices into an overall corporate IFE Matrix for J&J.

Assurance of Learning Exercise 4B

Should J&J Deploy More Resources or Less Outside of the USA?

Purpose

Note in the opening chapter boxed case that J&J receives more revenue from outside the United States than from inside. This exercise gives you practice analyzing this domestic versus global revenue base so that more effective strategies can be formulated and implemented.

Instructions

Step 1	Go the J&J's website and review the company's most recent *Form 10K*. Be careful to note the financial, management, and marketing information available by geographic region.
Step 2	Go to www.finance.yahoo.com and review the last 45 days of Headlines for J&J. Take note of public information related to J&J doing business outside the United States.
Step 3	Prepare a 3-page executive summary to reveal whether you feel J&J should be placing more or less emphasis on operations outside the Unites States. Provide supporting tables, #'s, ratios, and narrative.

Assurance of Learning Exercise 4C

Apply Breakeven Analysis

Purpose

Breakeven analysis is one of the simplest yet underused analytical tools in management. It helps to provide a dynamic view of the relationships between sales, costs and profits. A better understanding of breakeven analysis can enable an organization to formulate and implement strategies more effectively. This exercise will show you how to calculate breakeven points mathematically.

The formula for calculating breakeven point is BE Quantity = TFC/P – VC. In other words, the Quantity (Q) or units of product that need to be sold for a firm to breakeven is Total Fixed Costs divided by (Price per Unit − Variable Costs per Unit).

Instructions

Step 1	Lets say an airplane company has Fixed Costs of $100 million and Variable Costs per Unit of $2 million. Planes sell for $3 million each. What is the company's breakeven point in terms of the number of planes that need to be sold just to breakeven?

Step 2   If the airplane company wants to make a profit of $99 million annually, how many planes will it have to sell?

Step 3   If the company can sell 200 airplanes in a year, how much annual profit will the firm make?

Assurance of Learning Exercise 4D

Performing a Financial Ratio Analysis for Adidas AG

Purpose

Financial ratio analysis is one of the best techniques for identifying and evaluating internal strengths and weaknesses. Potential investors and current shareholders look closely at firms' financial ratios, making detailed comparisons to industry averages and to previous periods of time. Financial ratio analysis provides vital input information for developing an IFE Matrix.

Instructions

Step 1   On a separate sheet of paper, write down numbers 1 to 20. Referring to Adidas AG's income statement and balance sheet, calculate 20 financial ratios for 2011.

Step 2   In a second column, indicate whether you consider each ratio to be a strength, weakness, or neutral factor for Adidas.

Assurance of Learning Exercise 4E

Constructing an IFE Matrix for Adidas AG

Purpose

This exercise will give you experience developing an IFE Matrix. Identifying and prioritizing factors to include in an IFE Matrix fosters communication among functional and divisional managers. Preparing an IFE Matrix allows human resource, marketing, production/operations, finance/accounting, R&D, and management information systems managers to articulate their concerns and thoughts regarding the business condition of the firm. This results in an improved collective understanding of the business.

Instructions

Step 1   Join with two other individuals to form a three-person team. Develop a IFE Matrix for Adidas. Be sure to include information on Reebok and TaylorMade.

Step 2   Compare your team's IFE Matrix to other teams' IFE Matrices. Discuss any major differences.

Step 3   What strategies do you think would allow Adidas to capitalize on its major strengths? What strategies would allow Adidas to improve upon its major weaknesses?

Assurance of Learning Exercise 4F

Analyzing Your College or University's Internal Strategic Situation

Purpose

This exercise is excellent for doing together as a class.

Instruction

As a class, determine your college or university's major internal strengths and weaknesses. List 10 strengths and 10 weaknesses. Then, get everyone in class to rank order their factors with 1 being most important and 10 being least important. Then, gather up everyone's paper, count the numbers, and in that manner create a prioritized list of the key internal strengths and weaknesses facing your college.

"NOTABLE QUOTES"

"Alice said, 'Would you please tell me which way to go from here?' The cat said, 'That depends on where you want to get to.'"
—*Lewis Carroll*

"Tomorrow always arrives. It is always different. And even the mightiest company is in trouble if it has not worked on the future. Being surprised by what happens is a risk that even the largest and richest company cannot afford, and even the smallest business need not run."
—*Peter Drucker*

"Planning. Doing things today to make us better tomorrow. Because the future belongs to those who make the hard decisions today."
—*Eaton Corporation*

"One big problem with American business is that when it gets into trouble, it redoubles its effort. It's like digging for gold. If you dig down twenty feet and haven't found it, one of the strategies you could use is to dig twice as deep. But if the gold is twenty feet to the side, you could dig a long time and not find it."
—*Edward De Bono*

"Even if you're on the right track, you'll get run over if you just sit there."
—*Will Rogers*

"Strategies for taking the hill won't necessarily hold it."
—*Amar Bhide*

"The early bird may get the worm, but the second mouse gets the cheese."
—*Unknown*

Strategies in Action

CHAPTER OBJECTIVES

After studying this chapter, you should be able to do the following:

1. Discuss the value of establishing long-term objectives.
2. Identify 16 types of business strategies.
3. Identify numerous examples of organizations pursuing different types of strategies.
4. Discuss guidelines when particular strategies are most appropriate to pursue.
5. Discuss Porter's five generic strategies.
6. Describe strategic management in nonprofit, governmental, and small organizations.
7. Discuss joint ventures as a way to enter the Russian market.
8. Discuss the Balanced Scorecard.
9. Compare and contrast financial with strategic objectives.
10. Discuss the levels of strategies in large versus small firms.
11. Explain the First Mover Advantages concept.
12. Discuss recent trends in outsourcing.
13. Discuss strategies for competing in turbulent, high-velocity markets.

ASSURANCE OF LEARNING EXERCISES

Assurance of Learning Exercise 5A
Market Development: Procter & Gamble (P&G)

Assurance of Learning Exercise 5B
Alternative Strategies for P&G

Assurance of Learning Exercise 5C
Private-Equity Acquisitions

Assurance of Learning Exercise 5D
Adidas AG: 2011–2013

Assurance of Learning Exercise 5E
Lessons in Doing Business Globally

Assurance of Learning Exercise 5F
Procter & Gamble (P&G): Pursuing 2011–2013

Assurance of Learning Exercise 5G
What Strategies Are Most Risky?

Assurance of Learning Exercise 5H
Exploring Bankruptcy

Assurance of Learning Exercise 5I
Examining Strategy Articles

Assurance of Learning Exercise 5J
Classifying Some Strategies

Hundreds of companies today, including Sears, IBM, Searle, and Hewlett-Packard, have embraced strategic planning fully in their quest for higher revenues and profits. Kent Nelson, former chair of UPS, explains why his company has created a new strategic-planning department: "Because we're making bigger bets on investments in technology, we can't afford to spend a whole lot of money in one direction and then find out five years later it was the wrong direction."[1]

This chapter brings strategic management to life with many contemporary examples. Sixteen types of strategies are defined and exemplified, including Michael Porter's generic strategies: cost leadership, differentiation, and focus. Guidelines are presented for determining when it is most appropriate to pursue different types of strategies. An overview of strategic management in nonprofit organizations, governmental agencies, and small firms is provided. Proctor & Gamble (P&G) is an example company that for many years has exemplified excellent strategic management.

Long-Term Objectives

Long-term objectives represent the results expected from pursuing certain strategies. Strategies represent the actions to be taken to accomplish long-term objectives. The time frame for objectives and strategies should be consistent, usually from two to five years.

Excellent Strategic Management Showcased

PROCTER & GAMBLE (P&G)

Headquartered in Cincinnati, Ohio, P&G is the world's top producer of household products, pet food, and water filters. Two dozen P&G brands are global, billion-dollar sellers, including Febreze, Fusion, Always, Braun, Bounty, Charmin, Crest, Downy, Gillette, Mach3, Iams, Olay, Pampers, Pantene, Gain, Wella, and Head & Shoulders. P&G has manufacturing operations in 80 countries and P&G brands are sold in more than 180 countries worldwide. magazine, P&G made $82.6 billion in sales. In 2011, *Fortune Magazine* ranked P&G at fifth place in the "World's Most Admired Companies" list, up from sixth place in 2010. P&G utilizes excellent strategic management.

P&G's net sales grew 10 percent to $20.9 billion in the fourth quarter of 2011 and five percent to $82.6 billion for fiscal 2011. Unit volume of P&G products was up three percent in the fourth quarter of 2011 and six percent for the fiscal year, where volume grew in all business segments, all geographic regions, and in 15 of 17 key countries. P&G products are available in North America, Latin America, Europe, the Middle East, Africa, Asia, Australia, and New Zealand. The company owns 31 factories in China.

P&G's operations are categorized into two "Global Business Units" with each Global Business Unit divided into six business segments: 1) beauty, 2) grooming, 3) health care, 4) snacks & pet care, 5) fabric care & home care, and 6) baby care & family care. Dimitri Panayotopoulos is Vice Chairman of Global Business Units.

In April 2011, P&G was fined 211.2 million euro by the European Commission for price fixing cartel in Europe along with Unilever, who was fined 104 million euro. Though the fine was set higher at first, it

was discounted by 10 percent after P&G and Unilever admitted to running the cartel.

P&G recently filed a lawsuit against Luhns GmbH, a private-label manufacturer and distributor of hand dish washing liquids, in the District Court of Düsseldorf, Germany (Landgericht Düsseldorf). The lawsuit alleges that Luhns GmbH is violating P&G's intellectual property by manufacturing and selling certain Magnum[TM] private label hand dish washing detergents to a retailer in the United Kingdom of Great Britain and Northern Ireland. P&G alleges that Luhns's dish detergent products, specifically the bottle shape and its overall product appearance, infringe P&G's European Community Design Rights relating to its Fairy hand dish washing liquids. Luhns's use of P&G's intellectual property without P&G's consent is prohibited by law, and can cause consumer confusion. P&G is suing Luhns in order to protect its business and to prevent consumer confusion in the marketplace.

Source: Based on information at www.pg.com.

The Nature of Long-Term Objectives

Objectives should be quantitative, measurable, realistic, understandable, challenging, hierarchical, obtainable, and congruent among organizational units. Each objective should also be associated with a timeline. Objectives are commonly stated in terms such as growth in assets, growth in sales, profitability, market share, degree and nature of diversification, degree and nature of vertical integration, earnings per share, and social responsibility. Clearly established objectives offer many benefits. They provide direction, allow synergy, aid in evaluation, establish priorities, reduce uncertainty, minimize conflicts, stimulate exertion, and aid in both the allocation of resources and the design of jobs. Objectives provide a basis for consistent decision making by managers whose values and attitudes differ. Objectives serve as standards by which individuals, groups, departments, divisions, and entire organizations can be evaluated.

Long-term objectives are needed at the corporate, divisional, and functional levels of an organization. They are an important measure of managerial performance. Many practitioners and academicians attribute a significant part of U.S. industry's competitive decline to the short-term, rather than long-term, strategy orientation of managers in the United States. Arthur D. Little argues that bonuses or merit pay for managers today must be based to a greater extent on long-term objectives and strategies. A general framework for relating objectives to performance evaluation is provided in Table 5-1. A particular organization could tailor these guidelines to meet its own needs, but incentives should be attached to both long-term and annual objectives.

Without long-term objectives, an organization would drift aimlessly toward some unknown end. It is hard to imagine an organization or individual being successful without clear objectives (see Tables 5-2 and 5-3). Success only rarely occurs by accident; rather, it is the result of hard work directed toward achieving certain objectives.

Financial versus Strategic Objectives

Two types of objectives are especially common in organizations: financial and strategic objectives. *Financial objectives* include those associated with growth in revenues, growth in earnings, higher dividends, larger profit margins, greater return on investment, higher earnings per share, a rising stock price, improved cash flow, and so on; while *strategic objectives* include things such as a larger market share, quicker on-time delivery than rivals, shorter design-to-market times

TABLE 5-1 Varying Performance Measures by Organizational Level

Organizational Level	Basis for Annual Bonus or Merit Pay
Corporate	75% based on long-term objectives
	25% based on annual objectives
Division	50% based on long-term objectives
	50% based on annual objectives
Function	25% based on long-term objectives
	75% based on annual objectives

TABLE 5-2 The Desired Characteristics of Objectives

1. Quantitative
2. Measurable
3. Realistic
4. Understandable
5. Challenging
6. Hierarchical
7. Obtainable
8. Congruent across departments

TABLE 5-3   The Benefits of Having Clear Objectives

1. Provide direction by revealing expectations
2. Allow synergy
3. Aid in evaluation by serving as standards
4. Establish priorities
5. Reduce uncertainty
6. Minimize conflicts
7. Stimulate exertion
8. Aid in allocation of resources
9. Aid in design of jobs
10. Provide basis for consistent decision making

than rivals, lower costs than rivals, higher product quality than rivals, wider geographic coverage than rivals, achieving technological leadership, consistently getting new or improved products to market ahead of rivals, and so on.

Although financial objectives are especially important in firms, oftentimes there is a trade-off between financial and strategic objectives such that crucial decisions have to be made. For example, a firm can do certain things to maximize short-term financial objectives that would harm long-term strategic objectives. To improve financial position in the short run through higher prices may, for example, jeopardize long-term market share. The dangers associated with trading off long-term strategic objectives with near-term bottom-line performance are especially severe if competitors relentlessly pursue increased market share at the expense of short-term profitability. And there are other trade-offs between financial and strategic objectives, related to riskiness of actions, concern for business ethics, need to preserve the natural environment, and social responsibility issues. Both financial and strategic objectives should include both annual and long-term performance targets. Ultimately, the best way to sustain competitive advantage over the long run is to relentlessly pursue strategic objectives that strengthen a firm's business position over rivals. Financial objectives can best be met by focusing first and foremost on achieving on strategic objectives that improve a firm's competitiveness and market strength.

Not Managing by Objectives

An unidentified educator once said, "If you think education is expensive, try ignorance." The idea behind this saying also applies to establishing objectives. Strategists should avoid the following alternative ways of "not managing by objectives."

- *Managing by Extrapolation*—adheres to the principle "If it ain't broke, don't fix it." The idea is to keep on doing the same things in the same ways because things are going well.
- *Managing by Crisis*—based on the belief that the true measure of a really good strategist is the ability to solve problems. Because there are plenty of crises and problems to go around for every person and every organization, strategists ought to bring their time and creative energy to bear on solving the most pressing problems of the day. Managing by crisis is actually a form of reacting rather than acting and of letting events dictate the what and when of management decisions.
- *Managing by Subjectives*—built on the idea that there is no general plan for which way to go and what to do; just do the best you can to accomplish what you think should be done. In short, "Do your own thing, the best way you know how" (sometimes referred to as *the mystery approach to decision making* because subordinates are left to figure out what is happening and why).
- *Managing by Hope*—based on the fact that the future is laden with great uncertainty and that if we try and do not succeed, then we hope our second (or third) attempt will succeed. Decisions are predicated on the hope that they will work and that good times are just around the corner, especially if luck and good fortune are on our side![2]

The Balanced Scorecard

Developed in 1993 by Harvard Business School professors Robert Kaplan and David Norton, and refined continually through today, the Balanced Scorecard is a strategy evaluation and control technique.[3] *Balanced Scorecard* derives its name from the perceived need of firms to "balance" financial measures that are oftentimes used exclusively in strategy evaluation and control with nonfinancial measures such as product quality and customer service. An effective Balanced Scorecard contains a carefully chosen combination of strategic and financial objectives tailored to the company's business.

As a tool to manage and evaluate strategy, the Balanced Scorecard is currently in use at Sears, United Parcel Service, 3M Corporation, Heinz, and hundreds of other firms. For example, 3M Corporation has a financial objective to achieve annual growth in earnings per share of 10 percent or better, as well as a strategic objective to have at least 30 percent of sales come from products introduced in the past four years. The overall aim of the Balanced Scorecard is to "balance" shareholder objectives with customer and operational objectives. Obviously, these sets of objectives interrelate and many even conflict. For example, customers want low price and high service, which may conflict with shareholders' desire for a high return on their investment. The Balanced Scorecard concept is consistent with the notions of continuous improvement in management (CIM) and total quality management (TQM).

Although the Balanced Scorecard concept is covered in more detail in Chapter 9 as it relates to evaluating strategies, firms should establish objectives and evaluate strategies on criteria other than financial measures. Financial measures and ratios are vitally important in strategic planning, but of equal importance are factors such as customer service, employee morale, product quality, pollution abatement, business ethics, social responsibility, community involvement, and other such items. In conjunction with financial measures, these "softer" factors comprise an integral part of both the objective-setting process and the strategy-evaluation process. A Balanced Scorecard for a firm is simply a listing of all key objectives to work toward, along with an associated time dimension of when each objective is to be accomplished, as well as a primary responsibility or contact person, department, or division for each objective.

Types of Strategies

The model illustrated in Figure 5-1 provides a conceptual basis for applying strategic management. Defined and exemplified in Table 5-4, alternative strategies that an enterprise could pursue can be categorized into 11 actions: forward integration, backward integration, horizontal integration, market penetration, market development, product development, related diversification, unrelated diversification, retrenchment, divestiture, and liquidation. Each alternative strategy has countless variations. For example, market penetration can include adding salespersons, increasing advertising expenditures, couponing, and using similar actions to increase market share in a given geographic area.

Many, if not most, organizations simultaneously pursue a combination of two or more strategies, but a *combination strategy* can be exceptionally risky if carried too far. No organization can afford to pursue all the strategies that might benefit the firm. Difficult decisions must be made. Priority must be established. Organizations, like individuals, have limited resources. Both organizations and individuals must choose among alternative strategies and avoid excessive indebtedness.

Hansen and Smith explain that strategic planning involves "choices that risk resources" and "trade-offs that sacrifice opportunity." In other words, if you have a strategy to go north, then you must buy snowshoes and warm jackets (spend resources) and forgo the opportunity of "faster population growth in southern states." You cannot have a strategy to go north and then take a step east, south, or west "just to be on the safe side." Firms spend resources and focus on a finite number of opportunities in pursuing strategies to achieve an uncertain outcome in the future. Strategic planning is much more than a roll of the dice; it is a wager based on predictions and hypotheses that are continually tested and refined by knowledge, research, experience, and learning. Survival of the firm itself may hinge on your strategic plan.[4]

FIGURE 5-1

A Comprehensive Strategic-Management Model

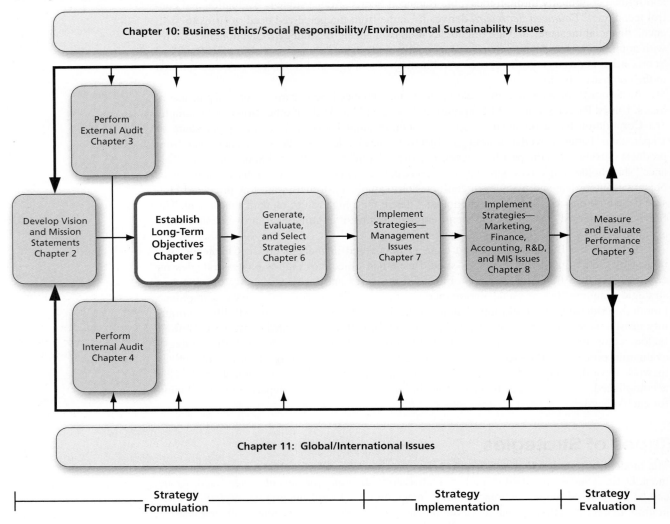

Source: Fred R. David, "How Companies Define Their Mission," *Long Range Planning* 22, no. 3 (June 1988): 40.

Organizations cannot do too many things well because resources and talents get spread thin and competitors gain advantage. In large, diversified companies, a combination strategy is commonly employed when different divisions pursue different strategies. Also, organizations struggling to survive may simultaneously employ a combination of several defensive strategies, such as divestiture, liquidation, and retrenchment.

Levels of Strategies

Strategy making is not just a task for top executives. Middle-and lower-level managers also must be involved in the strategic-planning process to the extent possible. In large firms, there are actually four levels of strategies: corporate, divisional, functional, and operational—as illustrated in Figure 5-2. However, in small firms, there are actually three levels of strategies: company, functional, and operational.

In large firms, the persons primarily responsible for having effective strategies at the various levels include the CEO at the corporate level; the president or executive vice president at the

TABLE 5-4   Alternative Strategies Defined and Exemplified

Strategy	Definition	2011 Examples
Forward Integration	Gaining ownership or increased control over distributors or retailers	Forward Integration—Starbucks reached a deal with Green Mountain Coffee Roasters for that firm to sell packs of Starbucks Tazo-branded coffee and tea in their brewers
Backward Integration	Seeking ownership or increased control of a firm's suppliers	Backward Integration—Dell Inc. acquired network security (virus protection) producer Secure Works Inc.
Horizontal Integration	Seeking ownership or increased control over competitors	Horizontal Integration—French drugmaker SanofiAventis purchased U.S. biotech drugmaker Genzyme for $20.1 billion
Market Penetration	Seeking increased market share for present products or services in present markets through greater marketing efforts	Market Penetration—Neiman Marcus (NM) launched NM Daily to attract less-affluent customers and hired a new "Managing Editor of Social Media" (Jean Scheidnes) to tweet and post for NM
Market Development	Introducing present products or services into new geographic area	Market Development—Hawaiian Airlines began offering flights from Hawaii to Seoul, Korea, and Tokyo, Japan—rather than mostly flying to and from the U.S. mainland
Product Development	Seeking increased sales by improving present products or services or developing new ones	Product Development—Apple introduced the new iPad 2
Related Diversification	Adding new but related products or services	Related Diversification—Amazon.com began allowing users to pay $79 per year for "Amazon Prime," which allows users to stream over 5,000 movies and TV shows
Unrelated Diversification	Adding new, unrelated products or services	Unrelated Diversification—Many banks now own, by default, many properties, putting many banks reluctantly in the real estate and/or property management business
Retrenchment	Regrouping through cost and asset reduction to reverse declining sales and profit	Retrenchment—Borders closed 200 of its 488 superstores and laid off 6,000 of its 19,500 employees
Divestiture	Selling a division or part of an organization	Divestiture—Marriott sold its timeshare business, creating the world's largest autonomous timeshare business, consisting of 71 properties with 33,000 rooms
Liquidation	Selling all of a company's assets, in parts, for their tangible worth	Liquidation—Blockbuster Inc. barely escaped liquidation in March 2011

divisional level; the respective chief finance officer (CFO), chief information officer (CIO), human resource manager (HRM), chief marketing officer (CMO), and so on at the functional level; and the plant manager, regional sales manager, and so on at the operational level. In small firms, the persons primarily responsible for having effective strategies at the various levels include the business owner or president at the company level and then the same range of persons at the lower two levels, as with a large firm.

It is important that all managers at all levels participate and understand the firm's strategic plan to help ensure coordination, facilitation, and commitment while avoiding inconsistency, inefficiency, and miscommunication. Plant managers, for example, need to understand and be supportive of the overall strategic plan (game plan), while the president and the CEO need to be knowledgeable of strategies being employed in various sales territories and manufacturing plants.

FIGURE 5-2

Levels of Strategies with Persons Most Responsible

Corporate Level—chief executive officer

Division Level—division president or executive vice president

Functional Level—finance, marketing, R&D, manufacturing, information systems, and human resource managers

Operational Level—plant managers, sales managers, production and department managers

Large Company

Company Level—owner or president

Functional Level—finance, marketing, R&D, manufacturing, information systems, and human resource managers

Operational Level—plant managers, sales managers, production and department managers

Small Company

Integration Strategies

Forward integration, backward integration, and horizontal integration are sometimes collectively referred to as *vertical integration* strategies. Vertical integration strategies allow a firm to gain control over distributors, suppliers, and/or competitors.

Forward Integration

Forward integration involves gaining ownership or increased control over distributors or retailers. Increasing numbers of manufacturers (suppliers) today are pursuing a forward integration strategy by establishing websites to directly sell products to consumers. This strategy is causing turmoil in some industries. For example, Apple Inc. recently began selling its iPad and iPhone through Verizon Wireless's 2,000 stores and AT&T's 2,200 stores. Apple's forward integration strategy aims to capitalize on its lead in tablets before the rival BlackBerry and Motorola versions are released.

Based in Herzogenaurach, Germany, Adidas plans to add 2,500 stores in China between 2011 and 2015 as the company widens its distribution in that country from 500 cities currently to over 1,400. As part of its new forward integration strategy in China, Adidas plans also to boost its presence in basketball, a sport that Adidas emphasizes less than competitors such as Nike and Li Ning Company, China's leading sports-apparel maker. Adidas recently sponsored the Beijing Marathon, the company's first running competition in China.

Chrysler Group LLC in 2011 opened its first company-owned dealership, Motor Village of Los Angeles, a four-level facility in downtown Los Angeles that houses all of Chrysler's brands, including Fiat. This dealership sells and services all Chrysler vehicles and is a test facility for showroom innovations.

Wal-Mart Stores recently began allowing customers to buy merchandise online at www.walmart.com and have it delivered free of charge to urban FedEx Corp. locations. Wal-Mart has never been very successful in large cities, and the company sees this new forward integration strategy as beneficial. Wal-Mart is test marketing this new strategy in Boston and Los Angeles, where the company has no stores.

The Washington Post Co. recently launched a free news-aggregation website called Trove that lets readers build their own news site based on particular topics they choose. Battered by declining revenues, newspaper companies are using forward integration to provide services that tailor the news experience to each individual reader. Trove sifts through more than 10,000 news sources and delivers articles to a personalized customer page.

An effective means of implementing forward integration is *franchising*. Approximately 2,000 companies in about 50 different industries in the United States use franchising to distribute their products or services. Businesses can expand rapidly by franchising because costs and opportunities are spread among many individuals. Total sales by franchises in the United States are annually about $1 trillion.

The International Franchise Association Educational Foundations reports that the number of franchise businesses in the United States is expected to grow 2.5 percent in 2011 to 784,802. However, a growing trend is for franchisees, who for example may operate 10 franchised restaurants, stores, or whatever, to buy out their part of the business from their franchiser (corporate owner). There is a growing rift between franchisees and franchisers as the segment often outperforms the parent. For example, McDonald's today owns only about 20 percent of its 32,800 restaurants. Restaurant chains are increasingly being pressured to own fewer of their locations. Companies such as McDonald's are using proceeds from the sale of company stores/restaurants to franchisees to buy back company stock, pay higher dividends, and make other investments to benefit shareholders.

The following six guidelines indicate when forward integration may be an especially effective strategy:[5]

- When an organization's present distributors are especially expensive, or unreliable, or incapable of meeting the firm's distribution needs.
- When the availability of quality distributors is so limited as to offer a competitive advantage to those firms that integrate forward.
- When an organization competes in an industry that is growing and is expected to continue to grow markedly; this is a factor because forward integration reduces an organization's ability to diversify if its basic industry falters.
- When an organization has both the capital and human resources needed to manage the new business of distributing its own products.
- When the advantages of stable production are particularly high; this is a consideration because an organization can increase the predictability of the demand for its output through forward integration.
- When present distributors or retailers have high profit margins; this situation suggests that a company could profitably distribute its own products and price them more competitively by integrating forward.

Backward Integration

Both manufacturers and retailers purchase needed materials from suppliers. *Backward integration* is a strategy of seeking ownership or increased control of a firm's suppliers. This strategy can be especially appropriate when a firm's current suppliers are unreliable, too costly, or cannot meet the firm's needs.

Wal-Mart recently announced that over the next five years the company will double the amount of food bought from local farmers in the United States. This backward integration strategy complements the company's plan to build hundreds of new, smaller Wal-Mart Express stores in small towns across the U.S. Wal-Mart hopes to reverse the booming business of Family Dollar, Dollar General, and Dollar Tree—which together have caused Wal-Mart's U.S. revenues to decline.

The largest coffee company in the world and, based in Switzerland, Nestle is training thousands of farmers over the next 10 years and providing them with new coffee trees. With this backward integration strategy, Nestle does not own the plantations or bind farmers into long-term contracts, but CEO Paul Bulcke says the relationship the firm develops with farmers will lead them to sell to Nestle. This may be a wise strategy for Nestle because rival firms such as Unilever and Kraft Foods struggle to obtain better control of raw materials. Nestle's coffee strategy comes just after the firm's backward integration strategy of recently spending $106 million to replant cocoa trees in Ivory Coast in West Africa.

Some industries in the United States, such as the automotive and aluminum industries, are reducing their historical pursuit of backward integration. Instead of owning their suppliers, companies negotiate with several outside suppliers. Ford and Chrysler buy over half of their component parts from outside suppliers such as TRW, Eaton, General Electric, and Johnson Controls. *De-integration* makes sense in industries that have global sources of supply. Companies today shop around, play one seller against another, and go with the best deal.

Global competition is also spurring firms to reduce their number of suppliers and to demand higher levels of service and quality from those they keep. Although traditionally relying on many suppliers to ensure uninterrupted supplies and low prices, American firms now are following the lead of Japanese firms, which have far fewer suppliers and closer, long-term relationships with those few. "Keeping track of so many suppliers is onerous," says Mark Shimelonis, formerly of Xerox.

Seven guidelines when backward integration may be an especially effective strategy are:[6]

- When an organization's present suppliers are especially expensive, or unreliable, or incapable of meeting the firm's needs for parts, components, assemblies, or raw materials.
- When the number of suppliers is small and the number of competitors is large.
- When an organization competes in an industry that is growing rapidly; this is a factor because integrative-type strategies (forward, backward, and horizontal) reduce an organization's ability to diversify in a declining industry.
- When an organization has both capital and human resources to manage the new business of supplying its own raw materials.
- When the advantages of stable prices are particularly important; this is a factor because an organization can stabilize the cost of its raw materials and the associated price of its product(s) through backward integration.
- When present supplies have high profit margins, which suggests that the business of supplying products or services in the given industry is a worthwhile venture.
- When an organization needs to quickly acquire a needed resource.

Horizontal Integration

Horizontal integration refers to a strategy of seeking ownership of or increased control over a firm's competitors. One of the most significant trends in strategic management today is the increased use of horizontal integration as a growth strategy. Mergers, acquisitions, and takeovers among competitors allow for increased economies of scale and enhanced transfer of resources and competencies. Kenneth Davidson makes the following observation about horizontal integration:

> The trend towards horizontal integration seems to reflect strategists' misgivings about their ability to operate many unrelated businesses. Mergers between direct competitors are more likely to create efficiencies than mergers between unrelated businesses, both because there is a greater potential for eliminating duplicate facilities and because the management of the acquiring firm is more likely to understand the business of the target.[7]

Consolidation is intensifying weekly in the airline industry. Dallas, Texas-based Southwest Airlines recently paid $1.4 billion in cash and stock to acquire AirTran Holdings based in Orlando, Florida. AirTran also had a hub at the world's largest airport—Atlanta International Airport in Georgia. Fierce rivals United Airlines and Continental Airlines recently combined forces to eclipse Delta as the world's largest airline. Southwest now flies more passengers inside the United States (105 million) annually than any other airline.

Horizontal integration is becoming the strategy of choice in countless industries to achieve economies of scale and efficiencies. Unilever PLC, for example, just acquired the U.S. hair-care firm Alberto Culver, moving into direct competition with Procter & Gamble and L'Oreal SA in shampoo and other personal products. Although known primarily for food products such as Ben & Jerry's ice cream and Lipton tea, Unilever is a huge personal-care products firm having months earlier purchased Sara Lee Corp.'s deodorant and body care products for $1.73 billion.

Canadian banks in general came through the recession in excellent shape and are aggressively looking to acquire U.S. banks. The Bank of Montreal recently purchased Milwaukee-based Marshall & Ilsley Corp. for $4.1 billion and there are many similar examples. Unlike U.S. banks, Canada's banks did not require bailout funds and avoided the subprime-mortgage crisis due to conservative lending practices and tight regulations.

These five guidelines indicate when horizontal integration may be an especially effective strategy:[8]

- When an organization can gain monopolistic characteristics in a particular area or region without being challenged by the federal government for "tending substantially" to reduce competition.
- When an organization competes in a growing industry.
- When increased economies of scale provide major competitive advantages.
- When an organization has both the capital and human talent needed to successfully manage an expanded organization.
- When competitors are faltering due to a lack of managerial expertise or a need for particular resources that an organization possesses; note that horizontal integration would not be appropriate if competitors are doing poorly, because in that case overall industry sales are declining.

Intensive Strategies

Market penetration, market development, and product development are sometimes referred to as *intensive strategies* because they require intensive efforts if a firm's competitive position with existing products is to improve.

Market Penetration

A *market penetration* strategy seeks to increase market share for present products or services in present markets through greater marketing efforts. This strategy is widely used alone and in combination with other strategies. Market penetration includes increasing the number of salespersons, increasing advertising expenditures, offering extensive sales promotion items, or increasing publicity efforts. United Parcel Service (UPS) recently launched its largest marketing campaign ever, replacing its memorable slogan "What can Brown do for you?' with the slogan "We [Heart] Logistics". Advertisements promoting this new slogan are running worldwide on both television and digital-media outlets. The television ads feature a new UPS jingle set to the tune of the Dean Martin classic "That's Amore" sung in Mandarin, Spanish, or English as appropriate.

The maker of Guinness beer recently launched its largest marketing push ever in the United States, including a sports-themed advertising campaign that features ex-footballer Jerome Bettis and ex-NFL coach Bill Cowher. Guinness has long been associated with soccer and rugby, but now wants to be associated with football and basketball.

Starbucks is tripling its number of outlets in China. Dunkin'Brands, which owns both Dunkin' Donuts and Baskin-Robbins, also is opening thousands of new outlets in China.

These five guidelines indicate when market penetration may be an especially effective strategy:[9]

- When current markets are not saturated with a particular product or service.
- When the usage rate of present customers could be increased significantly.
- When the market shares of major competitors have been declining while total industry sales have been increasing.
- When the correlation between dollar sales and dollar marketing expenditures historically has been high.
- When increased economies of scale provide major competitive advantages.

Market Development

Market development involves introducing present products or services into new geographic areas. For example, Ford Motor is introducing eight new vehicles in India between 2011 and 2015 to capitalize on increasing demand in the fast-expanding car market. Ford also has begun exporting its new Figo small car from India to 50 new markets, including Mexico, North Africa, and the Middle East. Ford's new market development strategy is aimed at taking advantage of fast-growing emerging markets while insulating the firm from slow-growing U.S. and European markets.

The oldest American beer brewer, D.G. Yuengling & Son, recently expanded beyond its 13-state footprint in the Eastern U.S. Pronounced ying-ling, the 181-year-old regional beer brewer bought a former Coors brewery in Memphis, Tennessee, more than doubling its overall capacity and enabling an aggressive market development strategy. Yuengling has about 250 employees compared to about 700 at rival firm Samuel Adams.

Based in Sweden, Volvo is building three new assembly plants in China and increasing its number of vehicles in that country from 24,000 to 300,000 in the next three years. Volvo desires to become one of China's largest car manufacturers and is launching 24 new models in that country between 2011 and 2015. Volvo used to be owned by Ford.

Las Vegas Sands Corp. recently built the only casino in Singapore, the famous city-state that has a global reputation for being crime-free and family-friendly. Called the Marina Bay Sands, this casino was a booming success in 2010–2011 and expectations are that as early as 2012, Singapore may take in more gaming revenues than Las Vegas. Another new casino in Singapore is the $4.4 billion Resorts World Sentosa owned by Malaysia's Genting Bhd.

Both Subway and Dunkin' Brands recently opened their first restaurants in Vietnam. Subway also just opened its first outlet in Bahrain. Subway expects its number of international restaurants to surpass its number of U.S. restaurants by 2020. Many customers say it is hard to beat Subway's $5 foot-long sandwiches in terms of value and nutrition. Starbucks expects to open its first restaurants in India within 12 months.

These six guidelines indicate when market development may be an especially effective strategy:[10]

- When new channels of distribution are available that are reliable, inexpensive, and of good quality.
- When an organization is very successful at what it does.
- When new untapped or unsaturated markets exist.
- When an organization has the needed capital and human resources to manage expanded operations.
- When an organization has excess production capacity.
- When an organization's basic industry is rapidly becoming global in scope.

Product Development

Product development is a strategy that seeks increased sales by improving or modifying present products or services. Product development usually entails large research and development expenditures. Google's new Chrome OS operating system illuminates years of monies spent on product development. Google expects Chrome OS to overtake Microsoft Windows by 2015.

Product development is perhaps the most important strategy for high-tech firms such as Acer. To compete with Apple's iPad and tablets, the world's second-largest PC maker by shipments, Acer, released in 2011 a tablet running Microsoft Windows software with a 10.1- inch screen. Acer also released two tablets using Google's Android software. Acer expects to sell about 50 million tablets worldwide in 2011. Historically, Acer had relied on netbooks (tiny, low-priced laptops). Also recently, Acer released a smartphone with a 4.8-inch screen running on Android software.

The world's largest hotel chain, Holiday Inn, recently completed a $1 billion upgrade to all of its 3,400 hotels. The mandatory upgrades includes new bedding, flat-screen TVs, better shower fixtures, and sleeker roadside signs. The product development strategy also includes closing 700 older, outdated hotels and adding 1,100 new, deluxe Holiday Inn hotels so the average age of Holiday Inn hotels is now 15 years.

Hilton Worldwide recently opened its first new hotel brand in 20 years—a Home2 Suites in Fayetteville, North Carolina. Home2 Suites moves Hilton into the mid-tier extended-stay market, although the company already owns Homewood Suites, aimed at the upscale extended-stay segment. Hilton opened about 10 new Home2 Suites in the U.S. in 2011.

In total, there were 40,820 new products introduced in the United States in 2010, up from 38,738 in 2009, and expected to exceed 45,000 in 2011.[11] Social media, especially Facebook, Twitter, and YouTube, is being used extensively by companies to both generate new ideas and market resultant new products, such as Colgate's new foaming toothpaste called Colgate MaxClean SmartFoam.

These five guidelines indicate when product development may be an especially effective strategy to pursue:[12]

- When an organization has successful products that are in the maturity stage of the product life cycle; the idea here is to attract satisfied customers to try new (improved) products as a result of their positive experience with the organization's present products or services.
- When an organization competes in an industry that is characterized by rapid technological developments.
- When major competitors offer better-quality products at comparable prices.
- When an organization competes in a high-growth industry.
- When an organization has especially strong research and development capabilities.

Diversification Strategies

There are two general types of *diversification strategies:* related and unrelated. Businesses are said to be *related* when their value chains possesses competitively valuable cross-business strategic fits; businesses are said to be *unrelated* when their value chains are so dissimilar that no competitively valuable cross-business relationships exist.[13] Most companies favor related diversification strategies in order to capitalize on synergies as follows:

- Transferring competitively valuable expertise, technological know-how, or other capabilities from one business to another.
- Combining the related activities of separate businesses into a single operation to achieve lower costs.
- Exploiting common use of a well-known brand name.
- Cross-business collaboration to create competitively valuable resource strengths and capabilities.[14]

Diversification strategies are becoming less popular as organizations are finding it more difficult to manage diverse business activities. In the 1960s and 1970s, the trend was to diversify to avoid being dependent on any single industry, but the 1980s saw a general reversal of that thinking. Diversification is now on the retreat. Michael Porter, of the Harvard Business School, says, "Management found it couldn't manage the beast." Hence businesses are selling, or closing, less profitable divisions to focus on core businesses.

The greatest risk of being in a single industry is having all of the firm's eggs in one basket. Although many firms are successful operating in a single industry, new technologies, new products, or fast-shifting buyer preferences can decimate a particular business.

Diversification must do more than simply spread business risk across different industries, however, because shareholders could accomplish this by simply purchasing equity in different firms across different industries or by investing in mutual funds. Diversification makes sense only to the extent the strategy adds more to shareholder value than what shareholders could accomplish acting individually. Thus, the chosen industry for diversification must be attractive enough to yield consistently high returns on investment and offer potential across the operating divisions for synergies greater than those entities could achieve alone.

A few companies today, however, pride themselves on being conglomerates, from small firms such as Pentair Inc. and Blount International to huge companies such as Textron, Allied Signal, Emerson Electric, General Electric, Viacom, and Samsung. Conglomerates prove that focus and diversity are not always mutually exclusive.

Many strategists contend that firms should "stick to the knitting" and not stray too far from the firms' basic areas of competence. However, diversification is still sometimes an appropriate strategy, especially when the company is competing in an unattractive industry. Hamish Maxwell, Philip Morris's former CEO, says, "We want to become a consumer-products company." Diversification makes sense for Philip Morris because cigarette consumption is declining, product liability suits are a risk, and some investors reject tobacco stocks on principle.

Related Diversification

In the 2010–2015 era, firms are generally moving away from diversification to focus. That dismantling is a clear trend. For example, ITT Corp. recently divided itself into three separate, specialized companies. ITT once owned everything from Sheraton hotels and Hartford Insurance to the maker of Wonder bread and Hostess Twinkies. About the ITT breakup, analyst Barry Knap said, "Companies generally are not very efficient diversifiers; investors usually can do a better job of that by purchasing stock in a variety of companies."

Bucking the trend however is Berkshire Hathaway, a holding company for diverse companies that include Dairy Queen, Burlington Northern Santa Fe Railroad, and Geico Insurance. Also bucking the trend, Panasonic Corp. recently diversified into hand-held, online videogames with a new product called the Jungle. Panasonic for years had focused on rechargeable batteries for electric cars as well as solar cells for home and industry, but with the Jungle, the firm is re-entering a business that it abandoned more than a decade ago.

PepsiCo in 2011 diversified into the dairy market by acquiring the Russian firm Wimm-Bill-Dann for $5.4 billion. This acquisition establishes PepsiCo as the largest food-and-beverage firm in Russia, and that country becomes PepsiCo's largest revenue generator outside of the United States. This acquisition comes soon after PepsiCo's $2 billion acquisition of the Russian fruit-juice maker OAO Lebedyansky. PepsiCo and Coke are fierce rivals in Russia, and of course around the world.

Electricity producer, NRG Energy Inc., recently entered the car-charging business, creating a network of 150 public charging points in Houston, Texas, and New York City. This is a "first mover" strategy because it signals that car charging may follow a subscription-based business model, rather than the price-per-unit model that has been used for decades to sell gasoline. NRG's customers will have a choice of three subscription plans, each with a three-year contract, beginning with a $49 monthly fee.

Based in Peoria, Illinois, Caterpillar recently diversified beyond its core areas of construction and mining machinery by acquiring a maker of railroad locomotives, Electro-Motive Diesel, and by also acquiring MWM Holding GmbH, a German maker of power-generation equipment. Caterpillar had cash and short-term investments of $2.27 billion and preferred to use those monies "to fund attractive growth initiatives" rather than to repurchase stock or increase dividend payouts.

Intel Corp. recently diversified beyond providing chips for personal computers by acquiring for $7.68 billion the security-software company McAfee, well known for its virus protection software. As part of this diversification strategy away from personal computer chips, Intel also acquired a Texas Instruments division that sells cable-modem chips as well as Infineon Technologies, AG's wireless chip business. Intel is also working with Google to supply chips that enable people to more easily navigate through websites and TV programs.

In a related diversification move, Tyson Foods recently entered the dog food business, selling refrigerated pet food targeted to consumers who give their pets everything from clothes and car seats to cemetery graves. Prior to this move by Tyson, meatpacking companies had been content to sell scraps such as chicken fat and by-products to makers of canned and dry pet food. Scott Morris of Freshpet Company in Secaucus, New Jersey, says this move by Tyson will change the fact that "pet food today looks the same as it did 30 years ago."

Six guidelines for when related diversification may be an effective strategy are as follows.[15]

- When an organization competes in a no-growth or a slow-growth industry.
- When adding new, but related, products would significantly enhance the sales of current products.
- When new, but related, products could be offered at highly competitive prices.
- When new, but related, products have seasonal sales levels that counterbalance an organization's existing peaks and valleys.
- When an organization's products are currently in the declining stage of the product's life cycle.
- When an organization has a strong management team.

Unrelated Diversification

An unrelated diversification strategy favors capitalizing on a portfolio of businesses that are capable of delivering excellent financial performance in their respective industries, rather than striving to capitalize on value chain strategic fits among the businesses. Firms that employ unrelated diversification continually search across different industries for companies that can be acquired for a deal and yet have potential to provide a high return on investment. Pursuing unrelated diversification entails being on the hunt to acquire companies whose assets are undervalued, or companies that are financially distressed, or companies that have high growth prospects but are short on investment capital. An obvious drawback of unrelated diversification is that the parent firm must have an excellent top management team that plans, organizes, motivates, delegates, and controls effectively. It is much more difficult to manage businesses in many industries than in a single industry. However, some firms are successful pursuing unrelated diversification, such as Walt Disney, which owns ABC, and General Electric, which owns NBC Universal. GE also produces locomotives, airplanes, appliances, and MRI machines and offers consumer finance, media, entertainment, oil, gas, and lighting products and services.

Tyson Foods recently launched a new diversification strategy, successfully opening a manufacturing plant that makes diesel and jet fuel from chicken fat, beef tallow, and leftover food grease from the firm's meat-processing plants. Tyson's new Louisiana factory can produce 75 million gallons of fat-based fuel annually. Working with Syntroleum Corp, Tyson is using heat to change the molecular structure of fats and oils so their new product performs like conventional fuels rather than similar biodiesel products.

In early 2011, Deutsche Bank opened a $4 billion, 3,000-room casino called the Cosmopolitan on the Las Vegas Strip. The huge German bank was originally just funding the project, but when developers defaulted on their loans, Deutsche decided to finish the last two years of work on the project and own and operate the new casino themselves. The new Cosmopolitan features a three-story, crystal-strewn bar meant to evoke the inside of a chandelier. Other financial institutions worldwide perhaps should consider unrelated diversification also by taking over some of their gone-bad projects rather than taking huge losses. Many more firms have failed at unrelated diversification than have succeeded due to immense management challenges.

Ten guidelines for when unrelated diversification may be an especially effective strategy are:[16]

- When revenues derived from an organization's current products or services would increase significantly by adding the new, unrelated products.
- When an organization competes in a highly competitive and/or a no-growth industry, as indicated by low industry profit margins and returns.
- When an organization's present channels of distribution can be used to market the new products to current customers.
- When the new products have countercyclical sales patterns compared to an organization's present products.
- When an organization's basic industry is experiencing declining annual sales and profits.
- When an organization has the capital and managerial talent needed to compete successfully in a new industry.
- When an organization has the opportunity to purchase an unrelated business that is an attractive investment opportunity.
- When there exists financial synergy between the acquired and acquiring firm. (Note that a key difference between related and unrelated diversification is that the former should be based on some commonality in markets, products, or technology, whereas the latter is based more on profit considerations.)
- When existing markets for an organization's present products are saturated.
- When antitrust action could be charged against an organization that historically has concentrated on a single industry.

Defensive Strategies

In addition to integrative, intensive, and diversification strategies, organizations also could pursue retrenchment, divestiture, or liquidation.

Retrenchment

Retrenchment occurs when an organization regroups through cost and asset reduction to reverse declining sales and profits. Sometimes called a *turnaround* or *reorganizational strategy,* retrenchment is designed to fortify an organization's basic distinctive competence. During retrenchment, strategists work with limited resources and face pressure from shareholders, employees, and the media. Retrenchment can entail selling off land and buildings to raise needed cash, pruning product lines, closing marginal businesses, closing obsolete factories, automating processes, reducing the number of employees, and instituting expense control systems.

Abbott Laboratories in 2011 cut about 3,000 jobs, or 3 percent of its workforce, as part of a major retrenchment strategy to streamline operations and improve efficiencies. Based in Abbott Park, Illinois, the company says most of the layoffs will be in its European operations. Abbott recently acquired Solvay SA's pharmaceutical division for about $6.1 billion. Abbott restructuring included closure of the Solvay facility in Marietta, Georgia.

A total of 157 banks in the United States ceased operations in 2010 due to financial insolvency. Many more banks followed suit in 2011, such as First Tier Bank in Louisville, Colorado and Enterprise Banking in McDonough, Georgia.

In some cases, *bankruptcy* can be an effective type of retrenchment strategy. Bankruptcy can allow a firm to avoid major debt obligations and to void union contracts. There are five major types of bankruptcy: Chapter 7, Chapter 9, Chapter 11, Chapter 12, and Chapter 13.

Chapter 7 bankruptcy is a liquidation procedure used only when a corporation sees no hope of being able to operate successfully or to obtain the necessary creditor agreement. All the organization's assets are sold in parts for their tangible worth. Chapter 7 is also the bankruptcy provision most frequently used by individuals to wipe out many types of unsecured debt.

Chapter 9 bankruptcy applies to municipalities. Prichard, Alabama (near Mobile), recently declared Chapter 9 bankruptcy when it "simply ran out of money to pay its pension obligations." Five municipalities in the United States filed Chapter 9 bankruptcy in 2010, but this part of the bankruptcy code is largely untested in courts. In fact, 21 states currently do not allow municipalities to file Chapter 9 bankruptcy. More than a dozen towns/cities in California, however, are expected to declare bankruptcy in the next 12 months., including San Diego, San Jose, and San Francisco.

Jefferson County in Alabama is home to Birmingham. The county is on the verge of declaring bankruptcy, as its fiscal soundness has deteriorated way beyond repair. Several Jefferson County former officials have been convicted of corruption charges related to sewer-bond dealings, which, coupled with inept management over many years, has led to the County's predicament. Norfolk, Virginia is in serious financial trouble, as is Reno, New York City, and Detroit.

Chapter 11 bankruptcy allows organizations to reorganize and come back after filing a petition for protection.

Chapter 12 bankruptcy was created by the Family Farmer Bankruptcy Act of 1986. This law became effective in 1987 and provides special relief to family farmers with debt equal to or less than $1.5 million.

Chapter 13 bankruptcy is a reorganization plan similar to Chapter 11, but it is available only to small businesses owned by individuals with unsecured debts of less than $100,000 and secured debts of less than $350,000. The Chapter 13 debtor is allowed to operate the business while a plan is being developed to provide for the successful operation of the business in the future.

Based in Los Angeles, California, Metro-Goldwyn-Mayer (MGM) Inc. recently declared Chapter 11 bankruptcy. MGM owns more than 4,100 movie titles, including the *James Bond* and *Rocky* franchises, but the firm's huge debt situation became too high to service.

Publisher of the *National Enquirer* and the *Star and Men's Fitness* magazines, American Media Inc. recently declared Chapter 11 bankruptcy. Based in Boca Raton, Florida, American Media told its advertisers, employees, customers, and vendors to expect "business as usual" during its restructuring.

Based in Secaucus, New Jersey, Urban Brands recently filed bankruptcy and is closing most of its 210 Ashley Stewart stores in 26 states. The stores primarily provide apparel for plus-size urban women.

The fast-food pizza chain, Sbarro Inc., recently declared Chapter 11 bankruptcy. Founded in the late 1950s by the Sbarro family, the company had grown to operate more than 1,000 stores in 40 countries, becoming a common sight in malls. Based in Melville, New York, Sbarro employs about 5,000 people.

Some of the largest bankruptcies in the United States in 2010 were: Ambac Financial Group, Corus Bankshares, FirstFed Financial, Blockbuster, Great Atlantic & Pacific (A&P) Tea, Mesa Air Group, and Affiliated Media. However, there were only 106 public U.S. companies filing bankruptcy in 2010, less than half the 211 public firms that filed the prior year, according to BankruptcyData.com. Owners of the Viceroy resort on the Caribbean island of Anguilla recently declared Chapter 11 bankruptcy protection in Delaware.

Five guidelines for when retrenchment may be an especially effective strategy to pursue are as follows:[17]

- When an organization has a clearly distinctive competence but has failed consistently to meet its objectives and goals over time.
- When an organization is one of the weaker competitors in a given industry.
- When an organization is plagued by inefficiency, low profitability, poor employee morale, and pressure from stockholders to improve performance.
- When an organization has failed to capitalize on external opportunities, minimize external threats, take advantage of internal strengths, and overcome internal weaknesses over time; that is, when the organization's strategic managers have failed (and possibly will be replaced by more competent individuals).
- When an organization has grown so large so quickly that major internal reorganization is needed.

Divestiture

Selling a division or part of an organization is called *divestiture*. Divestiture often is used to raise capital for further strategic acquisitions or investments. Divestiture can be part of an overall retrenchment strategy to rid an organization of businesses that are unprofitable, that require too much capital, or that do not fit well with the firm's other activities. Divestiture has also become a popular strategy for firms to focus on their core businesses and become less diversified. For example, the New York-based entertainment company, Viacom, recently divested of its Harmonix videogame division, which had produced the popular "Rock Band" line of games. Harmonix's "Rock Band" had been locked in brutal competition with a rival video game, "Guitar Hero," from Activision Blizzard, which is 60 percent owned by Vivendi SA.

Based in Downers Grove, Illinois, Sara Lee Corp. recently divested its North American bread division to Mexican bakery giant Grupo Bimbo for nearly $1 billion. Sara Lee continues to divest nonfood and low-margin units in order to focus on top brands such as Jimmy Dean, Ballpark hot dogs, and Hillshire Farm. Sara Lee is using much of those proceeds to buy back 2.5 million shares of their own stock (because the smaller, more focused company is a candidate for a takeover).

Based in Louisville, Kentucky, the maker of Jack Daniel's whiskey, Brown-Forman Corp., is trying to divest its wine business, which consists of eight wine brands that generated $310 million in sales in fiscal 2011. The company's flagship wines include Fetzer, Boneterra, and Sonoma-Cutrer. The wine business is challenging because it is capital intensive and wine consumers commonly experiment with different brands.

The private-equity fund Cerberus Capital Management LP recently sold its Chrysler Financial Corp. division to Toronto, Canada-based Toronto-Dominion Bank for roughly $80 billion. The acquisition by Canada's second-largest bank makes it one of the five biggest auto lenders in the U.S.

Clorox Company recently divested its auto-care division to private-equity firm Avista Capital Partners for about $780 million. Clorox desires to focus on its health-and-wellness products and desires to buy back some of its own stock. Clorox's auto-care brands that included STP and Armor All generated global sales of about $300 million.

Yum Brands is trying to divest its Long John Silver's and A&W Restaurants chains so the firm can focus on its KFC, Pizza Hut, and Taco Bell international businesses.

Historically firms have divested their unwanted or poorly performing divisions, but the global recession has witnessed firms simply closing such operations. For example, Home Depot is shutting down its Expo home-design stores; defense and aerospace manufacturer Textron Corp is closing groups that financed real estate deals; Pioneer Corp. will soon stop making televisions; Praxair Inc. is closing some of its service-related businesses outside the United States; even Google recently halted efforts to sell advertising on radio stations and in newspapers. Saks, the luxury clothing chain, recently closed 16 of its 18 bridal salons, leaving open only its departments in Manhattan and Beverly Hills.

Six guidelines for when divestiture may be an especially effective strategy to pursue follow:[18]

- When an organization has pursued a retrenchment strategy and failed to accomplish needed improvements.
- When a division needs more resources to be competitive than the company can provide.
- When a division is responsible for an organization's overall poor performance.
- When a division is a misfit with the rest of an organization; this can result from radically different markets, customers, managers, employees, values, or needs.
- When a large amount of cash is needed quickly and cannot be obtained reasonably from other sources.
- When government antitrust action threatens an organization.

Liquidation

Selling all of a company's assets, in parts, for their tangible worth is called *liquidation*. Liquidation is a recognition of defeat and consequently can be an emotionally difficult strategy. However, it may be better to cease operating than to continue losing large sums of money. For example, based in Mayodan, North Carolina, General Tobacco (GT) liquidated in 2011, as the maker of low-priced cigarettes failed to make payments owed to states under a massive industry settlement. Some GT brands were Bronco, Silver, and GT One.

Thousands of small businesses in the United States liquidate annually without ever making the news. It is tough to start and successfully operate a small business. In China and Russia, thousands of government-owned businesses liquidate annually as those countries try to privatize and consolidate industries.

These three guidelines indicate when liquidation may be an especially effective strategy to pursue:[19]

- When an organization has pursued both a retrenchment strategy and a divestitute strategy, and neither has been successful.
- When an organization's only alternative is bankruptcy. Liquidation represents an orderly and planned means of obtaining the greatest possible cash for an organization's assets. A company can legally declare bankruptcy first and then liquidate various divisions to raise needed capital.
- When the stockholders of a firm can minimize their losses by selling the organization's assets.

Michael Porter's Five Generic Strategies

Probably the three most widely read books on competitive analysis in the 1980s were Michael Porter's *Competitive Strategy* (Free Press, 1980), *Competitive Advantage* (Free Press, 1985), and *Competitive Advantage of Nations* (Free Press, 1989). According to Porter, strategies allow organizations to gain competitive advantage from three different bases: cost leadership, differentiation, and focus. Porter calls these bases *generic strategies*.

Cost leadership emphasizes producing standardized products at a very low per-unit cost for consumers who are price-sensitive. Two alternative types of cost leadership strategies can be defined. Type 1 is a *low-cost* strategy that offers products or services to a wide range of customers at the lowest price available on the market. Type 2 is a *best-value* strategy that offers products or services to a wide range of customers at the best price-value available on the market; the best-value strategy aims to offer customers a range of products or services at the lowest price available compared to a rival's products with similar attributes. Both Type 1 and Type 2 strategies target a large market.

Porter's Type 3 generic strategy is *differentiation,* a strategy aimed at producing products and services considered unique industrywide and directed at consumers who are relatively price-insensitive.

Focus means producing products and services that fulfill the needs of small groups of consumers. Two alternative types of focus strategies are Type 4 and Type 5. Type 4 is a *low-cost focus* strategy that offers products or services to a small range (niche group) of customers at the lowest price available on the market. Examples of firms that use the Type 4 strategy include Jiffy Lube International and Pizza Hut, as well as local used car dealers and hot dog restaurants. Type 5 is a *best-value focus* strategy that offers products or services to a small range of customers at the best price-value available on the market. Sometimes called "focused differentiation," the best-value focus strategy aims to offer a niche group of customers products or services that meet their tastes and requirements better than rivals' products do. Both Type 4 and Type 5 focus strategies target a small market. However, the difference is that Type 4 strategies offer products or services to a niche group at the lowest price, whereas Type 5 offers products/services to a niche group at higher prices but loaded with features so the offerings are perceived as the best value. Examples of firms that use the Type 5 strategy include Cannondale (top-of-the-line mountain bikes), Maytag (washing machines), and Lone Star Restaurants (steak house), as well as bed-and-breakfast inns and local retail boutiques.

Porter's five strategies imply different organizational arrangements, control procedures, and incentive systems. Larger firms with greater access to resources typically compete on a cost leadership and/or differentiation basis, whereas smaller firms often compete on a focus basis. Porter's five generic strategies are illustrated in Figure 5-3. Note that a differentiation strategy (Type 3) can be pursued with either a small target market or a large target market. However, it is not effective to pursue a cost leadership strategy in a small market because profits margins are generally too small. Likewise, it is not effective to pursue a focus strategy in a large market because economies of scale would generally favor a low-cost or best-value cost leadership strategy to gain and/or sustain competitive advantage.

Porter stresses the need for strategists to perform cost-benefit analyses to evaluate "sharing opportunities" among a firm's existing and potential business units. Sharing activities and resources enhances competitive advantage by lowering costs or increasing differentiation.

FIGURE 5-3

Porter's Five Generic Strategies

Type 1: Cost Leadership—Low Cost
Type 2: Cost Leadership—Best Value
Type 3: Differentiation
Type 4: Focus—Low Cost
Type 5: Focus—Best Value

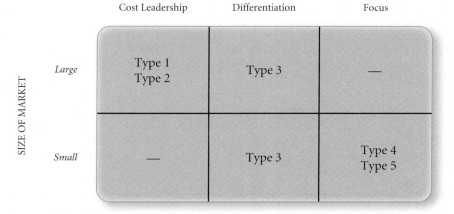

Source: Based on Michael E. Porter, *Competitive Strategy: Techniques for Analyzing Industries and Competitors* (New York: Free Press, 1980), 35–40.

In addition to prompting sharing, Porter stresses the need for firms to effectively "transfer" skills and expertise among autonomous business units to gain competitive advantage. Depending on factors such as type of industry, size of firm, and nature of competition, various strategies could yield advantages in cost leadership, differentiation, and focus.

Cost Leadership Strategies (Type 1 and Type 2)

A primary reason for pursuing forward, backward, and horizontal integration strategies is to gain low-cost or best-value cost leadership benefits. But cost leadership generally must be pursued in conjunction with differentiation. A number of cost elements affect the relative attractiveness of generic strategies, including economies or diseconomies of scale achieved, learning and experience curve effects, the percentage of capacity utilization achieved, and linkages with suppliers and distributors. Other cost elements to consider in choosing among alternative strategies include the potential for sharing costs and knowledge within the organization, R&D costs associated with new product development or modification of existing products, labor costs, tax rates, energy costs, and shipping costs.

Striving to be the low-cost producer in an industry can be especially effective when the market is composed of many price-sensitive buyers, when there are few ways to achieve product differentiation, when buyers do not care much about differences from brand to brand, or when there are a large number of buyers with significant bargaining power. The basic idea is to underprice competitors and thereby gain market share and sales, entirely driving some competitors out of the market. Companies employing a low-cost (Type 1) or best-value (Type 2) cost leadership strategy must achieve their competitive advantage in ways that are difficult for competitors to copy or match. If rivals find it relatively easy or inexpensive to imitate the leader's cost leadership methods, the leaders' advantage will not last long enough to yield a valuable edge in the marketplace. Recall that for a resource to be valuable, it must be either rare, hard to imitate, or not easily substitutable. To employ a cost leadership strategy successfully, a firm must ensure that its total costs across its overall value chain are lower than competitors' total costs. There are two ways to accomplish this:[20]

1. Perform value chain activities more efficiently than rivals and control the factors that drive the costs of value chain activities. Such activities could include altering the plant layout, mastering newly introduced technologies, using common parts or components in different products, simplifying product design, finding ways to operate close to full capacity year-round, and so on.
2. Revamp the firm's overall value chain to eliminate or bypass some cost-producing activities. Such activities could include securing new suppliers or distributors, selling products online, relocating manufacturing facilities, avoiding the use of union labor, and so on.

When employing a cost leadership strategy, a firm must be careful not to use such aggressive price cuts that their own profits are low or nonexistent. Constantly be mindful of cost-saving technological breakthroughs or any other value chain advancements that could erode or destroy the firm's competitive advantage. A Type 1 or Type 2 cost leadership strategy can be especially effective under the following conditions:[21]

1. When price competition among rival sellers is especially vigorous.
2. When the products of rival sellers are essentially identical and supplies are readily available from any of several eager sellers.
3. When there are few ways to achieve product differentiation that have value to buyers.
4. When most buyers use the product in the same ways.
5. When buyers incur low costs in switching their purchases from one seller to another.
6. When buyers are large and have significant power to bargain down prices.
7. When industry newcomers use introductory low prices to attract buyers and build a customer base.

A successful cost leadership strategy usually permeates the entire firm, as evidenced by high efficiency, low overhead, limited perks, intolerance of waste, intensive screening of budget requests, wide spans of control, rewards linked to cost containment, and broad employee participation in cost control efforts. Some risks of pursuing cost leadership are that competitors may imitate the strategy, thus driving overall industry profits down; that technological breakthroughs in the industry may make the strategy ineffective; or that buyer interest may swing to other differentiating features besides price. Several example firms that are well known for their low-cost leadership strategies are Wal-Mart, BIC, McDonald's, Black & Decker, Lincoln Electric, and Briggs & Stratton.

Differentiation Strategies (Type 3)

Different strategies offer different degrees of differentiation. Differentiation does not guarantee competitive advantage, especially if standard products sufficiently meet customer needs or if rapid imitation by competitors is possible. Durable products protected by barriers to quick copying by competitors are best. Successful differentiation can mean greater product flexibility, greater compatibility, lower costs, improved service, less maintenance, greater convenience, or more features. Product development is an example of a strategy that offers the advantages of differentiation.

A differentiation strategy should be pursued only after a careful study of buyers' needs and preferences to determine the feasibility of incorporating one or more differentiating features into a unique product that features the desired attributes. A successful differentiation strategy allows a firm to charge a higher price for its product and to gain customer loyalty because consumers may become strongly attached to the differentiation features. Special features that differentiate one's product can include superior service, spare parts availability, engineering design, product performance, useful life, gas mileage, or ease of use.

A risk of pursuing a differentiation strategy is that the unique product may not be valued highly enough by customers to justify the higher price. When this happens, a cost leadership strategy easily will defeat a differentiation strategy. Another risk of pursuing a differentiation strategy is that competitors may quickly develop ways to copy the differentiating features. Firms thus must find durable sources of uniqueness that cannot be imitated quickly or cheaply by rival firms.

Common organizational requirements for a successful differentiation strategy include strong coordination among the R&D and marketing functions and substantial amenities to attract scientists and creative people. Firms can pursue a differentiation (Type 3) strategy based on many different competitive aspects. For example, Mountain Dew and root beer have a unique taste; Lowe's, Home Depot, and Wal-Mart offer wide selection and one-stop shopping; Dell Computer and FedEx offer superior service; BMW and Porsche offer engineering design and performance; IBM and Hewlett-Packard offer a wide range of products; and E*Trade and Ameritrade offer Internet convenience. Differentiation opportunities exist or can potentially be developed anywhere along the firm's value chain, including supply chain activities, product R&D activities, production and technological activities, manufacturing activities, human resource management activities, distribution activities, or marketing activities.

The most effective differentiation bases are those that are hard or expensive for rivals to duplicate. Competitors are continually trying to imitate, duplicate, and outperform rivals along any differentiation variable that has yielded competitive advantage. For example, when U.S. Airways cut its prices, Delta quickly followed suit. When Caterpillar instituted its quick-delivery-of-spare-parts policy, John Deere soon followed suit. To the extent that differentiating attributes are tough for rivals to copy, a differentiation strategy will be especially effective, but the sources of uniqueness must be time-consuming, cost prohibitive, and simply too burdensome for rivals to match. A firm, therefore, must be careful when employing a differentiation (Type 3) strategy. Buyers will not pay the higher differentiation price unless their perceived value exceeds the price they are paying.[22] Based on such matters as attractive packaging, extensive advertising, quality of sales presentations, quality of website, list of customers, professionalism, size of the firm, and/or profitability of the company, perceived value may be more important to customers than actual value.

A Type 3 differentiation strategy can be especially effective under the following conditions:[23]

1. When there are many ways to differentiate the product or service and many buyers perceive these differences as having value.
2. When buyer needs and uses are diverse.

3. When few rival firms are following a similar differentiation approach.
4. When technological change is fast paced and competition revolves around rapidly evolving product features.

Focus Strategies (Type 4 and Type 5)

A successful focus strategy depends on an industry segment that is of sufficient size, has good growth potential, and is not crucial to the success of other major competitors. Strategies such as market penetration and market development offer substantial focusing advantages. Midsize and large firms can effectively pursue focus-based strategies only in conjunction with differentiation or cost leadership–based strategies. All firms in essence follow a differentiated strategy. Because only one firm can differentiate itself with the lowest cost, the remaining firms in the industry must find other ways to differentiate their products.

Focus strategies are most effective when consumers have distinctive preferences or requirements and when rival firms are not attempting to specialize in the same target segment. Milwaukee, Wisconsin-based Johnson Controls focuses on being a supplier of car interior products. Johnson Controls recently purchased Germany's Keiper Recaro Group's auto-parts business, which added 4,750 employees in seven countries producing devices that recline and adjust automobile seats. Johnson Controls now sells about $18 billion in auto-related products annually, although it also has a heating and ventilation equipment segment of the business.

Risks of pursuing a focus strategy include the possibility that numerous competitors will recognize the successful focus strategy and copy it or that consumer preferences will drift toward the product attributes desired by the market as a whole. An organization using a focus strategy may concentrate on a particular group of customers, geographic markets, or on particular product-line segments to serve a well-defined but narrow market better than competitors who serve a broader market.

A low-cost (Type 4) or best-value (Type 5) focus strategy can be especially attractive under the following conditions:[24]

1. When the target market niche is large, profitable, and growing.
2. When industry leaders do not consider the niche to be crucial to their own success.
3. When industry leaders consider it too costly or difficult to meet the specialized needs of the target market niche while taking care of their mainstream customers.
4. When the industry has many different niches and segments, thereby allowing a focuser to pick a competitively attractive niche suited to its own resources.
5. When few, if any, other rivals are attempting to specialize in the same target segment.

Strategies for Competing in Turbulent, High-Velocity Markets

The world is changing more and more rapidly, and consequently industries and firms themselves are changing faster than ever. Some industries are changing so fast that researchers call them *turbulent, high-velocity markets,* such as telecommunications, medical, biotechnology, pharmaceuticals, computer hardware, software, and virtually all Internet-based industries. High-velocity change is clearly becoming more and more the rule rather than the exception, even in such industries as toys, phones, banking, defense, publishing, and communication.

Meeting the challenge of high-velocity change presents the firm with a choice of whether to react, anticipate, or lead the market in terms of its own strategies. To primarily react to changes in the industry would be a defensive strategy used to counter, for example, unexpected shifts in buyer tastes and technological breakthroughs. The react-to-change strategy would not be as effective as the anticipate-change strategy, which would entail devising and following through with plans for dealing with the expected changes. However, firms ideally strive to be in a position to lead the changes in high-velocity markets, whereby they pioneer new and better technologies and products and set industry standards. Being the leader or pioneer of change in a high-velocity market is an aggressive, offensive strategy that includes rushing next-generation products to market ahead of rivals and being continually proactive in shaping the market to one's own benefit. Although a lead-change strategy is best whenever the firm has the resources to pursue this approach, on occasion even the strongest firms in turbulent industries have to employ the react-to-the-market strategy and the anticipate-the-market strategy.

An example turbulent, high-velocity market is the tablet computer, with more than 100 companies trying to emulate Apple's iPad and tablet products. Sales of tablet computers exceeded 20 million units in 2010 and 60 million units in 2011. A version of Google's Android operating system is now powering tablets, including Google's Honeycomb system. Apple utilizes a lead-change strategy as one of the strongest firms in the turbulent computer tablet industry, with firms such as Samsung and Toshiba aggressively pursuing a react-to-change strategy. The first laptop computers running on Google's Chrome OS were manufactured by Acer Inc. and Samsung Electronics and went on sale in mid-2011. Google is working with Verizon Wireless to ensure that Chrome laptops always stay online.

One strategy to compete in a turbulent industry is to acquire rivals, thus gaining economies of scale and improved efficiencies. For example, AT&T just acquired rival T-Mobile USA for $39 billion, creating the largest U.S. cellphone company, and Charles Schwab Corp. acquired online brokerage services provider OptionsXpress for $1 billion.

Means for Achieving Strategies

Cooperation Among Competitors

Strategies that stress cooperation among competitors are being used more. For collaboration between competitors to succeed, both firms must contribute something distinctive, such as technology, distribution, basic research, or manufacturing capacity. But a major risk is that unintended transfers of important skills or technology may occur at organizational levels below where the deal was signed.[25] Information not covered in the formal agreement often gets traded in the day-to-day interactions and dealings of engineers, marketers, and product developers. Firms often give away too much information to rival firms when operating under cooperative agreements! Tighter formal agreements are needed.

Perhaps the best example of rival firms in an industry forming alliances to compete against each other is the airline industry. Today there are three major alliances: Star, SkyTeam, and Oneworld, but other alliances are forming, such as the new trans-Atlantic joint venture among American Air, British Air, and Iberia Air formed by Oneworld. There is also a new trans-Pacific joint venture among American, Japan Air, United Continental, and All Nippon Air.

The idea of joining forces with a competitor is not easily accepted by Americans, who often view cooperation and partnerships with skepticism and suspicion. Indeed, joint ventures and cooperative arrangements among competitors demand a certain amount of trust if companies are to combat paranoia about whether one firm will injure the other. However, multinational firms are becoming more globally cooperative, and increasing numbers of domestic firms are joining forces with competitive foreign firms to reap mutual benefits. Kathryn Harrigan at Columbia University says, "Within a decade, most companies will be members of teams that compete against each other." Once major rivals, Google's YouTube and Vivendi SA's Universal Music Group have formed a partnership called Vevo to provide a new music-video service. Google provides the technology and Universal Music provides the content, and both firms share the revenues. The two firms now operate the stand-alone site Vevo.com.

U.S. companies often enter alliances primarily to avoid investments, being more interested in reducing the costs and risks of entering new businesses or markets than in acquiring new skills. In contrast, *learning from the partner* is a major reason why Asian and European firms enter into cooperative agreements. U.S. firms, too, should place learning high on the list of reasons to be cooperative with competitors. U.S. companies often form alliances with Asian firms to gain an understanding of their manufacturing excellence, but Asian competence in this area is not easily transferable. Manufacturing excellence is a complex system that includes employee training and involvement, integration with suppliers, statistical process controls, value engineering, and design. In contrast, U.S. know-how in technology and related areas can be imitated more easily. U.S. firms thus need to be careful not to give away more intelligence than they receive in cooperative agreements with rival Asian firms.

Joint Venture/Partnering

Joint venture is a popular strategy that occurs when two or more companies form a temporary partnership or consortium for the purpose of capitalizing on some opportunity. Often, the two or more sponsoring firms form a separate organization and have shared equity ownership in the new entity. Other types of *cooperative arrangements* include research and development partnerships, cross-distribution agreements, cross-licensing agreements, cross-manufacturing agreements, and joint-bidding consortia. Facebook Inc. and Skype SA recently combined their communications services more closely under a new partnership that allows Facebook members to sign into Skype through their Facebook Connect account and then send text messages or set up voice chats and video chats with their Facebook friends from within Skype. The partnership puts pressure on Google because it links Skype's 580 million registered users with Facebook's 500 million members. For the first time ever, U.S. Internet users spent 41.1 billion minutes on Facebook in August 2010, surpassing Google's 39.8 billion minutes.[26]

The world's largest cellphone maker, Nokia Corp., recently formed a partnership with the world's largest software company, Microsoft, whereby the Finnish company will receive billions of dollars from Microsoft to develop and market smartphones using Microsoft's operating system. Nokia still has the largest market share in the handset business but is losing ground. The partnership is designed to compete with Google's Android mobile-phone operating system and with Apple Inc.'s iPhone. Nokia's new smartphones will use Window Phone as their principal operating system, replacing its own Symbian software and Intel's MeeGo operating system. About the Nokia-Microsoft partnership, Google executive Vic Gundrota said, "Two turkeys do not make an eagle."

Joint ventures and cooperative arrangements are being used increasingly because they allow companies to improve communications and networking, to globalize operations, and to minimize risk. Joint ventures and partnerships are often used to pursue an opportunity that is too complex, uneconomical, or risky for a single firm to pursue alone. Such business creations also are used when achieving and sustaining competitive advantage when an industry requires a broader range of competencies and know-how than any one firm can marshal. Kathryn Rudie Harrigan, summarizes the trend toward increased joint venturing:

> In today's global business environment of scarce resources, rapid rates of technological change, and rising capital requirements, the important question is no longer "Shall we form a joint venture?" Now the question is "Which joint ventures and cooperative arrangements are most appropriate for our needs and expectations?" followed by "How do we manage these ventures most effectively?"[27]

In a global market tied together by the Internet, joint ventures, and partnerships, alliances are proving to be a more effective way to enhance corporate growth than mergers and acquisitions.[28] Strategic partnering takes many forms, including outsourcing, information sharing, joint marketing, and joint research and development. Many companies, such as Eli Lilly, now host partnership training classes for their managers and partners. There are today more than 10,000 joint ventures formed annually, more than all mergers and acquisitions. There are countless examples of successful strategic alliances, such as Internet coverage.

A major reason why firms are using partnering as a means to achieve strategies is globalization. Wal-Mart's successful joint venture with Mexico's Cifra is indicative of how a domestic firm can benefit immensely by partnering with a foreign company to gain substantial presence in that new country. Technology also is a major reason behind the need to form strategic alliances, with the Internet linking widely dispersed partners. The Internet paved the way and legitimized the need for alliances to serve as the primary means for corporate growth.

Striving to compete with Google, Microsoft and Facebook recently unveiled a plan to improve the results of Microsoft's Bing search engine by including peoples's social connections on Facebook. The sharing of personal data between Micorsoft and Facebook raises privacy concerns because the partnership gives Bing access to all public information about a Facebook user, including their friends' names and photos. Bing powers both Microsoft searches (11.2 percent) and Yahoo searches (16.7 percent), but Google's share of U.S. searches is 66.1 percent.

Evidence is mounting that firms should use partnering as a means for achieving strategies. However, the sad fact is that most U.S. firms in many industries—such as financial services, forest products, metals, and retailing—still operate in a merger or acquire mode to obtain growth. Partnering is not yet taught at most business schools and is often viewed within companies as a financial issue rather than a strategic issue. However, partnering has become a core competency, a strategic issue of such importance that top management involvement initially and throughout the life of an alliance is vital.[29]

Joint ventures among once rival firms are commonly being used to pursue strategies ranging from retrenchment to market development. Although ventures and partnerships are preferred over mergers as a means for achieving strategies, certainly they are not all successful. The good news is that joint ventures and partnerships are less risky for companies than mergers, but the bad news is that many alliances fail. There are countless examples of failed joint ventures. A few common problems that cause joint ventures to fail are as follows:

1. Managers who must collaborate daily in operating the venture are not involved in forming or shaping the venture.
2. The venture may benefit the partnering companies but may not benefit customers, who then complain about poorer service or criticize the companies in other ways.
3. The venture may not be supported equally by both partners. If supported unequally, problems arise.
4. The venture may begin to compete more with one of the partners than the other.[30]

Six guidelines for when a joint venture may be an especially effective means for pursuing strategies are:[31]

- When a privately owned organization is forming a joint venture with a publicly owned organization; there are some advantages to being privately held, such as closed ownership; there are some advantages of being publicly held, such as access to stock issuances as a source of capital. Sometimes, the unique advantages of being privately and publicly held can be synergistically combined in a joint venture.
- When a domestic organization is forming a joint venture with a foreign company; a joint venture can provide a domestic company with the opportunity for obtaining local management in a foreign country, thereby reducing risks such as expropriation and harassment by host country officials.
- When the distinct competencies of two or more firms complement each other especially well.
- When some project is potentially very profitable but requires overwhelming resources and risks.
- When two or more smaller firms have trouble competing with a large firm.
- When there exists a need to quickly introduce a new technology.

Merger/Acquisition

Google acquired 48 companies in 2010 and is on pace to eclipse that number in 2011, as the firm seeks ways to boost revenue growth and compete more aggressively in social networking. That may be a record annual number of acquisitions for any company ever. Cisco had 23 acquisitions back in 2000, Microsoft had 18 in 2008, and Oracle had 13 in 2005, but 48 is unreal. Despite Google's 48 acquisitions, the company's stock price dropped 4 percent in 2010—even when the stock market was roaring back.

Merger and acquisition are two commonly used ways to pursue strategies. A *merger* occurs when two organizations of about equal size unite to form one enterprise. An *acquisition* occurs when a large organization purchases (acquires) a smaller firm, or vice versa. When a merger or acquisition is not desired by both parties, it can be called a *takeover* or *hostile takeover*. In contrast, if the acquisition is desired by both firms, it is termed a *friendly merger*. Most mergers are friendly. For example, two Japanese steel producers, Nippon Steel Corp. and Sumitomo Metal Industries Ltd., recently merged in friendly fashion to form the world's second largest steel producer behind ArcelorMittal. Canada's Valeant Pharmaceuticals International recently made a hostile takeover bid of $5.7 billion for smaller rival Cephalon, or $73 per share, a 24.5 percent premium to Cephalon's stock price of $58.

There were numerous examples in 2011 of hostile takeover attempts. For example, the French pharmaceutical giant Sanofi-Aventis SA recently launched an $18.5 billion hostile takeover bid for the U.S. biotech company Genzyme Corp. Sanofi has offered $69 per share for Genzyme, but analysts say that bid may have to increase to $85 to seal the deal.

Nasdaq, with help from IntercontinentalExchange (ICE), which operates a global futures exchange and over-the-counter (OTC) markets and derivatives clearing houses, plans to place a hostile takeover bid for the New York Stock Exchange (NYSE) Euronext. Any Nasdaq bid, however, would face significant obstacles, including possible antitrust problems, since nearly every U.S. stock is listed on either the NYSE or Nasdaq. There has been a recent merger frenzy in the stock exchange business. Deutsche Boerse and NYSE Euronext desire to merge to create the world's largest exchange operator in a deal worth $10.2 billion. There is speculation that Nasdaq might even merge with another international exchange, such as the London Stock Exchange (LSE). The LSE is eyeing a takeover of Nasdaq after recently merging with the Canadian TMX Group, which operates the Toronto and Montreal stock exchanges.

With hundreds of companies flush with excess cash, the year 2010 saw a 13 percent increase in mergers and acquisitions in the United States; 2011 is on pace to exceed that percentage as firms increasingly use mergers to quickly tap into new businesses and reach new markets, both top priorities as companies were previously hunkered down during the recession.

General Electric continues to acquire diverse firms, including its recent purchase of oil-and-gas equipment maker Dresser Inc. for $3 billion. Based in Dallas, Texas, about 60 percent of Dresser's revenues come from outside the United States. General Electric desires to scale back its big finance business at GE Capital and beef up its industrial and infrastructure operations.

White knight is a term that refers to a firm that agrees to acquire another firm when that other firm is facing a hostile takeover by some company. For example, recently Palo Alto, California–based CV Thereapeutics Inc., a heart-drug maker, was fighting a hostile takeover bid by Japan's Astellas Pharma. Then CVT struck a friendly deal to be acquired by Forest City, California–based Gilead Sciences at a higher price of $1.4 billion in cash. Gilead is known for its HIV drugs, so its move into the heart-drug business surprised many analysts.

Not all mergers are effective and successful. For example, even 12 months after PulteGroup recently bought rival Centex Corp. for $1.3 billion in stock, creating the largest home builder in the United States, PulteGroup's profits are still negative and the company's stock price is 30 percent lower than the week of the acquisition. PulteGroup's dismal performance is in sharp contrast to rival firms such as Toll Brothers and Lennar Corp., whose stock price is up 22 percent during the same period. Many analysts say that PulteGroup's acquisition of Centex was poorly timed and a mistake. So a merger between two firms can yield great benefits, but the price and reasoning must be right. Some key reasons why many mergers and acquisitions fail are provided in Table 5-5.

Among mergers, acquisitions, and takeovers in recent years, same-industry combinations have predominated. A general market consolidation is occurring in many industries, especially banking, insurance, defense, and health care, but also in pharmaceuticals, food, airlines, accounting, publishing, computers, retailing, financial services, and biotechnology. For example, There are many potential benefits of merging with or acquiring another firm, as indicated in Table 5-6.

TABLE 5-5 Key Reasons Why Many Mergers and Acquisitions Fail

- Integration difficulties
- Inadequate evaluation of target
- Large or extraordinary debt
- Inability to achieve synergy
- Too much diversification
- Managers overly focused on acquisitions
- Too large an acquisition
- Difficult to integrate different organizational cultures
- Reduced employee morale due to layoffs and relocations

TABLE 5-6   Potential Benefits of Merging With or Acquiring Another Firm

- To provide improved capacity utilization
- To make better use of the existing sales force
- To reduce managerial staff
- To gain economies of scale
- To smooth out seasonal trends in sales
- To gain access to new suppliers, distributors, customers, products, and creditors
- To gain new technology
- To reduce tax obligations

The volume of mergers completed annually worldwide is growing dramatically and exceeds $1 trillion. There are annually more than 10,000 mergers in the United States that total more than $700 billion. The proliferation of mergers is fueled by companies' drive for market share, efficiency, and pricing power, as well as by globalization, the need for greater economies of scale, reduced regulation and antitrust concerns, the Internet, and e-commerce.

A *leveraged buyout (LBO)* occurs when a corporation's shareholders are bought (hence *buyout*) by the company's management and other private investors using borrowed funds (hence *leverage*).[32] Besides trying to avoid a hostile takeover, other reasons for initiating an LBO are senior management decisions that particular divisions do not fit into an overall corporate strategy or must be sold to raise cash, or receipt of an attractive offering price. An LBO takes a corporation private.

Private-Equity Acquisitions

As stock prices increased and companies became cash-rich in 2010–2012, private-equity firms such as Kohlberg Kravis Roberts (KKR) jumped aggressively back into the business of acquiring and selling firms. Private-equity firms have unleashed a wave of new initial public offerings (IPO), such as the IPO of Nielsen Holdings BV, the largest private-equity-backed IPO in the United States in five years. Apollo Global Management is a large private-equity firm that owns many companies. Some private-equity owned firms expected to go public soon include BankUnited Inc., Kinder Morgan Inc., and Toys "R" Us Inc.

The intent of virtually all private-equity acquisitions is to buy firms at a low price and sell them later at a high price, arguably just good business. Many if not most acquisitions in 2010–2012 were by large private-investment firms. For example, 3G Capital Management acquired Burger King Holdings for about $3.3 billion. CKE Restaurants, owner of the Carl's Jr. and Hardee's burger chains, was acquired by an affiliate of Apollo Management LLC for almost $700 million. Goldman Sachs's private-equity arm acquired Apple American Group, the largest franchisee (269 restaurants) of Applebee's Neighborhood Grill and Bar based in Independence, Ohio.

First Mover Advantages

First mover advantages refer to the benefits a firm may achieve by entering a new market or developing a new product or service prior to rival firms.[33] As indicated in Table 5-7, some advantages of being a first mover include securing access to rare resources, gaining new

TABLE 5-7   Benefits of a Firm Being the First Mover

1. Secure access and commitments to rare resources
2. Gain new knowledge of critical success factors and issues
3. Gain market share and position in the best locations
4. Establish and secure long-term relationships with customers, suppliers, distributors, and investors
5. Gain customer loyalty and commitments

knowledge of key factors and issues, and carving out market share and a position that is easy to defend and costly for rival firms to overtake. First mover advantages are analogous to taking the high ground first, which puts one in an excellent strategic position to launch aggressive campaigns and to defend territory. Being the first mover can be especially wise when such actions (1) build a firm's image and reputation with buyers, (2) produce cost advantages over rivals in terms of new technologies, new components, new distribution channels, and so on, (3) create strongly loyal customers, and (4) make imitation or duplication by a rival hard or unlikely.[34]

To sustain the competitive advantage gained by being the first mover, a firm needs to be a fast learner. There are, however, risks associated with being the first mover, such as unexpected and unanticipated problems and costs that occur from being the first firm doing business in the new market. Therefore, being a slow mover (also called *fast follower* or *late mover*) can be effective when a firm can easily copy or imitate the lead firm's products or services. If technology is advancing rapidly, slow movers can often leapfrog a first mover's products with improved second-generation products. However, slow movers often are relegated to relying on the first mover being a slow mover and making strategic and tactical mistakes. This situation does not occur often, so first mover advantages clearly offset the first mover disadvantages most of the time. Apple Inc. has always been a good example of a first mover firm.

Nokia, the world's largest mobile phone maker by units, has been a late mover in the smartphone industry, following Apple, by introducing the Nokia N8 smartphone. The N8 is a sleek phone with a 12-megapixel camera and high-definition video recording feature. Also a late mover, Hewlett-Packard (H-P) introduced its first tablet computer and first smartphone in 2011, well behind Apple and Google. Apple sold 14 million iPad computers before the H-P announcement. Sales of iPads are forecasted to reach 24.1 million in 2011 and eclipse 44 million annually by 2015 according to Forrester Research.

Based in Santa Clara, California, Intel is a first mover firm in terms of introducing new production processes sooner than competitors. Intel is investing $7 billion between 2011 and 2014 to upgrade its manufacturing plants in the United States and build a new research facility in Oregon. Intel is moving beyond PCs into chips for smartphones and other products.

First mover advantages tend to be greatest when competitors are roughly the same size and possess similar resources. If competitors are not similar in size, then larger competitors can wait while others make initial investments and mistakes, and then respond with greater effectiveness and resources.

Outsourcing

Business-process outsourcing (BPO) involves companies taking over the functional operations, such as human resources, information systems, payroll, accounting, customer service, and even marketing of other firms. Companies are choosing to outsource their functional operations more and more for several reasons: (1) it is less expensive, (2) it allows the firm to focus on its core businesses, and (3) it enables the firm to provide better services. Other advantages of outsourcing are that the strategy (1) allows the firm to align itself with "best-in-world" suppliers who focus on performing the special task, (2) provides the firm flexibility should customer needs shift unexpectedly, and (3) allows the firm to concentrate on other internal value chain activities critical to sustaining competitive advantage. BPO is a means for achieving strategies that are similar to partnering and joint venturing. The worldwide BPO market exceeds $173 billion.

Many firms, such as Dearborn, Michigan–based Visteon Corp. and J.P. Morgan Chase & Co., outsource their computer operations to IBM, which competes with firms such as Electronic Data Systems and Computer Sciences Corp. in the computer outsourcing business. 3M Corp. is outsourcing all of its manufacturing operations to Flextronics International Ltd. of Singapore or Jabil Circuit in Florida. 3M is also outsourcing all design and manufacturing of low-end standardized volume products by building a new design center in Taiwan.

U.S. and European companies for more than a decade have been outsourcing their manufacturing, tech support, and back-office work, but most insisted on keeping research and development activities in-house. However, an ever-growing number of firms today are outsourcing their product design to Asian developers. China and India are becoming increasingly important suppliers of intellectual property. For companies that include Hewlett-Packard, PalmOne, Dell, Sony, Apple, Kodak, Motorola, Nokia, Ericsson, Lucent, Cisco, and Nortel, the design of personal computers and cameras is mostly outsourced to China and India.

Companies pay about $68 billion annually in outsourcing operations to other firms, but the details of what work to outsource, to whom, where, and for how much can challenge even the biggest, most sophisticated companies.[35] And some outsourcing deals do not work out, such as the J.P. Morgan Chase deal with IBM and Dow Chemical's deal with Electronic Data Systems. Both outsourcing deals were abandoned after several years. Lehman Brothers Holdings and Dell Inc. both recently reversed decisions to move customer call centers to India after a customer rebellion. India has become a booming place for outsourcing. A recent *Wall Street Journal* article reported that roughly 85 percent of all Americans believe "outsourcing of production and manufacturing work to foreign countries is a major reason the U.S. economy is struggling and more people are not being hired."[36] However, organizations that outsource are seeking to realize benefits or address the following issues:[37]

- Cost savings — Access lower wages in foreign countries.
- Focus on core business — Focus resources on developing the core business rather than being distracted by other functions.
- Cost restructuring — Outsourcing changes the balance of fixed costs to variable costs by moving the firm more to variable costs. Outsourcing also makes variable costs more predictable.
- Improve quality — Improve quality by contracting out various business functions to specialists.
- Knowledge — Gain access to intellectual property and wider experience and knowledge.
- Contract — Gain access to services within a legally binding contract with financial penalties and legal redress. This is not the case with services performed internally.
- Operational expertise — Gain access to operational best practice that would be too difficult or time consuming to develop in-house.
- Access to talent — Gain access to a larger talent pool and a sustainable source of skills, especially science and engineering.
- Catalyst for change — Use an outsourcing agreement as a catalyst for major change that cannot be achieved alone.
- Enhance capacity for innovation — Use external knowledge to supplement limited in-house capacity for product innovation.
- Reduce time to market — Accelerate development and/or production of a product through additional capability brought by the supplier.
- Risk management — Manage risk by partnering with an outside firm.
- Tax benefit — Capitalize on tax incentives to locate manufacturing plants to avoid high taxes in various countries.

Strategic Management in Nonprofit and Governmental Organizations

Nonprofit organizations are basically just like for-profit companies except for two major differences: 1) nonprofits do not pay taxes and 2) nonprofits do not have shareholders to provide capital. In virtually all other ways, nonprofits are just like for-profits. Nonprofits have competitors that want to put them out of business. Nonprofits have employees, customers, creditors, suppliers, and distributors as well as financial budgets, income statements, balance sheets, cash flow statements, and so on. Nonprofit organizations embrace strategic planning just as much as for-profit firms, and perhaps even more, since equity capital is not an alternative source of financing.

The strategic-management process is being used effectively by countless nonprofit and governmental organizations, such as the Girl Scouts, Boy Scouts, the Red Cross, chambers of commerce, educational institutions, medical institutions, public utilities, libraries, government agencies, and churches. The nonprofit sector, surprisingly, is by far America's largest employer. Many nonprofit and governmental organizations outperform private firms and corporations on innovativeness, motivation, productivity, and strategic management.

Compared to for-profit firms, nonprofit and governmental organizations may be totally dependent on outside financing. Especially for these organizations, strategic management provides an excellent vehicle for developing and justifying requests for needed financial support.

Religious Facilities

A recent *Wall Street Journal* article reveals that the number of religious facilities having to close their doors is surging as many borrowed too much and built too big during boom times.[38] Chris Macke, a real-estate strategist at CoStar, recently said, "religious organizations may be subject to the laws of God but they are also subject to the laws of economics." Religious denominations of all kinds have suffered in recent years from consumer hardships, including high unemployment and underemployment, which translates into less money in the offering plate and declining attendance.

Six states in particular had 15 or more religious facilities foreclosed upon in the 2006–2010 period: California (29), Michigan (23), Florida (23), Georgia (19), Texas (17), and Ohio (15). Religious facilities are like businesses in many ways, including: 1) they can be foreclosed upon if their finances fall into disarray, and 2) they need effective strategic planning.

Educational Institutions

Educational institutions are more frequently using strategic-management techniques and concepts. Richard Cyert, former president of Carnegie Mellon University, said, "I believe we do a far better job of strategic management than any company I know." Population shifts nationally from the Northeast and Midwest to the Southeast and West are but one factor causing trauma for educational institutions that have not planned for changing enrollments. Ivy League schools in the Northeast are recruiting more heavily in the Southeast and West. This trend represents a significant change in the competitive climate for attracting the best high school graduates each year.

Online college degrees are common place and represent a threat to traditional colleges and universities. "You can put the kids to bed and go to law school," says Andrew Rosen, chief operating officer of Kaplan Education Centers, a subsidiary of the Washington Post Company.

Many American colleges and universities have now established campuses outside the United States. For example, Yale University and the National University of Singapore will establish a joint campus in Singapore in 2013. The institution will be Singapore's first liberal-arts college and Yale's first campus outside the Ivy League institution's New Haven, Connecticut home.

Medical Organizations

The $200 billion U.S. hospital industry is experiencing declining margins, excess capacity, bureaucratic overburdening, poorly planned and executed diversification strategies, soaring health care costs, reduced federal support, and high administrator turnover. The seriousness of this problem is accented by a 20 percent annual decline in use by inpatients nationwide. Declining occupancy rates, deregulation, and accelerating growth of health maintenance organizations, preferred provider organizations, urgent care centers, outpatient surgery centers, diagnostic centers, specialized clinics, and group practices are other major threats facing hospitals today. Many private and state-supported medical institutions are in financial trouble as a result of traditionally taking a reactive rather than a proactive approach in dealing with their industry.

Hospitals—originally intended to be warehouses for people dying of tuberculosis, smallpox, cancer, pneumonia, and infectious diseases—are creating new strategies today as advances in the diagnosis and treatment of chronic diseases are undercutting that earlier mission. Hospitals are beginning to bring services to the patient as much as bringing the patient to the hospital; health care is more and more being concentrated in the home and in the residential community, not on the hospital campus. Chronic care will require day-treatment facilities, electronic monitoring at home, user-friendly ambulatory services, decentralized service networks, and laboratory testing. A successful hospital strategy for the future will require renewed and deepened collaboration with physicians, who are central to hospitals' well-being, and a reallocation of resources from acute to chronic care in home and community settings.

Current strategies being pursued by many hospitals include creating home health services, establishing nursing homes, and forming rehabilitation centers. Backward integration strategies that some hospitals are pursuing include acquiring ambulance services, waste disposal services, and diagnostic services. Millions of persons annually research medical ailments online, which is causing a dramatic shift in the balance of power between doctor, patient, and hospitals. The number of persons using the Internet to obtain medical information is skyrocketing. A motivated patient using the Internet can gain knowledge on a particular subject far beyond his or her doctor's knowledge, because no person can keep up with the results and implications of billions of dollars' worth of medical research reported weekly. Patients today often walk into the doctor's office with a file folder of the latest articles detailing research and treatment options for their ailments.

Governmental Agencies and Departments

Federal, state, county, and municipal agencies and departments, such as police departments, chambers of commerce, forestry associations, and health departments, are responsible for formulating, implementing, and evaluating strategies that use taxpayers' dollars in the most cost-effective way to provide services and programs. Strategic-management concepts are generally required and thus widely used to enable governmental organizations to be more effective and efficient.

Strategists in governmental organizations operate with less strategic autonomy than their counterparts in private firms. Public enterprises generally cannot diversify into unrelated businesses or merge with other firms. Governmental strategists usually enjoy little freedom in altering the organizations' missions or redirecting objectives. Legislators and politicians often have direct or indirect control over major decisions and resources. Strategic issues get discussed and debated in the media and legislatures. Issues become politicized, resulting in fewer strategic choice alternatives. There is now more predictability in the management of public sector enterprises.

Government agencies and departments are finding that their employees get excited about the opportunity to participate in the strategic-management process and thereby have an effect on the organization's mission, objectives, strategies, and policies. In addition, government agencies are using a strategic-management approach to develop and substantiate formal requests for additional funding.

Strategic Management in Small Firms

The reason why "becoming your own boss" has become a national obsession is that entrepreneurs are America's role models. Almost everyone wants to own a business—from teens and college students, who are signing up for entrepreneurial courses in record numbers, to those over age 65, who are forming more companies every year.

As hundreds of thousands of people have been laid off from work in the last two years, many of these individuals have started small businesses. The *Wall Street Journal* recently provided a 10-page article on how to be a successful entrepreneur.[39] Not only laid off employees but also college graduates are seeking more and more to open their own businesses.[40]

Strategic management is vital for large firms' success, but what about small firms? The strategic-management process is just as vital for small companies. From their inception, all organizations have a strategy, even if the strategy just evolves from day-to-day operations. Even if conducted informally or by a single owner/entrepreneur, the strategic-management process can significantly enhance small firms' growth and prosperity. Because an ever-increasing number of men and women in the United States are starting their own businesses, more individuals are becoming strategists. Widespread corporate layoffs have contributed to an explosion in small businesses and new ideas.

Numerous magazine and journal articles have focused on applying strategic-management concepts to small businesses. A major conclusion of these articles is that a lack of strategic-management knowledge is a serious obstacle for many small business owners. Other problems often encountered in applying strategic-management concepts to small businesses are a lack of both sufficient capital to exploit external opportunities and a day-to-day cognitive frame of reference. Research also indicates that strategic management in small firms is more informal than in large firms, but small firms that engage in strategic management outperform those that do not.

Special Note to Students

There are numerous alternative strategies that could benefit any firm, but your strategic management case analysis should result in specific recommendations that you decide will best provide the firm competitive advantages. Since company recommendations with costs comprise the most important pages/slides in your case project, introduce bits of that information early in the presentation as relevant supporting material is presented to justify your expenditures. Your recommendations page(s) itself should therefore be a summary of suggestions mentioned throughout your paper or presentation, rather than being a surprise shock to your reader or audience. You may even want to include with your recommendations insight as to why certain other feasible strategies were not chosen for implementation. That information too should be anchored in the notion of competitive advantage and disadvantage with respect to perceived costs and benefits.

Conclusion

The main appeal of any managerial approach is the expectation that it will enhance organizational performance. This is especially true of strategic management. Through involvement in strategic-management activities, managers and employees achieve a better understanding of an organization's priorities and operations. Strategic management allows organizations to be efficient, but more important, it allows them to be effective. Although strategic management does not guarantee organizational success, the process allows proactive rather than reactive decision making. Strategic management may represent a radical change in philosophy for some organizations, so strategists must be trained to anticipate and constructively respond to questions and issues as they arise. The strategies discussed in this chapter can represent a new beginning for many firms, especially if managers and employees in the organization understand and support the plan for action.

Key Terms and Concepts

Acquisition (p. 185)
Backward Integration (p. 169)
Balanced Scorecard (p. 165)
Bankruptcy (p. 176)
Business-Process Outsourcing (BPO) (p. 188)
Combination Strategy (p. 165)
Cooperative Arrangements (p. 184)
Cost Leadership (p. 178)
De-integration (p. 169)
Differentiation (p. 179)
Diversification Strategies (p. 173)
Divestiture (p. 177)
Financial Objectives (p. 163)
First Mover Advantages (p. 187)
Focus (p. 179)
Forward Integration (p. 168)
Franchising (p. 168)
Friendly Merger (p. 185)
Generic Strategies (p. 178)
Horizontal Integration (p. 170)

Hostile Takeover (p. 185)
Integration Strategies (p. 168)
Intensive Strategies (p. 171)
Joint Venture (p. 183)
Leveraged Buyout (LBO) (p. 187)
Liquidation (p. 178)
Long-Term Objectives (p. 162)
Market Development (p. 171)
Market Penetration (p. 171)
Merger (p. 185)
Product Development (p. 172)
Related Diversification (p. 173)
Retrenchment (p. 176)
Strategic Objectives (p. 163)
Takeover (p. 185)
Turbulent, High-Velocity Markets (p. 182)
Unrelated Diversification (p. 173)
Vertical Integration (p. 168)
White Knight (p. 186)

Issues for Review and Discussion

1. For Procter & Gamble (P&G) featured at the beginning of the chapter, give a hypothetical strategy for each of the following categories: market penetration, related diversification, divestiture, and retrenchment.

2. For P&G featured at the beginning of the chapter, give a hypothetical strategy for each of the following categories: market development, unrelated diversification, backward integration, and product development.

3. Identify five situations when forward integration is a particularly good strategy.
4. What three strategies defined in the chapter do you feel are most widely used by small businesses?
5. Should non-profit organizations post their strategic plan on their website? What about corporations? Why?
6. Give some guidelines of when divestiture is a particularly effective strategy.
7. For Adidas, what two strategies do you feel is best for that company to pursue going forward? Why?
8. Give some examples of Type 4 and Type 5 focus strategies according to Porter's generic strategy approach.
9. List three industries when cooperation among competitors is most likely and explain why.
10. Do a Google search on joint ventures. What important new concepts did you learn that were not presented in the chapter?
11. Identify three joint ventures that have worked especially well in the past.
12. List four important reasons why many mergers and acquisitions fail.
13. Explain how strategic management differs in governmental organizations as compared to educational institutions.
14. Explain how and why P&G has been so successful in recent years.
15. List six characteristics of objectives and an example of each.
16. In order of importance, rank six major benefits of a firm having objectives.
17. Give a hypothetical example of forward integration, backward integration, and horizontal integration for Volkswagen.
18. Give a hypothetical example of market penetration, market development, and product development for Toyota Motors.
19. Give a hypothetical example of related diversification and an example of unrelated diversification for Google.
20. Give a hypothetical example of retrenchment and divestiture for Wal-Mart.
21. When would market development generally be the preferred strategy over backward or forward integration?
22. Why can firms generally not pursue several or many of the strategies presented in this chapter?
23. When should a firm diversify?
24. List and describe the five types of bankruptcy. If your college or university had to declare bankruptcy, which type would be appropriate?
25. Explain why you believe some analysts consider Michael Porter's generic strategies to be too few and too vague.
26. Explain the difference between joint ventures and partnerships as a means for achieving various strategies.
27. List the pros and cons of a hostile versus friendly takeover of another firm.
28. In order of importance, list six reasons why many mergers and acquisitions fail.
29. In order of importance, list six potential benefits of two firms merging.
30. Give three hypothetical examples of firms being a "first mover."
31. List three ways a country could prevent its companies from outsourcing jobs to other countries.
32. Explain how strategic planning differs across types and sizes of firms.
33. Identify three local businesses in your city. What three strategies do these three firms pursue? List the strategies in order of prevalence.
34. What strategies are best for turbulent, high-velocity markets?
35. Based on the information given for P&G, what three strategies are being pursued by the firm?
36. Elaborate on this chapter's "Special Note to Students" at the end, in terms of giving a case analysis presentation.
37. Identify three companies that use outsourcing effectively and explain how and why those firms utilize this management approach.

Notes

1. John Byrne, "Strategic Planning—It's Back," *BusinessWeek*, August 26, 1996, 46.
2. Steven C. Brandt, *Strategic Planning in Emerging Companies* (Reading, MA: Addison-Wesley, 1981). Reprinted with permission of the publisher.
3. R. Kaplan and D. Norton, "Putting the Balanced Scorecard to Work," *Harvard Business Review*, September–October, 1993, 147.
4. F. Hansen and M. Smith, "Crisis in Corporate America: The Role of Strategy," *Business Horizons* (January–February 2003, 9.
5. Adapted from F. R. David, "How Do We Choose Among Alternative Growth Strategies?" *Managerial Planning* 33, no. 4 (January–February 1985): 14–17, 22.
6. Ibid.
7. Kenneth Davidson, "Do Megamergers Make Sense?" *Journal of Business Strategy* 7, no. 3 (Winter 1987): 45.
8. David, "How Do We Choose."
9. Ibid.
10. Ibid.
11. Bruce Horovitz, "Marketing Trends Popping Up in 2011," *USA Today*, January 24, 2011, B1–B2.
12. Bruce Horovitz, "Marketing Trends Popping Up in 2011," *USA Today*, January 24, 2011, B1–B2.
13. David, "How Do we Choose."
14. Arthur Thompson Jr., A. J. Strickland III, and John Gamble, *Crafting and Executing Strategy: Text and Readings* (New York: McGraw-Hill/Irwin, 2005, 241.

15. Michael E. Porter, *Competitive Strategy: Techniques for Analyzing Industries and Competitors* (New York: Free Press, 1980, 53–57, 318–319.
16. Sheila Muto, "Seeing a Boost, Hospitals Turn to Retail Stores," *Wall Street Journal*, November 7, 2001, B1, B8.
17. David, "How Do We Choose."
18. Ibid.
19. Ibid.
20. Ibid.
21. Michael Porter, *Competitive Advantage* (New York: Free Press, 1985), 97. Also, Arthur Thompson Jr., A. J. Strickland III, and John Gamble, *Crafting and Executing Strategy: Text and Readings* (New York: McGraw-Hill/Irwin, 2005), 117.
22. Arthur Thompson Jr., A. J. Strickland III, and John Gamble, *Crafting and Executing Strategy: Text and Readings* (New York: McGraw-Hill/Irwin, 2005), 125–126.
23. Porter, *Competitive Advantage,* 160–162.
24. Thompson, Strickland, and Gamble, 129–130.
25. Ibid., 134.
26. Gary Hamel, Yves Doz, and C. K. Prahalad, "Collaborate with Your Competitors—and Win," *Harvard Business Review* 67, no. 1 (January–February 1989): 133.
27. Scott Morrison, "Facebook, Skype Ponder Alliance," *Wall Street Journal*, September 30, 2010, B4.
28. Kathryn Rudie Harrigan, "Joint Ventures: Linking for a Leap Forward," *Planning Review* 14, no. 4 (July–August 1986): 10.
29. Matthew Schifrin, "Partner or Perish," *Forbes* (May 21, 2001): 26.
30. Ibid., 28.
31. Ibid., 32.
32. Steven Rattner, "Mergers: Windfalls or Pitfalls?" *Wall Street Journal*, October 11, 1999, A22; Nikhil Deogun, "Merger Wave Spurs More Stock Wipeouts," *Wall Street Journal*, November 29, 1999, C1.
33. Joel Millman, "Mexican Mergers/Acquisitions Triple from 2001," *Wall Street Journal*, December 27, 2002, A2.
34. Robert Davis, "Net Empowering Patients," *USA Today*, July 14, 1999, 1A.
35. M. J. Gannon, K. G. Smith, and C. Grimm, "An Organizational Information-Processing Profile of First Movers," *Journal of Business Research* 25 (1992): 231–241; M. B. Lieberman and D. B. Montgomery, "First Mover Advantages," *Strategic Management Journal* 9 (Summer 1988): 41–58.
36. Scott Thurm, "Behind Outsourcing: Promise and Pitfalls," *Wall Street Journal*, February 26, 2007, B3.
37. Louise Radnofsky and Jim Carlton, "Recession-Weary Americans Sour on Free Trade," *Wall Street Journal*, October 4, 2010, A2.
38. http://en.wikipedia.org/wiki/Outsourcing. Also, R. Gareiss, "Analyzing The Outsourcers," *Information Week*, Nov. 18, 2002; D.W. Drezner, "The Outsourcing Bogeyman," 2004, www.foreignaffairs.org; P. Engardio, (2006). "Outsourcing: Job Killer or Innovation Boost?" *Business Week*, 2006; Justin Chakma, Jeff L. Calcagno, Ali Behbahani, and Shawn Moitahedian, "Is it Virtuous to be Virtual? The VC Viewpoint." *Nature Biotechnology* 27, no. 10 (October 2009).
39. Shelly Banjo, "Churches Find End is Nigh," *Wall Street Journal*, January 25, 2011, A3.
40. Kelly Spors, "So, You Want to Be an Entrepreneur," *Wall Street Journal*, February 28, 2009, R1.

Current Readings

Adegbesan, J. Adetunji, and Matthew J. Higgins. "The Intra-Alliance of Value Created Through Collaboration." *Strategic Management Journal* 32, no. 2 (February 2011): 187–211.

Bruton, Garry D., Igor Filatotchev, Salim Chahine, and Mike Wright. "Governance, Ownership Structure, and Performance of IPO Firms: The Impact of Different Types of Private Equity Investors and Institutional Environments." *Strategic Management Journal* 31, no. 5 (May 2010): 491–509.

Cedergren, Stefan, Anders Wall, and Christer Norstrom. "Evaluation of Performance in a Product Development Context." *Business Horizons* 53, no. 4 (July–August 2010): 359–370.

Combs, James G., David J. Ketchen Jr., Christopher L. Shook, and Jeremy C. Short. "Antecedents and Consequences of Franchising: Past Accomplishments and Future Challenges." *Journal of Management* 37, no. 1 (January 2011): 99–126.

Datta, Deepak K., James P. Guthrie, Dynah Basuil, and Alankrita Pandey. "Causes and Effects of Employee Downsizing: A Review and Synthesis." *Journal of Management* 36, no. 1 (January 2010): 281–348.

David, Parthiban, Jonathan P. O'Brien, Toru Yoshikawa, and Andrew Delios. "Do Shareholders or Stakeholders Appropriate the Rents from Corporate Diversification? The Influence of Ownership Structure." *The Academy of Management Journal* 53, no. 3 (June 2010): 636–648.

Graebner, Melissa E., Kathleen M. Eisenhardt, and Philip T. Roundy. "Success and Failure in Technology Acquisitions: Lessons for Buyers and Sellers." *The Academy of Management Perspectives* 24, no. 3 (August 2010): 73–92.

Kaplan, Robert S., David P. Norton, and Bjarne Rugelsjoen. "Managing Alliances with the Balanced Scorecard." *Harvard Business Review*, January–February 2010, 114–124.

Kumar, M. V. Shyam. "Are Joint Ventures Positive Sum Games? The Relative Effects of Cooperative and Noncooperative Behavior." *Strategic Management Journal* 32, no. 1 (January 2011): 32–54.

Lee, Gwendolyn K., and Marvin Lieberman. "Acquisition vs. Internal Development As Modes of Market Entry." *Strategic Management Journal* 31, no. 2 (February 2010): 140–158.

Lansiluoto, Aapo, and Marko Jarvenpaa. "Greening the Balanced Scorecard." *Business Horizons* 53, no. 4 (July–August 2010): 385–396.

Martin, John A., and Kevin J. Davis. "Learning of Hubris? Why CEOs Create Less Value in Successive Acquisitions." *The Academy of Management Perspectives* 24, no. 1 (February 2010): 79.

Rawley, Evan. "Diversification, Coordination Costs, and Organizational Rigidity: Evidence From Microdata." *Strategic Management Journal* 31, no. 8 (August 2010): 873–891.

Reitzig, Markus, and Stefan Wagner. "The Hidden Costs of Outsourcing: Evidence From Patent Data." *Strategic Management Journal* 31, no. 11 (November 2010): 1183–1201.

Salomon, Robert, and Byungchae Jin. "Do Leading or Lagging Firms Learn More From Exporting?" *Strategic Management Journal* 31, no. 10 (October 2010): 1088–1113.

Siegel, Donald S., and Kenneth L. Simons. "Assessing the Effects of Mergers and Acquisitions on Firm Performance, Plant Productivity, and Workers: New Evidence From Matched Employer-Employee Data." *Strategic Management Journal* 31, no. 8 (August 2010): 903–916.

Upson, John W., and Annette L. Ranft. "When Strategies Collide: Divergent Multipoint Strategies Within Competitive Triads." *Business Horizons* 53, no. 1 (January–February 2010): 49–58.

Yu, Jifeng, Brett Anitra Gilbert, and Benjamin M. Oviatt. "Effects of Alliances, Time, and Network Cohesion on the Initiation of Foreign Sales by New Ventures." *Strategic Management Journal* 32, no. 4 (April 2011): 424–446.

Wassmer, Ulrich. "Alliance Portfolios: A Review and Research Agenda." *Journal of Management* 36, no. 1 (January 2010): 141–171.

Wassmer, Ulrich, Pierre Dussauge, and Marcel Planellas. "How to Manage Alliances Better Than One at a Time." *MIT Sloan Management Review* 51, no. 3 (Spring 2010): 77–84.

ASSURANCE OF LEARNING EXERCISES

Assurance of Learning Exercise 5A

Market Development: Procter & Gamble (P&G)

Purpose

P&G is featured in the opening chapter case as a firm that engages in excellent strategic planning. P&G's net sales grew 10 percent to $20.9 billion in the fourth quarter of 2011 and 5 percent to $82.6 billion for fiscal 2011. Unit volume of P&G products was up 3 percent in the fourth quarter of 2011 and 6 percent for the fiscal year, where volume grew in all business segments, all geographic regions, and in 15 of 17 key countries. P&G products are available in North America, Latin America, Europe, the Middle East, Africa, Asia, Australia and New Zealand. The company owns 31 factories in China.

The purpose of this exercise is to give you practice extending a company's global strategy into new geographic regions.

Instructions

Step 1	Visit the P&G website and review the company's latest *Form 10K*. Especially assess where and in what respect does P&G do business in Asia, Australia, and the Middle East. Identify six countries that P&G currently does not do business with.
Step 2	Based on your analysis in Step 1, evaluate the six countries identified in terms of their business culture, environment, and attractiveness for P&G to begin doing business there.
Step 3	Rank order the six countries identified and evaluated in terms of a proposed plan for P&G to begin doing business in these places. Prepare a two-page executive summary to support your suggested plan.

Assurance of Learning 5B

Alternative Strategies for P&G

Purpose

P&G is the world's top producer of household products. Two dozen P&G brands are global, billion-dollar sellers, including Febreze, Fusion, Always, Braun, Bounty, Charmin, Crest, Downy, Gillette, Mach3, Iams, Olay, Pampers, Pantene, Gain, and Wella, Head & Shoulders, among others. P&G has manufacturing operations in 80 countries and P&G brands are sold in more than 180 countries worldwide. In 2011, P&G made $82.6 billion in sales. P&G is featured in the opening chapter case as a firm that engages in excellent strategic planning.

This exercise will give you practice labeling hypothetical strategies that a firm could pursue.

Instruction

For each of the strategies listed below, identify a hypothetical strategy that you believe may be good for P&G to pursue. Refer to Chapter 5 for a description of the strategies.

Forward Integration
Backward Integration
Horizontal Integration
Market Penetration
Market Development
Product Development
Related Diversification
Unrelated Diversification
Retrenchment
Divestiture
Liquidation

Assurance of Learning Exercise 5C

Private-Equity Acquisitions

Purpose

As stock prices increase and companies become more cash-rich, private-equity firms such as Kohlberg Kravis Roberts (KKR) have jumped aggressively back into the business of acquiring and selling firms. Private-equity firms have unleashed a wave of new initial public offerings (IPO), such as the IPO of Nielsen Holdings BV, the largest private-equity-backed IPO in the United States in five years. Apollo Global Management is a large private-equity firms that owns many companies. Some private-equity owned firms expected to go public soon include Bank United Inc., Kinder Morgan Inc., and Toys "R" Us Inc.

The purpose of this exercise is to give you practice identifying and evaluating the nature and role of private-equity acquisitions in Europe.

Instructions

Step 1	Identify the top five IPO's in Europe in the last 12 months.
Step 2	Identify the top five private-equity firms in Europe.
Step 3	Prepare a two-page executive summary of the nature and role of private-equity acquisitions in Europe in the last 12 months. Include your expectations over the next 12 months for this activity to increase or decrease across Europe. Give supporting rationales.

Assurance of Learning Exercise 5D

Adidas AG: 2011–2013

Purpose

In performing strategic management case analysis, you can find information about the company's actual and planned strategies. Comparing what is planned versus what you recommend is an important part of case analysis. Do not recommend what the firm actually plans, unless in-depth analysis of the situation reveals those strategies to be the best among all feasible alternatives. This exercise gives you experience conducting library and Internet research to determine what Adidas AG plans to do in 2011–2013.

Instructions

Step 1   Go to Reebok's and TaylorMade's websites. Find some recent articles about these subsidiaries and the parent—Adidas AG. Review Adidas' website also.

Step 2   Prepare a three-page report titled "Strategies Being Pursued By Adidas in 2011–2013."

Assurance of Learning Exercise 5E

Lessons in Doing Business Globally

Purpose

The purpose of this exercise is to discover some important lessons learned by local businesses that do business internationally.

Instruction

Contact several local business leaders by telephone. Find at least three firms that engage in international or export operations. Visit the owner or manager of each business in person. Ask the business person to give you several important lessons that his or her firm has learned in globally doing business. Record the lessons on paper and report your findings to the class.

Assurance of Learning Exercise 5F

Procter & Gamble (P&G): 2011–2013

Purpose

In performing strategic management case analysis, you should find information about the company's actual and planned strategies. Comparing what is planned versus what you recommend is an important part of case analysis. Do not recommend what the firm actually plans, unless in-depth analysis of the situation reveals those strategies to be the best among all feasible alternatives. This exercise gives you experience conducting library and Internet research to determine what P&G plans to do in 2011–2013.

Instructions

Step 1   Go to the P&G web site. Study the information provided there.

Step 2   Prepare a three-page report titled "Strategies Being Pursued by P&G in 2011–2013."

Assurance of Learning Exercise 5G

What Strategies Are Most Risky?

Purpose

This exercise encourages you to think about the relative riskiness of various strategies.

Instructions

Step 1   List the strategies defined in Chapter 5 in order of low risk to high risk.
Step 2   Write a synopsis that explains your rankings.

Assurance of Learning Exercise 5H

Exploring Bankruptcy

Purpose

Bankruptcy is becoming more and more common among business firms. This exercise is designed to enhance your knowledge of bankruptcy.

Instruction

Identify five firms in your country that are operating under bankruptcy. Compare and contrast the nature of the bankruptcy among these firms.

Assurance of Learning Exercise 5I

Examining Strategy Articles

Purpose

Strategy articles can be found weekly in journals, magazines, and newspapers. By reading and studying strategy articles, you can gain a better understanding of the strategic management process. Several of the best journals in which to find corporate strategy articles are: *Advanced Management Journal, Business Horizons, Long Range Planning, Journal of Business Strategy*, and *Strategic Management Journal*. These journals are devoted to reporting the results of empirical research in management. They apply strategic management concepts to specific organizations and industries. They introduce new strategic management techniques and provide short case studies on selected firms.

Other good journals in which to find strategic management articles are *Harvard Business Review, Sloan Management Review, California Management Review, Academy of Management Review, Academy of Management Journal, Academy of Management Executive, Journal of Management*, and *Journal of Small Business Management*.

In addition to journals, many magazines regularly publish articles that focus on business strategies. Several of the best magazines in which to find applied strategy articles are: *Dun's Business Month, Fortune, Forbes, BusinessWeek, Inc*, and *Industry Week*. Newspapers such as *USA Today, Wall Street Journal, New York Times*, and *Barrons* cover strategy events when they occur—for example, a joint venture announcement, a bankruptcy declaration, a new advertising campaign start, acquisition of a company, divestiture of a division, a chief executive officer's hiring or firing, or a hostile takeover attempt.

In combination, journal, magazine, and newspaper articles can make the strategic management course more exciting. These sources provide information about the strategies of for-profit and non-profit organizations.

Instructions

Step 1   Go to your college library and find a recent journal article that focuses on a strategic management topic. Select your article from one of the journals listed previously, not from a magazine. Copy the article and bring it to class.

Step 2   Give a three-minute oral report summarizing the most important information in your article. Include comments giving your personal reaction to the article. Pass your article around in class.

Assurance of Learning Exercise 5J

Classifying Some Strategies

Purpose

This exercise can improve your understanding of various strategies by giving you experience classifying strategies. This skill will help you use the strategy-formulation tools presented later. Consider the following 12 (actual or possible) strategies by various firms:

1. Dunkin' Donuts is increasing the number of its U.S. stores from 5,500 to 15,000.
2. Brown-Forman Corp. sold its Hartmann luggage and leather-goods business.
3. Motorola, which makes TVs, acquired Terayon Communication, a supplier of TV equipment.
4. Macy's department stores is adding bistros and Starbucks coffee shops at many of its stores.
5. Dell just allowed Wal-Mart to begin selling its computers. This was its first move away from direct mail order selling of computers.
6. Motorola cut 7,500 additional jobs.
7. Hilton Hotels is building 55 new properties in Russia, the United Kingdom, and Central America.
8. Video-sharing website YouTube launched its services into nine new countries.
9. Cadbury Schweppes PLC is slashing 7,500 jobs, shedding product variations, and closing factories globally.
10. General Electric sold its plastics division for $11.6 million to Saudi Basic Industries Corp. of Saudi Arabia.
11. Cadbury Schweppes PLC, the maker of Trident gum, just bought Turkish gum maker Intergum.
12. Limited Brands is selling its Express and Limited divisions to focus on its Victoria's Secret and Bath & Body Works divisions.

Instructions

Step 1   On a separate sheet of paper, write down numbers 1 to 12. These numbers correspond to the strategies described.

Step 2   What type of strategy best describes the 12 actions cited? Indicate your answers.

Step 3   Exchange papers with a classmate, and grade each other's paper as your instructor gives the right answers.

"NOTABLE QUOTES"

"Strategic management is not a box of tricks or a bundle of techniques. It is analytical thinking and commitment of resources to action. But quantification alone is not planning. Some of the most important issues in strategic management cannot be quantified at all."
—*Peter Drucker*

"Objectives are not commands; they are commitments. They do not determine the future; they are the means to mobilize resources and energies of an organization for the making of the future."
—*Peter Drucker*

"Life is full of lousy options."
—*General P. X. Kelley*

"When a crisis forces choosing among alternatives, most people will choose the worst possible one."
—*Rudin's Law*

"Strategy isn't something you can nail together in slapdash fashion by sitting around a conference table."
—*Terry Haller*

"Planning is often doomed before it ever starts, either because too much is expected of it or because not enough is put into it."
—*T. J. Cartwright*

"Whether it's broke or not, fix it—make it better. Not just products, but the whole company if necessary."
—*Bill Saporito*

Strategy Analysis and Choice

CHAPTER OBJECTIVES

After studying this chapter, you should be able to do the following:

1. Describe a three-stage framework for choosing among alternative strategies.

2. Explain how to develop a SWOT Matrix, SPACE Matrix, BCG Matrix, IE Matrix, and QSPM.

3. Identify important behavioral, political, ethical, and social responsibility considerations in strategy analysis and choice.

4. Discuss the role of intuition in strategic analysis and choice.

5. Discuss the role of organizational culture in strategic analysis and choice.

6. Discuss the role of a board of directors in choosing among alternative strategies.

ASSURANCE OF LEARNING EXERCISES

Assurance of Learning Exercise 6A
Should the Coca-Cola Company (TCCC) Penetrate Russia Further?

Assurance of Learning Exercise 6B
Perform a SWOT Analysis for TCCC's Global Operations

Assurance of Learning Exercise 6C
Preparing a BCG Matrix for TCCC

Assurance of Learning Exercise 6D
Developing a SWOT Matrix for Adidas AG

Assurance of Learning Exercise 6E
Developing a SPACE Matrix for Adidas AG

Assurance of Learning Exercise 6F
Developing a BCG Matrix for Adidas AG

Assurance of Learning Exercise 6G
Developing a QSPM for Adidas AG

Assurance of Learning Exercise 6H
Developing a SWOT Matrix for TCCC

Assurance of Learning Exercise 6I
Developing a SPACE Matrix for TCCC

Assurance of Learning Exercise 6J
Developing a BCG Matrix for your College or University

Assurance of Learning Exercise 6K
Developing a QSPM for a Company that You Are Familiar With

Assurance of Learning Exercise 6L
Formulating Individual Strategies

Assurance of Learning Exercise 6M
The Mach Test

Strategy analysis and choice largely involve making subjective decisions based on objective information. This chapter introduces important concepts that can help strategists generate feasible alternatives, evaluate those alternatives, and choose a specific course of action. Behavioral aspects of strategy formulation are described, including politics, culture, ethics, and social responsibility considerations. Modern tools for formulating strategies are described, and the appropriate role of a board of directors is discussed. The Coca-Cola Company (TCCC) is an example company that for many years has exemplified excellent strategic management.

The Nature of Strategy Analysis and Choice

As indicated by Figure 6-1, this chapter focuses on generating and evaluating alternative strategies, as well as selecting strategies to pursue. Strategy analysis and choice seek to determine alternative courses of action that could best enable the firm to achieve its mission and objectives. The firm's present strategies, objectives, and mission, coupled with the external and internal audit information, provide a basis for generating and evaluating feasible alternative strategies.

Excellent Strategic Management Showcased

THE COCA-COLA COMPANY (TCCC)

Headquartered in Atlanta, Georgia, TCCC is the world's largest global manufacturer, retailer, and marketer of non-alcoholic beverage concentrates and syrups. TCCC has operated using excellent strategic management for many decades. In addition to the famous Coca-Cola and Diet Coke beverages, TCCC offers more than 500 brands in over 200 countries or territories and serves over 1.6 billion servings each day.

TCCC owns four of the top five soft-drink brands in the world: Coca-Cola, Diet Coke, Fanta, and Sprite. Other major TCCC brands include Minute Maid, Powerade, and Dasani water. In North America it sells Groupe Danone's Evian mineral water. The company also sells brands from rival Dr. Pepper Snapple Group (Crush, Dr. Pepper, and Schweppes) outside Australia, Europe, and North America. TCCC makes or licenses more than 3,500 drinks for sale in 200-plus countries. In late 2010, TCCC bought out its leading bottler, Coca-Cola Enterprises (CCE), and renamed it Coca-Cola Refreshments USA.

TCCC and partner Coca-Cola Hellenic will spend $3 billion over the next five years to boost growth in Russia. TCCC in late 2011 opened a new $120 million Coca-Cola plant in the Rostov region— the company's 15th plant in Russia. Rostov is in southwest Russia near the Black Sea. The $3 billion commitment includes new infrastructure, brand building, and sustainability programs.

Coca-Cola Femsa SAB, Latin America's largest Coke bottler, now accounts for half of Mexico's Coca-Cola sales after buying the bottling operations of Grupo Cimsa for 11 billion pesos ($837 million) in stock and assumed debt. The acquisition of Cimsa, a closely held company that sells Coca-Cola products mostly in the central states near Morelos,

marks the second transaction this year in which Coca-Cola Femsa offered shares instead of cash.

In September 2011, TCCC opened its first concentrate manufacturing plant in Singapore to supply the Asia-Pacific region. For the second quarter of 2011, TCCC reported that worldwide volume grew 6 percent in both the quarter and year-to-date. TCCC achieved broad-based volume growth in the quarter across each of their five geographic operating groups, with growth of 7 percent in Eurasia and Africa, 7 percent in Pacific, 6 percent in Latin America, 5 percent in Europe, and 4 percent in North America. TCCC also reported an overall 5 percent growth in sparkling beverages, with worldwide brand Coca-Cola volume growth of 4 percent in the quarter driven by a number of global markets, including 24 percent growth in China, 17 percent in Russia, 7 percent in Mexico, 7 percent in France, 6 percent in Germany, and 2 percent in Japan.

Source: Based on information at www.thecoca-colacompany.com.

FIGURE 6-1

A Comprehensive Strategic-Management Model

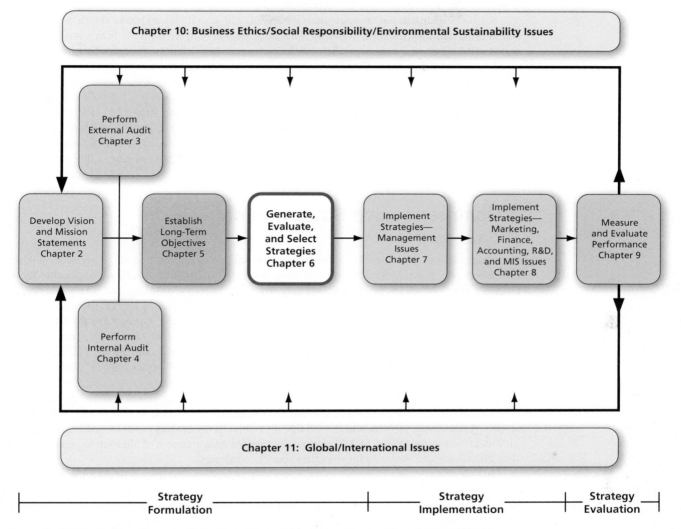

Source: Fred R. David, "How Companies Define Their Mission," *Long Range Planning* 22, no. 3 (June 1988): 40.

Unless a desperate situation confronts the firm, alternative strategies will likely represent incremental steps that move the firm from its present position to a desired future position. Alternative strategies do not come out of the wild blue yonder; they are derived from the firm's vision, mission, objectives, external audit, and internal audit; they are consistent with, or build on, past strategies that have worked well.

The Process of Generating and Selecting Strategies

Strategists never consider all feasible alternatives that could benefit the firm because there are an infinite number of possible actions and an infinite number of ways to implement those actions. Therefore, a manageable set of the most attractive alternative strategies must be developed. The advantages, disadvantages, trade-offs, costs, and benefits of these strategies should be determined. This section discusses the process that many firms use to determine an appropriate set of alternative strategies.

Identifying and evaluating alternative strategies should involve many of the managers and employees who earlier assembled the organizational vision and mission statements, performed the external audit, and conducted the internal audit. Representatives from each department and division of the firm should be included in this process, as was the case in previous strategy-formulation activities. Recall that involvement provides the best opportunity for managers and employees to gain an understanding of what the firm is doing and why and to become committed to helping the firm accomplish its objectives.

All participants in the strategy analysis and choice activity should have the firm's external and internal audit information available. This information, coupled with the firm's mission statement, will help participants crystallize in their own minds particular strategies that they believe could benefit the firm most. Creativity should be encouraged in this thought process.

Alternative strategies proposed by participants should be considered and discussed in a meeting or series of meetings. Proposed strategies should be listed in writing. When all feasible strategies identified by participants are given and understood, the strategies should be ranked in order of attractiveness by all participants, with 1 = should not be implemented, 2 = possibly should be implemented, 3 = probably should be implemented, and 4 = definitely should be implemented. This process will result in a prioritized list of best strategies that reflects the collective wisdom of the group.

A Comprehensive Strategy-Formulation Framework

Important strategy-formulation techniques can be integrated into a three-stage decision-making framework, as shown in Figure 6-2. The tools presented in this framework are applicable to all sizes and types of organizations and can help strategists identify, evaluate, and select strategies.

Stage 1 of the formulation framework consists of the EFE Matrix, the IFE Matrix, and the Competitive Profile Matrix (CPM). Called the *Input Stage,* Stage 1 summarizes the basic input information needed to formulate strategies. Stage 2, called the *Matching Stage,* focuses upon generating feasible alternative strategies by aligning key external and internal factors. Stage 2 techniques include the Strengths-Weaknesses-Opportunities-Threats (SWOT) Matrix, the Strategic Position and Action Evaluation (SPACE) Matrix, the Boston Consulting Group (BCG) Matrix, the Internal-External (IE) Matrix, and the Grand Strategy Matrix. Stage 3, called the *Decision Stage,* involves a single technique, the Quantitative Strategic Planning Matrix (QSPM). A QSPM uses input information from Stage 1 to objectively evaluate feasible alternative strategies identified in Stage 2. A QSPM reveals the relative attractiveness of alternative strategies and thus provides objective basis for selecting specific strategies.

All nine techniques included in the *strategy-formulation framework* require the integration of intuition and analysis. Autonomous divisions in an organization commonly use strategy-formulation techniques to develop strategies and objectives. Divisional analyses provide a basis for identifying, evaluating, and selecting among alternative corporate-level strategies.

FIGURE 6-2

The Strategy-Formulation Analytical Framework

STAGE 1: THE INPUT STAGE		
External Factor Evaluation (EFE) Matrix	Competitive Profile Matrix (CPM)	Internal Factor Evaluation (IFE) Matrix

STAGE 2: THE MATCHING STAGE				
Strengths-Weaknesses-Opportunities-Threats (SWOT) Matrix	Strategic Position and Action Evaluation (SPACE) Matrix	Boston Consulting Group (BCG) Matrix	Internal-External (IE) Matrix	Grand Strategy Matrix

STAGE 3: THE DECISION STAGE
Quantitative Strategic Planning Matrix (QSPM)

Strategists themselves, not analytic tools, are always responsible and accountable for strategic decisions. Lenz emphasized that the shift from a words-oriented to a numbers-oriented planning process can give rise to a false sense of certainty; it can reduce dialogue, discussion, and argument as a means for exploring understandings, testing assumptions, and fostering organizational learning.[1] Strategists, therefore, must be wary of this possibility and use analytical tools to facilitate, rather than to diminish, communication. Without objective information and analysis, personal biases, politics, emotions, personalities, and *halo error* (the tendency to put too much weight on a single factor) unfortunately may play a dominant role in the strategy-formulation process.

The Input Stage

Procedures for developing an EFE Matrix, an IFE Matrix, and a CPM were presented in Chapters 3 and 4. The information derived from these three matrices provides basic input information for the matching and decision stage matrices described later in this chapter.

The input tools require strategists to quantify subjectivity during early stages of the strategy-formulation process. Making small decisions in the input matrices regarding the relative importance of external and internal factors allows strategists to more effectively generate and evaluate alternative strategies. Good intuitive judgment is always needed in determining appropriate weights and ratings.

The Matching Stage

Strategy is sometimes defined as the match an organization makes between its internal resources and skills and the opportunities and risks created by its external factors.[2] The matching stage of the strategy-formulation framework consists of five techniques that can be used in any sequence: the SWOT Matrix, the SPACE Matrix, the BCG Matrix, the IE Matrix, and the Grand Strategy Matrix. These tools rely upon information derived from the input stage to match external opportunities and threats with internal strengths and weaknesses. *Matching* external and internal critical success factors is the key to effectively generating feasible alternative strategies. For example, a firm with excess working capital (an internal strength) could take advantage of the cell phone industry's 20 percent annual growth rate (an external opportunity) by acquiring Cellfone, Inc., a firm in the cell phone industry. This example portrays simple one-to-one matching. In most situations, external and internal relationships are more complex, and the matching requires multiple alignments for each strategy generated. The basic concept of matching is illustrated in Table 6-1.

Any organization, whether military, product-oriented, service-oriented, governmental, or even athletic, must develop and execute good strategies to win. A good offense without a good defense, or vice versa, usually leads to defeat. Developing strategies that use strengths to capitalize on opportunities could be considered an offense, whereas strategies designed to improve upon weaknesses while avoiding threats could be termed defensive. Every organization has some external opportunities and threats and internal strengths and weaknesses that can be aligned to formulate feasible alternative strategies.

TABLE 6-1   Matching Key External and Internal Factors to Formulate Alternative Strategies

Key Internal Factor	Key External Factor	Resultant Strategy
Excess working capital (an internal strength)	+ 20 percent annual growth in the cell phone industry (an external opportunity)	= Acquire Cellfone, Inc.
Insufficient capacity (an internal weakness)	+ Exit of two major foreign competitors from the industry (an external opportunity)	= Pursue horizontal integration by buying competitors' facilities
Strong R&D expertise (an internal strength)	+ Decreasing numbers of younger adults (an external threat)	= Develop new products for older adults
Poor employee morale (an internal weakness)	+ Rising health care costs (an external threat)	= Develop a new wellness program

The *Strengths-Weaknesses-Opportunities-Threats (SWOT) Matrix* is an important matching tool that helps managers develop four types of strategies: SO (strengths-opportunities) Strategies, WO (weaknesses-opportunities) Strategies, ST (strengths-threats) Strategies, and WT (weaknesses-threats) Strategies.[3] Matching key external and internal factors is the most difficult part of developing a SWOT Matrix and requires good judgment—and there is no one best set of matches. Note in Table 6-1 that the first, second, third, and fourth strategies are SO, WO, ST, and WT strategies, respectively.

SO Strategies use a firm's internal strengths to take advantage of external opportunities. All managers would like their organizations to be in a position in which internal strengths can be used to take advantage of external trends and events. Organizations generally will pursue WO, ST, or WT strategies to get into a situation in which they can apply SO Strategies. When a firm has major weaknesses, it will strive to overcome them and make them strengths. When an organization faces major threats, it will seek to avoid them to concentrate on opportunities.

WO Strategies aim at improving internal weaknesses by taking advantage of external opportunities. Sometimes key external opportunities exist, but a firm has internal weaknesses that prevent it from exploiting those opportunities. For example, there may be a high demand for electronic devices to control the amount and timing of fuel injection in automobile engines (opportunity), but a certain auto parts manufacturer may lack the technology required for producing these devices (weakness). One possible WO Strategy would be to acquire this technology by forming a joint venture with a firm having competency in this area. An alternative WO Strategy would be to hire and train people with the required technical capabilities.

ST Strategies use a firm's strengths to avoid or reduce the impact of external threats. This does not mean that a strong organization should always meet threats in the external environment head-on. An example ST Strategy occurred when Texas Instruments used an excellent legal department (a strength) to collect nearly $700 million in damages and royalties from nine Japanese and Korean firms that infringed on patents for semiconductor memory chips (threat). Rival firms that copy ideas, innovations, and patented products are a major threat in many industries. This is still a major problem for U.S. firms selling products in China.

WT Strategies are defensive tactics directed at reducing internal weakness and avoiding external threats. An organization faced with numerous external threats and internal weaknesses may indeed be in a precarious position. In fact, such a firm may have to fight for its survival, merge, retrench, declare bankruptcy, or choose liquidation.

A schematic representation of the SWOT Matrix is provided in Figure 6-3. Note that a SWOT Matrix is composed of nine cells. As shown, there are four key factor cells, four strategy cells, and one cell that is always left blank (the upper-left cell). The four strategy cells, labeled *SO, WO, ST,* and *WT,* are developed after completing four key factor cells, labeled *S, W, O,* and *T.* There are eight steps involved in constructing a SWOT Matrix:

1. List the firm's key external opportunities.
2. List the firm's key external threats.
3. List the firm's key internal strengths.
4. List the firm's key internal weaknesses.
5. Match internal strengths with external opportunities, and record the resultant SO Strategies in the appropriate cell.
6. Match internal weaknesses with external opportunities, and record the resultant WO Strategies.
7. Match internal strengths with external threats, and record the resultant ST Strategies.
8. Match internal weaknesses with external threats, and record the resultant WT Strategies.

Some important aspects of a SWOT Matrix are evidenced in Figure 6-3. For example, note that both the internal/external factors and the SO/ST/WO/WT Strategies are stated in quantitative terms to the extent possible. This is important. For example, regarding the second SO #2 and ST #1 strategies, if the analyst just said, "Add new repair/service persons," the reader might think that 20 new repair/service persons are needed. Actually only two are needed. Always *be specific* to the extent possible in stating factors and strategies.

It is also important to include the "S1, O2" type notation after each strategy in a SWOT Matrix. This notation reveals the rationale for each alternative strategy. Strategies do not rise out of the blue. Note in Figure 6-3 how this notation reveals the internal/external factors that were matched to formulate desirable strategies. For example, note that this retail computer store business may need to "purchase land to build new store" because a new Highway 34 will make its location less desirable. The notation (W2, O2) and (S8, T3) in Figure 6-3 exemplifies this matching process.

FIGURE 6-3

A SWOT Matrix for a Retail Computer Store

	Strengths	Weaknesses
	1. Inventory turnover up 5.8 to 6.7 2. Average customer purchase up $97 to $128 3. Employee morale is excellent 4. In-store promotions = 20% increase in sales 5. Newspaper advertising expenditures down 10% 6. Revenues from repair/service in store up 16% 7. In-store technical support persons have MIS degrees 8. Store's debt-to-total-assets ratio down 34%	1. Software revenues in store down 12% 2. Location of store hurt by new Hwy 34 3. Carpet and paint in store in disrepair 4. Bathroom in store needs refurbishing 5. Total store revenues down 8% 6. Store has no website 7. Supplier on-time-delivery up to 2.4 days 8. Customer checkout process too slow 9. Revenues per employee up 19%
Opportunities	**SO Strategies**	**WO Strategies**
1. Population of city growing 10% 2. Rival computer store opening 1 mile away 3. Vehicle traffic passing store up 12% 4. Vendors average six new products/yr 5. Senior citizen use of computers up 8% 6. Small business growth in area up 10% 7. Desire for websites up 18% by realtors 8. Desire for websites up 12% by small firms	1. Add 4 new in-store promotions monthly (S4, O3) 2. Add 2 new repair/service persons (S6, O5) 3. Send flyer to all seniors over age 55 (S5, O5)	1. Purchase land to build new store (W2, O2) 2. Install new carpet/paint/bath (W3, W4, O1) 3. Up website services by 50% (W6, O7, O8) 4. Launch mailout to all realtors in city (W5, O7)
Threats	**ST Strategies**	**WT Strategies**
1. Best Buy opening new store in 1 yr nearby 2. Local university offers computer repair 3. New bypass Hwy 34 in 1 yr will divert traffic 4. New mall being built nearby 5. Gas prices up 14% 6. Vendors raising prices 8%	1. Hire 2 more repair persons and market these new services (S6, S7, T1) 2. Purchase land to build new store (S8, T3) 3. Raise out-of-store service calls from $60 to $80 (S6, T5)	1. Hire 2 new cashiers (W8, T1, T4) 2. Install new carpet/paint/bath (W3, W4, T1)

The purpose of each Stage 2 matching tool is to generate feasible alternative strategies, not to select or determine which strategies are best. Not all of the strategies developed in the SWOT Matrix, therefore, will be selected for implementation.

The strategy-formulation guidelines provided in Chapter 5 can enhance the process of matching key external and internal factors. For example, when an organization has both the capital and human resources needed to distribute its own products (internal strength) and distributors are unreliable, costly, or incapable of meeting the firm's needs (external threat), forward integration can be an attractive ST Strategy. When a firm has excess production capacity (internal weakness) and its basic industry is experiencing declining annual sales and profits (external threat), related diversification can be an effective WT Strategy.

Although the SWOT matrix is widely used in strategic planning, the analysis does have some limitations.[4] First, SWOT does not show how to achieve a competitive advantage, so it must not be an end in itself. The matrix should be the starting point for a discussion on how proposed strategies could be implemented as well as cost-benefit considerations that ultimately could lead to competitive advantage. Second, SWOT is a static assessment (or snapshot) in time. A SWOT matrix can be like studying a single frame of a motion picture where you see the lead characters and the setting but have no clue as to the plot. As circumstances, capabilities, threats, and strategies change, the dynamics of a competitive environment may not be revealed in a single matrix. Third, SWOT analysis may lead the firm to overemphasize a single internal or external factor in formulating strategies. There are interrelationships among the key internal and external factors that SWOT does not reveal that may be important in devising strategies.

The Strategic Position and Action Evaluation (SPACE) Matrix

The *Strategic Position and Action Evaluation (SPACE) Matrix,* another important Stage 2 matching tool, is illustrated in Figure 6-4. Its four-quadrant framework indicates whether aggressive, conservative, defensive, or competitive strategies are most appropriate for a given organization. The axes of the SPACE Matrix represent two internal dimensions (*financial position [FP]* and *competitive position [CP]*) and two external dimensions (*stability position [SP]* and *industry position [IP]*). These four factors are perhaps the most important determinants of an organization's overall strategic position.[5]

Depending on the type of organization, numerous variables could make up each of the dimensions represented on the axes of the SPACE Matrix. Factors that were included earlier in the firm's EFE and IFE Matrices should be considered in developing a SPACE Matrix. Other variables commonly included are given in Table 6-2. For example, return on investment, leverage,

FIGURE 6-4

The SPACE Matrix

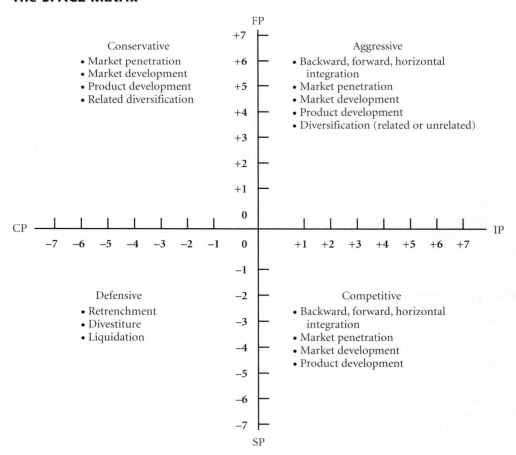

Source: Adapted from H. Rowe, R. Mason, and K. Dickel, *Strategic Management and Business Policy: A Methodological Approach* (Reading, MA: Addison-Wesley Publishing Co. Inc., © 1982), 155.

TABLE 6-2   Example Factors That Make Up the SPACE Matrix Axes

Internal Strategic Position	External Strategic Position
Financial Position (FP)	*Stability Position (SP)*
Return on investment	Technological changes
Leverage	Rate of inflation
Liquidity	Demand variability
Working capital	Price range of competing products
Cash flow	Barriers to entry into market
Inventory turnover	Competitive pressure
Earnings per share	Ease of exit from market
Price earnings ratio	Price elasticity of demand
	Risk involved in business
Competitive Position (CP)	*Industry Position (IP)*
Market share	Growth potential
Product quality	Profit potential
Product life cycle	Financial stability
Customer loyalty	Extent leveraged
Capacity utilization	Resource utilization
Technological know-how	Ease of entry into market
Control over suppliers and distributors	Productivity, capacity utilization

Source: Adapted from H. Rowe, R. Mason, and K. Dickel, *Strategic Management and Business Policy: A Methodological Approach* (Reading, MA: Addison-Wesley Publishing Co. Inc., © 1982), 155–156.

liquidity, working capital, and cash flow are commonly considered to be determining factors of an organization's financial strength. Like the SWOT Matrix, the SPACE Matrix should be both tailored to the particular organization being studied and based on factual information as much as possible.

The steps required to develop a SPACE Matrix are as follows:

1. Select a set of variables to define financial position (FP), competitive position (CP), stability position (SP), and industry position (IP).
2. Assign a numerical value ranging from +1 (worst) to +7 (best) to each of the variables that make up the FP and IP dimensions. Assign a numerical value ranging from –1 (best) to –7 (worst) to each of the variables that make up the SP and CP dimensions. On the FP and CP axes, make comparison to competitors. On the IP and SP axes, make comparison to other industries.
3. Compute an average score for FP, CP, IP, and SP by summing the values given to the variables of each dimension and then by dividing by the number of variables included in the respective dimension.
4. Plot the average scores for FP, IP, SP, and CP on the appropriate axis in the SPACE Matrix.
5. Add the two scores on the *x*-axis and plot the resultant point on X. Add the two scores on the *y*-axis and plot the resultant point on Y. Plot the intersection of the new *xy* point.
6. Draw a *directional vector* from the origin of the SPACE Matrix through the new intersection point. This vector reveals the type of strategies recommended for the organization: aggressive, competitive, defensive, or conservative.

Some examples of strategy profiles that can emerge from a SPACE analysis are shown in Figure 6-5. The directional vector associated with each profile suggests the type of strategies to pursue: aggressive, conservative, defensive, or competitive. When a firm's directional vector is located in the *aggressive quadrant* (upper-right quadrant) of the SPACE Matrix, an organization is in an excellent position to use its internal strengths to (1) take advantage of external opportunities, (2) overcome internal weaknesses, and (3) avoid external threats. Therefore, market penetration, market development, product development, backward integration, forward integration, horizontal integration, or diversification, can be feasible, depending on the specific circumstances that face the firm.

FIGURE 6-5

Example Strategy Profiles

Aggressive Profiles

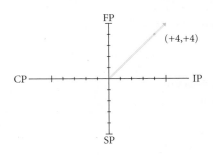

A financially strong firm that has achieved major competitive advantages in a growing and stable industry

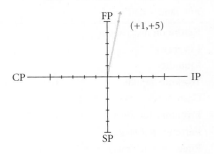

A firm whose financial strength is a dominating factor in the industry

Conservative Profiles

A firm that has achieved financial strength in a stable industry that is not growing; the firm has few competitive advantages

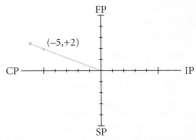

A firm that suffers from major competitive disadvantages in an industry that is technologically stable but declining in sales

Competitive Profiles

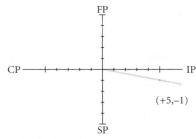

A firm with major competitive advantages in a high-growth industry

An organization that is competing fairly well in an unstable industry

Defensive Profiles

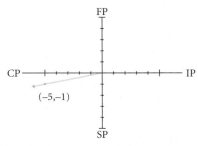

A firm that has a very weak competitive position in a negative growth, stable industry

A financially troubled firm in a very unstable industry

Source: Adapted from H. Rowe, R. Mason, and K. Dickel, *Strategic Management and Business Policy: A Methodological Approach* (Reading, MA: Addison-Wesley Publishing Co. Inc., © 1982), 155.

When a particular company is known, the analyst must be much more specific in terms of recommended strategies. For example, instead of saying market penetration is a recommended strategy when your vector goes in the Conservative quadrant, say that adding 34 new stores in India is a recommended strategy. This is a very important point for students doing case analyses because a particular company is generally known, and terms such as *market development* are too vague to use. That term could refer to adding a manufacturing plant in Thailand or Mexico or South Africa—so students—*Be specific to the extent possible regarding implications of all the matrices presented in Chapter 6.*

The directional vector may appear in the *conservative quadrant* (upper-left quadrant) of the SPACE Matrix, which implies staying close to the firm's basic competencies and not taking excessive risks. Conservative strategies most often include market penetration, market development, product development, and related diversification. The directional vector may be located in the lower-left or *defensive quadrant* of the SPACE Matrix, which suggests that the firm should focus on rectifying internal weaknesses and avoiding external threats. Defensive strategies include retrenchment, divestiture, liquidation, and related diversification. Finally, the directional vector may be located in the lower-right or *competitive quadrant* of the SPACE Matrix, indicating competitive strategies. Competitive strategies include backward, forward, and horizontal integration; market penetration; market development; and product development.

A SPACE Matrix analysis for a bank is provided in Table 6-3. Note that competitive type strategies are recommended. Headquartered in Winston-Salem, North Carolina, Krispy

TABLE 6-3   A SPACE Matrix for a Bank

Financial Position (FP)	Ratings
The bank's primary capital ratio is 7.23 percent, which is 1.23 percentage points over the generally required ratio of 6 percent.	1.0
The bank's return on assets is negative 0.77, compared to a bank industry average ratio of positive 0.70.	1.0
The bank's net income was $183 million, down 9 percent from a year earlier.	3.0
The bank's revenues increased 7 percent to $3.46 billion.	4.0
	9.0

Industry Position (IP)	
Deregulation provides geographic and product freedom.	4.0
Deregulation increases competition in the banking industry.	2.0
Pennsylvania's interstate banking law allows the bank to acquire other banks in New Jersey, Ohio, Kentucky, the District of Columbia, and West Virginia.	4.0
	10.0

Stability Position (SP)	
Less-developed countries are experiencing high inflation and political instability.	−4.0
Headquartered in Pittsburgh, the bank historically has been heavily dependent on the steel, oil, and gas industries. These industries are depressed.	−5.0
Banking deregulation has created instability throughout the industry.	−4.0
	−13.0

Competitive Position (CP)	
The bank provides data processing services for more than 450 institutions in 38 states.	−2.0
Superregional banks, international banks, and nonbanks are becoming increasingly competitive.	−5.0
The bank has a large customer base.	−2.0
	−9.0

Conclusion	

SP Average is −13.0 ÷ 3 = −4.33   IP Average is +10.0 ÷ 3 = 3.33

CP Average is −9.0 ÷ 3 = −3.00   FP Average is +9.0 ÷ 4 = 2.25

Directional Vector Coordinates: x-axis: −3.00 + (+3.33) = +0.33

y-axis: −4.33 + (+2.25) = −2.08

The bank should pursue Competitive Strategies.

Kreme Doughnut (KKD) Corp. has offered delicious doughnuts and coffee since 1937. Today, Krispy Kreme's "Hot Light" stores can be found in approximately 649 locations in 20 countries, including the United States, Australia, Bahrain, Canada, China, Dominican Republic, Indonesia, Japan, Kuwait, Lebanon, Malaysia, Mexico, the Philippines, Puerto Rico, the Republic of Korea, Qatar, the Kingdom of Saudi Arabia, Thailand, Turkey, the United Arab Emirates, and the United Kingdom. The company's mission statement is "To touch and enhance lives through the joy that is Krispy Kreme," and its vision statement is "To be the worldwide leader in sharing delicious tastes and creating joyful memories." A SPACE Matrix for KKD is given in Table 6-4 followed by the KKD SPACE diagram in Figure 6-6. Note that KKD is in a precarious defensive position, struggling to compete against Dunkin Donuts, Starbucks, and Tim Hortons.

The Boston Consulting Group (BCG) Matrix

Based in Boston and having 1,713 employees, the Boston Consulting Group (BCG) is a large consulting firm that endured the recent economic downturn without laying off any employees and in 2010 hired the most new consultants ever. BCG ranks #2 in *Fortune*'s recent list of the "100 Best Companies To Work For."

Autonomous divisions (or profit centers) of an organization make up what is called a *business portfolio*. When a firm's divisions compete in different industries, a separate strategy often must be developed for each business. The *Boston Consulting Group (BCG) Matrix* and the *Internal-External (IE) Matrix* are designed specifically to enhance a multidivisional firm's efforts to formulate strategies. (BCG is a private management consulting firm based in Boston that currently employs about 4,400 consultants in 40 countries.)

TABLE 6-4   An Actual SPACE Matrix for Krispy Kreme

Internal Analysis		*External Analysis*	
Financial Position (FP)		Stability Position (SP)	
Return on Investment (ROI)	1	Rate of Inflation	−2
Leverage	4	Technological Changes	−6
Liquidity	2	Price Elasticity of Demand	−3
Working Capital	1	Competitive Pressure	−7
Cash Flow	2	Barriers to Entry into Market	−4
Financial Position (FP) Average	**2**	**Stability Position (SP) Average**	**−4.4**
Internal Analysis		*External Analysis*	
Competitive Position (CP)		Industry Position (IP)	
Market Share	−7	Growth Potential	6
Product Quality	−2	Financial Stability	2
Customer Loyalty	−3	Ease of Entry into Market	4
Technological Know-how	−4	Resource Utilization	1
Control over Suppliers/Distributors	−5	Profit Potential	2
Competitive Position (CP) Average	**−4.2**	**Industry Position (IP) Average**	**3.0**

2.0+(−4.4)=−2.4   y-axis

3.0+(−4.2)=−1.2   x-axis

Coordinate (−1.2, −2.4)

Conclusion: Vector points in Defensive Quadrant

FIGURE 6-6

A SPACE Matrix for Krispy Kreme

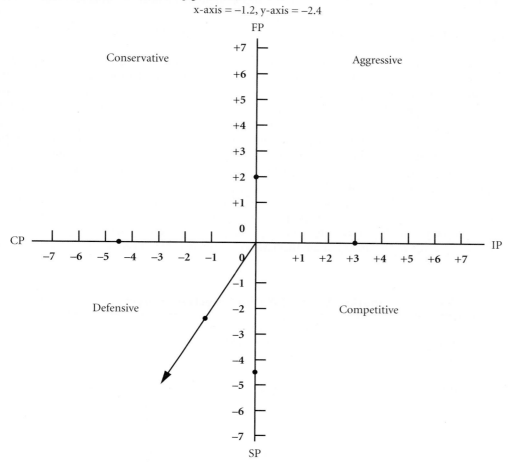

x-axis = −1.2, y-axis = −2.4

In a *Form 10K* or *Annual Report*, some companies do not disclose financial information by segment, so a BCG portfolio analysis is not possible by external entities. Reasons to disclose by-division financial information in the author's view, however, more than offset the reasons not to disclose, as indicated in Table 6-5.

The BCG Matrix graphically portrays differences among divisions in terms of relative market share position and industry growth rate. The BCG Matrix allows a multidivisional organization to manage its portfolio of businesses by examining the relative market share position and the industry growth rate of each division relative to all other divisions in the organization. *Relative market share position* is defined as the ratio of a division's own market share (or revenues) in a particular

TABLE 6-5   Reasons to (or Not to) Disclose Financial Information by Segment (by Division)

Reasons to Disclose	Reasons Not to Disclose
1. Transparency is a good thing in today's world of Sarbanes-Oxley	1. Can become free competitive information for rival firms
2. Investors will better understand the firm, which can lead to greater support	2. Can hide performance failures
3. Managers/employees will better understand the firm, which should lead to greater commitment	3. Can reduce rivalry among segments
4. Disclosure enhances the communication process both within the firm and with outsiders	

industry to the market share (or revenues) held by the largest rival firm in that industry. Note in Table 6-6 that other variables can be in this analysis besides revenues. For example, number of stores, or number of restaurants, or in the airline industry number of airplanes could be used for comparative purposes to determine relative market share position. Relative market share position for Heineken could also be determined by dividing Heineken's revenues by the leader Corona Extra's revenues.

Relative market share position is given on the *x*-axis of the BCG Matrix. The midpoint on the *x*-axis usually is set at .50, corresponding to a division that has half the market share of the leading firm in the industry. The *y*-axis represents the industry growth rate in sales, measured in percentage terms. The growth rate percentages on the *y*-axis could range from −20 to +20 percent, with 0.0 being the midpoint. The average annual increase in revenues for several leading firms in the industry would be a good estimate of the value. Also, various sources such as the S&P Industry Survey would provide this value. These numerical ranges on the *x*- and *y*-axes are often used, but other numerical values could be established as deemed appropriate for particular organizations, such as −10 to +10 percent.

The basic BCG Matrix appears in Figure 6-7. Each circle represents a separate division. The size of the circle corresponds to the proportion of corporate revenue generated by that business unit, and the pie slice indicates the proportion of corporate profits generated by that division. Divisions located in Quadrant I of the BCG Matrix are called "Question Marks," those located in

TABLE 6-6 Marker Share Data for Selected Industries

Business Analytics (using software to mine huge volumes of data to enhance decision-making; *WSJ*, 1/18/11, B4)—Market Share Leaders

Oracle	18.3%
SAP	13.6%
IBM	12.4%
SAS	7.8%
Microsoft	7.5%

Book Sales (*USA Today*, 2/10/11, 2A)

Amazon	22.6%
Barnes & Noble	17.3%
Borders	8.1%
Books-A-Million	3.0%
Independents	6.0%

Ready-to-Drink Beverages (*WSJ*, 2/10/11, B4)

Soft drinks	46.6%
Bottled water	19.9%
Non-refrigerated juice	9.0%
Refrigerated juice	9.0%
Sports drinks	6.2%
Tea	4.2%
Enhanced water	2.5%
Energy drinks	2.4%
Coffee	0.2%

U.S. Carbonated Soft Drinks (*WSJ*, 3/18/11, B5)

BY COMPANY		BY BRAND	
Coca-Cola	42.0%	Coke	17.0%
PepsiCo	29.3%	Diet Coke	9.9%
Dr Pepper/Snapple	16.7%	Pepsi-Cola	9.5%
Cott	4.8%	Mt. Dew	6.8%
National Beverage	2.8%	Dr Pepper	6.3%

Quadrant II are called "Stars," those located in Quadrant III are called "Cash Cows," and those divisions located in Quadrant IV are called "Dogs."

- *Question Marks*—Divisions in Quadrant I have a low relative market share position, yet they compete in a high-growth industry. Generally these firms' cash needs are high and their cash generation is low. These businesses are called *Question Marks* because the organization must decide whether to strengthen them by pursuing an intensive strategy (market penetration, market development, or product development) or to sell them.
- *Stars*—Quadrant II businesses (*Stars*) represent the organization's best long-run opportunities for growth and profitability. Divisions with a high relative market share and a high industry growth rate should receive substantial investment to maintain or strengthen their dominant positions. Forward, backward, and horizontal integration; market penetration; market development; and product development are appropriate strategies for these divisions to consider, as indicated in Figure 6-7.
- *Cash Cows*—Divisions positioned in Quadrant III have a high relative market share position but compete in a low-growth industry. Called *Cash Cows* because they generate cash in excess of their needs, they are often milked. Many of today's Cash Cows were yesterday's Stars. Cash Cow divisions should be managed to maintain their strong position for as long as possible. Product development or diversification may be attractive strategies for strong Cash Cows. However, as a Cash Cow division becomes weak, retrenchment or divestiture can become more appropriate.
- *Dogs*—Quadrant IV divisions of the organization have a low relative market share position and compete in a slow- or no-market-growth industry; they are *Dogs* in the firm's portfolio. Because of their weak internal and external position, these businesses are often liquidated, divested, or trimmed down through retrenchment. When a division first becomes a Dog, retrenchment can be the best strategy to pursue because many Dogs have bounced back, after strenuous asset and cost reduction, to become viable, profitable divisions.

The major benefit of the BCG Matrix is that it draws attention to the cash flow, investment characteristics, and needs of an organization's various divisions. The divisions of many firms evolve over time: Dogs become Question Marks, Question Marks become Stars, Stars become Cash Cows, and Cash Cows become Dogs in an ongoing counterclockwise motion. Less frequently, Stars become Question Marks, Question Marks become Dogs, Dogs become Cash Cows, and Cash Cows become Stars (in a clockwise motion). In some organizations, no cyclical motion is apparent. Over time, organizations should strive to achieve a portfolio of divisions that are Stars.

FIGURE 6-7

The BCG Matrix

Source: Based on the BCG Portfolio Matrix from the Product Portfolio Matrix, © 1970, The Boston Consulting Group.

FIGURE 6-8

An Example BCG Matrix

Division	Revenues	Percent Revenues	Profits	Percent Profits	Relative Market Share	Industry Growth Rate (%)
1	$60,000	37	$10,000	39	.80	+15
2	40,000	24	5,000	20	.40	+10
3	40,000	24	2,000	8	.10	+1
4	20,000	12	8,000	31	.60	−20
5	5,000	3	500	2	.05	−10
Total	**$165,000**	**100**	**$25,500**	**100**	—	—

An example BCG Matrix is provided in Figure 6-8, which illustrates an organization composed of five divisions with annual sales ranging from $5,000 to $60,000. Division 1 has the greatest sales volume, so the circle representing that division is the largest one in the matrix. The circle corresponding to Division 5 is the smallest because its sales volume ($5,000) is least among all the divisions. The pie slices within the circles reveal the percent of corporate profits contributed by each division. As shown, Division 1 contributes the highest profit percentage, 39 percent. Notice in the diagram that Division 1 is considered a Star, Division 2 is a Question Mark, Division 3 is also a Question Mark, Division 4 is a Cash Cow, and Division 5 is a Dog.

The BCG Matrix, like all analytical techniques, has some limitations. For example, viewing every business as either a Star, Cash Cow, Dog, or Question Mark is an oversimplification; many businesses fall right in the middle of the BCG Matrix and thus are not easily classified. Furthermore, the BCG Matrix does not reflect whether or not various divisions or their industries are growing over time; that is, the matrix has no temporal qualities, but rather it is a snapshot of an organization at a given point in time. Finally, other variables besides relative market share position and industry growth rate in sales, such as size of the market and competitive advantages, are important in making strategic decisions about various divisions.

An example BCG Matrix is provided in Figure 6-9. Note in Figure 6-9 that Division 5 had an operating loss of $188 million. Take note how the percent profit column is still calculated because oftentimes a firm will have a division that incurs a loss for a year. In terms of the pie slice in circle 5 of the diagram, note that it is a *different color* from the positive profit segments in the other circles.

The Internal-External (IE) Matrix

The *Internal-External (IE) Matrix* positions an organization's various divisions in a nine-cell display, illustrated in Figure 6-10. The IE Matrix is similar to the BCG Matrix in that both tools involve plotting organization divisions in a schematic diagram; this is why they are both called "portfolio matrices." Also, the size of each circle represents the percentage sales contribution of each division, and pie slices reveal the percentage profit contribution of each division in both the BCG and IE Matrix.

But there are some important differences between the BCG Matrix and the IE Matrix. First, the axes are different. Also, the IE Matrix requires more information about the divisions than the

FIGURE 6-9

An Example BCG Matrix

Division	$ Sales (millions)	% Sales	$ Profits (millions)	% Profits	RMSP	IG Rate %
1.	$5,139	51.5	$799	68.0	0.8	10
2.	2,556	25.6	400	39.0	0.4	05
3.	1,749	17.5	12	1.2	0.2	00
4.	493	4.9	4	0.1	0.5	−05
5.	42	0.5	−188	(18.3)	.02	−10
Total	**$9,979**	**100.0**	**$1,027**	**100.0**		

FIGURE 6-10

The Internal–External (IE) Matrix

Source: Adapted. The IE Matrix was developed from the General Electric (GE) Business Screen Matrix. For a description of the GE Matrix see Michael Allen, "Diagramming GE's Planning for What's WATT," in R. Allio and M. Pennington, eds., *Corporate Planning: Techniques and Applications* lpar;New York: AMACOM, 1979).

BCG Matrix. Furthermore, the strategic implications of each matrix are different. For these reasons, strategists in multidivisional firms often develop both the BCG Matrix and the IE Matrix in formulating alternative strategies. A common practice is to develop a BCG Matrix and an IE Matrix for the present and then develop projected matrices to reflect expectations of the future. This before-and-after analysis forecasts the expected effect of strategic decisions on an organization's portfolio of divisions.

The IE Matrix is based on two key dimensions: the IFE total weighted scores on the x-axis and the EFE total weighted scores on the y-axis. Recall that each division of an organization should construct an IFE Matrix and an EFE Matrix for its part of the organization. The total weighted scores derived from the divisions allow construction of the corporate-level IE Matrix. On the x-axis of the IE Matrix, an IFE total weighted score of 1.0 to 1.99 represents a weak internal position; a score of 2.0 to 2.99 is considered average; and a score of 3.0 to 4.0 is strong. Similarly, on the y-axis, an EFE total weighted score of 1.0 to 1.99 is considered low; a score of 2.0 to 2.99 is medium; and a score of 3.0 to 4.0 is high.

The IE Matrix can be divided into three major regions that have different strategy implications. First, the prescription for divisions that fall into cells I, II, or IV can be described as *grow and build*. Intensive (market penetration, market development, and product development) or integrative (backward integration, forward integration, and horizontal integration) strategies can be most appropriate for these divisions. Second, divisions that fall into cells III, V, or VII can be managed best with *hold and maintain* strategies; market penetration and product development are two commonly employed strategies for these types of divisions. Third, a common prescription for divisions that fall into cells VI, VIII, or IX is *harvest or divest*. Successful organizations are able to achieve a portfolio of businesses positioned in or around cell I in the IE Matrix.

An example of a completed IE Matrix is given in Figure 6-11, which depicts an organization composed of four divisions. As indicated by the positioning of the circles, *grow and build* strategies are appropriate for Division 1, Division 2, and Division 3. Division 4 is a candidate for *harvest or divest*. Division 2 contributes the greatest percentage of company sales and thus is represented by the largest circle. Division 1 contributes the greatest proportion of total profits; it has the largest-percentage pie slice.

FIGURE 6-11

An Example IE Matrix

Division	Sales	Percent Sales	Profits	Percent Profits	IFE Scores	EFE Scores
1	$100	25.0	10	50	3.6	3.2
2	200	50.0	5	25	2.1	3.5
3	50	12.5	4	20	3.1	2.1
4	50	12.5	1	5	1.8	2.5
Total	**400**	**100.0**	**20**	**100**		

FIGURE 6-12

The IE Matrix

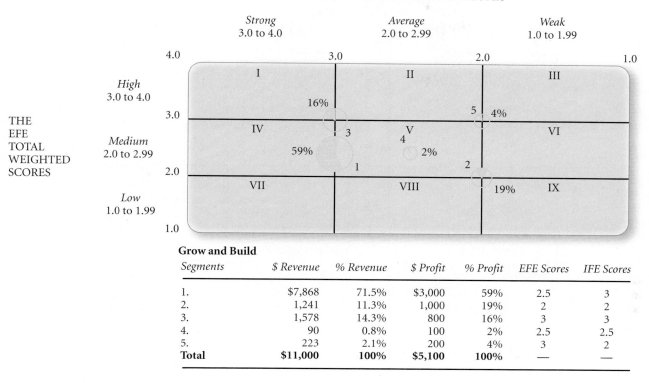

THE IFE TOTAL WEIGHTED SCORES

Grow and Build

Segments	$ Revenue	% Revenue	$ Profit	% Profit	EFE Scores	IFE Scores
1.	$7,868	71.5%	$3,000	59%	2.5	3
2.	1,241	11.3%	1,000	19%	2	2
3.	1,578	14.3%	800	16%	3	3
4.	90	0.8%	100	2%	2.5	2.5
5.	223	2.1%	200	4%	3	2
Total	**$11,000**	**100%**	**$5,100**	**100%**	—	—

As indicated in Figure 6-12, the IE Matrix has five product segments. Note that Division 1 has the largest revenues (as indicated by the largest circle) and the largest profits (as indicated by the largest pie slice) in the matrix. It is common for organizations to develop both geographic and product-based IE Matrices to more effectively formulate strategies and allocate resources among divisions. In addition, firms often prepare an IE (or BCG) Matrix for competitors. Furthermore, firms will often prepare "before and after" IE (or BCG) Matrices to reveal the situation at present versus the expected situation after one year. This latter idea minimizes the limitation of these matrices being a "snapshot in time." In performing case analysis, feel free to estimate the IFE and EFE scores for the various divisions based upon your research into the company and industry—rather than preparing a separate IE Matrix for each division.

The Grand Strategy Matrix

In addition to the SWOT Matrix, SPACE Matrix, BCG Matrix, and IE Matrix, the *Grand Strategy Matrix* has become a popular tool for formulating alternative strategies. All organizations can be positioned in one of the Grand Strategy Matrix's four strategy quadrants. A firm's divisions likewise could be positioned. As illustrated in Figure 6-13, the Grand Strategy Matrix is based on two evaluative dimensions: competitive position and market (industry) growth. Any industry whose annual growth in sales exceeds 5 percent could be considered to have rapid growth. Appropriate strategies for an organization to consider are listed in sequential order of attractiveness in each quadrant of the matrix.

Firms located in Quadrant I of the Grand Strategy Matrix are in an excellent strategic position. For these firms, continued concentration on current markets (market penetration and market development) and products (product development) is an appropriate strategy. It is unwise for a Quadrant I firm to shift notably from its established competitive advantages. When a Quadrant I organization has excessive resources, then backward, forward, or horizontal integration may be effective strategies. When a Quadrant I firm is too heavily committed to a single product, then related diversification may reduce the risks associated with a narrow product line. Quadrant I firms can afford to take advantage of external opportunities in several areas. They can take risks aggressively when necessary.

FIGURE 6-13

The Grand Strategy Matrix

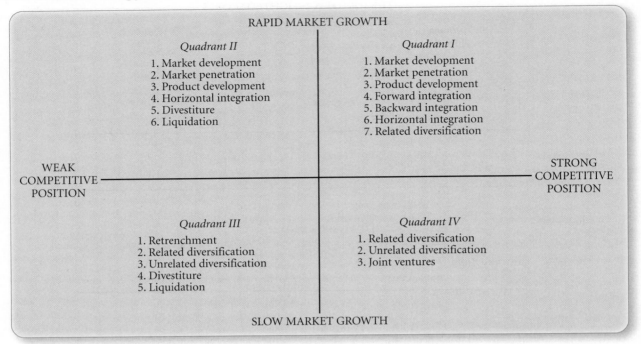

Source: Based on Roland Christensen, Norman Berg, and Malcolm Salter, *Policy Formulation and Administration* (Homewood, IL: Richard D. Irwin, 1976), 16–18.

Firms positioned in Quadrant II need to evaluate their present approach to the marketplace seriously. Although their industry is growing, they are unable to compete effectively, and they need to determine why the firm's current approach is ineffective and how the company can best change to improve its competitiveness. Because Quadrant II firms are in a rapid-market-growth industry, an intensive strategy (as opposed to integrative or diversification) is usually the first option that should be considered. However, if the firm is lacking a distinctive competence or competitive advantage, then horizontal integration is often a desirable alternative. As a last resort, divestiture or liquidation should be considered. Divestiture can provide funds needed to acquire other businesses or buy back shares of stock.

Quadrant III organizations compete in slow-growth industries and have weak competitive positions. These firms must make some drastic changes quickly to avoid further decline and possible liquidation. Extensive cost and asset reduction (retrenchment) should be pursued first. An alternative strategy is to shift resources away from the current business into different areas (diversify). If all else fails, the final options for Quadrant III businesses are divestiture or liquidation.

Finally, Quadrant IV businesses have a strong competitive position but are in a slow-growth industry. These firms have the strength to launch diversified programs into more promising growth areas: Quadrant IV firms have characteristically high cash-flow levels and limited internal growth needs and often can pursue related or unrelated diversification successfully. Quadrant IV firms also may pursue joint ventures.

The Decision Stage

Analysis and intuition provide a basis for making strategy-formulation decisions. The matching techniques just discussed reveal feasible alternative strategies. Many of these strategies will likely have been proposed by managers and employees participating in the strategy analysis and choice activity. Any additional strategies resulting from the matching analyses could be discussed and added to the list of feasible alternative options. As indicated earlier in this chapter, participants could rate these strategies on a 1 to 4 scale so that a prioritized list of the best strategies could be achieved.

The Quantitative Strategic Planning Matrix (QSPM)

Other than ranking strategies to achieve the prioritized list, there is only one analytical technique in the literature designed to determine the relative attractiveness of feasible alternative actions. This technique is the *Quantitative Strategic Planning Matrix (QSPM),* which comprises Stage 3 of the strategy-formulation analytical framework.[6] This technique objectively indicates which alternative strategies are best. The QSPM uses input from Stage 1 analyses and matching results from Stage 2 analyses to decide objectively among alternative strategies. That is, the EFE Matrix, IFE Matrix, and Competitive Profile Matrix that comprise Stage 1, coupled with the SWOT Matrix, SPACE Matrix, BCG Matrix, IE Matrix, and Grand Strategy Matrix that comprise Stage 2, provide the needed information for setting up the QSPM (Stage 3). The QSPM is a tool that allows strategists to evaluate alternative strategies objectively, based on previously identified external and internal critical success factors. Like other strategy-formulation analytical tools, the QSPM requires good intuitive judgment.

The basic format of the QSPM is illustrated in Table 6-7. Note that the left column of a QSPM consists of key external and internal factors (from Stage 1), and the top row consists of feasible alternative strategies (from Stage 2). Specifically, the left column of a QSPM consists of information obtained directly from the EFE Matrix and IFE Matrix. In a column adjacent to the critical success factors, the respective weights received by each factor in the EFE Matrix and the IFE Matrix are recorded.

The top row of a QSPM consists of alternative strategies derived from the SWOT Matrix, SPACE Matrix, BCG Matrix, IE Matrix, and Grand Strategy Matrix. These matching tools usually generate similar feasible alternatives. However, not every strategy suggested by the matching techniques has to be evaluated in a QSPM. Strategists should use good intuitive judgment in selecting strategies to include in a QSPM.

Conceptually, the QSPM determines the relative attractiveness of various strategies based on the extent to which key external and internal critical success factors are capitalized upon or improved. The relative attractiveness of each strategy within a set of alternatives is computed by determining the cumulative impact of each external and internal critical success factor. Any number of sets of alternative strategies can be included in the QSPM, and any number of strategies can make up a given set, but only strategies within a given set are evaluated relative to each other. For example, one set of strategies may include diversification, whereas another set may include issuing stock and selling a division to raise needed capital. These two sets of strategies are totally different, and the QSPM evaluates strategies only within sets. Note in Table 6-7 that three strategies are included, and they make up just one set.

A QSPM for a retail computer store is provided in Table 6-8. This example illustrates all the components of the QSPM: Strategic Alternatives, Key Factors, Weights, Attractiveness Scores (AS), Total Attractiveness Scores (TAS), and the Sum Total Attractiveness Score. The three new

TABLE 6-7   The Quantitative Strategic Planning Matrix—QSPM

		Strategic Alternatives		
Key Factors	Weight	Strategy 1	Strategy 2	Strategy 3
Key External Factors				
Economy				
Political/Legal/Governmental				
Social/Cultural/Demographic/Environmental				
Technological				
Competitive				
Key Internal Factors				
Management				
Marketing				
Finance/Accounting				
Production/Operations				
Research and Development				
Management Information Systems				

TABLE 6-8 A QSPM for a Retail Computer Store

		STRATEGIC ALTERNATIVES			
		1		2	
		Buy New Land and Build New Larger Store		Fully Renovate Existing Store	
Key Factors	Weight	AS	TAS	AS	TAS
Opportunities					
1. Population of city growing 10%	0.10	4	0.40	2	0.20
2. Rival computer store opening 1 mile away	0.10	2	0.20	4	0.40
3. Vehicle traffic passing store up 12%	0.08	1	0.08	4	0.32
4. Vendors average six new products/year	0.05	—		—	
5. Senior citizen use of computers up 8%	0.05	—		—	
6. Small business growth in area up 10%	0.10	—		—	
7. Desire for websites up 18% by Realtors	0.06	—		—	
8. Desire for websites up 12% by small firms	0.06	—		—	
Threats					
1. Best Buy opening new store nearby in 1 year	0.15	4	0.60	3	0.45
2. Local university offers computer repair	0.08	—		—	
3. New bypass for Hwy 34 in 1 year will divert traffic	0.12	4	0.48	1	0.12
4. New mall being built nearby	0.08	2	0.16	4	0.32
5. Gas prices up 14%	0.04	—		—	
6. Vendors raising prices 8%	0.03	—		—	
Total	**1.00**				
Strengths					
1. Inventory turnover increased from 5.8 to 6.7	0.05	—		—	
2. Average customer purchase increased from $97 to $128	0.07	2	0.14	4	0.28
3. Employee morale is excellent	0.10	—		—	
4. In-store promotions resulted in 20% increase in sales	0.05	—		—	
5. Newspaper advertising expenditures increased 10%	0.02	—		—	
6. Revenues from repair/service segment of store up 16%	0.15	4	0.60	3	0.45
7. In-store technical support personnel have MIS college degrees	0.05	—		—	
8. Store's debt-to-total-assets ratio declined to 34%	0.03	4	0.12	2	0.06
9. Revenues per employee up 19%	0.02	—		—	
Weaknesses					
1. Revenues from software segment of store down 12%	0.10	—		—	
2. Location of store negatively impacted by new Hwy 34	0.15	4	0.60	1	0.15
3. Carpet and paint in store somewhat in disrepair	0.02	1	0.02	4	0.08
4. Bathroom in store needs refurbishing	0.02	1	0.02	4	0.08
5. Revenues from businesses down 8%	0.04	3	0.12	4	0.16
6. Store has no website	0.05	—		—	
7. Supplier on-time delivery increased to 2.4 days	0.03	—		—	
8. Often customers have to wait to check out	0.05	2	0.10	4	0.20
Total	**1.00**		**4.36**		**3.27**

terms just introduced—(1) Attractiveness Scores, (2) Total Attractiveness Scores, and (3) the Sum Total Attractiveness Score—are defined and explained as the six steps required to develop a QSPM are discussed:

Step 1 *Make a list of the firm's key external opportunities/threats and internal strengths/ weaknesses in the left column of the QSPM.* This information should be taken directly from the EFE Matrix and IFE Matrix. A minimum of 10 external key success factors and 10 internal key success factors should be included in the QSPM.

Step 2 *Assign weights to each key external and internal factor.* These weights are identical to those in the EFE Matrix and the IFE Matrix. The weights are presented in a straight column just to the right of the external and internal critical success factors.

Step 3 *Examine the Stage 2 (matching) matrices, and identify alternative strategies that the organization should consider implementing.* Record these strategies in the top row of the QSPM. Group the strategies into mutually exclusive sets if possible.

Step 4 *Determine the Attractiveness Scores (AS)* defined as numerical values that indicate the relative attractiveness of each strategy in a given set of alternatives. *Attractiveness Scores (AS)* are determined by examining each key external or internal factor, one at a time, and asking the question "Does this factor affect the choice of strategies being made?" If the answer to this question is yes, then the strategies should be compared relative to that key factor. Specifically, Attractiveness Scores should be assigned to each strategy to indicate the relative attractiveness of one strategy over others, considering the particular factor. The range for Attractiveness Scores is 1 = not attractive, 2 = somewhat attractive, 3 = reasonably attractive, and 4 = highly attractive. By attractive, we mean the extent that one strategy, compared to others, enables the firm to either capitalize on the strength, improve on the weakness, exploit the opportunity, or avoid the threat. Work row by row in developing a QSPM. If the answer to the previous question is *no,* indicating that the respective key factor has no effect upon the specific choice being made, then do not assign Attractiveness Scores to the strategies in that set. Use a dash to indicate that the key factor does not affect the choice being made. *Note:* If you assign an AS score to one strategy, then assign AS score(s) to the other. In other words, if one strategy receives a dash, then all others must receive a dash in a given row.

Step 5 *Compute the Total Attractiveness Scores.* Total Attractiveness Scores (TAS) are defined as the product of multiplying the weights (Step 2) by the Attractiveness Scores (Step 4) in each row. The Total Attractiveness Scores indicate the relative attractiveness of each alternative strategy, considering only the impact of the adjacent external or internal critical success factor. The higher the Total Attractiveness Score, the more attractive the strategic alternative (considering only the adjacent critical success factor).

Step 6 *Compute the Sum Total Attractiveness Score.* Add Total Attractiveness Scores in each strategy column of the QSPM. The *Sum Total Attractiveness Scores (STAS)* reveal which strategy is most attractive in each set of alternatives. Higher scores indicate more attractive strategies, considering all the relevant external and internal factors that could affect the strategic decisions. The magnitude of the difference between the Sum Total Attractiveness Scores in a given set of strategic alternatives indicates the relative desirability of one strategy over another.

In Table 6-8, two alternative strategies—(1) buy new land and build new larger store and (2) fully renovate existing store—are being considered by a computer retail store. Note by sum total attractiveness scores of 4.63 versus 3.27 that the analysis indicates the business should buy new land and build a new larger store. Note the use of dashes to indicate which factors do not affect the strategy choice being considered. If a particular factor affects one strategy but not the other, it affects the choice being made, so attractiveness scores should be recorded for both strategies. Never rate one strategy and not the other. Note also in Table 6-8 that there are no double 1's, 2's, 3's, or 4's in a row. Never duplicate scores in a row. Never work column by column; always prepare a QSPM working row by row. If you have more than one strategy in the QSPM, then let the AS scores range from 1 to "the number of strategies being evaluated." This will enable you to have a different AS score for each strategy. These are all important guidelines to follow in developing a QSPM. In actual practice, the store did purchase the new land and build a new store; the business also did some minor refurbishing until the new store was operational.

There should be a rationale for each AS score assigned. Note in Table 6-8 in the first row that the "city population growing 10 percent annually" opportunity could be capitalized on best by strategy 1, "building the new, larger store," so an AS score of 4 was assigned to Strategy 1. AS scores, therefore, are not mere guesses; they should be rational, defensible, and reasonable.

An example QSPM for UPS is given in Table 6-9. UPS owns its own airline, based in Louisville, Kentucky. Note in the analysis that UPS is considering converting all its trucks to green technology and also is considering extending services deeper into Africa. Note that the "Africa" strategy is most attractive as indicated by the sum total attractiveness score of 3.78 versus 2.37.

Positive Features and Limitations of the QSPM

A positive feature of the QSPM is that sets of strategies can be examined sequentially or simultaneously. For example, corporate-level strategies could be evaluated first, followed by division-level strategies, and then function-level strategies. There is no limit to the number of strategies that can be evaluated or the number of sets of strategies that can be examined at once using the QSPM.

Another positive feature of the QSPM is that it requires strategists to integrate pertinent external and internal factors into the decision process. Developing a QSPM makes it less likely that key factors will be overlooked or weighted inappropriately. A QSPM draws attention to important relationships that affect strategy decisions. Although developing a QSPM requires a number of subjective decisions, making small decisions along the way enhances the probability that the final strategic decisions will be best for the organization. A QSPM can be adapted for use by small and large for-profit and nonprofit organizations so can be applied to virtually any type of organization. A QSPM can especially enhance strategic choice in multinational firms because many key factors and strategies can be considered at once. It also has been applied successfully by a number of small businesses.[7]

The QSPM is not without some limitations. First, it always requires intuitive judgments and educated assumptions. The ratings and attractiveness scores require judgmental decisions, even though they should be based on objective information. Discussion among strategists, managers, and

TABLE 6-9 An Actual QSPM for UPS

	Convert All UPS Trucks to Green Technology			Extend UPS Service in Africa	
	Weight	AS	TAS	AS	TAS
Strengths					0.36
1. Completed first phase of Worldport expansion, increasing sorting capacity by 15%, going to 37%	0.09	1	0.09	4	
2. 1st major airline to successfully operate a 100% Stage III fleet >3 years in advance of Fed regulations	0.07	1	0.07	4	0.28
3. Five out of every 6 UPS drivers come from part-timeranks (promotion within)	0.07	0	0.00	0	0.00
4. Over 4,000 UPS drivers have driven >25 years without an avoidable accident	0.06	0	0.00	0	0.00
5. Dividend of $0.47 per share paid and increasing	0.06	0	0.00	0	0.00
6. Average daily volume for Next Day Air and Deferred Products increased 2.8% and 4.3% respectively	0.06	3	0.18	4	0.24
7. Have yielded 1.71% cost and production efficiencies, improving profits	0.06	0	0.00	0	0.00
8. Owns 80% of joint venture headquartered in Dubai with 20% option to purchase	0.08	2	0.16	4	0.32
9. Streamlining Domestic Package segment, reducing U.S. regions from 5 to 3 and U.S. Districts from 46 to 20	0.07	0	0.00	0	0.00
10. Purchased 130 hybrid vehicles adding to UPS alternative-fuel vehicle (AFV) fleet	0.07	4	0.28	1	0.07

	Convert All UPS Trucks to Green Technology			Extend UPS Service in Africa	
Weaknesses	Weight	AS	TAS	AS	TAS
11. Approximately 254,000 UPS employees are members of a union	0.03	0	0.00	0	0.00
12. Approximately 2,800 UPS pilots	0.03	1	0.03	4	0.12
13. Approximately 3,400 UPS truck mechanics	0.03	4	0.12	1	0.03
14. Inability to identify sufficient operating cost savings to result in at least 300 furloughs for airline pilots	0.04	4	0.16	1	0.04
15. Top executives diversity percentage (25%) is low compared to rival firms	0.03	0	0.00	0	0.00
16. Over 4,000 UPS drivers have driven for 25 years or more and are eligible for retirement	0.04	0	0.00	0	0.00
17. Top executives' tenure 5 years or less	0.03	0	0.00	0	0.00
18. 80% of all U.S. small package delivery services guaranteed	0.02	0	0.00	0	0.00
19. With ~408,000 employees, expenses relating to health and pension benefits are high	0.03	0	0.00	0	0.00
20. 41.7% of top UPS executives have more than one role	0.03	0	0.00	0	0.00
Subtotal	**1.00**		**1.09**		**1.46**

	Weight	AS	TAS	AS	TAS
Opportunities					
1. Europe accounts for ~50% of international revenue	0.04	1	0.04	4	0.16
2. Africa is becoming commercially developed	0.03	1	0.03	4	0.12
3. >24 alliances with Asian delivery companies	0.07	1	0.07	4	0.28
4. International market growing 10% faster than U.S.	0.03	1	0.03	4	0.12
5. Customers outsourcing up to 100% of supply chain to lower costs	0.10	0	0.00	0	0.00
6. Increase internationally in use of wireless access tracking information	0.03	1	0.03	4	0.12
7. Telematics technology in ~12,000 U.S. UPS vehicles	0.03	3	0.09	1	0.03
8. Hybrid vehicles are available to add to UPS alternative fuel vehicle (AFV) fleet	0.06	4	0.24	1	0.06
9. Only 43.2% of employees are not union member	0.07	0	0.00	0	0.00
10. Direct-to-consumer business models require delivery services to be 100% effective	0.03	1	0.03	4	0.12

	Weight	AS	TAS	AS	TAS
Threats					
11. Incurred $77 million foreign currency charge	0.10	1	0.10	4	0.40
12. Jet and diesel fuel price variations cause fuel surcharges (13% increase to a 21.2% decrease)	0.08	2	0.16	4	0.32
13. Adverse currency exchange rate fluctuation (7.2% decline for the year)	0.03	4	0.12	1	0.03
14. FASB guidance requires re-measurement of pension plan = $44 million reduction to earnings	0.04	0	0.00	0	0.00
15. 1% change in health care cost trend = increase in post-retirement benefit obligation $83 million	0.06	0	0.00	0	0.00
16. Joint venture partner in Dubai owns 20% put option	0.03	1	0.03	4	0.12
17. Undistributed earnings of non-U.S. subsidiaries ~$2.2 billion	0.05	2	0.10	4	0.20
18. Consumers expect "green business operations"	0.04	4	0.16	1	0.04
19. U.S. unemployment rates holding around 10%	0.03	0	0.00	0	0.00
20. FedEx has greater international presence (27% as compared to UPS 24% of total revenues)	0.05	1	0.05	4	0.20
Subtotal	1.00		1.28		2.32
Grand Total	**2.00**		**2.37**		**3.78**

employees throughout the strategy-formulation process, including development of a QSPM, is constructive and improves strategic decisions. Constructive discussion during strategy analysis and choice may arise because of genuine differences of interpretation of information and varying opinions. Another limitation of the QSPM is that it can be only as good as the prerequisite information and matching analyses upon which it is based.

Cultural Aspects of Strategy Choice

All organizations have a culture. *Culture* includes the set of shared values, beliefs, attitudes, customs, norms, personalities, heroes, and heroines that describe a firm. Culture is the unique way an organization does business. It is the human dimension that creates solidarity and meaning, and it inspires commitment and productivity in an organization when strategy changes are made. All human beings have a basic need to make sense of the world, to feel in control, and to make meaning. When events threaten meaning, individuals react defensively. Managers and employees may even sabotage new strategies in an effort to recapture the status quo.

It is beneficial to view strategic management from a cultural perspective because success often rests upon the degree of support that strategies receive from a firm's culture. If a firm's strategies are supported by cultural products such as values, beliefs, rites, rituals, ceremonies, stories, symbols, language, heroes, and heroines, then managers often can implement changes swiftly and easily. However, if a supportive culture does not exist and is not cultivated, then strategy changes may be ineffective or even counterproductive. A firm's culture can become antagonistic to new strategies, and the result of that antagonism may be confusion and disarray.

Strategies that require fewer cultural changes may be more attractive because extensive changes can take considerable time and effort. Whenever two firms merge, it becomes especially important to evaluate and consider culture-strategy linkages.

Culture provides an explanation for the difficulties a firm encounters when it attempts to shift its strategic direction, as the following statement explains:

> Not only has the "right" corporate culture become the essence and foundation of corporate excellence, but success or failure of needed corporate reforms hinges on management's sagacity and ability to change the firm's driving culture in time and in tune with required changes in strategies.[8]

The Politics of Strategy Choice

All organizations are political. Unless managed, political maneuvering consumes valuable time, subverts organizational objectives, diverts human energy, and results in the loss of some valuable employees. Sometimes political biases and personal preferences get unduly embedded in strategy choice decisions. Internal politics affect the choice of strategies in all organizations. The hierarchy of command in an organization, combined with the career aspirations of different people and the need to allocate scarce resources, guarantees the formation of coalitions of individuals who strive to take care of themselves first and the organization second, third, or fourth. Coalitions of individuals often form around key strategy issues that face an enterprise. A major responsibility of strategists is to guide the development of coalitions, to nurture an overall team concept, and to gain the support of key individuals and groups of individuals.

In the absence of objective analyses, strategy decisions too often are based on the politics of the moment. With development of improved strategy-formation tools, political factors become less important in making strategic decisions. In the absence of objectivity, political factors sometimes dictate strategies, and this is unfortunate. Managing political relationships is an integral part of building enthusiasm and esprit de corps in an organization.

A classic study of strategic management in nine large corporations examined the political tactics of successful and unsuccessful strategists.[9] Successful strategists were found to let weakly supported ideas and proposals die through inaction and to establish additional hurdles or tests for strongly supported ideas considered unacceptable but not openly opposed. Successful strategists kept a low political profile on unacceptable proposals and strived to let most negative decisions come from subordinates or a group consensus, thereby reserving their personal vetoes for big issues and crucial moments. Successful strategists did a lot of chatting and informal questioning to stay abreast of how things were progressing and to know when to intervene. They led strategy but did not dictate it. They gave few orders, announced few decisions, depended heavily on informal questioning, and sought to probe and clarify until a consensus emerged.

Successful strategists generously and visibly rewarded key thrusts that succeeded. They assigned responsibility for major new thrusts to *champions,* the individuals most strongly identified with the idea or product and whose futures were linked to its success. They stayed alert to the symbolic impact of their own actions and statements so as not to send false signals that could stimulate movements in unwanted directions.

Successful strategists ensured that all major power bases within an organization were represented in, or had access to, top management. They interjected new faces and new views into considerations of major changes. This is important because new employees and managers generally have more enthusiasm and drive than employees who have been with the firm a long time. New employees do not see the world the same old way; nor do they act as screens against changes. Successful strategists minimized their own political exposure on highly controversial issues and in circumstances in which major opposition from key power centers was likely. In combination, these findings provide a basis for managing political relationships in an organization.

Because strategies must be effective in the marketplace and capable of gaining internal commitment, the following tactics used by politicians for centuries can aid strategists:

- *Equifinality*—It is often possible to achieve similar results using different means or paths. Strategists should recognize that achieving a successful outcome is more important than imposing the method of achieving it. It may be possible to generate new alternatives that give equal results but with far greater potential for gaining commitment.
- *Satisfying*—Achieving satisfactory results with an acceptable strategy is far better than failing to achieve optimal results with an unpopular strategy.
- *Generalization*—Shifting focus from specific issues to more general ones may increase strategists' options for gaining organizational commitment.
- *Focus on Higher-Order Issues*—By raising an issue to a higher level, many short-term interests can be postponed in favor of long-term interests. For instance, by focusing on issues of survival, the airline and automotive industries were able to persuade unions to make concessions on wage increases.
- *Provide Political Access on Important Issues*—Strategy and policy decisions with significant negative consequences for middle managers will motivate intervention behavior from them. If middle managers do not have an opportunity to take a position on such decisions in appropriate political forums, they are capable of successfully resisting the decisions after they are made. Providing such political access provides strategists with information that otherwise might not be available and that could be useful in managing intervention behavior.[10]

Governance Issues

A "director," according to Webster's Dictionary, is "one of a group of persons entrusted with the overall direction of a corporate enterprise." A *board of directors* is a group of individuals who are elected by the ownership of a corporation to have oversight and guidance over management and who look out for shareholders' interests. The act of oversight and direction is referred to as *governance.* The National Association of Corporate Directors defines governance as "the characteristic of ensuring that long-term strategic objectives and plans are established and that the proper management structure is in place to achieve those objectives, while at the same time making sure that the structure functions to maintain the corporation's integrity, reputation, and responsibility to its various constituencies." This broad scope of responsibility for the board shows how boards are being held accountable for the entire performance of the firm. In the Worldcom, Tyco, and Enron bankruptcies and scandals, the firms' boards of directors were sued by shareholders for mismanaging their interests. New accounting rules in the United States and Europe now enhance corporate-governance codes and require much more extensive financial disclosure among publicly held firms. The roles and duties of a board of directors can be divided into four broad categories, as indicated in Table 6-10.

The recent recession and credit crunch prompted shareholders to become more wary of boards of directors. Shareholders of hundreds of firms are demanding that their boards do a better job of governing corporate America.[11] New compensation policies are needed as well as direct shareholder involvement in some director activities. For example, boards could require CEOs to groom possible replacements from inside the firm because exorbitant compensation is most often paid to new CEOs coming from outside the firm.

Shareholders are also upset at boards for allowing CEOs to receive huge end-of-year bonuses when the firm's stock price drops drastically during the year.[12] For example, Chesapeake Energy Corp. and its board of directors came under fire from shareholders for paying Chairman and CEO Aubrey McClendon $112 million as the firm's stock price plummeted. Investor Jeffrey Bronchick wrote in a letter to the Chesapeake board that the CEO's compensation was a "near perfect illustration of the complete collapse of appropriate corporate governance."

Until recently, boards of directors did most of their work sitting around polished wooden tables. However, Hewlett-Packard's directors, among many others, now log on to their own special board website twice a week and conduct business based on extensive confidential briefing information posted there by the firm's top management team. Then the board members meet face to face and fully informed every two months to discuss the biggest issues facing the firm. Even the decision of whether to locate operations in countries with low corporate tax rates would be reviewed by a board of directors.

Today, boards of directors are composed mostly of outsiders who are becoming more involved in organizations' strategic management. The trend in the United States is toward much

TABLE 6-10 Board of Director Duties and Responsibilities

1. CONTROL AND OVERSIGHT OVER MANAGEMENT
   a. Select the Chief Executive Officer (CEO).
   b. Sanction the CEO's team.
   c. Provide the CEO with a forum.
   d. Ensure managerial competency.
   e. Evaluate management's performance.
   f. Set management's salary levels, including fringe benefits.
   g. Guarantee managerial integrity through continuous auditing.
   h. Chart the corporate course.
   i. Devise and revise policies to be implemented by management.

2. ADHERENCE TO LEGAL PRESCRIPTIONS
   a. Keep abreast of new laws.
   b. Ensure the entire organization fulfills legal prescriptions.
   c. Pass bylaws and related resolutions.
   d. Select new directors.
   e. Approve capital budgets.
   f. Authorize borrowing, new stock issues, bonds, and so on.

3. CONSIDERATION OF STAKEHOLDERS' INTERESTS
   a. Monitor product quality.
   b. Facilitate upward progression in employee quality of work life.
   c. Review labor policies and practices.
   d. Improve the customer climate.
   e. Keep community relations at the highest level.
   f. Use influence to better governmental, professional association, and educational contacts.
   g. Maintain good public image.

4. ADVANCEMENT OF STOCKHOLDERS' RIGHTS
   a. Preserve stockholders' equity.
   b. Stimulate corporate growth so that the firm will survive and flourish.
   c. Guard against equity dilution.
   d. Ensure equitable stockholder representation.
   e. Inform stockholders through letters, reports, and meetings.
   f. Declare proper dividends.
   g. Guarantee corporate survival.

greater board member accountability with smaller boards, now averaging 12 members rather than 18 as they did a few years ago. *BusinessWeek* recently evaluated the boards of most large U.S. companies and provided the following "principles of good governance":

1. No more than two directors are current or former company executives.
2. The audit, compensation, and nominating committees are made up solely of outside directors.
3. Each director owns a large equity stake in the company, excluding stock options.
4. Each director attends at least 75 percent of all meetings.
5. The board meets regularly without management present and evaluates its own performance annually.
6. The CEO is not also the chairperson of the board.
7. Stock options are considered a corporate expense.
8. There are no interlocking directorships (where a director or CEO sits on another director's board).[13]

Being a member of a board of directors today requires much more time, is much more difficult, and requires much more technical knowledge and financial commitment than in the past. Jeff Sonnerfeld, associate dean of the Yale School of Management, says, "Boards of directors are now rolling up their sleeves and becoming much more closely involved with management decision making." Since the Enron and Worldcom scandals, company CEOs and boards are required to personally certify financial statements; company loans to company executives and directors are illegal; and there is faster reporting of insider stock transactions.

Just as directors are beginning to place more emphasis on staying informed about an organization's health and operations, they are also taking a more active role in ensuring that publicly issued documents are accurate representations of a firm's status. It is becoming widely recognized that a board of directors has legal responsibilities to stockholders and society for all company activities, for corporate performance, and for ensuring that a firm has an effective strategy. Failure to accept responsibility for auditing or evaluating a firm's strategy is considered a serious breach of a director's duties. Stockholders, government agencies, and customers are filing legal suits against directors for fraud, omissions, inaccurate disclosures, lack of due diligence, and culpable ignorance about a firm's operations with increasing frequency. Liability insurance for directors has become exceptionally expensive and has caused numerous directors to resign.

The Sarbanes-Oxley Act resulted in scores of boardroom overhauls among publicly traded companies. The jobs of chief executive and chairman are now held by separate persons, and board audit committees must now have at least one financial expert as a member. Board audit committees now meet 10 or more times per year, rather than three or four times as they did prior to the act. The act put an end to the "country club" atmosphere of most boards and has shifted power from CEOs to directors. Although aimed at public companies, the act has also had a similar impact on privately owned companies.[14]

In Sweden, a new law has recently been passed requiring 25 percent female representation in boardrooms. The Norwegian government has passed a similar law that requires 40 percent of corporate director seats to go to women. In the United States, women currently hold about 13 percent of board seats at S&P 500 firms and 10 percent at S&P 1,500 firms. The Investor Responsibility Research Center in Washington, D.C., reports that minorities hold just 8.8 percent of board seats of S&P 1,500 companies. Progressive firms realize that women and minorities ask different questions and make different suggestions in boardrooms than white men, which is helpful because women and minorities comprise much of the consumer base everywhere.

A direct response to increased pressure on directors to stay informed and execute their responsibilities is that audit committees are becoming commonplace. A board of directors should conduct an annual strategy audit in much the same fashion that it reviews the annual financial audit. In performing such an audit, a board could work jointly with operating management and/or seek outside counsel. Boards should play a role beyond that of performing a strategic audit. They should provide greater input and advice in the strategy-formulation process to ensure that strategists are providing for the long-term needs of the firm. This is being done through the formation of three particular board committees: nominating committees to propose candidates for the board and senior officers of the firm; compensation committees to evaluate the performance of top executives and determine the terms and conditions of their employment; and audit committees to give board-level attention to company accounting and financial policies and performance.

Special Note to Students

Your SWOT, SPACE, BCG, IE, GRAND, and QSPM need to be developed accurately, but in covering those matrices in an oral presentation, focus more on the implications of those analyses than the nuts-and-bolts calculations. In other words, as you go through those matrices in a presentation, your goal is not to prove to the class that you did the calculations correctly. They expect accuracy and clarity and certainly you should have that covered. It is the implications of each matrix that your audience will be most interested in, so use these Chapter 6 matrices to pave the way for your recommendations with costs, which generally come just a page or two deeper into the project. A good rule of thumb is to spend at least an equal amount of time on the implications as the actual calculations of each matrix when presented. This approach will improve the delivery aspect of your presentation or paper by maintaining the high interest level of your audience. Focusing on implications rather than calculations will also encourage questions from the audience when you finish. Questions upon completion are a good thing. Silence upon completion is a bad thing, since silence could mean your audience was asleep, disinterested, or did not feel you did a good job.

Conclusion

The essence of strategy formulation is an assessment of whether an organization is doing the right things and how it can be more effective in what it does. Every organization should be wary of becoming a prisoner of its own strategy, because even the best strategies become obsolete sooner or later. Regular reappraisal of strategy helps management avoid complacency. Objectives and strategies should be consciously developed and coordinated and should not merely evolve out of day-to-day operating decisions.

An organization with no sense of direction and no coherent strategy precipitates its own demise. When an organization does not know where it wants to go, it usually ends up some place it does not want to be. Every organization needs to consciously establish and communicate clear objectives and strategies.

Modern strategy-formulation tools and concepts are described in this chapter and integrated into a practical three-stage framework. Tools such as the SWOT Matrix, SPACE Matrix, BCG Matrix, IE Matrix, and QSPM can significantly enhance the quality of strategic decisions, but they should never be used to dictate the choice of strategies. Behavioral, cultural, and political aspects of strategy generation and selection are always important to consider and manage. Because of increased legal pressure from outside groups, boards of directors are assuming a more active role in strategy analysis and choice. This is a positive trend for organizations.

Key Terms and Concepts

Aggressive Quadrant (p. 209)
Attractiveness Scores (AS) (p. 223)
Board of Directors (p. 227)
Boston Consulting Group (BCG) Matrix (p. 212)
Business Portfolio (p. 212)
Cash Cows (p. 215)
Champions (p. 227)
Competitive Position (CP) (p. 208)
Competitive Quadrant (p. 211)
Conservative Quadrant (p. 211)
Culture (p. 226)
Decision Stage (p. 204)
Defensive Quadrant (p. 211)
Directional Vector (p. 209)
Dogs (p. 215)

Equifinality (p. 227)
Financial Position (FP) (p. 208)
Governance (p. 227)
Grand Strategy Matrix (p. 219)
Halo Error (p. 205)
Industry Position (IP) (p. 208)
Input Stage (p. 204)
Internal-External (IE) Matrix (p. 212)
Matching (p. 205)
Matching Stage (p. 204)
Quantitative Strategic Planning Matrix (QSPM) (p. 221)
Question Marks (p. 215)
Relative Market Share Position (p. 213)
SO Strategies (p. 206)
Stability Position (SP) (p. 208)

Issues for Review and Discussion

1. The Coca-Cola Company (TCCC) has done really well for decades. How does TCCC do so well and how can they continue to prosper?
2. Give an internal and external strength of TCCC and show how those two factors can be matched to reveal a feasible alternative strategy.
3. What do you believe are the three major external opportunities facing TCCC?
4. Develop a SPACE Matrix for TCCC. Explain the implications of your Matrix.
5. Develop a BCG Matrix for TCCC. Explain the implications of your Matrix.
6. Develop a QSPM for TCCC that includes two strategies, six internal factors, and six external factors. What strategy appears to be best for TCCC to pursue?
7. Do a Google search using the key terms "boards of directors." What new information did you learn that was not given in the chapter?
8. In preparing a SPACE Matrix, which axis would the European political and economic unrest fall under?
9. In preparing a BCG Matrix, what would be the best range for the IGR axis as applied to the beverage industry?
10. List four reasons why the IE Matrix is widely considered to be superior to the BCG Matrix.
11. Is there a limit to the number of strategies that could be examined in a QSPM? Why?
12. Go to Adidas' website and examine what you can find about the company's board of directors. Evaluate Adidas' board based on guidelines presented in the chapter.
13. Explain why the CEO of a firm should not also be chairperson of the board of directors.
14. In preparing a QSPM, what should be done if the TAS for each strategy turn out to be identical?
15. Summarize in your own words the "Special Note to Students" section given at the end of the chapter.
16. Develop a Grand Strategy Matrix for TCCC and include PepsiCo and Dr. Pepper Snapple.
17. Explain what should be done if the SPACE vector coordinate point is (0,0).
18. Why on a QSPM should you work row by row instead of column by column?
19. When constructing a SPACE Matrix, would it be appropriate to use a 1 to 10 scale for all axes?
20. If TCCC has the leading market share in Russia, where along the top axis of a BCG would their Russia Operations be plotted?
21. Develop a SWOT Matrix for yourself.
22. Why is "matching" internal with external factors such an important strategic management activity?
23. Diagram the strategy formulation framework that includes three stages and nine analytical tools. Which stage and tool do you feel is most important? Why?
24. Develop an example SWOT Matrix for your college or university with two items in each quadrant. Make sure your strategies clearly exemplify "matching" and show this with (S1, T2) type notation.
25. Develop an example SPACE Matrix for a global company that you are familiar with. Include two factors for each of the four axes (SP, IP, SP, and CP).
26. What would be an appropriate SP rating for TCCC?
27. Discuss the pros and cons of divulging divisional information to stakeholders.
28. Develop an example BCG Matrix for a company that has three divisions with revenues of 4, 8, and 12 and profits of 5, 3, and 2, respectively.
29. Develop a SPACE Matrix for a firm that is a weak competitor competing in a slow growing and unstable industry. Label axes and quadrants clearly.
30. Discuss the limitations of a BCG analysis and the limitations of a SPACE analysis.
31. Prepare an IE Matrix for a company with two divisions that have 30 and 60 in revenues to go with 10 and 15 in profits.
32. Develop a Grand Strategy Matrix with two example companies in each quadrant, i.e., companies that you know something about and that you would place in those quadrants.
33. Develop a QSPM for yourself—given two strategies: 1) go to graduate school or 2) begin working full-time.
34. Would a QSPM analysis be useful without the weight column? Why or why not?
35. Discuss the characteristics of successful strategists in terms of political actions within the firm.
36. In order of attractiveness to you, rank the political tactics presented on page 227.
37. For a business in your city, list in order of importance the top eight board-of-director duties and responsibilities listed in the chapter.
38. Discuss the pros and cons of Sweden's new board-of-director rule regarding women.
39. Develop a SPACE Matrix for your college or university.
40. Develop a BCG Matrix for your college or university.
41. Explain the limitations of the BCG, SPACE, and SWOT.

42. Develop a QSPM for a local company that you are familiar with.
43. Write a short essay that reveals your recommendation to firms regarding disclosure of financial information.
44. Explain why a before and after BCG and IE analysis can be so useful in presenting a strategic plan for consideration.
45. Find an example company on the Internet that has both a Cash Cow and a Question Mark division.

46. Regarding a Grand Strategy Matrix, identify two companies that would be located in your judgment in each quadrant—identify eight firms total.
47. For a non-profit company, list in order of importance the top 10 board-of-director duties and responsibilities.
48. Regarding the principles of good governance in the chapter, list in order of importance the top seven guidelines.

Notes

1. R. T. Lenz, "Managing the Evolution of the Strategic Planning Process," *Business Horizons* 30, no. 1 (January–February 1987): 37.
2. Robert Grant, "The Resource-Based Theory of Competitive Advantage: Implications for Strategy Formulation," *California Management Review*, Spring 1991, 114.
3. Heinz Weihrich, "The TOWS Matrix: A Tool for Situational Analysis," *Long Range Planning* 15, no. 2 (April 1982): 61. Note: Although Dr. Weihrich first modified SWOT analysis to form the TOWS matrix, the acronym SWOT is much more widely used than TOWS in practice.
4. Greg Dess, G. T. Lumpkin, and Alan Eisner, *Strategic Management: Text and Cases* (New York: McGraw-Hill/Irwin, 2006), 72.
5. Adapted from H. Rowe, R. Mason, and K. Dickel, *Strategic Management and Business Policy: A Methodological Approach* (Reading, MA: Addison-Wesley, 1982), 155–156.
6. Fred David, "The Strategic Planning Matrix—A Quantitative Approach," *Long Range Planning* 19, no. 5 (October 1986): 102; Andre Gib and Robert Margulies, "Making Competitive Intelligence Relevant to the User," *Planning Review* 19, no. 3 (May–June 1991): 21.

7. Fred David, "Computer-Assisted Strategic Planning in Small Businesses," *Journal of Systems Management* 36, no. 7 (July 1985): 24–34.
8. Y. Allarie and M. Firsirotu, "How to Implement Radical Strategies in Large Organizations," *Sloan Management Review* 26, no. 3 (Spring 1985): 19. Another excellent article is P. Shrivastava, "Integrating Strategy Formulation with Organizational Culture," *Journal of Business Strategy* 5, no. 3 (Winter 1985): 103–111.
9. James Brian Quinn, *Strategies for Changes: Logical Incrementalism* (Homewood, IL: Richard D. Irwin, 1980), 128–145. These political tactics are listed in A. Thompson and A. Strickland, *Strategic Management: Concepts and Cases* (Plano, TX: Business Publications, 1984), 261.
10. William Guth and Ian MacMillan, "Strategy Implementation Versus Middle Management Self-Interest," *Strategic Management Journal* 7, no. 4 (July–August 1986): 321.
11. Joann Lublin, "Corporate Directors' Group Gives Repair Plan to Boards," *Wall Street Journal*, March 24, 2009, B4.
12. Phred Dvorak, "Poor Year Doesn't Stop CEO Bonuses," *Wall Street Journal*, March 18, 2009, B1.
13. Louis Lavelle, "The Best and Worst Boards," *BusinessWeek*, October 7, 2002, 104–110.
14. Matt Murray, "Private Companies Also Feel Pressure to Clean Up Acts," *Wall Street Journal*, July 22, 2003, B1.

Current Readings

Buytendijk, Frank, Toby Hatch, and Pietro Micheli. "Scenario-Based Strategy Maps." *Business Horizons* 53, no. 4 (July–August 2010): 335–348.
Cooper, Tim, Mark Purdy, and Mark Foster. "A Portfolio Strategy for Locating Operations in the New 'Multi-Polar World.' *Strategy & Leadership* 38, no. 4 (2010): 42.

Dalton, Dan R., and Catherine M. Dalton. "Women and Corporate Boards of Directors: The Promise of Increased, and Substantive, Participation in the Post Sarbanes-Oxley Era." *Business Horizons* 53, no. 3 (May–June 2010): 257–268.
Deutsch, Yuval, Thomas Keil, and Tomi Laamanen. "A Dual Agency View of Board Compensation: The Joint Effects of

Outside Director and CEO Stock Options on Firm Risk." *Strategic Management Journal* 32, no. 2 (February 2011): 212–227.

Fong, Eric A., Vilmos F. Misangyi, and Henry L. Tosi. "The Effect of CEO Pay Deviations on CEO Withdrawal, Firm Size, and Firm Profits." *Strategic Management Journal* 31, no. 6 (June 2010): 629–651.

McDonald, Michael L., and James D. Westphal. "A Little Help Here? Board Control, CEO Identification with the Corporate Elite, and Strategic Help Provided to CEOs at Other Firms." *The Academy of Management Journal* 53, no. 2 (April 2010): 343–370.

Pozen, Robert C. "The Case for Professional Boards." *Harvard Business Review*, December 2010, 50.

"Succeeding at Succession." *Harvard Business Review*, November 2010, 29–35.

Tuggle, Christopher S., Karen Schnatterly, and Richard A. Johnson. "Attention Patterns in the Boardroom: How Board Composition and Processes Affect Discussion of Entrepreneurial Issues." *The Academy of Management Journal* 53, no. 3 (June 2010): 550–571.

Walters, Bruce A., Mark Kroll, and Peter Wright. "The Impact of TMT Board Member Control and Environment on Post-IPO Performance." *The Academy of Management Journal* 53, no. 3 (June 2010): 572–595.

ASSURANCE OF LEARNING EXERCISES

Assurance of Learning Exercise 6A

Should the Coca-Cola Company (TCCC) Penetrate Russia Further?

Purpose

The Coca-Cola Company (TCCC) is featured in the opening chapter case as a firm that engages in excellent strategic planning. TCCC is the world's largest global manufacturer, retailer, and marketer of non-alcoholic beverage concentrates and syrups.

TCCC and partner Coca-Cola Hellenic will spend $3 billion over the next five years to boost growth in Russia. In late 2011, TCCC opened a new $120 million Coca-Cola plant in the Rostov region—the company's 15th plant in Russia. Rostov is in southwest Russia near the Black Sea. The $3 billion commitment includes new infrastructure, brand building, and sustainability programs.

The purpose of this exercise is to give you experience investigating a country to determine whether a firm should expand more deeply into that region of the world.

Instructions

Step 1   Go to TCCC's corporate website and print the company's most recent *Form 10K*. Examine the narrative and tables related to their operations in Russia.

Step 2   Research the competitive climate and business culture of Russia as well as the operations of rival PepsiCo.

Step 3   Develop six recommendations for TCCC based on your assessment of their present and potential operations in Russia.

Assurance of Learning Exercise 6B

Perform a SWOT Analysis for TCCC's Global Operations

Purpose

TCCC's global and domestic business segments could be required annually to submit a SWOT analysis to corporate top executives who merge divisional analyses into an overall corporate analysis. This exercise will give you practice performing a SWOT analysis.

TCCC owns four of the top five soft-drink brands in the world: Coca-Cola, Diet Coke, Fanta, and Sprite. Other major TCCC brands include Minute Maid, Powerade, and Dasani water. In North America it sells Groupe Danone's Evian mineral water. The company also sells brands from rival Dr. Pepper Snapple Group (Crush, Dr. Pepper, and Schweppes) outside Australia, Europe, and North America. TCCC makes or licenses more than 3,500 drinks for sale in 200-plus countries.

Instructions

Step 1	Review TCCC's global operations as described in the company's most recent *Annual Report* and *Form 10K*.
Step 2	Review industry and competitive information pertaining to TCCC's global operations, including competitors such as PepsiCo and Dr. Pepper Snapple.
Step 3	Join with two other students in class. Together, develop a global SWOT Matrix for TCCC's global business segment. Follow all the SWOT guidelines provided in the chapter, including (S4, T3)-type notation at the end of each strategy. Include three strategies in each of the four (SO, ST, WT, WO) quadrants. Be specific regarding your strategies, avoiding generic terms such as Forward Integration.
Step 4	Turn in your team-developed SWOT Matrix to your professor for a classwork grade.

Assurance of Learning Exercise 6C

Preparing a BCG Matrix for TCCC

Purpose

For the second quarter of 2011, TCCC reported that worldwide volume grew 6 percent in both the quarter and year-to-date. TCCC achieved broad-based volume growth in the quarter across each of their five geographic operating groups, with growth of 7 percent in Eurasia and Africa, 7 percent in Pacific, 6 percent in Latin America, 5 percent in Europe, and 4 percent in North America. TCCC also reported an overall 5 percent growth in sparkling beverages, with worldwide brand Coca-Cola volume growth of 4 percent in the quarter driven by a number of global markets, including 24 percent growth in China, 17 percent in Russia, 7 percent in Mexico, 7 percent in France, 6 percent in Germany and 2 percent in Japan.

This exercise will give you practice preparing a geographic-based BCG Matrix.

Instructions

Step 1	Review TCCC's global operations as described in the company's most recent *Annual Report* and *Form 10K*.
Step 2	Prepare an up-to-date BCG Matrix for TCCC. Include as many countries in your matrix as you reasonably can.
Step 3	Write a two-page executive summary to reveal the strategic implications of your BCG Matrix.

Assurance of Learning Exercise 6D

Developing a SWOT Matrix for Adidas AG

Purpose

The most widely used strategy formulation technique among firms worldwide is the SWOT Matrix. This exercise requires development of a SWOT Matrix for Adidas. Matching key external and internal factors in a SWOT Matrix requires good intuitive and conceptual skills. You will improve with practice in developing a SWOT Matrix.

Instructions

Recall from Exercise 1B that you already may have determined Adidas' external opportunities/threats and internal strengths/weaknesses. This information could be used to complete this exercise. Follow the steps outlined as follows:

Step 1   On a separate sheet of paper, construct a large nine-cell diagram that will represent your SWOT Matrix. Appropriately label the cells.

Step 2   Appropriately record Adidas' opportunities/threats and strengths/weaknesses in your diagram.

Step 3   Match external and internal factors to generate feasible alternative strategies for Adidas. Record SO, WO, ST, and WT strategies in appropriate cells of the SWOT Matrix. Use the proper notation to indicate the rationale for the strategies. Try to include four strategies in each of the four strategy cells.

Step 4   Compare your SWOT Matrix to another students' SWOT Matrices. Discuss any major differences.

Assurance of Learning Exercise 6E

Developing a SPACE Matrix for Adidas AG

Purpose

Should Adidas pursue aggressive, conservative, competitive, or defensive strategies? Develop a SPACE Matrix for Adidas to answer this question. Elaborate on the strategic implications of your directional vector. Be specific in terms of strategies that could benefit Adidas.

Instructions

Step 1   Join with two other persons in your class and develop a joint SPACE Matrix for Adidas.

Step 2   Diagram your SPACE Matrix on the board. Compare your Matrix with other teams' matrices.

Step 3   Discuss the implications of your SPACE Matrix.

Assurance of Learning Exercise 6F

Developing a BCG Matrix for Adidas AG

Purpose

Portfolio matrices are widely used by multidivisional organizations to help identify and select strategies to pursue. A BCG analysis identifies particular divisions that should receive fewer resources than others. It may identify some divisions to be divested. This exercise can give you practice developing a BCG Matrix.

Instructions

Step 1   Place the following five column headings at the top of a separate sheet of paper: Divisions, Revenues, Profits, Relative Market Share Position, and Industry Growth Rate. Down the far left of your page, list Adidas, Reebok, and TaylorMade. Turn back to the Cohesion Case and find information to fill in all the cells in your data table.

Step 2   Complete two BCG Matrices for Adidas: 1) Include Reebok, TaylorMade, and Adidas and 2) include Geographic Regions of the World.

Step 3   Compare your BCG Matrix to other students' matrices. Discuss any major differences.

Assurance of Learning Exercise 6G

Developing a QSPM for Adidas AG

Purpose

This exercise can give you practice developing a Quantitative Strategic Planning Matrix (QSPM) to determine the relative attractiveness of various strategic alternatives.

Instructions

Step 1	Join with two other students in class to develop a joint QSPM for Adidas.
Step 2	Go to the board and record your strategies and their Sum Total Attractiveness Scores. Compare your team's strategies and sum total attractiveness scores to those of other teams. Be sure not to assign the same AS score in a given row. Recall that dashes should be inserted all the way across a given row when used.
Step 3	Discuss any major differences.

Assurance of Learning Exercise 6H

Developing a SWOT Matrix for TCCC

Purpose

The most widely used strategy formulation technique among American firms is the SWOT Matrix. This exercise requires development of a SWOT Matrix for TCCC. Matching key external and internal factors in a SWOT Matrix requires good intuitive and conceptual skills. You will improve with practice in developing a SWOT Matrix.

Instructions

Step 1	On a separate sheet of paper, construct a large nine-cell diagram that will represent your SWOT matrix. Appropriately label the cells.
Step 2	Determine six opportunities and six threats, and six strengths and six weaknesses for TCCC.
Step 3	Match external and internal factors to generate feasible alternative strategies for Starbucks. Record SO, WO, ST, and WT strategies in appropriate cells of the SWOT Matrix. Use the proper notation to indicate the rationale for the strategies. Try to include two strategies in each of the four strategy cells. Compare your SWOT Matrix to another student's SWOT Matrix. Discuss any major differences.

Assurance of Learning Exercise 6I

Developing a SPACE Matrix for TCCC

Purpose

Should TCCC pursue aggressive, conservative, competitive, or defensive strategies? Develop a SPACE Matrix for TCCC to answer this question. Elaborate on the strategic implications of your directional vector. Be specific in terms of strategies that could benefit Starbucks.

Instructions

Step 1	Join with two other persons in class and develop a joint SPACE Matrix for TCCC.
Step 2	Diagram your SPACE Matrix on the board. Compare your matrix with other teams' matrices.
Step 3	Discuss the implications of your SPACE Matrix.

Assurance of Learning Exercise 6J

Developing a BCG Matrix for your College or University

Purpose

Portfolio matrices are widely used by multidivisional organizations to help identify and select strategies to pursue. A BCG analysis identifies particular divisions that should receive fewer resources than others; or it may identify some divisions to be divested. This exercise can give you practice developing a BCG Matrix for a college or university.

Instructions

Step 1   Place the following five column headings at the top of a separate sheet of paper: Divisions, Revenues, Profits, Relative Market Share Position, and Industry Growth Rate. Down the far left of your page, list Schools at your college.

Step 2   Complete two BCG Matrices for your college or university. Include the School of Business, the School of Education, and the School of Nursing—or any other three Schools.

Step 3   Compare your BCG Matrix to other students' Matrices. Discuss any major differences.

Assurance of Learning Exercise 6K

Developing a QSPM for a Company that You Are Familiar With

Purpose

This exercise can give you practice developing a Quantitative Strategic Planning Matrix (QSPM) to determine the relative attractiveness of various strategic alternatives.

Instructions

Step 1   Join with two other students in class to develop a joint QSPM for a company that all of you are familiar with.

Step 2   Record your strategies and their Sum Total Attractiveness Scores. Compare your team's strategies and sum total attractiveness scores to those of other teams. Be sure not to assign the same AS score in a given row. Recall that dashes should be inserted all the way across a given row when used. Discuss any major differences.

Assurance of Learning Exercise 6L

Formulating Individual Strategies

Purpose

Individuals and organizations are alike in many ways. Each has competitors, and each should plan for the future. Every individual and organization faces some external opportunities and threats and has some internal strengths and weaknesses. Both individuals and organizations establish objectives and allocate resources. These and other similarities make it possible for individuals to use many strategic-management concepts and tools. This exercise is designed to demonstrate how the SWOT Matrix can be used by individuals to plan their futures. As one nears completion of a college degree and begins interviewing for jobs, planning can be particularly important.

Instructions

On a separate sheet of paper, construct a SWOT Matrix. Include what you consider to be your major external opportunities, your major external threats, your major strengths, and your major weaknesses. An internal weakness may be a low grade point average. An external opportunity may be that your university offers a graduate program that interests you. Match key external and internal factors by recording in the appropriate cell of the matrix alternative strategies or actions that would allow you to capitalize upon your strengths, overcome your weaknesses, take advantage of your external opportunities, and minimize the impact of external threats. Be sure to use the appropriate matching notation in the strategy cells of the matrix. Because every individual (and organization) is unique, there is no one right answer to this exercise.

Assurance of Learning Exercise 6M

The Mach Test

Purpose

The purpose of this exercise is to enhance your understanding and awareness of the impact that behavioral and political factors can have on strategy analysis and choice.

Instructions

Step 1   On a separate sheet of paper, write down numbers 1 to 10. For each of the 10 statements given as follows, record a *1, 2, 3, 4,* or *5* to indicate your attitude, where

1 = I disagree a lot.
2 = I disagree a little.
3 = My attitude is neutral.
4 = I agree a little.
5 = I agree a lot.

1. The best way to handle people is to tell them what they want to hear.
2. When you ask someone to do something for you, it is best to give the real reason for wanting it, rather than a reason that might carry more weight.
3. Anyone who completely trusts anyone else is asking for trouble.
4. It is hard to get ahead without cutting corners here and there.
5. It is safest to assume that all people have a vicious streak, and it will come out when they are given a chance.
6. One should take action only when it is morally right.
7. Most people are basically good and kind.
8. There is no excuse for lying to someone else.
9. Most people forget more easily the death of their father than the loss of their property.
10. Generally speaking, people won't work hard unless they're forced to do so.

Step 2   Add up the numbers you recorded beside statements 1, 3, 4, 5, 9, and 10. This sum is Subtotal One. For the other four statements, reverse the numbers you recorded, so a 5 becomes a *1, 4* becomes *2, 2* becomes *4, 1* becomes *5,* and *3* remains *3.* Then add those four numbers to get Subtotal Two. Finally, add Subtotal One and Subtotal Two to get your Final Score.

Your Final Score

Your Final Score is your Machiavellian Score. Machiavellian principles are defined in a dictionary as "manipulative, dishonest, deceiving, and favoring political expediency over morality." These tactics are not desirable, are not ethical, and are not recommended in the strategic management process! You may, however, encounter some highly Machiavellian individuals in your career, so beware. It is important for strategists not to manipulate others in the pursuit of organizational objectives. Individuals today recognize and resent manipulative tactics more than ever before. The National

Opinion Research Center used this short quiz in a random sample of U.S. adults and found the national average Final Score to be 25.[1] The higher your score, the more Machiavellian (manipulative) you tend to be. The following scale is descriptive of individual scores on this test:

- Below 16: Never uses manipulation as a tool.
- 16 to 20: Rarely uses manipulation as a tool.
- 21 to 25: Sometimes uses manipulation as a tool.
- 26 to 30: Often uses manipulation as a tool.
- Over 30: Always uses manipulation as a tool.

Test Development

The Mach (Machiavellian) test was developed by Dr. Richard Christie, whose research suggests the following tendencies:

1. Men generally are more Machiavellian than women.
2. There is no significant difference between high Machs and low Machs on measures of intelligence or ability.
3. Although high Machs are detached from others, they are detached in a pathological sense.
4. Machiavellian scores are not statistically related to authoritarian values.
5. High Machs tend to be in professions that emphasize the control and manipulation of individuals—for example law, psychiatry, and behavioral science.
6. Machiavellianism is not significantly related to major demographic characteristics such as educational level or marital status.
7. High Machs tend to come from a city or have urban backgrounds.
8. Older adults tend to have lower Mach scores than younger adults.[2]

Notes
1. Richard Christie and Florence Geis, *Studies in Machiavellianism* (Orlando, FL: Academic Press, 1970). Material in this exercise adapted with permission of the authors and Academic Press.
2. Ibid. 82–83.

"NOTABLE QUOTES"

"You want your people to run the business as if it were their own."
—William Fulmer

"Poor Ike; when he was a general, he gave an order and it was carried out. Now, he's going to sit in that office and give an order and not a damn thing is going to happen."
—Harry Truman

"Changing your pay plan is a big risk, but not changing it could be a bigger one."
—Nancy Perry

"Objectives can be compared to a compass bearing by which a ship navigates. A compass bearing is firm, but "in actual navigation, a ship may veer off its course for many miles. Without a compass bearing, a ship would neither find its port nor be able to estimate the time required to get there."
—Peter Drucker

"The best game plan in the world never blocked or tackled anybody."
—Vince Lombardi

"Pretend that every single person you meet has a sign around his or her neck that says, 'Make me feel important.'"
—Mary Kay Ash

Implementing Strategies: Management and Operations Issues

CHAPTER OBJECTIVES

After studying this chapter, you should be able to do the following:

1. Explain why strategy implementation is more difficult than strategy formulation.

2. Discuss the importance of annual objectives and policies in achieving organizational commitment for strategies to be implemented.

3. Explain why organizational structure is so important in strategy implementation.

4. Compare and contrast restructuring and reengineering.

5. Describe the relationships between production/operations and strategy implementation.

6. Explain how a firm can effectively link performance and pay to strategies.

7. Discuss employee stock ownership plans (ESOPs) as a strategic-management concept.

8. Describe how to modify an organizational culture to support new strategies.

ASSURANCE OF LEARNING EXERCISES

Assurance of Learning Exercise 7A
Developing an Organizational Chart
for IKEA

Assurance of Learning Exercise 7B
Assessing IKEA's Sustainability Efforts

Assurance of Learning Exercise 7C
Revising Adidas AG's Organizational Chart

Assurance of Learning Exercise 7D
Exploring Objectives

Assurance of Learning Exercise 7E
Understanding My University's Culture

The strategic-management process does not end upon deciding what strategy or strategies to pursue. There must be a translation of strategic thought into strategic action. This translation is much easier if managers and employees of the firm understand the business, feel a part of the company, and through involvement in strategy-formulation activities have become committed to helping the organization succeed. Without understanding and commitment, strategy-implementation efforts face major problems.

Implementing strategy affects an organization from top to bottom, including all the functional and divisional areas of a business. It is beyond the purpose and scope of this text to examine all of the business administration concepts and tools important in strategy implementation. This chapter focuses on management issues most central to implementing strategies in 2012–2013 and Chapter 8 focuses on marketing, finance/accounting, R&D, and management information systems issues. IKEA is an example firm with excellent management practices.

Even the most technically perfect strategic plan will serve little purpose if it is not implemented. Many organizations tend to spend an inordinate amount of time, money, and effort on developing the strategic plan, treating the means and circumstances under which it will be implemented as afterthoughts! Change comes through implementation and evaluation, not through the plan. A technically imperfect plan that is implemented well will achieve more than the perfect plan that never gets off the paper on which it is typed.[1]

Excellent Strategic Management Showcased

IKEA

IKEA is a very well-managed, privately held, international home products company that designs and sells ready-to-assemble furniture such as beds, desks, appliances, and home accessories. IKEA is the world's largest furniture retailer. Founded in 1943 in Sweden, IKEA is an acronym comprising the initials of the founder's name (Ingvar Kamprad), the farm where he grew up (Elmtaryd), and his home parish (Aqunnaryd in Smaland, South Sweden).

IKEA is well known for the attention it gives to cost control, operational details, and continuous product development, allowing it to lower its prices by an of average 2–3 percent over the decade to 2010, while continuing its global expansion. IKEA is operated and controlled by INGKA Holding B.V., a Dutch corporation, which is controlled by a tax-exempt, not-for-profit Dutch foundation. INGKA Holding B.V. owns the industrial group Swedwood, which manufactures IKEA furniture and operates IKEA stores, as well as purchasing and supply functions, and IKEA of Sweden, which is responsible for the design and development of products in the IKEA range. IKEA's European logistics center is located in Dortmund, Germany while the company's Asian logistics center is located in Singapore.

IKEA has about 320 stores in 38 countries, most of them in Europe, North America, Asia, and Australia. The IKEA Group itself owns 276 stores in 25 countries and the other 37 stores are owned and run by franchisees outside the IKEA Group in 16 countries/territories. On February 17, 2011, IKEA announced its plans for a wind farm in Dalarna County, Sweden, furthering the furniture giant's goal of running on 100 percent renewable energy.

The first Möbel-IKÉA store was opened in Almhult, Smaland, in 1958, while the first stores outside Sweden were opened in Norway (1963)

and Denmark (1969). Today, Germany, with 44 stores, is IKEA's biggest market, followed by the United States, with 37. The first IKEA store in Latin America opened on February 2010 in Santo Domingo, Dominican Republic, although the company has thus far not shown much of a presence in the developing countries. The world's three largest IKEA stores are in Stockholm Kungens Kurva, Sweden; Shenyang, China; and Malmo Svagertorp, Sweden. There also is a very large IKEA store in Campbell field, Melbourne, Australia.

In 2012, IKEA plans to open its first shopping center in Croatia that will be one of the five biggest in Europe and among ten biggest IKEA stores in the world. IKEA stores are usually very large blue buildings with yellow accents (also Sweden's national colors) and few windows. Newer IKEA stores, like the one in Monchengladbach, Germany, make more use of glass, both for aesthetics and functionality.

Source: Based on information at www.wikipedia.com and www.ikea.com.

The Nature of Strategy Implementation

The strategy-implementation stage of strategic management is revealed in Figure 7-1. Successful strategy formulation does not guarantee successful strategy implementation. It is always more difficult to do something (strategy implementation) than to say you are going to do it (strategy formulation)! Although inextricably linked, strategy implementation is fundamentally different from strategy formulation. Strategy formulation and implementation can be contrasted in the following ways:

- Strategy formulation is positioning forces before the action.
- Strategy implementation is managing forces during the action.
- Strategy formulation focuses on effectiveness.
- Strategy implementation focuses on efficiency.
- Strategy formulation is primarily an intellectual process.
- Strategy implementation is primarily an operational process.
- Strategy formulation requires good intuitive and analytical skills.
- Strategy implementation requires special motivation and leadership skills.
- Strategy formulation requires coordination among a few individuals.
- Strategy implementation requires coordination among many individuals.

FIGURE 7-1

Comprehensive Strategic-Management Model

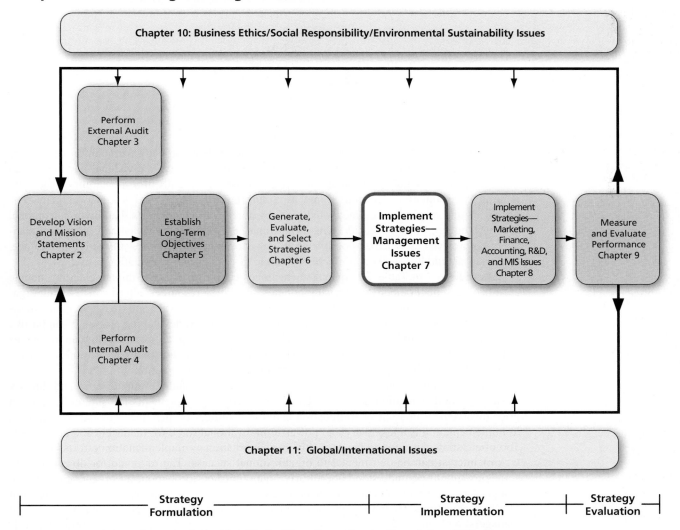

Source: Fred R. David, "How Companies Define Their Mission," *Long Range Planning* 22, no. 3 (June 1988): 40.

Strategy-formulation concepts and tools do not differ greatly for small, large, for-profit, or nonprofit organizations. However, strategy implementation varies substantially among different types and sizes of organizations. Implementing strategies requires such actions as altering sales territories, adding new departments, closing facilities, hiring new employees, changing an organization's pricing strategy, developing financial budgets, developing new employee benefits, establishing cost-control procedures, changing advertising strategies, building new facilities, training new employees, transferring managers among divisions, and building a better management information system. These types of activities obviously differ greatly among manufacturing, service, and governmental organizations.

Management Perspectives

In terms of "Quality of Management," *Fortune* in 2011 ranked the following companies as best in the world:

Rank	Company
1	McDonald's
2	ExxonMobil
3*	W.W. Grainger
3*	Walt Disney
5	U.S. Bancorp
6	Amazon.com
7	Apple
8	Nestlé
9	Nike
10	Occidental Petroleum

Source: Based on: http://money.cnn.com/magazines/fortune/mostadmired/2011/best_worst/best5.html

In all but the smallest organizations, the transition from strategy formulation to strategy implementation requires a shift in responsibility from strategists to divisional and functional managers. Implementation problems can arise because of this shift in responsibility, especially if strategy-formulation decisions come as a surprise to middle- and lower-level managers. Managers and employees are motivated more by perceived self-interests than by organizational interests, unless the two coincide. This is a primary reason why divisional and functional managers be involved as much as possible in strategy-formulation activities. Of equal importance, strategists should be involved as much as possible in strategy-implementation activities.

As indicated in Table 7-1, management issues central to strategy implementation include establishing annual objectives, devising policies, allocating resources, altering an existing organizational structure, restructuring and reengineering, revising reward and incentive plans, minimizing resistance to change, matching managers with strategy, developing a strategy-supportive culture, adapting production/operations processes, developing an effective human resources function, and, if necessary, downsizing. Management changes are necessarily more extensive when strategies to be implemented move a firm in a major new direction.

Managers and employees throughout an organization should participate early and directly in strategy-implementation decisions. Their role in strategy implementation should build upon prior involvement in strategy-formulation activities. Strategists' genuine personal commitment to implementation is a necessary and powerful motivational force for managers and employees. Too often, strategists are too busy to actively support strategy-implementation efforts, and their lack of interest can be detrimental to organizational success. The rationale for objectives and strategies should be understood and clearly communicated throughout an organization. Major competitors' accomplishments, products, plans, actions, and performance should be apparent to all organizational members. Major external opportunities and threats should be clear, and managers' and employees' questions should be answered. Top-down flow of communication is essential for developing bottom-up support.

TABLE 7-1   Some Management Issues Central to Strategy Implementation

Establish annual objectives

Devise policies

Allocate resources

Alter an existing organizational structure

Restructure and reengineer

Revise reward and incentive plans

Minimize resistance to change

Match managers with strategy

Develop a strategy-supportive culture

Adapt production/operations processes

Develop an effective human resources function

Downsize and furlough as needed

Link performance and pay to strategies

Firms need to develop a competitor focus at all hierarchical levels by gathering and widely distributing competitive intelligence; every employee should be able to benchmark her or his efforts against best-in-class competitors so that the challenge becomes personal. For example, Starbucks Corp. recently instituted "lean production/operations" at its 11,000 U.S. stores. This system eliminates idle employee time and unnecessary employee motions, such as walking, reaching, and bending. Starbucks says 30 percent of employees' time is motion and the company wants to reduce that. They say "motion and work are two different things."

Annual Objectives

Establishing annual objectives is a decentralized activity that directly involves all managers in an organization. Active participation in establishing annual objectives can lead to acceptance and commitment. *Annual objectives* are essential for strategy implementation because they (1) represent the basis for allocating resources; (2) are a primary mechanism for evaluating managers; (3) are the major instrument for monitoring progress toward achieving long-term objectives; and (4) establish organizational, divisional, and departmental priorities. Considerable time and effort should be devoted to ensuring that annual objectives are well conceived, consistent with long-term objectives, and supportive of strategies to be implemented. Approving, revising, or rejecting annual objectives is much more than a rubber-stamp activity. The purpose of annual objectives can be summarized as follows:

> Annual objectives serve as guidelines for action, directing and channeling efforts and activities of organization members. They provide a source of legitimacy in an enterprise by justifying activities to stakeholders. They serve as standards of performance. They serve as an important source of employee motivation and identification. They give incentives for managers and employees to perform. They provide a basis for organizational design.[2]

Clearly stated and communicated objectives are critical to success in all types and sizes of firms. Annual objectives, stated in terms of profitability, growth, and market share by business segment, geographic area, customer groups, and product, are common in organizations. Figure 7-2 illustrates how the Stamus Company could establish annual objectives based on long-term objectives. Table 7-2 reveals associated revenue figures that correspond to the objectives outlined in Figure 7-2. Note that, according to plan, the Stamus Company will slightly exceed its long-term objective of doubling company revenues between 2012 and 2014.

FIGURE 7-2

The Stamus Company's Hierarchy of Aims

```
                    ┌─────────────────────────────────────┐
                    │ LONG-TERM COMPANY OBJECTIVE          │
                    │                                      │
                    │ Double company revenues in two years │
                    │ through market development and       │
                    │ market penetration.                  │
                    │ (Current revenues are $2 million.)   │
                    └─────────────────────────────────────┘
```

DIVISION I ANNUAL OBJECTIVE	DIVISION II ANNUAL OBJECTIVE	DIVISION III ANNUAL OBJECTIVE
Increase divisional revenues by 40% this year and 40% next year. (Current revenues are $1 million.)	Increase divisional revenues by 40% this year and 40% next year. (Current revenues are $0.5 million.)	Increase divisional revenues by 50% this year and 50% next year. (Current revenues are $0.5 million.)

R&D annual objective	*Production annual objective*	*Marketing annual objective*	*Finance annual objective*	*Personnel annual objective*
Develop two new products this year that are succesfully marketed.	Increase production efficiency by 30% this year.	Increase the number of salespeople by 40 this year.	Obtain long-term financing of $400,000 in the next six months.	Reduce employee absenteeism from 10% to 5% this year.
	Purchasing Shipping Quality Control	Advertising Promotion Research Public Relations	Auditing Accounting Investments Collections Working Capital	

Figure 7-2 also reflects how a hierarchy of annual objectives can be established based on an organization's structure. Objectives should be consistent across hierarchical levels and form a network of supportive aims. *Horizontal consistency of objectives* is as important as *vertical consistency of objectives.* For instance, it would not be effective for manufacturing to achieve more than its annual objective of units produced if marketing could not sell the additional units.

Annual objectives should be measurable, consistent, reasonable, challenging, clear, communicated throughout the organization, characterized by an appropriate time dimension, and accompanied by commensurate rewards and sanctions. Too often, objectives are stated in generalities, with little operational usefulness. Annual objectives, such as "to

TABLE 7-2   The Stamus Company's Revenue Expectations (in $millions)

	2012	2013	2014
Division I Revenues	1.0	1.400	1.960
Division II Revenues	0.5	0.700	0.980
Division III Revenues	0.5	0.750	1.125
Total Company Revenues	**2.0**	**2.850**	**4.065**

improve communication" or "to improve performance," are not clear, specific, or measurable. Objectives should state quantity, quality, cost, and time—and also be verifiable. Terms and phrases such as *maximize, minimize, as soon as possible*, and *adequate* should be avoided.

Annual objectives should be compatible with employees' and managers' values and supported by clearly stated policies. More of something is not always better. Improved quality or reduced cost may, for example, be more important than quantity. It is important to tie rewards and sanctions to annual objectives so that employees and managers understand that achieving objectives is critical to successful strategy implementation. Clear annual objectives do not guarantee successful strategy implementation, but they do increase the likelihood that personal and organizational aims can be accomplished. Overemphasis on achieving objectives can result in undesirable conduct, such as faking the numbers, distorting the records, and letting objectives become ends in themselves. Managers must be alert to these potential problems.

Policies

Changes in a firm's strategic direction do not occur automatically. On a day-to-day basis, policies are needed to make a strategy work. Policies facilitate solving recurring problems and guide the implementation of strategy. Broadly defined, *policy* refers to specific guidelines, methods, procedures, rules, forms, and administrative practices established to support and encourage work toward stated goals. Policies are instruments for strategy implementation. Policies set boundaries, constraints, and limits on the kinds of administrative actions that can be taken to reward and sanction behavior; they clarify what can and cannot be done in pursuit of an organization's objectives. For example, Carnival's *Paradise* ship has a no smoking policy anywhere, anytime aboard ship. It was the first cruise ship to ban smoking comprehensively. Another example of corporate policy relates to surfing the web while at work. About 40 percent of companies today do not have a formal policy preventing employees from surfing the Internet, but software is being marketed now that allows firms to monitor how, when, where, and how long various employees use the Internet at work.

Policies let both employees and managers know what is expected of them, thereby increasing the likelihood that strategies will be implemented successfully. They provide a basis for management control, allow coordination across organizational units, and reduce the amount of time managers spend making decisions. Policies also clarify what work is to be done and by whom. They promote delegation of decision making to appropriate managerial levels where various problems usually arise. Many organizations have a policy manual that serves to guide and direct behavior. Wal-Mart has a policy that it calls the "10 Foot" Rule, whereby customers can find assistance within 10 feet of anywhere in the store. This is a welcomed policy in Japan, where Wal-Mart is trying to gain a foothold; 58 percent of all retailers in Japan are mom-and-pop stores and consumers historically have had to pay "top yen" rather than "discounted prices" for merchandise.

Policies can apply to all divisions and departments (for example, "We are an equal opportunity employer"). Some policies apply to a single department ("Employees in this department must take at least one training and development course each year"). Whatever their scope and form, policies serve as a mechanism for implementing strategies and obtaining objectives. Policies should be stated in writing whenever possible. They represent the means for carrying out strategic decisions. Examples of policies that support a company strategy, a divisional objective, and a departmental objective are given in Table 7-3.

Some example issues that may require a management policy are provided in Table 7-4.

TABLE 7-3 A Hierarchy of Policies

Company Strategy

Acquire a chain of retail stores to meet our sales growth and profitability objectives.

Supporting Policies

1. "All stores will be open from 8 a.m. to 8 p.m. Monday through Saturday." (This policy could increase retail sales if stores currently are open only 40 hours a week.)
2. "All stores must submit a Monthly Control Data Report." (This policy could reduce expense-to-sales ratios.)
3. "All stores must support company advertising by contributing 5 percent of their total monthly revenues for this purpose." (This policy could allow the company to establish a national reputation.)
4. "All stores must adhere to the uniform pricing guidelines set forth in the Company Handbook." (This policy could help assure customers that the company offers a consistent product in terms of price and quality in all its stores.)

Divisional Objective

Increase the division's revenues from $10 million in 2012 to $15 million in 2013.

Supporting Policies

1. "Beginning in January 2012, each one of this division's salespersons must file a weekly activity report that includes the number of calls made, the number of miles traveled, the number of units sold, the dollar volume sold, and the number of new accounts opened." (This policy could ensure that salespersons do not place too great an emphasis in certain areas.)
2. "Beginning in January 2012, this division will return to its employees 5 percent of its gross revenues in the form of a Christmas bonus." (This policy could increase employee productivity.)
3. "Beginning in January 2012, inventory levels carried in warehouses will be decreased by 30 percent in accordance with a just-in-time (JIT) manufacturing approach." (This policy could reduce production expenses and thus free funds for increased marketing efforts.)

Production Department Objective

Increase production from 20,000 units in 2012 to 30,000 units in 2013.

Supporting Policies

1. "Beginning in January 2012, employees will have the option of working up to 20 hours of overtime per week." (This policy could minimize the need to hire additional employees.)
2. "Beginning in January 2012, perfect attendance awards in the amount of $100 will be given to all employees who do not miss a workday in a given year." (This policy could decrease absenteeism and increase productivity.)
3. "Beginning in January 2012, new equipment must be leased rather than purchased." (This policy could reduce tax liabilities and thus allow more funds to be invested in modernizing production processes.)

TABLE 7-4 Some Issues That May Require a Management Policy

- To offer extensive or limited management development workshops and seminars
- To centralize or decentralize employee-training activities
- To recruit through employment agencies, college campuses, and/or newspapers
- To promote from within or to hire from the outside
- To promote on the basis of merit or on the basis of seniority
- To tie executive compensation to long-term and/or annual objectives
- To offer numerous or few employee benefits
- To negotiate directly or indirectly with labor unions
- To delegate authority for large expenditures or to centrally retain this authority
- To allow much, some, or no overtime work
- To establish a high- or low-safety stock of inventory
- To use one or more suppliers
- To buy, lease, or rent new production equipment
- To greatly or somewhat stress quality control
- To establish many or only a few production standards
- To operate one, two, or three shifts
- To discourage using insider information for personal gain
- To discourage sexual harassment
- To discourage smoking at work
- To discourage insider trading
- To discourage moonlighting

Resource Allocation

Resource allocation is a central management activity that allows for strategy execution. In organizations that do not use a strategic-management approach to decision making, resource allocation is often based on political or personal factors. Strategic management enables resources to be allocated according to priorities established by annual objectives.

Nothing could be more detrimental to strategic management and to organizational success than for resources to be allocated in ways not consistent with priorities indicated by approved annual objectives.

All organizations have at least four types of resources that can be used to achieve desired objectives: financial resources, physical resources, human resources, and technological resources. Allocating resources to particular divisions and departments does not mean that strategies will be successfully implemented. A number of factors commonly prohibit effective resource allocation, including an overprotection of resources, too great an emphasis on short-run financial criteria, organizational politics, vague strategy targets, a reluctance to take risks, and a lack of sufficient knowledge.

Below the corporate level, there often exists an absence of systematic thinking about resources allocated and strategies of the firm. Yavitz and Newman explain why:

> Managers normally have many more tasks than they can do. Managers must allocate time and resources among these tasks. Pressure builds up. Expenses are too high. The CEO wants a good financial report for the third quarter. Strategy formulation and implementation activities often get deferred. Today's problems soak up available energies and resources. Scrambled accounts and budgets fail to reveal the shift in allocation away from strategic needs to currently squeaking wheels.[3]

The real value of any resource allocation program lies in the resulting accomplishment of an organization's objectives. Effective resource allocation does not guarantee successful strategy implementation because programs, personnel, controls, and commitment must breathe life into the resources provided. Strategic management itself is sometimes referred to as a "resource allocation process."

Managing Conflict

Interdependency of objectives and competition for limited resources often leads to conflict. *Conflict* can be defined as a disagreement between two or more parties on one or more issues. Establishing annual objectives can lead to conflict because individuals have different expectations and perceptions, schedules create pressure, personalities are incompatible, and misunderstandings between line managers (such as production supervisors) and staff managers (such as human resource specialists) occur. For example, a collection manager's objective of reducing bad debts by 50 percent in a given year may conflict with a divisional objective to increase sales by 20 percent.

Establishing objectives can lead to conflict because managers and strategists must make trade-offs, such as whether to emphasize short-term profits or long-term growth, profit margin or market share, market penetration or market development, growth or stability, high risk or low risk, and social responsiveness or profit maximization. Trade-offs are necessary because no firm has sufficient resources to pursue all strategies that would benefit the firm. Table 7-5 reveals some important management trade-off decisions required in strategy implementation.

Conflict is unavoidable in organizations, so it is important that conflict be managed and resolved before dysfunctional consequences affect organizational performance. Conflict is not always bad. An absence of conflict can signal indifference and apathy. Conflict can serve to energize opposing groups into action and may help managers identify problems.

Various approaches for managing and resolving conflict can be classified into three categories: avoidance, defusion, and confrontation. *Avoidance* includes such actions as ignoring the problem in hopes that the conflict will resolve itself or physically separating the conflicting individuals (or groups). *Defusion* can include playing down differences between conflicting parties while accentuating similarities and common interests, compromising so that there is neither a clear winner nor loser, resorting to majority rule, appealing to a higher authority, or redesigning

TABLE 7-5 Some Management Trade-Off Decisions
Required in Strategy Implementation

To emphasize short-term profits or long-term growth

To emphasize profit margin or market share

To emphasize market development or market penetration

To lay off or furlough

To seek growth or stability

To take high risk or low risk

To be more socially responsible or more profitable

To outsource jobs or pay more to keep jobs at home

To acquire externally or to build internally

To restructure or reengineer

To use leverage or equity to raise funds

To use part-time or full-time employees

present positions. *Confrontation* is exemplified by exchanging members of conflicting parties so that each can gain an appreciation of the other's point of view or holding a meeting at which conflicting parties present their views and work through their differences.

Matching Structure with Strategy

Changes in strategy often require changes in the way an organization is structured for two major reasons. First, structure largely dictates how objectives and policies will be established. For example, objectives and policies established under a geographic organizational structure are couched in geographic terms. Objectives and policies are stated largely in terms of products in an organization whose structure is based on product groups. The structural format for developing objectives and policies can significantly impact all other strategy-implementation activities.

The second major reason why changes in strategy often require changes in structure is that structure dictates how resources will be allocated. If an organization's structure is based on customer groups, then resources will be allocated in that manner. Similarly, if an organization's structure is set up along functional business lines, then resources are allocated by functional areas. Unless new or revised strategies place emphasis in the same areas as old strategies, structural reorientation commonly becomes a part of strategy implementation.

Changes in strategy lead to changes in organizational structure. Structure should be designed to facilitate the strategic pursuit of a firm and, therefore, follow strategy. Without a strategy or reasons for being (mission), companies find it difficult to design an effective structure. Chandler found a particular structure sequence to be repeated often as organizations grow and change strategy over time.

There is no one optimal organizational design or structure for a given strategy or type of organization. What is appropriate for one organization may not be appropriate for a similar firm, although successful firms in a given industry do tend to organize themselves in a similar way. For example, consumer goods companies tend to emulate the divisional structure-by-product form of organization. Small firms tend to be functionally structured (centralized). Medium-sized firms tend to be divisionally structured (decentralized). Large firms tend to use a strategic business unit (SBU) or matrix structure. As organizations grow, their structures generally change from simple to complex as a result of concatenation, or the linking together of several basic strategies.

Numerous external and internal forces affect an organization; no firm could change its structure in response to every one of these forces, because to do so would lead to chaos. However, when a firm changes its strategy, the existing organizational structure may become ineffective. As indicated in Table 7-6, symptoms of an ineffective organizational structure include too many levels of management, too many meetings attended by too many people, too much attention being directed toward solving interdepartmental conflicts, too large a span of control, and too many unachieved objectives. Changes in structure can facilitate strategy-implementation efforts, but changes in structure should not be expected to make a bad strategy good, to make bad managers good, or to make bad products sell.

TABLE 7-6   Symptoms of an Ineffective Organizational Structure

1. Too many levels of management
2. Too many meetings attended by too many people
3. Too much attention being directed toward solving interdepartmental conflicts
4. Too large a span of control
5. Too many unachieved objectives
6. Declining corporate or business performance
7. Losing ground to rival firms
8. Revenue and/or earnings divided by number of employees and/or number of managers is low compared to rival firms

Structure undeniably can and does influence strategy. Strategies formulated must be workable, so if a certain new strategy required massive structural changes it would not be an attractive choice. In this way, structure can shape the choice of strategies. But a more important concern is determining what types of structural changes are needed to implement new strategies and how these changes can best be accomplished. We examine this issue by focusing on seven basic types of organizational structure: functional, divisional by geographic area, divisional by product, divisional by customer, divisional process, strategic business unit (SBU), and matrix.

The Functional Structure

The most widely used structure is the functional or centralized type because this structure is the simplest and least expensive of the seven alternatives. A *functional structure* groups tasks and activities by business function, such as production/operations, marketing, finance/accounting, research and development, and management information systems. A university may structure its activities by major functions that include academic affairs, student services, alumni relations, athletics, maintenance, and accounting. Besides being simple and inexpensive, a functional structure also promotes specialization of labor, encourages efficient use of managerial and technical talent, minimizes the need for an elaborate control system, and allows rapid decision making.

Some disadvantages of a functional structure are that it forces accountability to the top, minimizes career development opportunities, and is sometimes characterized by low employee morale, line/staff conflicts, poor delegation of authority, and inadequate planning for products and markets.

A functional structure often leads to short-term and narrow thinking that may undermine what is best for the firm as a whole. For example, the research and development department may strive to overdesign products and components to achieve technical elegance, while manufacturing may argue for low-frills products that can be mass produced more easily. Thus, communication is often not as good in a functional structure. Schein gives an example of a communication problem in a functional structure:

> The word "marketing" will mean product development to the engineer, studying customers through market research to the product manager, merchandising to the salesperson, and constant change in design to the manufacturing manager. Then when these managers try to work together, they often attribute disagreements to personalities and fail to notice the deeper, shared assumptions that vary and dictate how each function thinks.[4]

Most large companies have abandoned the functional structure in favor of decentralization and improved accountability. However, a large firm that still successfully uses a functional structure is Nucor Steel, based in Charlotte, North Carolina. Netflix, the company showcased for excellent strategic management in the prior chapter, also operates from a functional structure—as illustrated in Figure 7-3.

Table 7-7 summarizes the advantages and disadvantages of a functional organizational structure.

FIGURE 7-3

Netflix's Organizational Structure

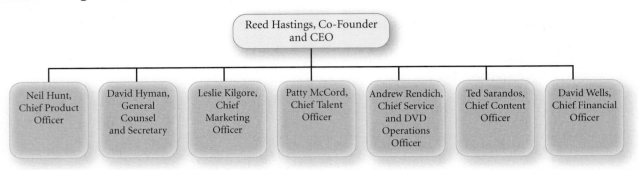

The Divisional Structure

The *divisional* or *decentralized structure* is the second most common type used by U.S. businesses. As a small organization grows, it has more difficulty managing different products and services in different markets. Some form of divisional structure generally becomes necessary to motivate employees, control operations, and compete successfully in diverse locations. The divisional structure can be organized in one of four ways: *by geographic area, by product* or *service, by customer,* or *by process.* With a divisional structure, functional activities are performed both centrally and in each separate division.

Cisco Systems recently discarded its divisional structure by customer and reorganized into a functional structure. CEO John Chambers replaced the three-customer structure based on big businesses, small businesses, and telecoms, and now the company has five functional executive vice presidents (EVPs). Chambers says the goal was to eliminate duplication, but the change should not be viewed as a shift in strategy. Chambers's span of control in the new structure is reduced from 15 to 12 managers reporting directly to him.

Sun Microsystems recently reduced the number of its business units from seven to four. Kodak recently reduced its number of business units from seven by-customer divisions to five by-product divisions. As consumption patterns become increasingly similar worldwide, a by-product structure is becoming more effective than a by-customer or a by-geographic type divisional structure. In the restructuring, Kodak eliminated its global operations division and distributed those responsibilities across the new by-product divisions.

A divisional structure has some clear advantages. First and perhaps foremost, accountability is clear. That is, divisional managers can be held responsible for sales and profit levels. Because a divisional structure is based on extensive delegation of authority, managers and employees can easily see the results of their good or bad performances. As a result, employee morale is generally higher in a divisional structure than it is in a centralized structure. Other advantages of

TABLE 7-7   Advantages and Disadvantages of a Functional Organizational Structure

Advantages	Disadvantages
1. Simple and inexpensive	1. Accountability forced to the top
2. Capitalizes on specialization of business activities such as marketing and finance	2. Delegation of authority and responsibility not encouraged
3. Minimizes need for elaborate control system	3. Minimizes career development
4. Allows for rapid decision making	4. Low employee/manager morale
	5. Inadequate planning for products and markets
	6. Leads to short-term, narrow thinking
	7. Leads to communication problems

TABLE 7-8   Advantages and Disadvantages of a Divisional Organizational Structure

Advantages	Disadvantages
1. Accountability is clear	1. Can be costly
2. Allows local control of local situations	2. Duplication of functional activities
3. Creates career development chances	3. Requires a skilled management force
4. Promotes delegation of authority	4. Requires an elaborate control system
5. Leads to competitive climate internally	5. Competition among divisions can become so intense as to be dysfunctional
6. Allows easy adding of new products or regions	6. Can lead to limited sharing of ideas and resources
7. Allows strict control and attention to products, customers, and/or regions	7. Some regions/products/customers may receive special treatment

the divisional design are that it creates career development opportunities for managers, allows local control of situations, leads to a competitive climate within an organization, and allows new businesses and products to be added easily.

The divisional design is not without some limitations, however. Perhaps the most important limitation is that a divisional structure is costly, for a number of reasons. First, each division requires functional specialists who must be paid. Second, there exists some duplication of staff services, facilities, and personnel; for instance, functional specialists are also needed centrally (at headquarters) to coordinate divisional activities. Third, managers must be well qualified because the divisional design forces delegation of authority; better-qualified individuals require higher salaries. A divisional structure can also be costly because it requires an elaborate, head-quarters-driven control system. Fourth, competition between divisions may become so intense that it is dysfunctional and leads to limited sharing of ideas and resources for the common good of the firm. Table 7-8 summarizes the advantages and disadvantages of divisional organizational structure.

Ghoshal and Bartlett, two leading scholars in strategic management, note the following:

> As their label clearly warns, divisions divide. The divisional model fragments companies' resources; it creates vertical communication channels that insulate business units and prevents them from sharing their strengths with one another. Consequently, the whole of the corporation is often less than the sum of its parts. A final limitation of the divisional design is that certain regions, products, or customers may sometimes receive special treatment, and it may be difficult to maintain consistent, companywide practices. Nonetheless, for most large organizations and many small firms, the advantages of a divisional structure more than offset the potential limitations.[5]

A *divisional structure by geographic area* is appropriate for organizations whose strategies need to be tailored to fit the particular needs and characteristics of customers in different geographic areas. This type of structure can be most appropriate for organizations that have similar branch facilities located in widely dispersed areas. A divisional structure by geographic area allows local participation in decision making and improved coordination within a region. Hershey Foods is an example company organized using the divisional-by geographic region type of structure. Hershey's divisions are United States, Canada, Mexico, Brazil, and Other. Analysts contend that this type of structure may not be best for Hershey because consumption patterns for candy are quite similar worldwide. An alternative—and perhaps better—type of structure for Hershey would be divisional by product because the company produces, and sells three types of products worldwide: (1) chocolate, (2) nonchocolate, and (3) grocery.

Coca-Cola Company operates from a divisional-by-geographic region type organizational structure, as illustrated in Figure 7-4.

FIGURE 7-4

Coca-Cola Company Executive Officers

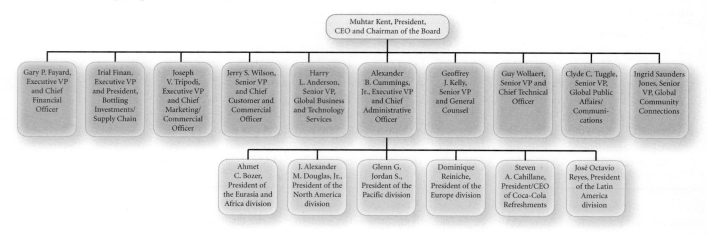

Source: Coke's 2010 *Annual Report.*

The *divisional structure by product (or services)* is most effective for implementing strategies when specific products or services need special emphasis. Also, this type of structure is widely used when an organization offers only a few products or services or when an organization's products or services differ substantially. The divisional structure allows strict control over and attention to product lines, but it may also require a more skilled management force and reduced top management control. General Motors, DuPont, and Procter & Gamble use a divisional structure by product to implement strategies. Huffy, the largest bicycle company in the world, is another firm that is highly decentralized based on a divisional-by-product structure. Based in Ohio, Huffy's divisions are the Bicycle division, the Gerry Baby Products division, the Huffy Sports division, YLC Enterprises, and Washington Inventory Service. Harry Shaw, Huffy's chairman, believes decentralization is one of the keys to Huffy's success.

Eastman Chemical established a new by-product divisional organizational structure. The company's two new divisions, Eastman Company and Voridian Company, focus on chemicals and polymers, respectively. The Eastman division focuses on coatings, adhesives, inks, and plastics, whereas the Voridian division focuses on fibers, polyethylene, and other polymers. Microsoft recently reorganized the whole corporation into three large divisions-by-product. Headed by a president, the new divisions are (1) platform products and services, (2) business, and (3) entertainment and devices. The Swiss electrical-engineering company ABB Ltd. recently scrapped its two core divisions, (1) power technologies and (2) automation technologies, and replaced them with five new divisions: (1) power products, (2) power systems, (3) automation products, (4) process automation, and (5) robotics.

When a few major customers are of paramount importance and many different services are provided to these customers, then a *divisional structure by customer* can be the most effective way to implement strategies. This structure allows an organization to cater effectively to the requirements of clearly defined customer groups. For example, book publishing companies often organize their activities around customer groups, such as colleges, secondary schools, and private commercial schools. Some airline companies have two major customer divisions: passengers and freight or cargo services. Utility companies often use (1) commercial, (2) residential, and (3) industrial as their divisions-by-customer.

Merrill Lynch is organized into separate divisions that cater to different groups of customers, including wealthy individuals, institutional investors, and small corporations. Motorola's semiconductor chip division is also organized divisionally by customer, having three separate segments that sell to (1) the automotive and industrial market, (2) the mobile phone market, and (3) the data-networking market. The automotive and industrial segment is doing well, but the other two segments are faltering, which is a reason why Motorola is trying to divest its semiconductor operations.

A *divisional structure by process* is similar to a functional structure, because activities are organized according to the way work is actually performed. However, a key difference between these two designs is that functional departments are not accountable for profits or revenues, whereas divisional process departments are evaluated on these criteria. An example of a divisional structure by process is a manufacturing business organized into six divisions: electrical work, glass cutting, welding, grinding, painting, and foundry work. In this case, all operations related to these specific processes would be grouped under the separate divisions. Each process (division) would be responsible for generating revenues and profits. The divisional structure by process can be particularly effective in achieving objectives when distinct production processes represent the thrust of competitiveness in an industry. Halliburton's organizational chart illustrated on the next page features aspects of the division-by-process design.

The Strategic Business Unit (SBU) Structure

As the number, size, and diversity of divisions in an organization increase, controlling and evaluating divisional operations become increasingly difficult for strategists. Increases in sales often are not accompanied by similar increases in profitability. The span of control becomes too large at top levels of the firm. For example, in a large conglomerate organization composed of 90 divisions, such as ConAgra, the chief executive officer could have difficulty even remembering the first names of divisional presidents. In multidivisional organizations, an SBU structure can greatly facilitate strategy-implementation efforts. ConAgra has put its many divisions into three primary SBUs: (1) food service (restaurants), (2) retail (grocery stores), and (3) agricultural products.

The SBU structure groups similar divisions into strategic business units and delegates authority and responsibility for each unit to a senior executive who reports directly to the chief executive officer. This change in structure can facilitate strategy implementation by improving coordination between similar divisions and channeling accountability to distinct business units. In a 100-division conglomerate, the divisions could perhaps be regrouped into 10 SBUs according to certain common characteristics, such as competing in the same industry, being located in the same area, or having the same customers.

Two disadvantages of an SBU structure are that it requires an additional layer of management, which increases salary expenses. Also, the role of the group vice president is often ambiguous. However, these limitations often do not outweigh the advantages of improved coordination and accountability. Another advantage of the SBU structure is that it makes the tasks of planning and control by the corporate office more manageable.

Citigroup recently reorganized the whole company into two SBUs: (1) Citigroup, which includes the retail bank, the corporate and investment bank, the private bank, and global transaction services; and (2) Citi Holdings, which includes Citi's asset management and consumer finance segments, CitiMortgage, CitiFinancial, and the joint brokerage operations with Morgan Stanley. Citigroup's CEO, Vikram Pandit, says the restructuring will allow the company to reduce operating costs and to divest (spin off) Citi Holdings.

The huge computer firm Dell Inc. recently reorganized into two SBUs. One SBU is Consumer Products and the other is Commercial. As part of its reorganization, Dell deleted the geographic divisions within its Consumer Products segment. However within its Commercial segment, there are now three worldwide units: (1) large enterprise, (2) public sector, and (3) small and midsize businesses. Dell is also closing a manufacturing facility in Austin, Texas, and laying off more employees as the company struggles to compete. Computer prices and demand are falling as competition increases. Atlantic Richfield Fairchild Industries, and Honeywell International are examples of firms that successfully use an SBU-type structure.

As illustrated in Figure 7-5, Sonoco Products Corporation, based in Hartsville, South Carolina, utilizes an SBU organizational structure. Note that Sonoco's SBUs—Industrial Products and Consumer Products—each have four autonomous divisions that have their own sales, manufacturing, R&D, finance, HRM, and MIS functions.

An excellent example of an SBU organizational chart is the one posted at the Halliburton Company website and shown in Figure 7-6. Note that six division executives report to the Drilling and Evaluation top executive, while four division heads report to the Completion and Production top executive. It is interesting and somewhat unusual that the 10 Halliburton divisions are organized by process rather than by geographic region or product.

FIGURE 7-5

Sonoco Products' SBU Organizational Chart

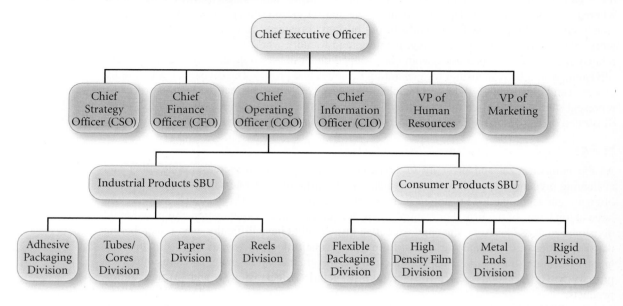

FIGURE 7-6

Halliburton Company's SBU Organizational Chart

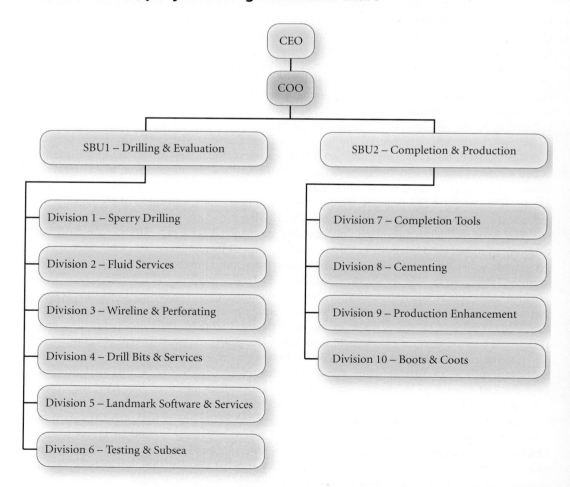

Source: Based on http://www.halliburton.com/AboutUs/default.aspx?pageid=2458&navid=966

The Matrix Structure

A *matrix structure* is the most complex of all designs because it depends upon both vertical and horizontal flows of authority and communication (hence the term *matrix*). In contrast, functional and divisional structures depend primarily on vertical flows of authority and communication. A matrix structure can result in higher overhead because it creates more management positions. Other disadvantages of a matrix structure that contribute to overall complexity include dual lines of budget authority (a violation of the unity-of-command principle), dual sources of reward and punishment, shared authority, dual reporting channels, and a need for an extensive and effective communication system.

Despite its complexity, the matrix structure is widely used in many industries, including construction, health care, research, and defense. As indicated in Table 7-9, some advantages of a matrix structure are that project objectives are clear, there are many channels of communication, workers can see the visible results of their work, and shutting down a project can be accomplished relatively easily. Another advantage of a matrix structure is that it facilitates the use of specialized personnel, equipment, and facilities. Functional resources are shared in a matrix structure, rather than duplicated as in a divisional structure. Individuals with a high degree of expertise can divide their time as needed among projects, and they in turn develop their own skills and competencies more than in other structures.

A typical matrix structure is illustrated in Figure 7-7. Note that the letters (A through Z4) refer to managers. For example, if you were manager A, you would be responsible for financial aspects of Project 1, and you would have two bosses: the Project 1 Manager onsite and the CFO off site.

For a matrix structure to be effective, organizations need participative planning, training, clear mutual understanding of roles and responsibilities, excellent internal communication, and mutual trust and confidence. The matrix structure is being used more frequently by U.S. businesses because firms are pursuing strategies that add new products, customer groups, and technology to their range of activities. Out of these changes are coming product managers, functional managers, and geographic-area managers, all of whom have important strategic responsibilities. When several variables, such as product, customer, technology, geography, functional area, and line of business, have roughly equal strategic priorities, a matrix organization can be an effective structural form.

Some Do's and Don'ts in Developing Organizational Charts

Students analyzing strategic-management cases are often asked to revise and develop a firm's organizational structure. This section provides some basic guidelines for this endeavor. There are some basic do's and don'ts in regard to devising or constructing organizational charts, especially for midsize to large firms. First of all, reserve the title CEO for the top executive of the firm. Don't use the title "president" for the top person; use it for the division top managers if there are divisions within the firm. Also, do not use the title "president" for functional business executives. They should have the title "chief," or "vice president," or "manager," or "officer," such as "Chief Information Officer," or "VP of Human Resources." Further, do not recommend a dual

TABLE 7-9   Advantages and Disadvantages of a Matrix Structure

Advantages	Disadvantages
1. Project objectives are clear	1. Requires excellent vertical and horizontal flows of communication
2. Employees can clearly see results of their work	2. Costly because creates more manager positions
3. Shutting down a project is easily accomplished	3. Violates unity of command principle
4. Facilitates uses of special equipment/personnel/facilities	4. Creates dual lines of budget authority
5. Functional resources are shared instead of duplicated as in a divisional structure	5. Creates dual sources of reward/punishment
	6. Creates shared authority and reporting
	7. Requires mutual trust and understanding

FIGURE 7-7

An Example Matrix Structure

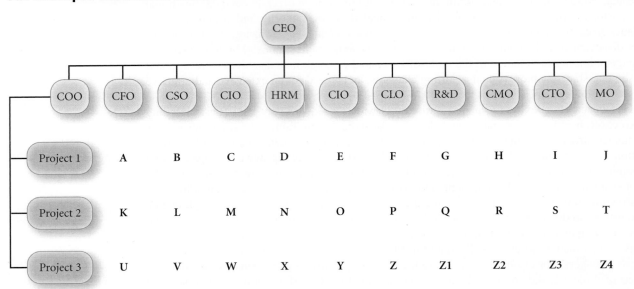

Note: Titles spelled out as follows.

Chief Executive Officer (CEO)
Chief Finance Officer (CFO)
Chief Strategy Officer (CSO)
Chief Information Officer (CIO)
Human Resources Manager (HRM)
Chief Operating Officer (COO)
Chief Legal Officer (CLO)
Research & Development Officer (R&D)
Chief Marketing Officer (CMO)
Chief Technology Officer (CTO)
Competitive Intelligence Officer (CIO)
Maintenance Officer (MO)

title (such as "CEO and president") for just one executive. The chairman of the board and CEO of Bristol-Myers Squibb, Peter Dolan, recently gave up his title as chairman. However, Pfizer's CEO, Jeffrey Kindler, recently added chairman of the board to his title when he succeeded Hank McKinnell as chairman of Pfizer's board. And Comverse Technology recently named Andre Dahan as its president, chief executive officer, and board director. Actually, "chairperson" is much better than "chairman" for this title.

A significant movement began among corporate America in mid-2009 to split the chairperson of the board and the CEO positions in publicly-held companies.[6] The movement includes asking the New York Stock Exchange and Nasdaq to adopt listing rules that would require separate positions. About 37 percent of companies in the S&P 500 stock index have separate positions, up from 22 percent in 2002, but this still leaves plenty of room for improvement. Among European and Asian companies, the split in these two positions is much more common. For example, 79 percent of British companies split the positions, and all German and Dutch companies split the position.

Directly below the CEO, it is best to have a COO (chief operating officer) with any division presidents reporting directly to the COO. On the same level as the COO and also reporting to the CEO, draw in your functional business executives, such as a CFO (chief financial officer), VP of human resources, a CSO (chief strategy officer), a CIO (chief information officer), a CMO (chief marketing officer), a VP of R&D, a VP of legal affairs, an investment relations officer, maintenance officer, and so on. Note in Figure 7-8 that these positions are labeled and placed appropriately. Note that a controller and/or treasurer would normally report to the CFO.

FIGURE 7-8

Typical Top Managers of a Large Firm

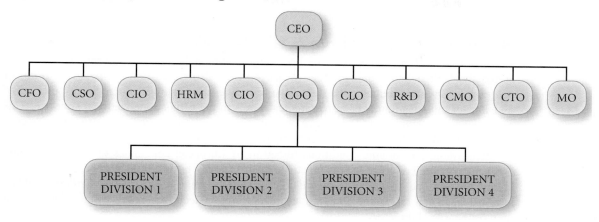

Note: Titles spelled out as follows.

Chief Executive Officer (CEO)
Chief Finance Officer (CFO)
Chief Strategy Officer (CSO)
Chief Information Officer (CIO)
Human Resources Manager (HRM)
Chief Operating Officer (COO)
Chief Legal Officer (CLO)
Research & Development Officer (R&D)
Chief Marketing Officer (CMO)
Chief Technology Officer (CTO)
Competitive Intelligence Officer (CIO)
Maintenance Officer (MO)

In developing an organizational chart, avoid having a particular person reporting to more than one person in the chain of command. This would violate the unity-of-command principle of management that "every employee should have just one boss." Also, do not have the CFO, CIO, CSO, human resource officer, or other functional positions report to the COO. All these positions report directly to the CEO.

A key consideration in devising an organizational structure concerns the divisions. Note whether the divisions (if any) of a firm presently are established based upon geography, customer, product, or process. If the firm's organizational chart is not available, you often can devise a chart based on the titles of executives. An important case analysis activity is for you to decide how the divisions of a firm should be organized for maximum effectiveness. Even if the firm presently has no divisions, determine whether the firm would operate better with divisions. In other words, which type of divisional breakdown do you (or your group or team) feel would be best for the firm in allocating resources, establishing objectives, and devising compensation incentives? This important strategic decision faces many midsize and large firms (and teams of students analyzing a strategic-management case).

As consumption patterns become more and more similar worldwide, the divisional-by-product form of structure is increasingly the most effective. Be mindful that all firms have functional staff below their top executive and often readily provide this information, so be wary of concluding prematurely that a particular firm utilizes a functional structure. If you see the word "president" in the titles of executives, coupled with financial-reporting segments, such as by product or geographic region, then the firm is divisionally structured.

If the firm is large with numerous divisions, decide whether an SBU type of structure would be more appropriate to reduce the span of control reporting to the COO. Note in Figure 7-5 that the Sonoco Products' strategic business units (SBUs) are based on product groupings. An alternative SBU structure would have been to base the division groupings on location. One never knows for sure if a proposed or actual structure is indeed most effective for a particular firm. According to Alfred Chandler, declining financial performance signals a need for altering the structure.

Restructuring and Reengineering

Restructuring and reengineering are becoming commonplace on the corporate landscape across the United States and Europe. *Restructuring*—also called *downsizing, rightsizing,* or *delayering*—involves reducing the size of the firm in terms of number of employees, number of divisions or units, and number of hierarchical levels in the firm's organizational structure. This reduction in size is intended to improve both efficiency and effectiveness. Restructuring is concerned primarily with shareholder well-being rather than employee well-being.

Recessionary economic conditions forced many European companies to downsize, laying off managers and employees. This practice has historically been rare in Europe. because labor unions and laws required lengthy negotiations or huge severance checks before workers could be terminated. In contrast to the United States, labor union executives of large European firms sit on most boards of directors.

Job security in European companies is slowly moving toward a U.S. scenario, in which firms lay off almost at will. From banks in Milan to factories in Mannheim, European employers are starting to show people the door in an effort to streamline operations, increase efficiency, and compete against already slim and trim U.S. firms. Massive U.S.-style layoffs are still rare in Europe, but unemployment rates throughout the continent are rising quite rapidly. European firms still prefer to downsize by attrition and retirement rather than by blanket layoffs because of culture, laws, and unions.

In contrast, *reengineering* is concerned more with employee and customer well-being than shareholder well-being. Reengineering—also called process management, process innovation, or process redesign—involves reconfiguring or redesigning work, jobs, and processes for the purpose of improving cost, quality, service, and speed. Reengineering does not usually affect the organizational structure or chart, nor does it imply job loss or employee layoffs. Whereas restructuring is concerned with eliminating or establishing, shrinking or enlarging, and moving organizational departments and divisions, the focus of reengineering is changing the way work is actually carried out. Reengineering is characterized by many tactical (short-term, business-function-specific) decisions, whereas restructuring is characterized by strategic (long-term, affecting all business functions) decisions.

Developed by Motorola in 1986 and made famous by CEO Jack Welch at General Electric and more recently by Robert Nardelli, former CEO of Home Depot, *Six Sigma* is a quality-boosting process improvement technique that entails training several key persons in the firm in the techniques to monitor, measure, and improve processes and eliminate defects. Six Sigma has been widely applied across industries from retailing to financial services. CEO Dave Cote at Honeywell and CEO Jeff Immelt at General Electric spurred acceptance of Six Sigma, which aims to improve work processes and eliminate waste by training "select" employees who are given judo titles such as Master Black Belts, Black Belts, and Green Belts.

Six Sigma was criticized in a *Wall Street Journal* article that cited many example firms whose stock price fell for a number of years after adoption of Six Sigma. The technique's reliance on the special group of trained employees is problematic and its use within retail firms such as Home Depot has not been as successful as in manufacturing firms.[7]

Restructuring

Firms often employ restructuring when various ratios appear out of line with competitors as determined through benchmarking exercises. Recall that *benchmarking* simply involves comparing a firm against the best firms in the industry on a wide variety of performance-related criteria. Some benchmarking ratios commonly used in rationalizing the need for restructuring are head-count-to-sales-volume, or corporate-staff-to-operating-employees, or span-of-control figures.

The primary benefit sought from restructuring is cost reduction. For some highly bureaucratic firms, restructuring can actually rescue the firm from global competition and demise. But the downside of restructuring can be reduced employee commitment, creativity, and innovation that accompanies the uncertainty and trauma associated with pending and actual employee layoffs. Avon Products restructured in 2011 partly due to corruption investigations in its Russia and Brazil operations. The company reduced its six commercial business units down to two—(1) Developed Markets and (2) Developing Markets—in essence going to a divisional by geographic region type structure. Avon has been reporting lower sales and profits amid missteps in key markets. CEO Andrea Jung is installing five new regional heads and new presidents in Avon's U.S. and Russia markets.

Another downside of restructuring is that many people today do not aspire to become managers, and many present-day managers are trying to get off the management track.[8] Sentiment against joining management ranks is higher today than ever. About 80 percent of employees say they want nothing to do with management, a major shift from just a decade ago when 60 to 70 percent hoped to become managers. Managing others historically led to enhanced career mobility, financial rewards, and executive perks; but in today's global, more competitive, restructured arena, managerial jobs demand more hours and headaches with fewer financial rewards. Managers today manage more people spread over different locations, travel more, manage diverse functions, and are change agents even when they have nothing to do with the creation of the plan or disagree with its approach. *Employers today are looking for people who can do things, not for people who make other people do things.* Restructuring in many firms has made a manager's job an invisible, thankless role. More workers today are self-managed, entrepreneurs, interpreneurs, or team-managed. Managers today need to be counselors, motivators, financial advisors, and psychologists. They also run the risk of becoming technologically behind in their areas of expertise. "Dilbert" cartoons commonly portray managers as enemies or as morons.

Reengineering

The argument for a firm engaging in reengineering usually goes as follows: Many companies historically have been organized vertically by business function. This arrangement has led over time to managers' and employees' mind-sets being defined by their particular functions rather than by overall customer service, product quality, or corporate performance. The logic is that all firms tend to bureaucratize over time. As routines become entrenched, turf becomes delineated and defended, and politics takes precedence over performance. Walls that exist in the physical workplace can be reflections of "mental" walls.

In reengineering, a firm uses information technology to break down functional barriers and create a work system based on business processes, products, or outputs rather than on functions or inputs. Cornerstones of reengineering are decentralization, reciprocal interdependence, and information sharing. A firm that exemplifies complete information sharing is Springfield Remanufacturing Corporation, which provides to all employees a weekly income statement of the firm, as well as extensive information on other companies' performances.

The *Wall Street Journal* noted that reengineering today must go beyond knocking down internal walls that keep parts of a company from cooperating effectively; it must also knock down the external walls that prohibit or discourage cooperation with other firms—even rival firms.[9] A maker of disposable diapers echoes this need differently when it says that to be successful "cooperation at the firm must stretch from stump to rump."

Hewlett-Packard is a good example of a company that has knocked down the external barriers to cooperation and practices modern reengineering. The HP of today shares its forecasts with all of its supply-chain partners and shares other critical information with its distributors and other stakeholders. HP does all the buying of resin for its many manufacturers, giving it a volume discount of up to 5 percent. HP has established many alliances and cooperative agreements of the kind discussed in Chapter 5.

A benefit of reengineering is that it offers employees the opportunity to see more clearly how their particular jobs affect the final product or service being marketed by the firm. However, reengineering can also raise manager and employee anxiety, which, unless calmed, can lead to corporate trauma.

Linking Performance and Pay to Strategies

With so many people out of work and executive salaries so large, politicians are more and more giving shareholders greater control over executive pay. The new Dodd-Frank Wall Street Reform and Consumer Protection Act grants shareholders advisory votes on compensation. A recent

Bloomberg Businessweek article says companies should install five policies to improve their compensation practices:

1. Provide full transparency to all stakeholders. Novartis does an excellent job on this.
2. Reward long-term performance with long-term pay, rather than annual incentives. ExxonMobil does an excellent job on this.
3. Base executive compensation on actual company performance, rather than on stock price. Target, for example, bases executive pay on same-store sales growth rather than stock price.
4. Extend the time-horizon for bonuses. Replace short-term with long-term incentives. Goldman Sachs does an excellent job on this.
5. Increase equity between workers and executives. Delete many special perks and benefits for executives. Be more consistent across levels, although employees with greater responsibility must receive greater compensation.[10]

CEOs at Japanese companies with more than $10 billion in annual revenues are paid about $1.3 million annually, including bonuses and stock options.[11] This compares to an average CEO pay among European firms of $6 million and an average among U.S. firms of $12 million. As firms acquire other firms in other countries, these pay differences can cause resentment and even turmoil. Larger pay packages of American CEOs are socially less acceptable in many other countries. For example, in Japan, seniority rather than performance has been the key factor in determining pay, and harmony among managers is emphasized over individual excellence.

How can an organization's reward system be more closely linked to strategic performance? How can decisions on salary increases, promotions, merit pay, and bonuses be more closely aligned to support the long-term strategic objectives of the organization? There are no widely accepted answers to these questions, but a dual bonus system based on both annual objectives and long-term objectives is becoming common. The percentage of a manager's annual bonus attributable to short-term versus long-term results should vary by hierarchical level in the organization. A chief executive officer's annual bonus could, for example, be determined on a 75 percent short-term and 25 percent long-term basis. It is important that bonuses not be based solely on short-term results because such a system ignores long-term company strategies and objectives.

One result of the global recession was that companies instituted policies to allow their shareholders to vote on executive compensation policies. Aflac was the first U.S. corporation to voluntarily give shareholders an advisory vote on executive compensation. Aflac did this back in 2007. Apple did this in 2008, as did H&R Block. Several companies that instituted say-on-pay policies more recently were Ingersoll-Rand, Verizon, Motorola, Occidental Petroleum, and Hewlett-Packard. These new policies underscore how the financial crisis and shareholder outrage about top executive pay has affected compensation practice. None of the shareholder votes are binding on the companies, however, at least not so far. The U.S. House of Representatives recently passed a bill to formalize this shareholder tactic, which is gaining steam across the country as a means to combat exorbitant executive pay.

In an effort to cut costs and increase productivity, more and more Japanese companies are switching from seniority-based pay to performance-based approaches. Toyota has switched to a full merit system for 20,000 of its 70,000 white-collar workers. Fujitsu, Sony, Matsushita Electric Industrial, and Kao also have switched to merit pay systems. This switching is hurting morale at some Japanese companies, which have trained workers for decades to cooperate rather than to compete and to work in groups rather than individually.

Richard Brown, CEO of Electronic Data Systems (EDS), once said,

---

You have to start with an appraisal system that gives genuine feedback and differentiates performance. Some call it ranking people. That seems a little harsh. But you can't have a manager checking a box that says you're either stupendous, magnificent, very good, good, or average. Concise, constructive feedback is the fuel workers use to get better. A company that doesn't differentiate performance risks losing its best people.[12]

Profit sharing is another widely used form of incentive compensation. More than 30 percent of U.S. companies have profit sharing plans, but critics emphasize that too many factors affect profits for this to be a good criterion. Taxes, pricing, or an acquisition would wipe out profits, for example. Also, firms try to minimize profits in a sense to reduce taxes.

General Motors paid its 45,000 hourly workers in the United States $3,000 each in profit-sharing payouts in 2011, the largest amount ever for the company. In comparison, Ford Motor paid its U.S. hourly workers $5,000 in profit sharing, more than the company was required to pay under the profit-sharing formula in its United Auto Workers contract. Unlike GM and Ford, Chrysler Group LLC did not make money in 2010 but in early 2011 still paid its hourly workers a $750 bonus in recognition of their contribution to the firm's progress toward recovery.

Still another criterion widely used to link performance and pay to strategies is gain sharing. *Gain sharing* requires employees or departments to establish performance targets; if actual results exceed objectives, all members get bonuses. More than 26 percent of U.S. companies use some form of gain sharing; about 75 percent of gain sharing plans have been adopted since 1980. Carrier, a subsidiary of United Technologies, has had excellent success with gain sharing in its six plants in Syracuse, New York; Firestone's tire plant in Wilson, North Carolina, has experienced similar success with gain sharing.

Criteria such as sales, profit, production efficiency, quality, and safety could also serve as bases for an effective *bonus system.* If an organization meets certain understood, agreed-upon profit objectives, every member of the enterprise should share in the harvest. A bonus system can be an effective tool for motivating individuals to support strategy-implementation efforts. BankAmerica, for example, recently overhauled its incentive system to link pay to sales of the bank's most profitable products and services. Branch managers receive a base salary plus a bonus based both on the number of new customers and on sales of bank products. Every employee in each branch is also eligible for a bonus if the branch exceeds its goals. Thomas Peterson, a top BankAmerica executive, says, "We want to make people responsible for meeting their goals, so we pay incentives on sales, not on controlling costs or on being sure the parking lot is swept."

Five tests are often used to determine whether a performance-pay plan will benefit an organization:

1. ***Does the plan capture attention?*** Are people talking more about their activities and taking pride in early successes under the plan?
2. ***Do employees understand the plan?*** Can participants explain how it works and what they need to do to earn the incentive?
3. ***Is the plan improving communication?*** Do employees know more than they used to about the company's mission, plans, and objectives?
4. ***Does the plan pay out when it should?*** Are incentives being paid for desired results—and being withheld when objectives are not met?
5. ***Is the company or unit performing better?*** Are profits up? Has market share grown? Have gains resulted in part from the incentives?[13]

In addition to a dual bonus system, a combination of reward strategy incentives, such as salary raises, stock options, fringe benefits, promotions, praise, recognition, criticism, fear, increased job autonomy, and awards, can be used to encourage managers and employees to push hard for successful strategic implementation. The range of options for getting people, departments, and divisions to actively support strategy-implementation activities in a particular organization is almost limitless. Merck, for example, recently gave each of its 37,000 employees a 10-year option to buy 100 shares of Merck stock at a set price of $127. Steven Darien, Merck's vice president of human resources, says, "We needed to find ways to get everyone in the workforce on board in terms of our goals and objectives. Company executives will begin meeting with all Merck workers to explore ways in which employees can contribute more."

There is rising public resentment over executive pay. The Associated Press (AP), using data provided by Equilar, recently revealed that the average pay package for CEOs in the United States in 2010 was 24 percent higher than a year earlier, reversing two years of declines. In contrast, employees' pay only grew 3 percent in 2010, to an average of about $40,500. CEOs received more pay of all types—salaries, bonuses, stock options, and perks. The biggest gains came in cash bonuses, typically based on corporate profits, which rose 41 percent last year.

The highest-paid CEO in 2010 was Philippe Dauman of Viacom, the entertainment company that owns MTV, Nickelodeon, and Paramount Pictures. He received a 2010 pay package valued at $84.5 million, two and a half times what he made the year before. Besides

Dauman, other top paid CEOs included Leslie Moonves of CBS, $56.9 million; David Zaslav of Discovery Communications, $42.6 million; Brian Roberts of Comcast, $31.1 million; Robert Iger of Walt Disney, $28 million; and Jeff Bewkes of Time Warner, $26.1 million. The 10 highest-paid CEOs made $440 million in 2010, a third more than the top 10 made in 2009.

To calculate CEO pay, the AP adds an executive's salary, bonuses, perks, any interest on deferred pay that's above market interest rates, and the value a company places on stock and stock options awarded during the year. The median pay value of $9 million, calculated by Equilar, is the midpoint of the companies used in the AP analysis; half of the CEOs made more and half made less. In 2007, the median pay was $8.4 million. In 2008 it was $7.6 million, and in 2009 it was $7.2 million. The $9 million median for 2010 is the highest since the AP began the analysis in 2006.

The *Wall Street Journal's* late 2010 CEO pay survey revealed that annual bonuses rose 11 percent to a median of $1.67 million in 2010, compared with a 3.4 percent rise the previous year.[14] The top paid U.S. CEOs in that survey were Gregory Maffei at Liberty Media with $87.1 million, followed by Larry Ellison at Oracle ($68.6 million), Ray Irani at Occidental Petroleum ($52.2 million), and Carol Bartz at Yahoo ($44.6 million).

Managing Resistance to Change

No organization or individual can escape change. But the thought of change raises anxieties because people fear economic loss, inconvenience, uncertainty, and a break in normal social patterns. Almost any change in structure, technology, people, or strategies has the potential to disrupt comfortable interaction patterns. For this reason, people resist change. The strategic-management process itself can impose major changes on individuals and processes. Reorienting an organization to get people to think and act strategically is not an easy task.

Resistance to change can be considered the single greatest threat to successful strategy implementation. Resistance regularly occurs in organizations in the form of sabotaging production machines, absenteeism, filing unfounded grievances, and an unwillingness to cooperate. People often resist strategy implementation because they do not understand what is happening or why changes are taking place. In that case, employees may simply need accurate information. Successful strategy implementation hinges upon managers' ability to develop an organizational climate conducive to change. Change must be viewed as an opportunity rather than as a threat by managers and employees.

Resistance to change can emerge at any stage or level of the strategy-implementation process. Although there are various approaches for implementing changes, three commonly used strategies are a force change strategy, an educative change strategy, and a rational or self-interest change strategy. A *force change strategy* involves giving orders and enforcing those orders; this strategy has the advantage of being fast, but it is plagued by low commitment and high resistance. The *educative change strategy* is one that presents information to convince people of the need for change; the disadvantage of an educative change strategy is that implementation becomes slow and difficult. However, this type of strategy evokes greater commitment and less resistance than does the force change strategy. Finally, a *rational* or *self-interest change strategy* is one that attempts to convince individuals that the change is to their personal advantage. When this appeal is successful, strategy implementation can be relatively easy. However, implementation changes are seldom to everyone's advantage.

The rational change strategy is the most desirable, so this approach is examined a bit further. Managers can improve the likelihood of successfully implementing change by carefully designing change efforts. Jack Duncan described a rational or self-interest change strategy as consisting of four steps. First, employees are invited to participate in the process of change and in the details of transition; participation allows everyone to give opinions, to feel a part of the change process, and to identify their own self-interests regarding the recommended change. Second, some motivation or incentive to change is required; self-interest can be the most important motivator. Third, communication is needed so that people can understand the purpose for the changes. Giving and receiving feedback is the fourth step: everyone enjoys knowing how things are going and how much progress is being made.[15]

Because of diverse external and internal forces, change is a fact of life in organizations. The rate, speed, magnitude, and direction of changes vary over time by industry and organization. Strategists should strive to create a work environment in which change is recognized as necessary and beneficial so that individuals can more easily adapt to change. Adopting a strategic-management approach to decision making can itself require major changes in the philosophy and operations of a firm.

Strategists can take a number of positive actions to minimize managers' and employees' resistance to change. For example, individuals who will be affected by a change should be involved in the decision to make the change and in decisions about how to implement the change. Strategists should anticipate changes and develop and offer training and development workshops so that managers and employees can adapt to those changes. They also need to effectively communicate the need for changes. The strategic-management process can be described as a process of managing change.

Organizational change should be viewed today as a continuous process rather than as a project or event. The most successful organizations today continuously adapt to changes in the competitive environment, which themselves continue to change at an accelerating rate. It is not sufficient today to simply react to change. Managers need to anticipate change and ideally be the creator of change. Viewing change as a continuous process is in stark contrast to an old management doctrine regarding change, which was to unfreeze behavior, change the behavior, and then refreeze the new behavior. The new "continuous organizational change" philosophy should mirror the popular "continuous quality improvement philosophy."

Creating a Strategy-Supportive Culture

Strategists should strive to preserve, emphasize, and build upon aspects of an existing *culture* that support proposed new strategies. Aspects of an existing culture that are antagonistic to a proposed strategy should be identified and changed. Substantial research indicates that new strategies are often market-driven and dictated by competitive forces. For this reason, changing a firm's culture to fit a new strategy is usually more effective than changing a strategy to fit an existing culture. As indicated in Table 7-10, numerous techniques are available to alter an organization's culture, including recruitment, training, transfer, promotion, restructure of an organization's design, role modeling, positive reinforcement, and mentoring.

Schein indicated that the following elements are most useful in linking culture to strategy:

1. Formal statements of organizational philosophy, charters, creeds, materials used for recruitment and selection, and socialization
2. Designing of physical spaces, facades, buildings
3. Deliberate role modeling, teaching, and coaching by leaders
4. Explicit reward and status system, promotion criteria

TABLE 7-10   Ways and Means for Altering an Organization's Culture

1. Recruitment
2. Training
3. Transfer
4. Promotion
5. Restructuring
6. Reengineering
7. Role modeling
8. Positive reinforcement
9. Mentoring
10. Revising vision and/or mission
11. Redesigning physical spaces/facades
12. Altering reward system
13. Altering organizational policies/procedures/practices

5. Stories, legends, myths, and parables about key people and events
6. What leaders pay attention to, measure, and control
7. Leader reactions to critical incidents and organizational crises
8. How the organization is designed and structured
9. Organizational systems and procedures
10. Criteria used for recruitment, selection, promotion, leveling off, retirement, and "excommunication" of people[16]

In the personal and religious side of life, the impact of loss and change is easy to see.[17] Memories of loss and change often haunt individuals and organizations for years. Ibsen wrote, "Rob the average man of his life illusion and you rob him of his happiness at the same stroke."[18] When attachments to a culture are severed in an organization's attempt to change direction, employees and managers often experience deep feelings of grief. This phenomenon commonly occurs when external conditions dictate the need for a new strategy. Managers and employees often struggle to find meaning in a situation that changed many years before. Some people find comfort in memories; others find solace in the present. Weak linkages between strategic management and organizational culture can jeopardize performance and success. Deal and Kennedy emphasized that making strategic changes in an organization always threatens a culture:

> People form strong attachments to heroes, legends, the rituals of daily life, the hoopla of extravaganza and ceremonies, and all the symbols of the workplace. Change strips relationships and leaves employees confused, insecure, and often angry. Unless something can be done to provide support for transitions from old to new, the force of a culture can neutralize and emasculate strategy changes.[19]

Production/Operations Concerns When Implementing Strategies

Production/operations capabilities, limitations, and policies can significantly enhance or inhibit the attainment of objectives. Production processes typically constitute more than 70 percent of a firm's total assets. A major part of the strategy-implementation process takes place at the production site. Production-related decisions on plant size, plant location, product design, choice of equipment, kind of tooling, size of inventory, inventory control, quality control, cost control, use of standards, job specialization, employee training, equipment and resource utilization, shipping and packaging, and technological innovation can have a dramatic impact on the success or failure of strategy-implementation efforts.

Examples of adjustments in production systems that could be required to implement various strategies are provided in Table 7-11 for both for-profit and nonprofit organizations. For instance, note that when a bank formulates and selects a strategy to add 10 new branches, a production-related implementation concern is site location. The largest bicycle company in the

TABLE 7-11   Production Management and Strategy Implementation

Type of Organization	Strategy Being Implemented	Production System Adjustments
Hospital	Adding a cancer center (Product Development)	Purchase specialized equipment and add specialized people.
Bank	Adding 10 new branches (Market Development)	Perform site location analysis.
Beer brewery	Purchasing a barley farm operation (Backward Integration)	Revise the inventory control system.
Steel manufacturer	Acquiring a fast-food chain (Unrelated Diversification)	Improve the quality control system.
Computer company	Purchasing a retail distribution chain (Forward Integration)	Alter the shipping, packaging, and transportation systems.

United States, Huffy, recently ended its own production of bikes and now contracts out those services to Asian and Mexican manufacturers. Huffy focuses instead on the design, marketing, and distribution of bikes, but it no longer produces bikes itself. The Dayton, Ohio, company closed its plants in Ohio, Missouri, and Mississippi.

Just-in-time (JIT) production approaches have withstood the test of time. JIT significantly reduces the costs of implementing strategies. With JIT, parts and materials are delivered to a production site just as they are needed, rather than being stockpiled as a hedge against later deliveries. Harley-Davidson reports that at one plant alone, JIT freed $22 million previously tied up in inventory and greatly reduced reorder lead time.

Factors that should be studied before locating production facilities include the availability of major resources, the prevailing wage rates in the area, transportation costs related to shipping and receiving, the location of major markets, political risks in the area or country, and the availability of trainable employees.

For high-technology companies, production costs may not be as important as production flexibility because major product changes can be needed often. Industries such as biogenetics and plastics rely on production systems that must be flexible enough to allow frequent changes and the rapid introduction of new products. An article in the *Harvard Business Review* explained why some organizations get into trouble:

> They too slowly realize that a change in product strategy alters the tasks of a production system. These tasks, which can be stated in terms of requirements for cost, product flexibility, volume flexibility, product performance, and product consistency, determine which manufacturing policies are appropriate. As strategies shift over time, so must production policies covering the location and scale of manufacturing facilities, the choice of manufacturing process, the degree of vertical integration of each manufacturing facility, the use of R&D units, the control of the production system, and the licensing of technology.[20]

A common management practice, cross-training of employees, can facilitate strategy implementation and can yield many benefits. Employees gain a better understanding of the whole business and can contribute better ideas in planning sessions. Cross-training employees can, however, thrust managers into roles that emphasize counseling and coaching over directing and enforcing and can necessitate substantial investments in training and incentives.

Human Resource Concerns When Implementing Strategies

In terms of Human Resource or "People Management," *Fortune* in 2011 ranked the following companies as best in the world:

Rank	Company
1	Goldman Sachs Group
2	Apple
3	Walt Disney
4	Google
5	Nike
6	Royal Dutch Shell
7	Nestlé
8	Amazon.com
9	Accenture
9	Procter & Gamble

Source: Based on: http://money.cnn.com/magazines/fortune/mostadmired/2011/best_worst/best2.html

More and more companies are instituting furloughs to cut costs as an alternative to laying off employees. *Furloughs* are temporary layoffs and even white-collar managers are being given furloughs, once confined to blue-collar workers. A few organizations furloughing professional workers include Gulfstream Aerospace, Media General, Gannett, the University of Maryland, Clemson University, and Spansion. Most companies are still using temporary and part-time workers rather than hiring full-time employees, which suggests that high unemployment rates may be a long-term trend. More and more companies may follow Harley-Davidson's lead when that firm signed a new union contract in late 2010 that creates a tier of "casual workers" with no benefits and no minimum number of hours, allowing Harley to call up workers only as needed.[21] Table 7-12 lists ways that companies today are reducing labor costs to stay financially sound.

The job of human resource manager is changing rapidly as companies continue to downsize and reorganize. Strategic responsibilities of the human resource manager include assessing the staffing needs and costs for alternative strategies proposed during strategy formulation and developing a staffing plan for effectively implementing strategies. This plan must consider how best to manage spiraling health care insurance costs. Employers' health coverage expenses consume an average 26 percent of firms' net profits, even though most companies now require employees to pay part of their health insurance premiums. The plan must also include how to motivate employees and managers during a time when layoffs are common and workloads are high.

The human resource department must develop performance incentives that clearly link performance and pay to strategies. The process of empowering managers and employees through their involvement in strategic-management activities yields the greatest benefits when all organizational members understand clearly how they will benefit personally if the firm does well. Linking company and personal benefits is a major new strategic responsibility of human resource managers. Other new responsibilities for human resource managers may include establishing and administering an *employee stock ownership plan (ESOP)*, instituting an effective child-care policy, and providing leadership for managers and employees in a way that allows them to balance work and family.

A well-designed strategic-management system can fail if insufficient attention is given to the human resource dimension. Human resource problems that arise when businesses implement strategies can usually be traced to one of three causes: (1) disruption of social and political structures, (2) failure to match individuals' aptitudes with implementation tasks, and (3) inadequate top management support for implementation activities.[22]

TABLE 7-12   Labor Cost-Saving Tactics

Salary freeze

Hiring freeze

Salary reductions

Reduce employee benefits

Raise employee contribution to health-care premiums

Reduce employee 401(k)/403(b) match

Reduce employee workweek

Mandatory furlough

Voluntary furlough

Hire temporary instead of full-time employees

Hire contract employees instead of full-time employees

Volunteer buyouts (Walt Disney is doing this)

Halt production for 3 days a week (Toyota Motor is doing this)

Layoffs

Early retirement

Reducing/eliminating bonuses

Source: Based on Dana Mattioli, "Employers Make Cuts Despite Belief Upturn Is Near," *Wall Street Journal*, April 23, 2009, B4.

Strategy implementation poses a threat to many managers and employees in an organization. New power and status relationships are anticipated and realized. New formal and informal groups' values, beliefs, and priorities may be largely unknown. Managers and employees may become engaged in resistance behavior as their roles, prerogatives, and power in the firm change. Disruption of social and political structures that accompany strategy execution must be anticipated and considered during strategy formulation and managed during strategy implementation.

A concern in matching managers with strategy is that jobs have specific and relatively static responsibilities, although people are dynamic in their personal development. Commonly used methods that match managers with strategies to be implemented include transferring managers, developing leadership workshops, offering career development activities, promotions, job enlargement, and job enrichment.

A number of other guidelines can help ensure that human relationships facilitate rather than disrupt strategy-implementation efforts. Specifically, managers should do a lot of chatting and informal questioning to stay abreast of how things are progressing and to know when to intervene. Managers can build support for strategy-implementation efforts by giving few orders, announcing few decisions, depending heavily on informal questioning, and seeking to probe and clarify until a consensus emerges. Key thrusts that succeed should be rewarded generously and visibly.

It is surprising that so often during strategy formulation, individual values, skills, and abilities needed for successful strategy implementation are not considered. It is rare that a firm selecting new strategies or significantly altering existing strategies possesses the right line and staff personnel in the right positions for successful strategy implementation. The need to match individual aptitudes with strategy-implementation tasks should be considered in strategy choice.

Inadequate support from strategists for implementation activities often undermines organizational success. Chief executive officers, small business owners, and government agency heads must be personally committed to strategy implementation and express this commitment in highly visible ways. Strategists' formal statements about the importance of strategic management must be consistent with actual support and rewards given for activities completed and objectives reached. Otherwise, stress created by inconsistency can cause uncertainty among managers and employees at all levels.

Perhaps the best method for preventing and overcoming human resource problems in strategic management is to actively involve as many managers and employees as possible in the process. Although time consuming, this approach builds understanding, trust, commitment, and ownership and reduces resentment and hostility. The true potential of strategy formulation and implementation resides in people.

Employee Stock Ownership Plans (ESOPs)

An *ESOP* is a tax-qualified, defined-contribution, employee-benefit plan whereby employees purchase stock of the company through borrowed money or cash contributions. ESOPs empower employees to work as owners; this is a primary reason why the number of ESOPs have grown dramatically to more than 10,000 firms covering more than 14 million employees. ESOPs now control more than $600 billion in corporate stock in the United States.

Some ESOP companies include:

- W. L. Gore & Associates—maker of medical and industrial products as well as Gore-Tex
- Herman Miller—famous for making innovative office furniture
- KCI—a civil engineering firm
- HCSS—a software manufacturer for the heavy construction industry

Besides reducing worker alienation and stimulating productivity, ESOPs allow firms other benefits, such as substantial tax savings. Principal, interest, and dividend payments on ESOP-funded debt are tax deductible. Banks lend money to ESOPs at interest rates below prime. This money can be repaid in pretax dollars, lowering the debt service as much as 30 percent in some cases. "The ownership culture really makes a difference, when management is a facilitator, not a dictator," says Corey Rosen, executive director of the National Center for Employee Ownership. Fifteen employee-owned companies are listed in Table 7-13.

TABLE 7-13   Fifteen Example ESOP Firms

Firm	Headquarters Location
Publix Supermarkets	Florida
Tribune Company	Illinois
Lifetouch	Minnesota
John Lewis Partnership	United Kingdom
Mondragon Cooperative	Spain
Houchens Industries	Kentucky
Amsted Industries	Illinois
Mast General Store	North Carolina
HDR, Inc.	Nebraska
Yoke's Fresh Market	Washington
SPARTA, Inc.	California
Hy-Vee	Iowa
Bi-Mart	Washington
Ferrellgas Partners	Kansas

Source: Based on Edward Iwata, "ESOPs Can Offer Both Upsides, Drawbacks,"
USA Today, April 3, 2007, 2B.

If an ESOP owns more than 50 percent of the firm, those who lend money to the ESOP are taxed on only 50 percent of the income received on the loans. ESOPs are not for every firm, however, because the initial legal, accounting, actuarial, and appraisal fees to set up an ESOP are about $50,000 for a small or midsized firm, with annual administration expenses of about $15,000. Analysts say ESOPs also do not work well in firms that have fluctuating payrolls and profits. Human resource managers in many firms conduct preliminary research to determine the desirability of an ESOP, and then they facilitate its establishment and administration if benefits outweigh the costs.

Wyatt Cafeterias, a southwestern United States operator of 120 cafeterias, also adopted the ESOP concept to prevent a hostile takeover. Employee productivity at Wyatt greatly increased since the ESOP began, as illustrated in the following quote:

> The key employee in our entire organization is the person serving the customer on the cafeteria line. We now tell the tea cart server, "Don't wait for the manager to tell you how to do your job better or how to provide better service. You take care of it." Sure, we're looking for productivity increases, but since we began pushing decisions down to the level of people who deal directly with customers, we've discovered an awesome side effect—suddenly the work crews have this "happy to be here" attitude that the customers really love.[23]

Balancing Work Life and Home Life

More women earn both undergraduate and graduate degrees in the United States than men, but a wage disparity still persists between men and women at all education levels.[24] Women on average make 25 percent less than men. The average age today for women to get married in the United States is 30 for those with a college degree, and 26 for those with just a high school degree. About 29 percent of both men and women in the United States today have a college degree, whereas in 1970 only 8 percent of women and 14 percent of men had college degrees.

Work/family strategies have become so popular among companies today that the strategies now represent a competitive advantage for those firms that offer such benefits as elder care assistance, flexible scheduling, job sharing, adoption benefits, an on-site summer camp, employee help lines, pet care, and even lawn service referrals. New corporate titles such as work/life coordinator and director of diversity are becoming common.

Working Mother magazine annually published its listing of "The 100 Best Companies for Working Mothers" (www.workingmother.com). Three especially important variables used in the ranking were availability of flextime, advancement opportunities, and equitable distribution of benefits among companies. Other important criteria are compressed weeks, telecommuting, job sharing, childcare facilities, maternity leave for both parents, mentoring, career development, and promotion for women. *Working Mother's* top 10 best companies for working women in 2011 are provided in Table 7-14. *Working Mother* also conducts extensive research to determine the best U.S. firms for women of color.

Human resource managers need to foster a more effective balancing of professional and private lives because nearly 60 million people in the United States are now part of two-career families. A corporate objective to become more lean and mean must today include consideration for the fact that a good home life contributes immensely to a good work life.

The work/family issue is no longer just a women's issue. Some specific measures that firms are taking to address this issue are providing spouse relocation assistance as an employee benefit; providing company resources for family recreational and educational use; establishing employee country clubs, such as those at IBM and Bethlehem Steel; and creating family/work interaction opportunities. A study by Joseph Pleck of Wheaton College found that in companies that do not offer paternity leave for fathers as a benefit, most men take short, informal paternity leaves anyway by combining vacation time and sick days.

Some organizations have developed family days, when family members are invited into the workplace, taken on plant or office tours, dined by management, and given a chance to see exactly what other family members do each day. Family days are inexpensive and increase the employee's pride in working for the organization. Flexible working hours during the week are another human resource response to the need for individuals to balance work life and home life. The work/family topic is being made part of the agenda at meetings and thus is being discussed in many organizations.

There is great room for improvement in removing the *glass ceiling* domestically, especially considering that women make up 47 percent of the U.S. labor force. *Glass ceiling* refers to the invisible barrier in many firms that bars women and minorities from top-level management positions. The United States leads the world in promoting women and minorities into mid- and top-level managerial positions in business. Only 2.6 percent of Fortune 500 firms have a woman CEO. Table 7-15 gives the 18 Fortune 500 Women CEOs in 2012.

Boeing's firing of CEO Harry Stonecipher for having an extramarital affair raised public awareness of office romance. However, just 12 percent of 391 companies surveyed by the American Management Association have written guidelines on office dating.[25] The fact of the matter is that most employers in the United States turn a blind eye to marital cheating. Some employers, such as Southwest Airlines, which employs more than 1,000 married couples, explicitly allow consensual office relationships. Research suggests that more men than women engage in extramarital affairs at work, roughly 22 percent to 15 percent; however, the percentage of women having extramarital affairs is increasing steadily, whereas the percentage of men having

TABLE 7-14   Top Ten Companies for Working Women

1. Bank of America—allows employees to define how they work
2. Deloitte—grants employees four unpaid weeks off annually
3. Discovery Communications—maternity leave is with full pay and consists of nine weeks for moms and three weeks for dads
4. Ernst & Young—up to 75 percent of its employees work outside E&Y offices
5. General Mills—women head five of the seven US. retail divisions
6. IBM—offers outstanding assistance to children of employees through its Special Care for Children program
7. KPMG—employees may take 26 (job guaranteed, partially paid) weeks off following the birth or adoption of a child
8. PricewaterhouseCoopers—many female partners go through the Breakthrough Leadership Development Program and achieve top executive positions
9. University of Wisconsin Hospital and Clinics—spends about $1.6 million annually on tuition to help employees further their education
10. WellStar Health System—has an in-house concierge service to help moms get things done

Source: Based on 2011: http://www.workingmother.com/BestCompanies/node/7818/list/4767

TABLE 7-15 Fortune 500 Women CEOs in 2012

CEO	Company
Angela Braly	WellPoint
Patricia Woertz	Archer Daniels Midland
Lynn Elsenhans	Sunoco
Indra Nooyi	PepsiCo
Irene Rosenfeld	Kraft Foods
Carol Meyrowitz	TJX
Mary Sammons	Rite Aid
Anne Mulcahy	Xerox
Brenda Barnes	Sara Lee
Andrea Jung	Avon Products
Susan Ivey	Reynolds American
Christina Gold	Western Union
Cathie Lesjak	Hewlett-Packard
Susan Ivey	Reynolds American
Carol Meyrowitz	TJX Cos.
Oprah Winfrey	Harpo and Own
Ellen Kullman	DuPont
Ursula Burns	Xerox

affairs with co-workers is holding steady.[26] If an affair is disrupting your work, then "the first step is to go to the offending person privately and try to resolve the matter. If that fails, then go to the human-resources manager seeking assistance."[27] Filing a discrimination lawsuit based on the affair is recommended only as a last resort because courts generally rule that co-workers' injuries are not pervasive enough to warrant any damages.

Benefits of a Diverse Workforce

Advertising agencies are an example industry transitioning from being specialist Hispanic, African American, and Asian agencies to becoming multicultural, generalist agencies. Leading executives of culturally specialized agencies are defecting in large numbers to generalist agencies as companies increasingly embrace multicultural marketing using multicultural ad agencies. Companies such as Burger King are shifting their Hispanic and African American ad agencies to generalist firms such as Crispin. Church's Chicken says pooling everything at a generalist agency helps reinforce the multicultural component of its overall market strategy.[28]

In Latin and South America, the number of women in high office has increased dramatically in recent years. Brazil recently elected its first woman president, Dilma Rouseff. Both Argentina and Chile already have a woman president, Cristina Kirchner and Michelle Bachelet respectively. Regarding the percent of national congressional seats held by women, Argentina has 38.3 percent followed by Honduras with 23.4 percent, as compared to Europe with 20.0 percent, Nordic countries at 41.6 percent, and Arab states at 11.1 percent.[29] Women now make up 53 percent of the work force in Latin and South America.

An organization can perhaps be most effective when its workforce mirrors the diversity of its customers. For global companies, this goal can be optimistic, but it is a worthwhile goal.

Corporate Wellness Programs

A recent *Harvard Business Review* article details how companies such as Johnson & Johnson (J&J), Lowe's Home-Improvement, the supermarket chain H-E-B, and Healthwise report impressive returns on investment of comprehensive, well-run employee wellness programs, sometimes as high as six to one.[30] J&J estimates that wellness programs have cumulatively saved the company $250 million on health care costs over the past decade. All J&J facilities around the world are tobacco free. At the software firm SAS Institute headquartered in Cary, North Carolina, voluntary turnover of employees has dropped to just 4 percent, largely, the firm says, due to its effective wellness program. On the SAS main campus, 70 percent of employees use the recreation center at least twice a week. SAS has maintained its #1 ranking in recent years among *Fortune*'s "100 Best Companies to Work For." At Healthwise, CEO Don Kemper's personal commitment to wellness permeates the entire culture of the firm, from monthly staff meetings to an annual Wellness Day. Starting in January 2011, Lowe's offered employees a monthly $50 discount on medical insurance if they pledge that they and covered dependents will not use any tobacco products.

Chevron is also a model corporate wellness company that sponsors many internal and external wellness activities. Chevron and other companies such as Biltmore that provide exemplary wellness programs think beyond diet and exercise and focus also on stress management by assisting employees with such issues as divorce, serious illness, death and grief recovery, child rearing, and care of aging parents. Biltmore's two-day health fairs twice a year focus on physical, financial, and spiritual wellness. At Lowe's headquarters, an impressive spiral staircase in the lobby makes climbing the stairs more appealing than riding the elevator. Such practices as "providing abundant bicycle racks," "conducting walking meetings," and "offering five minute stress breaks" are becoming common at companies to promote a corporate wellness culture.

Whole Foods Market headquartered in Austin, Texas, is another outstanding corporate wellness company with their employees receiving a 30 percent discount card on all products sold in their stores "if they maintain and document a healthy lifestyle." In addition, Wegman's Food Markets, headquartered in Rochester, New York, is another supermarket chain with an excellent corporate wellness program. More than 11,000 of Wegman's 39,000 employees recently took part in a challenge to eat five cups of fruit and vegetables and walk up to 10,000 steps a day for eight weeks. Wegman recently ranked #2 among *Fortune*'s "100 Best Companies to Work For."

Firms are striving to lower the accelerating costs of employees' health-care insurance premiums. Many firms such as Scotts Miracle-Gro Company (based in Marysville, Ohio), IBM, and Microsoft are implementing wellness programs, requiring employees to get healthier or pay higher insurance premiums. Employees that do get healthier win bonuses, free trips, and pay lower premiums; nonconforming employees pay higher premiums and receive no "healthy" benefits. Wellness of employees has become a strategic issue for many firms. Most firms require a health examination as a part of an employment application, and healthiness is more and more becoming a hiring factor. Michael Porter, coauthor of *Redefining Health Care*, says, "We have this notion that you can gorge on hot dogs, be in a pie-eating contest, and drink every day, and society will take care of you. We can't afford to let individuals drive up company costs because they're not willing to address their own health problems."

Wellness programs provide counseling to employees and seek lifestyle changes to achieve healthier living. For example, trans fats are a major cause of heart disease. Near elimination of trans fats in one's diet will reduce one's risk for heart attack by as much as 19 percent, according to a recent article.

Saturated fats are also bad, so one should avoid eating too much red meat and dairy products, which are high in saturated fats. Seven key lifestyle habits listed in Table 7-16 may significantly improve health and longevity.

TABLE 7-16 The Key to Staying Healthy, Living to 100, and Being a "Well" Employee

1. Eat nutritiously—eat a variety of fruits and vegetables daily because they have ingredients that the body uses to repair and strengthen itself.

2. Stay hydrated—drink plenty of water to aid the body in eliminating toxins and to enable body organs to function efficiently; the body is mostly water.

3. Get plenty of rest—the body repairs itself during rest, so get at least seven hours of sleep nightly, preferably eight hours.

4. Get plenty of exercise—exercise vigorously at least 30 minutes daily so the body can release toxins and strengthen vital organs.

5. Reduce stress—the body's immune system is weakened when one is under stress, making the body vulnerable to many ailments, so keep stress to a minimum.

6. Do not smoke—smoking kills, no doubt about it anymore.

7. Take vitamin supplements—consult your physician, but because it is difficult for diet alone to supply all the nutrients and vitamins needed, supplements can be helpful in achieving good health and longevity.

Source: Based on Lauren Etter, "Trans Fats: Will They Get Shelved?" *Wall Street Journal*, December 8, 2006, A6; Joel Fuhrman, MD, *Eat to Live* (Boston: Little, Brown, 2003).

Special Note to Students

An integral part of managing a firm is continually and systematically seeking to gain and sustain competitive advantage through effective planning, organizing, motivating, staffing, and controlling. Rival firms engage in these same activities, so emphasize in your strategic-management case analysis how your firm implementing your recommendations will outperform rival firms. Remember to be prescriptive rather than descriptive on every page or slide in your project, meaning to be insightful, forward-looking, and analytical rather than just describing operations. It is easy to *describe* a company but is difficult to *analyze* a company. Strategic-management case analysis is about *analyzing* a company and its industry, uncovering ways and means for the firm to best gain and sustain competitive advantage. So communicate throughout your project how your firm, and especially your recommendations, will lead to improved growth and profitability versus rival firms. Avoid vagueness and generalities throughout your project, as your audience or reader seeks great ideas backed up by great analyses. Use an analytical rather than descriptive approach in highlighting every slide you show an audience.

Conclusion

Successful strategy formulation does not at all guarantee successful strategy implementation. Although inextricably interdependent, strategy formulation and strategy implementation are characteristically different. In a single word, strategy implementation means *change*. It is widely agreed that "the real work begins after strategies are formulated." Successful strategy implementation requires the support of, as well as discipline and hard work from, motivated managers and employees. It is sometimes frightening to think that a single individual can irreparably sabotage strategy-implementation efforts.

Formulating the right strategies is not enough, because managers and employees must be motivated to implement those strategies. Management issues considered central to strategy implementation include matching organizational structure with strategy, linking performance and pay to strategies, creating an organizational climate conducive to change, managing political relationships, creating a strategy-supportive culture, adapting production/ operations processes, and managing human resources. Establishing annual objectives, devising policies, and allocating resources are central strategy-implementation activities common to all organizations. Depending on the size and type of the organization, other management issues could be equally important to successful strategy implementation.

Key Terms and Concepts

Annual Objectives (p. 245)
Avoidance (p. 249)
Benchmarking (p. 260)
Bonus System (p. 263)
Conflict (p. 249)
Confrontation (p. 250)
Culture (p. 265)
Decentralized Structure (p. 252)
Defusion (p. 249)
Delayering (p. 260)
Divisional Structure by Geographic Area, Product, Customer, or Process (p. 253)
Downsizing (p. 260)
Educative Change Strategy (p. 264)
Employee Stock Ownership Plans (ESOP) (p. 268)
Establishing Annual Objectives (p. 245)
Force Change Strategy (p. 264)
Functional Structure (p. 251)

Furloughs (p. 268)
Gain Sharing (p. 263)
Glass Ceiling (p. 271)
Horizontal Consistency of Objectives (p. 246)
Just-in-Time (JIT) (p. 267)
Matrix Structure (p. 257)
Policy (p. 247)
Profit Sharing (p. 262)
Rational Change Strategy (p. 264)
Reengineering (p. 260)
Resistance to Change (p. 264)
Resource Allocation (p. 249)
Restructuring (p. 260)
Rightsizing (p. 260)
Self-Interest Change Strategy (p. 264)
Six Sigma (p. 260)
Strategic Business Unit (SBU) Structure (p. 255)
Vertical Consistency of Objectives (p. 246)

Issues for Review and Discussion

1. IKEA is a globally strong firm. What are the three major threats you see that face IKEA in your country?
2. List in order of importance the six management issues you feel are most central to strategy implementation. Give your rationale.
3. List the five major benefits of a firm having clearly defined annual objectives.
4. Which approach to conflict resolution would you use to resolve a disagreement between top-level managers regarding a firm's strategic plan?
5. Diagram a functional organizational chart.
6. Diagram a divisional organizational chart.
7. Diagram a strategic business unit organizational chart.
8. Diagram a matrix organizational chart.
9. List ten do's and dont's regarding development of organizational charts.
10. Compare and contrast restructuring and reengineering.
11. Describe five ways a firm could link performance and pay to strategies.
12. List in order of importance eight ways and means for altering an organization's culture. Explain why.
13. Why are so many firms today installing corporate wellness programs?
14. Discuss how business attitudes towards "balancing work life and home life" vary across three countries that you are familiar with today.
15. Discuss the glass ceiling in your country versus the United States.
16. Discuss ESOPs in your country versus the United States.
17. In order of importance in your opinion, list six advantages of a matrix organizational structure.
18. Determine whether your college or university has a corporate wellness program. Give several policies that could be instituted to implement such a program.
19. Do you think horizontal consistency of objectives is as important as vertical consistency? Explain and give an example.
20. Define policies. Give four examples of policies for a bank.
21. Discuss your preference on each of the trade-off decisions required for strategy implementation. Explain why.
22. List three categories or approaches for conflict resolution. Which approach would you use for a salesperson who has a disagreement with a client regarding value of a property to be listed for sale.
23. In order of importance, list six symptoms of an ineffective organizational structure.
24. Explain why the functional organizational structure is the most widely used globally.
25. List the advantages versus disadvantages of a functional versus divisional structure.
26. How should a firm decide between a divisional-by-product versus divisional-by-geographic region type organizational chart?
27. A divisional-structure-by-process organizational chart is quite uncommon. Give two examples of the type of companies when this would be appropriate.
28. Diagram a matrix-type structure for a hospital.
29. Compare and contrast restructuring versus reengineering.
30. Explain why it is so important to link performance and pay to strategies.
31. Describe five tests that often are used to determine whether a performance-pay plan will benefit an organization.
32. Describe three commonly used strategies to minimize employee resistance to change. Which approach would you most often use? Why?
33. Give a hypothetical example of each labor cost-saving tactic listed in the chapter.
34. Do some research on the Internet to find five companies in your country that operate based on an ESOP. Bring your list to class.
35. Give some advantages and disadvantages of a firm operating based on an ESOP.
36. Go to www.workingmother.com and find five example firms that are outstanding for working mothers to work for and that have business locations in your city.
37. There were only 12 *Fortune 500* women CEOs in 2009. Conduct Internet research to identify five companies in your country that have women CEOs. Why are there so few women CEOs?
38. List four benefits of having a diverse workforce.
39. Explain why corporate wellness programs are becoming more and more popular.
40. Define and give an example of Six Sigma.
41. Define and give an example of a glass ceiling.
42. How many divisions would a firm have to have for you to recommend an SBU type structure? Why?
43. Explain when a matrix type structure may be the most effective.
44. How would you link compensation of your employees to performance of your business?

Notes

1. Dale McConkey, "Planning in a Changing Environment," *Business Horizons*, September–October 1988, 66.

2. A. G. Bedeian and W. F. Glueck, *Management*, 3rd ed. (Chicago: The Dryden Press, 1983), 212.

3. Boris Yavitz and William Newman, *Strategy in Action: The Execution, Politics, and Payoff of Business Planning* (New York: The Free Press, 1982), 195.

4. E. H. Schein, "Three Cultures of Management: The Key to Organizational Learning," *Sloan Management Review* 38, 1 (1996): 9–20.

5. S. Ghoshal and C. A. Bartlett, "Changing the Role of Management: Beyond Structure to Processes." *Harvard Business Review* 73, 1 (1995): 88.

6. Joann Lublin, "Chairman-CEO Split Gains Allies," *Wall Street Journal*, March 30, 2009, B4.

7. Karen Richardson, "The 'Six Sigma' Factor for Home Depot," *Wall Street Journal*, January 4, 2007, C3.

8. "Want to Be a Manager? Many People Say No, Calling Job Miserable," *Wall Street Journal*, April 4, 1997, 1; Stephanie Armour, "Management Loses Its Allure," *USA Today*, October 10, 1997, 1B.

9. Paul Carroll, "No More Business as Usual, Please. Time to Try Something Different," *Wall Street Journal*, October 23, 2001, A24.

10. Bill George, "Executive Pay: Rebuilding Trust in an Era of Rage," *Bloomberg Businessweek*, September 13–19, 2010, 56.

11. Yuka Hayashi and Phred Dvorak, "Japanese Wrestle with CEO Pay as They Go Global," *Wall Street Journal*, November 28, 2008, B1.

12. Richard Brown, "Outsider CEO: Inspiring Change with Force and Grace," *USA Today* (July 19, 1999): 3B.

13. Yavitz and Newman, 58.

14. Joann Lublin, "Pay Survey Shuffles Top CEOs," *Wall Street Journal*, November 15, 2010, B1.

15. Jack Duncan, *Management* (New York: Random House, 1983): 381–390.

16. E. H. Schein, "The Role of the Founder in Creating Organizational Culture," *Organizational Dynamics* (Summer 1983): 13–28.

17. T. Deal and A. Kennedy, "Culture: A New Look Through Old Lenses," *Journal of Applied Behavioral Science* 19, no. 4 (1983): 498–504.

18. H. Ibsen, "The Wild Duck," in O. G. Brochett and L. Brochett (eds.), *Plays for the Theater* (New York: Holt, Rinehart & Winston, 1967); R. Pascale, "The Paradox of 'Corporate Culture': Reconciling Ourselves to Socialization," *California Management Review* 28, no. 2 (1985): 26, 37–40.

19. T. Deal and A. Kennedy, *Corporate Cultures: The Rites and Rituals of Corporate Life* (Reading, MA: Addison-Wesley, 1982): 256.

20. Robert Stobaugh and Piero Telesio, "Match Manufacturing Policies and Product Strategy," *Harvard Business Review* 61, no. 2 (March–April 1983): 113.

21. Sudeep Reddy, "Employers Increasingly Rely on Temps, Part-Timers," *Wall Street Journal*, October 11, 2010, A4.

22. R. T. Lenz and Marjorie Lyles, "Managing Human Resource Problems in Strategy Planning Systems," *Journal of Business Strategy* 60, no. 4 (Spring 1986): 58.

23. J. Warren Henry, "ESOPs with Productivity Payoffs," *Journal of Business Strategy* (July–August 1989): 33.

24. Conor Dougherty, "Strides by Women, Still a Wage Gap," *Wall Street Journal*, March 1, 2011, A3. Also, David Jackson and Mimi Hall, "Women Gain in Education and Longevity," *USA Today*, March 2, 2011, 5A.

25. Sue Shellenbarger, "Employers Often Ignore Office Affairs, Leaving Co-workers in Difficult Spot," *Wall Street Journal* (March 10, 2005): D1.

26. Ibid.

27. Ibid.

28. Suzanne Vranica, "Ad Firms Heed Diversity," *Wall Street Journal*, November 29, 2010, B7.

29. Paulo Prada, "Women Ascend in Latin America," *Wall Street Journal*, December 24, 2010, A10.

30. Berry, Leonard L,, Ann Mirabito, and William Baun, "What's The Hard Return On Employee Wellness Programs?" *Harvard Business Review*, December 2010, 104–112.

Current Readings

Kulich, Clara, Grzegors Trojanowski, Michelle K. Ryan, S. Alexander Haslam, and Luc D. R. Renneboog. "Who Gets the Carrot and Who Gets the Stick? Evidence of Gender Disparities in Executive Remuneration." *Strategic Management Journal* 32, no. 3 (March 2011): 301–321.

Berry, Leonard L., Ann M. Mirabito, and William B. Baun. "What's the Hard Return On Employee Wellness Programs?" *Harvard Business Review*, December 2010, 104–114.

Blenko, Marcia W., Michael C. Mankins, and Paul Rogers. "The Decision-Driven Organization." *Harvard Business Review*, June 2010, 54–63.

Core, John E., and Wayne R. Guay. "Is CEO Pay Too High and Are Incentives Too Low? A Wealth-Based Contracting Framework." *The Academy of Management Perspectives* 24, no. 1 (February 2010): 5–19.

Davenport, Thomas H., Jeanne Harris, and Jeremy Shapiro. "Competing on Talent Analytics," *Harvard Business Review*, October 2010, 52–89.

Filatotchev, Igor, and Deborah Allcock. "Corporate Governance and Executive Remuneration: A Contingency Framework." *The Academy of Management Perspectives* 24, no. 1 (February 2010): 20–33.

Fredrickson, James W., Alison Davis-Blake, and Gerard Sanders. "Sharing the Wealth: Social Comparisons and Pay Dispersion in the CEO's Top Team." *Strategic Management Journal* 31, no. 10 (October 2010): 1031–1053.

Gaines-Ross, Leslie. "Reputation Warfare." *Harvard Business Review*, December 2010, 70–77.

Moschieri, Caterina. "The Implementation and Structuring of Divestitures: The Unit's Perspective." *Strategic Management Journal* 32, no. 4 (April 2011): 368–401.

Mossholder, Kevin W., Hettie A. Richardson, and Randall P. Settoon. "Human Resource Systems and Helping in Organizations: A Relational Perspective." *The Academy of Management Review* 36, no. 1 (January 2011): 33–52.

Pearce, John A. II. "What Execs Don't Get About Office Romance." *MIT Sloan Management Review* 51, no. 3 (Spring 2010): 39–40.

Santora, Joseph C., and Mark Esposito. "Do Competitive Work Environments Help or Hurt Employees?" *The Academy of Management Perspectives* 24, no. 1 (February 2010): 81.

Shook, John. "How to Change a Culture: Lessons From NUMMI." *MIT Sloan Management Review* 51, no. 2 (Winter 2010): 63–68.

Sonenshein, Scott. "We're Changning—Or Are We? Untangling the Role of Progressive, Regressive, and Stability Narratives During Strategic Change Implementation." *The Academy of Management Journal* 53, no. 3 (June 2010): 477–512.

"Women in Management: Delusions of Progress" *Harvard Business Review*, March 2010, 19–27.

Wowak, Adam J., and Donald C. Hambrick. "A Model of Person-Pay Interaction: How Executives Vary in Their Responses to Compensation Arrangements." *Strategic Management Journal* 31, no. 8 (August 2010): 803–821.

Yuan, Feirong, and Richard W. Woodman. "Innovative Behavior in the Workplace: The Role of Performance and Image Outcome Expectations." *The Academy of Management Journal* 53, no. 2 (April 2010): 323–342.

ASSURANCE OF LEARNING EXERCISES

Assurance of Learning Exercise 7A

Developing an Organizational Chart for IKEA

Purpose
IKEA is featured in the opening chapter case as a firm that engages in excellent strategic planning. IKEA is a very well-managed, privately held, international home products company that designs and sells ready-to-assemble furniture such as beds, desks, appliances, and home accessories. IKEA is the world's largest furniture retailer. Founded in 1943 in Sweden, IKEA is an acronym comprising the initials of the founder's name (Ingvar Kamprad), the farm where he grew up (Elmtaryd), and his home parish (Aqunnaryd in Smaland, South Sweden).

IKEA is operated and controlled by INGKA Holding B.V., a Dutch corporation, which is controlled by a tax-exempt, not-for-profit Dutch foundation. INGKA Holding B.V. owns the industrial group Swedwood which manufactures IKEA furniture and operates IKEA stores, as well as purchasing and supply functions, and IKEA of Sweden, which is responsible for the design and development of products in the IKEA range. IKEA's European logistics center is located in Dortmund, Germany while the company's Asian logistics center is located in Singapore.

This exercise gives you practice developing an organizational chart.

Instructions

Step 1   Visit IKEA's website. Review the company's most recent *Annual Report*. Note the list of top managers of IKEA.
Step 2   Develop an organizational chart for IKEA based on the titles of their top executives.
Step 3   Develop a recommended organizational chart for IKEA based on the guidelines presented in Chapter 7.

Assurance of Learning Exercise 7B

Assessing IKEA's Sustainability Efforts

Purpose
IKEA has about 320 stores in 38 countries, most of them in Europe, North America, Asia and Australia. The IKEA Group itself owns 276 stores in 25 countries and the other 37 stores are owned and run by franchisees outside the IKEA Group in 16 countries/territories. On February 17, 2011, IKEA announced its plans for a wind farm in Dalarna County, Sweden, furthering the furniture giant's goal of running on 100 percent renewable energy. IKEA strives to be a model firm in regards to sustainability efforts.

Instructions

Step 1   Visit IKEA's web site and review its sustainability efforts.
Step 2   Identify IKEA's major competitors.
Step 3   Compare and contrast IKEA's sustainability efforts versus its two major competitors.

Assurance of Learning Exercise 7C

Revising Adidas AG's Organizational Chart

Purpose
Developing and altering organizational charts is an important skill for strategists to possess. This exercise can improve your skill in altering an organization's hierarchical structure in response to new strategies being formed.

Instructions

Step 1   Turn back to the Adidas Cohesion Case and visit the Adidas website. Develop an organizational chart for Adidas. On a separate sheet of paper, answer the following questions:

1. What type of organizational chart have you illustrated for Adidas?
2. What improvements could you recommend for the Adidas organizational chart?

Give your reasoning for each suggestion.

Step 2   Now consider the following:

1. What aspects of your Adidas chart do you especially like?
2. What type of organizational chart do you believe would best suit Adidas? Why?

Assurance of Learning Exercise 7D

Exploring Objectives

Purpose

The purpose of this exercise is to bridge the gap between key topics in Chapter 7 versus what companies are doing in your area with regard to having clearly defined objectives.

Instruction

Do sufficient research to discover five businesses in your local area that have clearly defined objectives. Discuss the nature and role of objectives in these firms.

Assurance of Learning Exercise 7E

Understanding My University's Culture

Purpose

It is something of an art to uncover the basic values and beliefs that are buried deeply in an organization's rich collection of stories, language, heroes, heroines, and rituals. Yet culture can be the most important factor in implementing strategies.

Instructions

Step 1   On a separate sheet of paper, list the following terms: hero/heroine, belief, metaphor, language, value, symbol, story, legend, saga, folktale, myth, ceremony, rite, and ritual.

Step 2   For your college or university, give examples of each term. If necessary, speak with faculty, staff, alumni, administration, or fellow students of the institution to identify examples of each term.

Step 3   Report your findings to the class. Tell the class how you feel regarding cultural products being consciously used to help implement strategies.

Source: MTP/Alamy

"NOTABLE QUOTES"

"The greatest strategy is doomed if it's implemented badly."
—*Bernard Reimann*

"There is no 'perfect' strategic decision. One always has to pay a price. One always has to balance conflicting objectives, conflicting opinions, and conflicting priorities. The best strategic decision is only an approximation—and a risk."
—*Peter Drucker*

"The real question isn't how well you're doing today against your own history, but how you're doing against your competitors."
—*Donald Kress*

"As market windows open and close more quickly, it is important that R&D be tied more closely to corporate strategy."
—*William Spenser*

"Most of the time, strategists should not be formulating strategy at all; they should be getting on with implementing strategies they already have."
—*Henry Mintzberg*

"It is human nature to make decisions based on emotion, rather than on fact. But nothing could be more illogical."
—*Toshiba Corporation*

"No business can do everything. Even if it has the money, it will never have enough good people. It has to set priorities. The worst thing to do is a little bit of everything. This makes sure that nothing is being accomplished. It is better to pick the wrong priority than none at all."
—*Peter Drucker*

Implementing Strategies: Marketing, Finance/Accounting, R&D, and MIS Issues

CHAPTER OBJECTIVES

After studying this chapter, you should be able to do the following:

1. Explain market segmentation and product positioning as strategy-implementation tools.

2. Discuss procedures for determining the worth of a business.

3. Explain why projected financial statement analysis is a central strategy-implementation tool.

4. Explain how to evaluate the attractiveness of debt versus stock as a source of capital to implement strategies.

5. Discuss the nature and role of research and development in strategy implementation.

6. Explain how management information systems can determine the success of strategy-implementation efforts.

7. Explain business analytics and data mining.

ASSURANCE OF LEARNING EXERCISES

Assurance of Learning Exercise 8A
Preparing an EPS/EBIT Analysis for Hewlett-Packard (HP)

Assurance of Learning Exercise 8B
Developing a Product-Positioning Map for Adidas AG

Assurance of Learning Exercise 8C
Performing an EPS/EBIT Analysis for Adidas AG

Assurance of Learning Exercise 8D
Preparing Projected Financial Statements for Adidas AG

Assurance of Learning Exercise 8E
Determining the Cash Value of Adidas AG

Assurance of Learning Exercise 8F
Developing a Product-Positioning Map for My College

Assurance of Learning Exercise 8G
Do Banks Require Projected Financial Statements?

Strategies have no chance of being implemented successfully in organizations that do not market goods and services well, in firms that cannot raise needed working capital, in firms that produce technologically inferior products, or in firms that have a weak information system. This chapter examines marketing, finance/accounting, R&D, and management information systems (MIS) issues that are central to effective strategy implementation. Special topics include market segmentation, market positioning, evaluating the worth of a business, determining to what extent debt and/or stock should be used as a source of capital, developing projected financial statements, contracting R&D outside the firm, and creating an information support system. Manager and employee involvement and participation are essential for success in marketing, finance/accounting, R&D, and MIS activities.

The Nature of Strategy Implementation

The quarterback can call the best play possible in the huddle, but that does not mean the play will go for a touchdown. The team may even lose yardage unless the play is executed (implemented) well. Less than 10 percent of strategies formulated are successfully implemented! There are many reasons for this low success rate, including failing to appropriately segment markets, paying too much for a new acquisition, and falling behind competitors in R&D. Hewlitt-Packard (HP) HP implements strategies especially well.

Excellent Strategic Management Showcased

HEWLETT-PACKARD (HP)

Headquartered in Palo Alto, California, HP is a very well-managed global information technology corporation that operates worldwide. It specializes in developing and manufacturing computing, data storage, and networking hardware, designing software, and delivering services. Major product lines include personal computing devices, enterprise, and industry standard servers, related storage devices, networking products, software, and a diverse range of printers and other imaging products.

HP markets its products to households, small- to medium-sized businesses and enterprises directly as well as via online distribution, consumer-electronics and office-supply retailers, software partners, and major technology vendors. It also has strong services and consulting business around its products and partner products.

On April 28, 2010, HP announced the buyout of Palm for $1.2 billion. On September 2, 2010, HP won its bidding war for 3PAR with a $33-a-share offer ($2.07 billion) which Dell declined to match. On August 18, 2011, HP announced that it would strategically exit the smartphone and tablet computer business, focusing on higher-margin strategic priorities of cloud, solutions, and software with an emphasis on enterprise, commercial, and government markets. HP plans to spin off their personal computer division into a separate company. HP's restructuring to quit the PC business, while continuing to sell servers and other equipment to business customers, was similar to what IBM did years earlier. On September 22, 2011, HP named former eBay Inc. chief executive Meg Whitman its president and CEO, replacing Léo Apotheker.

HP has globally successful lines of printers, scanners, digital cameras, calculators, PDAs, servers, workstation computers, and computers for home and small business use. HP's Imaging and Printing Group (IPG) is the leading imaging and printing systems provider in the world. Products and technology associated with IPG include: ink-

jet and laserjet printers, consumables and related products, Officejet all in-one multifunction printer/scanner/faxes, HP Photosmart digital cameras and photo printers, and Snapfish a photo sharing and photo products service to name a few.

HP also provides IT-support solutions for other companies and organizations. For example, a large activity is HP offering "Professional Support" and desktop "Premier Support" for Microsoft in the EMEA marketplace. This is done from the Leixlip campus. Support is also offered for Microsoft operation systems, Exchange, Sharepoint and some office applications. HP also offers outsourced services for companies like the Bank of Ireland, some UK banks, and the U.S. defense forces.

Source: Based on information at www.wikipedia.com and www.hp.com.

Strategy implementation directly affects the lives of plant managers, division managers, department managers, sales managers, product managers, project managers, personnel managers, staff managers, supervisors, and all employees. In some situations, individuals may not have participated in the strategy-formulation process at all and may not appreciate, understand, or even accept the work and thought that went into strategy formulation. There may even be foot dragging or resistance on their part. Managers and employees who do not understand the business and are not committed to the business may attempt to sabotage strategy-implementation efforts in hopes that the organization will return to its old ways. The strategy-implementation stage of the strategic-management process is highlighted in Figure 8-1.

Current Marketing Issues

Countless marketing variables affect the success or failure of strategy implementation, and the scope of this text does not allow us to address all those issues. Some examples of marketing decisions that may require policies are as follows:

1. How to make advertisements more interactive to be more effective.
2. How to best take advantage of Facebook and Twitter conservations about the company and industry.

FIGURE 8-1

A Comprehensive Strategic-Management Model

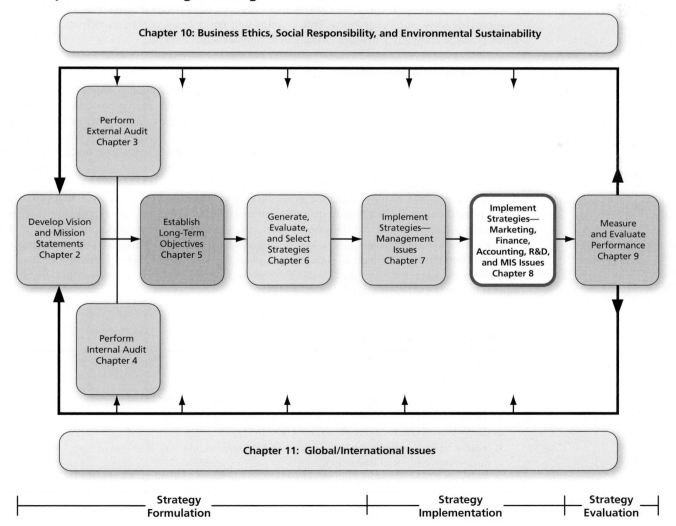

Source: Fred R. David, "How Companies Define Their Mission," *Long Range Planning* 22, no. 3 (June 1988): 40.

3. To use exclusive dealerships or multiple channels of distribution
4. To use heavy, light, or no TV advertising versus online advertising
5. To limit (or not) the share of business done with a single customer
6. To be a price leader or a price follower
7. To offer a complete or limited warranty
8. To reward salespeople based on straight salary, straight commission, or a combination salary/commission

Marketing of late has become more about building a two-way relationship with consumers than just informing consumers about a product or service. Marketers today must get their customers involved in their company website and solicit suggestions from customers in terms of product development, customer service, and ideas. The online community is much quicker, cheaper, and effective than traditional focus groups and surveys.

Companies and organizations should encourage their employees to create *wikis*—websites that allows users to add, delete, and edit content regarding frequently asked questions and information across the firm's whole value chain of activities. The most common wiki is Wikipedia, but think of wikis as user-generated content. Know that anyone can change the content in a wiki but the group and other editors can change the content or changes that you submit.

Firms should provide incentives to consumers to share their thoughts, opinions, and experiences on the company website. Encourage consumers to network among themselves on topics of their choosing on the company website. So the company website must not be all about the company—it must be all about the customer too. Perhaps offer points or discounts for customers who provide ideas and suggestions. This practice will not only encourage participation but will allow both the company and other customers to interact with "experts."

New Principles of Marketing

Today a business or organization's website must provide clear and simple instructions for customers to set up a blog and/or contribute to a wiki. Customers trust each others' opinions more than a company's marketing pitch, and the more they talk freely, the more the firm can learn how to improve its product, service, and marketing. Marketers today monitor blogs daily to determine, evaluate, and influence opinions being formed by customers. Customers must not feel like they are a captive audience for advertising at a firm's website. Table 8-1 provides new principles of marketing according to Parise, Guinan, and Weinberg.[1]

Wells Fargo and Bank of America *tweet* customers, meaning they posted messages of 140 characters or less on Twitter.com to describe features of bank products. Some banks are placing marketing videos on YouTube. Discover Financial, American Express, and Citigroup all now have Facebook or Myspace pages. UMB Financial of Kansas City, Missouri, tweets about everything from the bank's financial stability to the industry's prospects. Steve Furman, Discover's director of e-commerce, says the appeal of social networking is that it provides "pure, instant" communication with customers.[2]

TABLE 8-1   The New Principles of Marketing

1. Don't just talk at consumers—work with them throughout the marketing process.
2. Give consumers a reason to participate.
3. Listen to—and join—the conversation outside your company's website.
4. Resist the temptation to sell, sell, sell. Instead attract, attract, attract.
5. Don't control online conversations; let it flow freely.
6. Find a "marketing technologist," a person who has three excellent skill sets (marketing, technology, and social interaction).
7. Embrace instant messaging and chatting.

Source: Based on Salvatore Parise, Patricia Guinan, and Bruce Weinberg, "The Secrets of Marketing in a Web 2.0 World," *Wall Street Journal*, December 15, 2008, R1.

PepsiCo recently established a "Mission Control" staffed with social marketing employees promoting the company's long-time product Gatorade, which had been on a three-year sales slide. PepsiCo employees staff Mission Control 24/7 to tweet encouragement to high-school athletes and respond to Facebook questions.[3] Whenever anybody uses Twitter or Facebook to comment on Gatorade, that message pops up on a screen in Mission Control and a PepsiCo employee joins that person's social circle. PepsiCo is a leading company that tracks social media, tracks online-ad traffic, heads off potential crises, builds support for products, and monitors consumer behavior in depth. Gatorade is under intense pressure from Coca-Cola's Powerade, whose sales increased 16.8 percent in the first half of 2010 compared to Gatorade's 2.4 percent increase.

Although the exponential increase in social networking and business online has created huge opportunities for marketers, it also has produced some severe threats. Perhaps the greatest threat is that any kind of negative publicity travels fast online. For example, Dr Pepper recently suffered immensely when an attorney for the rock band Guns N' Roses accused the company of not following through on giving every American a soft drink if they released their album *Chinese Democracy*. Other examples abound, such as Motrin ads that lightheartedly talked about Mom's back pain from holding babies in slings, and Burger King's Whopper Virgin campaign, which featured a taste test of a Whopper versus a McDonald's Big Mac in remote areas of the world. Even Taco Bell suffered from its ads that featured asking 50 Cent (aka Curtis Jackson) if he would change his name to 79 Cent or 89 Cent for a day in exchange for a $10,000 donation to charity. Seemingly minor ethical and questionable actions can catapult these days into huge public relations problems for companies as a result of the monumental online social and business communications.

In increasing numbers, people living in underdeveloped and poor nations around the world have cell phones but no computers, so the Internet is rapidly moving to cell phone platforms. This is opening up even larger markets to online marketing. People in remote parts of Indonesia, Egypt, and Africa represent the fastest growing customer base for Opera Software ASA, a Norwegian maker of Internet browsers for mobile devices. Actually, persons who cannot afford computers live everywhere in every country, and many of these persons will soon be on the Internet on their cell phones. Cell phones are rapidly becoming used for data transfer, not just for phone calls. Companies such as Nokia, AT&T, Purple Labs SA of France, Japan's Access, Vodafone Group PLC, Siemens AG, Research in Motion, and Apple are spurring this transition by developing new and improved web-capable mobile products every day.[4]

Advertising Media

Recent research by Forrester Research reveals that people ages 18 to 27 spend more time weekly on the Internet than watching television, listening to the radio, or watching DVDs or VHS tapes. Companies are rapidly coming to the realization that social networking sites and video sites are better means of reaching their customers than spending so many marketing dollars on traditional yellow pages or television, magazine, radio, or newspaper ads. People spend time on the Internet. And it is not just the time. Television viewers are passive viewers of ads, whereas Internet users take an active role in choosing what to look at—so customers on the Internet are tougher for marketers to reach.[5]

According to analysts at Corporate Eye, advertising investments are expected to decrease or stay fairly even through 2013 with one exception—Internet advertising is expected to increase 27.9 percent between 2010 and 2013, as indicated in the table found at http://www .corporate-eye.com/blog/2010/12/ad-spending-forecasts-highlight-china-and-the-internet/. That website also notes that television advertising is by far the most commonly relied upon medium and is expected to slightly increase its share of total dollars spent. When it comes to regional investments, Corporate Eye says the Asia Pacific region will see advertising expenditures increase by 31.0 percent between 2009 and 2013. That's not as high, however, as increases in Latin America (43.3%), Central Europe (39.8%), or Africa and the Middle East (32.2%). Considering that China accounts for 20 percent of the world's population, the return on advertising investments in the Asia Pacific region could be exponentially higher than in any other area of the world.[6]

New companies such as Autonet Mobile based in San Francisco are selling new technology equipment for cars so the front passenger may conduct an iChat video conference while persons in the back each have a laptop and watch a YouTube video or download music or wirelessly transfer pictures from a digital camera. Everyone in the vehicle can be online except, of course, the driver. This technology is now available for installation in nearly all cars and is accelerating the movement from hard media to web-based media. With this technology also, when the vehicle drives into a new location, you may instantly download information on shows, museums, hotels, and other attractions around you.

Internet advertising is growing so rapidly that marketers are more and more allowed to create bigger, more intrusive ads that take up more space on the web page. Web sites are allowing lengthier ads to run before short video clips play. And blogs are creating more content that doubles also as an ad. Companies are also waiving minimum ad purchases. Companies are redesigning their websites to be much more interactive and are building new sponsorship programs and other enticements on their sites. Editorial content and advertising content are increasingly being mixed on blogs.

J.C. Penney CEO Myron Ullman says, "Consumers now shop for what they 'need' and less for what they 'want.' And they don't need much." Essentials, such as food, health-care products, and beauty aids are selling, but even in those industries, consumers are shifting to less costly brands and stores. There is a need for marketers to convince consumers that their brand will make life easier or better. Consumers now often wait until prices are slashed 75 percent or more to buy. Consumers today are very cautious about how they spend their money. Gone are the days when retailers could convince consumers to buy something they do not need.

J.C. Penney is among many firms that today have revamped their marketing to be more digital related. Penney's is segmenting its e-mail databases according to customers' shopping behaviors and then sending out relevant messages. Penney's corporate director of brand communications recently said, "Tailoring the e-mail insures that our customers are receiving timely, relevant information."

Purpose-Based Marketing

The former global marketing chief at Procter & Gamble, Jim Stengel, recently started his own LLC business to try to persuade companies that the best way to sell in a weak economy is to "show customers how they can improve their lives" with your product or service. Stengel calls this "*purpose-based marketing,*" and hundreds of firms have now adopted this approach successfully. He says there is need in an ad to build trust and an emotional connection to the customer in order to differentiate your product or service.[7]

In a weak economy when consumers are more interested in buying cheaper brands, Stengel acknowledges that ads must promote price, but he says ads must also show the intrinsic value of the product or service to be cost effective. Stengel contends that ads should do both: promote low price and build emotional equity through "purpose-based appeal."

As an example of purpose-based marketing, the second-largest department-store chain in the United States, Macy's, introduced 2,200 local-themed tree ornaments in late 2010 as part of its "My Macy's" program, to better customize merchandise to local shoppers. You can buy Chicago Blackhawk ornaments in Illinois or Elvis ornaments in Memphis. Sales at Macy's 810 stores were up 5 percent in 2010.

The Coca-Cola Company is leading the way to another new kind of selling in a weak economy. CEO Muhtar Kent at Coke says marketing today must "employ optimism." That is why Coca-Cola recently launched a new global ad campaign appealing to consumers' longing for comfort and optimism. The new campaign features the new slogan "Open Happiness," which replaced Coke's prior popular slogan of three years, "The Coke Side of Life." The Coke CEO says marketers must use feel-good messages to counter the fallout from the economic crisis. Firms must today project to customers that their products or services offer a beacon of comfort and optimism.

Market Segmentation

Two variables are of central importance to strategy implementation: *market segmentation* and *product positioning*. Market segmentation and product positioning rank as marketing's most important contributions to strategic management.

TABLE 8-2 The Marketing Mix Component Variables

Product	Place	Promotion	Price
Quality	Distribution channels	Advertising	Level
Features and options	Distribution coverage	Personal selling	Discounts and allowances
Style	Outlet location	Sales promotion	Payment terms
Brand name	Sales territories	Publicity	
Packaging	Inventory levels and locations		
Product line	Transportation carriers		
Warranty			
Service level			
Other services			

Source: Based on E. Jerome McCarthy, *Basic Marketing: A Managerial Approach,* 9th ed. (Homewood, IL: Richard D. Irwin, Inc., 1987), 37–44. Used with permission.

Market segmentation is widely used in implementing strategies, especially for small and specialized firms. Market segmentation can be defined as the subdividing of a market into distinct subsets of customers according to needs and buying habits.

Market segmentation is an important variable in strategy implementation for at least three major reasons. First, strategies such as market development, product development, market penetration, and diversification require increased sales through new markets and products. To implement these strategies successfully, new or improved market-segmentation approaches are required. Second, market segmentation allows a firm to operate with limited resources because mass production, mass distribution, and mass advertising are not required. Market segmentation enables a small firm to compete successfully with a large firm by maximizing per-unit profits and per-segment sales. Finally, market segmentation decisions directly affect *marketing mix variables:* product, place, promotion, and price, as indicated in Table 8-2.

Perhaps the most dramatic new market-segmentation strategy is the targeting of regional tastes. Firms from Pizza Hut to Honda Motors are increasingly modifying their products to meet different regional preferences of customers around the world. Campbell's has a spicier version of its nacho cheese soup for the Southwest, and Burger King offers breakfast burritos in New Mexico but not in South Carolina. Geographic and demographic bases for segmenting markets are the most commonly employed, as illustrated in Table 8-3.

Evaluating potential market segments requires strategists to determine the characteristics and needs of consumers, to analyze consumer similarities and differences, and to develop consumer group profiles. Segmenting consumer markets is generally much simpler and easier than segmenting industrial markets, because industrial products, such as electronic circuits and forklifts, have multiple applications and appeal to diverse customer groups.

Segmentation is a key to matching supply and demand, which is one of the thorniest problems in customer service. Segmentation often reveals that large, random fluctuations in demand actually consist of several small, predictable, and manageable patterns. Matching supply and demand allows factories to produce desirable levels without extra shifts, overtime, and subcontracting. Matching supply and demand also minimizes the number and severity of stock-outs. The demand for hotel rooms, for example, can be dependent on foreign tourists, businesspersons, and vacationers. Focusing separately on these three market segments, however, can allow hotel firms to more effectively predict overall supply and demand.

Banks now are segmenting markets to increase effectiveness. "You're dead in the water if you aren't segmenting the market," says Anne Moore, president of a bank consulting firm in Atlanta. The Internet makes market segmentation easier today because consumers naturally form "communities" on the web.

Retention-Based Segmentation

To aid in more effective and efficient deployment of marketing resources, companies commonly tag each of their active customers with three values:

TABLE 8-3   Alternative Bases for Market Segmentation

Variable	Typical Breakdowns
Geographic	
Region	Pacific, Mountain, West North Central, West South Central, East North Central, East South Central, South Atlantic, Middle Atlantic, New England
County Size	A, B, C, D
City Size	Under 5,000; 5,000–20,000; 20,001–50,000; 50,001–100,000; 100,001–250,000; 250,001–500,000; 500,001–1,000,000; 1,000,001–4,000,000; 4,000,001 or over
Density	Urban, suburban, rural
Climate	Northern, southern
Demographic	
Age	Under 6, 6–11, 12–19, 20–34, 35–49, 50–64, 65+
Gender	Male, female
Family Size	1–2, 3–4, 5+
Family Life Cycle	Young, single; young, married, no children; young, married, youngest child under 6; young, married, youngest child 6 or over; older, married, with children; older, married, no children under 18; older, single; other
Income	Under $10,000; $10,001–$15,000; $15,001–$20,000; $20,001–$30,000; $30,001–$50,000; $50,001–$70,000; $70,001–$100,000; over $100,000
Occupation	Professional and technical; managers, officials, and proprietors; clerical and sales; craftspeople; foremen; operatives; farmers; retirees; students; housewives; unemployed
Education	Grade school or less; some high school; high school graduate; some college; college graduate
Religion	Catholic, Protestant, Jewish, Islamic, other
Race	White, Asian, Hispanic, African American
Nationality	American, British, French, German, Scandinavian, Italian, Latin American, Middle Eastern, Japanese
Psychographic	
Social Class	Lower lowers, upper lowers, lower middles, upper middles, lower uppers, upper uppers
Personality	Compulsive, gregarious, authoritarian, ambitious
Behavioral	
Use Occasion	Regular occasion, special occasion
Benefits Sought	Quality, service, economy
User Status	Nonuser, ex-user, potential user, first-time user, regular user
Usage Rate	Light user, medium user, heavy user
Loyalty Status	None, medium, strong, absolute
Readiness Stage	Unaware, aware, informed, interested, desirous, intending to buy
Attitude Toward Product	Enthusiastic, positive, indifferent, negative, hostile

Source: Adapted from Philip Kotler, *Marketing Management: Analysis, Planning and Control,* © 1984: 256. Adapted by permission of Prentice-Hall, Inc., Upper Saddle River, New Jersey.

Tag #1: Is this customer at high risk of canceling the company's service? One of the most common indicators of high-risk customers is a drop off in usage of the company's service. For example, in the credit card industry this could be signaled through a customer's decline in spending on his or her card.

Tag #2: Is this customer worth retaining? This determination boils down to whether the post-retention profit generated from the customer is predicted to be greater than the cost incurred to retain the customer. Customers need to be managed as investments.

Tag #3: What retention tactics should be used to retain this customer? For customers who are deemed "save-worthy," it's essential for the company to know which save tactics are most likely to be successful. Tactics commonly used range from providing "special" customer discounts to sending customers communications that reinforce the value proposition of the given service.[8]

The basic approach to tagging customers is to utilize historical retention data to make predictions about active customers regarding:

- Whether they are at high risk of canceling their service
- Whether they are profitable to retain
- What retention tactics are likely to be most effective

The idea with retention-based segmentation is to match up active customers with customers from historic retention data who share similar attributes. Using the theory that "birds of a feather flock together," the approach is based on the assumption that active customers will have similar retention outcomes as those of their comparable predecessor. This whole process is possible through business analytics or data mining (discussed later in this chapter).

Does the Internet Make Market Segmentation Easier?

Yes. The segments of people whom marketers want to reach online are much more precisely defined than the segments of people reached through traditional forms of media, such as television, radio, and magazines. For example, Quepasa.com is widely visited by Hispanics. Marketers aiming to reach college students, who are notoriously difficult to reach via traditional media, focus on sites such as collegeclub.com and studentadvantage.com. The gay and lesbian population, which is estimated to comprise about 5 percent of the population worldwide, has always been difficult to reach via traditional media but now can be focused on at sites such as gay.com. Marketers can reach persons interested in specific topics, such as travel or fishing, by placing banners on related websites.

People all over the world are congregating into virtual communities on the web by becoming members/customers/visitors of websites that focus on an endless range of topics. People in essence segment themselves by nature of the websites that comprise their "favorite places," and many of these websites sell information regarding their "visitors." Businesses and groups of individuals all over the world pool their purchasing power in websites to get volume discounts.

Product Positioning

After markets have been segmented so that the firm can target particular customer groups, the next step is to find out what customers want and expect. This takes analysis and research. A severe mistake is to assume the firm knows what customers want and expect. Countless research studies reveal large differences between how customers define service and rank the importance of different service activities and how producers view services. Many firms have become successful by filling the gap between what customers and producers see as good service. What the customer believes is good service is paramount, not what the producer believes service should be.

Identifying target customers to focus marketing efforts on sets the stage for deciding how to meet the needs and wants of particular consumer groups. Product positioning is widely used for this purpose. Positioning entails developing schematic representations that reflect how your products or services compare to competitors' on dimensions most important to success in the industry. The following steps are required in product positioning:

1. Select key criteria that effectively differentiate products or services in the industry.
2. Diagram a two-dimensional product-positioning map with specified criteria on each axis.
3. Plot major competitors' products or services in the resultant four-quadrant matrix.
4. Identify areas in the positioning map where the company's products or services could be most competitive in the given target market. Look for vacant areas (niches).
5. Develop a marketing plan to position the company's products or services appropriately.

Because just two criteria can be examined on a single product-positioning map, multiple maps are often developed to assess various approaches to strategy implementation. *Multidimensional scaling* could be used to examine three or more criteria simultaneously, but this technique requires computer assistance and is beyond the scope of this text. Some examples of product-positioning maps are illustrated in Figure 8-2.

Some rules for using product positioning as a strategy-implementation tool are the following:

1. Look for the hole or *vacant niche*. The best strategic opportunity might be an unserved segment.
2. Don't serve two segments with the same strategy. Usually, a strategy successful with one segment cannot be directly transferred to another segment.
3. Don't position yourself in the middle of the map. The middle usually means a strategy that is not clearly perceived to have any distinguishing characteristics. This rule can vary with the number of competitors. For example, when there are only two competitors, as in U.S. presidential elections, the middle becomes the preferred strategic position.[9]

An effective product-positioning strategy meets two criteria: (1) it uniquely distinguishes a company from the competition, and (2) it leads customers to expect slightly less service than a company can deliver. Firms should not create expectations that exceed the service the firm

FIGURE 8-2

Examples of Product-Positioning Maps

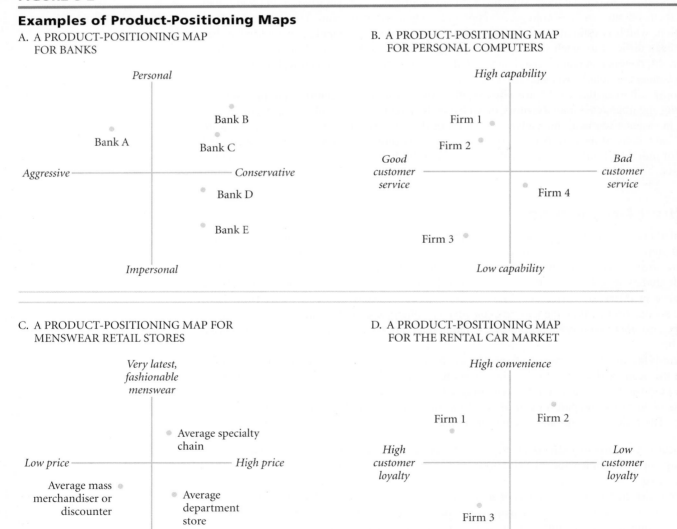

A. A PRODUCT-POSITIONING MAP FOR BANKS

B. A PRODUCT-POSITIONING MAP FOR PERSONAL COMPUTERS

C. A PRODUCT-POSITIONING MAP FOR MENSWEAR RETAIL STORES

D. A PRODUCT-POSITIONING MAP FOR THE RENTAL CAR MARKET

can or will deliver. Network Equipment Technology is an example of a company that keeps customer expectations slightly below perceived performance. This is a constant challenge for marketers. Firms need to inform customers about what to expect and then exceed the promise. Underpromise and then overdeliver is the key!

Finance/Accounting Issues

In terms of "Financial Soundness," *Fortune* in 2011 ranked the following companies as best in the world:

Rank	Company
1	Google
2	Apple
3	McDonald's
4	Occidental Petroleum
5	W.W. Grainger
6	Nestlé
7	Amazon.com
8	Wal-Mart Stores
9	Microsoft
10	Walt Disney

Source: Based on http://money.cnn.com/magazines/fortune/mostad-mired/2011/best_worst/best6.html

In this section, we examine several finance/accounting concepts considered to be central to strategy implementation: acquiring needed capital, developing projected financial statements, preparing financial budgets, and evaluating the worth of a business. Some examples of decisions that may require finance/accounting policies are these:

1. To raise capital with short-term debt, long-term debt, preferred stock, or common stock
2. To lease or buy fixed assets
3. To determine an appropriate dividend payout ratio
4. To use LIFO (Last-in, First-out), FIFO (First-in, First-out), or a market-value accounting approach
5. To extend the time of accounts receivable
6. To establish a certain percentage discount on accounts within a specified period of time
7. To determine the amount of cash that should be kept on hand

Acquiring Capital to Implement Strategies

When students complete their Recommendations Page as part of a case analysis, or in actual company practice when a firm decides what strategies to pursue, it is necessary to address the question: Where should the company obtain needed capital?

Successful strategy implementation often requires additional capital. Besides net profit from operations and the sale of assets, two basic sources of capital for an organization are debt and equity. Determining an appropriate mix of debt and equity in a firm's capital structure can be vital to successful strategy implementation. An *Earnings Per Share/Earnings Before Interest and Taxes (EPS/EBIT) analysis* is the most widely used technique for determining whether debt, stock, or a combination of debt and stock is the best alternative for raising capital to implement strategies. This technique involves an examination of the impact that debt versus stock financing has on earnings per share under various assumptions as to EBIT.

Theoretically, an enterprise should have enough debt in its capital structure to boost its return on investment by applying debt to products and projects earning more than the cost of the debt. In low earning periods, too much debt in the capital structure of an organization can endanger stockholders' returns and jeopardize company survival. Fixed debt obligations generally must be met, regardless of circumstances. This does not mean that stock issuances are always better than debt for raising capital. Some special concerns with stock issuances are dilution of ownership, effect on stock price, and the need to share future earnings with all new shareholders.

Before explaining EPS/EBIT analysis, it is important to know that EPS = Earnings per Share, which is Net Income divided by # of Shares Outstanding. Another term for Shares Outstanding is Shares Issued. Also know that EBIT = Earnings Before Interest and Taxes. Another name for EBIT is Operating Income. EBT = Earnings Before Tax. EAT = Earnings After Tax.

The purpose of EPS/EBIT analysis is to determine whether All Debt, or All Stock, or some combination of debt and stock yields the highest EPS values for the firm. EPS is perhaps the best measure of success of a company, so it is widely used in making the capital acquisition decision. EPS reflects the common "maximizing shareholders' wealth" overarching corporate objective. By chance if profit maximization is the company's goal, then in performing an EPS/EBIT analysis, you may focus more on the EAT row more than the EPS row. Large companies may have millions of shares outstanding, so even small differences in EPS across different financing options can equate to large sums of money saved by using that highest EPS value alternative. Any number of combination debt/stock scenarios, such as 70/30 D/S or 30/70 D/S, may be examined in an EPS/EBIT analysis.

EPS/EBIT analysis may best be explained by working through an example for the XYZ Company, as provided in Table 8-4. Note that 100% Stock is the best financing alternative as indicated by the EPS values of 0.279 and 0.056. An EPS/EBIT chart can be constructed to determine the break-even point, where one financing alternative becomes more attractive than another. Figure 8-3 reveals that issuing common stock is the best financing alternative for the XYZ Company. As noted in Figure 8-3, you simply graph the top row (EBIT) on the x-axis with the bottom row (EPS) on the y-axis and the highest plotted line reveals the best method. Sometimes the plotted lines will interact, so a graph is especially helpful in making the capital acquisition decision, rather than solely relying on a table of numbers.

TABLE 8-4 EPS/EBIT Analysis for the XYZ Company

Input Data	The Number	How Determined
$Amount of Capital Needed	$100 million	Estimated $cost of recommendations
EBIT Range	$20 to $40 million	Estimate based on prior year EBIT and recommendations for the coming year(s)
Interest Rate	5 percent	Estimate based on cost of capital
Tax Rate	30 percent	Use prior year %: taxes divided by income before taxes, as given on income statement
Stock Price	$50	Use most recent stock price
#Shares Outstanding	500 million	For the debt columns, enter the existing #shares outstanding. For stock columns, use the existing #shares outstanding + the #new shares that must be issued to raise the needed capital, i.e., based on stock price. So divide the stock price into the $amount of capital needed.

	100% Debt		100% Stock		50/50 Debt/Stock Combo	
$ EBIT	20,000,000	40,000,000	20,000,000	40,000,000	20,000,000	40,000,000
$ Interest	5,000,000	5,000,000	0	0	2,500,000	2,500,000
$ EBT	15,000,000	35,000,000	20,000,000	40,000,000	17,500,000	37,500,000
$ Taxes	4,500,000	10,500,000	6,000,000	12,000,000	5,250,000	11,250,000
$ EAT	10,500,000	24,500,000	14,000,000	28,000,000	12,250,000	26,250,000
# Shares	500,000,000	500,000,000	502,000,000	502,000,000	501,000,000	501,000,000
$ EPS	0.210	0.049	0.279	0.056	0.245	0.0523

Conclusion—the best financing alternative is 100% Stock since the EPS values are largest; the worst financing alternative is 100% Debt since the EPS values are lowest.

FIGURE 8-3

An EPS/EBIT Chart for the XYZ Company

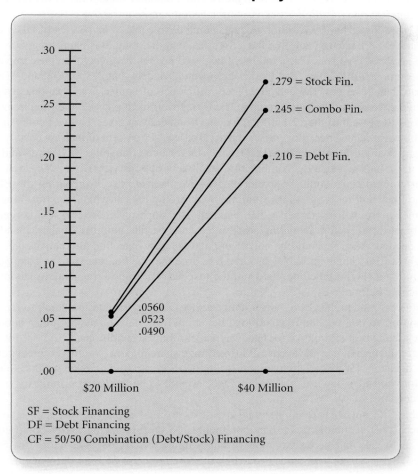

SF = Stock Financing
DF = Debt Financing
CF = 50/50 Combination (Debt/Stock) Financing

A consideration when using EPS/EBIT analysis is flexibility. As an organization's capital structure changes, so does its flexibility for considering future capital needs. Using all debt or all stock to raise capital in the present may impose fixed obligations, restrictive covenants, or other constraints that could severely reduce a firm's ability to raise additional capital in the future. Control is also a concern. When additional stock is issued to finance strategy implementation, ownership and control of the enterprise are diluted. This can be a serious concern in today's business environment of hostile takeovers, mergers, and acquisitions.

IBM has in fact bought back on average $10 billion worth of its own stock per year during the 2009 to 2012 years, dropping its number of outstanding shares from a high of 1.72 billion in 2003 to less than 1.0 billion in 2012. IBM is buying back its stock because it believes the stock price is going up and thus it is a better investment of company monies than some other strategic alternatives.

For all of 2010, companies bought back $299 billion of their own stock, up a record 117 percent from the prior year. However, that total was roughly half of the record total in 2007. Many analysts say buyouts reflect optimism among companies and say it is a good sign. However, other analysts argue that buybacks eat cash that a firm could better utilize to grow the firm.

Dilution of ownership can be an overriding concern in closely held corporations in which stock issuances affect the decision-making power of majority stockholders. For example, the Smucker family owns 30 percent of the stock in Smucker's, a well-known jam and jelly company. When Smucker's acquired Dickson Family, Inc., the company used mostly debt rather than stock in order not to dilute the family ownership.

When using EPS/EBIT analysis, timing in relation to movements of stock prices, interest rates, and bond prices becomes important. In times of depressed stock prices, debt may prove to be the most suitable alternative from both a cost and a demand standpoint. However, when cost of capital (interest rates) is high, stock issuances become more attractive.

The United States has $9.7 trillion in outstanding debt, equal to 63 percent of GDP. Based on that percentage, S&P recently lowered the USA's AAA credit rating. It is interesting, however, that 147 of the S&P 500 companies have total debt that is 63 percent or greater than the company's revenue. For example, GE, Lennar, and Harley-Davidson have debt that is 300, 131, and 116 percent greater than their revenues, respectively. A key difference of course is that companies generate money while governments consume money. The U.S. government pays $210 billion in interest annually, about 10 percent of the $2.1 trillion it collects annually in taxes. Only 24 companies in the S&P 500 however incur interest payments that total at least 10 percent of their revenue.

Tables 8-5 and 8-6 provide EPS/EBIT analyses for two companies—Gateway and Boeing. Notice in those analyses that the combination stock/debt options vary from 30/70 to 70/30. Any number of combinations could be explored. However, sometimes in preparing the EPS/EBIT graphs, the lines will intersect, thus revealing break-even points at which one financing alternative becomes more or less attractive than another. The slope of these lines will be determined by a combination of factors including stock price, interest rate, number of shares, and amount of capital needed. Also, it should be noted here that the best financing alternatives are indicated by the highest EPS values. In Tables 8-5 and 8-6, note that the tax rates for the companies vary considerably and should be computed from the respective income statements by dividing taxes paid by income before taxes.

In Table 8-5, the higher EPS values indicate that Gateway should use stock to raise capital in recession or normal economic conditions but should use debt financing under boom conditions. Stock is the best alternative for Gateway under all three conditions if EAT (profit maximization) were the decision criteria, but EPS (maximize shareholders' wealth) is the better ratio to make this decision. Firms can do many things in the short run to maximize profits, so investors and creditors consider maximizing shareholders' wealth to be the better criteria for making financing decisions.

In Table 8-6, note that Boeing should use stock to raise capital in recession (see 0.92) or normal (see 2.29) economic conditions but should use debt financing under boom conditions (see 5.07). Let's calculate here the number of shares figure of 1014.68 given under Boeing's stock alternative. Divide $10,000 M funds needed by the stock price of $53 = 188.68 M new shares to be issued + the 826 M shares outstanding already = 1014.68 M shares under the stock scenario. Along the final row, EPS is the number of shares outstanding divided by EAT in all columns.

Note in Table 8-5 and Table 8-6 that a dividends row is absent from both the Gateway and Boeing analyses. The more shares outstanding, the more dividends to be paid (if the firm indeed pays dividends). To consider dividends in an EPS/EBIT analysis, simply insert another row for "Dividends" right below the "EAT" row and then insert an "Earnings After Taxes and Dividends" row. Considering dividends would make the analysis more robust.

Note in both the Gateway and Boeing graphs, there is a break-even point between the normal and boom range of EBIT where the debt option overtakes the 70% Debt/30% Stock option as the best financing alternative. A break-even point is where two lines cross each other. A break-even point is the EBIT level where various financing alternative represented by lines crossing are equally attractive in terms of EPS. Both the Gateway and Boeing graphs indicate that EPS values are highest for the 100 percent debt option at high EBIT levels. The two graphs also reveal that the EPS values for 100 percent debt increase faster than the other financing options as EBIT levels increase beyond the break-even point. At low levels of EBIT however, both the Gateway and Boeing graphs indicate that 100 percent stock is the best financing alternative because the EPS values are highest.

Projected Financial Statements

Projected financial statement analysis is a central strategy-implementation technique because it allows an organization to examine the expected results of various actions and approaches. This type of analysis can be used to forecast the impact of various implementation decisions (for example, to increase promotion expenditures by 50 percent to support a market-development strategy, to increase salaries by 25 percent to support a market-penetration strategy, to increase

TABLE 8-5   EPS/EBIT Analysis for Gateway (M = in millions)

Amount Needed: $1,000 M

EBIT Range: – $500 M to + $100 M to + $500 M

Interest Rate: 5%

Tax Rate: 0% (because the firm has been incurring a loss annually)

Stock Price: $6.00

# of Shares Outstanding: 371 M

	Common Stock Financing			Debt Financing		
	Recession	*Normal*	*Boom*	*Recession*	*Normal*	*Boom*
EBIT	(500.00)	100.00	500.00	(500.00)	100.00	500.00
Interest	0.00	0.00	0.00	50.00	50.00	50.00
EBT	(500.00)	100.00	500.00	(550.00)	50.00	450.00
Taxes	0.00	0.00	0.00	0.00	0.00	0.00
EAT	(500.00)	100.00	500.00	(550.00)	50.00	450.00
#Shares	537.67	537.67	537.67	371.00	371.00	371.00
EPS	**(0.93)**	**0.19**	**0.93**	**(1.48)**	**0.13**	**1.21**

	70 Percent Stock—30 Percent Debt			70 Percent Debt—30 Percent Stock		
	Recession	*Normal*	*Boom*	*Recession*	*Normal*	*Boom*
EBIT	(500.00)	100.00	500.00	(500.00)	100.00	500.00
Interest	15.00	15.00	15.00	35.00	35.00	35.00
EBT	(515.00)	85.00	485.00	(535.00)	65.00	465.00
Taxes	0.00	0.00	0.00	0.00	0.00	0.00
EAT	(515.00)	85.00	485.00	(535.00)	65.00	465.00
#Shares	487.67	487.67	487.67	421.00	421.00	421.00
EPS	**(1.06)**	**0.17**	**0.99**	**(1.27)**	**0.15**	**1.10**

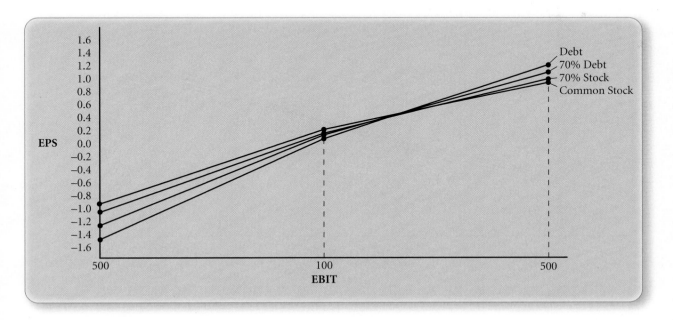

Conclusion: Gateway should use common stock to raise capital in recession or normal economic conditions but should use debt financing under boom conditions. Note that stock is the best alternative under all three conditions according to EAT (profit maximization), but EPS (maximize shareholders' wealth) is the better ratio to make this decision.

TABLE 8-6 EPS/EBIT Analysis for Boeing (M = in millions)

Amount Needed: $10,000 M
Interest Rate: 5%
Tax Rate: 7%
Stock Price: $53.00
# of Shares Outstanding: 826 M

	Common Stock Financing			Debt Financing		
	Recession	*Normal*	*Boom*	*Recession*	*Normal*	*Boom*
EBIT	1,000.00	2,500.00	5,000.00	1,000.00	2,500.00	5,000.00
Interest	0.00	0.00	0.00	500.00	500.00	500.00
EBT	1,000.00	2,500.00	5,000.00	500.00	2,000.00	4,500.00
Taxes	70.00	175.00	350.00	35.00	140.00	315.00
EAT	930.00	2,325.00	4,650.00	465.00	1,860.00	4,185.00
# Shares	1,014.68	1,014.68	1,014.68	826.00	826.00	826.00
EPS	**0.92**	**2.2 9**	**4.58**	**0.56**	**2.25**	**5.07**

	70% Stock—30% Debt			70% Debt—30% Stock		
	Recession	*Normal*	*Boom*	*Recession*	*Normal*	*Boom*
EBIT	1,000.00	2,500.00	5,000.00	1,000.00	2,500.00	5,000.00
Interest	150.00	150.00	150.00	350.00	350.00	350.00
EBT	850.00	2,350.00	4,850.00	650.00	2,150.00	4,650.00
Taxes	59.50	164.50	339.50	45.50	150.50	325.50
EAT	790.50	2,185.50	4,510.50	604.50	1,999.50	4,324.50
# Shares	958.08	958.08	958.08	882.60	882.60	882.60
EPS	**0.83**	**2.28**	**4.71**	**0.68**	**2.27**	**4.90**

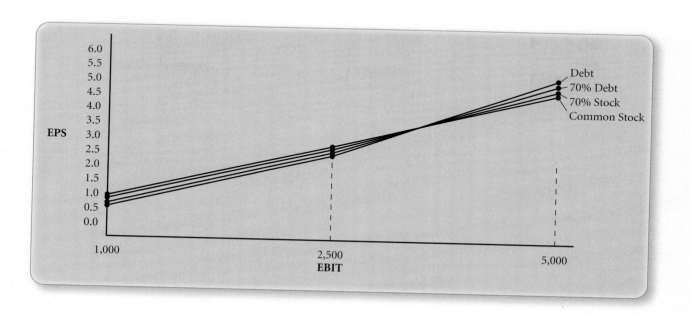

Conclusion: Boeing should use common stock to raise capital in recession (see 0.92) or normal (see 2.29) economic conditions but should use debt financing under boom conditions (see 5.07). Note that a dividends row is absent from this analysis. The more shares outstanding, the more dividends to be paid (if the firm pays dividends), which would lower the common stock EPS values.

research and development expenditures by 70 percent to support product development, or to sell $1 million of common stock to raise capital for diversification). Nearly all financial institutions require at least three years of projected financial statements whenever a business seeks capital. A projected income statement and balance sheet allow an organization to compute projected financial ratios under various strategy-implementation scenarios. When compared to prior years and to industry averages, financial ratios provide valuable insights into the feasibility of various strategy-implementation approaches.

Primarily as a result of the Sarbanes-Oxley Act, companies today are being much more diligent in preparing projected financial statements to "reasonably rather than too optimistically" project future expenses and earnings. There is much more care not to mislead shareholders and other constituencies.

A 2013 projected income statement and a balance sheet for the Litten Company are provided in Table 8-7. The projected statements for Litten are based on five assumptions: (1) The company needs to raise $45 million to finance expansion into foreign markets; (2) $30 million of

TABLE 8-7 A Projected Income Statement and Balance Sheet for the Litten Company (in millions)

	Prior Year 2012	Projected Year 2013	Remarks
PROJECTED INCOME STATEMENT			
Sales	$100	$150.00	50% increase
Cost of Goods Sold	70	105.00	70% of sales
Gross Margin	30	45.00	
Selling Expense	10	15.00	10% of sales
Administrative Expense	5	7.50	5% of sales
Earnings Before Interest and Taxes	15	22.50	
Interest	3	3.00	
Earnings Before Taxes	12	19.50	
Taxes	6	9.75	50% rate
Net Income	**6**	**9.75**	
Dividends	2	5.00	
Retained Earnings	4	4.75	
PROJECTED BALANCE SHEET			
Assets			
Cash	5	7.75	Plug figure
Accounts Receivable	2	4.00	100% increase
Inventory	20	45.00	
Total Current Assets	27	56.75	
Land	15	15.00	
Plant and Equipment	50	80.00	Add three new plants at $10 million each
Less Depreciation	10	20.00	
Net Plant and Equipment	40	60.00	
Total Fixed Assets	55	75.00	
Total Assets	**82**	**131.75**	
Liabilities			
Accounts Payable	10	10.00	
Notes Payable	10	10.00	
Total Current Liabilities	20	20.00	
Long-term Debt	40	70.00	Borrowed $30 million
Additional Paid-in-Capital	20	35.00	Issued 100,000 shares at $150 each
Retained Earnings	2	6.75	$2 + $4.75
Total Liabilities and Net Worth	**82**	**131.75**	

this total will be raised through increased debt and $15 million through common stock; (3) sales are expected to increase 50 percent; (4) three new facilities, costing a total of $30 million, will be constructed in foreign markets; and (5) land for the new facilities is already owned by the company. Note in Table 8-7 that Litten's strategies and their implementation are expected to result in a sales increase from $100 million to $150 million and in a net increase in income from $6 million to $9.75 million in the forecasted year.

There are six steps in performing projected financial analysis:

1. Prepare the projected income statement before the balance sheet. Start by forecasting sales as accurately as possible. Be careful not to blindly push historical percentages into the future with regard to revenue (sales) increases. Be mindful of what the firm did to achieve those past sales increases, which may not be appropriate for the future unless the firm takes similar or analogous actions (such as opening a similar number of stores, for example). If dealing with a manufacturing firm, also be mindful that if the firm is operating at 100 percent capacity running three eight-hour shifts per day, then probably new manufacturing facilities (land, plant, and equipment) will be needed to increase sales further.

2. Use the percentage-of-sales method to project cost of goods sold (CGS) and the expense items in the income statement. For example, if CGS is 70 percent of sales in the prior year (as it is in Table 8-7), then use that same percentage to calculate CGS in the future year—unless there is a reason to use a different percentage. Items such as interest, dividends, and taxes must be treated independently and cannot be forecasted using the percentage-of-sales method.

3. Calculate the projected net income.

4. Subtract from the net income any dividends to be paid for that year. This remaining net income is retained earnings (RE). Bring this retained earnings amount for that year (NI - DIV = RE) over to the balance sheet by adding it to the prior year's RE shown on the balance sheet. In other words, every year a firm adds its RE for that particular year (from the income statement) to its historical RE total on the balance sheet. Therefore, the RE amount on the balance sheet is a cumulative number rather than money available for strategy implementation! Note that RE is the first projected balance sheet item to be entered. Due to this accounting procedure in developing projected financial statements, the RE amount on the balance sheet is usually a large number. However, it also can be a low or even negative number if the firm has been incurring losses. The only way for RE to decrease from one year to the next on the balance sheet is (1) if the firm incurred an earnings loss that year or (2) the firm had positive net income for the year but paid out dividends more than the net income. Be mindful that RE is the key link between a projected income statement and balance sheet, so be careful to make this calculation correctly.

5. Project the balance sheet items, beginning with retained earnings and then forecasting stockholders' equity, long-term liabilities, current liabilities, total liabilities, total assets, fixed assets, and current assets (in that order). Use the cash account as the plug figure—that is, use the cash account to make the assets total the liabilities and net worth. Then make appropriate adjustments. For example, if the cash needed to balance the statements is too small (or too large), make appropriate changes to borrow more (or less) money than planned.

6. List comments (remarks) on the projected statements. Any time a significant change is made in an item from a prior year to the projected year, an explanation (remark) should be provided. Remarks are essential because otherwise pro formas are meaningless.

Projected Financial Statement Analysis for Whole Foods Market

Because so many strategic management students have limited experience developing projected financial statements, let's apply the steps outlined on the previous pages to Whole Foods Market, the company showcased at the beginning of this chapter for excellent strategic management.

Whole Foods Market opened 16 stores in fiscal 2010. The projected statements given on the next page(s) are based on the following recommendations:

1. WFMI opens 40 new stores in 2011 and 60 new stores in 2012.
2. WFMI uses a 50/50 debt/stock combination to finance the 100 new stores.
3. After paying almost no dividends in 2010, WFMI starts paying dividends at $1.00 per share in 2011 and 2012.
4. WFMI boosts its advertising expenses by $20 million per year.
5. WFMI installs a new inventory control system that increases the company's low gross margin from 34.8 percent to 40.0 percent.
6. WFMI's per store revenues will increase 10 percent annually in 2011–2013 due to the new ad campaign and the improving economy.
7. Total cost of recommendations for two years are $800 million = $200 million per year to be raised through both debt and equity.

Whole Food's actual consolidated income statements and balance sheets are provided in Table 8-8 and Table 8-9 respectively. The projected statements, based on the above recommendations, are provided in Table 8-10 and 8-11 respectively. Read carefully the notes (a through f), which reveal the rationale for various changes and exemplify the pro forma process. Note in Table 8-10 that Whole Foods' operating margin with the proposed strategic plan increases from 4.9 percent in 2010 to 16.9 percent in 2012. Note in Table 8-11 that Whole Foods' current ratio would be $3,580.3/$400 = 8.95, which is high. Thus in 2012 the company could better use that money to perhaps pay down some of its $908 million in long-term debt.

The projected financial statements were prepared using the six steps outlined on prior pages and the above seven strategy statements. Note the cash account is used as the plug figure, and it is too high, so WFMI could reduce this number and concurrently reduce a liability and/or equity account the same amount to keep the statement in balance. Rarely is the cash account perfect on the first pass through, so adjustments are needed and made. However, these adjustments are *not* made on the projected statements given in Tables 8-10 and 8-11, so that the five strategy statements above can be more readily seen on respective rows. Note the author's comments on Tables 8-10 and 8-11 that help explain changes in the numbers.

TABLE 8-8   Actual Whole Foods Market Income Statements (in millions)

	2010	2009
Revenue (a)	$9,005.8	$8,031.6
Cost of Goods Sold	5,870.4	5,277.3
Gross Profit	3,135.4	2,754.3
Gross Profit Margin	34.8%	34.3%
SG&A Expense	2,697.4	2,470.0
Depreciation & Amortization	275.6	266.7
Operating Income	438.0	284.3
Operating Margin	4.9%	3.5%
Nonoperating Income	6.9	3.4
Nonoperating Expenses	(33.0)	(36.9)
Income Before Taxes	411.8	250.9
Income Taxes (b)	165.9	104.1
Net Income After Taxes	245.8	146.8
Net Income	$245.8	$146.8

(a) – Note that the 16 news stores in 2010 resulted in ($9,005.8 – 8,031.6 = 974.2 revenue increase = an average of $974.2 / 16 = $60.89) $60.89 million as the average revenue per new store.

(b) – Note WFMI's effective tax rate is $165.9 / 411.8 = 40.3%.

TABLE 8-9   Actual Whole Foods Market Balance Sheets (in millions)

	2010	2009
Assets		
Current Assets		
Cash	$132.0	$430.1
Net Receivables	133.3	104.7
Inventories	323.5	310.6
Other Current Assets	572.7	209.9
Total Current Assets	1,161.5	1,055.4
Net Fixed Assets (a)	1,886.1	1,897.9
Other Noncurrent Assets	938.9	830.2
Total Assets	**3,986.5**	**3,783.4**
Liabilities		
Current Liabilities		
Accounts Payable	213.2	189.6
Short-Term Debt	0.4	0.4
Other Current Liabilities	534.3	494.0
Total Current Liabilities	747.9	684.0
Long-Term Debt	508.3	738.8
Other Noncurrent Liabilities	357.0	732.6
Total Liabilities	**1,613.2**	**2,155.5**
Shareholders' Equity		
Common Stock	500	400
Additional-paid-in-capital	1,274.7	869.7
Retained Earnings (b)	598.6	358.2
Total Shareholders' Equity	2,373.3	1,627.9
Total Liabilities and SE	**$3,986.5**	**$3,783.4**
Shares Outstanding (thou.)	172,033	140,542

(a) – Since WFMI operated 300 stores in 2010, we can estimate cost per store = $1,886 / 300 = $6.3 million and use that cost # for each new store to be built.

(b) – Note that WFMI reinvested back into the company $240.4 million of its total $245.8 million in net income, so in 2010 the company paid out only $5.4 million in dividends. We know that because $598.6 – $358.2 = $240.4.

The U.S. Securities and Exchange Commission (SEC) conducts fraud investigations if projected numbers are misleading or if they omit information that's important to investors. Projected statements must conform with generally accepted accounting principles (GAAP) and must not be designed to hide poor expected results. The Sarbanes-Oxley Act requires CEOs and CFOs of corporations to personally sign their firms' financial statements attesting to their accuracy. These executives could thus be held personally liable for misleading or inaccurate statements. The collapse of the Arthur Andersen accounting firm, along with its client Enron, fostered a "zero tolerance" policy among auditors and shareholders with regard to a firm's financial statements. But plenty of firms still "inflate" their financial projections and call them "pro formas," so investors, shareholders, and other stakeholders must still be wary of different companies' financial projections.[10]

On financial statements, different companies use different terms for various items, such as *revenues* or *sales* used for the same item by different companies. For net income, many firms use the term *earnings*, and many others use the term *profits*.

Financial Budgets

A *financial budget* is a document that details how funds will be obtained and spent for a specified period of time. Annual budgets are most common, although the period of time for a budget

TABLE 8-10 Projected Whole Foods Market Income Statements (in millions)

	2010	2011	2012
Revenue (a)	$9,005.8	12,584.0	17,860.0
Cost of Goods Sold	5,870.4	7,550.0	10,716.0
Gross Profit	3,135.4	5,034.0	7,144.0
Gross Profit Margin (b)	34.8%	40%	40%
SG&A Expense (c)	2,697.4	3,782.0	4,109.0
Depreciation & Amortization	275.6	290	310.0
Operating Income	438.0	1,252.0	3,035.0
Operating Margin	4.9%	9.9%	16.9%
Nonoperating Income	6.9	0	0
Nonoperating Expenses	(33.0)	0	0
Income Before Taxes	411.8	1,252.0	3,035.0
Income Taxes (d)	165.9	504.0	1,223.0
Net Income After Taxes	245.8	748.0	1,812.0
Net Income	$245.8	748.0	1,812.0
Dividends	5.4	175.0	180.0
Retained Earnings	$240.4	573.0	1,632.0

(a) - $60.89 million per new store + 10% increase for all stores, so in 2011 we have $60.89 x 40 = $2,435 + 9,005 = $11,440 + 10% = $12,584. In 2012 we have $60.89 x 60 = 3,653 + 12,584 = $16,237 + 10% = $17,860.

(b) increases to 40% due to better inventory control; note that 5,034/12,584 = 40% and 7,144/17,860 = 40%.

(c) same 29.9% of revenue + $20 million per year, new ad campaign; note that $12,584 × .299 + $20 = $3,782.

(d) same 40.3% rate as in 2010.

can range from one day to more than 10 years. Fundamentally, financial budgeting is a method for specifying what must be done to complete strategy implementation successfully. Financial budgeting should not be thought of as a tool for limiting expenditures but rather as a method for obtaining the most productive and profitable use of an organization's resources. Financial budgets can be viewed as the planned allocation of a firm's resources based on forecasts of the future.

There are almost as many different types of financial budgets as there are types of organizations. Some common types of budgets include cash budgets, operating budgets, sales budgets, profit budgets, factory budgets, capital budgets, expense budgets, divisional budgets, variable budgets, flexible budgets, and fixed budgets. When an organization is experiencing financial difficulties, budgets are especially important in guiding strategy implementation.

Perhaps the most common type of financial budget is the *cash budget*. The Financial Accounting Standards Board (FASB) has mandated that every publicly-held company in the United States must issue an annual cash-flow statement in addition to the usual financial reports. The statement includes all receipts and disbursements of cash in operations, investments, and financing. It supplements the Statement on Changes in Financial Position formerly included in the annual reports of all publicly held companies. A cash budget for the year 2013 for the Toddler Toy Company is provided in Table 8-12. Note that Toddler is not expecting to have surplus cash until November 2013.

Financial budgets have some limitations. First, budgetary programs can become so detailed that they are cumbersome and overly expensive. Overbudgeting or underbudgeting can cause problems. Second, financial budgets can become a substitute for objectives. A budget is a tool and not an end in itself. Third, budgets can hide inefficiencies if based solely on precedent rather than on periodic evaluation of circumstances and standards. Finally, budgets are sometimes used as instruments of tyranny that result in frustration, resentment, absenteeism, and high turnover. To minimize the effect of this last concern, managers should increase the participation of subordinates in preparing budgets.

TABLE 8-11 Projected Whole Foods Market Balance Sheets (in millions)

	2010	2011	2012
Assets			
Current Assets			
Cash	$132.0	$1,55.3	$3,260.3
Net Receivables	133.3	140.0	160.0
Inventories	323.5	330.0	360.0
Other Current Assets	572.7	0	0
Total Current Assets	1,161.5	2,020.3	3,580.3
Net Fixed Assets (a)	1,886.1	2,138.0	2,516.0
Other Noncurrent Assets	938.9	0	0
Total Assets	**$3,986.5**	**$4,159.3**	**$6,296.3**
Liabilities			
Current Liabilities			
Accounts Payable	213.2	300.0	400.0
Short-Term Debt	0.4	0	0
Other Current Liabilities	534.3	0	0
Total Current Liabilities	747.9	300.0	400.0
Long-Term Debt (b)	508.3	708.0	908.0
Other Noncurrent Liabilities	357.0	0	0
Total Liabilities	1,613.2	1,008.0	1,308.0
Shareholders' Equity			
Common Stock (c)	500.0	505.0	510.0
Additional-paid-in-capital (d)	1,247.7	1,474.7	1,674.7
Retained Earnings (e)	598.6	1,171.6	2,803.6
Total Shareholders' Equity	2,373.3	3151.3	4,988.3
Total Liabilities and SE	**$3,986.5**	**$4,159.3**	**$6,296.3**
Shares Outstanding (in thousands) (f)	172,033	177,033	182,033

(a) $6.3 M per store × 40 stores = 252 + 1,886 = 2,138; 6.3 × 60 = 378 + 2,139 = 2,516

(b) $200 M to be raised by debt annually

(c) add 5 M new shares annually since $40 per share and need $200 M to be raised by equity annually

(d) add $200 M annually thru stock issuance

(e) $ 598.6 + $ 573.0 = $1,171.6 + 1,632.0 = $2,803.6

(f) stock price = $40, $200 M needed per year thru equity, so 5 M new shares to be issued annually; thus 172,033 + 5 M = 177,033

Evaluating the Worth of a Business

Evaluating the worth of a business is central to strategy implementation because integrative, intensive, and diversification strategies are often implemented by acquiring other firms. Other strategies, such as retrenchment and divestiture, may result in the sale of a division of an organization or of the firm itself. Thousands of transactions occur each year in which businesses are bought or sold in the United States. In all these cases, it is necessary to establish the financial worth or cash value of a business to successfully implement strategies.

All the various methods for determining a business's worth can be grouped into three main approaches: what a firm owns, what a firm earns, or what a firm will bring in the market. But it is important to realize that valuation is not an exact science. The valuation of a firm's worth is based on financial facts, but common sense and intuitive judgment must enter into the process. It is difficult to assign a monetary value to some factors—such as a loyal customer base,

TABLE 8-12   Six-Month Cash Budget for the Toddler Toy Company in 2013

Cash Budget (in thousands)	July	Aug.	Sept.	Oct.	Nov.	Dec.	Jan.
Receipts							
Collections	$12,000	$21,000	$31,000	$35,000	$22,000	$18,000	$11,000
Payments							
Purchases	14,000	21,000	28,000	14,000	14,000	7,000	
Wages and Salaries	1,500	2,000	2,500	1,500	1,500	1,000	
Rent	500	500	500	500	500	500	
Other Expenses	200	300	400	200	—	100	
Taxes	—	8,000	—	—	—	—	
Payment on Machine	—	—	10,000	—	—	—	
Total Payments	$16,200	$31,800	$41,400	$16,200	$16,000	$8,600	
Net Cash Gain (Loss) During Month	–4,200	–10,800	–10,400	18,800	6,000	9,400	
Cash at Start of Month if No Borrowing Is Done	6,000	1,800	–9,000	–19,400	-600	5,400	
Cumulative Cash (Cash at start plus gains or minus losses)	1,800	–9,000	–19,400	–600	5,400	14,800	
Less Desired Level of Cash	–5,000	–5,000	–5,000	–5,000	–5,000	–5,000	
Total Loans Outstanding to Maintain $5,000 Cash Balance	$3,200	$14,000	$24,400	$5,600	—	—	
Surplus Cash	—	—	—	—	400	9,800	

a history of growth, legal suits pending, dedicated employees, a favorable lease, a bad credit rating, or good patents—that may not be reflected in a firm's financial statements. Also, different valuation methods will yield different totals for a firm's worth, and no prescribed approach is best for a certain situation. Evaluating the worth of a business truly requires both qualitative and quantitative skills.

The first approach in evaluating the worth of a business is determining its net worth or stockholders' equity. Net worth represents the sum of common stock, additional paid-in capital, and retained earnings. After calculating net worth, subtract an appropriate amount for goodwill and intangibles. Whereas intangibles include copyrights, patents, and trademarks, goodwill arises only if a firm acquires another firm and pays more than the book value for that firm.

It should be noted that Financial Accounting Standards Board (FASB) Rule 142 requires companies to admit once a year if the premiums they paid for acquisitions, called goodwill, were a waste of money. Goodwill is not a good thing to have on a balance sheet. Note in Table 8-13 that Merck is worth almost eight times the value of Hershey. Note also that Home Depot's $Goodwill to $Total Assets ratio (2.86%) is significantly better (lower) than either Hershey or Merck.

The second approach to measuring the value of a firm grows out of the belief that the worth of any business should be based largely on the future benefits its owners may derive through net profits. A conservative rule of thumb is to establish a business's worth as five times the firm's current annual profit. A five-year average profit level could also be used. When using this approach, remember that firms normally suppress earnings in their financial statements to minimize taxes.

The third approach is called the *price-earnings ratio method.* To use this method, divide the market price of the firm's common stock by the annual earnings per share and multiply this number by the firm's average net income for the past five years.

The fourth method can be called the *outstanding shares method.* To use this method, simply multiply the number of shares outstanding by the market price per share. If the purchase price is more than this amount, the additional dollars are called a *premium.* The outstanding

TABLE 8-13   **Company Worth Analysis for Hershey Co., Home Depot, and Merck (year-end 2010, in millions, except stock price and EPS)**

Input Data	Hershey Co.	Home Depot	Merck
$ Shareholders' Equity (SE)	902	19,393	54,376
$ Net Income (NI)	509	2,661	861
$ Stock Price (SP)	50	35	32
$ EPS	2.21	2.30	0.28
# of Shares Outstanding	227	1,610	3,080
$ Goodwill	524	1,171	12,378
$ Intangibles	123	0.0	39,456
$ Total Assets	4,270	40,877	105,781
Company Worth Analyses			
1. SE – Goodwill – Intangibles	$255	$18,222	$2,542
2. Net Income x 5	2,545	13,305	4,305
3. (SP / EPS) x NI	11,510	40,493	98,399
4. # of Shares Out x Stock Price	11,350	56,350	98,560
5. Four Method Average	$6,415	$32,092	$50,951
$ Goodwill / $ Total Assets	12.27%	2.86%	11.7%

shares method may be called the book value of the firm. The premium is a per-share dollar amount that a person or firm is willing to pay beyond the book value of the firmal to control (acquire) the other company.

When Chevron Corp. acquired Atlas Energy in 2011 for $3.2 billion, that price represented a 37 percent premium over and above Atlas's closing stock price. Based in Moon Township, Pennsylvania, Atlas was a leading producer of natural gas, whereas the much larger Chevron, based in San Ramon, California, was weak in natural gas reserves. Similarly, J. Crew Group Inc. was acquired recently by two private-equity firms for $43.50 a share in cash, or about $3 billion. That price represented a 16 percent premium to the stock's closing price, but J. Crew's shares jumped 17 percent the next business day. When Danaher Corp. purchased Beckman Coulter in 2011 for $5.87 billion, that was a 45 percent premium over Beckman's $83.50 stock price.

If the purchase price is less than the stock price times # of shares outstanding, rather than more, that difference is called a *discount*. For example, when Clayton Doubilier & Rice LLC recently acquired Emergency Medical Services (EMS) Corp. for $2.9 billion, that was a 9.4 percent discount below EMS's stock price of $64.00.

Business evaluations are becoming routine in many situations. Businesses have many strategy-implementation reasons for determining their worth in addition to preparing to be sold or to buy other companies. Employee plans, taxes, retirement packages, mergers, acquisitions, expansion plans, banking relationships, death of a principal, divorce, partnership agreements, and IRS audits are other reasons for a periodic valuation. It is just good business to have a reasonable understanding of what your firm is worth. This knowledge protects the interests of all parties involved.

Table 8-13 provides the cash value analyses for three companies—Hershey, Home Depot, and Merck—for year-end 2010. Notice that there is significant variation among the four methods used to determine cash value. For example, the worth of Hershey ranged from $255 million to $11.5 billion. Obviously, if you were selling your company, you would seek the larger values, while if purchasing a company you would seek the lower values. In practice, substantial negotiation takes place in reaching a final compromise (or averaged) amount. Also recognize that if a firm's net income is negative, theoretically the approaches involving that figure would result in a negative number, implying that the firm would pay you to acquire them. Of course, you obtain all of the firm's debt and liabilities in an acquisition, so theoretically this would be possible.

Deciding Whether to Go Public

Hundreds of companies in 2011 held *initial public offerings* (IPOs) to move from being private to being public. These firms took advantage of high stock market prices. For example, the Internet phone company Skype Ltd. was set to hold its IPO in 2011 in what would have been one of the biggest initial public offerings in the technology sector since Google went public in 2004 raising $1.67 billion. Having over 600 million registered users, Skype expected to raise close to $1 billion through its IPO.

Going public means selling off a percentage of your company to others in order to raise capital; consequently, it dilutes the owners' control of the firm. Going public is not recommended for companies with less than $10 million in sales because the initial costs can be too high for the firm to generate sufficient cash flow to make going public worthwhile. One dollar in four is the average total cost paid to lawyers, accountants, and underwriters when an initial stock issuance is under $1 million; 1 dollar in 20 will go to cover these costs for issuances over $20 million.

In addition to initial costs involved with a stock offering, there are costs and obligations associated with reporting and management in a publicly held firm. For firms with more than $10 million in sales, going public can provide major advantages. It can allow the firm to raise capital to develop new products, build plants, expand, grow, and market products and services more effectively.

Research and Development (R&D) Issues

In terms of "Innovation," *Fortune* in 2011 ranked the following companies as best in the world. Note that Whole Foods Market was # 10 in the world.

Rank	Company
1	Apple
2	Google
3	Nike
4	Amazon.com
5	Charles Schwab
6	3M
7	Statoil
8	ExxonMobil
9	Walt Disney
10	Whole Foods Market

Source: Based on http://money.cnn.com/magazines/fortune/mostadmired/2011/best_worst/best1.html

Research and development (R&D) personnel can play an integral part in strategy implementation. These individuals are generally charged with developing new products and improving old products in a way that will allow effective strategy implementation. R&D employees and managers perform tasks that include transferring complex technology, adjusting processes to local raw materials, adapting processes to local markets, and altering products to particular tastes and specifications. Strategies such as product development, market penetration, and related diversification require that new products be successfully developed and that old products be significantly improved. But the level of management support for R&D is often constrained by resource availability.

Technological improvements that affect consumer and industrial products and services shorten product life cycles. Companies in virtually every industry are relying on the development of new products and services to fuel profitability and growth.[11] Surveys suggest that the most successful organizations use an R&D strategy that ties external opportunities to internal strengths and is linked with objectives. Well-formulated R&D policies match market opportunities with internal capabilities. R&D policies can enhance strategy implementation efforts to:

1. Emphasize product or process improvements.
2. Stress basic or applied research.

3. Be leaders or followers in R&D.
4. Develop robotics or manual-type processes.
5. Spend a high, average, or low amount of money on R&D.
6. Perform R&D within the firm or to contract R&D to outside firms.
7. Use university researchers or private-sector researchers.

R&D policy among rival firms often varies dramatically. For example, Pfizer spent $9.4 billion on R&D in 2010 but slashed that to $5.0 billion in 2011. In contrast, rival Merck spent $11 billion on R&D in 2010 and increased that amount further in 2011. Underlying this difference in strategy between the two pharmaceutical giants is a philosophical dispute over the merits of heavy investment to discover new drugs versus waiting for others to spend the money and discover and then follow up with similar products. Pfizer and Merck "are going in different directions," said Les Funtleyder, portfolio manager of the Miller Tabak Health Care Transformation mutual fund.

There must be effective interactions between R&D departments and other functional departments in implementing different types of generic business strategies. Conflicts between marketing, finance/accounting, R&D, and information systems departments can be minimized with clear policies and objectives. Table 8-14 gives some examples of R&D activities that could be required for successful implementation of various strategies. Many U.S. utility, energy, and automotive companies are employing their research and development departments to determine how the firm can effectively reduce its gas emissions.

Many firms wrestle with the decision to acquire R&D expertise from external firms or to develop R&D expertise internally. The following guidelines can be used to help make this decision:

1. If the rate of technical progress is slow, the rate of market growth is moderate, and there are significant barriers to possible new entrants, then in-house R&D is the preferred solution. The reason is that R&D, if successful, will result in a temporary product or process monopoly that the company can exploit.
2. If technology is changing rapidly and the market is growing slowly, then a major effort in R&D may be very risky, because it may lead to the development of an ultimately obsolete technology or one for which there is no market.
3. If technology is changing slowly but the market is growing quickly, there generally is not enough time for in-house development. The prescribed approach is to obtain R&D expertise on an exclusive or nonexclusive basis from an outside firm.
4. If both technical progress and market growth are fast, R&D expertise should be obtained through acquisition of a well-established firm in the industry.[12]

There are at least three major R&D approaches for implementing strategies. The first strategy is to be the first firm to market new technological products. This is a glamorous and exciting strategy but also a dangerous one. Firms such as 3M and General Electric have been successful with this approach, but many other pioneering firms have fallen, with rival firms seizing the initiative.

A second R&D approach is to be an innovative imitator of successful products, thus minimizing the risks and costs of start-up. This approach entails allowing a pioneer firm to develop the first version of the new product and to demonstrate that a market exists. Then, laggard firms develop a similar product. This strategy requires excellent R&D personnel and an excellent marketing department.

TABLE 8-14 Research and Development Involvement in Selected Strategy-Implementation Situations

Type of Organization	Strategy Being Implemented	R&D Activity
Pharmaceutical company	Product development	Test the effects of a new drug on different subgroups.
Boat manufacturer	Related diversification	Test the performance of various keel designs under various conditions.
Plastic container manufacturer	Market penetration	Develop a biodegradable container.
Electronics company	Market development	Develop a telecommunications system in a foreign country.

A third R&D strategy is to be a low-cost producer by mass-producing products similar to but less expensive than products recently introduced. As a new product is accepted by customers, price becomes increasingly important in the buying decision. Also, mass marketing replaces personal selling as the dominant selling strategy. This R&D strategy, requires substantial investment in plant and equipment but fewer expenditures in R&D than the two approaches described previously.

R&D activities among U.S. firms need to be more closely aligned to business objectives. There needs to be expanded communication between R&D managers and strategists. Corporations are experimenting with various methods to achieve this improved communication climate, including different roles and reporting arrangements for managers and new methods to reduce the time it takes research ideas to become reality.

Perhaps the most current trend in R&D management has been lifting the veil of secrecy whereby firms, even major competitors, are joining forces to develop new products. Collaboration is on the rise due to new competitive pressures, rising research costs, increasing regulatory issues, and accelerated product development schedules. Companies not only are working more closely with each other on R&D, but they are also turning to consortia at universities for their R&D needs. More than 600 research consortia are now in operation in the United States. Lifting of R&D secrecy among many firms through collaboration has allowed the marketing of new technologies and products even before they are available for sale. For example, some firms are collaborating on the efficient design of solar panels to power homes and businesses.

Management Information Systems (MIS) Issues

Firms that gather, assimilate, and evaluate external and internal information most effectively are gaining competitive advantages over other firms. Having an effective *management information system (MIS)* may be the most important factor in differentiating successful from unsuccessful firms. The process of strategic management is facilitated immensely in firms that have an effective information system.

Information collection, retrieval, and storage can be used to create competitive advantages in ways such as cross-selling to customers, monitoring suppliers, keeping managers and employees informed, coordinating activities among divisions, and managing funds. Like inventory and human resources, information is now recognized as a valuable organizational asset that can be controlled and managed. Firms that implement strategies using the best information will reap competitive advantages in the twenty-first century.

A good information system can allow a firm to reduce costs. For example, online orders from salespersons to production facilities can shorten materials ordering time and reduce inventory costs. Direct communications between suppliers, manufacturers, marketers, and customers can link together elements of the value chain as though they were one organization. Improved quality and service often result from an improved information system.

Firms must increasingly be concerned about computer hackers and take specific measures to secure and safeguard corporate communications, files, orders, and business conducted over the Internet. Thousands of companies today are plagued by computer hackers who include disgruntled employees, competitors, bored teens, sociopaths, thieves, spies, and hired agents. Computer vulnerability is a giant, expensive headache.

Dun & Bradstreet is an example company that has an excellent information system. Every D&B customer and client in the world has a separate nine-digit number. The database of information associated with each number has become so widely used that it is like a business Social Security number. D&B reaps great competitive advantages from its information system.

In many firms, information technology is doing away with the workplace and allowing employees to work at home or anywhere, anytime. The mobile concept of work allows employees to work the traditional 9-to-5 workday across any of the 24 time zones around the globe. Affordable desktop videoconferencing software allows employees to "beam in" whenever needed. Any manager or employee who travels a lot away from the office is a good candidate for working at home rather than in an office provided by the firm. Salespersons or consultants are good examples, but any person whose job largely involves talking to others or handling information could easily operate at home with the proper computer system and software.

Many people see the officeless office trend as leading to a resurgence of family togetherness in U.S. society. Even the design of homes may change from having large open areas to having more private small areas conducive to getting work done.[13]

Business Analytics

Business analytics is a management information systems technique that involves using software to mine huge volumes of data to help executives make decisions. Sometimes called predictive analytics, machine learning, or data mining, this software enables a researcher to assess and utilize the aggregate experience of an organization, a priceless strategic asset for a firm. The history of a firm's interaction with its customers, suppliers, distributors, employees, rival firms, and more can all be tapped with *data mining* to generate predictive models. Business analytics is very similar to the actuarial methods used by insurance companies to rate customers by the chance of positive or negative outcomes. Every business is basically a risk management endeavor! Therefore, like insurance companies, all businesses can benefit from measuring, tracking, and computing the risk associated with hundreds of strategic and tactical decisions made everyday. Business analytics enables a company to benefit from measuring and managing risk.

As more and more products become commoditized (so similar as to be indistinguishable), competitive advantage more and more hinges on improvements to business processes. Business analytics can provide a firm with proprietary business intelligence regarding, for example, which segment(s) of customers choose your firm versus those who defer, delay, or defect to a competitor and why. Business analytics can reveal where your competitors are weak so that marketing and sales activities can be directly targeted to take advantage of resultant opportunities (knowledge). In addition to understanding consumer behavior better, which yields more effective and efficient marketing, business analytics also is being used to slash expenses by, for example, withholding retention offers from customers who are going to stay with the firm anyway, or managing fraudulent transactions involving invoices, credit care purchases, tax returns insurance claims, mobile phone calls, online ad clicks, and more.

A key distinguishing feature of business analytics is that it is predictive rather than retrospective, in that it enables a firm to learn from experience and make current and future decisions based on prior information. Deriving robust predictive models from data mining to support hundreds of commonly occurring business decisions is the essence of learning from experience. The mathematical models associated with business analytics can dramatically enhance decision-making at all organizational levels and all stages of strategic management. In a sense, art becomes science with business analytics due to the mathematical generalization of thousands, millions, or even billions of prior data points to discover patterns of behavior for optimizing the deployment of resources.

IBM's CEO Samuel Palmisano recently announced that IBM is moving aggressively into business analytics, trying to overtake Oracle's market share lead.[14] IBM's annual business analytics revenues of about $40 billion are growing about 15 percent every quarter compared to the industry growing about 15 percent annually. IBM's acquisition of SPSS for $1.2 billion, among other recent acquisitions, launched the firm heavily into the business analytics consulting business. Microsoft currently has a software program called PowerPivot that offers data-mining capability in a spreadsheet-like way, but this is not nearly as powerful as business analytics software. IBM recently completed a business analytics project for the New York City Fire Department whereby buildings in the city were assessed for risk.

Special Note to Students

Regardless of your business major, be sure to capitalize on that special knowledge in delivering your strategic management case analysis. Whenever the opportunity arises in your oral or written project, reveal how your firm can gain and sustain competitive advantage using your marketing, finance/accounting, and/or MIS recommendations. Continuously compare your firm to rivals and draw insights and conclusions so that your recommendations come across as well conceived. Never shy away from the EPS/EBIT or projected financial statement analyses because your audience must be convinced that what you recommend is financially feasible and worth the dollars to be spent. Spend sufficient time on the nuts-and-bolts of those analyses, so fellow students (and your professor) will be assured that you did them correctly and reasonably. Too often, when students rush at the end, it means their financial statements are overly optimistic or incorrectly developed—so avoid that issue. The marketing, finance/accounting, and MIS aspects of your recommended strategies must ultimately work together to gain and sustain competitive advantage for the firm—so point that out frequently.

Conclusion

Successful strategy implementation depends on cooperation among all functional and divisional managers in an organization. Marketing departments are commonly charged with implementing strategies that require significant increases in sales revenues in new areas and with new or improved products. Finance and accounting managers must devise effective strategy-implementation approaches at low cost and minimum risk to that firm. R&D managers have to transfer complex technologies or develop new technologies to successfully implement strategies. Information systems managers are being called upon more and more to provide leadership and training for all individuals in the firm. The nature and role of marketing, finance/accounting, R&D, and management information systems activities, coupled with the management activities described in Chapter 7, largely determine organizational success.

Key Terms and Concepts

Business Analytics (p. 308)
Cash Budget (p. 301)
Data mining (p. 308)
EPS/EBIT Analysis (p. 291)
Financial Budget (p. 300)
Initial Public Offering (p. 305)
Management Information System (MIS) (p. 307)
Market Segmentation (p. 286)
Marketing Mix Variables (p. 287)
Multidimensional Scaling (p. 290)

Outstanding Shares Method (p. 303)
Premium (p. 303)
Price-Earnings Ratio Method (p. 303)
Product Positioning (p. 286)
Projected Financial Statement Analysis (p. 294)
Purpose-Based Marketing (p. 286)
Research and Development (R&D) (p. 305)
Tweet (p. 284)
Vacant Niche (p. 290)
Wikis (p. 284)

Issues for Review and Discussion

1. Hewlett-Packard (HP) has been successful for decades. Analyze their year-end 2011 financials. List six points that reveal HP's performance in 2011.
2. Explain how to develop an advertising strategy?
3. Diagram a product-positioning map for HP. Include three rival firms in your matrix.
4. Diagram a product-positioning map for your college or university.
5. List and explain the advantages versus disadvantages of using debt versus equity as a means of raising capital.
6. List in order of importance the limitations of the EPS/EBIT analysis.
7. Turn back to the Cohesion Case on Adidas AG. Calculate that company's tax rate, which is a common calculation needed in performing EPS/EBIT analysis.
8. Review the website of a company that you are familiar with. Discuss the extent to which that organization has instituted the new principles of marketing according to Parise, Guinan, and Weinberg.
9. For companies in general, identify and discuss three opportunities and three threats associated with social networking activities on the Internet.
10. Do you agree or disagree with the following statement? Explain your reasoning. "Television viewers are passive viewers of ads whereas Internet users take an active role in choosing what to look at—so customers on the Internet are tougher for marketers to reach."
11. How important or relevant do you believe purpose-based marketing is for organizations today?
12. Why is it essential for organizations to segment markets and target particular groups of consumers?
13. Explain how and why the Internet makes market segmentation easier?
14. A product-positioning rule given in the chapter is that "when there are only two competitors, the middle becomes the preferred strategic position." Illustrate this for the cruise ship industry where two firms, Carnival and Royal Caribbean, dominate. Illustrate this for the commercial airliner building industry where Boeing and Airbus dominate.
15. How could/would dividends affect an EPS/EBIT analysis? Would it be correct to refer to "earnings after taxes, interest, and dividends" as retained earnings for a given year?
16. In performing an EPS/EBIT analysis, where does the first row of (EBIT) numbers come from?

17. In performing an EPS/EBIT analysis, where does the tax rate percentage come from?
18. What amount of dividends did HP pay in 2011? How much of 2011's earnings did HP reinvest back into the company?
19. Show algebraically that the price earnings ratio formula is identical to the number of shares outstanding multiplied by the stock price formula? Why are the values obtained from these two methods sometimes different?
20. In accounting terms, distinguish between intangibles and goodwill on a balance sheet. Why do these two items generally stay the same on projected financial statements?
21. What are the three major R&D approaches to implementing strategies? Which approach would you prefer as owner of a small software company? Why?
22. Explain in your own words the process of developing projected financial statement analysis.
23. In developing projected financial statements, why should the preparer not use historical percentages too heavily?
24. Explain five methods for determining the cash value of a company.
25. Given the seven R&D policies mentioned in the chapter, which four do you feel would be best for Audi to utilize? Why?
26. Diagram an EPS/EBIT chart that reflects negative EPS values.
27. Define and give an example of a vacant niche.
28. Define and give an example of wikis and tweets.
29. List the marketing mix variables and give an example of each.
30. Show algebraically that the price earnings ratio method of calculating the cash value of a company is identical to the number of shares outstanding multiplied by the stock price method.
31. Define and give an example of goodwill and intangibles.
32. What is the difference between capital surplus and additional paid in capital on a balance sheet?
33. What transaction is the link between the projected income statement and the projected balance sheet?
34. Explain the benefits of a before-and-after product-positioning map.
35. Explain how HP should conduct market segmentation.
36. Determine the cash value of HP using the methods described in this chapter.

Notes

1. Salvatore Parise, Patricia Guinan, and Bruce Weinberg, "The Secrets of Marketing in a Web 2.0 World," *Wall Street Journal*, December 15, 2008, R1.
2. Kathy Chu and Kim Thai, "Banks Jump on Twitter Wagon," *USA Today*, May 12, 2009, B1.
3. Valerie Bauerlein, "Gatorade's Mission: Sell More Drinks," *Wall Street Journal*, September 14, 2010, B6.
4. Tom Wright, "Poor Nations Go Online on Cell Phones," *Wall Street Journal*, December 5, 2008, B8.
5. http://www.corporate-eye.com/blog/2010/12/ad-spending-forecasts-highlight-china-and-the-internet/
6. Ellen Byron, "A New Odd Couple: Google, P&G Swap Workers to Spur Innovation," *Wall Street Journal*, November 19, 2008, A1.
7. Susanne Vranica, "Veteran Marketer Promotes a New Kind of Selling," *Wall Street Journal*, October 31, 2008, B4.
8. Gupta, Sunil, and Donald R. Lehmann, *Managing Customers as Investments: The Strategic Value of Customers in the Long Run* ("Customer Retention" section) (Upper Saddle River, NJ: Pearson Education/Wharton School Publishing, 2005).
9. Ralph Biggadike, "The Contributions of Marketing to Strategic Management," *Academy of Management Review* 6, no. 4 (October 1981): 627.
10. Michael Rapoport, "Pro Forma Is a Hard Habit to Break," *Wall Street Journal*, September 18, 2003, B3A.
11. Amy Merrick, "U.S. Research Spending to Rise Only 3.2 Percent," *Wall Street Journal*, December 28, 2001, A2.
12. Pier Abetti, "Technology: A Key Strategic Resource," *Management Review* 78, no. 2 (February 1989): 38.
13. Adapted from Edward Baig, "Welcome to the Officeless Office," *BusinessWeek*, June 26, 1995.
14. Spencer Ante, "IBM Ready for Close-Up," *Wall Street Journal*, January 18, 2011, B4.

Current Readings

Bertini, Marco, and Luc Wathieu. "How to Stop Customers from Fixating on Price." *Harvard Business Review*, May 2010, 84–91.

Comstock, Beth, Ranjay Culati, and Stephen Liguori. "Unleashing the Power of Marketing." *Harvard Business Review*, October 2010, 90–99.

Cuervo-Cazurra, Alvaro, and C. Annique Un. "Why Some Firms Never Invest in Formal R&D." *Strategic Management Journal* 31, no. 7 (July 2010): 759–779.

Dixon, Matthew, Karen Freeman, and Nicholas Toman. "Stop Trying to Delight Your Customers." *Harvard Business Review*, July–August 2010, 116–123.

Dunn, Brian J. "Best Buy's CEO on Learning To Love Social Media." *Harvard Business Review*, December 2010, 43–50.

Hayashi, Alden M. "How Not to Market On the Web." *MIT Sloan Management Review* 51, no. 2 (Winter 2010): 14–16.

Hey, Tony. "The Next Scientific Revolutions." *Harvard Business Review*, November 2010, 56–91.

Hopkins, Michael S., and Leslie Brokaw. "Matchmaking With Math: How Analytics Beats Intuition to Win Customers." *MIT Sloan Management Review* 52, no. 2 (Winter 2011): 35–42.

Kaplan, Andreas M., and Michael Haenlein. "Users of the World, Unite! The Challenges and Opportunities of Social Media." *Business Horizons* 53, no. 1 (January–February 2010): 59–68.

Kruschwitz, Nina, and Rebecca Shockley. "10 Data Points: Information and Analytics at Work." *MIT Sloan Management Review* 52, no. 1 (Fall 2010): 28–32.

Lavalle, Steve, Eric Lesser, Rebecca Shockley, Michael S. Hopkins, and Nina Kruschwitz. "Big Data, Analytics and the Path From Insights to Value."

MIT Sloan Management Review 52, no. 2 (Winter 2011): 21–34.

Roy, Abhijit, and Satya P. Chattopadhyay. "Stealth Marketing as a Strategy." *Business Horizons* 53, no. 1 (January–February 2010): 69–77.

Rust, Roland T., Christine Moorman, and Gaurav Bhalla. "Rethinking Marketing." *Harvard Business Review*, January–February 2010, 94–101.

Slater, Stanley F., Eric M. Olson, and G. Thomas M. Hult. "Worried About Strategy Implementation? Don't Overlook Marketing's Role." *Business Horizons* 53, no. 5 (September–October 2010): 469–480.

Yujuico, Emmanuel, and Betsy D. Gelb. "Better Marketing to Developing Countries: Why and How." *Business Horizons* 53, no. 5 (September–October 2010): 501–510.

ASSURANCE OF LEARNING EXERCISES

Assurance of Learning Exercise 8A

Preparing an EPS/EBIT Analysis for Hewlett-Packard (HP)

Purpose

HP is featured in the opening chapter case as a firm that engages in excellent strategic planning. An important part of effective strategic management is wisely using debt versus equity for raising capital. Headquartered in Palo Alto, California, HP is a very well managed global information technology corporation that operates in nearly every country. HP's Latin America operations are based in Miami, Florida, its European offices are based in Meyrin, Switzerland, and its Asia-Pacific offices are based in Singapore. In the UK, HP is based in Bracknell, Berkshire.

This exercise gives you practice preparing an EPS/EBIT analysis for a company to determine whether debt versus equity or some combination of the two is best for the firm to expand and grow.

Instructions

Step 1	HP needs to raise $600 million to expand its Asia-Pacific operations from its Singapore headquarters.
Step 2	Prepare an EPS/EBIT analysis to determine whether HP should use stock or debt to raise the needed capital.
Step 3	Prepare a two-page executive summary to provide justification for your financing decision.

Assurance of Learning Exercise 8B

Developing a Product-Positioning Map for Adidas AG

Purpose

Organizations continually monitor how their products and services are positioned relative to competitors. This information is especially useful for marketing managers, but is also used by other managers and strategists.

Instructions

Step 1   On a separate sheet of paper, develop two product-positioning maps that include Reebok, Adidas, Nike, Puma, Converse, and Under Armour. Let one map focus on athletic footwear and one map focus on apparel.

Step 2   At the board, diagram your product-positioning maps.

Step 3   Compare your product-positioning maps with those diagrammed by other students. Discuss any major differences.

Assurance of Learning Exercise 8C

Performing an EPS/EBIT Analysis for Adidas AG

Purpose

An EPS/EBIT analysis is one of the most widely used techniques for determining the extent that debt and/or stock should be used to finance strategies to be implemented. This exercise can give you practice performing EPS/EBIT analysis.

Instruction

Adidas needs to raise $1 billion to expand into Africa. Determine whether Adidas should use all debt, all stock, or a 50–50 combination of debt and stock to finance this market-development strategy. Assume a 20 percent tax rate, 5 percent interest rate, Adidas stock price of $30 per share, and an annual dividend of $0.50 per share of common stock. The EBIT range for 2011 is between $1.0 billion and $2 billion. A total of 500 million shares of common stock are outstanding. Develop an EPS/EBIT chart to reflect your analysis.

Assurance of Learning Exercise 8D

Preparing Projected Financial Statements for Adidas AG

Purpose

This exercise is designed to give you experience preparing projected financial statements. Pro forma analysis is a central strategy-implementation technique because it allows managers to anticipate and evaluate the expected results of various strategy-implementation approaches.

Instructions

Step 1   Work with a classmate. Develop a 2012 projected income statement and balance sheet for Adidas. Assume that Adidas plans to raise $900 million in 2012 to begin serving Africa, and plans to obtain 50 percent financing from a bank and 50 percent financing from a stock issuance. Make other assumptions as needed, and state them clearly in written form. Use Adidas' website as needed.

Step 2   Compute Adidas' current ratio, debt-to-equity ratio, and return on investment for 2010 and 2011. How do your 2012 projected ratios compare to the 2010 and 2011 ratios? Why is it important to make this comparison?

Step 3   Bring your projected statements to class and discuss any problems or questions you encountered.

Step 4   Compare your projected statements to the statements of other students. What major differences exist between your analysis and the work of other students?

Assurance of Learning Exercise 8E

Determining the Cash Value of Adidas AG

Purpose

It is simply good business practice to periodically determine the financial worth or cash value of your company. This exercise gives you practice determining the total worth of a company using several methods. Use year-end 2010 data as given in the Cohesion Case or the 2011 data from the Adidas website.

Instructions

Step 1   Calculate the financial worth of Adidas based on four methods: 1) the net worth or stock-holders' equity, 2) the future value of Adidas' earnings, 3) the price-earnings ratio, and 4) the outstanding shares method. In dollars, how much is Adidas worth?

Step 2   Compare your analyses and conclusions with those of other students.

Assurance of Learning Exercise 8F

Developing a Product-Positioning Map for My College

Purpose

Organizations continually monitor how their products and services are positioned relative to competitors. This information is especially useful for marketing managers, but is also used by other managers and strategists.

Instructions

Step 1   On a separate sheet of paper, develop a product-positioning map for your college or university.

Step 2   At the board, diagram your product-positioning map. Compare your product-positioning map with those diagrammed by other students. Discuss any major differences.

Assurance of Learning Exercise 8G

Do Banks Require Projected Financial Statements?

Purpose

This exercise will allow you to explore the practical importance and use of projected financial statements among banks in your city.

Instruction

Contact several local banks and ask managers about the nature and role of projected financial statements in determining whether to make commercial loans to businesses. Report back to your class on your findings.

"NOTABLE QUOTES"

"Complicated controls do not work. They confuse. They misdirect attention from what is to be controlled to the mechanics and methodology of the control." —*Seymour Tilles*

"Although Plan A may be selected as the most realistic … the other major alternatives should not be forgotten. They may well serve as contingency plans." —*Dale McConkey*

"Organizations are most vulnerable when they are at the peak of their success." —*R. T. Lenz*

"Strategy evaluation must make it as easy as possible for managers to revise their plans and reach quick agreement on the changes." —*Dale McConkey*

"While strategy is a word that is usually associated with the future, its link to the past is no less central. Life is lived forward but understood backward. Managers may live strategy in the future, but they understand it through the past." —*Henry Mintzberg*

"Unless strategy evaluation is performed seriously and systematically, and unless strategists are willing to act on the results, energy will be used up defending yesterday. No one will have the time, resources, or will to work on exploiting today, let alone to work on making tomorrow." —*Peter Drucker*

"Executives, consultants, and B-school professors all agree that strategic planning is now the single most important management issue and will remain so for the next five years. Strategy has become a part of the main agenda at lots of organizations today. Strategic planning is back with a vengeance." —*John Byrne*

"Planners should not plan, but serve as facilitators, catalysts, inquirers, educators, and synthesizers to guide the planning process effectively." —*A. Hax and N. Majluf*

9

Strategy Review, Evaluation, and Control

CHAPTER OBJECTIVES

After studying this chapter, you should be able to do the following:

1. Describe a practical framework for evaluating strategies.

2. Explain why strategy evaluation is complex, sensitive, and yet essential for organizational success.

3. Discuss the importance of contingency planning in strategy evaluation.

4. Discuss the role of auditing in strategy evaluation.

5. Discuss the Balanced Scorecard.

6. Discuss three twenty-first-century challenges in strategic management.

ASSURANCE OF LEARNING EXERCISES

Assurance of Learning Exercise 9A
Evaluating Google's Strategies

Assurance of Learning Exercise 9B
Preparing a Strategy-Evaluation Report for Adidas AG

Assurance of Learning Exercise 9C
Preparing a Balanced Scorecard for Adidas AG

Assurance of Learning Exercise 9D
Evaluate My University's Strategies

The best formulated and best implemented strategies become obsolete as a firm's external and internal environments change. It is essential, therefore, that strategists systematically review, evaluate, and control the execution of strategies. This chapter presents a framework that can guide managers' efforts to evaluate strategic-management activities, to make sure they are working, and to make timely changes. Management information systems being used to evaluate strategies are discussed. Guidelines are presented for formulating, implementing, and evaluating strategies. Google evaluates strategies really well and takes corrective actions promptly as needed.

The Nature of Strategy Evaluation

The strategic-management process results in decisions that can have significant, long-lasting consequences. Erroneous strategic decisions can inflict severe penalties and can be exceedingly difficult, if not impossible, to reverse. Most strategists agree, therefore, that strategy evaluation is vital to an organization's well-being; timely evaluations can alert management to problems

Excellent Strategic Management Showcased

GOOGLE INC.

Headquartered in Mountain View, California, Google is the world's leading Internet search engine company, offering targeted search results from billions of Web pages every day to customers on all continents. The company also is invested heavily in cloud computing and advertising technology. In May 2011, unique visitors of Google surpassed 1 billion for the first time, an 8.4 percent increase from 2010 with 931 million unique visitors. Google recently donated 1 million euro to the International Mathematical Olympiad to support that organization's next five annual International Mathematical Olympiads (2011–2015). Google has physical offices in nearly every country in the world, including European offices in Brussels, Prague, Copenhagen, Helsinki, Paris, Hamburg, Munich, Athens, Budapest, Dublin, Milan, Amsterdam, Oslo, Krakow, Warszawa, Lisboa, Stockholm, Zurich, Kyiv, London, Madrid, and Manchester.

Ninety-nine percent of Google's revenue is derived from its advertising programs, primarily through AdWords. Advertisers can purchase relevant ads targeted to search queries or Web content. The Google Network is a network of third-party customers that use Google's ad programs to deliver relevant ads to their own sites. Google subsidiaries include YouTube and DoubleClick. Founders Sergey Brin and Larry Page (CEOs) each have nearly 30 percent voting control of the firm.

Google's mission statement from its inception has been to organize the world's information and make it universally available. Google's main site, www.google.com, is the Internet's most visited website, and numerous international Google sites, such as in India, www.google.co.in, and the UK, www.google.co.uk, are in the top hundred websites visited.

In 2011, Google announced Gmail Motion, an interactive way of controlling Gmail and the computer with body movements via the user's webcam. Until March 2010, Google adhered to the Internet censorship policies of China. There were reports in 2010 from leaked diplomatic cables that the Chinese Politburo had hacked into Google's computers as part of a worldwide coordinated campaign of computer sabotage carried out by "government operatives, private security experts and Internet outlaws recruited by the Chinese government."

Google reported revenues of $9.03 billion in the second quarter of 2011, a 32 percent increase over second quarter 2010 revenues of $6.82 billion. Google-owned websites generated revenues of $6.23 billion, or 69 percent of total revenues, in the second quarter of 2011. This represents a 39 percent increase over second quarter 2010 revenues of $4.50 billion. Also for the second quarter of 2011, Google's partner sites generated revenues, through AdSense programs, of $2.48 billion, or 28 percent of total revenues. This represented a 20 percent increase from second quarter 2010 network revenues of $2.06 billion. Google revenues from outside of the United States totaled $4.87 billion in the second quarter of 2011, representing 54 percent of total revenues in the second quarter of 2011, compared to 53 percent in the first quarter of 2011. Among that total, revenues from the United Kingdom totaled $976 million, representing 11 percent of revenues.

Source: Based on information at www.google.com.

or potential problems before a situation becomes critical. Strategy evaluation includes three basic activities: (1) examining the underlying bases of a firm's strategy, (2) comparing expected results with actual results, and (3) taking corrective actions to ensure that performance conforms to plans. The strategy-evaluation stage of the strategic-management process is illustrated in Figure 9-1.

Adequate and timely feedback is the cornerstone of effective strategy evaluation. Strategy evaluation can be no better than the information on which it is based. Too much pressure from top managers may result in lower managers contriving numbers they think will be satisfactory.

Strategy evaluation can be a complex and sensitive undertaking. Too much emphasis on evaluating strategies may be expensive and counterproductive. No one likes to be evaluated too closely! The more managers attempt to evaluate the behavior of others, the less control they have. Yet too little or no evaluation can create even worse problems. Strategy evaluation is essential to ensure that stated objectives are being achieved.

In many organizations, strategy evaluation is simply an appraisal of how well an organization has performed. Have the firm's assets increased? Has there been an increase in profitability? Have sales increased? Have productivity levels increased? Have profit margin,

FIGURE 9-1

A Comprehensive Strategic-Management Model

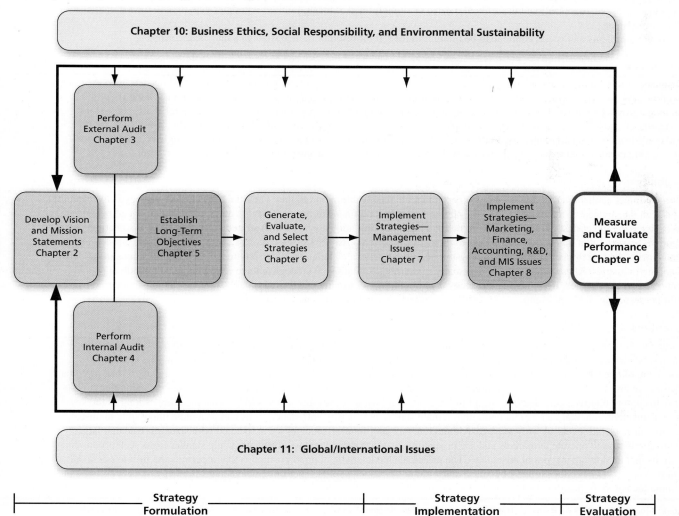

Source: Fred R. David, "How Companies Define Their Mission," *Long Range Planning* 22, no. 3 (June 1988): 40.

return on investment, and earnings-per-share ratios increased? Some firms argue that their strategy must have been correct if the answers to these types of questions are affirmative. Well, the strategy or strategies may have been correct, but this type of reasoning can be misleading because strategy evaluation must have both a long-run and short-run focus. Strategies often do not affect short-term operating results until it is too late to make needed changes.

It is impossible to demonstrate conclusively that a particular strategy is optimal or even to guarantee that it will work. One can, however, evaluate it for critical flaws. Richard Rumelt offered four criteria that could be used to evaluate a strategy: consistency, consonance, feasibility, and advantage. Described in Table 9-1, *consonance* and *advantage* are mostly based on a firm's external assessment, whereas *consistency* and *feasibility* are largely based on an internal assessment.

Strategy evaluation is important because organizations face dynamic environments in which key external and internal factors often change quickly and dramatically. Success today is no guarantee of success tomorrow! An organization should never be lulled into complacency with

TABLE 9-1   Rumelt's Criteria for Evaluating Strategies

Consistency

A strategy should not present inconsistent goals and policies. Organizational conflict and interdepartmental bickering are often symptoms of managerial disorder, but these problems may also be a sign of strategic inconsistency. Three guidelines help determine if organizational problems are due to inconsistencies in strategy:

- If managerial problems continue despite changes in personnel and if they tend to be issue-based rather than people-based, then strategies may be inconsistent.
- If success for one organizational department means, or is interpreted to mean, failure for another department, then strategies may be inconsistent.
- If policy problems and issues continue to be brought to the top for resolution, then strategies may be inconsistent.

Consonance

Consonance refers to the need for strategists to examine *sets of trends*, as well as individual trends, in evaluating strategies. A strategy must represent an adaptive response to the external environment and to the critical changes occurring within it. One difficulty in matching a firm's key internal and external factors in the formulation of strategy is that most trends are the result of interactions among other trends. For example, the daycare explosion came about as a combined result of many trends that included a rise in the average level of education, increased inflation, and an increase in women in the workforce. Although single economic or demographic trends might appear steady for many years, there are waves of change going on at the interaction level.

Feasibility

A strategy must neither overtax available resources nor create unsolvable subproblems. The final broad test of strategy is its feasibility; that is, can the strategy be attempted within the physical, human, and financial resources of the enterprise? The financial resources of a business are the easiest to quantify and are normally the first limitation against which strategy is evaluated. It is sometimes forgotten, however, that innovative approaches to financing are often possible. Devices, such as captive subsidiaries, sale-leaseback arrangements, and tying plant mortgages to long-term contracts, have all been used effectively to help win key positions in suddenly expanding industries. A less quantifiable, but actually more rigid, limitation on strategic choice is that imposed by individual and organizational capabilities. In evaluating a strategy, it is important to examine whether an organization has demonstrated in the past that it possesses the abilities, competencies, skills, and talents needed to carry out a given strategy.

Advantage

A strategy must provide for the creation and/or maintenance of a competitive advantage in a selected area of activity. Competitive advantages normally are the result of superiority in one of three areas: (1) resources, (2) skills, or (3) position. The idea that the positioning of one's resources can enhance their combined effectiveness is familiar to military theorists, chess players, and diplomats. Position can also play a crucial role in an organization's strategy. Once gained, a good position is defensible—meaning that it is so costly to capture that rivals are deterred from full-scale attacks. Positional advantage tends to be self-sustaining as long as the key internal and environmental factors that underlie it remain stable. This is why entrenched firms can be almost impossible to unseat, even if their raw skill levels are only average. Although not all positional advantages are associated with size, it is true that larger organizations tend to operate in markets and use procedures that turn their size into advantage, while smaller firms seek product/market positions that exploit other types of advantage. The principal characteristic of good position is that it permits the firm to obtain advantage from policies that would not similarly benefit rivals without the same position. Therefore, in evaluating strategy, organizations should examine the nature of positional advantages associated with a given strategy.

Source: Adapted from Richard Rumelt, "The Evaluation of Business Strategy," in W. F. Glueck (ed.), *Business Policy and Strategic Management* (New York: McGraw-Hill, 1980), 359–367. Used with permission.

success. Countless firms have thrived one year only to struggle for survival the following year. Organizational trouble can come swiftly, as evidenced by the many Fortune 400 companies listed in Table 9-2 that had negative profits for 2010.

The world's largest cellphone maker, Nokia Corp., based in Finland, watched its profits drop 21 percent in the last quarter of 2010 alone as rival firms gained market share and customer loyalty on Nokia. Nokia's operating margins on devices and services dropped in 2011 to below 7 percent from 12.1 percent early in 2010. Nokia is hoping their recent partnership with Microsoft will be a lifesaver.

Strategy evaluation is becoming increasingly difficult with the passage of time, for many reasons. Domestic and world economies were more stable in years past, product life cycles were longer, product development cycles were longer, technological advancement was slower, change

TABLE 9-2   Fortune 400 Companies That Had Negative Profits in 2010

Fortune Rank	Company	2010 Profits ($)
5	Fannie Mae	− 14.01 B
9	Bank of America	− 2.24 B
20	Freddie Mac	− 14.03 B
85	Sprint Nextel	− 3.47 B
118	AMR	− 471 M
128	Tesoro	− 29 M
138	Manpower	− 263 M
148	US Steel	− 482 M
209	Qwest Communications	− 55 M
216	Smithfield Foods	− 101 M
236	First Data	− 1.02 B
257	Wiliams	− 1.10 B
277	Caesars Entertainment	− 831 M
292	Energy Future Holdings	− 2.81 B
293	Regions Financial	− 539 M
294	Kinder Morgan	− 41 M
298	Western Refining	− 17 M
305	Boston Scientific	− 1.10 B
309	Elbridge Energy Partners	− 198 M
314	Masco	− 1.04 B
327	Eastman Kodak	− 687 M
333	Charter Communications	− 237 M
341	Dole Food	− 34 M
345	Owens-Illinois	− 47 M
361	Commercial Metals	− 205 M
363	Pantry	− 166 M
371	Omnicare	− 106 M
374	Virgin Metal	− 218 M
380	MGM Resorts Int.	− 1.44 B
381	Spectrum Group Int.	− 1.1 M
383	AK Steel Holding	− 128 M
385	TravelCenters of America	− 66 M
391	CC Media Holdings	− 479 M
399	Mutual of Omaha Ins.	− 45 M

Source: Based on company documents.

TABLE 9-3   A Few Big Company Household Names That Disappeared Over Past Years

Compaq

Compaq was one of the largest sellers of PCs in the world until, under duress, the company was acquired by Hewlett-Packard and their name dissolved.

E.F. Hutton

"When E.F. Hutton speaks, people listen," claimed the well-known slogan from the 1970s and 1980s. But money laundering and fraud scandals caused people to stop listening. What barely remains of the once proud firm is today part of Citigroup.

PaineWebber

Founded in 1880 by William Alfred Paine and Wallace G. Webber, PaineWebber by 1990 had 200 brokerage branch offices in 42 states and six offices in Asia and Europe. But in 2000, it merged with UBS AG to become UBS PaineWebber. Then in 2003, "PaineWebber" was dropped and replaced with UBS Wealth Management USA.

Eastern Airlines

Eastern Airlines once dominated much of the domestic travel industry along the profitable East Coast U.S. corridor, but deteriorating labor relations forced the firm into bankruptcy, and it ceased operations in 1991.

Woolworth's

Founded in 1879, Woolworth's became the model for five-and-dime stores throughout the United States. The rise of Wal-Mart and K-mart ended Woolworth's reign.

Arthur Andersen

Arthur Andersen was once a member of the "Big 8" accounting firms, which later became the "Big 5." Andersen's downfall was its role as Enron's auditor, whereby it had approved a whole host of illegal accounting.

TransWorld Airlines (TWA)

Founded in 1930, TWA once dominated airline travel in the United States but eventually declared bankruptcy and was absorbed into American Airlines in 2001.

Source: Based on http://www.walletpop.com/2011/01/10/remember-them-15-most-memorable-companies-that-vanished/

occurred less frequently, there were fewer competitors, foreign companies were weak, and there were more regulated industries. Other reasons why strategy evaluation is more difficult today include the following trends:

1. A dramatic increase in the environment's complexity
2. The increasing difficulty of predicting the future with accuracy
3. The increasing number of variables
4. The rapid rate of obsolescence of even the best plans
5. The increase in the number of both domestic and world events affecting organizations
6. The decreasing time span for which planning can be done with any degree of certainty[1]

A fundamental problem facing managers today is how to control employees effectively in light of modern organizational demands for greater flexibility, innovation, creativity, and initiative from employees.[2] How can managers today ensure that empowered employees acting in an entrepreneurial manner do not put the well-being of the business at risk? The costs to companies in terms of damaged reputations, fines, missed opportunities, and diversion of management's attention are enormous.

When empowered employees are held accountable for and pressured to achieve specific goals and are given wide latitude in their actions to achieve them, there can be dysfunctional behavior. For example, Nordstrom, the upscale fashion retailer known for outstanding customer service, was subjected to lawsuits and fines when employees underreported hours worked in order to increase their sales per hour—the company's primary performance criterion.

The Process of Evaluating Strategies

Strategy evaluation is necessary for all sizes and kinds of organizations. Strategy evaluation should initiate managerial questioning of expectations and assumptions, should trigger a review of objectives and values, and should stimulate creativity in generating alternatives and formulating criteria of evaluation.[3] Regardless of the size of the organization, a certain amount of *management by wandering around* at all levels is essential to effective strategy evaluation. Strategy-evaluation activities should be performed on a continuing basis, rather than at the end of specified periods of time or just after problems occur. Waiting until the end of the year, for example, could result in a firm closing the barn door after the horses have already escaped.

Evaluating strategies on a continuous rather than on a periodic basis allows benchmarks of progress to be established and more effectively monitored. Some strategies take years to implement; consequently, associated results may not become apparent for years. Successful strategies combine patience with a willingness to promptly take corrective actions when necessary. There always comes a time when corrective actions are needed in an organization! Centuries ago, a writer (perhaps Solomon) made the following observations about change:

There is a time for everything,
A time to be born and a time to die,
A time to plant and a time to uproot,
A time to kill and a time to heal,
A time to tear down and a time to build,
A time to weep and a time to laugh,
A time to mourn and a time to dance,
A time to scatter stones and a time to gather them,
A time to embrace and a time to refrain,
A time to search and a time to give up,
A time to keep and a time to throw away,
A time to tear and a time to mend,
A time to be silent and a time to speak,
A time to love and a time to hate,
A time for war and a time for peace.[4]

Managers and employees of the firm should be continually aware of progress being made toward achieving the firm's objectives. As critical success factors change, organizational members should be involved in determining appropriate corrective actions. If assumptions and expectations deviate significantly from forecasts, then the firm should renew strategy-formulation activities, perhaps sooner than planned. In strategy evaluation, like strategy formulation and strategy implementation, people make the difference. Through involvement in the process of evaluating strategies, managers and employees become committed to keeping the firm moving steadily toward achieving objectives.

A Strategy-Evaluation Framework

Table 9-4 summarizes strategy-evaluation activities in terms of key questions that should be addressed, alternative answers to those questions, and appropriate actions for an organization to take. Notice that corrective actions are almost always needed except when (1) external and internal factors have not significantly changed and (2) the firm is progressing satisfactorily toward achieving stated objectives. Relationships among strategy-evaluation activities are illustrated in Figure 9-2.

Reviewing Bases of Strategy

As shown in Figure 9-2, *reviewing the underlying bases of an organization's strategy* could be approached by developing a revised EFE Matrix and IFE Matrix. A *revised IFE Matrix* should focus on changes in the organization's management, marketing, finance/accounting, production/operations, R&D, and management information systems strengths and weaknesses. A *revised EFE Matrix* should indicate how effective a firm's strategies have been in response to key opportunities and threats. This analysis could also address such questions as the following:

1. How have competitors reacted to our strategies?
2. How have competitors' strategies changed?

TABLE 9-4   A Strategy-Evaluation Assessment Matrix

Have Major Changes Occurred in the Firm's Internal Strategic Position?	Have Major Changes Occurred in the Firm's External Strategic Position?	Has the Firm Progressed Satisfactorily Toward Achieving Its Stated Objectives?	Result
No	No	No	Take corrective actions
Yes	Yes	Yes	Take corrective actions
Yes	Yes	No	Take corrective actions
Yes	No	Yes	Take corrective actions
Yes	No	No	Take corrective actions
No	Yes	Yes	Take corrective actions
No	Yes	No	Take corrective actions
No	No	Yes	Continue present strategic course

3. Have major competitors' strengths and weaknesses changed?
4. Why are competitors making certain strategic changes?
5. Why are some competitors' strategies more successful than others?
6. How satisfied are our competitors with their present market positions and profitability?
7. How far can our major competitors be pushed before retaliating?
8. How could we more effectively cooperate with our competitors?

Numerous external and internal factors can prevent firms from achieving long-term and annual objectives. Externally, actions by competitors, changes in demand, changes in technology, economic changes, demographic shifts, and governmental actions may prevent objectives from being accomplished. Internally, ineffective strategies may have been chosen or implementation activities may have been poor. Objectives may have been too optimistic. Thus, failure to achieve objectives may not be the result of unsatisfactory work by managers and employees. All organizational members need to know this to encourage their support for strategy-evaluation activities. Organizations desperately need to know as soon as possible when their strategies are not effective. Sometimes managers and employees on the front lines discover this well before strategists.

External opportunities and threats and internal strengths and weaknesses that represent the bases of current strategies should continually be monitored for change. It is not really a question of whether these factors will change but rather when they will change and in what ways. Here are some key questions to address in evaluating strategies:

1. Are our internal strengths still strengths?
2. Have we added other internal strengths? If so, what are they?
3. Are our internal weaknesses still weaknesses?
4. Do we now have other internal weaknesses? If so, what are they?
5. Are our external opportunities still opportunities?
6. Are there now other external opportunities? If so, what are they?
7. Are our external threats still threats?
8. Are there now other external threats? If so, what are they?
9. Are we vulnerable to a hostile takeover?

Measuring Organizational Performance

Another important strategy-evaluation activity is *measuring organizational performance.* This activity includes comparing expected results to actual results, investigating deviations from plans, evaluating individual performance, and examining progress being made toward meeting stated objectives. Both long-term and annual objectives are commonly used in this process. Criteria for evaluating strategies should be measurable and easily verifiable. Criteria that predict results may be more important than those that reveal what already has happened. For example, rather than simply being informed that sales in the last quarter were 20 percent under what was

FIGURE 9-2

A Strategy-Evaluation Framework

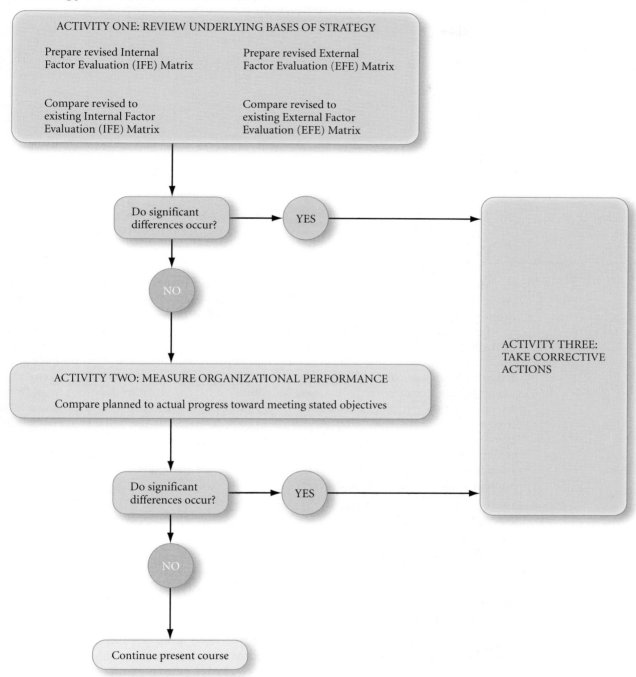

expected, strategists need to know that sales in the next quarter may be 20 percent below stan-dard unless some action is taken to counter the trend. Really effective control requires accurate forecasting.

Failure to make satisfactory progress toward accomplishing long-term or annual objectives signals a need for corrective actions. Many factors, such as unreasonable policies, unexpected turns in the economy, unreliable suppliers or distributors, or ineffective strategies, can result in unsatisfactory progress toward meeting objectives. Problems can result from ineffectiveness (not doing the right things) or inefficiency (poorly doing the right things).

TABLE 9-5 A Sample Framework for Measuring Organizational Performance

Factor	Actual Result	Expected Result	Variance	Action Needed
Corporate Revenues				
Corporate Profits				
Corporate ROI				
Region 1 Revenues				
Region 1 Profits				
Region 1 ROI				
Region 2 Revenues				
Region 2 Profits				
Region 2 ROI				
Product 1 Revenues				
Product 1 Profits				
Product 1 ROI				
Product 2 Revenues				
Product 2 Profits				
Product 2 ROI				

Many variables can and should be included in measuring organizational performance. As indicated in Table 9-5, typically a favorable or unfavorable variance is recorded monthly, quarterly, and annually, and resultant actions needed are then determined.

Determining which objectives are most important in the evaluation of strategies can be difficult. Strategy evaluation is based on both quantitative and qualitative criteria. Selecting the exact set of criteria for evaluating strategies depends on a particular organization's size, industry, strategies, and management philosophy. An organization pursuing a retrenchment strategy, for example, could have an entirely different set of evaluative criteria from an organization pursuing a market-development strategy. Quantitative criteria commonly used to evaluate strategies are financial ratios, which strategists use to make three critical comparisons: (1) comparing the firm's performance over different time periods, (2) comparing the firm's performance to competitors', and (3) comparing the firm's performance to industry averages. Some key financial ratios that are particularly useful as criteria for strategy evaluation are as follows:

1. Return on investment (ROI)
2. Return on equity (ROE)
3. Profit margin
4. Market share
5. Debt to equity
6. Earnings per share (EPS)
7. Sales growth
8. Asset growth

But some potential problems are associated with using quantitative criteria for evaluating strategies. First, most quantitative criteria are geared to annual objectives rather than long-term objectives. Also, different accounting methods can provide different results on many quantitative criteria. Third, intuitive judgments are almost always involved in deriving quantitative criteria. For these and other reasons, qualitative criteria are also important in evaluating strategies. Human factors such as high absenteeism and turnover rates, poor production quality and quantity rates, or low employee satisfaction can be underlying causes of declining performance. Marketing, finance/accounting, R&D, or management information systems factors can also cause financial problems.

Some additional key questions that reveal the need for qualitative or intuitive judgments in strategy evaluation are as follows:

1. How good is the firm's balance of investments between high-risk and low-risk projects?
2. How good is the firm's balance of investments between long-term and short-term projects?

3. How good is the firm's balance of investments between slow-growing markets and fast-growing markets?
4. How good is the firm's balance of investments among different divisions?
5. To what extent are the firm's alternative strategies socially responsible?
6. What are the relationships among the firm's key internal and external strategic factors?
7. How are major competitors likely to respond to particular strategies?

Taking Corrective Actions

The final strategy-evaluation activity, *taking corrective actions,* requires making changes to competitively reposition a firm for the future. As indicated in Table 9-6, examples of changes that may be needed are altering an organization's structure, replacing one or more key individuals, selling a division, or revising a business mission. Other changes could include establishing or revising objectives, devising new policies, issuing stock to raise capital, adding additional salespersons, differently allocating resources, or developing new performance incentives. Taking corrective actions does not necessarily mean that existing strategies will be abandoned or even that new strategies must be formulated.

> The probabilities and possibilities for incorrect or inappropriate actions increase geometrically with an arithmetic increase in personnel. Any person directing an overall undertaking must check on the actions of the participants as well as the results that they have achieved. If either the actions or results do not comply with preconceived or planned achievements, then corrective actions are needed.[5]

No organization can survive as an island; no organization can escape change. Taking corrective actions is necessary to keep an organization on track toward achieving stated objectives. In his thought-provoking books *Future Shock* and *The Third Wave,* Alvin Toffler argued that business environments are becoming so dynamic and complex that they threaten people and organizations with *future shock*, which occurs when the nature, types, and speed of changes overpower an individual's or organization's ability and capacity to adapt. Strategy evaluation enhances an organization's ability to adapt successfully to changing circumstances.

Taking corrective actions raises employees' and managers' anxieties. Research suggests that participation in strategy-evaluation activities is one of the best ways to overcome individuals' resistance to change. According to Erez and Kanfer, individuals accept change best when they have a cognitive understanding of the changes, a sense of control over the situation, and an awareness that necessary actions are going to be taken to implement the changes.[6]

Strategy evaluation can lead to strategy-formulation changes, strategy-implementation changes, both formulation and implementation changes, or no changes at all. Strategists cannot escape having to revise strategies and implementation approaches sooner or later. Hussey and Langham offered the following insight on taking corrective actions:

TABLE 9-6   Corrective Actions Possibly Needed to Correct Unfavorable Variances

1. Alter the firm's structure
2. Replace one or more key individuals
3. Divest a division
4. Alter the firm's vision and/or mission
5. Revise objectives
6. Alter strategies
7. Devise new policies
8. Install new performance incentives
9. Raise capital with stock or debt
10. Add or terminate salespersons, employees, or managers
11. Allocate resources differently
12. Outsource (or rein in) business functions

Resistance to change is often emotionally based and not easily overcome by rational argument. Resistance may be based on such feelings as loss of status, implied criticism of present competence, fear of failure in the new situation, annoyance at not being consulted, lack of understanding of the need for change, or insecurity in changing from well-known and fixed methods. It is necessary, therefore, to overcome such resistance by creating situations of participation and full explanation when changes are envisaged.[7]

Corrective actions should place an organization in a better position to capitalize upon internal strengths; to take advantage of key external opportunities; to avoid, reduce, or mitigate external threats; and to improve internal weaknesses. Corrective actions should have a proper time horizon and an appropriate amount of risk. They should be internally consistent and socially responsible. Perhaps most important, corrective actions strengthen an organization's competitive position in its basic industry. Continuous strategy evaluation keeps strategists close to the pulse of an organization and provides information needed for an effective strategic-management system. Carter Bayles described the benefits of strategy evaluation as follows:

Evaluation activities may renew confidence in the current business strategy or point to the need for actions to correct some weaknesses, such as erosion of product superiority or technological edge. In many cases, the benefits of strategy evaluation are much more far-reaching, for the outcome of the process may be a fundamentally new strategy that will lead, even in a business that is already turning a respectable profit, to substantially increased earnings. It is this possibility that justifies strategy evaluation, for the payoff can be very large.[8]

The Balanced Scorecard

Introduced earlier in the Chapter 5 discussion of objectives, the Balanced Scorecard is an important strategy-evaluation tool. It is a process that allows firms to evaluate strategies from four perspectives: financial performance, customer knowledge, internal business processes, and learning and growth. The *Balanced Scorecard* analysis requires that firms seek answers to the following questions and utilize that information, in conjunction with financial measures, to adequately and more effectively evaluate strategies being implemented:

1. How well is the firm continually improving and creating value along measures such as innovation, technological leadership, product quality, operational process efficiencies, and so on?
2. How well is the firm sustaining and even improving upon its core competencies and competitive advantages?
3. How satisfied are the firm's customers?

A sample Balanced Scorecard is provided in Table 9-7. Notice that the firm examines six key issues in evaluating its strategies: (1) Customers, (2) Managers/Employees, (3) Operations/Processes, (4) Community/Social Responsibility, (5) Business Ethics/Natural Environment, and (6) Financial. The basic form of a Balanced Scorecard may differ for different organizations. The Balanced Scorecard approach to strategy evaluation aims to balance long-term with short-term concerns, to balance financial with nonfinancial concerns, and to balance internal with external concerns. It can be an excellent management tool, and it is used successfully today by Chemical Bank, ExxonMobil Corporation, CIGNA Property and Casualty Insurance, and numerous other firms. The Balanced Scorecard would be constructed differently, that is, adapted to particular firms in various industries with the underlying theme or thrust being the same, which is to evaluate the firm's strategies based upon both key quantitative and qualitative measures.

TABLE 9-7   An Example Balanced Scorecard

Area of Objectives	Measure or Target	Time Expectation	Primary Responsibility
Customers			
1.			
2.			
3.			
4.			
Managers/Employees			
1.			
2.			
3.			
4.			
Operations/Processes			
1.			
2.			
3.			
4.			
Community/Social Responsibility			
1.			
2.			
3.			
4.			
Business Ethics/Natural Environment			
1.			
2.			
3.			
4.			
Financial			
1.			
2.			
3.			
4.			

The Balanced Scorecard Institute has a Certification Program that includes two levels of certification: *Balanced Scorecard Master Professional (BSMP)* and *Balanced Scorecard Professional (BSP)*, both of which are offered in association with George Washington University and are achievable through public workshop participation. The website for this program is http:// www.balancedscorecard.org/.

Published Sources of Strategy-Evaluation Information

A number of publications are helpful in evaluating a firm's strategies. For example, *Fortune* annually identifies and evaluates the Fortune 1,000 (the largest manufacturers) and the Fortune 50 (the largest retailers, transportation companies, utilities, banks, insurance companies, and diversified financial corporations in the United States). *Fortune* ranks the best and worst performers on various factors, such as return on investment, sales volume, and profitability. *Fortune* annually publishes its strategy-evaluation research in an article entitled "America's Most Admired Companies." Eight key attributes serve as evaluative criteria: people management; innovativeness; quality of products or services; financial soundness; social responsibility; use of corporate assets; long-term investment; and quality of management. Every year, *Fortune*

TABLE 9-8 The Most and Least Admired Company in Various Industries (2011)

Industry	Most Admired	Least Admired
Pharmaceuticals	Abbott Laboratories	Pfizer
Metals	Alcoa	Hebel Iron and Steel
Computers	Apple	NEC
Food Production	Archer Daniels Midland	Pilgrim's Pride
Chemicals	BASF	ChemChina
Industrial and Farm Equipment	Caterpillar	Alstom
Specialty Retailers	Costco Wholesale	Office Depot
Food and Drug Stores	CVS/Caremark	Supervalu
Petroleum Refining	Exxon Mobil	PDVSA
Electronics	General Electric	Tyco International

Source: Based on information accessed March 15, 2011, at the websites http://money.cnn.com/magazines/fortune/mostadmired/2010/champions/ and http://money.cnn.com/magazines/fortune/mostadmired/2010/industries/42.html.

publishes additional strategy-evaluation research in an article entitled "The World's Most Admired Companies." *Fortune's* 2011 evaluation in Table 9-8 reveals the firms most admired (best managed) in their industry. The most admired company in the world in 2011 was Nike, followed by Anheuser-Busch, Nestle, and Procter & Gamble.[9]

BusinessWeek, Industry Week, and *Dun's Business Month* periodically publish detailed evaluations of U.S. businesses and industries. Although published sources of strategy-evaluation information focus primarily on large, publicly-held businesses, the comparative ratios and related information are widely used to evaluate small businesses and privately owned firms as well.

Characteristics of an Effective Evaluation System

Strategy evaluation must meet several basic requirements to be effective. First, strategy-evaluation activities must be economical; too much information can be just as bad as too little information, and too many controls can do more harm than good. Strategy-evaluation activities also should be meaningful; they should specifically relate to a firm's objectives. They should provide managers with useful information about tasks over which they have control and influence. Strategy-evaluation activities should provide timely information; on occasion and in some areas, managers may daily need information. For example, when a firm has diversified by acquiring another firm, evaluative information may be needed frequently. However, in an R&D department, daily or even weekly evaluative information could be dysfunctional. Approximate information that is timely is generally more desirable as a basis for strategy evaluation than accurate information that does not depict the present. Frequent measurement and rapid reporting may frustrate control rather than give better control. The time dimension of control must coincide with the time span of the event being measured.

Strategy evaluation should be designed to provide a true picture of what is happening. For example, in a severe economic downturn, productivity and profitability ratios may drop alarmingly, although employees and managers are actually working harder. Strategy evaluations should fairly portray this type of situation. Information derived from the strategy-evaluation process should facilitate action and should be directed to those individuals in the organization who need to take action based on it. Managers commonly ignore evaluative reports that are provided only for informational purposes; not all managers need to receive all reports. Controls need to be action-oriented rather than information-oriented.

The strategy-evaluation process should not dominate decisions; it should foster mutual understanding, trust, and common sense. No department should fail to cooperate with another in evaluating strategies. Strategy evaluations should be simple, not too cumbersome, and not too restrictive. Complex strategy-evaluation systems often confuse people and accomplish little. The test of an effective evaluation system is its usefulness, not its complexity.

Large organizations require a more elaborate and detailed strategy-evaluation system because it is more difficult to coordinate efforts among different divisions and functional areas. Managers in small companies often communicate daily with each other and their employees and do not need extensive evaluative reporting systems. Familiarity with local environments usually makes gathering and evaluating information much easier for small organizations than for large businesses. But the key to an effective strategy-evaluation system may be the ability to convince participants that failure to accomplish certain objectives within a prescribed time is not necessarily a reflection of their performance.

There is no one ideal strategy-evaluation system. The unique characteristics of an organization, including its size, management style, purpose, problems, and strengths, can determine a strategy-evaluation and control system's final design. Robert Waterman offered the following observation about successful organizations' strategy-evaluation and control systems:

> Successful companies treat facts as friends and controls as liberating. Morgan Guaranty and Wells Fargo not only survive but thrive in the troubled waters of bank deregulation, because their strategy evaluation and control systems are sound, their risk is contained, and they know themselves and the competitive situation so well. Successful companies have a voracious hunger for facts. They see information where others see only data. Successful companies maintain tight, accurate financial controls. Their people don't regard controls as an imposition of autocracy but as the benign checks and balances that allow them to be creative and free.[10]

Contingency Planning

A basic premise of good strategic management is that firms plan ways to deal with unfavorable and favorable events before they occur. Too many organizations prepare contingency plans just for unfavorable events; this is a mistake, because both minimizing threats and capitalizing on opportunities can improve a firm's competitive position.

Regardless of how carefully strategies are formulated, implemented, and evaluated, unforeseen events, such as strikes, boycotts, natural disasters, arrival of foreign competitors, and government actions, can make a strategy obsolete. To minimize the impact of potential threats, organizations should develop contingency plans as part of their strategy-evaluation process. *Contingency plans* can be defined as alternative plans that can be put into effect if certain key events do not occur as expected. Only high-priority areas require the insurance of contingency plans. Strategists cannot and should not try to cover all bases by planning for all possible contingencies. But in any case, contingency plans should be as simple as possible.

Some contingency plans commonly established by firms include the following:

1. If a major competitor withdraws from particular markets as intelligence reports indicate, what actions should our firm take?
2. If our sales objectives are not reached, what actions should our firm take to avoid profit losses?
3. If demand for our new product exceeds plans, what actions should our firm take to meet the higher demand?
4. If certain disasters occur—such as loss of computer capabilities; a hostile takeover attempt; loss of patent protection; or destruction of manufacturing facilities because of earthquakes, tornadoes, or hurricanes—what actions should our firm take?
5. If a new technological advancement makes our new product obsolete sooner than expected, what actions should our firm take?

Too many organizations discard alternative strategies not selected for implementation although the work devoted to analyzing these options would render valuable information.

Alternative strategies not selected for implementation can serve as contingency plans in case the strategy or strategies selected do not work. U.S. companies and governments are increasingly considering nuclear-generated electricity as the most efficient means of power generation. Many contingency plans certainly call for nuclear power rather than for coal- and gas-derived electricity.

When strategy-evaluation activities reveal the need for a major change quickly, an appropriate contingency plan can be executed in a timely way. Contingency plans can promote a strategist's ability to respond quickly to key changes in the internal and external bases of an organization's current strategy. For example, if underlying assumptions about the economy turn out to be wrong and contingency plans are ready, then managers can make appropriate changes promptly.

In some cases, external or internal conditions present unexpected opportunities. When such opportunities occur, contingency plans could allow an organization to quickly capitalize on them. Linneman and Chandran reported that contingency planning gave users, such as DuPont, Dow Chemical, Consolidated Foods, and Emerson Electric, three major benefits: (1) It permitted quick response to change, (2) it prevented panic in crisis situations, and (3) it made managers more adaptable by encouraging them to appreciate just how variable the future can be. They suggested that effective contingency planning involves a seven-step process:

1. Identify both beneficial and unfavorable events that could possibly derail the strategy or strategies.
2. Specify trigger points. Calculate about when contingent events are likely to occur.
3. Assess the impact of each contingent event. Estimate the potential benefit or harm of each contingent event.
4. Develop contingency plans. Be sure that contingency plans are compatible with current strategy and are economically feasible.
5. Assess the counterimpact of each contingency plan. That is, estimate how much each contingency plan will capitalize on or cancel out its associated contingent event. Doing this will quantify the potential value of each contingency plan.
6. Determine early warning signals for key contingent events. Monitor the early warning signals.
7. For contingent events with reliable early warning signals, develop advance action plans to take advantage of the available lead time.[11]

Auditing

A frequently used tool in strategy evaluation is the audit. *Auditing* is defined by the American Accounting Association (AAA) as "a systematic process of objectively obtaining and evaluating evidence regarding assertions about economic actions and events to ascertain the degree of correspondence between these assertions and established criteria, and communicating the results to interested users."[12]

Auditors examine the financial statement of firms to determine whether they have been prepared according to generally accepted accounting principles (*GAAP*) and whether they fairly represent the activities of the firm. Independent auditors use a set of standards called generally accepted auditing standards *(GAAS)*. Public accounting firms often have a consulting arm that provides strategy-evaluation services.

The new era of international financial reporting standards *(IFRS)* appears unstoppable, and businesses need to go ahead and get ready to use IFRS. Many U.S. companies now report their finances using both the old generally accepted accounting standards (GAAP) and the new IFRS. "If companies don't prepare, if they don't start three years in advance," warns business professor Donna Street at the University of Dayton, "they're going to be in big trouble." GAAP standards comprised 25,000 pages, whereas IFRS comprises only 5,000 pages, so in that sense IFRS is less cumbersome.

This accounting switch from GAAP to IFRS in the United States is going to cost businesses millions of dollars in fees and upgraded software systems and training. U.S. CPAs need to study global accounting principles intensely, and business schools should go ahead and begin teaching students the new accounting standards.

At the American Institute of CPAs (AICPA) annual conference in December 2010, Security Exchange Commission (SEC) Chairman Mary Schapiro indicated that an important IFRS decision would likely come in late 2011. She mentioned that the wide-ranging Dodd-Frank Act would have little or no bearing on the IFRS decision, and that the SEC would allow a "minimum of four years" for any transition to IFRS. When the SEC does incorporate IFRS into the U.S. domestic reporting system, the first time U.S. issuers would report under that system would be approximately 2015 or 2016. Implementation dates may still be staggered thereafter.

The U.S. Chamber of Commerce supports the change, saying it will lead to much more cross-border commerce and will help the United States compete in the world economy. Already the European Union and 113 nations have adopted or soon plan to use international rules, including Australia, China, India, Mexico, and Canada. So the United States likely will also adopt IFRS rules, but this switch could unleash a legal and regulatory nightmare. A few U.S. multinational firms already use IFRS for their foreign subsidiaries, such as United Technologies (UT). UT derives more than 60 percent of its revenues from abroad and is already training its entire staff to use IFRS. UT has redone its 2007 through 2009 financial statements in the IFRS format.

Movement to IFRS from GAAP encompasses a company's entire operations, including auditing, oversight, cash management, taxes, technology, software, investing, acquiring, merging, importing, exporting, pension planning, and partnering. Switching from GAAP to IFRS is also likely to be plagued by gaping differences in business customs, financial regulations, tax laws, politics, and other factors. One critic of the upcoming switch is Charles Niemeier of the Public Company Accounting Oversight Board, who says the switch "has the potential to be a Tower of Babel," costing firms millions when they do not even have thousands to spend.

Others say the switch will help U.S. companies raise capital abroad and do business with firms abroad. Perhaps the biggest upside of the switch is that IFRS rules are more streamlined and less complex than GAAP. Lenovo, the China-based technology firm that bought IBM's personal computer business, is a big advocate of IFRS. Lenovo's view is that they desire to be a world company rather than a U.S. or Chinese company, so the faster the switch to IFRS, the better for them. The bottom line is that IFRS is coming to the United States, sooner rather than later, so we all need to gear up for this switch as soon as possible.[13]

Twenty-First-Century Challenges in Strategic Management

Three particular challenges or decisions that face all strategists today are (1) deciding whether the process should be more an art or a science, (2) deciding whether strategies should be visible or hidden from stakeholders, and (3) deciding whether the process should be more top-down or bottom-up in their firm.[14]

The Art or Science Issue

This textbook is consistent with most of the strategy literature in advocating that strategic management be viewed more as a science than an art. This perspective contends that firms need to systematically assess their external and internal environments, conduct research, carefully evaluate the pros and cons of various alternatives, perform analyses, and then decide upon a particular course of action. In contrast, Mintzberg's notion of "crafting" strategies embodies the artistic model, which suggests that strategic decision making be based primarily on holistic thinking, intuition, creativity, and imagination.[15] Mintzberg and his followers reject strategies that result from objective analysis, preferring instead subjective imagination. "Strategy scientists" reject strategies that emerge from emotion, hunch, creativity, and politics. Proponents of the artistic view often consider strategic planning exercises to be time poorly spent. The Mintzberg philosophy insists on informality, whereas strategy scientists (and this text) insist on more formality. Mintzberg refers to strategic planning as an "emergent" process whereas strategy scientists use the term "deliberate" process.[16]

The answer to the art versus science question is one that strategists must decide for themselves, and certainly the two approaches are not mutually exclusive. In deciding which approach is more effective, however, consider that the business world today has become increasingly complex and more intensely competitive. There is less room for error in strategic planning. Recall that Chapter 1 discussed the importance of intuition, experience, and subjectivity in strategic planning, and even the weights and ratings discussed in Chapters 3, 4, and 6 certainly require good judgment. But the idea of deciding on strategies for any firm without thorough research and analysis, at least in the mind of this writer, is unwise. Certainly, in smaller firms there can be more informality in the process compared to larger firms, but even for smaller firms, a wealth of competitive information is available on the Internet and elsewhere and should be collected, assimilated, and evaluated before deciding on a course of action upon which survival of the firm may hinge. The livelihood of countless employees and shareholders may hinge on the effectiveness of strategies selected. Too much is at stake to be less than thorough in formulating strategies. It is not wise for a strategist to rely too heavily on gut feeling and opinion instead of research data, competitive intelligence, and analysis in formulating strategies.

The Visible or Hidden Issue

An interesting aspect of any competitive analysis discussion is whether strategies themselves should be secret or open within firms. The Chinese warrior Sun Tzu and military leaders today strive to keep strategies secret, as war is based on deception. However, for a business organization, secrecy may not be best. Keeping strategies secret from employees and stakeholders at large could severely inhibit employee and stakeholder communication, understanding, and commitment and also forgo valuable input that these persons could have regarding formulation and/or implementation of that strategy. Thus strategists in a particular firm must decide for themselves whether the risk of rival firms easily knowing and exploiting a firm's strategies is worth the benefit of improved employee and stakeholder motivation and input. Most executives agree that some strategic information should remain confidential to top managers, and that steps should be taken to ensure that such information is not disseminated beyond the inner circle. For a firm that you may own or manage, would you advocate openness or secrecy in regard to strategies being formulated and implemented?

An excellent example of a totally transparent company is Great Little Box, located in Richmond, British Columbia, in Canada. All 213 employees of that company know exactly how profitable the firm is; 15 percent of all pretax earnings are split equally among everyone at that firm. Employees at Great Little Box work harder because they can readily see how their work matters, and they actively try to increase the company's profits—and their own income. In contrast, *CFO Magazine* reports that only 1 percent of American companies use open-book finances.[17] Among *Inc. Magazine's* 500 fastest growing companies in the United States, fully 40 percent are like Great Little Box in that they use open-book management and clearly visible profit sharing practices.

There are certainly good reasons to keep the strategy process and strategies themselves visible and open rather than hidden and secret. There are also good reasons to keep strategies hidden from all but top-level executives. Strategists must decide for themselves what is best for their firms. This text comes down largely on the side of being visible and open, but certainly this may not be best for all strategists and all firms. As pointed out in Chapter 1, Sun Tzu argued that all war is based on deception and that the best maneuvers are those not easily predicted by rivals. Business and war are analogous.

Some reasons to be completely open with the strategy process and resultant decisions are these:

1. Managers, employees, and other stakeholders can readily contribute to the process. They often have excellent ideas. Secrecy would forgo many excellent ideas.
2. Investors, creditors, and other stakeholders have greater basis for supporting a firm when they know what the firm is doing and where the firm is going.
3. Visibility promotes democracy, whereas secrecy promotes autocracy. Domestic firms and most foreign firms prefer democracy over autocracy as a management style.
4. Participation and openness enhance understanding, commitment, and communication within the firm.

Reasons why some firms prefer to conduct strategic planning in secret and keep strategies hidden from all but the highest-level executives are as follows:

1. Free dissemination of a firm's strategies may easily translate into competitive intelligence for rival firms who could exploit the firm given that information.
2. Secrecy limits criticism, second guessing, and hindsight.
3. Participants in a visible strategy process become more attractive to rival firms who may lure them away.
4. Secrecy limits rival firms from imitating or duplicating the firm's strategies and undermining the firm.

The obvious benefits of the visible versus hidden extremes suggest that a working balance must be sought between the apparent contradictions. Parnell says that in a perfect world all key individuals both inside and outside the firm should be involved in strategic planning, but in practice particularly sensitive and confidential information should always remain strictly confidential to top managers.[18] This balancing act is difficult but essential for survival of the firm.

The Top-Down or Bottom-Up Approach

Proponents of the top-down approach contend that top executives are the only persons in the firm with the collective experience, acumen, and fiduciary responsibility to make key strategy decisions. In contrast, bottom-up advocates argue that lower- and middle-level managers and employees who will be implementing the strategies need to be actively involved in the process of formulating the strategies to ensure their support and commitment. Recent strategy research and this textbook emphasize the bottom-up approach, but earlier work by Schendel and Hofer stressed the need for firms to rely on perceptions of their top managers in strategic planning.[19] Strategists must reach a working balance of the two approaches in a manner deemed best for their firms at a particular time, while cognizant of the fact that current research supports the bottom-up approach, at least among U.S. firms. Increased education and diversity of the workforce at all levels are reasons why middle- and lower-level managers—and even nonmanagers—should be invited to participate in the firm's strategic planning process, at least to the extent that they are willing and able to contribute.

A recent example of "top-down strategic planning" is the approach used by former Hewlett-Packard CEO Leo Apotheker. A recent *Wall Street Journal* article describes how Mr. Apotheker was working with the H-P Board of Directors to develop a new strategic plan for the company.[20] CEO Apotheker made public the new H-P Strategic Plan at the firm's March 2011 shareholders' meeting. Apotheker, in conjunction with the H-P Board, crafted the new strategy aimed at placing greater emphasis on software, networking, storage, and cloud computing—rather than traditional personal computers and accessories.

Special Note to Students

Just Google the words "balanced scorecard images" and you will see more than 100 actual Balanced Scorecards being used as a tool by various organizations to gain and sustain competitive advantage. Note the variation in format. In performing your case analysis, develop and present a Balanced Scorecard that you recommend to help your firm monitor and evaluate progress toward stated objectives. Effective, timely evaluation of strategies can enable a firm to adapt quickly to changing conditions, and a Balanced Scorecard can assist in this endeavor. Couch your discussion of the Balanced Scorecard in terms of competitive advantage versus rival firms.

Conclusion

This chapter presents a strategy-evaluation framework that can facilitate accomplishment of annual and long-term objectives. Effective strategy evaluation allows an organization to capitalize on internal strengths as they develop, to exploit external opportunities as they emerge, to recognize and defend against threats, and to mitigate internal weaknesses before they become detrimental.

Strategists in successful organizations take the time to formulate, implement, and then evaluate strategies deliberately and systematically. Good strategists move their organization forward with purpose and direction, continually evaluating and improving the firm's external and internal strategic positions. Strategy evaluation allows an organization to shape its own future rather than allowing it to be constantly shaped by remote forces that have little or no vested interest in the well-being of the enterprise.

Although not a guarantee for success, strategic management allows organizations to make effective long-term decisions, to execute those decisions efficiently, and to take corrective actions as needed to ensure success. Computer networks and the Internet help to coordinate strategic-management activities and to ensure that decisions are based on good information. A key to effective strategy evaluation and to successful strategic management is an integration of intuition and analysis:

> A potentially fatal problem is the tendency for analytical and intuitive issues to polarize. This polarization leads to strategy evaluation that is dominated by either analysis or intuition, or to strategy evaluation that is discontinuous, with a lack of coordination among analytical and intuitive issues.[21]

Strategists in successful organizations realize that strategic management is first and foremost a people process. It is an excellent vehicle for fostering organizational communication. People are what make the difference in organizations.

> The real key to effective strategic management is to accept the premise that the planning process is more important than the written plan, that the manager is continuously planning and does not stop planning when the written plan is finished. The written plan is only a snapshot as of the moment it is approved. If the manager is not planning on a continuous basis—planning, measuring, and revising—the written plan can become obsolete the day it is finished. This obsolescence becomes more of a certainty as the increasingly rapid rate of change makes the business environment more uncertain.[22]

Key Terms and Concepts

Advantage (p. 318)
Auditing (p. 330)
Balanced Scorecard (p. 326)
Consistency (p. 318)
Consonance (p. 318)
Contingency Plans (p. 329)
Feasibility (p. 318)
Future Shock (p. 325)

GAAS, GAAP, and IFRS (p. 330)
Management by Wandering Around (p. 321)
Measuring Organizational Performance (p. 322)
Reviewing the Underlying Bases of an Organization's Strategy (p. 321)
Revised EFE Matrix (p. 321)
Revised IFE Matrix (p. 321)
Taking Corrective Actions (p. 325)

Issues for Review and Discussion

1. Google has been very successful in the last decade. What is the major reason why?
2. Visit Google's website and evaluate the firm's strategies currently being implemented.
3. Discuss the nature and implications of the upcoming accounting switch from GAAP to IFRS in the United States.

4. Ask an accounting professor at your college or university the following question and report back to the class—"To what extent would my learning the IFRS standards on my own give me a competitive advantage in the job market?"
5. Give an example of "consonance" other than the one provided by Rumelt in the chapter.

6. "Evaluating strategies on a continuous rather than a periodic basis is desired." Discuss the pros and cons of this statement.
7. How often should an organization's vision/mission be changed in light of strategy evaluation activities?
8. Compare Mintzberg's notion of "crafting" strategies with this textbook's notion of "gathering and assimilating information" to formulate strategies.
9. Do you believe strategic management is more of an art or a science? Explain.
10. Do you feel strategic management should be more a top-down or bottom-up process in a firm? Explain.
11. Do you believe strategic management should be more visible or hidden as a process in a firm? Explain.
12. Develop a Balanced Scorecard for Google.
13. Develop a Balanced Scorecard for your college or university.
14. Discuss contingency planning.
15. Identify some important financial ratios useful in evaluating a firm's strategies.
16. How often should a firm formally evaluate its strategies?
17. Under what conditions are corrective actions not required in the strategy-evaluation process?
18. Define and discuss auditing as it relates to strategy evaluation.
19. List 10 characteristics of an effective evaluation system.
20. Go to *Fortune* magazine's website and identify several firms in your city that are listed among the most admired companies in the world according to *Fortune*.
21. Ask the dean of your School of Business to describe for you how his/her department evaluates strategies.
22. Identify four firms that provide their strategic plans on their websites and four that do not. Should firms do this or not? Why?

Notes

1. Dale McConkey, "Planning in a Changing Environment," *Business Horizons*, September–October 1988, 64.
2. Robert Simons, "Control in an Age of Empowerment," *Harvard Business Review*, March–April 1995, 80.
3. Dale Zand, "Reviewing the Policy Process," *California Management Review* 21, no. 1 (Fall 1978): 37.
4. Eccles. 3:1–8.
5. Claude George Jr., *The History of Management Thought* (Upper Saddle River, New Jersey: Prentice Hall, 1968), 165–166.
6. M. Erez and F. Kanfer, "The Role of Goal Acceptance in Goal Setting and Task Performance," *Academy of Management Review* 8, no. 3 (July 1983): 457.
7. D. Hussey and M. Langham, *Corporate Planning: The Human Factor* (Oxford, England: Pergamon Press, 1979), 138.
8. Carter Bayles, "Strategic Control: The President's Paradox," *Business Horizons* 20, no. 4 (August 1977): 18.
9. Adam Lashinsky, "The World's Most Admired Companies," *Fortune*, March 16, 2009, 81–91.
10. Robert Waterman, Jr., "How the Best Get Better," *BusinessWeek*, September 14, 1987, 105.
11. Robert Linneman and Rajan Chandran, "Contingency Planning: A Key to Swift Managerial Action in the Uncertain Tomorrow," *Managerial Planning* 29, no. 4 (January–February 1981): 23–27.
12. American Accounting Association, *Report of Committee on Basic Auditing Concepts*, 1971, 15–74.
13. Edward Iwata, "Will Going Global Extend to Accounting?" *USA Today*, January 6, 2009, B1.
14. John Parnell, "Five Critical Challenges in Strategy Making," *SAM Advanced Management Journal* 68, no. 2 (Spring 2003): 15–22.
15. Henry Mintzberg, "Crafting Strategy," *Harvard Business Review*, July–August 1987, 66–75.
16. Henry Mintzberg and J. Waters, "Of Strategies, Deliberate and Emergent," *Strategic Management Journal* 6, no. 2: 257–272.
17. Jody Heymann, "Bootstrapping Profits by Opening the Books," *Bloomberg Businessweek*, September 27–October 3, 2010, 62.
18. Parnell, 15–22.
19. D. E. Schendel and C. W. Hofer (Eds.), *Strategic Management* (Boston: Little, Brown, 1979).
20. Ben Worthen and JoAnn Lublin, "New H-P CEO Reprograms Strategy," *Wall Street Journal*, January 15–16, 2011, B5.
21. Michael McGinnis, "The Key to Strategic Planning: Integrating Analysis and Intuition," *Sloan Management Review* 26, no. 1 (Fall 1984): 49.
22. McConkey, 72.

Current Readings

Haynes, Katalin Takacs, and Amy Hillman. "The Effect of Board Capital and CEO Power on Strategic Change." *Strategic Management Journal* 31, no. 11 (November 2010): 1145–1163.

Kaplan, Robert S., David P. Norton, and Bjarne Rugelsjoen. "Managing Alliances with the Balanced Scorecard." *Harvard Business Review*, January–February 2010, 114–124.

Lansiluoto, Aapo, and Marko Jarvenpaa. "Greening the Balanced Scorecard." *Business Horizons* 53, no. 4 (July–August 2010): 385–396.

Shaojie, Anna Cui, Roger J. Calantone, and David A. Griffith. "Strategic Change and Termination of Interfirm Partnerships." *Strategic Management Journal* 32, no. 4 (April 2011): 402–423.

Simons, Robert. "Stress-Test Your Strategy: The 7 Questions to Ask." *Harvard Business Review*, November 2010, 92–101.

ASSURANCE OF LEARNING EXERCISES

Assurance of Learning Exercise 9A

Evaluating Google's Strategies

Purpose

Google is featured in the opening chapter example as a firm that engages in excellent strategic planning. Google is the leading Internet search engine company in the world, offering targeted search results from billions of Web pages every day to customers on all continents. The company also is invested heavily in cloud computing and advertising technology. In May 2011, unique visitors of Google surpassed 1 billion for the first time, an 8.4 percent increase from a year ago with 931 million unique visitors.

This exercise can give you practice evaluating a company's strategies.

Instructions

Step 1   Go to www.finance.yahoo.com and review recent headlines for Google.
Step 2   Determine what new strategies Google is pursuing.
Step 3   Evaluate Google's newest strategies based on concepts presented in Chapter 9.
Step 4   Prepare a strategy evaluation report for Google.

Assurance of Learning Exercise 9B

Preparing a Strategy-Evaluation Report for Adidas AG

Purpose

This exercise can give you experience locating strategy-evaluation information. Use of the Internet coupled with published sources of information can significantly enhance the strategy-evaluation process. Performance information on competitors, for example, can help put into perspective a firm's own performance.

Instructions

Step 1   Search the Internet for information on Adidas. Prepare a strategy-evaluation report for your instructor. Include in your report a summary of Adidas' strategies and performance in 2011 and a summary of your conclusions regarding the effectiveness of Adidas' strategies.
Step 2   Based on your analysis, do you feel that Adidas is pursuing effective strategies? What recommendations would you offer to Adidas' chief executive officer?

Assurance of Learning Exercise 9C

Preparing a Balanced Scorecard for Adidas AG

Purpose

This exercise can give you experience developing a Balanced Scorecard for a corporation.

Instructions

Step 1	Compile all information that you have collected on Adidas.
Step 2	Join with three other students in class. Jointly develop a 20-item Balanced Scorecard for the company.
Step 3	Appoint a spokesperson for your team to give a three-minute overview to the class regarding the substance of your Balanced Scorecard.

Assurance of Learning Exercise 9D

Evaluate My University's Strategies

Purpose

An important part of evaluating strategies is determining the nature and extent of changes in an organization's external opportunities/threats and internal strengths/weaknesses. Changes in these underlying critical success factors can indicate a need to change or modify the firm's strategies.

Instruction

As a class, discuss positive and negative changes in your university's external and internal factors during your college career. Begin by listing on the board new or emerging opportunities and threats. Then identify strengths and weaknesses that have changed significantly during your college career. In light of the external and internal changes that were identified, discuss whether your university's strategies need modifying. Are there any new strategies that you would recommend? Make a list to recommend to your department chair, dean, president, or chancellor.

"NOTABLE QUOTES"

"If you have integrity, nothing else matters. If you don't have integrity, nothing else matters."
—*Alan K. Simpson*

"If business is not based on ethical grounds, it is of no benefit to society and will, like all other unethical combinations, pass into oblivion."
—*C. Max Killan*

"Good ethics is good business."

"Do unto others as you would have them do unto you."

"Be joyful when you do things to conserve, preserve, and enhance the natural environment."

Business Ethics/ Social Responsibility/ Environmental Sustainability

10

CHAPTER OBJECTIVES

After studying this chapter, you should be able to do the following:

1. Explain why good ethics is good business in strategic management.

2. Explain how firms can best ensure that their code of business ethics guides decision making instead of being ignored.

3. Explain why whistle-blowing is important to encourage in a firm.

4. Discuss the nature and role of corporate sustainability reports.

5. Discuss specific ways that firms can be good stewards of the natural environment.

6. Explain ISO 14000 and 14001.

7. Discuss recent trends in bribery law.

ASSURANCE OF LEARNING EXERCISES

Assurance of Learning Exercise 10A
Sustainability and Goldman Sachs

Assurance of Learning Exercise 10B
How Does My Municipality Compare To Others on Being Pollution-Safe?

Assurance of Learning Exercise 10C
Compare Adidas AG versus Nike on Social Responsibility

Assurance of Learning Exercise 10D
How Do You Rate Adidas AG's Sustainability Efforts?

Assurance of Learning Exercise 10E
How Do You Rate Goldman Sach's Sustainability Efforts?

Assurance of Learning Exercise 10F
The Ethics of Spying on Competitors

Although the three sections of this chapter (Business Ethics, Social Responsibility, and Sustainability) are distinct, the topics are quite related. Many people, for example, consider it unethical for a firm to be socially irresponsible. *Social responsibility* refers to actions an organization takes beyond what is legally required to protect or enhance the well-being of living things. *Sustainability* refers to the extent that an organization's operations and actions protect, mend, and preserve rather than harm or destroy the natural environment. Polluting the environment, for example, is unethical, irresponsible, and in many cases illegal. Business ethics, social responsibility, and sustainability issues therefore are interrelated and impact all areas of the comprehensive strategic-management model, as illustrated in Figure 10-1.

Goldman Sachs has an outstanding commitment to corporate sustainability as described an their website.

Excellent Strategic Management Showcased

GOLDMAN SACHS GROUP

Founded in 1869, Goldman Sachs has numerous offices worldwide in major international financial centers. Headquartered in New York City, Goldman Sachs is a global leader in providing mergers and acquisitions advice and securities underwriting. The company offers investment banking and asset management services to corporate and government clients worldwide, as well as institutional and individual investors. Goldman Sachs Execution & Clearing is a leading market maker for fixed income products, currencies, and commodities. Through affiliates GS Capital Partners, GS Mezzanine Partners, and others, Goldman Sachs is also one of the largest private equity investors in the world.

Goldman Sachs is betting big on India, having recently agreed to acquire a majority stake in India's ReNew Wind Power Pvt. for 10 billion rupees ($200 million), extending the U.S. bank's investments in emerging economies. ReNew Wind plans to have 1,000 megawatts of wind-generation capacity by 2015. The Mumbai-based power producer is India's largest wind-turbine maker. Goldman has invested $1.5 billion worldwide in clean energy companies, but India is the biggest market for new wind park installations after China. Goldman now has representatives on the board of ReNew Wind, which has signed agreements with Suzlon, Kenersys GmbH and Regen Powertech Pvt. to build and operate wind farms in India. Goldman has invested more than $2 billion through private equity and its own funds in India since 2006.

Sometimes an excellent strategic plan includes retrenchment, and Goldman is also employing that strategy. The company recently said it would cut $1.2 billion in costs by mid-2012 and trim about 1,000 jobs, or 3 percent of its work force. Goldman is considering deeper job reductions as compensation and benefits have historically been Goldman's biggest line-item expense. Goldman's 35,700 employees received $15.4 billion in compensation and benefits in 2010—or about $430,700 per person—one of the highest rates on Wall Street. Compared to its chief rival, Morgan Stanley paid its 62,542 employees $16 billion, or about $256,596 per person.

Goldman Sachs is divided into three businesses units: Investment Banking, Trading and Principal Investments, and Asset Management

and Securities Services. Investment banking is further divided into two divisions and includes Finan-cial Advisory (mergers and acquisitions, investitures, corporate defense activities, restructuring and spin-offs) and Underwriting (public offerings and private placements of equity, equity-related and debt instruments). Goldman Sachs is one of the leading Merger &Acquisition advisory firms.

Trading and Principal Investments is the largest of Goldman's three segments, and is the company's primary profit center. That segment is divided into three divisions and includes Fixed Income, Currency, and Commodities. This segment consists of the revenues and profit gained from the bank's trading activities, both on behalf of its clients (known as flow trading) and for its own account (known as proprietary trading).

Goldman's Asset Management division provides investment advisory and financial planning services and offers investment products (primarily through separately managed accounts and commingled vehicles) across all major asset classes to a diverse group of institutions and individuals worldwide. The company's Securities Services division provides clearing, financing, custody, lending, and reporting services to institutional clients, including hedge funds, mutual funds, and pension funds. The division generates revenues primarily in the form of interest rate spreads or fees.

Source: www.goldmansachs.com.

FIGURE 10-1

A Comprehensive Strategic-Management Model

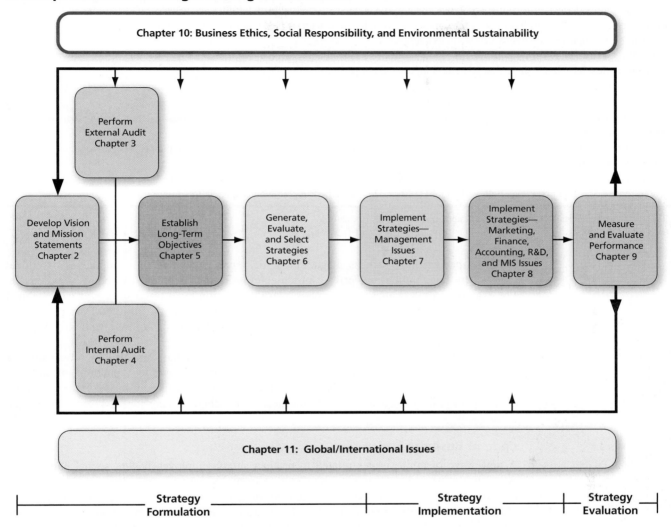

Source: Fred R. David, "How Companies Define Their Mission," *Long Range Planning* 22, no. 3 (June 1988): 40.

Business Ethics

The Institute of Business Ethics (IBE) recently did a study titled "Does Business Ethics Pay?" and concluded that companies displaying a "clear commitment to ethical conduct" consistently outperform companies that do not display ethical conduct. Philippa Foster Black of the IBE stated: "Not only is ethical behavior in business life the right thing to do in principle, it pays off in financial returns." Table 10-1 provides some results of the IBE study.

Good ethics is good business. Bad ethics can derail even the best strategic plans. This chapter provides an overview of the importance of business ethics in strategic management. *Business ethics* can be defined as principles of conduct within organizations that guide decision making and behavior. Good business ethics is a prerequisite for good strategic management; good ethics is just good business!

A rising tide of consciousness about the importance of business ethics is sweeping the United States and the rest of the world. Strategists such as CEOs and business owners are the individuals primarily responsible for ensuring that high ethical principles are espoused and practiced in an organization. All strategy formulation, implementation, and evaluation decisions have ethical ramifications.

TABLE 10-1   Seven Principles of Admirable Business Ethics

1. Be Trustful: Customers want to do business with a company they can trust. Customers can recognize when trust is at the core of a company. Simply defined, trust is assured reliance on the character, ability, strength, and truth of a business.

2. Keep an Open Mind: The leaders of an organization must be open to new ideas. Continually ask for opinions and feedback from both customers and employees to assure a good ethics culture.

3. Meet Obligations: Do everything possible to gain the trust of past customers and clients, particularly if something has gone awry. Reclaim any lost business by honoring all commitments and obligations.

4. Have Clear Documents: Make certain that all print materials such as advertising brochures and business documents are clear, precise, professional, and, most importantly, do not misrepresent or misinterpret.

5. Become Community Involved: Be actively involved in community-related issues and activities, continually demonstrating that your business is a responsible community citizen.

6. Maintain Accounting Control: View accounting and record keeping not only as a means for monitoring the progress of your company but as a resource for identifying and stopping any "questionable" activities.

7. Be Respectful: Treat others with the utmost of respect. Regardless of different positions, titles, ages, or beliefs, always treat others with professional respect and courtesy. Follow the Golden Rule: Do unto others as you would have them do unto you.

Source: Based on http://sbinformation.about.com/od/bestpractices/a/businessethics.htm.

Newspapers and business magazines daily report legal and moral breaches of ethical conduct by both public and private organizations. Being unethical can be very expensive. For example, some of the largest payouts for class-action legal fraud suits ever were against Enron ($7.16 billion), WorldCom ($6.16 billion), Cendant ($3.53 billion), Tyco ($2.98 billion), AOL Time Warner ($2.5 billion), Nortel Networks ($2.47 billion), and Royal Ahold ($1.09 billion).

Other business actions considered to be unethical include misleading advertising or labeling, causing environmental harm, poor product or service safety, padding expense accounts, insider trading, dumping banned or flawed products in foreign markets, not providing equal opportunities for women and minorities, overpricing, moving jobs overseas, and sexual harassment.

Code of Business Ethics

A new wave of ethics issues related to product safety, employee health, sexual harassment, AIDS in the workplace, smoking, acid rain, affirmative action, waste disposal, foreign business practices, cover-ups, takeover tactics, conflicts of interest, employee privacy, inappropriate gifts, and security of company records has accentuated the need for strategists to develop a clear *code of business ethics*. Internet fraud, hacking into company computers, spreading viruses, and identity theft are other unethical activities that plague every sector of online commerce.

Merely having a code of ethics, however, is not sufficient to ensure ethical business behavior. A code of ethics can be viewed as a public relations gimmick, a set of platitudes, or window dressing. To ensure that the code is read, understood, believed, and remembered, periodic ethics workshops are needed to sensitize people to workplace circumstances in which ethics issues may arise.[1] If employees see examples of punishment for violating the code as well as rewards for upholding the code, this reinforces the importance of a firm's code of ethics. The website www.ethicsweb.ca/codes provides guidelines on how to write an effective code of ethics.

An Ethics Culture

An ethics "culture" needs to permeate organizations! To help create an ethics culture, Citicorp developed a business ethics board game that is played by thousands of employees worldwide. Called "The Word Ethic," this game asks players business ethics questions, such as how do you deal with a customer who offers you football tickets in exchange for a new, backdated IRA? Diana Robertson at the Wharton School of Business believes the game is effective because it is interactive. Many organizations have developed a code-of-conduct manual outlining ethical expectations and giving examples of situations that commonly arise in their businesses.

Harris Corporation and other firms warn managers and employees that failing to report an ethical violation by others could bring discharge. The Securities and Exchange Commission (SEC) recently strengthened its whistle-blowing policies, virtually mandating that anyone seeing unethical activity report such behavior. *Whistle-blowing* refers to policies that require employees to report any unethical violations they discover or see in the firm.

Whistle-blowers in the corporate world receive up to 25 percent of the proceeds of legal proceedings against firms for wrongdoing. In the largest such whistle-blower payout ever, a quality-assurance manager, Cheryl Eckerd, with GlaxoSmithKline PLC received $96 million in 2010 for her role in helping the government secure a criminal guilty plea and a $750 million payment from that company to settle manufacturing deficiencies. Whistle-blower payouts are becoming more and more common. Pfizer paid out $2.3 billion in a whistle-blower settlement case earlier and Eli Lilly paid out $1.4 billion. Most firms have internal whistle-blowing incentives and policies and try to keep such matters internal, but recent laws and court cases are shifting disclosure and settlements outside the firm.[2]

An accountant recently tipped off the IRS that his employer was skimping on taxes and received $4.5 million in the first IRS whistle-blower award. The accountant's tip netted the IRS $20 million in taxes and interest from the errant financial-services firm. The award represented a 22 percent cut of the taxes recovered. The IRS program, designed to encourage tips in large-scale cases, mandates awards of 15 to 30 percent of the amount recouped. "It's a win-win for both the government and taxpayers. These are dollars that are being returned to the Treasury that otherwise wouldn't be," said lawyer Eric Young.

One reason strategists' salaries are high is that they must take the moral risks of the firm. Strategists are responsible for developing, communicating, and enforcing the code of business ethics for their organizations. Although primary responsibility for ensuring ethical behavior rests with a firm's strategists, an integral part of the responsibility of all managers is to provide ethics leadership by constant example and demonstration. Managers hold positions that enable them to influence and educate many people. This makes managers responsible for developing and implementing ethical decision making. Gellerman and Drucker, respectively, offer some good advice for managers:

All managers risk giving too much because of what their companies demand from them. But the same superiors, who keep pressing you to do more, or to do it better, or faster, or less expensively, will turn on you should you cross that fuzzy line between right and wrong. They will blame you for exceeding instructions or for ignoring their warnings. The smartest managers already know that the best answer to the question "How far is too far?" is don't try to find out.[3]

A man (or woman) might know too little, perform poorly, lack judgment and ability, and yet not do too much damage as a manager. But if that person lacks character and integrity—no matter how knowledgeable, how brilliant, how successful—he destroys. He destroys people, the most valuable resource of the enterprise. He destroys spirit. And he destroys performance. This is particularly true of the people at the head of an enterprise. For the spirit of an organization is created from the top. If an organization is great in spirit, it is because the spirit of its top people is great. If it decays, it does so because the top rots. As the proverb has it, "Trees die from the top." No one should ever become a strategist unless he or she is willing to have his or her character serve as the model for subordinates.[4]

No society anywhere in the world can compete very long or successfully with people stealing from one another or not trusting one another, with every bit of information requiring notarized confirmation, with every disagreement ending up in litigation, or with government having to regulate businesses to keep them honest. Being unethical is a recipe for headaches, inefficiency, and waste. History has proven that the greater the trust and confidence of people in the ethics of an institution or society, the greater its economic strength. Business relationships are built mostly on mutual trust and reputation. Short-term decisions based on greed and questionable ethics will preclude the necessary self-respect to gain the trust of others. More and more firms believe that ethics training and an ethics culture create strategic advantage.

Ethics training programs should include messages from the CEO or owner of the business emphasizing ethical business practices, the development and discussion of codes of ethics, and procedures for discussing and reporting unethical behavior. Firms can align ethical and strategic decision making by incorporating ethical considerations into long-term planning, by integrating ethical decision making into the performance appraisal process, by encouraging whistle-blowing or the reporting of unethical practices, and by monitoring departmental and corporate performance regarding ethical issues.

Bribes

Bribery is defined by *Black's Law Dictionary* as the offering, giving, receiving, or soliciting of any item of value to influence the actions of an official or other person in discharge of a public or legal duty. A *bribe* is a gift bestowed to influence a recipient's conduct. The gift may be any money, good, right in action, property, preferment, privilege, emolument, object of value, advantage, or merely a promise or undertaking to induce or influence the action, vote, or influence of a person in an official or public capacity. Bribery is a crime in most countries of the world, including the United States.[5]

The U.S. Foreign Corrupt Practices Act that governs bribery is being enforced more strictly. Eight of the top 10 largest settlements ever under the law occurred in 2010. The Las Vegas Sands Corp. is currently under bribery investigation regarding its three casinos in Macau. Macau has four times the gambling revenue of Las Vegas.

Royal Dutch Shell PLC recently paid $30 million in bribery penalties related to its association with Panalpina, which paid about $85 million in bribery fines. The U.S. Foreign Corrupt Practices Act and a new provision in the Dodd-Frank financial-regulation law allows company employees or others who bring cases of financial fraud, such as bribery, to the government's attention to receive up to 30 percent of any sum recovered. Bribery suits against a company also expose the firm to shareholder lawsuits.

Headquartered in Springdale, Arkansas, Tyson Foods recently paid $5.2 million in criminal and civil penalties to resolve bribery allegations involving two meat inspectors in Mexico. Tyson General Counsel David Van Bebber said, "While we are disappointed mistakes were made, corrective action has been taken and the improper payments were discontinued."

The United Kingdom instituted a new Bribery Law in April 2011 that forbids any company doing any business in the United Kingdom from bribing foreign or domestic officials to gain competitive advantage. The new British law is more stringent even than the similar U.S. Foreign Corrupt Practices Act. The British Bribery Law carries a maximum 10-year prison sentence for those convicted of bribery. The new law stipulates that "failure to prevent bribery" is an offense and stipulates that facilitation payments, or payments to gain access, are not a valid defense to prevent bribery.

Great Britain's new Bribery Act applies even to bribes between private businesspersons, and if the individual who makes the payment does not realize the transaction was a bribe, he/she is still liable. The new bribery law is being enforced by Britain's Serious Fraud Office (SFO) and boosts the maximum penalty for bribery to 10 years in prison from seven, and sets no limits on fines. More and more nations are taking a tougher stance against corruption, and companies worldwide are installing elaborate programs to avoid running afoul of the FCPA or the SFO.

In China, Zeng Jinchun was recently executed for accepting bribes of more than $4.7 million. Zeng had allegedly been accepting money over a nine-year period in return for awarding mining contracts and job promotions. A Chinese court found that Zeng was unable to account for about $1.4 million of his assets. A former secretary of the Chenzhou Municipal Commission for Discipline Inspection of the Communist Party of China, Mr. Zeng was executed by firing squad. The execution followed a pledge a day earlier by Communist Party officials in Beijing to "root out corruption that has caused civil unrest around the country."

Paying bribes is considered both illegal and unethical in the United States, but in some foreign countries, paying bribes and kickbacks is acceptable. Tipping is even considered bribery in some countries. Important antibribery and extortion initiatives are advocated by many organizations, including the World Bank, the International Monetary Fund, the European Union, the Council of Europe, the Organization of American States, the Pacific Basin Economic Council, the Global Coalition for Africa, and the United Nations.

The U.S. Justice Department recently increased its prosecutions of alleged acts of foreign bribery. Businesses have to be much more careful these days. For years, taking business associates to lavish dinners and giving them expensive holiday gifts and even outright cash may have been expected in many countries, such as South Korea and China, but there is now stepped-up enforcement of bribery laws. The SEC and Justice Department are investigating several pharmaceutical companies, including Merck, AstraZeneca PLC, Bristol-Myers Squibb, and GlaxoSmithKline PLC, for allegedly paying bribes in certain foreign countries to boost sales and speed approvals. Four types of violations are being reviewed: bribing government-employed doctors to purchase drugs; paying company sales agents commissions that are passed along to government doctors; paying hospital committees to approve drug purchases; and paying regulators to win drug approvals.

The SEC and the Justice Department are also investigating Hewlett-Packard for allegedly paying Russian government officials bribes to secure a $44.5 million information technology network. Similarly, the engineering giant Siemens AG is being investigated on bribery charges related to a $27 million traffic-control system installed in Moscow, Russia.

The U.S. Foreign Corrupt Practices Act (FCPA) prohibits U.S. companies from paying or offering to pay foreign government officials or employees of state companies to gain a business advantage. The oil-service company Schlumberger, which has major offices in Houston, Texas, is being investigated on bribery charges for violating these laws in Yemen. Under the U.S. Dodd-Frank Act, passed in 2010, employees are encouraged to report possible acts of bribery and whistle-blowers are rewarded between 10 percent and 30 percent of any financial sanctions against companies.

Royal Dutch Shell PLC and several other companies recently paid a combined $236 million settlement due to allegations that they or their contractors bribed foreign officials to assist in importing equipment and materials into various countries. At the center of this settlement was Panalpina World Transport Ltd., which admitted that it paid over the last few years $27 million in bribes on behalf of its clients, including Shell, to officials in Nigeria, Brazil, Azerbaijan, Russia, Turkmenistan, Kazakhstan, and Angola.

Love Affairs at Work

With 280 retail stores in 20 countries, American Apparel Inc. and its CEO, Dov Charney, currently face a $260 million lawsuit alleging that Mr. Charney pressured a teenage employee into performing sex acts in order to keep her job. The employee, New York City resident Irene Morales, now 20, alleges that Mr. Charney, 42, invited her to his New York apartment shortly after her 18th birthday and demanded fellatio as soon as she walked in the door. The alleged nonconsensual sex continued for eight months, until Morales resigned from her job as manager of an American Apparel store in the city's Chelsea neighborhood. The lawsuit contends that Morales was promised job security and advancement in exchange for sex. Also is 2011, four other women, Alyssa Ferguson, Marissa Wilson, Tesa Lubans-Dehaven, and Kimbra Lo, came forward with similar claims against CEO Charney. The 19-year-old, former American Apparel sales associate Lo said: "My main priority is to stop what's going on and to expose this man for who he is." Asked for details of her allegations, she stated: "When I went over to his house he attacked me. I made it very clear for him to stop. I said, 'No, please don't touch me,' and he became more aggressive. I didn't feel there was a way for me to leave safely. I was terrified." Mr. Charney's lawyer, Peter Schey, says: "I think all of these claims are contrived. The allegations are false. I think this is an effort to shake down American Apparel. These claims should be resolved in confidential arbitration."

Among colleges and universities, the federal Office of Civil Rights (OCR) has stepped up its investigation of sexual harassment cases brought forward by female students against professors. Yale University has been in the news in this regard as well as numerous other institutions currently being investigated. At no charge to the student, the OCR will investigate a female student's claim if evidence is compelling.

A recent *Wall Street Journal* article recapped current American standards regarding boss-subordinate love affairs at work.[6] Only 5 percent of all firms sampled had no restrictions on such relationships; 80 percent of firms have policies that prohibit relationships between a supervisor and a subordinate. Only 4 percent of firms strictly prohibited such relationships, but 39 percent of firms had policies that required individuals to inform their supervisors whenever a romantic relationship begins with a coworker. Only 24 percent of firms required the two persons to be in different departments.

In Europe, romantic relationships at work are largely viewed as private matters and most firms have no policies on the practice. However, European firms are increasingly adopting explicit, American-style sexual harassment laws. The U.S. military strictly bans officers from dating or having sexual relationships with enlistees. At the World Bank, sexual relations between a supervisor and an employee are considered "a de facto conflict of interest which must be resolved to avoid favoritism." World Bank president Paul Wolfowitz recently was forced to resign due to a relationship he had with a bank staff person.

A recent *Bloomberg Businessweek* article reports that in the sluggish job market, employees are filing sexual harassment complaints as a way to further their own job security. Many of these filings are increasingly third party individuals not even directly involved in the relationship but alleging their own job was impacted. Largely due to the rise of third party discrimination claims, the EEOC recovered $376 million on behalf of office romance victims in 2009.[7]

Social Responsibility

Fortune annually lists the most admired and least admired companies globally on social responsibility. *Fortune*'s 2011 top three most admired socially responsible companies are Statoil, Ferrovial, and Walt Disney. The top three least admired companies are Kirin Holdings, Carlsberg, and Asahi Breweries.[8] Chinese firms dominate the least admired list.

Wal-Mart was very socially responsible in the wake of the earthquake and tsunami that devastated Japan in 2011. Following the catastrophe, Wal-Mart mobilized a local relief effort to deliver supplies such as water and flashlights to survivors. Wal-Mart has a history of helping immensely in times of crisis—the retailer was also able to get supplies to people who needed them following Hurricane Katrina.

Some strategists agree with Ralph Nader, who proclaims that organizations have tremendous social obligations. Nader points out, for example, that ExxonMobil has more assets than most countries, and because of this such firms have an obligation to help society cure its many ills. Other people, however, agree with the economist Milton Friedman, who asserts that organizations have no obligation to do any more for society than is legally required. Friedman may contend that it is irresponsible for a firm to give monies to charity.

Do you agree more with Nader or Friedman? Surely we can all agree that the first social responsibility of any business must be to make enough profit to cover the costs of the future because if this is not achieved, no other social responsibility can be met. Indeed, no social need can be met by the firm if the firm fails.

Strategists should examine social problems in terms of potential costs and benefits to the firm and focus on social issues that could benefit the firm most. For example, should a firm avoid laying off employees so as to protect the employees' livelihood, when that decision may force the firm to liquidate?

Social Policy

The term *social policy* embraces managerial philosophy and thinking at the highest level of the firm, which is why the topic is covered in this textbook. Social policy concerns what responsibilities the firm has to employees, consumers, environmentalists, minorities, communities, shareholders, and other groups. After decades of debate, many firms still struggle to determine appropriate social policies.

The impact of society on business and vice versa is becoming more pronounced each year. Corporate social policy should be designed and articulated during strategy formulation, set and administered during strategy implementation, and reaffirmed or changed during strategy evaluation.[9]

Firms should strive to engage in social activities that have economic benefits. Merck & Co. once developed the drug ivermectin for treating river blindness, a disease caused by a fly-borne parasitic worm endemic in poor tropical areas of Africa, the Middle East, and Latin America.

In an unprecedented gesture that reflected its corporate commitment to social responsibility, Merck then made ivermectin available at no cost to medical personnel throughout the world. Merck's action highlights the dilemma of orphan drugs, which offer pharmaceutical companies no economic incentive for profitable development and distribution. Merck did however garner substantial goodwill among its stakeholders for its actions.

Social Policies on Retirement

Some countries around the world are facing severe workforce shortages associated with their aging populations. The percentage of persons age 65 or older exceeds 20 percent in Japan, Italy, and Germany—and will reach 20 percent in 2018 in France. In 2036, the percentage of persons age 65 or older will reach 20 percent in the United States and China. Unlike the United States, Japan is reluctant to rely on large-scale immigration to bolster its workforce. Instead, Japan provides incentives for its elderly to work until ages 65 to 75. Western European countries are doing the opposite, providing incentives for its elderly to retire at ages 55 to 60. The International Labor Organization says 71 percent of Japanese men ages 60 to 64 work, compared to 57 percent of American men and just 17 percent of French men in the same age group.

Sachiko Ichioka, a typical 67-year-old man in Japan, says, "I want to work as long as I'm healthy. The extra money means I can go on trips, and I'm not a burden on my children." Better diet and health care have raised Japan's life expectancy now to 82, the highest in the world. Japanese women are having on average only 1.28 children compared to 2.04 in the United States. Keeping the elderly at work, coupled with reversing the old-fashioned trend of keeping women at home, are Japan's two key remedies for sustaining its workforce in factories and businesses. This prescription for dealing with problems associated with an aging society should be considered by many countries around the world. The Japanese government is phasing in a shift from age 60 to age 65 as the date when a person may begin receiving a pension, and premiums paid by Japanese employees are rising while payouts are falling. Unlike the United States, Japan has no law against discrimination based on age.

Japan's huge national debt, 175 percent of gross domestic product (GDP) compared to 65 percent for the United States, is difficult to lower with a falling population because Japan has fewer taxpaying workers. Worker productivity increases in Japan are not able to offset declines in number of workers, thus resulting in a decline in overall economic production. Like many countries, Japan does not view immigration as a good way to solve this problem.

Japan's shrinking workforce has become such a concern that the government just recently allowed an unspecified number of Indonesian and Filipino nurses and caregivers to work in Japan for two years. The number of working-age Japanese—those between ages 15 and 64—is projected to shrink to 70 million by 2030. Using foreign workers is known as *gaikokujin roudousha* in Japanese. Many Filipinos have recently been hired now to work in agriculture and factories throughout Japan.

Environmental Sustainability

The Global 100 most sustainable corporations in the world are determined every year by the Corporate Knights Inc., an independent, Canadian organization based in Toronto, Ontario. Table 10-2 reveals Corporate Knights top 20 companies among the 100 identified in 2011 as being the best in the world for their sustainability efforts. Note that General Electric was determined to be the best in the world. Note that the United Kingdom led all countries with 5 companies in the top 20. Note the extension on the company names, such as Ag for Germany and Plc for the United Kingdom. These extensions denote where the firms are from.

The strategies of both companies and countries are increasingly scrutinized and evaluated from a natural environment perspective. Companies such as Wal-Mart now monitor not only the price its vendors offer for products, but also how those products are made in terms of environmental practices. A growing number of business schools offer separate courses and even a concentration in environmental management.

TABLE 10-2   The Top 20 Companies in the World on Sustainability

Company	Country
1. General Electric (GE) Corp. (#1)	USA
2. PG & E Corp.	USA
3. Tnt Nv	Netherlands
4. H&M Hennes & Mauritz Ab	Sweden
5. Nokia Corp.	Finland
6. Siemens Ag	Germany
7. Unilever Plc	United Kingdom
8. Vodafone Group Plc	United Kingdom
9. Smiths Group Plc	United Kingdom
10. Geberit	Switzerland
11. Henkel Ag	Germany
12. Inditex Sa	Spain
13. Procter & Gamble Co.	USA
14. Toyota Motor Corp.	Japan
15. Westpac Banking Corp.	Australia
16. Enbridge Inc.	Canada
17. Koninkiijke Phillips Electronics Na	Netherlands
18. Diageo Plc	United Kingdom
19. Nippon Yusen Kk	Japan
20. Royal Dutch Shell Plc	United Kingdom

Source: Based on http://www.global100.org/list/global-100-2010-review-results.html.

Businesses must not exploit and decimate the natural environment. Mark Starik at George Washington University says, "Halting and reversing worldwide ecological destruction and deterioration is a strategic issue that needs immediate and substantive attention by all businesses and managers. According to the International Standards Organization (ISO), the word *environment* is defined as "surroundings in which an organization operates, including air, water, land, natural resources, flora, fauna, humans, and their interrelation." This chapter illustrates how many firms are gaining competitive advantage by being good stewards of the natural environment.

Employees, consumers, governments, and society are especially resentful of firms that harm rather than protect the natural environment. Conversely people today are especially appreciative of firms that conduct operations in a way that mends, conserves, and preserves the natural environment. Consumer interest in businesses preserving nature's ecological balance and fostering a clean, healthy environment is high.

No business wants a reputation as being a polluter. A bad sustainability record will hurt the firm in the market, jeopardize its standing in the community, and invite scrutiny by regulators, investors, and environmentalists. Governments increasingly require businesses to behave responsibly and require, for example, that businesses publicly report the pollutants and wastes their facilities produce.

In terms of megawatts of wind power generated by various states in the United States, Iowa's 2,791 recently overtook California's 2,517, but Texas's 7,118 megawatts dwarfs all other states. Minnesota also is making substantial progress in wind power generation. New Jersey recently outfitted 200,000 utility poles with solar panels, which made it the nation's second-largest producer of solar energy behind California. New Jersey is also adding solar panels to corporate rooftops. The state's $514 million solar program will double its solar capacity to 160 megawatts by 2013. The state's goal is to obtain 3 percent of its electricity from the sun and 12 percent from offshore wind by 2020.

What Is a Sustainability Report?

Wal-Mart Stores is one among many companies today that annually provides a sustainability report that reveals how the firm's operations impact the natural environment. This document discloses to shareholders information about Wal-Mart's labor practices, product sourcing, energy efficiency, environmental impact, and business ethics practices.

It is good business for a company to provide a sustainability report annually to the public. With 60,000 suppliers and over $350 billion in annual sales, Wal-Mart works with its suppliers to make sure they provide such reports. Wal-Mart monitors not only prices its vendors offer for products, but also the vendors' social-responsibility and environmental practices. Many firms use the Wal-Mart sustainability report as a benchmark, guideline, and model to follow in preparing their own report.

The Global Reporting Initiative recently issued a set of detailed reporting guidelines specifying what information should go into sustainability reports. The proxy advisory firm Institutional Shareholder Services reports that an increasing number of shareholder groups are pushing firms to provide sustainability information annually.

Wal-Mart encourages and expects its 1.35 million U.S. employees to adopt what it calls Personal Sustainability Projects, which include such measures as organizing weight-loss or smoking-cessation support groups, biking to work, or starting recycling programs. Employee wellness can be a part of sustainability.

Wal-Mart is installing solar panels on its stores in California and Hawaii, providing as much as 30 percent of the power in some stores. Wal-Mart may go national with solar power if this test works well. Also moving to solar energy is department-store chain Kohl's Corp., which is converting 64 of its 80 California stores to use solar power. There are big subsidies for solar installations in some states.

Home Depot, the world's second largest retailer behind Wal-Mart, recently more than doubled its offering of environmentally friendly products such as all-natural insect repellent. Home Depot has made it much easier for consumers to find its organic products by using special labels similar to Timberland's (the outdoor company) Green Index tags. Another huge retailer, Target, now offers more than 500 choices of organic certified food and has 18 buildings in California alone powered only by solar energy. The largest solar power plant in North America is the one in Nevada that powers Nellis Air Force Base outside Las Vegas.[10]

Managers and employees of firms must be careful not to become scapegoats blamed for company environmental wrongdoings. Harming the natural environment can be unethical, illegal, and costly. When organizations today face criminal charges for polluting the environment, they increasingly turn on their managers and employees to win leniency. Employee firings and demotions are becoming common in pollution-related legal suits. Managers were fired at Darling International, Inc., and Niagara Mohawk Power Corporation for being indirectly responsible for their firms polluting water. Managers and employees today must be careful not to ignore, conceal, or disregard a pollution problem, or they may find themselves personally liable.

Lack of Standards Changing

A few years ago, firms could get away with placing "green" terminology on their products and labels using such terms as *organic*, *green*, *safe*, *earth-friendly*, *nontoxic*, and/or *natural* because there were no legal or generally accepted definitions. Today, however, such terms as these carry much more specific connotations and expectations. Uniform standards defining environmentally responsible company actions are rapidly being incorporated into our legal landscape. It has become more and more difficult for firms to make "green" claims when their actions are not substantive, comprehensive, or even true. Lack of standards once made consumers cynical about corporate environmental claims, but those claims today are increasingly being challenged in courts. Joel Makower says, "One of the main reasons to truly become a green firm is for your employees. They're the first group that needs assurance than any claims you make hold water."[11]

Around the world, political and corporate leaders now realize that the "business green" topic will not go away and in fact is gaining ground rapidly. Strategically, companies more than ever must demonstrate to their customers and stakeholders that their green efforts are substantive and set the firm apart from competitors. A firm's performance facts and figures must back up their rhetoric and be consistent with sustainability standards.

Federal Regulations

Strict regulations now require firms to conserve energy. Federal government buildings are being refitted with energy-efficient improvements. Alternative-energy firms are busy with new customers every day as the federal stimulus package includes adding alternative-energy infrastructure. Venture capitalists and lenders are funding new "clean technology" business start-ups, including solar power, wind power, biofuels, and insulation firms. Such firms are boosting marketing efforts, expanding geographically, and hiring more staff. Venture capital investments in clean technology companies are increasing dramatically.

General Electric achieved $20 billion in sales by 2011 in eco-friendly technologies that include cleaner coal-fired power plants, a diesel-and-electric hybrid locomotive, and agricultural silicon that cuts the amount of water and pesticide used in spraying fields. GE has a goal to improve its energy efficiency by 30 percent between 2005 and 2012.

The Environmental Protection Agency recently reported that U.S. citizens and organizations annually spend more than about $200 billion on pollution abatement. Environmental concerns touch all aspects of a business's operations, including workplace risk exposures, packaging, waste reduction, energy use, alternative fuels, environmental cost accounting, and recycling practices.

Managing Environmental Affairs in the Firm

The ecological challenge facing all organizations requires managers to formulate strategies that preserve and conserve natural resources and control pollution. Special natural environment issues include ozone depletion, global warming, depletion of rain forests, destruction of animal habitats, protecting endangered species, developing biodegradable products and packages, waste management, clean air, clean water, erosion, destruction of natural resources, and pollution control. Firms increasingly are developing green product lines that are biodegradable and/or are made from recycled products. Green products sell well.

Managing as if "health of the planet" matters requires an understanding of how international trade, competitiveness, and global resources are connected. Managing environmental affairs can no longer be simply a technical function performed by specialists in a firm; more emphasis must be placed on developing an environmental perspective among all employees and managers of the firm. Many companies are moving environmental affairs from the staff side of the organization to the line side, thus making the corporate environmental group report directly to the chief operating officer. Firms that manage environmental affairs will enhance relations with consumers, regulators, vendors, and other industry players, substantially improving their prospects of success.

Environmental strategies could include developing or acquiring green businesses, divesting or altering environment-damaging businesses, striving to become a low-cost producer through waste minimization and energy conservation, and pursuing a differentiation strategy through green-product features. In addition, firms could include an environmental representative on their board of directors, conduct regular envrionmental audits, implement bonuses for favorable environmental results, become involved in environmental issues and programs, incorporate environmental values in mission statements, establish environmentally oriented objectives, acquire environmental skills, and provide environmental training programs for company employees and managers.

Should Students Receive Environmental Training?

Most corporate recruiters indicate that it is important to hire students with an awareness of social and environmental responsibility. According to Ford Motor Company's director of corporate governance, "We want students who will help us find solutions to societal challenges and we have trouble hiring students with such skills."

The Aspen Institute contends that most business schools currently do not, but should, incorporate environmental training in all facets of their core curriculum, not just in special elective courses. The institute reports that the University of Texas, the University of North Carolina, and the University of Michigan, among others, are at the cutting edge in providing environmental coverage at their respective MBA levels. Companies favor hiring graduates from such universities.

Findings from research suggest that business schools at the undergraduate level are doing a poor job of educating students on environmental issues. Business students with limited knowledge on environmental issues may make poor decisions, so business schools should address environmental issues more in their curricula. Failure to do so could result in graduates making inappropriate business decisions in regard to the natural environment. Failing to provide adequate coverage of natural environment issues and decisions in their training could make those students less attractive to employers.[12]

Reasons Why Firms Should "Be Green"

Preserving the environment should be a permanent part of doing business for the following reasons:

1. Consumer demand for environmentally safe products and packages is high.
2. Public opinion demanding that firms conduct business in ways that preserve the natural environment is strong.
3. Environmental advocacy groups now have over 20 million Americans as members.
4. Federal and state environmental regulations are changing rapidly and becoming more complex.
5. More lenders are examining the environmental liabilities of businesses seeking loans.
6. Many consumers, suppliers, distributors, and investors shun doing business with environmentally weak firms.
7. Liability suits and fines against firms having environmental problems are on the rise.

Be Proactive, Not Reactive

More firms are becoming environmentally proactive—doing more than the bare minimum to develop and implement strategies that preserve the environment. The old undesirable alternative of being environmentally reactive—changing practices only when forced to do so by law or consumer pressure—more often today leads to high cleanup costs, liability suits, reduced market share, reduced customer loyalty, and higher medical costs. In contrast, a proactive policy views environmental pressures as opportunities and includes such actions as developing green products and packages, conserving energy, reducing waste, recycling, and creating a corporate culture that is environmentally sensitive.

New required diesel technology has reduced emissions by up to 98 percent in all new big trucks, at an average cost increase of $12,000 per truck. "Clean air is not free," says Rich Moskowitz, who handles regulatory affairs for the American Trucking Association, which supports the transition.[13]

ISO 14000/14001 Certification

Based in Geneva, Switzerland, the International Organization for Standardization (ISO) is a network of the national standards institutes of 147 countries, with one member per country. ISO is the world's largest developer of sustainability standards. Widely accepted all over the world, ISO standards are voluntary because ISO has no legal authority to enforce their implementation. ISO itself does not regulate or legislate.

Governmental agencies in various countries, such as the Environmental Protection Agency (EPA) in the United States, have adopted ISO standards as part of their regulatory framework, and the standards are the basis of much legislation. Adoptions are sovereign decisions by the regulatory authorities, governments, and/or companies concerned.

ISO 14000 refers to a series of voluntary standards in the environmental field. The ISO 14000 family of standards concerns the extent to which a firm minimizes harmful effects on the environment caused by its activities and continually monitors and improves its own environmental performance. Included in the ISO 14000 series are the ISO 14001 standards in fields such as environmental auditing, environmental performance evaluation, environmental labeling, and life-cycle assessment.

ISO 14001 is a set of standards adopted by thousands of firms worldwide to certify to their constituencies that they are conducting business in an environmentally friendly manner. ISO 14001 standards offer a universal technical standard for environmental compliance that more and more firms are requiring not only of themselves but also of their suppliers and distributors.

The ISO 14001 standard requires that a community or organization put in place and implement a series of practices and procedures that, when taken together, result in an *environmental management system (EMS)*. ISO 14001 is not a technical standard and as such does not in any way replace technical requirements embodied in statutes or regulations. It also does not set prescribed standards of performance for organizations. Not being ISO 14001 certified can be a strategic disadvantage for towns, counties, and companies because people today expect organizations to minimize or, even better, to eliminate environmental harm they cause.[14] The major requirements of an EMS under ISO 14001 include the following:

- Show commitments to prevention of pollution, continual improvement in overall environmental performance, and compliance with all applicable statutory and regulatory requirements.
- Identify all aspects of the organization's activities, products, and services that could have a significant impact on the environment, including those that are not regulated.
- Set performance objectives and targets for the management system that link back to three policies: (1) prevention of pollution, (2) continual improvement, and (3) compliance.
- Meet environmental objectives that include training employees, establishing work instructions and practices, and establishing the actual metrics by which the objectives and targets will be measured.
- Conduct an audit operation of the EMS.
- Take corrective actions when deviations from the EMS occur.

Electric Car Networks Are Here

GE is buying 25,000 electric vehicles between 2011 and 2015 to use in its fleet-services business, converting over half of the firm's total fleet of vehicles to electric. GE sells the popular WattStation electric-car recharger. The purchase included 12,000 GM Chevrolet Volt vehicles in 2011, and several thousand each year thereafter. The Volt can go 50 miles on a single charge before a gas generator needs to kick in for power. Ford now offers the electric Focus, Toyota Motor offers the electric RAV4, and Nissan Motor offers the 100-mile-range Leaf electric car.

Staples recently ordered 41 electric trucks from Smith Electric Vehicles of Kansas City, Missouri, and plans to order another 40. The Staples trucks have a top speed of 50 mph, can carry 16,000 pounds, and cost about $30,000 more than a comparable diesel truck—but Staples expects to recover that expense in 3.3 years. Other companies ordering electric trucks include Frito-Lay, FedEx, and AT&T.

The company Better Place is building a network of 250,000 electric car recharging stations in the San Francisco/Oakland Bay Area. Each station is about the size of a parking meter. The company has already built such networks in Denmark, Israel, and Australia. City officials in the Bay Area expect that region to lead the United States in electric cars in the near future. The stations are essential because most electric cars need recharging after about 40 miles. Better Place is also building about 200 stations in the Bay Area where electric car batteries can be switched out within 15 minutes, so no waiting is needed for recharging. Even with petroleum prices at low levels, expectations are for the United States and other countries to switch to electric cars quite aggressively over the next 10 years—for pollution minimization reasons and to take advantage of government incentives and eventual mandates.

The Chinese auto maker BYD Co. recently unveiled the country's first all-electric vehicle for mass market. The company's F3DM vehicle runs off batteries that can be charged from a regular electrical outlet. BYD is now selling this car in the United States. BYD is headquartered in Shenzhen.

Hawaii is creating an electric car network for the islands to greatly reduce the state's near-complete dependence on oil for its energy needs. The firm Better Place is creating 70,000 to 100,000 recharging points throughout the islands to support plug-in electric cars. Under the Hawaii Clean Energy Initiative, the state intends to cut its dependence on oil to 30 percent by 2030. Hawaiians pay very high electricity prices because costly oil is burned to produce power. Electric cars have a driving range of 40 miles between charges, which is suitable for Hawaii.[15]

Table 10-3 reveals the impact that bad environmental policies have on two of nature's many ecosystems.

TABLE 10-3   Songbirds and Coral Reefs Need Help

Songbirds

Be a good steward of the natural environment to save our songbirds. Bluebirds are one of 76 songbird species in the United States that have dramatically declined in numbers in the last two decades. Not all birds are considered songbirds, and why birds sing is not clear. Some scientists say they sing when calling for mates or warning of danger, but many scientists now contend that birds sing for sheer pleasure. Songbirds include chickadees, orioles, swallows, mockingbirds, warblers, sparrows, vireos, and the wood thrush. "These birds are telling us there's a problem, something's out of balance in our environment," says Jeff Wells, bird conservation director for the National Audubon Society. Songbirds may be telling us that their air or water is too dirty or that we are destroying too much of their habitat. People collect Picasso paintings and save historic buildings. "Songbirds are part of our natural heritage. Why should we be willing to watch songbirds destroyed any more than allowing a great work of art to be destroyed?" asks Wells. Whatever message songbirds are singing to us today about their natural environment, the message is becoming less and less heard nationwide. Listen when you go outside today. Each of us as individuals, companies, states, and countries should do what we reasonably can to help improve the natural environment for songbirds.[16] A recent study concludes that 67 of the 800 bird species in the United States are endangered, and another 184 species are designated of "conservation concern." The birds of Hawaii are in the greatest peril.

Coral Reefs

Be a good steward of the natural environment to save our coral reefs. The ocean covers more than 71 percent of the earth. The destructive effect of commercial fishing on ocean habitats coupled with increasing pollution runoff into the ocean and global warming of the ocean have decimated fisheries, marine life, and coral reefs around the world. The unfortunate consequence of fishing over the last century has been overfishing, with the principal reasons being politics and greed. Trawl fishing with nets destroys coral reefs and has been compared to catching squirrels by cutting down forests because bottom nets scour and destroy vast areas of the ocean. The great proportion of marine life caught in a trawl is "by-catch" juvenile fish and other life that are killed and discarded. Warming of the ocean due to carbon dioxide emissions also kills thousands of acres of coral reefs annually. The total area of fully protected marine habitats in the United States is only about 50 square miles, compared to some 93 million acres of national wildlife refuges and national parks on the nation's land. A healthy ocean is vital to the economic and social future of the nation—and, indeed, all countries of the world. Everything we do on land ends up in the ocean, so we all must become better stewards of this last frontier on earth in order to sustain human survival and the quality of life.[17]

Special Note to Students

No company or individual wants to do business with someone who is unethical or is insensitive to natural environment concerns. It is no longer just cool to be environmentally proactive, it is expected, and in many respects is the law. Firms are being compared to rival firms every day on sustainability and ethics behavior, actually every minute on Facebook, Twitter, Myspace, LinkedIn, and YouTube. Issues presented in this chapter therefore comprise a competitive advantage or disadvantage for all organizations. Thus you should include in your case analysis recommendations for your firm to exceed stakeholder expectations on ethics, sustainability, and social responsibility. Make comparisons to rival firms to show how your firm can gain or sustain competitive advantage on these issues. Reveal suggestions for the firm to be a good corporate citizen and promote that for competitive advantage. Be mindful that the first responsibility of any business is to stay in business, so utilize cost/benefit analysis as needed to present your recommendations effectively.

Conclusion

In a final analysis, ethical standards come out of history and heritage. Our predecessors have left us with an ethical foundation to build on. Even the legendary football coach Vince Lombardi knew that some things were worth more than winning, and he required his players to have three kinds of loyalty: to God, to their families, and to the Green Bay Packers, "in that order." Employees, customers, and shareholders have become less and less tolerant of business ethics violations in firms, and more and more appreciative of model ethical firms. Information sharing across the Internet increasingly reveals such model firms versus irresponsible firms.

Consumers across the country and around the world appreciate firms that do more than is legally required to be socially responsible. But staying in business while adhering to all laws and regulations must be a primary objective of any business. One of the best ways to be socially responsible is for the firm to proactively conserve and preserve the natural environment. For example, to develop a corporate sustainability report annually is not legally required, but such a report, based on concrete actions, goes a long way toward assuring stakeholders that the firm is worthy of their support. Business ethics, social responsibility, and environmental sustainability are interrelated and key strategic issues facing all organizations.

Key Terms and Concepts

Bribe (p. 344)
Bribery (p. 344)
Business Ethics (p. 341)
Code of Business Ethics (p. 342)
Environment (p. 348)
Environmental Management System (EMS) (p. 352)

ISO 14000 (p. 351)
ISO 14001 (p. 351)
Social policy (p. 346)
Social responsibility (p. 340)
Sustainability (p. 340)
Whistle-Blowing (p. 343)

Issues for Review and Discussion

1. Goldman Sachs has done really well in 2010–2011. Visit their corporate website and determine if business ethics and sustainability issues may be key reasons for their success.
2. If you owned a small business, would you develop a code of business conduct? If yes, what variables would you include? If no, how would you ensure that ethical business standards were being followed by your employees?
3. What do you feel is the relationship between personal ethics and business ethics? Are they or should they be the same?
4. How can firms best ensure that their code of business ethics is read, understood, believed, remembered, and acted upon—rather than ignored?
5. Why is it important not to view the concept of "whistle-blowing" as "tattle-telling" or "ratting" on another employee?
6. List six desired results of "ethics training programs" in terms of recommended business ethics policies or procedures in the firm.
7. Discuss bribery. Would actions such as politicians adding earmarks in legislation or pharmaceutical salespersons giving away drugs to physicians constitute bribery? Identify three business activities that would constitute bribery and three actions that would not.
8. How could a strategist's attitude toward social responsibility affect a firm's strategy? On a 1 to 10 scale ranging from Nader's view to Friedman's view, what is your attitude toward social responsibility?
9. How do social policies on retirement differ in various countries around the world?
10. Firms should formulate and implement strategies from an environmental perspective. List eight ways firms can do this.
11. Discuss the major requirements of an EMS under ISO 14001.

Notes

1. Joann Greco, "Privacy—Whose Right Is It Anyhow?" *Journal of Business Strategy*, January–February 2001, 32.
2. Ashby Jones and JoAnn Lublin, "New Law Prompts Blowing Whistle," *Wall Street Journal*, November 1, 2010, B1.
3. Saul Gellerman, "Why 'Good' Managers Make Bad Ethical Choices," *Harvard Business Review* 64, no. 4 (July–August 1986): 88.
4. Peter Drucker, *Management: Tasks, Responsibilities, and Practices* (New York: Harper & Row, 1974), 462, 463.
5. www.wikipedia.org.
6. Phred Dvorak, Bob Davis, and Louise Radnofsky, "Firms Confront Boss-Subordinate Love Affairs," *Wall Street Journal*, October 27, 2008, B5.
7. Spencer Morgan, "The End of the Office Affair,"

Bloomberg Businessweek, September 20–26, 2010, 74.
8. Based on http://money.cnn.com/magazines/fortune/mostadmired/2011/best_worst/best4.html.
9. Archie Carroll and Frank Hoy, "Integrating Corporate Social Policy into Strategic Management," *Journal of Business Strategy* 4, no. 3 (Winter 1984): 57.
10. Antonie Boessenkool, "Activists Push More Firms on Social Responsibility," *Wall Street Journal*, January 31, 2007, B13; Kris Hudson, "Wal-Mart Wants Supplies, Workers to Join Green Effort," *Wall Street Journal*, February 2, 2007, A14; Jayne O'Donnell and Christine Dugas, "More Retailers Go for Green—The Eco Kind," *USA Today*, April 18, 2007, 3B.
11. Kerry Hannon, "Businesses' Green Opportunities Are Wide, But Complex," *USA Today*, January 2, 2009, 5B.

12. R. Alsop, "Corporations Still Put Profits First, But Social Concerns Gain Ground," *Wall Street Journal*, 2001, B14; Jane Kim, "Business Schools Take a Page from Kinder, Gentler Textbook," *Wall Street Journal*, October 22, 2003, B2C; Beth Gardner, "Business Schools Going Green," *Wall Street Journal*, June 6, 2007, B5A.

13. Forest Reinhardt, "Bringing the Environment Down to Earth," *Harvard Business Review*, July–August 1999, 149–158; Christine Rosen, "Environmental Strategy and Competitive Advantage," *California Management Review* 43, no. 3 (Spring 2001): 8–15; Chris Woodyard, "Cleaner Diesel Engine Rules Take Effect," *USA Today*, December 29, 2006, 1B.

14. Adapted from the www.iso14000.com website and the www.epa.gov website.

15. Jim Carlton, "Electric-Car Network Planned," *Wall Street Journal*, November 21, 2008, B2. Also, "BYD to Introduce China's First Electric Car," *Wall Street Journal*, December 15, 2008, B2. Rebecca Smith, "Hawaii Makes Big Bet on Electric Cars," *Wall Street Journal*, December 3, 2008, A2.

16. Tom Brook, "Declining Numbers Mute Many Birds' Songs," *USA Today*, September 11, 2001, 4A.

17. John Ogden, "Maintaining Diversity in the Oceans," *Environment*, April 2001, 29–36.

Current Readings

Arino, Africa, and Peter Smith Ring. "The Role of Fairness in Alliance Formation." *Strategic Management Journal* 31, no. 10 (October 2010): 1054–1087.

Delmas, Magali A., and Maria J. Montes-Sancho. "Voluntary Agreements to Improve Environmental Quality: Symbolic and Substantive Cooperation." *Strategic Management Journal* 31, no. 6 (June 2010): 575–601.

Esty, Daniel C. "The Sustainability Imperative." *Harvard Business Review*, May 2010, 42–73.

Flynn, Francis J., and Scott S.Wiltermuth. "Who's With Me? False Consensus, Brokerage, and Ethical Decision Making in Organizations." *Academy of Management Journal* 53, no. 5 (October 2010): 1074.

Gentile, Mary C. "Keeping Your Colleagues Honest." *Harvard Business Review*, March 2010, 114–120.

Gilley, K. Matthew, Christopher J. Robertson, and Tim C. Mazur. "The Bottom-Line Benefits of Ethics Code Commitment." *Business Horizons* 53, no. 1 (January–February 2010): 31.

Golicic, Susan L., Courtney N. Boerstler, and Lisa M. Ellram. "'Greening' the Transportation in Your Supply Chain." *MIT Sloan Management Review* 51, no. 2 (Winter 2010): 47–56.

Haanaaes, Knut, Martin Reeves, Balu Balagopal, David Arthur, Nina Kruschwitz, and Michael S. Hopkins. "First Look: The Second Annual Sustainability & Innovation Survey." *Sloan Management Review* (Winter 2011): 77–85.

Hopkins, Michael S. "Bad Banking. Good Ethics. Discuss." *MIT Sloan Management Review* 51, no. 2 (Winter 2010): 96–104.

Hopkins, Michael S. "How SAP Made the Business Case for Sustainability." *MIT Sloan Management Review* 52, no. 1 (Fall 2010): 69–74.

Hopkins, Michael S. "How Sustainability Fuels Design Innovation." *MIT Sloan Management Review* 52, no. 1 (Fall 2010): 75–83.

Hopkins, Michael S. "The Four-Point Supply Chain Checklist (or, How Sustainability Creates New Opportunity)." *MIT Sloan Management Review* 51, no. 4 (Summer 2010): 65–70.

Lev, Baruch, Christine Petrovits, and Suresh Radhakrishnan. "Is Doing Good for You? How Corporate Charitable Contributions Enhance Revenue Growth." *Strategic Management Journal* 31, no. 2 (February 2010): 182–200.

Lubin, David A., and Daniel C. Esty. "The Sustainability Imperative." *Harvard Business Review*, May 2010, 42.

Lueneburger, Christoph, and Daniel Goleman. "The Change Leadership That Sustainability Demands." *MIT Sloan Management Review* 51, no. 4 (Summer 2010): 49–57.

McNutty, Eric J., and Rupert Davis. "Should the C-Suite Have a 'Green' Seat?" *Harvard Business Review*, December 2010, 133–137.

Mishina, Yuri, Bernadine J. Dykes, Emily S. Block, and Timothy G. Pollock. "Why 'Good' Firms Do Bad Things: The Effects of High Aspirations, High Expectations, and Prominence on the Incidence of Corporate Illegality." *The Academy of Management Journal* 53, no. 4 (August 2010): 701–722.

Surroca, Jordi, Josep A. Tribo, and Sandra Waddock. "Corporate Responsibility and Financial Performance: The Role of Intangible Resources." *Strategic Management Journal* 31, no. 5 (May 2010): 463–490.

Tenbrunsel, Ann. "Ethical Breakdowns." *Harvard Business Review*, April 2011, 58–67.

Unruh, Gregory, and Richard Ettenson. "Growing Green: Three Smart Paths to Developing Sustainable Products." *Harvard Business Review*, June 2010, 94–102.

Unruh, Gregory, and Richard Ettenson. "Winning in the Green Frenzy." *Harvard Business Review*, November 2010, 110–117.

ASSURANCE OF LEARNING EXERCISES

Assurance of Learning Exercise 10A

Sustainability and Goldman Sachs

Purpose

Goldman Sachs is the opening case at the beginning of Chapter 10. Goldman is a global leader in providing mergers and acquisitions advice and securities underwriting. The company offers investment banking and asset management services to corporate and government clients worldwide, as well as institutional and individual investors. Goldman Sachs is betting big on India, having recently agreed to acquire a majority stake in India's ReNew Wind Power Pvt. for 10 billion rupees ($200 million), extending the U.S. bank's investments in emerging economies. ReNew Wind plans to have 1,000 megawatts of wind-generation capacity by 2015.

This exercise can give you practice evaluating a company's sustainability efforts.

Instructions

Conduct research to determine whether Goldman Sachs and ReNew Wind are on target to meet their sustainability goals for 2015. Prepare a report to reveal your findings.

Assurance of Learning Exercise 10B

How Does My Municipality Compare To Others on Being Pollution-Safe?

Purpose

Sometimes it is difficult to know how safe a particular municipality or county is regarding industrial and agricultural pollutants. A website that provides consumers and businesses excellent information in this regard is http://scorecard.goodguide.com/. This type information is often used in assessing where to locate new business operations.

Instructions

Go to http://scorecard.goodguide.com/. Put in your zip code. Print off the information available for your city/county regarding pollutants. Prepare a comparative analysis of your municipality versus state and national norms on pollution issues. Does your locale receive an A, B, C, D, or F?

Assurance of Learning Exercise 10C

Compare Adidas AG versus Nike on Social Responsibility

Purpose

This exercise aims to familiarize you with corporate social responsibility programs.

Instructions

Step 1   Go to Adidas' Code of Conduct, which is provided at the website http://www.adidasgroup.com/en/sustainability/suppliers_and_workers/code_of_conduct/default.aspx.

Step 2   Go to Nike's website at http://www.nike.com/nikeos/p/nike/en_US/ and click on About Nike and then review Nike's Corporate Responsibility Report.

Step 3   Compare Adidas' social responsibility efforts with Nike's. Summarize your findings in a three-page report for your professor.

Assurance of Learning Exercise 10D

How Do You Rate Adidas AG's Sustainability Efforts?

Purpose
This exercise aims to familiarize you with corporate sustainability programs.

Instructions

Step 1   Go to http://www.adidas-group.com/en/home/Welcome.aspx Click on Sustainability. Then click on Sustainability Performance Review.

Step 2   On a separate sheet of paper, list six aspects that you like most and six aspects that you like least about Adidas' sustainability efforts.

Step 3   Provide a two-page executive summary of your assessment of Adidas' sustainability efforts.

Assurance of Learning Exercise 10E

How Do You Rate Goldman Sach's Sustainability Efforts?

Purpose
This exercise aims to familiarize you with corporate sustainability programs. Review the opening chapter company discussion. Review the material at Goldman Sach's corporate website.

Instructions

Step 1   On a separate sheet of paper, list six aspects that you like most and six aspects that you like least about Goldman Sach's sustainability efforts.

Step 2   Provide a two-page executive summary of your assessment of Goldman Sach's sustainability efforts.

Assurance of Learning Exercise 10F

The Ethics of Spying on Competitors

Purpose
This exercise gives you an opportunity to discuss in class ethical and legal issues related to methods being used by many companies to spy on competing firms. Gathering and using information about competitors is an area of strategic management that Japanese firms do more proficiently than American firms.

Instructions
On a separate sheet of paper, write down numbers 1 to 18. For the 18 spying activities that follow, indicate whether or not you believe the activity is ethical or unethical and legal or illegal. Place either an *E* for ethical or *U* for unethical, and either an *L* for legal or an *I* for illegal for each activity. Compare your answers to those of your classmates and discuss any differences.

1. Buying competitors' garbage
2. Dissecting competitors' products
3. Taking competitors' plant tours anonymously
4. Counting tractor-trailer trucks leaving competitors' loading bays
5. Studying aerial photographs of competitors' facilities
6. Analyzing competitors' labor contracts
7. Analyzing competitors' help-wanted ads
8. Quizzing customers and buyers about the sales of competitors' products
9. Infiltrating customers' and competitors' business operations
10. Quizzing suppliers about competitors' level of manufacturing
11. Using customers to buy out phony bids
12. Encouraging key customers to reveal competitive information
13. Quizzing competitors' former employees
14. Interviewing consultants who may have worked with competitors
15. Hiring key managers away from competitors
16. Conducting phony job interviews to get competitors' employees to reveal information
17. Sending engineers to trade meetings to quiz competitors' technical employees
18. Quizzing potential employees who worked for or with competitors

"NOTABLE QUOTES"

"Sad but true, U.S. businesspeople have the lowest foreign language proficiency of any major trading nation. U.S. business schools do not emphasize foreign languages, and students traditionally avoid them."
—*Ronald Dulek*

"America's economy has become much less American."

"In God we trust. All others bring data."
—*Edward Deming*

Global/ International Issues

CHAPTER OBJECTIVES

After studying this chapter, you should be able to do the following:

1. Explain the advantages and disadvantages of entering global markets.

2. Discuss protectionism as it impacts the world economy.

3. Explain when and why a firm (or industry) may need to become more or less global in nature to compete.

4. Discuss the global challenge facing American firms.

5. Compare and contrast business culture in the United States with many other countries.

6. Describe how management style varies globally.

7. Discuss communication differences across countries.

8. Discuss Africa as the newest hotspot for business entry.

ASSURANCE OF LEARNING EXERCISES

Assurance of Learning Exercise 11A
Adidas AG Wants to Enter Africa.
Help Them.

Assurance of Learning Exercise 11B
Assessing Differences in Culture Across
Countries

Assurance of Learning Exercise 11C
Pfizer Wants to Enter Vietnam.
Help Them.

Assurance of Learning Exercise 11D
Does My University Recruit in Foreign
Countries?

As illustrated in Figure 11-1, global considerations impact virtually all strategic decisions. The boundaries of countries no longer can define the limits of our imaginations. To see and appreciate the world from the perspective of others has become a matter of survival for businesses. The underpinnings of strategic management hinge on managers gaining an understanding of competitors, markets, prices, suppliers, distributors, governments, creditors, shareholders, and customers worldwide. The price and quality of a firm's products and services must be competitive on a worldwide basis, not just on a local basis. As indicated in the boxed insert, Pfizer is an example global business that formulates and implements excellent strategies.

Among the 30 companies in the Dow Jones Industrial Average, the 10 that obtained the largest share of their sales abroad expected to see their revenues grow by an average of 8.3 percent in 2011.[1] By contrast, the 10 companies that do the least business outside the United States expect average revenue gains of just 1.6 percent. Shareholders expect substantial revenue growth, so doing business globally is one of the best ways to achieve this end.

Although exports of goods and services from the United States were valued at $1.6 trillion in 2009, that accounted for only 11 percent of U.S. gross domestic product. Therefore the United States is still largely a domestic, continental economy, and what happens inside the U.S. largely

Excellent Strategic Management Showcased

PFIZER INC.

Based in New York City but with research headquarters in Groton, Connecticut, Pfizer produces hundreds of medicines including Lipitor to lower blood cholesterol; the neuropathic pain/fibromyalgia drug Lyrica; the oral antifungal medication Diflucan; the antibiotic Zithromax; and the anti-inflammatory Celebrex (known as Celebra in some countries outside the United States and Canada, mainly in South America). Very profitable and well managed, Pfizer is the world's largest research-based pharmaceutical firm with other well-known prescription medicines such as pneumonia vaccine Prevnar, arthritis drug Enbrel, depression treatment Effexor, and high-blood-pressure therapy Norvasc. Pfizer's consumer health products include such leading brands as Advil, Centrum, and Robitussin. Pfizer also sells Promil and Promise baby formula and keeps Fluffy and Fido in mind with its animal health products, including Revolution (anti-parasitic) and Convenia (anti-infective). On February 1, 2011 Pfizer announced that it would close its UK Research and Development center at Sandwich, Kent, with the loss of 2,400 jobs.

Private-equity firm KKR won EU approval in September 2011 to purchase Pfizer's Capsugel unit for $2.38 billion. The world's largest maker of hard capsules, Capsugel made about $750 million in revenues in 2010. The European Commission, the EU competition watchdog, said its investigation showed the acquisition would not hamper rivals. According to the Commission, the transaction would not cause overlaps since neither KKR nor any company that it controls have interests in the same field as Capsugel.

In late 2011, the European Medicines Agency (EMA) accepted Pfizer's regulatory submissions for review of two investigational compounds— crizotinib, an oral first-in-class anaplastic lymphoma kinase (ALK) inhibitor,

for the treatment of patients with previously treated ALK-positive advanced non-small cell lung cancer (NSCLC); and bosutinib, for the treatment of adult patients with newly diagnosed Philadelphia chromosome positive (Ph+) chronic myeloid leukemia (CML) in the chronic phase. With the EMA submissions for crizotinib and bosutinib, Pfizer are one step closer to potentially bringing two promising drugs to patients in desperate need.

Source: Based on information at www.pfizer.com.

FIGURE 11-1

A Comprehensive Strategic-Management Mode

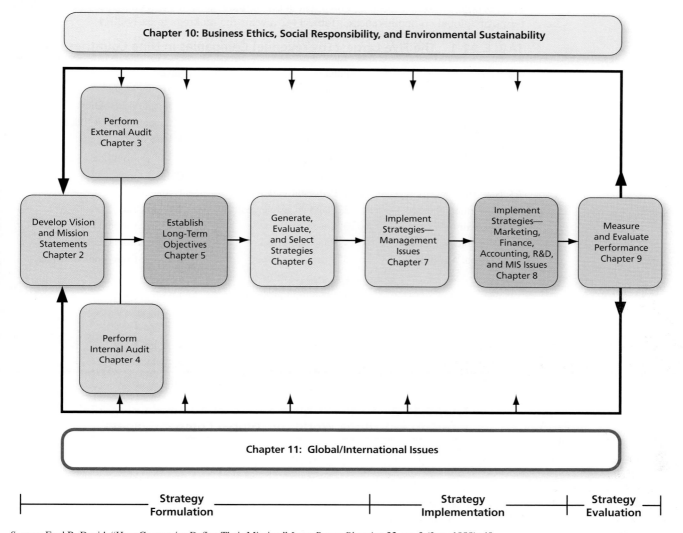

Source: Fred R. David, "How Companies Define Their Mission," *Long Range Planning* 22, no. 3 (June 1988): 40.

determines the strength of the economic recovery. In contrast, as a percent of GDP, exports comprise 35.3 percent of the German economy, 24.5 percent of the Chinese economy, and 156 percent of the Singapore economy. Singapore's number is so high because they import oil and other products and then re-export them globally. The point here is that the United States has substantial room for improvement in doing business globally based on the 11 percent exports to GDP number.

A world market has emerged from what previously was a multitude of distinct national markets, and the climate for international business today is more favorable than in years past. Mass communication and high technology have created similar patterns of consumption in diverse cultures worldwide. This means that many companies may find it difficult to survive by relying solely on domestic markets.

It is no exaggeration that in an industry that is, or is rapidly becoming global, the riskiest possible posture is to remain a domestic competitor. The domestic competitor will watch as more aggressive companies use this growth to capture economies of scale and learning. The domestic competitor will then be faced with an attack on domestic markets using different (and possibly superior) technology, product design, manufacturing, marketing approaches, and economies of scale.[2]

As a point of global reference, the five largest companies in nine different countries are listed in Table 11-1. The largest of all 45 companies listed is Wal-Mart Stores, headquartered in Bentonville, Arkansas, and employing 2.1 million people worldwide.

Fortune annually determines the most admired and least admired companies in the world in terms of "global competitiveness." Table 11-2 reveals the rankings in early 2011.

TABLE 11-1   The Five Largest (by revenue) Companies in Nine Countries (2011)

Britain	India	Japan
1. BP	1. Indian Oil	1. Toyota Motor
2. HSBC Holdings	2. Reliance Industries	2. Japan Post Holdings
3. Lloyds Banking Group	3. State Bank of India	3. Nippon TeleG & TeleP
4. Aviva	4. Bharat Petroleum	4. Hitachi
5. Royal Bank of Scotland	5. Hindustan Petroleum	5. Honda Motor
Australia	Brazil	China
1. BHP Billiton	1. Petrobras	1. Sinopec
2. Wesfarmers	2. Itausa-Investmentos	2. State Grid
3. Woolworths	3. Banco Bradesco	3. China National Petroleum
4. Commonwealth Bank	4. Banco do Brasil	4. China Mobile Communi.
5. National Australia Bank	5. Vale	5. Ind. & Com. Bank of China
USA	Canada	Germany
1. Wal-Mart Stores	1. Manulife Financial	1. Volkswagen
2. ExxonMobil	2. Royal Bank of Canada	2. Allianz
3. Chevron	3. Power Corp. of Canada	3. E.ON
4. General Electric	4. George Weston	4. Daimier
5. Bank of America	5. Sun Life Financial	5. Siemens

Source: Based on http://money.cnn.com/magazines/fortune/global500/2010/countries/US.html.

TABLE 11-2   *Fortune*'s Most and Least Admired Companies in the World for "Global Competitiveness"

MOST ADMIRED
1. McDonald's
2. Google
3. Nestlé
4. Nike
5. Yum Brands
6. Walt Disney
7. Colgate-Palmolive
8. IBM
9. Accenture
10. Manpower

LEAST ADMIRED
1. Asahi Breweries
2. Kirin Holdings
3. Winn-Dixie Stores
4. Hovnanian Enterprises
5. Carlsberg
6. Great Atlantic & Pacific Tea
7. Bob Evans Farms
8. Dongfeng Motor
9. D.R. Horton
10. Lennar

Source: http://money.cnn.com/magazines/fortune/mostadmired/2011/best_worst/best9.html.
Also, http://money.cnn.com/magazines/fortune/mostadmired/2011/best_worst/worst9.html.

Multinational Organizations

Organizations that conduct business operations across national borders are called *international firms* or *multinational corporations*. The strategic-management process is conceptually the same for multinational firms as for purely domestic firms; however, the process is more complex for international firms due to more variables and relationships. The social, cultural, demographic, environmental, political, governmental, legal, technological, and competitive opportunities and threats that face a multinational corporation are almost limitless, and the number and complexity of these factors increase dramatically with the number of products produced and the number of geographic areas served.

More time and effort are required to identify and evaluate external trends and events in multinational corporations than in domestic corporations. Geographic distance, cultural and national differences, and variations in business practices often make communication between domestic headquarters and overseas operations difficult. Strategy implementation can be more difficult because different cultures have different norms, values, and work ethics.

Multinational corporations (MNCs) face unique and diverse risks, such as expropriation of assets, currency losses through exchange rate fluctuations, unfavorable foreign court interpretations of contracts and agreements, social/political disturbances, import/export restrictions, tariffs, and trade barriers. Strategists in MNCs are often confronted with the need to be globally competitive and nationally responsive at the same time. With the rise in world commerce, government and regulatory bodies are more closely monitoring foreign business practices. The U.S. Foreign Corrupt Practices Act, for example, monitors business practices in many areas.

Before entering international markets, firms should scan relevant journals and patent reports, seek the advice of academic and research organizations, participate in international trade fairs, form partnerships, and conduct extensive research to broaden their contacts and diminish the risk of doing business in new markets. Firms can also offset some risks of doing business internationally by obtaining insurance from the U.S. government's Overseas Private Investment Corporation (OPIC).

Advantages and Disadvantages of International Operations

Firms have numerous reasons for formulating and implementing strategies that initiate, continue, or expand involvement in business operations across national borders. Perhaps the greatest advantage is that firms can gain new customers for their products and services, thus increasing revenues. Growth in revenues and profits is a common organizational objective and often an expectation of shareholders because it is a measure of organizational success.

Potential advantages to initiating, continuing, and/or expanding international operations are as follows:

1. Firms can gain new customers for their products.
2. Foreign operations can absorb excess capacity, reduce unit costs, and spread economic risks over a wider number of markets.
3. Foreign operations can allow firms to establish low-cost production facilities in locations close to raw materials and/or cheap labor.
4. Competitors in foreign markets may not exist, or competition may be less intense than in domestic markets.
5. Foreign operations may result in reduced tariffs, lower taxes, and favorable political treatment.
6. Joint ventures can enable firms to learn the technology, culture, and business practices of other people and to make contacts with potential customers, suppliers, creditors, and distributors in foreign countries.
7. Economies of scale can be achieved from operation in global rather than solely domestic markets. Larger-scale production and better efficiencies allow higher sales volumes and lower-price offerings.
8. A firm's power and prestige in domestic markets may be significantly enhanced if the firm competes globally. Enhanced prestige can translate into improved negotiating power among creditors, suppliers, distributors, and other important groups.

The availability, depth, and reliability of economic and marketing information in different countries vary extensively, as do industrial structures, business practices, and the number and nature of regional organizations. There are also numerous potential disadvantages of initiating, continuing, or expanding business across national borders, such as the following:

1. Foreign operations could be seized by nationalistic factions.
2. Firms confront different and often little-understood social, cultural, demographic, environmental, political, governmental, legal, technological, economic, and competitive forces when doing business internationally. These forces can make communication difficult in the firm.
3. Weaknesses of competitors in foreign lands are often overestimated, and strengths are often underestimated. Keeping informed about the number and nature of competitors is more difficult when doing business internationally.
4. Language, culture, and value systems differ among countries, which can create barriers to communication and problems managing people.
5. Gaining an understanding of regional organizations such as the European Economic Community, the Latin American Free Trade Area, the International Bank for Reconstruction and Development, and the International Finance Corporation is difficult but is often required in doing business internationally.
6. Dealing with two or more monetary systems can complicate international business operations.

The Global Challenge

Few companies can afford to ignore the presence of international competition. Firms that seem insulated and comfortable today may be vulnerable tomorrow; for example, foreign banks do not yet compete or operate in most of the United States, but this too is changing. China's largest commercial bank, Industrial & Commercial Bank of China Ltd., recently acquired an 80 percent stake in Bank of East Asia Ltd.'s U.S. subsidiary, putting the Chinese bank in position to become the first Beijing-controlled financial institution to operate retail banks in the United States.

America's economy is becoming much less American. A world economy and monetary system are emerging. Corporations in every corner of the globe are taking advantage of the opportunity to obtain customers globally. Markets are shifting rapidly and in many cases converging in tastes, trends, and prices. Innovative transport systems are accelerating the transfer of technology. Shifts in the nature and location of production systems, especially to China and India, are reducing the response time to changing market conditions. China has more than 1.3 billion residents and a dramatically growing middle class anxious to buy goods and services. Yum Brands, which owns KFC and Pizza Hut, reported in 2011 that its China division overtook the U.S. in profits generated. GM sales in China exceeded GM's U.S. sales for the first time ever in 2010. Wynn and Las Vegas Sands report their net revenue in China growing more than triple their U.S. properties. China is the fastest-growing market for pocket book maker Coach and the second-largest market for Dell.

Business in Brazil is booming, with that country having more than a 7 percent growth in GDP in 2011. The capital of Brazil, Rio de Janeiro, is making massive preparations for the 2016 Summer Olympics, including a $5 billion investment program to extend the subway system, improve railroads, and construct new highways. Two firms in Rio that are growing exponentially are Petrobras, the world's fourth-largest oil producer, and Vale, the world's largest iron-ore mining company. Rio de Janeiro is Brazil's second largest manufacturing center in the country, but its scenic beauty and elaborate port facilities are world renown.

More and more countries around the world are welcoming foreign investment and capital. As a result, labor markets have steadily become more international. East Asian countries are market leaders in labor-intensive industries, Brazil offers abundant natural resources and rapidly developing markets, and Germany offers skilled labor and technology. The drive to improve the efficiency of global business operations is leading to greater functional specialization. This is not limited to a search for the familiar low-cost labor in Latin America or Asia. Other considerations include the cost of energy, availability of resources, inflation rates, tax rates, and the nature of trade regulations.

Many countries became more protectionist during the recent global economic recession. *Protectionism* refers to countries imposing tariffs, taxes, and regulations on firms outside the country to favor their own companies and people. Most economists argue that protectionism harms the world economy because it inhibits trade among countries and invites retaliation.

Advancements in telecommunications are drawing countries, cultures, and organizations worldwide closer together. Foreign revenue as a percentage of total company revenues already exceeds 50 percent in hundreds of U.S. firms, including ExxonMobil, Gillette, Dow Chemical, Citicorp, Colgate-Palmolive, and Texaco.

A primary reason why most domestic firms do business globally is that growth in demand for goods and services outside the United States is considerably higher than inside. For example, the domestic food industry is growing just 3 percent per year, so Kraft Foods, the second largest food company in the world behind Nestlé, is focusing on foreign acquisitions.

Shareholders and investors expect sustained growth in revenues from firms; satisfactory growth for many firms can only be achieved by capitalizing on demand outside the United States. Joint ventures and partnerships between domestic and foreign firms are becoming the rule rather than the exception!

Fully 95 percent of the world's population lives outside the United States, and this group is growing 70 percent faster than the U.S. population. The lineup of competitors in virtually all industries is global. General Motors, Ford, and Chrysler compete with Toyota and Hyundai. General Electric and Westinghouse battle Siemens and Mitsubishi. Caterpillar and John Deere compete with Komatsu. Goodyear battles Michelin, Bridgestone/Firestone, and Pirelli. Boeing competes with Airbus. Only a few U.S. industries—such as furniture, printing, retailing, consumer packaged goods, and retail banking—are not yet greatly challenged by foreign competitors. But many products and components in these industries too are now manufactured in foreign countries. International operations can be as simple as exporting a product to a single foreign country or as complex as operating manufacturing, distribution, and marketing facilities in many countries.

Globalization

Globalization is a process of doing business worldwide, so strategic decisions are made based on global profitability of the firm rather than just domestic considerations. A global strategy seeks to meet the needs of customers worldwide, with the highest value at the lowest cost. This may mean locating production in countries with the lowest labor costs or abundant natural resources, locating research and complex engineering centers where skilled scientists and engineers can be found, and locating marketing activities close to the markets to be served.

A *global strategy* includes designing, producing, and marketing products with global needs in mind, instead of considering individual countries alone. A global strategy integrates actions against competitors into a worldwide plan. Today, there are global buyers and sellers and the instant transmission of money and information across continents.

It is clear that different industries become global for different reasons. The need to amortize massive R&D investments over many markets is a major reason why the aircraft manufacturing industry became global. Monitoring globalization in one's industry is an important strategic-management activity. Knowing how to use that information for one's competitive advantage is even more important. For example, firms may look around the world for the best technology and select one that has the most promise for the largest number of markets. When firms design a product, they design it to be marketable in as many countries as possible. When firms manufacture a product, they select the lowest-cost source, which may be Japan for semiconductors, Sri Lanka for textiles, Malaysia for simple electronics, and Europe for precision machinery.

Corporate Tax Rates Globally

Corporate tax rates vary considerably across countries and companies. Tax rates in countries are important in strategic decisions regarding where to build manufacturing facilities or retail stores or even where to acquire other firms. Japan recently cut its corporate tax rate by five percentage points, leaving the United States with the highest corporate tax rate among all nations in the world. Having the highest corporate tax rates is not a good position for the United States since it competes with other nations as a location for investment. High corporate tax rates deter investment in new factories and also provide strong incentives for corporations to avoid and evade taxes.

Since the 1980s, most countries have been steadily lowering their tax rates, but the United States has not cut its top statutory corporate tax rate since 1993. Top combined statutory rates among developed countries, excluding the United States, fell from an average of about 48 percent in the early 1980s to 25.5 percent in 2010. The main wave of reforms occurred in the mid- to late-1980s, but the average fell almost 9 percent from 2000 to 2010.

Even within countries there is significant variation in federal taxes paid. For example, General Electric paid almost no federal income taxes in the United States in 2010, thanks to various tax breaks and some innovative but legal accounting measures. GE paid nearly zero even though $5.1 billion of GE's total $14.2 billion in profits came from operations in the United States. Carnival, the world's largest cruise line company, is incorporated in Panama and paid an effective tax rate of 1.4 percent from 2005 through 2010. In comparison, the rate for Agilent Technologies was 10.7 percent over the same period, and it was 17.7 percent for Pfizer.

Forbes recently examined the 20 most profitable U.S. companies and found that the average 2010 income tax rate within the group was 25.4 percent.[3] America's three biggest oil companies, ExxonMobil, Chevron, and ConocoPhillips, all paid more than 40 percent—higher than the statutory U.S. rate of 35 percent. Exxon, with a 45 percent rate, paid $21.6 billion in worldwide income taxes for 2010. Wal-Mart Stores paid $7.1 billion (at a rate of 32.4 percent) in 2010 income taxes.

As indicated in Table 11-3, the top national statutory corporate tax rates in 2010 among sample countries ranged from 8.5 percent in Switzerland to 35 percent in the United States. Note the countries that have a flat tax, which often, upon adoption, triggers a surge in foreign direct investment.

TABLE 11-3 Corporate Tax Rates Across Countries in 2011 (from high to low)

Country	Statutory Corporate Income Tax Rate (%)
United States	35
France	34.43
Belgium	33
New Zealand	30
Spain	30
Australia	30
Mexico	30
Norway	28
United Kingdom	28
Italy	27.5
Finland	26
Netherlands	25.5
Portugal	25
Austria	25
Denmark	25
Greece	24
Ukraine	23 (flat tax)
Korea	22
Turkey	20
Czech Republic	19 (flat tax)
Hungary	19
Slovak Republic	19 (flat tax)
Poland	19
Canada	18
Chile	17
Russia	16 (flat tax)
Germany	15.83
Iceland	15
Ireland	12.5
Bulgaria	10 (flat tax)
Serbia	10 (flat tax)
Switzerland	8.5

Source: Varied sources on the Internet from a March 1, 2011 Google search for "Corporate Tax Rates Globally."

Other factors besides the corporate tax rate obviously affect companies' decisions of where to locate plants and facilities and whether to acquire other firms. For example, the large, affluent market and efficient infrastructure in both Germany and Britain attract companies, but the high labor costs and strict labor laws there keep other companies away. The rapidly growing GDP in Brazil and India attracts companies, but violence and political unrest in Middle East countries deter investment. The United States perhaps should lower its rate to reward companies that invest in jobs domestically. Lowering the U.S. corporate tax rate should also reduce unemployment and spur growth domestically.

United States versus Foreign Business Cultures

To compete successfully in world markets, U.S. managers must obtain a better knowledge of historical, cultural, and religious forces that motivate and drive people in other countries. In Japan, for example, business relations operate within the context of *Wa,* which stresses group harmony and social cohesion. In China, business behavior revolves around *guanxi,* or personal relations. In South Korea, activities involve concern for *inhwa,* or harmony based on respect of hierarchical relationships, including obedience to authority.[4]

In Europe, it is generally true that the farther north on the continent, the more participatory the management style. Most European workers are unionized and enjoy more frequent vacations and holidays than U.S. workers. A 90-minute lunch break plus 20-minute morning and afternoon breaks are common in European firms. Guaranteed permanent employment is typically a part of employment contracts in Europe. In socialist countries such as France, Belgium, and the United Kingdom, the only grounds for immediate dismissal from work is a criminal offense. A six-month trial period at the beginning of employment is usually part of the contract with a European firm. Many Europeans resent pay-for-performance, commission salaries, and objective measurement and reward systems. This is true especially of workers in southern Europe. Many Europeans also find the notion of team spirit difficult to grasp because the unionized environment has dichotomized worker–management relations throughout Europe.

A weakness of some U.S. firms in competing with Pacific Rim firms is a lack of understanding of Asian cultures, including how Asians think and behave. Spoken Chinese, for example, has more in common with spoken English than with spoken Japanese or Korean. U.S. managers consistently put more weight on being friendly and liked, whereas Asian and European managers often exercise authority without this concern. Americans tend to use first names instantly in business dealings with foreigners, but foreigners find this presumptuous. In Japan, for example, first names are used only among family members and intimate friends; even longtime business associates and coworkers shy away from the use of first names. Table 11-4 lists other cultural differences or pitfalls that U.S. managers need to know about.

TABLE 11-4   Cultural Pitfalls That May Help You Be a Better Manager

- Waving is a serious insult in Greece and Nigeria, particularly if the hand is near someone's face.
- Making a "good-bye" wave in Europe can mean "No," but it means "Come here" in Peru.
- In China, last names are written first.
- A man named Carlos Lopez-Garcia should be addressed as Mr. Lopez in Latin America but as Mr. Garcia in Brazil.
- Breakfast meetings are considered uncivilized in most foreign countries.
- Latin Americans are on average 20 minutes late to business appointments.
- Direct eye contact is impolite in Japan.
- Don't cross your legs in any Arab or many Asian countries—it's rude to show the sole of your shoe.
- In Brazil, touching your thumb and first finger—an American "Okay" sign—is the equivalent of raising your middle finger.
- Nodding or tossing your head back in southern Italy, Malta, Greece, and Tunisia means "No." In India, this body motion means "Yes."
- Snapping your fingers is vulgar in France and Belgium.
- Folding your arms across your chest is a sign of annoyance in Finland.
- In China, leave some food on your plate to show that your host was so generous that you couldn't finish.
- Do not eat with your left hand when dining with clients from Malaysia or India.
- One form of communication works the same worldwide. It's the smile—so take that along wherever you go.

U.S. managers have a low tolerance for silence, whereas Asian managers view extended periods of silence as important for organizing and evaluating one's thoughts. U.S. managers are much more action oriented than their counterparts around the world; they rush to appointments, conferences, and meetings—and then feel the day has been productive. But for many foreign managers, resting, listening, meditating, and thinking is considered productive. Sitting through a conference without talking is unproductive in the United States, but it is viewed as positive in Japan if one's silence helps preserve unity.

U.S. managers place greater emphasis on short-term results than foreign managers. In marketing, for example, Japanese managers strive to achieve "everlasting customers," whereas many Americans strive to make a onetime sale. Marketing managers in Japan see making a sale as the beginning, not the end, of the selling process. This is an important distinction. Japanese managers often criticize U.S. managers for worrying more about shareholders, whom they do not know, than employees, whom they do know. Americans refer to "hourly employees," whereas many Japanese companies still refer to "lifetime employees."

Rose Knotts recently summarized some important cultural differences between U.S. and foreign managers.[5] Awareness and consideration of these differences can enable a manager to be more effective, regardless of his/her own nationality.

1. Americans place an exceptionally high priority on time, viewing time as an asset. Many foreigners place more worth on relationships. This difference results in foreign managers often viewing U.S. managers as "more interested in business than people."

2. Personal touching and distance norms differ around the world. Americans generally stand about three feet from each other when carrying on business conversations, but Arabs and Africans stand about one foot apart. Touching another person with the left hand in business dealings is taboo in some countries.

3. Family roles and relationships vary in different countries. For example, males are valued more than females in some cultures, and peer pressure, work situations, and business interactions reinforce this phenomenon.

4. Business and daily life in some societies are governed by religious factors. Prayer times, holidays, daily events, and dietary restrictions, for example, need to be respected by managers not familiar with these practices in some countries.

5. Time spent with the family and the quality of relationships are more important in some cultures than the personal achievement and accomplishments espoused by the traditional U.S. manager.

6. Many cultures around the world value modesty, team spirit, collectivity, and patience much more than competitiveness and individualism, which are so important in the United States.

7. Punctuality is a valued personal trait when conducting business in the United States, but it is not revered in many of the world's societies. Eating habits also differ dramatically across cultures. For example, belching is acceptable in some countries as evidence of satisfaction with the food that has been prepared. Chinese culture considers it good manners to sample a portion of each food served.

8. To prevent social blunders when meeting with managers from other lands, one must learn and respect the rules of etiquette of others. Sitting on a toilet seat is viewed as unsanitary in most countries, but not in the United States. Leaving food or drink after dining is considered impolite in some countries, but not in China. Bowing instead of shaking hands is customary in many countries. Some cultures view Americans as unsanitary for locating toilet and bathing facilities in the same area, whereas Americans view people of some cultures as unsanitary for not taking a bath or shower every day.

9. Americans often do business with individuals they do not know, unlike businesspersons in many other cultures. In Mexico and Japan, for example, an amicable relationship is often mandatory before conducting business.

In many countries, effective managers are those who are best at negotiating with government bureaucrats rather than those who inspire workers. Many U.S. managers are uncomfortable with nepotism and bribery, which are practiced in some countries. The United States has gained a reputation for defending women from sexual harassment and minorities from discrimination, but not all countries embrace the same values.

American managers in China have to be careful about how they arrange office furniture because Chinese workers believe in *feng shui,* the practice of harnessing natural forces. U.S. managers in Japan have to be careful about *nemaswashio,* whereby Japanese workers expect supervisors to alert them privately of changes rather than informing them in a meeting. Japanese managers have little appreciation for versatility, expecting all managers to be the same. In Japan, "If a nail sticks out, you hit it into the wall," says Brad Lashbrook, an international consultant for Wilson Learning.

Probably the biggest obstacle to the effectiveness of U.S. managers—or managers from any country working in another—is the fact that it is almost impossible to change the attitude of a foreign workforce. "The system drives you; you cannot fight the system or culture," says Bill Parker, president of Phillips Petroleum in Norway.

Communication Differences Across Countries

Americans increasingly interact with managers in other countries, so it is important to understand foreign business cultures. Americans often come across as intrusive, manipulative, and garrulous; this impression may reduce their effectiveness in communication. *Forbes* provided the following cultural hints from Charis Intercultural Training:

1. Italians, Germans, and French generally do not soften up executives with praise before they criticize. Americans do soften up folks, and this practice seems manipulative to Europeans.
2. Israelis are accustomed to fast-paced meetings and have little patience for American informality and small talk.
3. British executives often complain that American executives chatter too much. Informality, egalitarianism, and spontaneity from Americans in business settings jolt many foreigners.
4. Europeans feel they are being treated like children when asked to wear name tags by Americans.
5. Executives in India are used to interrupting one another. Thus, when American executives listen without asking for clarification or posing questions, they are viewed by Indians as not paying attention.
6. When negotiating orally with Malaysian or Japanese executives, it is appropriate to allow periodically for a time of silence. However, no pause is needed when negotiating in Israel.
7. Refrain from asking foreign managers questions such as "How was your weekend?" That is intrusive to foreigners, who tend to regard their business and private lives as totally separate.[6]

Business Culture Across Countries

Mexico—Business Culture

Mexico is an authoritarian society in terms of schools, churches, businesses, and families. Employers seek workers who are agreeable, respectful, and obedient, rather than innovative, creative, and independent. Mexican workers tend to be activity oriented rather than problem solvers. When visitors walk into a Mexican business, they are impressed by the cordial, friendly atmosphere. This is almost always true because Mexicans desire harmony rather than conflict; desire for harmony is part of the social fabric in worker–manager relations. There is a much lower tolerance for adversarial relations or friction at work in Mexico as compared to the United States.

Mexican employers are paternalistic, providing workers with more than a paycheck, but in return they expect allegiance. Weekly food baskets, free meals, free bus service, and free day care are often part of compensation. The ideal working condition for a Mexican worker is the family model, with people all working together, doing their share, according to their designated roles. Mexican workers do not expect or desire a work environment in which self-expression and initiative are encouraged. Whereas U.S. business embodies individualism, achievement, competition, curiosity, pragmatism, informality, spontaneity, and doing more than expected on the job, Mexican businesses stress collectivism, continuity, cooperation, belongingness, formality, and doing exactly what you're told.

In Mexico, business associates rarely entertain each other at their homes, which are places reserved exclusively for close friends and family. Business meetings and entertaining are nearly always done at a restaurant. Preserving one's honor, saving face, and looking important are also exceptionally important in Mexico. This is why Mexicans do not accept criticism and change easily; many find it humiliating to acknowledge having made a mistake. A meeting among employees and managers in a business located in Mexico is a forum for giving orders and directions rather than for discussing problems or participating in decision making. Mexican workers want to be closely supervised, cared for, and corrected in a civil manner. Opinions expressed by employees are often regarded as back talk in Mexico. Mexican supervisors are viewed as weak if they explain the rationale for their orders to workers.

Mexicans do not feel compelled to follow rules that are not associated with a particular person in authority they work for or know well. Thus, signs to wear earplugs or safety glasses, or attendance or seniority policies, and even one-way street signs are often ignored. Whereas Americans follow the rules, Mexicans often do not.

Life is slower in Mexico than in the United States. The first priority is often assigned to the last request, rather than to the first. Telephone systems break down. Banks may suddenly not have pesos. Phone repair can take a month. Electricity for an entire plant or town can be down for hours or even days. Business and government offices may open and close at odd hours. Buses and taxis may be hours off schedule. Meeting times for appointments are not rigid. Tardiness is common everywhere. Effectively doing business in Mexico requires knowledge of the Mexican way of life, culture, beliefs, and customs.

In Mexico, when greeting others, it is customary for women to pat each other on the right forearm or shoulder, rather than shaking hands. Men shake hands or, if close friends, use the traditional hug and back slapping upon greeting. If visiting a Mexican home, bring a gift such as flowers or sweets. Avoid marigolds, as they symbolize death. Arrive up to 30 minutes late, but definitely not early. Avoid red flowers which have a negative connotation. White flowers are an excellent choice. If you receive a gift, open it immediately and react enthusiastically. At dinner, do not sit until you are invited to and wait to be told where to sit. This is true in most foreign countries and in the United States. Do not begin eating until the hostess starts. Only men give toasts in Mexico. It is also polite to leave some food on your plate after a meal. For business appointments, as opposed to home visits, it is best to arrive on time, although your Mexican counterparts may be up to 30 minutes late. Do not get irritated at their lack of punctuality.

Mexicans often judge or stereotype a person by who introduces them and changing that first impression is very difficult in business. Expect to answer questions about your personal background, family, and life interests—because Mexicans consider trustworthiness and character to be of upmost importance. Mexicans are very status conscious, so business titles and rank are important. Face-to-face meetings are preferred over telephone calls, letters, or e-mail. Negotiations in Mexico include a fair amount of haggling, so do not give your best offer first.

Japan—Business Culture

The Japanese place great importance on group loyalty and consensus, a concept called *Wa*. Nearly all corporate activities in Japan encourage *Wa* among managers and employees. *Wa* requires that all members of a group agree and cooperate; this results in constant discussion and compromise. Japanese managers evaluate the potential attractiveness of alternative business decisions in terms of the long-term effect on the group's *Wa*. This is why silence, used for pondering alternatives, can be a plus in a formal Japanese meeting. Discussions potentially disruptive to *Wa* are generally conducted in very informal settings, such as at a bar, so as to minimize harm to the group's *Wa*. Entertaining is an important business activity in Japan because it strengthens *Wa*. Formal meetings are often conducted in informal settings. When confronted with disturbing questions or opinions, Japanese managers tend to remain silent, whereas Americans tend to respond directly, defending themselves through explanation and argument.

Americans have more freedom to control their own fates than do the Japanese. Life in the United States and life in Japan are very different; the United States offers more upward mobility to its people. This is a great strength of the United States, as indicated here:

> America is not like Japan and can never be. America's strength is the opposite: It opens its doors and brings the world's disorder in. It tolerates social change that would tear most other societies apart. This openness encourages Americans to adapt as individuals rather than as a group. Americans go west to California to get a new start; they move east to Manhattan to try to make the big time; they move to Vermont or to a farm to get close to the soil. They break away from their parents' religions or values or class; they rediscover their ethnicity. They go to night school; they change their names.[7]

Most Japanese managers are reserved, quiet, distant, introspective, and other oriented, whereas most U.S. managers are talkative, insensitive, impulsive, direct, and individual oriented. Americans often perceive Japanese managers as wasting time and carrying on pointless conversations, whereas U.S. managers often use blunt criticism, ask prying questions, and make quick decisions. These kinds of cultural differences have disrupted many potentially productive Japanese–American business endeavors. Viewing the Japanese communication style as a prototype for all Asian cultures is a stereotype that must be avoided.

In Japan, a person's age and status are of paramount importance, whether in the family unit, the extended family, or a social or business situation. Schoolchildren learn early that the oldest person in the group is to be honored. Older folks are served first and their drinks are poured for them. Greetings in Japan are very formal and ritualized. Wait to be introduced because it may be viewed as impolite to introduce yourself, even in a large gathering. Foreigners may shake hands, but the traditional form of greeting is to bow. The deeper you bow, the more respect you show, but at least bow the head slightly in greetings.

In gift giving in Japan, chocolates or small cakes are excellent choices, but do not give lilies, camellias, lotus blossoms, or white flowers because they all are associated with funerals. Do not give potted plants as they encourage sickness, although a bonsai tree is always acceptable. Give items in odd numbers, but avoid the number 9. Gifts are not opened when received. If going to a Japanese home, remove your shoes before entering and put on the slippers left at the doorway. Leave your shoes pointing away from the doorway you are about to walk through. If going to the toilet in a Japanese home, put on the toilet slippers and remove them when you exit.

In Japan, when you finally are seated for dinner, never point your chopsticks. Learn how to use chopsticks before you visit Japan and do not pierce your food with chopsticks. Japanese oftentimes slurp their noodles and soup, but mixing other food with rice is inappropriate. Instead of mixing, eat a bit of rice and then a bit of food. To signify that you do not want more rice or drink, leave some in your bowl or glass. Conversation over dinner is generally subdued in Japan, because they prefer to savor their food.

Unlike Americans, Japanese prefer to do business on the basis of personal relationships rather than impersonally speaking over the phone or by written correspondence. Therefore, build and maintain relationships by sending greeting, thank you, birthday, and seasonal cards. You need to be a good "correspondent" to effectively do business with the Japanese. Punctuality is very important so arrive on time for meetings and be mindful that it may take several meetings to establish a good relationship. The Japanese are looking for a long-term relationship. Always give a small gift as a token of your appreciation, and present it to the most senior person at the end of any meeting.

Like many Asian and African cultures, the Japanese are nonconfrontational. They have a difficult time saying 'no,' so you must be vigilant at observing their nonverbal communication. Rarely refuse a request, no matter how difficult or nonprofitable it may appear at the time. In communicating with Japanese, phrase questions so that they can answer yes. For example, do you disagree with this? Group decision making and consensus are vitally important. The Japanese often remain silent in meetings for long periods of time and may even close their eyes when they want to listen intently.

Business cards are exchanged in Japan constantly and with excitement. Invest in quality business cards and keep them in pristine condition. Do not write on them. Have one side of your card translated in Japanese and give it to the person with the Japanese side facing the recipient. Business cards are generally given and received with two hands and a slight bow. Examine any business card you receive very carefully.

Brazil—Business Culture

In both Brazil and America, men greet each other by shaking hands while maintaining steady eye contact. Women greet each other with kisses in Brazil, starting with the left and alternating cheeks. Hugging and backslapping are also common greetings among Brazilian close friends. If a woman wishes to shake hands with a man, she should extend her hand first. Brazilians speak Portuguese. If going to someone's house in Brazil, bring the hostess flowers or a small gift. Orchids are nice, but avoid purple or black, as these are mourning colors. Arrive at least 30 minutes late if your invitation is for dinner and arrive up to an hour late for a party or large gathering. Never arrive early. Brazilians dress with a flair and judge others on their appearance, so even casual dress is more formal than in many other countries. Always err on the side of over-dressing in Brazil rather than under-dressing.

Avoid embarrassing a Brazilian by criticizing an individual publically. That causes that person to lose face with all others at a business meeting, and the person making the criticism also loses face, as they have disobeyed the unwritten Brazilian rule. It is considered acceptable, however, to interrupt someone who is speaking. Face-to-face, oral communication is preferred over written communication. As for business agreements, Brazilians insist on drawing up detailed legal contracts. They are more comfortable doing business with and negotiating with people than companies. Therefore, wait for your Brazilian colleagues to raise the business subject. Never rush the prebusiness relationship-building time. Brazilians take their time when negotiating. Use local lawyers and accountants for negotiations, because Brazilians resent an outside legal presence.

Appointments are commonly cancelled or changed at the last minute in Brazil, so do not be surprised or get upset. In the cities of Sao Paulo and Brasilia, arrive on time for meetings, but in Rio de Janeiro arrive a few minutes late for a meeting. Do not appear impatient if you are kept waiting, because relationship building always takes precedence over adhering to a strict schedule. Brazilians pride themselves on dressing well, so men should wear conservative, dark-colored business suits or even three-piece suits for executives. Women should wear suits or dresses that are elegant and feminine with good, quality accessories. And ladies, manicures are expected.

Germany—Business Culture

Business communication in Germany is very formal, so the home is a welcome, informal place. Germans take great pride in their home, which is generally neat and tidy inside and out. Only close friends and relatives are invited into the sanctity of a person's house, so consider that an honor if you get that invitation, and bring a gift, such as chocolates or yellow roses or tea roses—but not red roses, which symbolize romantic intentions. Also do not bring carnations, lilies, or chrysanthemums, which in Germany symbolize mourning. If you bring wine to a German's home, it should be imported, French or Italian. Always arrive on time but never early, and always send a handwritten note the following day to thank your hostess for her hospitality.

When it's time to have dinner, remain standing until invited to sit down. As is custom in many countries, you may be shown to a particular seat. Table manners in Germany are strictly Continental with the fork being held in the left hand and the knife in the right while eating. Do not begin eating until the hostess starts or someone says "guten appetit" (good appetite). Wait for the hostess to place her napkin in her lap before doing so yourself and do not rest your elbows on the table. Cut as much of your food with your fork as possible, since this compliments the cook by indicating the food is tender. Break bread or rolls apart by hand, but if a loaf is in the middle for all, then touch only what you extract to eat. This sanitary practice is a must in all countries including the United States. Finish everything on your plate and indicate you have finished eating by laying your knife and fork parallel across the right side of your plate, with the fork over the knife.

Germans are like Americans in that they do not need a personal relationship to do business. They are more interested in a businessperson's academic credentials and their company's credentials. A quick, firm handshake is the traditional greeting, even with children. At the office, Germans do not have an open-door policy and often work with their office door closed, so knock and wait to be invited to enter. Appointments are mandatory and should be made one to two weeks in advance. Germans are often very direct to the point of bluntness. Punctuality is extremely important in Germany, so if you are going to be delayed, telephone immediately and offer an explanation. It is very rude to cancel a meeting at the last minute and this could jeopardize your whole business relationship. German meetings adhere to strict agendas, including starting and ending times. Germans maintain direct eye contact while speaking.

There is a strict protocol to follow in Germany when entering a room—the eldest or highest-ranking person enters first and men enter before women if their age and status are roughly equivalent. Germans are detail oriented and want to understand every innuendo before coming to an agreement. Business decision making is autocratic and held at the top of the company. Final decisions will not be changed and are expected to be implemented by lower-level managers and employees with no questions asked. Americans are more flexible in many respects than Germans.

Egypt—Business Culture

In Egypt, greetings are based on both social class and religion, so follow the lead of others. Handshakes, although limp and prolonged, are the customary greeting among Egyptians of the same sex. Handshakes are always given with a hearty smile and direct eye contact. Once a relationship has developed, it is common to greet with a kiss on one cheek and then the other, while shaking hands, men with men and women with women. In greetings between men and women, the woman will extend her hand first. Otherwise, a man should bow his head in greeting.

If you are invited to an Egyptian's home, remove your shoes before entering, just as you would do in China and Japan. As a gift, bring chocolates, sweets, or pastries to the hostess. Do not give flowers, which are usually reserved for weddings or the ill, unless you know that the host will appreciate them. Always give gifts with the right hand or both hands if the gift is heavy. Gifts are not opened when received. Never sit at a dinner table until the host or hostess tells you where to sit. Eat with the right hand only and compliment the host by taking second helpings. Always show appreciation for the meal. Putting salt or pepper on your food is considered an insult to a cook. This is true to a lesser extent even in the United States. Leave a small amount of food on your plate when you have finished eating. Otherwise your Egyptian host may keep bringing you more food.

Egyptians prefer to do business with those they know and respect, so expect to spend time cultivating a personal relationship before business is conducted. Who you know is more important than what you know in Egypt, so network and cultivate a number of contracts. You should expect to be offered coffee or tea whenever you meet someone in Egypt, as this demonstrates hospitality. Even if you do not want the drink, always accept the beverage because declining the offer is viewed as rejecting the person.

In Egypt, appearance is important, so wear, conservative clothes and present yourself well at all times. For Egyptians, direct eye contact is a sign of honesty, so be prepared for overly intense stares. Hierarchy and rank are very important. Unlike in Germany, Egyptian business people do have an open-door policy, even when they are in a meeting, so you may experience frequent interruptions as others wander into the room and start a different discussion. It is best that you not try to bring the topic back to the original discussion until the new person leaves. Business meetings generally start after prolonged inquiries about health, family, etc.

Egyptians must know and like you to conduct business. Personal relationships are necessary for long-term business. The highest-ranking person makes decisions, after obtaining group consensus. Decisions are reached after great deliberation. In Egypt, business moves at a slow pace and society is extremely bureaucratic—even in the post-Hosin Mubarak era. Egyptians respect age and experience and engage in a fair amount of haggling. They are tough negotiators and do not like confrontation or having to say "no." Egyptian women must be careful to cover themselves appropriately. Skirts and dresses should cover the knee and sleeves should cover most of the arm. Women are daily gaining more rights, however, throughout the Middle East, and that is a good thing. In late 2011, women in Saudi Arabia were finally granted the right to vote, but women still are not allowed to drive cars in that country.

China—Business Culture

In China, greetings are formal and the oldest person is always greeted first. Like in the United States, handshakes are the most common form of greeting. Many Chinese will look toward the ground when greeting someone. The Chinese have an excellent sense of humor. They can easily laugh at themselves if they have a comfortable relationship with the other person. In terms of gifts, a food basket makes an excellent gift, but do not give scissors, knives, or other cutting utensils, as these objects indicate severing of the relationship. Never give clocks, handkerchiefs, flowers, or straw sandals, as they are associated with funerals. Do not wrap gifts in white, blue, or black paper. In China, the number 4 is unlucky, so do not give four of anything. Eight is the luckiest number, so giving eight of something is a great idea.

If invited to a Chinese person's home, consider this a great honor and arrive on time. Remove your shoes before entering the house and bring a small gift to the hostess. Eat heartily to demonstrate that you are enjoying the food. Use chopsticks and wait to be told where to sit. You should try everything that is offered and never eat the last piece from the serving tray. Hold the rice bowl close to your mouth while eating. Do not be offended if a Chinese person makes slurping or belching sounds; it merely indicates that they are enjoying their food.

The Chinese rarely do business with companies or people they do not know. Your position on an organizational chart is extremely important in business relationships. Gender bias is generally not an issue. Meals and social events are not the place for business discussions. There is a demarcation between business and socializing in China, so try to be careful not to intertwine the two.

Like in the United States and Germany, punctuality is very important in China. Arriving late to a meeting is an insult and could negatively affect your relationship. Meetings require patience because mobile phones ring frequently and conversations tend to be boisterous. Never ask the Chinese to turn off their mobile phones as this causes you both to lose face. The Chinese are nonconfrontational and virtually never overtly say "no." Rather, they will say "they will think about it" or "they will see." The Chinese are shrewd negotiators, so your initial offer or price should leave room for negotiation.

India—Business Culture

According to UN statistics, India's rate of female participation in the labor force is 34.2 percent, which is quite low, especially since women make up 42 percent of college graduates in India. But Indian women with a college degree are expected to let their careers take a back seat to caring for their husband, children, and elderly parents. "The measures of daughterly guilt are much higher in Indian women than in other countries," says Sylvia Ann Hewlett, president of the Center for Work-Life Policy, a Manhattan think tank, who headed a recent study on the challenges Indian women face in the workplace.[7] Sylvia says, "Since taking care of elderly parents usually becomes a reality later in a woman's career, it takes them out of the workplace just when they should be entering top management roles." That is why gender disparities at Indian companies unfortunately grow more pronounced at higher levels of management.

Like in many Asian cultures, people in India do not like to say "no," verbally or nonverbally. Rather than disappoint you, they often will say something is not available, or will offer you the response that they think you want to hear, or will be vague with you. This behavior should not be considered dishonest. Shaking hands is common in India, especially in the large cities among the more educated who are accustomed to dealing with westerners. Men may shake hands with other men and women may shake hands with other women; however, there are seldom handshakes between men and women because of religious beliefs.

Indians believe that giving gifts eases the transition into the next life. Gifts of cash are common, but do not give frangipani or white flowers as they represent mourning. Yellow, green, and red are lucky colors, so use them to wrap gifts. Since Hindus consider cows to be sacred, do not give gifts made of leather to Hindus. Muslims should not be given gifts made of pigskin or alcoholic products. Gifts are usually not opened when received.

Before entering an Indian's house, take off your shoes just as you would in China or Japan. Politely turn down the host's first offer of tea, coffee, or snacks. You will be asked again and again. Saying no to the first invitation is part of the protocol. Be mindful that neither Hindus nor Sikhs eat beef, and many are vegetarians. Muslims do not eat pork or drink alcohol. Lamb, chicken, and fish are the most commonly served main courses. Table manners are somewhat formal, but much Indian food is eaten with the fingers. Like most places in the world, wait to be told where and when to sit at dinner. Women in India typically serve the men and eat later. You may be asked to wash your hands before and after sitting down to a meal. Always use your right hand to eat, whether using utensils or your fingers. Leave a small amount of food on your plate to indicate that you are satisfied. Finishing all your food means that you are still hungry, which as true in Egypt, China, Mexico, and many countries.

Indians prefer to do business with those with whom they have established a relationship built upon mutual trust and respect. Punctuality is important. Indians generally do not trust the legal system, and someone's word is often sufficient to reach an agreement. Do not disagree publicly with anyone in India.

Titles such as professor, doctor, or engineer are very important in India, as is a person's age, university degree, caste, and profession. Use the right hand to give and receive business cards. Business cards need not be translated into Hindi but always present your business card so the recipient may read the card as it is handed to them. This is a nice, expected gesture in most countries around the world.

Nigeria—Business Culture

With the largest population of any country in Africa and located on the west coast bordering the Gulf of Guinea, Nigeria is a democratic country with English as its official language. With a growing economy, Nigeria's constitution guarantees religious freedom. Christians in Nigeria live mostly in the south, whereas Muslims live mostly in the north. Native religions in which people believe in deities, spirits, and ancestor worship are spread throughout Nigeria, as are different languages. Christmas and Easter are national holidays. Muslims observe Ramadan, the Islamic month of fasting, and the two Eids. Working hours in the north often vary from the south, primarily because Muslims do not work on their holy day—Friday.

Endowed with vast quantities of natural resources and being the sixth largest oil-producing nation on the planet, Nigeria has a well-educated and industrious people who are proud of their country. Nigerians are fond of the expression, "When Nigeria sneezes, the rest of Africa catches a cold (except South Africa)." Nigeria re-elected its president in April 2011, a zoology professor-turned-president, Goodluck Jonathan.

In Nigeria, extended families are still the backbone of social and business systems. Grandparents, cousins, aunts, uncles, sisters, brothers, and in-laws all work as a unit through life. Hierarchy and seniority within extended families are very important; the oldest person in a group is revered and honored, and is greeted and served first. In return, however, the most senior person has the responsibility to make good decisions for the extended family.

The most common greeting in Nigeria is a handshake with a warm, welcoming smile. Muslims will not generally shake hands with members of the opposite sex. Nigerians do not use first names readily, so wait to be invited to do this before engaging. Gift giving is common and even expected, but gifts from a man to a woman must be said to come from the man's mother, wife, sister, or other female relative, never from the man himself. Never rush a greeting because that is extremely rude; rather, spend time inquiring about the other person's general well-being. Foreigners who take the time to get to know a Nigerian as a person are often welcomed into the Nigerian's inner circle of family and close friends. Nigerians are generally outgoing and friendly, especially in the southwest, where the Yoruba often use humor even during business meetings and serious discussions.

To combat the AIDS epidemic in sub-Saharan Africa, the World Bank is now paying young girls cash to stop accepting gifts and cash from older men in exchange for sex. This "sugar daddy" relationship is common in many African countries and is fueling the AIDS problem, since the percent of men aged 30–34 that test positive for HIV is upward of 30 percent in countries such as Zimbabwe. The World Bank has a billboard in the Mbare vegetable market in Harare, Zimbabwe, that reads, "Your future is brighter without a sugar daddy."

Business Climate Across Countries/Continents[9]

The business climate for various countries is conveniently summarized at http://globaledge.msu.edu/countries/. This site provides comparative information for 183 countries in terms of per capita GDP, inflation rate, ease-of-doing-business ranking, and population, as well as narrative that describes the business situation in those countries. Business information about a select few countries is presented in this chapter.

African Countries

By 2020, McKinsey & Co. predicts that consumer spending in Africa will double to nearly $1.8 trillion, up from about $860 million in 2008—which will be equivalent to adding a consumer market the size of Brazil.[10] The expected growth has many firms globally acquiring firms in Africa, such as India's No. 2 tire maker, Apollo Tyres, recently buying South Africa's Dunlop Tyres for $62 million. Apollo plans to triple sales to $6 billion by 2015, with 60 percent of that revenue coming from outside India. Nearly 100 firms in India acquired firms in Africa between 2005 and 2011.

The McKinsey Global Institute reports that approximately 40 percent of Africans now live in urban areas and the number of households with discretionary income should increase 50 percent by the end of this decade.[11] Graham Allan, CEO of Yum Restaurants International, recently said, "A lot of companies, especially Chinese ones, have invested in Africa; we share the general view that Africa over the next 10 to 20 years will have massive potential." McKinsey & Co. says the number of consumers who can spend beyond bare necessities is greater now in Africa than India. From 2000 to 2009, foreign direct investment in Africa increased 600 percent to $58.56 billion.

Wal-Mart recently acquired South African retailer Massmart Holdings for $4.6 billion, providing the company with 290 stores in 13 African countries: Ghana, Nigeria, Zambia, Botswana, Namibia, South Africa, Lesotho, Mozambique, Zimbabwe, Mauritius, Malawi, Tanzania, and Uganda. The Wal-Mart acquisition paves the way for many firms now viewing Africa as a deal-making destination. For example, HSBC Holdings is trying to acquire a majority stake in Nedbank Group, South Africa's fourth-largest bank, and Nippon Telegraph and Telephone in Japan is buying Africa's largest technology company, Dimension Data. Huge purchases such as these have been a wake-up call to the rest of the world, which now views Africa as a growing, attractive new market.

Table 11-5 provides a summary of the economic situation in 12 African countries. Note that Angola is rated lowest in terms of doing business, whereas South Africa is rated highest. Recent regime changes in Egypt, Tunisia, Libya, and Algeria may spur further investment in Africa as democracy and capitalism strengthens. Many multinational companies are now gaining first mover advantages by engaging Africa at all levels. For example, Nokia and Coca-Cola have distribution networks in nearly every African country. Unilever has a presence in 20 of Africa's 50 countries. Nestlé is in 19 African countries, Barclays is in 12, Societe Generale is in 15, and Standard Chartered Bank is in 14. Africa has about 10 percent of the world's oil reserves, 40 percent of its gold ore, and 85 percent of the world's deposits of chromium and plantinum. Africa's population is young, growing, and moving into jobs in the cities. Forty percent of Africans today live in the cities, a proportion close to China and India. The general stereotype of Africa is rapidly changing from subsistence farmers avoiding lions, to millions of cell-phone carrying consumers in cities purchasing products.

TABLE 11-5   **Sampling of African Countries—Ease-of-Doing-Business Rankings**

	GDP per Capita ($)	Inflation Rate (%)	Population in Millions	Ease of Doing Business Among all Countries	Capital City
South Africa	10,116	07.2	49	34 out of 183	Pretoria
Tunisia	7,956	03.7	11	55 out of 183	Tunis
Ghana	1,463	19.6	24	67 out of 183	Accra
Egypt	5,425	10.1	79	94 out of 183	Cairo
Kenya	1,551	20.5	39	98 out of 183	Nairobi
Ethiopia	869	11.0	86	104 out of 183	Addis Ababa
Morocco	4,263	02.0	32	114 out of 183	Rabat
Uganda	1,166	12.6	33	122 out of 183	Kampala
Mozambique	838	03.5	22	126 out of 183	Maputo
Nigeria	2,099	11.5	150	137 out of 183	Abuja
Sudan	2,155	12.3	41	154 out of 183	Khartoum
Angola	5,820	13.1	13	163 out of 183	Luanda

Source: Based on information at http://globaledge.msu.edu/countries and other sources. Obtained March 1, 2011.

Africa has the world's largest deposits of platinum, chrome, and diamonds—and many Chinese companies in particular are investing there. Africa's largest food retailer, Shoprite Holdings, has more than 1,000 stores in 17 countries. Shoprite is a potential acquisition target being considered by European retailers Carrefour and Tesco. Diageo PLC sells Guinness beer, Smirnoff vodka, Baileys liqueur, and Johnnie Walker whiskey in more than 40 countries across Africa. Nestlé SA now has more than 25 factories in Africa.

From 2011 to 2014, Yum Brands is doubling the number of Kentucky Fried Chicken outlets in Africa to 1,200 and aims to double its revenue from the continent to $2 billion. "Africa wasn't even on our radar screen 10 years ago, but now we see it exploding with opportunity" says David Novak, Yum's chairman and CEO. Yum Brands is excited about Africa's growing middle class, vast population, and improving political stability of most African governments. Yum Brands is especially targeting Nigeria, Namibia, Mozambique, Ghana, Zambia, and South Africa. The company says it wants to reach more of Africa's one billion people than its current customer base of 180 million. But KFC currently has about 45 percent of South Africa's fast-food market, followed by Nando's with 6 percent and McDonald's with 5 percent.

Ghana recently became Africa's newest oil producing nation when the 1.5-billion-barrel Jubilee field began pumping oil. Although Ghana's estimated four billion barrels of reserves are about a third those of Nigeria, Ghana has a stable political and economic situation. Ethiopia is also doing very well economically. SABMiller PLC recently invested $20 million in a manufacturing plant in Ethiopia's large city, Ambo. That factory today produces 40,000 glass bottles of mineral water per hour. Ambo sells for about $6 a bottle in New York restaurants. Ambo water is part of the SABMiller portfolio that includes 45 African beers.[12]

Nairobi, Kenya, is the center of several major telecom companies trying to gain market share in the rapidly growing African cellphone business. Vodafone Safaricom Ltd. dominates the Kenyan telecommunications sector with 77 percent market share, but India's Bharti Airtel Ltd. boosted its market share in the last year to almost 20 percent. There are currently over 440 million mobile subscribers in Africa generating over $15 billion in telecom revenue annually. All of Africa is coming online, representing huge opportunities for countless companies. McKinsey & Co. estimates that within five years another 220 million Africans that today can meet only basic needs will join the middle class as consumers.[13] There are over 950 million people who live in Africa.

China

Although the United States is the world's largest economy with a gross domestic product (GDP) of about $14.62 trillion annually, China recently passed Japan to become the world's second-largest economy with a GDP of about $5.75 trillion annually, compared to Japan's $5.4 trillion. China, however, is still an emerging economy, as indicated by a per-capita GDP of $4,000, compared to the United States and Japan per-capita GDPs of $47,000 and $42,000 respectively. China's economic (GDP) growth of over 9 percent annually for several decades is, however, much faster than either the United States or Japan. Premier Wen Jiabao recently proclaimed that China's annual GDP growth will be held to 7.0 percent if possible to constrain inflation. Goldman Sachs predicts that China will overtake the United States as the world's largest economy by 2027.

China's rapid growth has created substantial pollution, extensive inequality, and deeply embedded corruption. In fact, China's communist government is concerned that political unrest in the Middle East may spread to China in a "Jasmine Revolution," as the masses in China barely make enough to survive. The World Bank estimates that more than 100 million Chinese citizens, nearly the size of Japan's entire population, live on less than $2 a day—but China's middle class is growing rapidly.

For many decades, low wage rates in China helped keep world prices low on hundreds of products—but that is changing, because all 31 Chinese provinces and regions recently boosted their minimum wage for the second consecutive year. Analysts expect demand for workers in China to outstrip supply by 2014, and this is contributing to rapidly rising wage rates and worldwide inflation. Commercial and industrial development in China's west has turned interior cities such as Chongqing into production centers that compete for labor with coastal factories. According to Credit Suisse in Hong Kong, pay to migrant laborers who fuel China's export industry rose 40 percent in 2010 and 30 percent in 2011, and similar increases are expected in 2012. Average monthly pay in 2009 in Shenzhen on the southern China coast was $235, compared to Seoul's $1,220, Taipei's $888, Ho Chi Minh City's $100, Jakarta's $148, and $47 in Dhaka, Bangladesh.[14]

China has become the biggest trading partner for Australia, Japan, Korea, India, Russia, and South Africa and has replaced the United States as the top export market for Brazil. The world's two fastest-growing major economies, China and India, recently announced that the two countries will more than double their bilateral trade between 2010 and 2015 to $100 billion.[15] China is opening its large consumer markets more to Indian goods. China may soon support India having a permanent seat on the United Nations Security Council. China has long opposed a permanent seat for India. The increased cooperation between China and India is good news for companies worldwide doing business in that part of Asia.

As indicated in Table 11-6, China ranks 79th out of 183 countries in terms of doing business, for a variety of reasons ranging from human rights issues to substantial disregard for copyright/patent/trademark rules of law. Best Buy and Home Depot are example companies that are closing stores in China. Both firms have not competed well in China due to being too "high priced" compared to home-grown, similar businesses. The Chinese are very price conscious.

China is gaining a stronger and stronger foothold into Japanese businesses. The five largest recent Chinese investments in Japan are Mitsubishi UFJ Financial (92 billion yen), Canon (74.5 billion yen), Sumitomo Mitsui (57.9 billion yen), Nippon T&T (49.2 billion yen), Mitsubishi (47.8 billion yen), Takeda Pharm (45.4 billion yen), and Sony (41.6 billion yen). The Japanese investment adviser Chibagin Asset Management says China state funds have recently more than doubled their investment in Japan to 1.62 trillion yen in 90 companies.

Note also in Table 11-6 that Singapore is rated the best country on the planet for doing business.

Philippines

A highly educated, English speaking country, the Philippines overtook India in early 2011 in call-center jobs, employing 350,000 compared with India's 330,000.[16] Call centers in the Philippines produced $7.4 billion in revenue in 2011, and that figure is growing about 15 percent annually. The Philippines recently also overtook Indonesia as the world's biggest supplier of voice-based call-center services.[17] Citigroup and Chase are just two companies outsourcing

TABLE 11-6   Sampling of Asian Countries—Ease-of-Doing-Business Rankings

	GDP per Capita ($)	Inflation Rate (%)	Population in Millions	Ease of Doing Business Among all Countries	Capital City
Singapore	49,321	00.2	5	1 out of 183	Singapore
South Korea	27,658	02.8	49	16 out of 183	Seoul
Japan	34,129	- 1.3	127	18 out of 183	Tokyo
Thailand	8,086	- 0.9	66	19 out of 183	Bangkok
Malaysia	14,215	00.5	26	21 out of 183	Kuala Lumpur
Taiwan	-	- 0.9	23	33 out of 183	Taipei
China	5,971	01.0	1,500	79 out of 183	Beijing
Pakistan	2,538	14.2	175	83 out of 183	Islamabad
Indonesia	3,994	05.0	241	121 out of 183	Jakarta
Russia	15,923	11.9	140	123 out of 183	Moscow
India	2,946	10.7	1,160	134 out of 183	New Delhi
Philippines	3,513	03.2	98	148 out of 183	Manila

Source: Based on information at http://globaledge.msu.edu/countries and other sources. Obtained March 1, 2011.

customer calls, back-office work, and other operations to the Philippines. A major reason why the Philippines is an attractive place for call centers is the country's overall business culture to "deliver absolutely fantastic service." An associate professor at the City University of Hong Kong, Jane Lockwood, says "Filipinos go out of their way, not just in call centers, but in tourism and events management, to ensure people are well looked after."[18]

As indicated in Table 11-6, the Philippines has about 98 million people, making the country the world's 12th largest in population. Located in Southeast Asia, the Philippines was a founding member of the United Nations and is very active in that organization. Filipinos love Americans who rescued them in WWII. Thousands of Filipinos today work all-night shifts to accommodate the normal 8 am-to-5 pm business time zone in the United States. Philippines president Benigno Aquino recently indicated that services outsourced to the Philippines from around the world will generate up to $100 billion in 2020, representing 20 percent of the global offshoring market share.

Unemployment is at 6.9 percent in the Philippines, but under-employment—defined as people who work only part-time or with minimal incomes—is 18 percent. The average per capita income of Filipinos is about $1,790 a year, so hundreds of thousands of Filipinos work outside the country. In fact, the Philippines' economy depends greatly on outside workers sending monies back to the country and also traveling to and from the country.

The television advertising market in the Philippines is nearly $4 billion annually, larger than India's and on par with Indonesia's.[19] Television is the most enjoyed media among the Philippines 7,100 island people, whereas newspapers are the most important media outlet in India. Television ads comprise 75 percent of advertising spending in the Philippines.

Among major emerging economies, the Philippines has only a 9 percent Internet penetration rate among its population, which is very low compared to China (28.9%), Nigeria (28.4%), Mexico (28.3%), and Russia (29.0%). But the Philippines' 9 percent rate is above the Internet penetration rate among Indonesia's population (8.7%) and India's population (5.1%).[20] These percentages reveal the percentage of the country's people that could shop online.

Taiwan

Located off the southeast coast of mainland China, Taiwan has a dynamic, capitalist, export-driven economy with gradually decreasing state involvement in investment and foreign trade. Many large, government-owned banks and industrial firms are being privatized in Taiwan. Real annual growth in GDP has averaged about 8 percent during the past three decades. Exports have provided the primary impetus for industrialization. The trade surplus is substantial, and foreign reserves are the world's fifth largest. As indicated in Table 11-6, Taiwan is rated 33rd among all countries in the world for doing business.

Taiwan's total trade in 2010 reached an all-time high of $526 billion, according to Taiwan's Ministry of Finance. Both exports and imports for the year reached record levels, totaling U.S. $274 billion and $251 billion, respectively. Agriculture constitutes only 2 percent of Taiwan's GDP, down from 35 percent in 1952. Some brands from Taiwan that are leaders globally include: Acer, HTC, ASUS, TrendMicro, MasterKong, Want-Want, Maxxis, Giant, Synnex, Transcend, Uni-President, Advantech, D-Link, ZyXel, Merida, Johnson, Gigabyte, CyberLink, Genius, and Depo.

India

President Obama recently said "India's progress in just two decades is one of the most stunning achievements in human history." India grew its GDP 8 percent in 2009–2010 and is on track for GDP growth of 8.6 percent in 2010–2011. With a medium age of 25, India has perhaps the youngest population among all large countries on the planet. About one third the geographic size of the United States, India's 1.21 billion people live in the world's largest democracy.

Note in Table 11-6 that India is rated 134 out of 183 in attractiveness for doing business, partly because that country still requires foreign firms to form a joint venture with an Indian firm in order to do business. Also note in Table 11-6 India's high inflation and low per capita GDP. India has been slow to allow 3G wireless, which allows for high-speed Internet access on cellphones. As the rest of Asia rolled out 4G in 2010/2011, India rolled out 3G in January 2011—and the signal quality is not that good, definitely not good enough to stream a movie.

4G will not become available in India until 2012. Japan and South Korea got 3G back in 2005, and China got 3G in 2009. Also, India's bureaucracy slows down all business. Telecom authorities for example are divided into several dozen areas and this creates problems. Still only one percent of India's population has access to broadband connections. G.V. Giri, an analyst in Mumbai with IIFL Securities, says, "People in India have been starved for high-speed Internet connections. The number of people in India with broadband access will however grow from 10 million in early 2011 to 100 million by 2014."

Various economic reports predict that by 2015, India will outpace China's annual GDP growth rate of 8.5–9.5 percent. Various trends in India lead to this conclusion, including a young, increasingly educated labor force, relatively few retired people to care for, a high savings rate, massive structural reforms the government continues to undertake, and increased infrastructure spending. The United Nations estimates that India's age dependency ratio (the number of working age people supporting children and the elderly) will decrease substantially, from 55.6 percent in 2010 to 47.2 percent in 2025; the lower the number the better. China, by contrast, has already reaped the benefit of a large working age population, which will soon begin to age and decline: its dependency ratio will rise from 39.1 percent in 2010 to 45.8 percent in 2025. The Indian government is slowly improving the country's education system, but an enormous amount of work remains. Only 74 percent of Indian men and 48 percent of Indian women are literate, compared to 96 percent of men and 88 percent of women in China. India's "knowledge economy" employs only about 2.23 million people out of 750 million available.

Prime Minister Manmohan Singh's government has instituted education reforms, so the number of Indian children out of school has dropped greatly from 18 million in 2000. Dropout ratios in primary schools have improved as well. However, at present only 12 percent of India's citizens enter higher education, and the government hopes to increase this to 21 percent by 2017. The Indian Institutes of Technology—a group of universities focused on engineering and technology—are world renowned but offer only a miniscule 7,000 places to students each year. There is elaborate red tape required to establish and operate any business in India. Also, India's tax code is archaic and many new sectors are not even open to foreign direct investment.

India's 2011 census revealed that the country will surpass China as the most populated country in 2030. The new census revealed that India's highest density growth and population is in the northwest and east-central areas of the country. India has a literacy rate now of 74 percent, up from 65 percent a decade ago.

Germany

Germany's economy in 2010 grew at 3.6 percent, the highest rate in more than two decades, as the country's cars, machinery, and other products were in high demand in Asia, especially China. As Europe's debt crisis has pushed the euro lower, German goods are more competitive abroad. The economic and fiscal crises in Greece, Ireland, Portugal, and Spain have only limited direct impact on Germany's $3.24 trillion economy. There is a growing north-south divide in Europe, with the north doing much better economically than the south. Germany's budget deficit was 3.5 percent in 2010, the first time in years that the country has exceeded the 3 percent limit set by EU budget rules, but that percent is well below the deficit in the U.S., UK, and Japan—so overall the German economy is very healthy. Note in Table 11-7 that Germany ranks 22nd out of 183 countries in ease of doing business.

German automobile producers such as Daimler AG, BMW AG, and Volkswagen AG have fallen behind rivals such as GM, Renault SA, and Nissan Motor in mass-producing electric cars. The German companies are playing catch up in this key area of industrial growth, partly because the German government has committed just $688 million in state support for electric battery research and infrastructure projects, such as car-charging stations. That amount is only a small fraction of the U.S. (and Chinese) government support for electric cars. Since one out of seven German jobs is connected to the country's car markers and domestic suppliers, this issue is very important. More than 15 percent of German exports stem from the automobile industry. Germany also fallen way behind in electric car lithium-ion battery development and production.

TABLE 11-7   Sampling of European Countries—Ease-of-Doing-Business Rankings

	GDP per Capita ($)	Inflation Rate (%)	Population in Millions	Ease of Doing Business Among All Countries	Capital City
United Kingdom	35,468	2.10	62	4 out of 183	London
Sweden	36,961	-0.50	9	14 out of 183	Stockholm
Germany	35,374	0.00	83	22 out of 183	Berlin
France	33,058	0.10	64	26 out of 183	Paris
Czech Republic	24,643	1.10	11	63 out of 183	Prague
Turkey	13,417	6.50	77	65 out of 183	Ankara
Italy	31,283	0.60	59	80 out of 183	Rome
Ukraine	7,277	12.30	46	145 out of 183	Kyiv

Source: Based on information at http://globaledge.msu.edu/countries and other sources. Obtained March 1, 2011.

The European Union is a single economic bloc with free movement of people, goods, and services among its 27 nations, but in matters such as taxes and labor costs, each country sets its own rules. Businesses entering Europe for the first time need to carefully research the various countries. Belgium, for example, has the highest labor costs in Europe with 53 percent of workers there being unionized, but that percent is only the fifth highest in Europe. In terms of employer-paid social security costs as a percentage of total labor costs, Belgium is at 30.8 percent, followed by France at 28.4 percent, Spain at 25.0 percent, Germany at 22.9 percent, and the Netherlands at 21 percent. A nonmember, the United Kingdom, is at 17.1 percent.

Germany has one of Europe's fastest aging and shrinking populations. Germany now faces shortages of skilled labor and aggressive recruiting from abroad for the country's top engineering and scientific talent.[21] More people emigrate from Germany than re-locate to Germany, especially highly educated professionals—partly because Germany has a restrictive labor code and inward-looking hiring practices. Germany might need to follow the lead of Italy, which has the same, albeit more severe, problem but has enacted excellent new laws and incentives to both keep and attract young, highly educated professionals.

Mexico

More and more companies such as Electrolux and Whirlpool have recently reduced their capital expenditures in Mexico because of spiraling drug-related violence. Electrolux AB recently chose Memphis, Tennessee, over locations in Mexico for its new $190 million appliance factor that will employ 1,200. Fights between rival drug cartels have claimed more than 31,000 lives in the past four years, including more than 11,000 in 2010.[22] Other crimes such as robbery, extortion, and kidnapping are climbing. Terex Corp. of Westport Connecticut recently said, "We won't put a factory in Mexico until some of this violence gets addressed. We just can't put our people at risk."

Based in Perrysburg, Ohio, Owens-Illinois Inc. recently said, "The escalating violence in Mexico has led us to be more cautious. We take the safety and security of our employees very seriously." Whirlpool recently chose Cleveland, Tennessee, over Mexico to build its new oven and cooktop factor that employs more than 1,600. J.P. Morgan's chief economist for Mexico, Gabriel Casillas, says drug-related violence in Mexico probably cost the country some $4 billion in foreign direct investment in 2010. Mexico's troubled interior states of Durango, Sinaloa, and Michoacan, as well as the border regions, have seen a drop in foreign investment to roughly $1.9 billion in 2010 from an average of about $5 billion in prior years. The drug-related death toll in Mexico climbed to 15,273 in 2010, the highest casualty rate in years. The most violent city in Mexico is Ciudad Juarez.

As indicated in Table 11-8, Mexico has fallen to 35th out of 183 countries in terms of doing business. Note Mexico's population is about 112 million people, more than three times Canada's population.

TABLE 11-8 Sampling of North and South American Countries—Ease-of-Doing-Business Rankings

	GDP per Capita ($)	Inflation Rate (%)	Population in Millions	Ease of Doing Business Among all Countries	Capital City
United States	46,350	00.7	308	5 out of 183	Washington, DC
Canada	39,078	00.2	34	7 out of 183	Ottawa
Mexico	14,570	03.6	112	35 out of 183	Mexico City
Argentina	14,313	07.7	41	115 out of 183	Buenos Aires
Brazil	10,304	04.2	199	127 out of 183	Brasilia
Chile	14,436	01.7	17	43 out of 183	Santiago
Ecuador	8,014	04.3	15	130 out of 183	Quito
Bolivia	4,277	04.3	10	149 out of 183	La Paz
Peru	8,509	01.2	30	36 out of 183	Lima
Venezuela	12,818	27.3	27	172 out of 183	Caracas

Source: Based on information at http://globaledge.msu.edu/countries and other sources. Obtained March 1, 2011.

Special Note to Students

Even the smallest businesses today regularly serve customers globally and gain competitive advantages and economies of scale doing so. Many iconic American businesses, such as Tupperware, obtain more than 80 percent of their revenue from outside the United States. Therefore, in performing a strategic management case analysis, you must evaluate the scope, magnitude, and nature of what your company is doing globally compared to rival firms. Then, determine what your company should be doing to garner global business. Continuously throughout your presentation or written report, compare your firm to rivals in terms of global business and make recommendations based on careful analysis. Be "prescriptive and insightful" rather than "descriptive and mundane" with every slide presented to pave the way for your specific recommendations with costs regarding global reach of your firm.

Conclusion

The population of the world surpassed 7 billion persons in 2011. Just as they did for centuries before Columbus reached America, businesses will search for new opportunities beyond their national boundaries for centuries to come. There has never been a more internationalized and economically competitive society than today's model. Some U.S. industries, such as automobiles, textiles, steel, and consumer electronics, are in complete disarray as a result of the international challenge.

Success in business increasingly depends on offering products and services that are competitive on a world basis, not just on a local basis. If the price and quality of a firm's products and services are not competitive with those available elsewhere in the world, the firm may soon face extinction. Global markets have become a reality in all but the most remote areas of the world. Certainly throughout the United States, even in small towns, firms feel the pressure of world competitors.

This chapter has provided some basic global information that can be essential to consider in developing a strategic plan for any organization. The advantages of engaging in international business may well offset the drawbacks for most firms. It is important in strategic planning to be effective, and the nature of global operations may be the key component in a plan's overall effectiveness.

Key Terms and Concepts

Feng Shui (p. 369)
Global Strategy (p. 365)
Globalization (p. 365)
Guanxi (p. 367)
International Firms (p. 363)

Inhwa (p. 367)
Multinational Corporations (p. 363)
Nemaswashio (p. 369)
Protectionism (p. 364)
Wa (p. 367)

Issues for Review and Discussion

1. Pfizer has been so successful in recent years. What percentage of Pfizer's revenues come from the United States versus Europe? How does this percentage compare to rival firms?
2. Explain why consumption patterns are becoming similar worldwide. What are the strategic implications of this trend?
3. What are the advantages and disadvantages of beginning export operations in a foreign country?
4. What are the major differences between U.S. and multinational operations that affect strategic management?
5. Why is globalization of industries a common factor today?
6. Compare and contrast U.S. versus foreign cultures in terms of doing business.
7. List six reasons why strategic management is more complex in a multinational firm.
8. Do you feel that protectionism is good or bad for the world economy? Why?
9. Why are some industries more "global" than others? Discuss.
10. *Wa*, *guanxi* and *inhwa* are important management terms in Japan, China, and Korea respectively. What would be analogous terms to describe American management practices?
11. Why do many Europeans also find the notion of "team spirit" in a work environment difficult to grasp?
12. In China, *feng shui*, is important in business, whereas in Japan *nemaswashio*, is important. What are analogous American terms and practices?
13. Describe the business culture in Mexico.
14. Describe the business culture in Japan.
15. Compare tax rates in the United States versus other countries. What impact could these differences have on "keeping jobs at home?"
16. Discuss requirements for doing business in India.
17. Select four countries. Evaluate Pfizer's operations in those countries.
18. Compare business practice and culture in northern Europe versus southern Europe.
19. Explain how the Arab Spring movement in the Middle East will likely impact Pfizer.
20. What five countries in Asia have the highest GDP? What are the implications for Adidas?
21. Africa is rapidly joining the world economic community. Give 10 examples of this.
22. What six countries in Africa do you feel are most attractive for foreign investment.
23. Compare business practice and culture in the USA versus your own country.
24. Explain in your own words the "Special Note to Students" section at the end of the chapter.
25. Select three countries in South America. Prepare a one-page summary for each to reveal their attractiveness for foreign direct investment.
26. Compare sexual harassment policies and practice across continents and countries.
27. Discuss Australia as a continent for doing business.
28. In terms of presenting flowers as business gifts, compare and contrast practice and custom across six countries.
29. Discuss how business etiquette at dinner varies across countries.

Notes

1. Justin Lahart, "Divided by Two-Track Economy," *Wall Street Journal*, September 8, 2010, B1.
2. Frederick Gluck, "Global Competition in the 1990s," *Journal of Business Strategy* (Spring 1983): 22–24.
3. http://finance.yahoo.com/taxes/article/112560/what-top-companies-pay-taxes-forbes.
4. Jon Alston, "Wa, Guanxi, and Inhwa: Managerial Principles in Japan, China and Korea," *Business Horizons* 32, no. 2 (March–April 1989): 26.
5. Rose Knotts, "Cross-Cultural Management: Transformations and Adaptations," *Business Horizons*, January–February 1989, 29–33.
6. Lalita Khosla, "You Say Tomato," *Forbes*, May 21, 2001, 36.
7. Mehul Srivastava, "Keeping Women on the Job in India," *Bloomberg Businessweek*, March 7–13, 2011, 11–12.
8. Stratford Sherman, "How to Beat the Japanese," *Fortune*, April 10, 1989, 145.
9. Based on information at http://www.kwintessential.co.uk/resources/country-profiles.html.
10. Mehul Srivastava and Subramaniam Sharma, "Corporate India Finds Greener Pastures—in Africa," *Bloomberg Businessweek*, November 8–14, 2010, 61–62. Also, McKinsey has excellent information for developing strategies to engage Africa at the website www.mckinsey.com/mgi. Also, there is an excellent *Harvard Business Review* article on engaging Africa (May 2011, pp. 117–122).
11. Julie Jargon, "KFC Savors Potential in Africa," *Wall Street Journal*, December 8, 2010, B1. Peter Wonacott, "A Continent of New Consumers Beckons," *Wall Street Journal*, January 13, 2011, B1.
12. Peter Wonacott, "SABMiller Taps Ethiopia's Holy Water," *Wall Street Journal*, January 13, 2011, B1.
13. Sarah Childress, "Telecom Giants Battle for Kenya," *Wall Street Journal*, January 14, 2011, B1.
14. Sophie Leung and Simon Kennedy with Cotton Timberlake and Chris Burritt, "Global Inflation Starts With Chinese Workers," *Bloomberg Businessweek*, March 7–13, 2011, 9–10.
15. Arpan Mukherjee and Abhrajit Gangopadhyay, "India, China Aim to Double Trade," *Wall Street Journal*, December 17, 2010, A15.
16. Michelle Yun and Kathy Chu, "Philippines May Answer Call," *USA Today*, January 10. 2011, 1–2B.
17. Ibid.
18. James Hookway, "Dollar's Fall Rocks Far-Flung Families," *Wall Street Journal*, February 25, 2011, A12.
19. James Hookway, "High Drama for Philippine TV," *Wall Street Journal*, March 3, 2011, B10.
20. Amol Sharma, "Dot-Coms Begin to Blossom in India," *Wall Street Journal*, April 12, 2011, B1.
21. Vanessa Fuhrmans, "Exodus of Skilled Labor Saps Germany," *Wall Street Journal*, March 11, 2011, A12.
22. Nicholas Casey and James Gagerty, "Violence Limits Mexico's Allure," *Wall Street Journal*, December 17, 2010, B1. Jose de Cordora and David Luhnow, "In Mexico, Death Toll in Drug War Hits Record,' *Wall Street Journal*, January 13, 2010, A8.

Current Readings

Abdelal, Rawi. "The Promise and Peril of Russia's Resurgent State." *Harvard Business Review*, January–February 2010, 125–130.

Becht, Bart. "Building a Company Without Borders." *Harvard Business Review*, April 2010, 103–109.

Bozionelos, Nikos, and Ioannis Nikolaou. "What Accounts for Job Satisfaction Differences Across Countries?" *The Academy of Management Perspectives* 24, no. 1 (February 2010): 82–83.

Cappelli, Peter, Harbir Singh, Jitendra V. Singh, and Michael Useem. "Leadership Lessons from India." *Harvard Business Review*, March 2010, 90–98.

Cappelli, Peter, Harbir Singh, Jitendra Singh, and Michael Useem. "The India Way: Lessons for the U.S." *The Academy of Management Perspectives* 24, no. 2 (May 2010): 6–24.

Chan, Christine M., Shige Makino, and Takehiko Isobe. "Does Subnational Region Matter? Foreign Affiliate Performance in the United States and China." *Strategic Management Journal* 31, no. 11 (November 2010): 1226–1243.

Chironga, Mutsa, Acha Leke, Susan Lund, and Arend van Wamelen. "Cracking the Next Growth Market: Africa," *Harvard Business Review*, May 2011, 117–122.

D'Andrea, Guillermo, David Marcotte, and Gwen Dixon Morrison. "Let Emerging Market Customers Be Your Teachers." *Harvard Business Review*, December 2010, 115–122.

Guler, Isin, and Mauro F. Guillèn. "Home Country Networks and Foreign Expansion: Evidence from the Venture Capital Industry." *The Academy of Management Journal* 53, no. 2 (April 2010): 390.

Henisz, Witold J., and Bennet A. Zelner. "The Hidden Risks in Emerging Markets." *Harvard Business Review*, April 2010, 88–95.

Hermelo, Francisco Diaz, and Roberto Vassolo. "Institutional Development and Hypercompetition in Emerging Economies." *Strategic Management Journal* 31, no. 13 (December 2010): 1457–1473.

Hewlett, Sylvia Ann, and Ripa Rashid. "The Battle for Female Talent in Emerging Markets." *Harvard Business Review*, May 2010, 101–107.

Hout, Thomas M., and Pankaj Ghemawat. "China vs the World: Whose Technology Is It?" *Harvard Business Review*, December 2010, 94–103.

Huang, Yasheng. "Debating China's Economic Growth: The Beijing Consensus or The Washington Consensus?" *The Academy of Management Perspectives* 24, no. 2 (May 2010): 31–47.

Javidan, Mansour, Mary Teagarden, and David Bowen. "Making It Overseas." *Harvard Business Review*, April 2010, 109–114.

Martin, John A., and Kevin J. Davis. "Stacked Deck: Can Governance Structures Explain CEO Compensation Differences Across Countries?" *The Academy of Management Perspectives* 24, no. 1 (February 2010): 78.

Morrison, Allen, and Cyril Bouquet. "Are You Giving Globalization the Right Amount of Attention?" *MIT Sloan Management Review* 52, no. 2 (Winter 2011): 15–16.

Numagami, Tsuyoshi, Masaru Karube, and Toshihiko Kato. "Organizational Deadweight: Learning From Japan." *The Academy of Management Perspectives* 24, no. 4 (November 2010): 25–37.

Spencer, Jennifer, and Carolina Gomez. "MNEs and Corruption: The Impact of National Institutions and Subsidiary Strategy." *Strategic Management Journal* 32, no. 3 (March 2011): 280–300.

Tharenou, Phyllis, and Natasha Caulfield. "Will I Stay or Will I Go? Explaining Repatriation by Self-Initiated Expatriates." *Academy of Management Journal* 53, no. 5 (October 2010): 1009–1028.

Tse, Edward. "Is It Too Late to Enter China?" *Harvard Business Review*, April 2010, 96–102.

Xia, Jun. "Mutual Dependence, Partner Substitutability, and Repeated Partnership: The Survival of Cross-Border Alliances." *Strategic Management Journal* 32, no. 3 (March 2011): 229–253.

ASSURANCE OF LEARNING EXERCISES

Assurance of Learning Exercise 11A

Adidas AG Wants to Enter Africa. Help Them.

Purpose

More and more companies every day decide to begin doing business in Africa. Research is necessary to determine the best strategy for being the first mover in many African countries (i.e., being the first competitor doing business in various countries).

Instructions

Step 1	Print a map of Africa.
Step 2	Print demographic data on 10 African countries.
Step 3	Gather competitive information regarding the presence of shoe companies doing business in Africa.
Step 4	List in prioritized order eight countries that you would recommend for Adidas to enter. Country 1 is your best, and Country 2 is your next best. Based on your research, indicate how many Adidas/Reebok/TaylorMade stores you would recommend building over the next three years in each country. List in prioritized order three cities in each of your eight African countries where you believe Adidas should build most of its stores.

Assurance of Learning Exercise 11B

Assessing Differences in Culture Across Countries

Purpose

Americans can be more effective in dealing with businesspeople from other countries if they have some awareness and understanding of differences in culture across countries. This is a fun exercise that provides information for your class regarding some of these key differences.

Instructions

Step 1	Identify four individuals who either grew up in a foreign country or have lived in a foreign country for more than one year. Interview those four persons. Try to have four different countries represented. During each interview, develop a list of eight key differences between American style/custom and that particular country's style/custom in terms of various aspects of speaking, meetings, meals, relationships, friendships, and communication that could impact business dealings.
Step 2	Develop a 15-minute PowerPoint presentation for your class and give a talk summarizing your findings. Identify in your talk the persons you interviewed as well as the length of time those persons lived in the respective countries. Give your professor a hard copy of your PowerPoint presentation.

Assurance of Learning Exercise 11C

Pfizer Wants to Enter Vietnam. Help Them.

Purpose

More and more companies every day decide to begin doing business in Vietnam. Research is necessary to determine the best strategy for being competitive in Vietnam. Review the opening chapter boxed insert and Pfizer's website.

Instructions

Step 1	Print off a map of Vietnam.
Step 2	Print off demographic data on 10 cities in Vietnam.
Step 3	Gather competitive information regarding the presence of pharmaceutical companies doing business in Vietnam.
Step 4	List in prioritized order the five cities that you would recommend for Pfizer to expand their business operations into.

Assurance of Learning Exercise 11D

Does My University Recruit in Foreign Countries?

Purpose

A competitive climate is emerging among colleges and universities around the world. Colleges and universities in Europe and Japan are increasingly recruiting U.S. students to offset declining enrollments. Foreign students already make up more than one-third of the student body at many U.S. universities. The purpose of this exercise is to identify particular colleges and universities in foreign countries that represent a competitive threat to your college.

Instructions

Step 1	Select a foreign country. Conduct research to determine the number and nature of colleges and universities in that country. What are the major educational institutions in that country? What programs are those institutions recognized for offering? What percentage of undergraduate and graduate students attending those institutions are citizens of your country? Do these institutions actively recruit students from your country? Are any of the Schools of Business at the various universities AACSB-International accredited?
Step 2	Prepare a report for the class that summarizes your research findings. Present your report to the class.

"NOTABLE QUOTES"

"Two heads are better than one."

—*Unknown Author*

"One reaction frequently heard is 'I don't have enough information.' In reality strategists never have enough information because some information is not available and some is too costly."

—*William Glueck*

"I keep six honest serving men. They taught me all I know. Their names are What, Why, When, How, Where, and Who."

—*Rudyard Kipling*

"Don't recommend anything you would not be prepared to do yourself if you were in the decision maker's shoes."

—*A. J. Strickland III*

"A picture is worth a thousand words."

—*Unknown Author*

How to Prepare and Present a Case Analysis

CHAPTER OBJECTIVES

After studying this chapter, you should be able to do the following:

1. Describe the case method for learning strategic-management concepts.
2. Identify the steps in preparing a comprehensive written case analysis.
3. Describe how to give an effective oral case analysis presentation.
4. Discuss special tips for doing a case analysis.

ASSURANCE OF LEARNING EXERCISES

Oral Presentation—
Step 1 Introduction (2 minutes)

Oral Presentation—
Step 2 Mission/Vision (4 minutes)

Oral Presentation—
Step 3 Internal Assessment (8 minutes)

Oral Presentation—
Step 4 External Assessment (8 minutes)

Oral Presentation—
Step 5 Strategy Formulation (14 minutes)

Oral Presentation—
Step 6 Strategy Implementation (8 minutes)

Oral Presentation—
Step 7 Strategy Evaluation (2 minutes)

Oral Presentation—
Step 8 Conclusion (4 minutes)

The purpose of this section is to help you analyze strategic-management cases. Guidelines for preparing written and oral case analyses are given, and suggestions for preparing cases for class discussion are presented. Steps to follow in preparing case analyses are provided. Guidelines for making an oral presentation are described.

What Is a Strategic-Management Case?

A *strategic-management case* describes an organization's external and internal conditions and raises issues concerning the firm's mission, strategies, objectives, and policies. Most of the information in a strategic-management case is established fact, but some information may be opinions, judgments, and beliefs. Strategic-management cases are more comprehensive than those you may have studied in other courses. They generally include a description of related management, marketing, finance/accounting, production/operations, R&D, information systems, and natural environment issues. A strategic-management case puts the reader at the scene of the action by describing a firm's situation at some point in time. Strategic-management cases are written to give you practice applying strategic-management concepts. The case method for studying strategic management is often called *learning by doing.*

Guidelines for Preparing Case Analyses

The Need for Practicality

There is no such thing as a complete case, and no case ever gives you all the information you need to conduct analyses and make recommendations. Likewise, in the business world, strategists never have all the information they need to make decisions: information may be unavailable or too costly to obtain, or it may take too much time to obtain. So in analyzing strategic-management cases, do what strategists do every day—make reasonable assumptions about unknowns, clearly state assumptions, perform appropriate analyses, and make decisions. *Be practical.* For example, in performing a projected financial analysis, make reasonable assumptions, appropriately state them, and proceed to show what impact your recommendations are expected to have on the organization's financial position. Avoid saying, "I don't have enough information." Always supplement the information provided in a case with Internet and library research.

The Need for Justification

The most important part of analyzing cases is not what strategies you recommend but rather how you support your decisions and how you propose that they be implemented. There is no single best solution or one right answer to a case, so give ample justification for your recommendations. This is important. In the business world, strategists usually do not know if their decisions are right until resources have been allocated and consumed. Then it is often too late to reverse a decision. This cold fact accents the need for careful integration of intuition and analysis in preparing business policy case analyses.

The Need for Realism

Avoid recommending a course of action beyond an organization's means. *Be realistic.* No organization can possibly pursue all the strategies that could potentially benefit the firm. Estimate how much capital will be required to implement what you recommended. Determine whether debt, stock, or a combination of debt and stock could be used to obtain the capital. Make sure your recommendations are feasible. Do not prepare a case analysis that omits all arguments and information not supportive of your recommendations. Rather, present the major advantages and disadvantages of several feasible alternatives. Try not to exaggerate, stereotype, prejudge, or overdramatize. Strive to demonstrate that your interpretation of the evidence is reasonable and objective.

The Need for Specificity

Do not make broad generalizations such as "The company should pursue a market penetration strategy." Be specific by telling *what, why, when, how, where,* and *who.* Failure to use specifics is the single major shortcoming of most oral and written case analyses. For example, in an internal audit say, "The firm's current ratio fell from 2.2 in 2011 to 1.3 in 2012, and this is considered to be a major weakness," instead of "The firm's financial condition is bad." Rather than concluding from a Strategic Position and Action Evaluation (SPACE) Matrix that a firm should be defensive, be more specific, saying, "The firm should consider closing three plants, laying off 280 employees, and divesting itself of its chemical division, for a net savings of $20.2 million in 2012." Use ratios, percentages, numbers, and dollar estimates. Businesspeople dislike generalities and vagueness.

The Need for Originality

Do not necessarily recommend the course of action that the firm plans to take or actually undertook, even if those actions resulted in improved revenues and earnings. The aim of case analysis is for you to consider all the facts and information relevant to the organization at the time, to generate feasible alternative strategies, to choose among those alternatives, and to defend your recommendations. Put yourself back in time to the point when strategic decisions were being made by the firm's strategists. Based on the information available then, what would you have done? Support your position with charts, graphs, ratios, analyses, and the like—not a revelation from the library. You can become a good strategist by thinking through situations, making management assessments, and proposing plans yourself. *Be original.* Compare and contrast what you recommend versus what the company plans to do or did.

The Need to Contribute

Strategy formulation, implementation, and evaluation decisions are commonly made by a group of individuals rather than by a single person. Therefore, your professor may divide the class into three- or four-person teams and ask you to prepare written or oral case analyses. Members of a strategic-management team, in class or in the business world, differ on their aversion to risk, their concern for short-run versus long-run benefits, their attitudes toward social responsibility, and their views concerning globalization. There are no perfect people, so there are no perfect strategies. Be open-minded to others' views. *Be a good listener and a good contributor.*

Preparing a Case for Class Discussion

Your professor may ask you to prepare a case for class discussion. Preparing a case for class discussion means that you need to read the case before class, make notes regarding the organization's external opportunities/threats and internal strengths/weaknesses, perform appropriate analyses, and come to class prepared to offer and defend some specific recommendations.

The Case Method versus Lecture Approach

The case method of teaching is radically different from the traditional lecture approach, in which little or no preparation is needed by students before class. The *case method* involves a classroom situation in which students do most of the talking; your professor facilitates discussion by asking questions and encouraging student interaction regarding ideas, analyses, and recommendations. Be prepared for a discussion along the lines of "What would you do, why would you do it, when would you do it, and how would you do it?" Prepare answers to the following types of questions:

- What are the firm's most important external opportunities and threats?
- What are the organization's major strengths and weaknesses?
- How would you describe the organization's financial condition?
- What are the firm's existing strategies and objectives?
- Who are the firm's competitors, and what are their strategies?
- What objectives and strategies do you recommend for this organization? Explain your reasoning. How does what you recommend compare to what the company plans?
- How could the organization best implement what you recommend? What implementation problems do you envision? How could the firm avoid or solve those problems?

The Cross-Examination

Do not hesitate to take a stand on the issues and to support your position with objective analyses and outside research. Strive to apply strategic-management concepts and tools in preparing your case for class discussion. Seek defensible arguments and positions. Support opinions and judgments with facts, reasons, and evidence. Crunch the numbers before class! Be willing to describe your recommendations to the class without fear of disapproval. Respect the ideas of others, but be willing to go against the majority opinion when you can justify a better position.

Strategic-management case analysis gives you the opportunity to learn more about yourself, your colleagues, strategic management, and the decision-making process in organizations. The rewards of this experience will depend on the effort you put forth, so do a good job. Discussing business policy cases in class is exciting and challenging. Expect views counter to those you present. Different students will place emphasis on different aspects of an organization's situation and submit different recommendations for scrutiny and rebuttal. Cross-examination discussions commonly arise, just as they occur in a real business organization. Avoid being a silent observer.

Preparing a Written Case Analysis

In addition to asking you to prepare a case for class discussion, your professor may ask you to prepare a written case analysis. Preparing a written case analysis is similar to preparing a case for class discussion, except written reports are generally more structured and more detailed. There is no ironclad procedure for preparing a written case analysis because cases differ in focus; the type, size, and complexity of the organizations being analyzed also vary.

When writing a strategic-management report or case analysis, avoid using jargon, vague or redundant words, acronyms, abbreviations, sexist language, and ethnic or racial slurs. And watch your spelling! Use short sentences and paragraphs and simple words and phrases. Use quite a few subheadings. Arrange issues and ideas from the most important to the least important. Arrange recommendations from the least controversial to the most controversial. Use the active voice rather than the passive voice for all verbs; for example, say "Our team recommends that the company diversify" rather than "It is recommended by our team to diversify." Use many examples to add specificity and clarity. Tables, figures, pie charts, bar charts, timelines, and other kinds of exhibits help communicate important points and ideas. Sometimes a picture *is* worth a thousand words.

The Executive Summary

Your professor may ask you to focus the written case analysis on a particular aspect of the strategic-management process, such as (1) to identify and evaluate the organization's existing mission, objectives, and strategies; or (2) to propose and defend specific recommendations for the company; or (3) to develop an industry analysis by describing the competitors, products, selling techniques, and market conditions in a given industry. These types of written reports are sometimes called *executive summaries*. An executive summary usually ranges from three to five pages of text in length, plus exhibits.

The Comprehensive Written Analysis

Your professor may ask you to prepare a *comprehensive written analysis*. This assignment requires you to apply the entire strategic-management process to the particular organization. When preparing a comprehensive written analysis, picture yourself as a consultant who has been asked by a company to conduct a study of its external and internal environment and to make specific recommendations for its future. Prepare exhibits to support your recommendations. Highlight exhibits with some discussion in the paper. Comprehensive written analyses are usually about 10 pages in length, plus exhibits. Throughout your written analysis, emphasize how your proposed strategies will enable the firm to gain and sustain competitive advantage.

Steps in Preparing a Comprehensive Written Analysis

In preparing a **written** case analysis, you could follow the steps outlined here, which correlate to the stages in the strategic-management process and the chapters in this text. (Note—The steps in presenting an **oral** case analysis are given on pages 397–399, are more detailed, and could be used here).

Step 1   Identify the firm's existing vision, mission, objectives, and strategies.

Step 2   Develop vision and mission statements for the organization.

Step 3   Identify the organization's external opportunities and threats.

Step 4   Construct a Competitive Profile Matrix (CPM).

Step 5   Construct an External Factor Evaluation (EFE) Matrix.

Step 6   Identify the organization's internal strengths and weaknesses.

Step 7   Construct an Internal Factor Evaluation (IFE) Matrix.

Step 8   Prepare a Strengths-Weaknesses-Opportunities-Threats (SWOT) Matrix, Strategic Position and Action Evaluation (SPACE) Matrix, Boston Consulting Group (BCG) Matrix, Internal-External (IE) Matrix, Grand Strategy Matrix, and Quantitative Strategic Planning Matrix (QSPM) as appropriate. Give advantages and disadvantages of alternative strategies.

Step 9   Recommend specific strategies and long-term objectives. Show how much your recommendations will cost. Clearly itemize these costs for each projected year. Compare your recommendations to actual strategies planned by the company.

Step 10   Specify how your recommendations can be implemented and what results you can expect. Prepare forecasted ratios and projected financial statements. Present a time-table or agenda for action.

Step 11   Recommend specific annual objectives and policies.

Step 12   Recommend procedures for strategy review and evaluation.

Making an Oral Presentation

Your professor may ask you to prepare a strategic-management case analysis, individually or as a group, and present your analysis to the class. Oral presentations are usually graded on two parts: content and delivery. *Content* refers to the quality, quantity, correctness, and appropriate-ness of analyses presented, including such dimensions as logical flow through the presentation, coverage of major issues, use of specifics, avoidance of generalities, absence of mistakes, and feasibility of recommendations. *Delivery* includes such dimensions as audience attentive-ness, clarity of visual aids, appropriate dress, persuasiveness of arguments, tone of voice, eye contact, and posture. Great ideas are of no value unless others can be convinced of their merit through clear communication. The guidelines presented here can help you make an effective oral presentation.

Organizing the Presentation

Begin your presentation by introducing yourself and giving a clear outline of topics to be covered. If a team is presenting, specify the sequence of speakers and the areas each person will address. At the beginning of an oral presentation, try to capture your audience's interest and attention. You could do this by displaying some products made by the company, telling an interesting short story about the company, or sharing an experience you had that is related to the company, its products, or its services. You could develop or obtain a video to show at the beginning of class; you could visit a local distributor of the firm's products and tape a personal interview with the business owner or manager. A light or humorous introduction can be effective at the beginning of a presentation.

Be sure the setting of your presentation is well organized, with seats for attendees, flip charts, a transparency projector, and whatever else you plan to use. Arrive at the classroom at least 15 minutes early to organize the setting, and be sure your materials are ready to go. Make sure everyone can see your visual aids well.

Controlling Your Voice

An effective rate of speaking ranges from 100 to 125 words per minute. Practice your presentation aloud to determine if you are going too fast. Individuals commonly speak too fast when nervous. Breathe deeply before and during the presentation to help yourself slow down. Have a cup of water available; pausing to take a drink will wet your throat, give you time to collect your thoughts, control your nervousness, slow you down, and signal to the audience a change in topic.

Avoid a monotone voice by placing emphasis on different words or sentences. Speak loudly and clearly, but don't shout. Silence can be used effectively to break a monotone voice. Stop at the end of each sentence, rather than running sentences together with *and* or *uh.*

Managing Body Language

Be sure not to fold your arms, lean on the podium, put your hands in your pockets, or put your hands behind you. Keep a straight posture, with one foot slightly in front of the other. Do not turn your back to the audience; doing so is not only rude, but it also prevents your voice from projecting well. Avoid using too many hand gestures. On occasion, leave the podium or table and walk toward your audience, but do not walk around too much. Never block the audience's view of your visual aids.

Maintain good eye contact throughout the presentation. This is the best way to persuade your audience. There is nothing more reassuring to a speaker than to see members of the audience nod in agreement or smile. Try to look everyone in the eye at least once during your presentation, but focus more on individuals who look interested than on those who seem bored. To stay in touch with your audience, use humor and smiles as appropriate throughout your presentation. A presentation should never be dull!

Speaking from Notes

Be sure not to read to your audience because reading puts people to sleep. Perhaps worse than reading is merely reciting what you have memorized. Do not try to memorize anything. Rather, practice unobtrusively using notes. Make sure your notes are written clearly so you will not flounder when trying to read your own writing. Include only main ideas on your note cards. Keep note cards on a podium or table if possible so that you won't drop them or get them out of order; walking with note cards tends to be distracting.

Constructing Visual Aids

Make sure your visual aids are legible to individuals in the back of the room. Use color to highlight special items. Avoid putting complete sentences on visual aids; rather, use short phrases and then orally elaborate on issues as you make your presentation. Generally, there should be no more than four to six lines of text on each visual aid. Use clear headings and subheadings. Be careful about spelling and grammar; use a consistent style of lettering. Use masking tape or an easel for posters—do not hold posters in your hand. Transparencies and handouts are excellent aids; however, be careful not to use too many handouts or your audience may concentrate on them instead of you during the presentation.

Answering Questions

It is best to field questions at the end of your presentation, rather than during the presentation itself. Encourage questions, and take your time to respond to each one. Answering questions can be persuasive because it involves you with the audience. If a team is giving the presentation, the audience should direct questions to a specific person. During the question-and-answer period, be polite, confident, and courteous. Avoid verbose responses. Do not get defensive with your answers, even if a hostile or confrontational question is asked. Staying calm during potentially disruptive situations, such as a cross-examination, reflects self-confidence, maturity, poise, and command of the particular company and its industry. Stand up throughout the question-and-answer period.

Tips for Success in Case Analysis

Strategic-management students who have used this text over 13 editions offer you the following tips for success in doing case analysis. The tips are grouped into two basic sections: (1) Content Tips and (2) Process Tips. Content tips relate especially to the content of your case analysis, whereas the Process tips relate mostly to the process that you and your group mates undergo in preparing and delivering your case analysis/presentation.

Content Tips

1. Use the www.strategyclub.com website resources. The software described there is especially useful.
2. In preparing your external assessment, use the S&P Industry Survey material in your college library.
3. Go to http://finance.yahoo.com or http://moneycentral.msn/investor/home.asp and enter your company's stock symbol.
4. View your case analysis and presentation as a product that must have some competitive factor to favorably differentiate it from the case analyses of other students.
5. Develop a mind-set of *why*, continually questioning your own and others' assumptions and assertions.
6. Because strategic management is a capstone course, seek the help of professors in other specialty areas when necessary.
7. Read your case frequently as work progresses so you don't overlook details.
8. At the end of each group session, assign each member of the group a task to be completed for the next meeting.
9. Become friends with the library and the Internet.
10. Be creative and innovative throughout the case analysis process.
11. A goal of case analysis is to improve your ability to think clearly in ambiguous and confusing situations; do not get frustrated that there is no single best answer.
12. Do not confuse symptoms with causes; do not develop conclusions and solutions prematurely; recognize that information may be misleading, conflicting, or wrong.
13. Work hard to develop the ability to formulate reasonable, consistent, and creative plans; put yourself in the strategist's position.
14. Develop confidence in using quantitative tools for analysis. They are not inherently difficult; it is just practice and familiarity you need.
15. Strive for excellence in writing and in the technical preparation of your case. Prepare nice charts, tables, diagrams, and graphs. Use color and unique pictures. No messy exhibits! Use PowerPoint.
16. Do not forget that the objective is to learn; explore areas with which you are not familiar.
17. Pay attention to detail.
18. Think through alternative implications fully and realistically. The consequences of decisions are not always apparent. They often affect many different aspects of a firm's operations.
19. Provide answers to such fundamental questions as *what, when, where, why, who,* and *how.*
20. Do not merely recite ratios or present figures. Rather, develop ideas and conclusions concerning the possible trends. Show the importance of these figures to the corporation.
21. Support reasoning and judgment with factual data whenever possible.
22. Your analysis should be as detailed and specific as possible.
23. A picture speaks a thousand words, and a creative picture gets you an A in many classes.
24. Emphasize the Recommendations and Strategy Implementation sections. A common mistake is to spend too much time on the external or internal analysis parts of your paper. The recommendations and implementation sections are the most important part of the paper or presentation.
25. Throughout your case analysis, emphasize how your proposed strategic plan will enable the firm to gain and sustain competitive advantage.

Process Tips

1. When working as a team, encourage most of the work to be done individually. Use team meetings mostly to assimilate work. This approach is most efficient.
2. If allowed to do so, invite questions throughout your presentation.
3. During the presentation, keep good posture, eye contact, and voice tone, and project confidence. Do not get defensive under any conditions or with any questions.

4. Prepare your case analysis in advance of the due date to allow time for reflection and practice. Do not procrastinate.
5. Maintain a positive attitude about the class, working *with* problems rather than against them.
6. Keep in tune with your professor, and understand his or her values and expectations.
7. Other students will have strengths in functional areas that will complement your weaknesses, so develop a cooperative spirit that moderates competitiveness in group work.
8. When preparing a case analysis as a group, divide into separate teams to work on the external analysis and internal analysis.
9. Have a good sense of humor.
10. Capitalize on the strengths of each member of the group; volunteer your services in your areas of strength.
11. Set goals for yourself and your team; budget your time to attain them.
12. Foster attitudes that encourage group participation and interaction. Do not be hasty to judge group members.
13. Be prepared to work. There will be times when you will have to do more than your share. Accept it, and do what you have to do to move the team forward.
14. Think of your case analysis as if it were really happening; do not reduce case analysis to a mechanical process.
15. To uncover flaws in your analysis and to prepare the group for questions during an oral presentation, assign one person in the group to actively play the devil's advocate.
16. Do not schedule excessively long group meetings; two-hour sessions are about right.
17. Push your ideas hard enough to get them listened to, but then let up; listen to others and try to follow their lines of thinking; follow the flow of group discussion, recognizing when you need to get back on track; do not repeat yourself or others unless clarity or progress demands repetition.
18. Develop a case-presentation style that is direct, assertive, and convincing; be concise, precise, fluent, and correct.
19. Have fun when at all possible. Preparing a case is frustrating at times, but enjoy it while you can; it may be several years before you are playing CEO again.
20. In group cases, do not allow personality differences to interfere. When they occur, they must be understood for what they are—and then put aside.
21. Get things written down (drafts) as soon as possible.
22. Read everything that other group members write, and comment on it in writing. This allows group input into all aspects of case preparation.
23. Adaptation and flexibility are keys to success; be creative and innovative.
24. Neatness is a real plus; your case analysis should look professional.
25. Let someone else read and critique your presentation several days before you present it.
26. Make special efforts to get to know your group members. This leads to more openness in the group and allows for more interchange of ideas. Put in the time and effort necessary to develop these relationships.
27. Be constructively critical of your group members' work. Do not dominate group discussions. Be a good listener and contributor.
28. Learn from past mistakes and deficiencies. Improve upon weak aspects of other case presentations.
29. Learn from the positive approaches and accomplishments of classmates.

Sample Case Analysis Outline

There are musicians who play wonderfully without notes and there are chefs who cook wonderfully without recipes, but most of us prefer a more orderly cookbook approach, at least in the first attempt at doing something new. Therefore the following eight steps may serve as a basic outline for you in presenting a strategic plan for your firm's future. This outline is not the only approach used in business and industry for communicating a strategic plan, but this approach is time-tested, it does work, and it does cover all of the basics. You may amend the content, tools, and concepts given to suit your own company, audience, assignment, and circumstances, but it helps to know and understand the rules before you start breaking them.

Depending on whether your class is 50 minutes or 75 minutes and how much time your professor allows for your case presentation, the following outlines what generally needs to be covered. A recommended time (in minutes) as part of the presentation is given for an overall 50-minute event. Of course, all cases are different, some being about for-profit and some about not-for-profit organizations, for example, so the scope and content of your analysis may vary. Even if you do not have time to cover all areas in your oral presentation, you may be asked to prepare these areas and give them to your professor as a "written case analysis." Be sure in an oral presentation to manage time knowing that your recommendations and associated costs are the most important part. You should go to www.strategyclub.com and utilize that information and software in preparing your case analysis. Good luck.

Current Readings

Kearney, Eric, Diether Gebert, and Sven Voelpel. "When Diversity Benefits Teams: The Importance of Team Members' Need for Cognition." *Academy of Management Journal*, June 2009, 581–598.

STEPS IN PRESENTING AN ORAL CASE ANALYSIS

Oral Presentation—Step 1

Introduction (2 minutes)

a. Introduce yourselves by name and major. Establish the time setting of your case and analysis. Prepare your strategic plan for the three years 2012–2014.
b. Introduce your company and its products/services; capture interest.
c. Show the outline of your presentation and tell who is doing what parts.
d. Let your audience know that the primary motivation/rationale/intent of every slide is to reveal how the firm can best gain and sustain competitive advantage.

Oral Presentation—Step 2

Mission/Vision (4 minutes)

a. Show existing mission and vision statements if available from the firm's website, or annual report, or elsewhere.
b. Show your "improved" mission and vision and tell why it is improved.
c. Compare your mission and vision to a leading competitor's statements.
d. Comment on your vision and mission in terms of how they support the strategies you envision for your firm.

Oral Presentation—Step 3

Internal Assessment (8 minutes)

a. Give your financial ratio analysis. Highlight especially good and bad ratios. Do not give definitions of the ratios and do not highlight all the ratios.

b. Show the firm's organizational chart found or "created based on executive titles." Identify the type of chart as well as good and bad aspects. Unless all white males comprise the chart, peoples' names are generally not important because positions reveal structure as people come and go.

c. Present your improved/recommended organizational chart. Tell why you feel it is improved over the existing chart.

d. Show a market positioning map with firm and competitors. Discuss the map in light of strategies you envision for firm versus competitors' strategies.

e. Identify the marketing strategy of the firm in terms of good and bad points versus competitors and in light of strategies you envision for the firm.

f. Show a map locating the firm's operations. Discuss in light of strategies you envision. Also, perhaps show a Value Chain Analysis chart.

g. Discuss (and perhaps show) the firm's website and Facebook page in terms of good and bad points compared to rival firms.

h. Show your "value of the firm" analysis.

i. List up to 20 of the firm's strengths and weaknesses. Go over each one listed without "reading" them verbatim.

j. Show and explain your Internal Factor Evaluation (IFE) Matrix.

Oral Presentation—Step 4

External Assessment (8 minutes)

a. Identify and discuss major competitors. Use pie charts, maps, tables, and/or figures to show the intensity of competition in the industry.

b. Show your Competitive Profile Matrix. Include at least 12 factors and two competitors.

c. Summarize key industry trends citing Standard & Poor's *Industry Survey* or Chamber of Commerce statistics, etc. Highlight key external trends as they impact the firm, including trends that are economic, social, cultural, demographic, geographic, technological, political, legal, governmental, and to do with the natural environment.

d. List up to 20 of the firm's opportunities and threats. Make sure your opportunities are not stated as strategies. Go over each one listed without "reading" them verbatim.

e. Show and explain your External Factor Evaluation (EFE) Matrix.

Oral Presentation—Step 5

Strategy Formulation (14 minutes)

a. Show and explain your SWOT Matrix, highlighting each of your strategies listed.

b. Show and explain your SPACE Matrix, using half of your "space time" on calculations and the other half on implications of those numbers. Strategy implications must be specific rather than generic. In other words, use of a term such as "market penetration" is not satisfactory alone as a strategy implication.

c. Show your Boston Consulting Group (BCG) Matrix. Again focus on both the numbers and the strategy implications. Do multiple BCG Matrices if possible, including domestic versus global, or another geographic breakdown. Develop a product BCG if at all possible. Comment on changes to this matrix as per strategies you envision. Develop this matrix even if you do not know the profits per division and even if you have to estimate the axes information. However, make no wild guesses on axes or revenue/profit information.

d. Show your Internal-External (IE) Matrix. Because this analysis is similar to the BCG, see the preceding comments.

e. Show your Grand Strategy Matrix. Again focus on implications after giving the quadrant selection. Reminder: Use of a term such as "market penetration" is not satisfactory alone as a strategy implication. Be more specific. Elaborate.

f. Show your Quantitative Strategic Planning Matrix (QSPM). Be sure to explain your strategies to start with here. Do not go back over the internal and external factors. Avoid having more than one 4, 3, 2, or 1 in a row. If you rate one strategy, you need to rate the other because that particular factor is affecting the choice. Work row by row rather than column by column on preparing the QSPM.

g. Present your Recommendations Page. This is the most important page in your presentation. Be specific in terms of both strategies and estimated costs of those strategies. *Total your estimated costs.* You should have 10 or more strategies. Divide your strategies into two groups: (1) Existing Strategies to Be Continued, and (2) New Strategies to Be Started.

Oral Presentation—Step 6

Strategy Implementation (8 minutes)

a. Show and explain your EPS/EBIT analysis to reveal whether stock, debt, or a combination is best to finance your recommendations. Graph the analysis. Decide which approach to use if there are any given limitations of the analysis.

b. Show your projected income statement. Relate changes in the items to your recommendations rather than blindly going with historical percentage changes.

c. Show your projected balance sheet. Relate changes in your items to your recommendations. Be sure to show the retained earnings calculation and the results of your EPS/EBIT decision.

d. Show your projected financial ratios and highlight several key ratios to show the benefits of your strategic plan.

Oral Presentation—Step 7

Strategy Evaluation (2 minutes)

a. Prepare a Balanced Scorecard to show your expected financial and nonfinancial objectives recommended for the firm.

Oral Presentation—Step 8

Conclusion (4 minutes)

a. Compare and contrast your strategic plan versus the company's own plans for the future.

b. Thank audience members for their attention. Genuinely seek and gladly answer questions.

Name Index

Subject Index